© VLADGRIN/Shutterstock.com

Practical Computer Literacy 4ᵗʰ Edition

Internet and Computing Core Certification

June Jamrich Parsons • Dan Oja

CONTAINS A **Digital Book** FOR A FULLY INTERACTIVE LEARNING EXPERIENCE

CENGAGE Learning

Australia • Brazil • Japan • Korea • Mexico • Singapore • Spain • United Kingdom • United States

CENGAGE
Learning

Practical Computer Literacy, 4th Edition

June Jamrich Parsons, Dan Oja

Product Director: Kathleen McMahon

Senior Director of Development:
  Marah Bellegarde

Senior Product Team Manager: Donna
  Gridley

Associate Product Manager: Amanda Lyons

Product Development Manager: Leigh
  Hefferon

Senior Content Developer: Kathy Finnegan

Content Developer: Julia Leroux-Lindsey

Product Assistant: Melissa Stehler

Marketing Director: Elinor Gregory

Senior Market Development Manager:
  Eric LaScola

Market Development Manager: Kristie Clark

Marketing Manager: Gretchen Swann

Marketing Coordinator: Elizabeth Murphy

Content Project Manager:
  Jennifer Feltri-George

Manufacturing Planner: Fola Orekoya

Proofreader: Suzanne Huizenga

Indexer: Alexandra Nickerson

Art Director: GEX Publishing Services

Cover Art: (C) VLADGRIN/Shutterstock.com

Electronic Publishing Specialist:
  Tensi Parsons

Digital Book Technician: Keefe Crowley

Digital Animator: Donna Mulder

Digital Book Development:
  MediaTechnics Corp.

Prepress Production: GEX Publishing Services

For product information and technology assistance, contact us at
Cengage Learning Customer & Sales Support, 1-800-354-9706

For permission to use material from this text or product,
submit all requests online at **cengage.com/permissions**.
Further permissions questions can be e-mailed to
permissionrequest@cengage.com.

Library of Congress Control Number: 2013942508
ISBN-13: 978-1-285-07677-5
ISBN-10: 1-285-07677-X

Cengage Learning
200 First Stamford Place, 4th Floor
Stamford, CT 06902
USA

Cengage Learning is a leading provider of customized learning solutions with office
locations around the globe, including Singapore, the United Kingdom, Australia,
Mexico, Brazil and Japan. Locate your local office at:
www.cengage.com/global

Cengage Learning products are represented in Canada by Nelson Education, Ltd.

To learn more about Cengage Learning, visit **www.cengage.com**

Purchase any of our products at your local college store or at our preferred online
store **www.cengagebrain.com**

Printed in the United States of America
6 7 8 9 10 11 12 23 22 21 20 19

Preface

Practical Computer Literacy provides a state-of-the-art introduction to computer concepts and software applications, written in an easy-to-read style. It encompasses productivity applications, browsers, and e-mail clients within the context of Microsoft Windows 7 and 8.

The action-packed, multimedia digital book contains every page of the printed textbook plus interactive elements such as guided software tours and end-of-chapter quizzes. The digital book is distributed on a CD and requires no installation, so it's easy to use at home, at school, or at work.

How does it work?

Practical Computer Literacy offers a unique, graduated learning environment where you see it, try it, and then apply it.

1. See It

The **book** provides background information and step-by-step screen illustrations to get you oriented to a task.

2. Try It

Use the **digital book** to work with hands-on, step-by-step task simulations that help you learn the basics even if you don't have access to Windows 8 or Microsoft Office 2013.

3. Apply It

Activities in the **Projects** section challenge you to try your skills on real-world examples using Microsoft Office and other application software.

Use this book because...

- **You want to learn about computers.** *Practical Computer Literacy* helps you understand enough "tech talk" so you can decipher computer ads and hold your own when the conversation turns to computers.

- **You want to learn Windows.** *Practical Computer Literacy* shows you how to use Windows 7 and 8 to manage files and customize your on-screen work area.

- **You want to learn Microsoft Office.** *Practical Computer Literacy* teaches you all the key skills for Microsoft Word, Excel, PowerPoint, and Access.

- **You want to learn how to use the Internet.** *Practical Computer Literacy* shows you how to get connected, use a browser, send e-mail, and work with search engines.

- **You want to prepare for a computer competency certification exam.** *Practical Computer Literacy* offers a visual, hands-on way to prepare for computer competency certification, such as Certiport's IC3 exam. The topics and activities in *Practical Computer Literacy* have been carefully structured to cover all of the objectives for globally recognized certification programs.

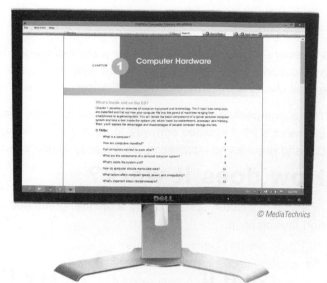

© MediaTechnics

The Digital Book

Every book includes a CD, which is a digital version of the printed textbook loaded with features to enhance and reinforce learning.

PLAYIT! On the CD, the Play It! button makes figures come to life as videos that show you exactly how computer hardware components work.

TRYIT! Try It! buttons produce step-by-step interactive software tutorials, which give you a chance to quickly hone your software skills.

CHECKIT! Interactive end-of-chapter QuickCheck questions provide instant feedback on what you've learned.

DEFINITIONS Clickable boldface terms display pop-up definitions. A Glossary button provides easy access to all definitions from any page.

SKILLTESTS Chapters about application software include Skill Tests so that you can test your ability to carry out software tasks. These activities are similar to the performance-based questions on the IC^3 exam; your performance on Skill Tests is scored and recorded.

Teaching Tools

With **ExamView**, our powerful testing software package, instructors can generate printed tests, create LAN-based tests, or administer tests over the Internet.

An **Instructor's Manual** outlines each chapter and provides valuable teaching tips.

WebTrack provides automated delivery of tracking data from any student directly to the instructor with minimal setup or administrative overhead.

Presentations for *Practical Computer Literacy* are easy. Just use the digital book along with a computer projection system to display software tours, QuickChecks, and Skill Tests.

Check with your Course Technology sales representative or go to **www.cengage.com/coursetechnology** to learn more about other valuable Teaching Tools.

INTERNET AND
COMPUTING CORE
CERTIFICATION

SETTING THE STANDARD

Certification

Learning materials provided by the *Practical Computer Literacy* book and digital book are designed to help you prepare for IC^3 certification exams.

IC^3...What is it?

IC^3 (Internet and Computing Core Certification) is a global training and certification program providing proof to the world that you are:

© MediaTechnics

- Equipped with the computer skills necessary to excel in a digital world

- Capable of using a broad range of computer technology—from basic hardware and software, to operating systems, applications, and the Internet

- Ready for the work employers, colleges, and universities want to throw your way

- Positioned to advance your career through additional computer certifications such as CompTIA's A+ and other desktop application exams as shown in the Certification Roadmap

IC^3...Why do you need it?

Employers, colleges, and universities now understand that exposure to computers does not equal understanding computers. So now more than ever, basic computer and Internet skills are being considered prerequisites for employment and higher education.

This is where IC^3 helps! IC^3 provides specific guidelines for the knowledge and skills required to be a functional user of computer hardware, networks, and the Internet. It does this through three exams:

- Computing Fundamentals

- Key Applications

- Living Online

By passing the three IC^3 exams, you'll have initiated yourself into today's digital world. You'll have also earned a globally accepted and validated credential that provides the proof employers and higher education institutions need.

Earn your IC^3 certification today. Visit **www.certiport.com/ic3** to learn how.

Acknowledgments

When you think about how a textbook is created, you might envision a lone author who produces a manuscript that is copyedited and then sent to the printer. If that was the case, textbooks might be less expensive, but they would certainly be less effective and far less interesting.

Today, creating a textbook is more like developing a computer game than penning a novel. It is a process that requires designers, script writers, narrators, animators, videographers, photographers, photo researchers, desktop publishers, programmers, testers, indexers, editors, reviewers—and, yes, somewhere in the middle of all this creative effort are the authors.

The successful launch of this textbook was possible only because of an extraordinary and diverse team of dedicated specialists who collaborate from geographically dispersed locations using the Internet. It is a team of disciplined professionals who do what it takes to meet deadlines with high-quality work and cheeriness, even after working all weekend.

We would like to acknowledge the members of our incredible team who helped to bring you this colorful, interactive textbook:

Keefe Crowley: Multi-talented Keefe produces the digital book by linking together the text, photos, videos, software tours, animations, and computer-scored quizzes. He also ushers the CD through the testing process and is responsible for producing many of the photos and video sequences. Keefe keeps in shape riding his mountain bike even during snowy northern winters.

Donna Mulder: As our senior animator, Donna works tirelessly to script and develop guided software tours from her office in Colorado, where we assume she has a cozy fireplace to keep her warm up there in the mountains.

Chris Robbert: The voice of the *Practical* series, Chris records narrations from his studio in the U.S. Virgin Islands, and he is a talented musician who specializes in classical and jazz guitar.

Tensi Parsons: Our layout and desktop publishing expert, Tensi, is responsible for tracking all the elements for the printed book. Each chapter goes through at least four revisions, and Tensi's job is to keep everything straight so the final product meets the highest standards. Tensi coaches community rowing in her free time.

Testers, testers, testers: Kevin Lappi, Joseph Smit, Kelsey Schuch, Nora Heikkinen, Michael Crowley, and the Course Technology Software Quality Assurance Team; they test the digital book, they test the instructions, and they test the tests.

Julia Leroux-Lindsey: As our content development manager, Julia oversees the manuscript from inception to publication.

Michelle Durgerian: As our content project manager, Michelle monitors the flow of chapters among the copyeditor, author, and desktop publisher. She makes sure that all the final copy is clean and error-free.

Sarah Fowler: Our schedule maven and project manager keeps everything on track with her weekly reports and production schedules.

Suzanne Huizenga: With today's technology, spelling errors are few and far between. But there are still a million and one grammar and style issues for the copyeditor to address, and Suzanne is a perfectionist with an eagle eye.

And that's not all! We simply cannot omit the editorial staff at Course Technology who make the executive decisions and work with customers: Donna Gridley, Amanda Lyons, Kathy Finnegan, and Melissa Stehler. They are this product's fairy godmothers who make the pumpkin turn into a coach.

Contents

Contents

Contents

Contents

Contents

Before You Begin

You are going to enjoy using *Practical Computer Literacy* and the accompanying digital version of the book. It's a snap to get started. The answers to the FAQs (frequently asked questions) in this section will help you begin.

FAQ Will the digital book work on my computer?

The easiest way to find out if the digital book works on your computer is to try it! Just follow the steps below to start the CD. If it works, you're all set. Otherwise, check with your local technical support person.

To run the digital book, your computer needs the Windows operating system (Windows 8, 7, Vista, or XP), a CD or DVD drive, and screen resolution of 1024 x 768 or better. If a CD or DVD drive is not built into your computer, you can use an external drive to access the digital book or transfer the book to your computer's hard disk.

The instructions below explain how to use the digital book from the CD. If you prefer to transfer the digital book to your computer's hard drive, refer to the instructions at the end of this section.

FAQ How do I start the CD?

The *Practical Computer Literacy* digital book is distributed on a CD, which is easy to use and requires no installation. Follow these simple steps to get started:

1. Make sure your computer is turned on.

2. Insert the CD into your computer's CD/ DVD drive.

3. If your computer displays an AutoPlay window similar to the one shown below, click the Run BookOnReader option.

© MediaTechnics

DVD RW Drive (D:) PLIT4

Choose what to do with this disc.

Install or run program from your media

Run BookOnReader.exe
Publisher not specified

Other choices

Open folder to view files
File Explorer

Take no action

Source: Microsoft Corporation

4. When you see the title screen below, your digital book is open. You can click the OK button to start reading, or you can set your tracking options. For information on tracking options, continue to the FAQ on the next page of your textbook.

The length of time your computer takes to start the digital book depends on your security settings. If you have security set to conduct a virus check on software running from CDs, you must wait for that process to be completed before the digital book opens.

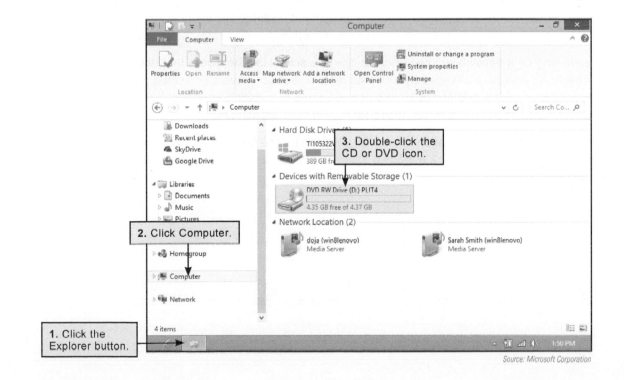

© MediaTechnics

Manual Start: Follow the instructions in the figure below only if you've waited a minute or two and the title screen has not appeared.

Source: Microsoft Corporation

FAQ How should I set my tracking options?

A Tracking file records your progress by saving your scores on assessment activities, such as QuickChecks, Skill Tests, and Practice Tests. You can access tracking options and create your personal tracking file by selecting File and then selecting Change Tracking Options. If you don't want to record your scores, simply make sure the Save Tracking data box is empty and then click the OK button to proceed straight to the first chapter

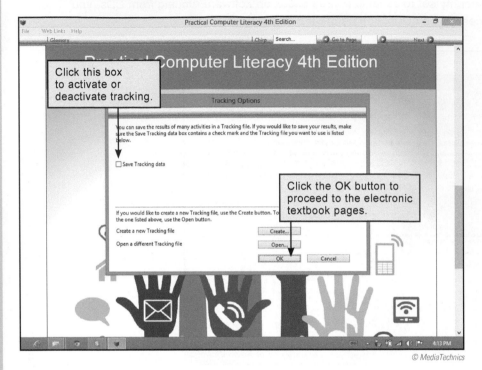

© MediaTechnics

If you prefer to track your scores, then you can create a Tracking file. It's easy! Click the Create button and then follow the on-screen prompts to enter your name, student ID, and class section.

When the Save As window appears, you can select the location for your Tracking file. If you are using your own computer, the default location in the My Documents folder is a great place to store your Tracking file, so just click the Save button and you're all set!

If you are working on a public computer, such as one in a school lab, be aware that data stored on the hard disk might be erased or changed by other students unless you have a protected personal storage area. When working on a public computer or when you need to transport your data from one computer to another, a USB flash drive is a better option for storing your Tracking file.

To save your Tracking file in a location other than your computer's My Documents folder, click the Computer icon and then double-click a storage location to select it. Click the Save button to finalize your storage selection.

FAQ How do I navigate through the digital book?

Each on-screen page exactly duplicates a page from the paper book. Tools on the menu bar help you navigate from page to page. If your computer screen does not show an entire page, use the scroll bar.

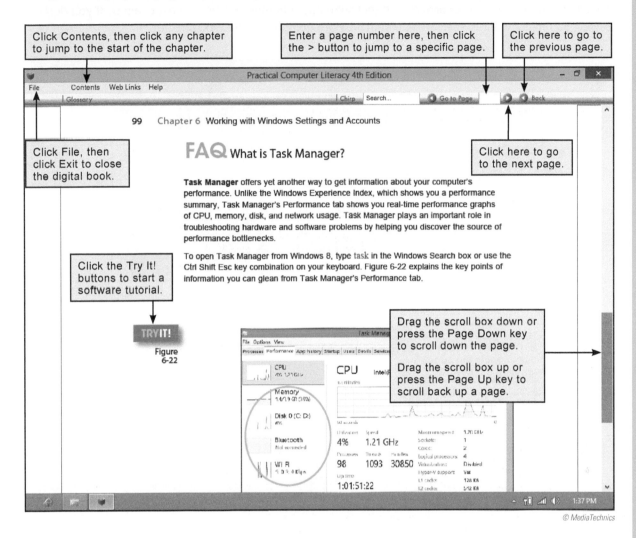

Click Contents, then click any chapter to jump to the start of the chapter.

Enter a page number here, then click the > button to jump to a specific page.

Click here to go to the previous page.

Click File, then click Exit to close the digital book.

Click here to go to the next page.

Click the Try It! buttons to start a software tutorial.

Drag the scroll box down or press the Page Down key to scroll down the page.

Drag the scroll box up or press the Page Up key to scroll back up a page.

© MediaTechnics

FAQ What should I know about the Projects?

The last chapter contains projects that help you review and apply the concepts presented in the book. All projects require the Windows 7 or 8 operating system. Other software and storage media that you'll need are listed at the beginning of each project.

If a project requires you to send an e-mail attachment to your instructor, use your usual e-mail software, such as Thunderbird, Microsoft Outlook, Windows Mail, Outlook.com, Gmail, Yahoo! Mail, or AOL mail. (If you don't have an e-mail account, see Chapter 20 for instructions on how to set one up.) First, make sure that you have saved the project file. Next, start your e-mail software. Then, follow your software's procedures for sending an e-mail attachment.

FAQ How does the interactive assessment page work?

Each chapter ends with an assessment page containing interactive activities. You can use these activities to evaluate how well you've mastered the concepts and skills covered in the chapter. If you do well on the end-of-chapter activities, then you're ready to move on to the next chapter. If you don't do well, you might want to review the material before going on to the next chapter.

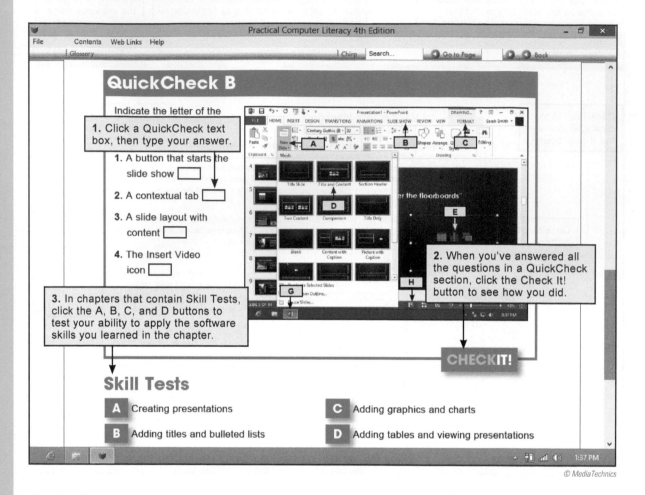

© MediaTechnics

FAQ Are all my scores tracked?

Your scores on QuickChecks and Skill Tests located at the end of each chapter, and the Get It? Practice Tests located at the beginning of each section, are tracked if you have activated tracking with a checkmark in the *Save Tracking data* box.

FAQ How can I change tracking options?

You can access the Tracking Options window at any time by clicking File on the menu bar and selecting Change Tracking Options. When the Tracking Options window appears, you can activate or deactivate tracking, create a new Tracking file, or select a different Tracking file.

FAQ What if the Tracking Options window shows the wrong Tracking file?

When working in a computer lab or using a computer where other students are using the *Practical Computer Literacy CD*, the Tracking Options window might show the name of a Tracking file that belongs to another person because that person was the last one to use the computer. You can use the Open button on the Tracking Options window to select a different Tracking file. Tracking files are usually stored in the Documents folder.

1. To change the Tracking file, open the Tracking Options dialog box by clicking File, then selecting Change Tracking Options.

Tracking Options

You can save the results of many activities in a Tracking file. If you would like to save your results, make sure the Save Tracking data box contains a check mark and the Tracking file you want to use is listed below.

☑ Save Tracking data

Use Tracking file for: Sarah Smith
Student ID: 12345   Class Section: CS101
Location: C:\Users\Sarah Smith\Documents\Tracking-12345.tk4

2. Click Open, select a storage device and folder, then select a Tracking file.

If you would like to create a new Tracking file, use the Create button. To select a Tracking file other than the one listed above, use the Open button.

Create a new Tracking file   [Create...]

Open a different Tracking file   [Open...]

[OK]   [Cancel]

© MediaTechnics

FAQ How do I submit my Tracking file?

In an academic setting, your instructor might request your Tracking file data to monitor your progress. Your instructor will tell you if you should submit your Tracking file using the WebTrack system, if you should hand in your Tracking file on a USB drive, or if you should send the Tracking file as an e-mail attachment.

FAQ How do I end a session?

Leave the *Practical Computer Literacy CD* in the CD drive while you're using it, or you will encounter an error message. Before you remove the CD from the drive, you must exit the program by clicking File on the menu bar, then clicking Exit. You can also exit by clicking the Close button in the upper-right corner of the window.

FAQ What about sound?

If your computer is equipped for sound, you should hear narrations during videos, screen tours, and interactive simulations. If you don't hear anything, check the volume control on your computer by clicking the speaker icon in the lower-right corner of your screen. If you're working in a lab or an office where sound would be disruptive, consider using headphones.

Before You Begin

FAQ What if my computer has no CD drive?

The *Practical Computer Literacy* digital book is distributed on a CD, but it can be transferred to your computer's hard disk. To do so, you will need to temporarily connect an external CD/DVD drive, which you can borrow from a friend, if necessary. Put the *Practical Computer Literacy CD* in the drive and then complete the following steps:

1. From the Windows 8 Start screen, click the Desktop tile.

2. Select the ▢ File Explorer icon that's at the bottom of the desktop.

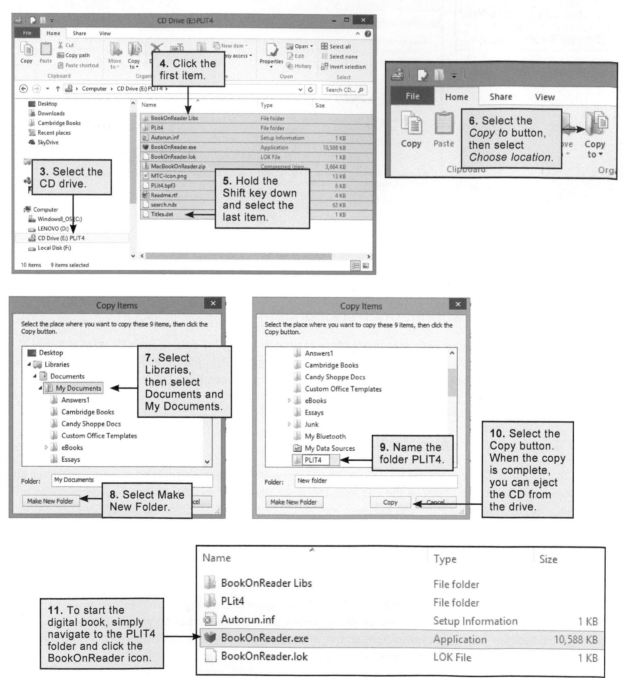

Section I

Computing Fundamentals

What's in this Section?

GETIT?

When you complete Section I, use the digital textbook to take Practice Tests by selecting the Get It? button.

Computer Hardware

What's Inside and on the CD?

Chapter 1 provides an overview of computer equipment and terminology. You'll learn how computers are classified and find out how your computer fits into the gamut of machines ranging from smartphones to supercomputers. You will review the basic components of a typical personal computer system and take a look inside the system unit, which holds the motherboard, processor, and memory. Then, you'll explore the advantages and disadvantages of several computer storage devices.

● **FAQs:**

FAQ What is a computer?

At its core, a **computer** is a multipurpose digital device that accepts input, processes data, stores data, and produces output, all according to a series of stored instructions.

Computer input is whatever is typed into, submitted to, or transmitted to a computer system. Input can be supplied by a person, by the environment, or by another computer. Examples of input that a computer can accept include words and symbols in a document, numbers for a calculation, photos from a digital camera, temperatures from a thermostat, audio signals from a microphone, and instructions from a computer program. An input device, such as a keyboard, mouse, or touchscreen, gathers data and transforms it into a series of electronic signals for the computer to store and manipulate.

In the context of computing, **data** refers to symbols that represent facts, objects, and ideas. Computers manipulate data in many ways, and this manipulation is called **processing**. In a computer, most processing takes place in a component called the **central processing unit** (CPU), which is sometimes described as the computer's "brain."

The series of instructions that tell a computer how to carry out a processing task is referred to as a **computer program**, or simply a program. These programs form the **software** that sets up a computer to do a specific task. An **operating system** is software that helps a computer control itself to operate efficiently and keep track of data. **Application software** helps users "apply" the computer to specific tasks, such as writing documents and editing photos.

A computer stores data so that it is available for processing. Most computers have more than one location for storing data, depending on how the data is being used. **Memory** is an area of a computer that temporarily holds data waiting to be processed, saved, or output. **Storage** is the area where data can be left on a permanent basis when it is not immediately needed for processing.

Computer output is the result produced by a computer. Some examples of computer output include reports, documents, music, graphs, and pictures. An output device displays, prints, or transmits the results of processing. Figure 1-1 can help you visualize the input, processing, storage, and output activities of a computer.

PLAY**IT!**

Figure
1-1

Computers produce output on devices such as screens and printers.

A computer accepts input from an input device, such as a keyboard, mouse, scanner, touchscreen, or digital camera.

Data is processed in the CPU according to instructions that have been loaded into the computer's memory.

A computer uses hard disks, CDs, DVDs, and flash drives to permanently store data.

© MediaTechnics

FAQ How are computers classified?

Computers are sometimes divided into categories. In order of size and computing power starting with the most powerful, these categories are: supercomputers, mainframes, servers, and personal computers.

Figure
1-2

Courtesy of Lawrence Livermore National Laboratory, used with permission

Supercomputers. A computer falls into the **supercomputer** category if it is, at the time of construction, one of the fastest computers in the world (Figure 1-2). Because of their speed, supercomputers can tackle complex tasks that just would not be practical for other computers. Typical uses for supercomputers include breaking codes, modeling worldwide weather systems, and simulating nuclear explosions.

Computer manufacturers such as IBM, Cray, and Fujitsu have in recent years held top honors for the world's fastest computer. Supercomputer speeds are measured in petaflops (PFLOPS). One petaflop is an astounding 1,000,000,000,000,000 mathematical calculations per second. That's about 20,000 times faster than your laptop computer.

Figure
1-3

Courtesy of IBM International Business Machines

Mainframes. A **mainframe computer** (or simply a mainframe) is a large and expensive computer capable of simultaneously processing data for hundreds or thousands of users. Its main processing circuitry is housed in a closet-sized cabinet like the one shown in Figure 1-3; but after large components are added for storage and output, a mainframe installation can fill a good-sized room.

Mainframes are generally used by businesses and government agencies to provide centralized storage, processing, and management for large amounts of data. Mainframes remain the computer of choice in situations, such as banking, where reliability, data security, and centralized control are necessary. The price of a mainframe computer typically starts at several hundred thousand dollars and can easily exceed US$ 1 million.

Figure
1-4

© dotshock/Shutterstock.com

Servers. The purpose of a **server** is to "serve" data to computers connected to a network. When you search Google or access a Web site, the information you obtain is provided by servers. At e-commerce sites, the store's merchandise information is housed in database servers. E-mail, chat, Skype, and online multiplayer games are all operated by servers.

Technically, just about any computer can be configured to perform the work of a server. Nonetheless, computer manufacturers such as IBM and Dell offer devices classified as servers that are especially suited for storing and distributing data on networks. These devices are about the size of a desk drawer and are often mounted in racks of multiple servers (Figure 1-4).

Figure
1-5

© MediaTechnics

Servers in small standalone units resemble old-style desktop tower units (Figure 1-5). Despite impressive performance on server-related tasks, these machines do not offer features such as sound cards, DVD players, and other fun accessories, so they are not a suitable alternative to a personal computer.

• How are computers classified? (continued)

Personal computers. A **personal computer** is designed to meet the computing needs of an individual. These computers were originally referred to as microcomputers. Personal computers provide access to a wide variety of computing applications, such as word processing, photo editing, e-mail, and Internet access. Personal computers can be further classified as desktop, portable, and mobile devices.

Figure 1-6

A **desktop computer** fits on a desk and runs on power from an electrical wall outlet. The keyboard is typically a separate component. Traditionally styled desktop computers are housed in a vertical case or in a horizontal case. In most modern desktops, called **all-in-one computers**, the computer circuitry is incorporated into the display device (Figure 1-6).

Desktop computers are popular for offices and schools where portability is not important. Their operating systems include Microsoft Windows, OS X, and Linux. The price of an entry-level desktop computer starts at $500 or a bit less.

Figure 1-7

A **portable computer** runs on battery power. Its screen, keyboard, camera, storage devices, and speakers are fully contained in a single case so that the device can be easily transported from one place to another. Portable computers include laptops, netbooks, tablets, and smartphones.

A **laptop computer** (also referred to as a notebook computer) is a small, lightweight personal computer designed like a clamshell with a keyboard as the base and a screen on the hinged cover (Figure 1-7).

Figure 1-8

Small laptop computers are sometimes called **netbooks**. Netbooks and laptops use the same operating systems as desktop computers. The price of an entry-level netbook computer starts at about $250. Larger laptops start at $300.

A **tablet computer** is a portable computing device featuring a touch-sensitive screen that can be used for input as well as for output. Tablet computers use specialized operating systems, such as iOS, Android, and Microsoft Windows RT.

Figure 1-9

A **slate tablet** configuration lacks a physical keyboard (although one can be attached) and resembles a high-tech clipboard (Figure 1-8). The Apple iPad and Samsung Galaxy are popular examples of slate tablets. A **convertible tablet** can be operated by using its touch-sensitive screen or with a physical keyboard that can be folded out of the way or removed (Figure 1-9).

When tablet computers were first introduced in 2002, they were priced significantly higher than laptop computers with similar specifications. Currently, however, tablet computers are priced only slightly higher than equivalent laptop computers.

• How are computers classified? (continued)

Figure
1-10

A **smartphone** features a small keyboard or touch-sensitive screen and is designed to fit into a pocket, run on batteries, and be used while you are holding it (Figure 1-10). It can connect to a cell phone network to make voice calls, send text messages, and access the Internet. Smartphones and tablet computers that have cellular connectivity are sometimes classified as **mobile devices**.

Smartphones evolved from basic cell phones and PDAs. A **PDA** (personal digital assistant) was a handheld device used as an electronic appointment book, calculator, and notepad. Modern smartphones include a similar suite of applications but also have access to a huge variety of mobile apps. Unlike a basic mobile phone, smartphones are programmable, so they can download, store, and run software.

Smartphones include GPS capability so that apps can provide location-based services, such as a list of nearby restaurants. Many smartphones also feature built-in speech recognition that allows you to ask questions and control the device using verbal commands.

The operating systems for smartphones are similar to those used for tablet computers. iOS is used on the iPad and iPhone. Microsoft Windows Phone 8 is used on smartphones that offer much the same user experience as Windows RT tablets. The Android operating system that is used on Samsung tablets is also used on Samsung Galaxy and Motorola Droid smartphones.

Figure
1-11

Other digital devices. A key feature of computers is their programmability. They can be used for many different tasks, depending on a set of program instructions carried out by their software. Other digital devices are not as flexible because their programming is limited. Nevertheless, several categories of these devices exist:

- Ebook readers. Popularized by the NOOK and Kindle, **ebook readers** are designed for displaying the content of digital publications, such as books, magazines, and newspapers. Dedicated ebook readers (Figure 1-11) are limited to digital books, but the Kindle Fire and NOOK Tablet include a browser for accessing the Internet and can be classified as tablet computers.

- Game consoles. Devices for playing computer games include Sony's PlayStation, Nintendo's Wii, and Microsoft's Xbox. Game consoles feature powerful processing capability and excellent graphics, but are generally used for dedicated game playing and have limited access to application software.

Figure
1-12

- Portable media players. Media players, such as the iPod Touch (Figure 1-12), revolutionized the music industry by providing a handheld device that could store and play thousands of songs. These devices are controlled by touchscreens or simple click-wheel mechanisms.

FAQ Can computers connect to each other?

A **computer network** is two or more computers linked together to share data and resources. Computers can connect to each other in a variety of ways. In a very simple computer-to-computer connection, a smartphone can connect to a desktop computer using a cable or wireless link to synchronize data between the two devices—for example, to update or back up your playlist.

Personal computers within a limited geographical area can link to each other and to larger computers over a computer network using wired or wireless connections. Such networks are in widespread use at schools, small businesses, and large enterprises. You'll find computer networks in homes, college computer labs, university administrative offices, government agencies, retail stores, and multi-location superstores.

The **Internet** is the world's largest network, connecting millions of personal computers, servers, mainframes, and supercomputers. You can connect your computer directly to an Internet service provider through a cable or phone connection. More commonly, you'll connect your computer to a home, school, or business network that offers Internet access as illustrated in Figure 1-13.

Figure
1-13

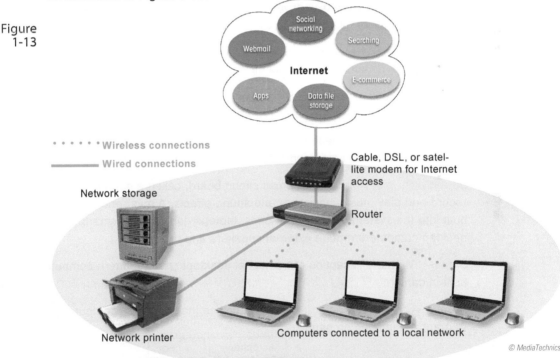

© MediaTechnics

The Internet is a source for a vast array of information, from Wikipedia to the iTunes Store. The process of copying files from a network server to your own computer is referred to as **downloading**. You might download music or movie files from iTunes, for example, so that you can store them on your computer and play them at any time. The process of copying files to a network is referred to as **uploading**. You can upload photo files to your Facebook page, for example, when you want to show them to your friends.

Today, most digital devices include circuitry and software to access networks. This capability is included in some printers and digital cameras, as well as in desktop computers, laptops, tablets, and smartphones. Desktop computers also typically include the necessary hardware and software for connecting to wired networks. You'll learn more details about networks in later chapters.

FAQ What are the components of a personal computer system?

The term **personal computer system** usually refers to a desktop or portable computer and all the input, output, and storage devices connected to it. A typical personal computer system (Figure 1-14) includes the following equipment:

- **System unit.** The system unit is the component that holds the computer's circuit boards, CPU, power supply, memory, and storage devices. Depending on the computer design, the system unit might also include other devices, such as a keyboard and speakers.

- **Display device.** Display devices, also referred to as monitors and screens, can be standalone units or incorporated into the system unit of a computer configured as an all-in-one, laptop, tablet, or smartphone.

- **Keyboard.** Desktop and laptop computers are equipped with a keyboard as the primary input device.

- **Mouse/touchpad.** A mouse is an input device designed to manipulate on-screen graphical objects and controls. A touchpad performs the same functions as a mouse.

- **Storage devices.** Hard disk drives, CD/DVD drives, and solid state drives are the most popular storage devices for personal computers.

- **Connection ports.** Most computers include sockets called ports into which you can plug the cables for components such as mice, keyboards, and external storage devices.

- **USB ports.** Sockets called USB ports on the system unit make it easy to plug in various devices, such as external hard disk drives and USB flash drives.

- **Memory card slots.** These slots can be used to transfer data from memory cards that contain data from cameras and other digital devices.

- **Sound card and speakers.** A small circuit board, called a sound card, is required to record and play music, narration, and sound effects. A microphone and speakers are built into the system units of all-in-ones, laptops, tablets, and smartphones. Traditional desktop computers require external speakers and mics.

- **Camera.** With the exception of traditional desktops, most modern computers include a built-in camera.

- **Printer.** A computer printer is an output device that produces computer-generated text or graphical images on paper.

Figure 1-14

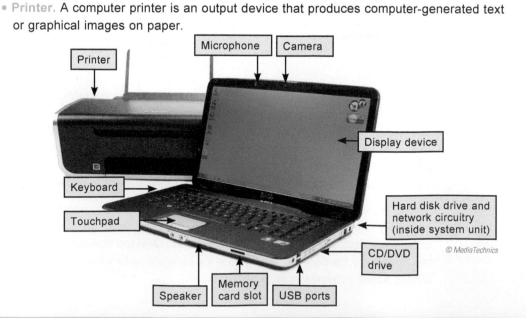

© MediaTechnics

FAQ What's inside the system unit?

The system unit contains storage devices, a power supply, and the computer's main circuit board, called a **motherboard**, system board, or mainboard. This circuit board houses all essential chips and provides connecting circuitry between them.

The terms "computer chip," "microchip," and "chip" originated as technical jargon for integrated circuits. An **integrated circuit** is a super-thin slice of semiconducting material packed with microscopic circuit elements, such as wires, transistors, capacitors, logic gates, and resistors.

An integrated circuit is usually encapsulated in a small, black plastic case that provides a series of metal connectors. These connectors plug into special chip sockets in the motherboard and other circuit boards. Multiple chips can be incorporated onto small circuit boards called expansion cards and memory modules, which slide easily into slots on the motherboard.

A **microprocessor** (sometimes simply referred to as a processor) is an integrated circuit designed to process instructions. Although a microprocessor is sometimes mistakenly referred to as "a computer on a chip," it can be more accurately described as "a CPU on a chip" because it contains—on a single chip—circuitry that performs essentially the same tasks as the CPU of a classic mainframe computer.

Figure 1-15 shows the motherboard, chips, and other components housed within a typical desktop computer system unit.

PLAYIT!

Figure
1-15

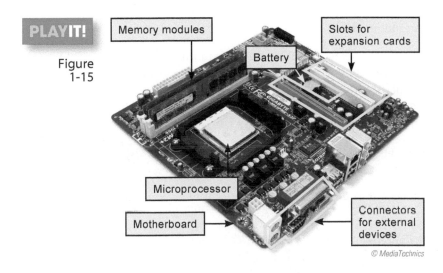

Memory modules

Slots for expansion cards

Battery

Microprocessor

Motherboard

Connectors for external devices

© MediaTechnics

FAQ How do computer circuits manipulate data?

Most computers are electronic, digital devices. A **digital device** works with discrete—distinct and separate—data, such as the digits 1 and 0. In contrast, an **analog device** works with continuous data. For example, a traditional light switch has two discrete states—on and off—so it is a digital device. In contrast, a dimmer switch has a rotating dial that controls a continuous range of brightness. It is, therefore, an analog device.

Most computers use the simplest type of digital technology—their circuits have only two possible states. For convenience, let's say that one of those states is "on" and the other state is "off." When discussing these states, we usually indicate the "on" state with 1 and the "off" state with 0. So the sequence "on" "on" "off" "off" would be written as 1100. These 1s and 0s are referred to as binary digits. This term has been shortened to **bit** (*bi*nary dig*it*). Computers use sequences of bits to digitally represent numbers, letters, punctuation marks, music, pictures, and videos.

The binary number system has only two digits: 0 and 1. No numeral like 2 exists in this system, so the number "2" is represented in binary as "10" (pronounced "one zero"). The important point to understand is that the binary number system allows computers to represent virtually any number simply by using 0s and 1s, which conveniently translate into electrical "on" and "off" signals. Using binary arithmetic, a computer can perform calculations.

Computers employ several types of codes to represent character data. **ASCII** (American Standard Code for Information Interchange, pronounced "ASK ee") requires only seven bits for each character. For example, the ASCII code for an uppercase "A" is 1000001. ASCII provides codes for 128 characters, including uppercase letters, lowercase letters, punctuation symbols, and numerals.

As shown in Figure 1-16, a superset of ASCII, called **Extended ASCII**, uses eight bits to represent each character. **Unicode** (pronounced "YOU ni code") uses 16 bits and provides codes for 65,000 characters—a real bonus for representing the alphabets of multiple languages. For example, Unicode represents an uppercase "A" in the Russian Cyrillic alphabet as 0000010000010000.

Figure
1-16

0	00110000	C	01000011	V	01010110	i	01101001
1	00110001	D	01000100	W	01010111	j	01101010
2	00110010	E	01000101	X	01011000	k	01101011
3	00110011	F	01000110	Y	01011001	l	01101100
4	00110100	G	01000111	Z	01011010	m	01101101
5	00110101	H	01001000	[	01011011	n	01101110
6	00110110	I	01001001	\	01011100	o	01101111
7	00110111	J	01001010	]	01011101	p	01110000
8	00111000	K	01001011	^	01011110	q	01110001
9	00111001	L	01001100	_	01011111	r	01110010
:	00111010	M	01001101	`	01100000	s	01110011
;	00111011	N	01001110	a	01100001	t	01110100
<	00111100	O	01001111	b	01100010	u	01110101
=	00111101	P	01010000	c	01100011	v	01110110
>	00111110	Q	01010001	d	01100100	w	01110111
?	00111111	R	01010010	e	01100101	x	01111000
@	01000000	S	01010011	f	01100110	y	01111001
A	01000001	T	01010100	g	01100111	z	01111010
B	01000010	U	01010101	h	01101000		

FAQ What factors affect computer speed, power, and compatibility?

Computers have three major components: a microprocessor, memory, and storage. In a nutshell, a computer keeps programs and data in storage when they are not immediately needed. When you start a program, it is moved from a storage device into memory.

The microprocessor then fetches a program instruction from memory and begins to execute it. If the instruction requires data, the computer fetches it from storage, loads it into memory, and then transfers it to the microprocessor. Results from processing the data are sent back to memory. From there, the results can be stored or output to a printer or screen (Figure 1-17).

Figure 1-17

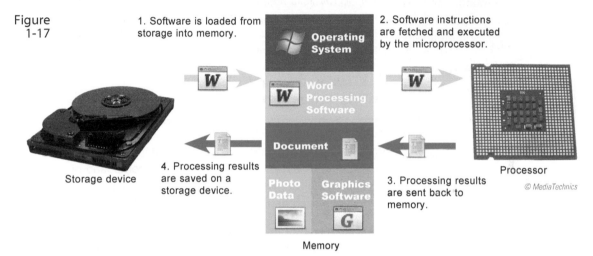

1. Software is loaded from storage into memory.

2. Software instructions are fetched and executed by the microprocessor.

4. Processing results are saved on a storage device.

Storage device

3. Processing results are sent back to memory.

Processor

© MediaTechnics

Memory

Processing speed and efficiency can be affected by the following factors:

- **Microprocessor type and speed.** Faster processors are able to execute more instructions and manipulate more data than slower processors.

- **Memory capacity.** Transferring data from disk to memory is slower than transferring data from memory to the processor. More memory capacity means your computer can load in lots of program instructions and data while other processing occurs. Once instructions and data are loaded into memory, the microprocessor doesn't have to wait for their arrival from a slow storage device.

- **Storage transfer speed and organization.** The faster a disk drive or other storage device transfers data to memory, the faster the data is available for processing. Also, data can be accessed quickly if it is well organized. As explained in a later chapter, running a defragmentation program optimizes disk performance.

- **Display capability and video memory.** When data is output to a display device, your computer has to draw every dot on the screen. As the image changes, the screen image is redrawn. When this process happens quickly, the screen appears crisp and steady. The data used to form the screen image is stored in special video memory. Your screen gives the best performance for videos and fast-action computer games when a large amount of video memory is supplied by the video circuitry.

- **Network and modem connection speed.** When you request data from a network, your computer cannot process the data until it arrives. A slow network connection makes your computer seem to operate slowly when dealing with transmitted data.

• What factors affect computer speed, power, and compatibility? (continued)

Figure
1-18 Computer ads, like the one in Figure 1-18, include several specifications for computer speed and capacity. Understanding a few key concepts about bits and bytes can help you use those specifications to compare computers before making a purchasing decision.

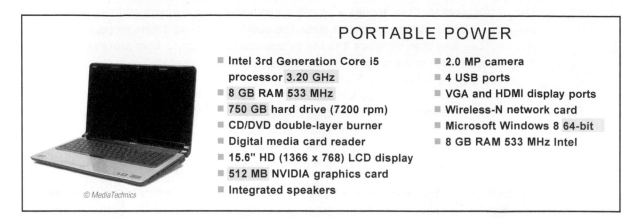

PORTABLE POWER

- Intel 3rd Generation Core i5 processor 3.20 GHz
- 8 GB RAM 533 MHz
- 750 GB hard drive (7200 rpm)
- CD/DVD double-layer burner
- Digital media card reader
- 15.6" HD (1366 x 768) LCD display
- 512 MB NVIDIA graphics card
- Integrated speakers

- 2.0 MP camera
- 4 USB ports
- VGA and HDMI display ports
- Wireless-N network card
- Microsoft Windows 8 64-bit
- 8 GB RAM 533 MHz Intel

© MediaTechnics

Even though the word "bit" is an abbreviation for "binary digit," it can be further abbreviated as a lowercase "b." A **byte**, on the other hand, is composed of eight bits and it is abbreviated as an uppercase "B." These abbreviations combine with prefixes such as "kilo" to produce specifications such as KB (kilobyte) and Kb (kilobit).

In common usage, "kilo," abbreviated as "K," means 1,000. In the world of computers, however, "kilo" means 1,024. A kilobit (abbreviated Kb or Kbit) is 1,024 bits. A kilobyte (abbreviated KB or Kbyte) is 1,024 bytes. Kilobytes are often used when referring to the size of small computer files.

The prefix "mega" means a million, or in the context of bits and bytes, precisely 1,048,576. A megabit (Mb or Mbit) is 1,048,576 bits. A megabyte (MB or MByte) is 1,048,576 bytes. Megabits are often used when referring to the speed of data transmission over a computer network connection. Megabytes are also used when referring to the size of medium to large computer files, CD capacity, or video card memory capacity.

The prefix "giga" refers to a billion, or precisely 1,073,741,824. As you might expect, a gigabit (Gb or Gbit) is approximately 1 billion bits. A gigabyte (GB or GByte) is 1 billion bytes. Gigabytes are typically used to refer to RAM, DVD, and hard disk capacity.

Computers—especially mainframes and supercomputers—sometimes work with huge amounts of data, and so terms such as "tera" (trillion), "peta" (quadrillion), and "exa" (quintillion) are also handy. Figure 1-19 summarizes the terms commonly used to quantify computer data.

Figure
1-19

Bit	1 binary digit	Megabit	1,048,576 bits	Terabyte	1 trillion bytes
Byte	8 bits	Megabyte	1,048,576 bytes	Petabyte	1 quadrillion bytes
Kilobit	1,024 bits	Gigabit	1 billion bits	Exabyte	1 quintillion bytes
Kilobyte	1,024 bytes	Gigabyte	1 billion bytes		

FAQ What's important about microprocessors?

The microprocessor is the most important, and usually the most expensive, component of a computer. Manufactured by several companies such as Intel, AMD, Motorola, and IBM, today's microprocessors are used in a variety of devices. Some microprocessors perform general computing tasks in personal computers, servers, mainframes, and supercomputers. Other microprocessors are built into non-computer machinery such as automobiles, appliances, and industrial equipment. These **embedded microprocessors** are designed for specialized tasks, such as monitoring the performance of automobile engines, controlling washing machine spin cycles, or running assembly-line robots.

The miniaturized circuitry in a microprocessor is grouped into important functional areas, such as the ALU and the control unit. The **ALU** (arithmetic logic unit) performs arithmetic operations, such as addition and subtraction. It also performs logical operations, such as comparing two numbers to see if they are the same. The **control unit** directs microprocessor tasks. The ALU uses **registers** to hold data that is being processed.

For a microprocessor analogy, consider the equipment and procedures you use to whip up a batch of brownies. Registers hold data just as a mixing bowl holds ingredients for a batch of brownies. The microprocessor's control unit fetches each instruction, just as you would get each ingredient out of a cupboard or the refrigerator. The computer loads data into the ALU's registers, just as you would add all the ingredients to the mixing bowl. Finally, the control unit gives the ALU the green light to begin processing, just as you would flip the switch on your electric mixer to begin blending the brownie ingredients.

Microprocessor speed is governed by an internal clock. During each clock cycle, the microprocessor executes instructions. All other factors being equal, the faster the clock speed, the more instructions your microprocessor can carry out in each second.

Processor speed used to be measured in megahertz (MHz), but today's processors operate at gigahertz (GHz) speeds. Hertz is a measurement of frequency used to quantify cycles for sound waves and other state changes. One hertz is one cycle per second. One megahertz is 1 million cycles per second. One gigahertz is 1 billion cycles per second. The original IBM PC, introduced in 1981, operated at 4.77 MHz. Today's computers with GHz speeds are almost 1,000 times faster.

Microprocessors are also rated by word size. Many of today's computers process a 32-bit word—a chunk of data up to 32 bits long. 64-bit computers are also popular. By handling more data in each clock cycle, these computers are faster than their 32-bit counterparts. Intel's powerful Core i7 shown in Figure 1-20 is a 64-bit processor.

Figure
1-20

Courtesy of Intel Corporation

FAQ What's important about computer memory?

All computers, from the largest supercomputer to the smallest smartphone, contain one or more types of memory circuitry that's directly connected to the motherboard. Memory plays one of two major roles: It can temporarily hold data that is scheduled to be processed, or it can permanently hold basic operating instructions that get a device powered up and running. Two major types of memory are RAM and ROM.

Figure
1-21

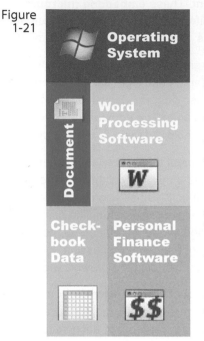

RAM (random access memory) is a temporary holding area for data, application program instructions, and the operating system. It is the "waiting room" for the computer's processor, where program instructions, raw data, and the results of processing are stored before and after processing. Figure 1-21 illustrates the contents of RAM while your computer is on and running application software.

When you start a program, it is loaded from disk into RAM. The program remains in RAM until you close it, which releases the RAM space it used.

RAM also holds data. For example, when using personal finance software to balance your checkbook, you enter raw data for check amounts. This data is held in RAM. The personal finance software sends the instructions for processing this data to RAM. The processor uses these instructions to calculate your checkbook balance and sends the results back to RAM. From RAM, your checkbook balance can be stored on disk, displayed, or printed.

RAM also stores the data used to display an image on the screen. Complex and quickly changing images, such as those generated by realistic 3D games and videos, require significant RAM capacity.

In addition to data and application software instructions, RAM also holds operating system instructions that control the basic functions of a computer system. These instructions are loaded into RAM every time you start your computer, and they remain there until you turn off your computer.

Unlike disk storage, most RAM is **volatile**, which means it requires electrical power to hold data. This factor is especially significant for desktop computers, which depend on power from a wall outlet. When the computer is turned off or the power goes out, all data stored in RAM instantly and permanently disappears. You can understand why it is important to frequently save your data in a more permanent storage area, such as the hard disk, as you work. The process of saving data copies it from RAM to a storage device.

Figure
1-22

RAM for a desktop computer

In a desktop or laptop computer, RAM is usually composed of several chips or small circuit boards that plug into the motherboard within the computer's system unit (Figure 1-22). RAM capacity is measured in megabytes or gigabytes. Today's computers typically feature between 512 MB and 8 GB of RAM. Most desktop computers and some laptops can be upgraded to add RAM. Applications that require lots of RAM to operate at peak efficiency include video editing, realistic gaming, and desktop publishing.

• What's important about computer memory? (continued)

In addition to RAM, most computers also contain **ROM** (read-only memory)—a type of memory circuitry that holds the computer's startup routine. Whereas RAM is temporary and volatile, ROM is more permanent and non-volatile. ROM circuitry holds instructions that remain in place even when the computer power is turned off.

Some ROM contains permanently hardwired instructions, similar to the square root and cosine functions built into a handheld calculator. This type of ROM contains instructions called the **ROM BIOS** (basic input/output system) that tell the computer how to access the hard disk, find the operating system, and load it into RAM.

ROM BIOS is important because when you turn on your computer, the microprocessor receives electrical power and is ready to begin executing instructions. As a result of the power being off, however, RAM is empty and doesn't contain any instructions for the microprocessor to execute. Now ROM plays its part. When ROM receives power, its ROM BIOS instructions are activated and they load the operating system into RAM. This startup sequence is referred to as the **boot process**. After the operating system is loaded, the computer can accept input, display output, run software, and access your data.

Today, the ROM in most computers can be reprogrammed so the instructions it contains can be changed. This capability accounts for the term "firmware" that is sometimes used to refer to ROM. In contrast to software that is stored on external devices, **firmware** is a set of instructions held semi-permanently in specialized ROM chips on the motherboard.

Figure 1-23

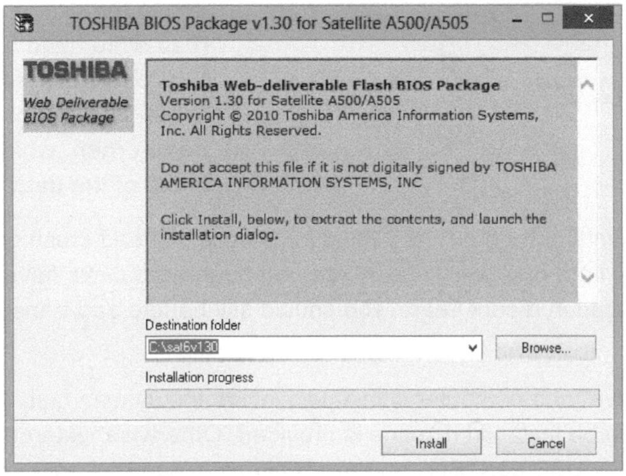

Source: Toshiba America, Inc.

The process of changing firmware is commonly called flashing. You may be familiar with the term and the process if you've ever flashed your smartphone or tablet to update to a new version of the operating system. The process is similar to updating the ROM BIOS on your desktop or laptop computer (Figure 1-23). Updates to the BIOS can correct hardware problems and compatibility problems with external devices.

The flash update process must be completed without interruption because a partial BIOS can render a device inoperable. When updating firmware, consider the following precautions:

- **Back up.** Be sure to back up your device before you begin the firmware update.

- **Plug in.** For battery-operated devices, such as laptops, tablets, and smartphones, connect the device to a power source to ensure continuous availability of power throughout the flashing process.

- **Do not disturb.** Do not interrupt the process by using the device or turning it off before the update is complete.

FAQ Why do computers use multiple storage devices?

The perfect storage device would be inexpensive, high-capacity, portable, and virtually indestructible. Unfortunately, such a device does not exist today. To cover everyone's storage needs, computers typically feature multiple storage devices, such as hard disk drives, DVD drives, and USB flash drives. Each one has advantages and disadvantages that make it useful for some tasks, but not appropriate for other tasks.

A **hard disk drive** is the main storage device in most desktop computers and many laptops. A hard disk provides economical, high-capacity storage—up to 2 terabytes. It also provides fast access to files. In computer ads, hard disk capacity is specified in gigabytes (GB), and its speed is measured in milliseconds (ms) or revolutions per minute (RPM). Higher GB numbers mean more capacity. Lower ms numbers mean faster speeds. Higher RPMs mean faster speeds.

PLAYIT!

Figure
1-24

A hard disk drive often contains more than one hard disk platter for data storage.

Read-write heads move in and out from the center of the disk to locate data.

© MediaTechnics

Hard disks are not the most durable type of storage. They use **magnetic storage technology** in which microscopic particles are magnetized to represent 0s and 1s. Hard disk read-write heads, shown in Figure 1-24, hover a microscopic distance above the disk surface. If a read-write head runs into a dust particle or some other contaminant, it can cause a **head crash**, which damages some of the data on the disk.

To eliminate contaminants, a hard disk is sealed in its case. A head crash can also be triggered by jarring the hard disk while it is in use. Although hard disks have become considerably more rugged in recent years, you should still handle and transport them with care.

The main hard disk drive for a computer is installed inside the system unit. Additional internal hard drives can be installed if space is provided. Otherwise, external hard drives can be connected to any USB port. Because external drives can be easily removed and stored in a safe place, they work well for holding backups of hard disk data.

Most computers include an **optical drive** that uses a small laser light to read data stored on plastic-coated CDs, DVDs, or Blu-ray discs. Figure 1-25 illustrates how these drives work.

Figure
1-25

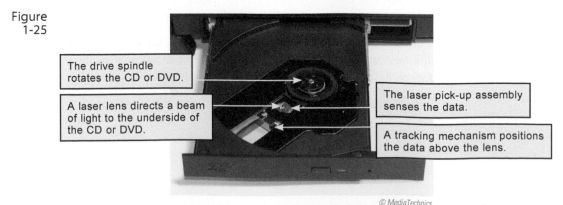

The drive spindle rotates the CD or DVD.

A laser lens directs a beam of light to the underside of the CD or DVD.

The laser pick-up assembly senses the data.

A tracking mechanism positions the data above the lens.

© MediaTechnics

•Why do computers use multiple storage devices? (continued)

A **CD** (compact disc) provides 650–700 MB of storage space for computer data. A **DVD** (digital video disc or digital versatile disc) is a variation of CD technology with a capacity of 4.7 GB. Storage capacity can be doubled if the DVD drive and DVD medium support dual-layer technology. A **Blu-ray disc** (BD) is a storage medium with 25 GB capacity in a single layer or 50 GB in dual layers. CDs, DVDs, and BDs are all a similar physical size, so you have to examine the labels to identify them (Figure 1-26).

Figure
1-26

CD   DVD   BD

© MediaTechnics

CDs, DVDs, and BDs are classified as removable storage technologies because they can be easily removed from the drive and transported to another device. This characteristic makes them handy for backing up or sharing data files, music, and movies.

CDs, DVDs, and BDs are durable because their **optical storage technology** essentially etches data onto the disc surface. The process of creating optical discs is sometimes referred to as "burning" and drives are referred to as "burners." Optical discs have a much higher tolerance for temperature fluctuations than hard disks. They are unaffected by magnetic fields. Dust and dirt can be cleaned off using a soft cloth. Scratches pose the biggest threat to the data stored on optical discs, so they should be stored in a case or jacket. Optical discs come in several varieties:

- Read-only (ROM) versions of CDs, DVDs, and BDs contain permanent data stored on the disc during the manufacturing process. Data on CD-ROMs, for example, cannot be changed or deleted. These discs are typically used to distribute software and movies.

- Recordable (R) discs contain a layer of color dye sandwiched beneath the clear plastic disc surfaces. A writable drive can store data on CD-R, DVD-R, and BD-R discs by changing the dye color. The change in the dye is permanent, so data cannot be modified after it has been recorded.

- Rewritable (RW or RE) discs contain a crystal structure on the disc surface. The crystal structure of CD-RW, DVD-RW, CD+RW, DVD+RW, and BD-RE discs can be changed many times, making it possible to record and modify data much like on a hard disk.

Optical drives are backward compatible, so DVD drives also handle CDs; Blu-ray drives handle CDs and DVDs. Although an optical drive is a fine addition to a computer system, it is not a good replacement for a hard disk drive because the process of accessing, saving, and modifying data on rewritable discs is relatively slow compared to the speed of hard disk access. A 24X DVD drive, for example, transfers data at 259 Mbps, compared to a hard disk drive's transfer rate of 2,560 Mbps.

Fewer new computers include optical drives, and their use seems to be declining as online storage, apps, music, movies, and downloads become more popular.

• Why do computers use multiple storage devices?
(continued)

Figure
1-27

© MediaTechnics

A **USB flash drive** ("flash drive" for short) is a popular removable, portable storage device featuring a built-in connector that plugs directly into a computer's USB port. Nicknamed "jump drives" or "thumb drives," USB flash drives like the one in Figure 1-27 are about the size of a highlighter pen and so durable that you can literally carry them on your key ring.

Data can be written onto a flash drive without a bulky drive or burner; and with capacity that ranges up to 256 GB, flash drives store lots of data.

You can open, edit, delete, and run files stored on a USB flash drive just as though those files were stored on your computer's hard disk. USB flash drives use **solid state storage technology**, which provides fast access to data, and holds data even when not connected to a power source.

Solid state technology is also used for **solid state drives** (SSDs), which are essentially high-capacity flash drives installed inside a computer's system unit. Solid state drives are popular for thin laptops, tablets, and smartphones because they can take rough handling that would ruin a magnetic hard drive.

In addition to popular storage devices directly connected to your computer, data can also be stored on remote devices, such as network hard disk drives and virtual drives located on the Internet.

Network drives offer an alternative to storing files on devices connected to your personal computer, but the speed at which you can access data depends on the network connection speed. Files stored on network drives are easily accessible to others for collaborative work. Network storage offers a potentially safe place to store data backups in case your computer is damaged or stolen.

Online storage provides space for your files on a server that can be accessed over the Internet (Figure 1-28). Such storage is handy for files you want to back up, share, or access while you are out and about, but be cautious about storing sensitive personal information online unless you are confident of the site's ability to maintain security.

Figure
1-28

Online storage services offer a place to store backups and files you want to share with others.

https://skydrive.live.com/

File   Edit   View   Favorites   Tools   Help

Page ▾   Safety ▾   Tools ▾

SkyDrive | ∨   (+) Create ∨   (↑) Upload   Sarah Mae Smith

Search SkyDrive 🔎   Files   Sarah Mae's SkyDrive   Sort by: Name ∨

Files   ☐ Name ↑   Date modified   Sharing   Size
Recent docs   ☐ ▪ Documents   8/28/2012   –   0 bytes
Shared   ☐ ▪ DOG   10/20/1998   –   844 KB
                        ☐ ▪ Environmental Study   8/28/2012   –   18.2 KB
Groups   ☐ ▪ Spooky Savannah   8/24/2012   –   57.0 MB

PCs
LaptopPC

26.9 GB available   © 2013 Microsoft   Terms   Privacy   Developers   Report abuse   English (United States)

🔍 85%

Source: Microsoft Corporation

QuickCheck A

1. [_____] is circuitry on a computer motherboard that temporarily holds data waiting to be processed, stored, or output. [_____] is the area where data can be left on a permanent basis when it is not immediately needed for processing.

2. [_____] is the process of copying a file from a network or Internet server to your personal computer.

3. A(n) [_____] circuit is a super-thin slice of semiconducting material packed with microscopic circuit elements, such as wires, transistors, capacitors, logic gates, and resistors.

4. In the world of computers, [_____] is abbreviated MB.

5. Unlike disk storage and solid state storage, most RAM is [_____], which means it requires electrical power to hold data.

CHECKIT!

QuickCheck B

Examine each specification indicated. If the specification is correct, enter C in the corresponding box below. For incorrect specifications, enter the correct measurement, such as MB, GHz, and so on.

1. [____]

2. [____]

3. [____]

4. [____]

5. [____]

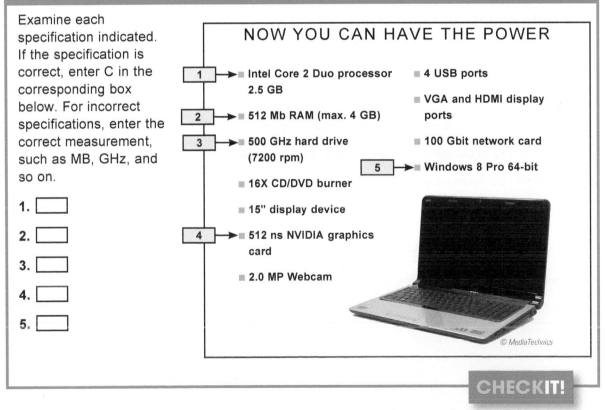

NOW YOU CAN HAVE THE POWER

1 → ■ Intel Core 2 Duo processor 2.5 GB

2 → ■ 512 Mb RAM (max. 4 GB)

3 → ■ 500 GHz hard drive (7200 rpm)

■ 16X CD/DVD burner

■ 15" display device

4 → ■ 512 ns NVIDIA graphics card

■ 2.0 MP Webcam

■ 4 USB ports

■ VGA and HDMI display ports

■ 100 Gbit network card

5 → ■ Windows 8 Pro 64-bit

© MediaTechnics

CHECKIT!

CHAPTER

2

Peripheral Devices

What's Inside and on the CD?

This chapter provides an overview of the most popular peripheral devices for personal computers. It begins with standard input devices—your computer's keyboard and mouse—and then takes a look at other popular peripherals, such as displays, printers, cameras, and audio equipment.

Peripheral devices can be connected to a computer system in a variety of ways. You'll find out which technologies provide the easiest connections.

The chapter winds up with an FAQ about keeping electronic equipment in good working order and some tips for troubleshooting equipment problems.

● **FAQs:**

FAQ What is a peripheral device?

The term **peripheral device** refers to any input, output, or storage equipment that might be added to a computer system to enhance its functionality. Because these devices handle input and output, they are sometimes called I/O devices or Input/Output devices. Keyboards, mice, display devices, and printers are standard peripherals for personal computers. Specialized peripheral devices include home monitoring systems, digitizing tablets, scanners, and game controllers. Smartphone peripherals include earbuds, credit card scanners, blood glucose meters, and roll-up keyboards.

Peripheral devices connect to computers, but computers can function without them. Although a microphone, speaker, camera, and touchpad are housed in the case of your laptop computer, the computer can function without them and so they are considered peripherals.

Most peripheral devices handle input, output, or storage; but a few devices, such as touchscreens handle both input and output. The table in Figure 2-1 summarizes the input, output, and storage capabilities of popular computer peripherals. Review the peripherals you commonly use and make sure you can classify them as input, output, or storage devices.

Figure 2-1

Device	Input	Output	Storage
Keyboard	●		
Mouse	●		
Touchpad	●		
Touchscreen	●	●	
Monitor		●	
Projector		●	
Printer		●	
Scanner	●		
Fax	●	●	
Camera	●		
Plotter		●	
Microphone	●		
Speakers		●	
Headphones		●	
Earbuds		●	
USB flash drive			●
Hard drive			●
CD/DVD drive			●
External hard drive			●
Credit card scanner	●		
Graphics tablet	●		

FAQ What's special about computer keyboards?

Most personal computer systems include a keyboard for entering data and issuing commands. The keyboard is the most important input device on desktop and laptop computers. You can also find tiny keyboards on some handheld devices, and many devices with a touch-sensitive screen can display a **virtual keyboard** (Figure 2-2).

Figure
2-2

© MediaTechnics

The design of most computer keyboards is based on the typewriter's QWERTY layout. This unusual arrangement of keys was not designed to maximize typing speed, but to keep a typewriter's mechanical keys from jamming. Computers inherited this layout because of its familiarity to millions of typists.

In addition to basic typing keys (Figure 2-3), computer keyboards can include an **editing keypad** with arrow keys to efficiently move the screen-based insertion point. They also include a collection of **function keys** designed for computer-specific tasks, such as putting the computer into sleep mode, adjusting screen brightness, and using a second display screen. Many computer keyboards also include a calculator-style **numeric keypad**.

PLAY**IT!**

Figure
2-3

Function keys

Windows
key

Arrow keys   Numeric keypad

© MediaTechnics

Computer keyboards include several special keys designed for the sometimes complex input tasks required when working with computers. The **Windows key** is essential for computers that run Windows 8. It calls up the Start screen used to select software applications and files. Other special keys include Esc, Ctrl, and Alt.

The **Esc (escape) key** is an all-purpose "go back" or undo key that hides menus and gets you out of various task modes. The **Ctrl (control) key** and **Alt (alternate) key** work in conjunction with other keys to invoke **keyboard shortcuts**. For example, holding down the Ctrl key along with the X key typically cuts or deletes something in the work area.

Keyboard shortcuts are generally listed on an application's command menus and in online help. The notation for keyboard shortcuts varies. The delete shortcut can be written as Ctrl X, Ctrl+X, or Ctrl-X, but there is no need to press the + or - keys.

FAQ What are the options for pointing devices?

A **pointing device** allows you to manipulate an on-screen pointer ↖ and other screen-based graphical controls. Popular pointing devices for personal computers include mice, touchpads, game controllers, touchscreens, and graphics tablets.

A standard desktop computer includes a **mouse** as its primary pointing device. Many computer owners also add a mouse to their laptop computers. A mouse is used to move an on-screen pointer, select various screen elements by clicking them, and move screen elements by dragging them—a process carried out by holding down one of the mouse buttons while moving the mouse at the same time.

Mice are available in wired and wireless varieties. The advantage of a wireless mouse is the lack of a cord, which can get in your way. Wired mice have slightly better response times, however, and are preferred for computer gaming where a split second can mean the difference between life and death for an on-screen character who is under attack.

Most mice use optical technology. An onboard chip emits a light beam that is tracked by an optical sensor as it bounces off the surface of a desk, clipboard, or mouse pad (Figure 2-4). Positioning data supplied by the mouse is processed by the computer so that movements of the on-screen pointer correspond to movements of the mouse.

Figure 2-4

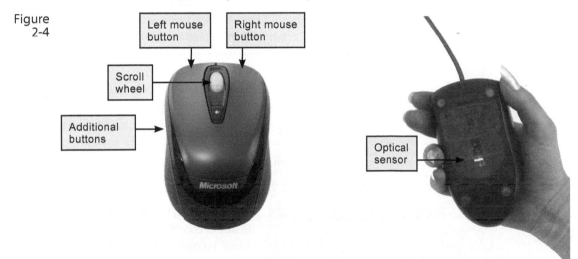

A **trackball** (left) looks like a mechanical mouse turned upside down. You use your fingers, thumb, or palm to roll the ball and move the pointer. Onboard buttons work just like mouse buttons for clicking and double-clicking on-screen objects. Trackballs perform the same input functions as a mouse, but require a different set of muscles for their use. Switching periodically between a mouse and a trackball can prevent some stress injuries.

A **game controller** (left) looks like a small version of a car's stick shift. Moving the stick provides input to on-screen objects, such as a pointer or a character in a computer game. Game controllers (also called joysticks) can include several sticks and buttons for arcade-like control when playing computer games. Game controllers can also be adapted for use by individuals who have difficulty using a keyboard.

• What are the options for pointing devices? (continued)

A **touchpad** (also called a trackpad) is a touch-sensitive surface on which you can tap and slide your fingers to manipulate the pointer, menus, and other objects on the screen. Touchpads use capacitance technology that senses the touch and movement of a virtual ground, such as a finger. Multi-touch touchpads can sense more than one point of contact, which increases input options for multiple finger swipes and taps. Swipes, taps, and other movements on a touchpad are called **gestures** (Figure 2-5).

Figure 2-5

  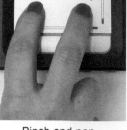 

| Tap | Rotate | Pinch and pan | Swipe |

Tablet computers, smartphones, retail store self-checkouts, and information kiosks collect input from a **touchscreen**, which overlays a display screen. The most commonly used touchscreen technology is a transparent panel coated with a thin layer of electrically conductive material that senses a change in the electrical current when touched. Processing technology can interpret a single touch or more complex input such as handwriting.

PLAYIT!

Figure 2-6

The coordinates for a touch event are processed in essentially the same way as on a touchpad. For example, if you touch the screen of your tablet computer at the location of a tile labeled Google, the area you touch generates coordinates and sends them to the processor. The processor compares the coordinates to the image displayed on the screen to find out what is at the coordinates, and then responds—in this case, by opening your list of contacts.

Most touchscreens respond to gestures from a stylus as well as from fingers. A **stylus** is a pen-shaped object with a tapered end that can be used for precise input and manipulation of small objects on the screen. Using a stylus also avoids the smudgy screen syndrome associated with touch devices.

Another gesture-based device is a **graphics tablet** (right), which features a pressure-sensitive surface and stylus for free-hand drawing. Pressing hard with the stylus creates a thick, dark line; light pressure reduces the line width. Some graphics tablets also support finger gestures just like a touchpad. Graphics tablets are peripheral devices; although they are called "tablets," they are not tablet computers.

FAQ What are the most popular display technologies?

Computer display devices for desktop computers are standalone units (sometimes called monitors). Laptops, tablets, and smartphones use integrated flat-panel screens. Another display option is a projection device that links to a computer to project images on a wall screen or other flat surface (Figure 2-7). Two technologies are commonly used for computer display devices: LCD and DLP.

Figure 2-7

LCD (liquid crystal display) technology produces on-screen images by manipulating light within a layer of liquid crystal cells. Devices that use LCD technology are compact in size and lightweight. The advantages of LCD technology include display clarity, low radiation emission, portability, and energy efficiency. LCD technology is used for computer monitors, integrated screens, and some projection devices.

DLP (digital light processing) technology creates an image by bouncing light off of microscopically small mirrors arranged on a semiconductor chip. Each mirror corresponds to a small dot of color on the projected image. DLP technology is used for most modern projection devices, for rear-projection televisions, and for digital billboards that change images every few seconds.

All © MediaTechnics

The performance of a display device is a factor of screen size, dot pitch, response time, color depth, brightness, resolution, and aspect ratio. When selecting a display device, it is important to keep these factors in mind:

- **Screen size** is the measurement in inches from one corner of the screen diagonally across to the opposite corner. Screen sizes for standalone displays range from 13" to 30". Laptop screens are typically 15" to 17". Tablet screens are usually 9" to 10".

- **Dot pitch** (or pixel pitch) is a measure of image clarity. Technically, dot pitch is the distance in millimeters between like-colored dots of light that form an image. A dot pitch between .28 mm and .22 mm is typical for today's display devices. The smaller the dot pitch, the crisper the image.

- **Response time** is the length of time required for a pixel to change color to keep pace with the image being displayed on the screen. For example, when playing an action game, the screen image is constantly changing. A display device with good response time will maintain a crisp image without the appearance of smearing or ghosting. Response time is measured in milliseconds, with lower numbers indicating better response times. Typical response times vary from 6 ms to 2 ms.

- **Color depth** (or bit depth) is the number of colors a device can display. Most display devices have the capability to display millions of colors. When set at 24-bit color depth (sometimes called True Color), your Windows computer can display more than 16 million colors and produce what are considered photographic-quality images.

• What are the most popular display technologies? (continued)

- **Luminance** is a measure of screen brightness usually expressed in candelas per square meter (cd/m²), with higher numbers indicating a brighter display. Another measure of brightness is **contrast ratio**, which is the difference between the luminance of white and black pixels. You can adjust a display's brightness level; but if you plan to use your computer outdoors, make sure the screen has a good brightness rating and contrast ratio.

- **Screen resolution** is the number of horizontal and vertical pixels that a device displays on a screen. A **pixel** is a small dot of color—one of many picture elements that form an image on a screen or paper. The resolution for many early PC displays was referred to as VGA (Video Graphics Array). Today's 1080i and 1080p display devices typically have 1920 x 1080 resolution, which makes them compatible with widescreen HDTV standards.

- **Aspect ratio** is the relationship between the width and height of a displayed image. Computer displays originally had a 3:4 aspect ratio, but modern widescreen devices have a 16:9 aspect ratio.

Your computer's display system includes ports used to connect display devices, and graphics circuitry that generates signals for displaying images on the screen (Figure 2-8).

Figure 2-8

© MediaTechnics

VGA, HDMI, and DVI ports

Graphics card

Monitors and projectors connect to computers using VGA, DVI, or HDMI ports. You can use these ports to connect a second monitor to your tablet, laptop, or desktop computer.

Graphics circuitry comes in two forms: integrated graphics and a graphics card. **Integrated graphics** is a type of graphics circuitry that's built into a computer's motherboard and uses system RAM for graphics processing.

A **graphics card** (also called a graphics board or video card) typically contains a graphics processing unit and special video memory. A **graphics processing unit** (GPU) executes graphics commands, leaving the main processor free for other tasks. **Video memory** stores screen images as they are processed but before they are displayed. A fast GPU and lots of video memory are the keys to lightning-fast screen updating for fast action games, 3D modeling, and graphics-intensive desktop publishing.

FAQ What are the most popular printer technologies?

Printers are one of the most popular output devices available for personal computers. Multifunction printers not only produce printed output; they can perform the same functions as a photocopier and they can scan documents and photos. Some printers even function as fax machines. Today's best-selling printers typically use ink jet or laser technology.

An **ink jet printer** has a nozzle-like print head that sprays ink onto paper to form characters and graphics. The print head in a color ink jet printer consists of a series of nozzles, each with its own ink cartridge. Most ink jet printers use CMYK color, which

Figure 2-9

requires only cyan (blue), magenta (pink), yellow, and black inks to create a printout that appears to have thousands of colors. Alternatively, some printers use six ink colors to print midtone shades that create slightly more realistic photographic images.

Ink jet printers, such as the one in Figure 2-9, outsell all other types of printers because they are inexpensive and produce both color and black-and-white printouts. They work well for most home and small business applications. Small, portable ink jet printers meet the needs of many mobile computer owners. Ink jet technology also powers many photo printers, which are optimized to print high-quality images produced by digital cameras and scanners.

A **laser printer**, such as the one in Figure 2-10, uses the same technology as a photocopier to paint dots of light on a light-sensitive drum. Electrostatically charged ink is applied to the drum and then transferred to paper. Laser technology is more complex than ink jet technology, which accounts for the higher price of laser printers.

A basic laser printer produces only black-and-white printouts. Color laser printers are available, but are somewhat more costly than basic black-and-white models. Laser printers are often the choice for business printers, particularly for applications that produce a high volume of printed material.

PLAYIT!

Figure 2-10

© MediaTechnics

What are the most popular printer technologies? (continued)

When selecting a printer for your personal computer system, you should consider if its resolution, speed, duty cycle, operating costs , and other factors meet your printing needs.

Printer resolution. The quality or sharpness of printed images and text depends on the printer's resolution—the density of dots that create an image. Printer resolution is measured by the number of dots per linear inch, abbreviated as dpi. At normal reading distance, a resolution of about 900 dpi appears solid to the human eye; but a close examination reveals a dot pattern. If you want magazine-quality printouts, 900 dpi is sufficient resolution. If you are aiming for resolution similar to expensive coffee-table books, look for printer resolution of 2,400 dpi or higher.

Print speed. Printer speeds are measured either by pages per minute (ppm) or characters per second (cps). Color printouts typically take longer than black-and-white printouts. Pages that contain mostly text tend to print more rapidly than pages that contain graphics. Typical speeds for personal computer printers range from 6 to 30 pages of text per minute. A full-page 8.5" x 11" photo can take about a minute to print.

Duty cycle. In addition to printer speed, a printer's **duty cycle** determines how many pages a printer is able to churn out. Printer duty cycle is usually measured in pages per month. For example, a personal laser printer has a duty cycle of about 3,000 pages per month—that means roughly 100 pages per day.

Operating costs. The initial cost of a printer is only one of the expenses associated with printed output. Ink jet printers require frequent replacement of relatively expensive print heads. Laser printers require toner cartridge refills or replacements. When shopping for a printer, you can check online resources to determine how often you can expect to replace printer supplies and how much they are likely to cost.

Recycling. Ink and toner cartridges are expensive and you can save some money by refilling them yourself or taking them to an ink refilling station at a local office store. If cartridge and toner refills are not available, find out how you can responsibly recycle them.

Duplex printing. The ability of a printer to print on both sides of the paper is referred to as **duplex printing**. The main advantage of duplex printing is cost: You use half the amount of paper required for single-sided printing. Saving paper is also good for the environment.

Networkability. Some printers can be connected directly to a network rather than to a computer. Network circuitry adds to the cost of a printer but is worth considering if you don't want to leave one of the computers on your network running all the time.

FAQ How do computers work with digital cameras?

A **digital camera** is a device that captures still or moving images by recording them on a chip-based image sensor. Digital cameras are available as standalone devices in sizes designed to fit in a shirt pocket and range up to large and expensive movie cameras used in Hollywood productions. Miniature cameras can be embedded in pens and other objects in true James Bond style.

Small digital cameras are built into many computers. Just about every smartphone has one, as do laptops, tablets, and desktop all-in-one units. These cameras can be used for photos, but they are more often used for video conferencing and Skyping.

Built-in cameras can be controlled by software, such as Windows Camera, to take photos. After taking a photo, the software may give you options for storing, posting, or e-mailing the image file.

Built-in cameras have become the subject of controversy because they can be turned on surreptitiously without the computer owner's knowledge. As a precautionary measure, a sticky note can be positioned over the camera lens when it is not in use.

The lens of a film camera captures the light from an image onto a light sensitive roll of film, which is developed to produce a photographic print. In a digital camera, the lens focuses light from an object onto a small image sensor called a **CCD** (charge-coupled device). A CCD like the one in Figure 2-11 contains a grid of tiny light-sensitive diodes called **photosites**.

Figure 2-11

© MediaTechnics

The number of photosites depends on the size of the CCD. A one-half-inch square CCD can contain more than 500,000 photosites. Each photosite detects the brightness and color for its tiny piece of the image.

The more photosites used to capture an image, the higher its resolution, and the better the resulting picture. Cameras with larger CCDs produce higher quality images.

Camera manufacturers sometimes express the resolution of digital cameras as megapixels. A **megapixel** is 1 million pixels. A camera with a resolution of 1600 x 1200 has the capability of producing photos containing 1.9 megapixels (1600 multiplied by 1200). A camera with 3888 x 2592 resolution is technically 10.1 megapixels, but might be rounded off and called a 10 megapixel camera by its manufacturer.

Photos taken with a standalone camera are stored on solid state memory cards, which can be removed from the camera and inserted into a card reader that's built-in or attached to a computer's USB port (right). Cameras can also be cabled to computers to transfer photos from the memory card to a hard disk.

© MediaTechnics

FAQ What are the options for audio peripherals?

Computers are not silent devices. Even the very first personal computers had a built-in speaker that emitted beeps and dings to warn users of errors. Today's personal computers are equipped with a standard suite of audio equipment that includes speakers and a microphone. Audio In and Audio Out ports (Figure 2-12) are included for connecting an external microphone, speakers, headphones, and earbuds. Additional audio devices can be added by connecting them to a USB port or a smartphone's dock port used for recharging.

Figure 2-12

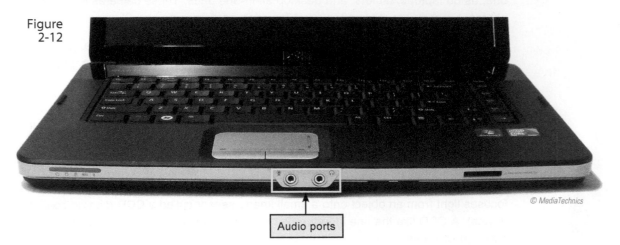

© MediaTechnics

Audio ports

A computer's ability to record and produce sound is handled by audio circuitry and software. Audio circuitry handles the conversion between the analog sounds that exist in the real world and the digital format in which sound is processed and stored by a computer. Audio software can be used to make recordings and edit them, play music, and control a computer with voice commands.

A **speech synthesizer** converts digital text into audio output. Many people are familiar with the synthesized voice that narrates weather reports on National Weather Service radio stations. Speech synthesizers are also an integral part of telephone directory assistance and other automated calling systems.

Speech synthesizers are used as adaptive devices on personal computers. They can read the text displayed in a word processor or on a Web page, making these computer services available to people with visual disabilities. For adaptive applications, speech synthesis has a great advantage over recorded audio files because the narration is generated on-the-fly and reflects exactly what appears on the screen. Windows includes an application called Narrator that reads the contents of the screen and names screen-based objects as the mouse pointer encounters them.

A computer uses a standard microphone to collect audio input. Some software applications include built-in **speech recognition**, which allows you to dictate commands and data using a microphone instead of a keyboard and mouse. Apple's Siri software accepts voice commands spoken into an iPhone or similar device. Voice Actions is a similar service available on Android phones.

Microphones are also handy for recording narrations designed to accompany Web sites and videos. You can even attach audio files to word processing documents, spreadsheets, and e-mail messages. Audio files tend to require lots of storage space, however, so you should refrain from recording long audio segments.

FAQ How do I connect peripheral devices to my computer?

All PCs have an internal expansion bus that provides a variety of ways to connect peripheral devices. An **expansion bus** is an electronic pathway that moves information between the microprocessor and RAM, and stretches to various ports and slots where data can be transferred to other electronic circuitry and devices. In many ways, an expansion bus is analogous to the transit system within an airport that transports people to different airline terminals where they can board flights.

The expansion bus leads from a computer's motherboard to connection points called **ports** that can be accessed outside the system unit. Standard expansion ports include USB, VGA, FireWire, and HDMI. When you install a peripheral device, you are basically creating a pathway for data to flow between the device and the computer. The channel that transmits data between these devices could be wired or wireless.

Today, **USB** (Universal Serial Bus) is the preferred way to connect peripheral devices. On most new computer models, USB ports are conveniently located on the front and sides of the system unit, so that peripherals can be easily connected and disconnected (Figure 2-13).

Figure
2-13

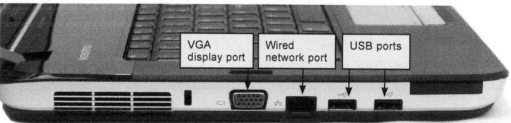

© MediaTechnics

If you want to connect more devices than the available number of USB ports, you can use USB hubs. A **USB hub** is an inexpensive device that turns one USB port into multiple ports. It also saves wear and tear on USB ports caused by repeatedly inserting and removing USB devices.

For devices such as printers and external hard disk drives that draw a fair amount of power, a **self-powered USB hub** plugs into an external power supply. When connecting low-power devices—such as a mouse, keyboard, or flash drive—you can use a **bus-powered hub** that draws all its power from the computer (Figure 2-14).

PLAY**IT!**

Figure
2-14

© MediaTechnics

• How do I connect peripheral devices to my computer? (continued)

Establishing a wireless connection between your computer and a peripheral device typically requires some type of transceiver on both devices. A **transceiver** transmits and receives signals. Those signals could be generated as **infrared** light, like those used on a television remote control. Signals could also be generated as radio waves by popular wireless technologies, such as Bluetooth and Wi-Fi, that you'll learn about in the Networks chapter.

Wireless peripheral devices have a built-in transceiver for a specific wireless technology. Your computer might have a matching built-in wireless transceiver. If not, you can usually connect a transceiver to one of your computer's USB ports.

In addition to a physical or wireless connection, some peripheral devices also require software called a **device driver** to establish communication with a computer. Device drivers are supplied on CDs by the device manufacturer or they can be downloaded from the manufacturer's Web site. If needed, directions for installing the device driver are supplied along with the device.

Windows includes built-in device drivers for many peripheral devices. This feature, sometimes called Plug and Play, makes it easy to connect devices without manually installing device drivers. These built-in device drivers are also referred to as in-OS drivers. When you connect a new peripheral device, Windows looks for an appropriate built-in driver; if one is not found, you'll be prompted to insert the driver disc supplied by the peripheral device manufacturer.

Device drivers work directly with a computer's operating system, and they work best when designed for the operating system installed in your computer. As operating systems are updated, some device drivers might stop working correctly and the device they control will malfunction. One of the first steps in troubleshooting a malfunctioning peripheral device is to access the manufacturer's Web site and look for a driver update. Updated driver downloads are usually available from the site's Support link (Figure 2-15).

Figure 2-15

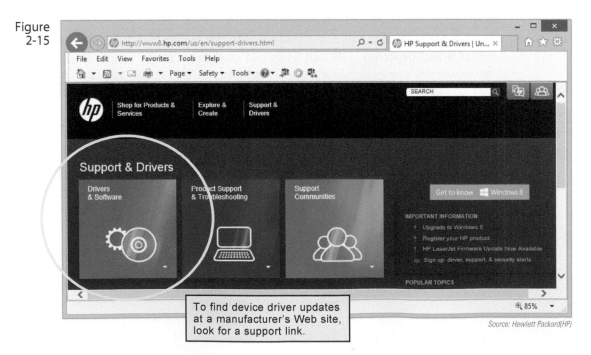

To find device driver updates at a manufacturer's Web site, look for a support link.

Source: Hewlett Packard(HP)

FAQ How do I keep computer and peripheral equipment in good working condition?

The data stored on your computer can be quite valuable. A malfunctioning computer or peripheral device might prevent you from accessing the data you need and the music, movies, and Facebook interactions that you enjoy.

Digital equipment is fairly durable, but even the tough Gorilla Glass on your smartphone screen can break if the device is dropped on a hard floor. Laptops are even more sensitive to breakage, and any device that contains a hard disk drive should be handled gently.

Environmental factors can damage computers. Extreme temperatures can damage circuitry. High humidity can corrode contacts and cables. Water leaks can short out circuits. Magnetic fields can erase data on disk drives. Dust, dirt, and air pollution can cause overheating and clog up mechanical parts.

Follow the manufacturer's instructions for the care and maintenance of all your digital gear. Printers might need periodic cleaning to prevent paper jams and clogged print heads. Routinely cleaning your mouse and keyboard can keep them working smoothly (Figure 2-16).

PLAYIT!

Figure 2-16

All © MediaTechnics

Digital equipment is vulnerable to power irregularities and outages. Before transporting a computer to another country that uses a different power system, check with the manufacturer for information on compatible power adapters.

At home, you should use a surge strip like the one at left to protect your electronic equipment from power spikes and surges that could overload circuits and cause permanent damage. A **surge strip** (also called a surge protector or surge suppressor) is a device that contains electrical outlets protected by circuitry that blocks surges. Some surge strips also have sockets for modem connections that prevent surges from traveling down telephone or cable lines and into your electronic equipment.

A big power surge can burn out a surge strip while it tries to protect your equipment. Some surge strips have an indicator light that warns you if the surge strip is no longer functioning properly. Check the manufacturer's documentation to determine if you should discard the depleted strip, reset it, or install a new fuse.

•How do I keep computer and peripheral equipment in good working condition? (continued)

A **UPS** (uninterruptible power supply) is a device that not only provides surge protection, but also furnishes desktop computers and network devices with battery backup power during a power outage.

If your desktop computer is connected to a UPS when a power outage occurs, the battery backup allows you to save what you're doing and properly shut down your computer. Depending on your system's configuration, a UPS with a high-performance battery might give you enough backup power to keep your computer up and running for several hours, allowing you to continue to work during the entire power outage.

Portable computers run on battery power and so the data you're working on is not immediately affected by a power outage. However, if you want to access your local area network or Internet connection, you might consider plugging your network devices and Internet modem into a UPS so that they continue to operate during an outage.

As shown in Figure 2-17, most UPSs have two types of sockets: One type offers battery backup plus surge protection, and the other offers only surge protection. The surge-only sockets are for printers, which use so much power that they can quickly drain the battery.

Figure
2-17

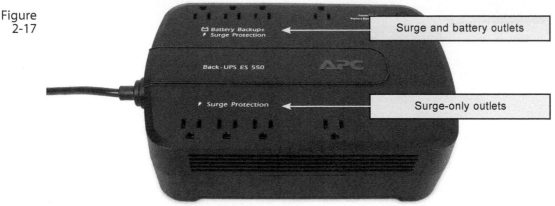

© MediaTechnics

High-performance processors, hard drives, graphics cards, and several other computer components generate a lot of heat. Overheating can shorten the lifespan of internal components and chips. Fans built into the system units of desktop and laptop computers help to keep their circuitry cool (Figure 2-18).

Figure
2-18

© MediaTechnics

Smartphones and tablets that have no fans should not be placed on hot surfaces. Make sure devices with fans are placed in an area where the fans are not blocked. Dust particles, dirt, and pet hair can collect on and around a computer's cooling fans and impede their performance. You should regularly use a can of compressed air or a vacuum cleaner hose to carefully clean out debris from the vents and fans.

FAQ How do I troubleshoot equipment problems?

Most computer owners can troubleshoot malfunctioning equipment and at least narrow down the source of the problem. Common problems include a computer that fails to power up, a "crashed" hard drive, newly installed hardware that doesn't work correctly, and a peripheral device that begins to behave erratically.

Let's start with the computer itself. There are several telltale signs that your computer is in trouble. Hardware problems can show up as unexpected restarts at random intervals. Some problems are intermittent and might seem to be resolved, only to come back when they are least convenient to deal with. The most obvious malfunction is failure to power up. A loud beep at startup time can also indicate a problem. If your computer's screen remains blank or error messages appear, you can correctly surmise that your computer might have a hardware problem (Figure 2-19).

Figure
2-19

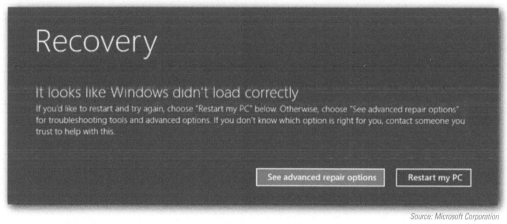

Source: Microsoft Corporation

From the Recovery screen, you can follow instructions to restart. If the problem is not hardware related, your computer will likely start up on the second try. If that does not happen, you may have to access the advanced repair options.

Most operating systems offer a **safe mode** designed for professional troubleshooting. When operating in this mode, your computer provides a limited version of the operating system that allows you to use your mouse, screen, and keyboard, but no other peripheral devices. Safe mode can be used to track down and uninstall programs or hardware that might be causing operational problems (Figure 2-20).

Figure
2-20

Source: Microsoft Corporation

● How do I troubleshoot equipment problems? (continued)

When peripheral devices malfunction, you have several tools available to uncover the problem. First, make sure that the device is properly connected to the computer and to a power supply. The next step in troubleshooting peripherals is to check for an updated device driver.

If the drivers are up to date, you can check your operating system for troubleshooting utilities. Windows includes troubleshooters for printers, recording devices, and networks (Figure 2-21).

Figure
2-21

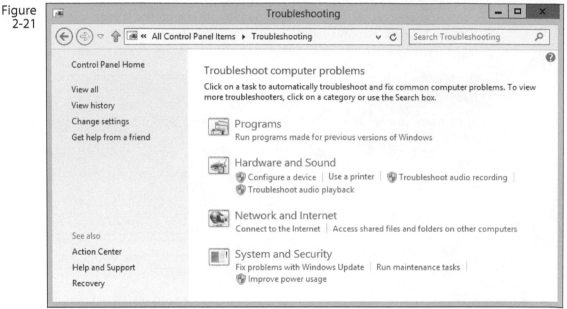

Source: Microsoft Corporation

You can check the manufacturer's Web site and online forums for possible solutions. Also consider the possibility that the device might have simply failed. Try swapping out the malfunctioning part with one that works; you can try a keyboard or printer from a friend's computer, for example. Let's summarize some of the key steps in the troubleshooting process:

● Make sure equipment is plugged in to a functioning wall outlet and turned on.

● Check all cables to make sure they are firmly connected.

● Get a clear idea of the problem by trying to isolate the component that malfunctioned.

● Try restarting the device or rebooting the computer.

● Write down relevant error messages.

● Check the manufacturer's site for solutions to the problem, such as updated device drivers.

● Conduct a general Web search for discussions about and solutions to similar problems. Make sure, however, that the site is reputable and the advice comes from a knowledgeable source.

● Before contacting technical support, make sure you know the brand and model of your equipment as well as the name and version number of your computer's operating system.

QuickCheck A

1. A(n) [_____] keyboard can be used to enter words and numbers on computers with touchscreens.

2. Touchpads and touchscreens are controlled by [_____] such as taps and swipes.

3. Screen [_____] is the number of horizontal and vertical pixels that a device displays.

4. True or false? Today, USB (Universal Serial Bus) is the preferred way to connect peripheral devices. [_____]

5. In a digital camera, the lens focuses light from an object onto a small image sensor called a(n) [_____] .

CHECKIT!

QuickCheck B

Enter Y for the ports that are shown in the photo; enter N if the port is not shown in the photo.

1. USB port [____]

2. Display port [____]

3. Network port [____]

4. Audio port [____]

5. FireWire port [____]

© MediaTechnics

CHECKIT!

3 Software

What's Inside and on the CD?

Operating systems are the foundation for all the activities that a computer can carry out. So which operating systems will you use? This chapter begins with an overview of today's popular operating systems to give you a taste of their features. The second part of the chapter delves into application software.

Choosing the right software to complete a task is sometimes tricky. Different types of software can help you accomplish similar tasks. For example, word processing software, spreadsheet software, database software, and personal finance software can all be used to create a table of numbers. How do you decide which to use to balance your checkbook?

Choosing the wrong software can cause problems as you try to complete a task. For example, although word processing software might allow you to create a nicely formatted table of numbers, it won't provide much flexibility for manipulating those numbers to produce totals and other calculations. For balancing your checkbook, spreadsheet or personal finance software would be more appropriate. In this chapter, you'll learn about many kinds of software and the types of tasks they can carry out.

● **FAQs:**

FAQ What is software?

The instructions that tell a computer how to carry out a task are referred to as a computer program. These programs form the software that prepares a computer to do a specific task, such as document production, video editing, graphic design, or Web browsing.

Software applies rules, also called algorithms, to process data. An **algorithm** is basically the steps necessary to complete a task. For example, when you listen to a playlist, your iTunes software follows an algorithm to start at the beginning of your list to play the first song, and then it steps down the list to play the next song. The instructions that specify this sequence are part of the iTunes algorithm.

Software is categorized as system software or application software. The primary purpose of **system software**—your computer's operating system, device drivers, players, and other utilities—is to help the computer carry out its basic operating functions. System software helps computers manage files, interact with peripheral devices, send data over networks, and filter out viruses.

In contrast to system software, the primary purpose of application software is to help people use a computer to carry out tasks, such as creating documents, tracking finances, and editing photos. Figure 3-1 illustrates the division between system software and application software, and lists some specific types of software included in each category.

Figure 3-1

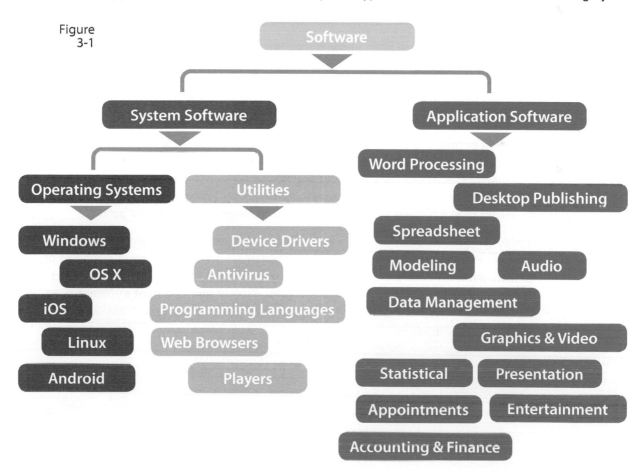

• What is software? (continued)

System and application software work together in a way that is similar to the chain of command in an army. When you issue a command using application software, it tells the operating system what to do. The operating system tells the device drivers, device drivers tell the hardware, and the hardware actually does the work. Figure 3-2 illustrates this chain of command for printing a document or photo.

Figure
3-2

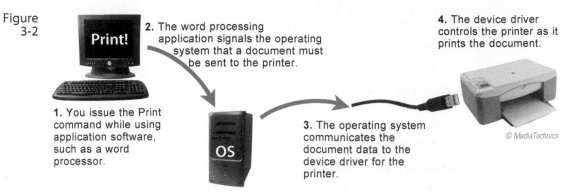

2. The word processing application signals the operating system that a document must be sent to the printer.

4. The device driver controls the printer as it prints the document.

1. You issue the Print command while using application software, such as a word processor.

3. The operating system communicates the document data to the device driver for the printer.

© MediaTechnics

Application software is subcategorized in a variety of ways. **Productivity software** refers to word processing, spreadsheet, presentation, and database applications, all of which are designed to increase individual productivity at home, school, and work.

Related applications are often bundled together in a **software suite**. Productivity applications are commonly bundled together as an **office suite**, such as Microsoft Office, LibreOffice, and Apache OpenOffice. You can purchase other types of suites such as the CorelDRAW Graphics Suite, which includes photo editing, drawing, and animation software.

Business software is a broad umbrella for applications designed to help businesses and organizations accomplish routine or specialized tasks. **Vertical market software** is designed to automate specialized tasks in a specific market or business. Examples include patient management and billing software specially designed for hospitals, job estimating software for construction businesses, and student record management software for schools.

Horizontal market software is generic software that just about any kind of business can use. Payroll, accounting, and project management software are good examples of horizontal market software. **Accounting software** helps a business keep track of the money flowing into and out of various accounts. **Project management software** is an important tool for planning large projects, scheduling project tasks, and tracking project costs.

FAQ What does an operating system do?

An operating system is essentially the master controller for all the activities that take place within a computer. Operating systems are classified as system software, not application software, because their primary purpose is to help the computer system run software and monitor itself in order to function efficiently. The most important operating system functions include:

- Storing files, opening them, and remembering their locations

- Managing the memory allocated for programs and data

- Providing a basic level of system security through passwords and encryption

- Regulating the flow of data to the processor

- Providing standards for the **user interface**, which encompasses input devices, screen elements, and other aspects related to how people interact with a computer system

Unlike application software, an operating system does not directly help people perform application-specific tasks, such as word processing. People do, however, interact with the operating system for certain operational and storage tasks, such as starting programs and locating data files.

Historically, Microsoft DOS was one of the first operating systems for personal computers. Installed on the original IBM PCs, DOS used a **command-line interface** that simply displayed a "prompt" such as C:\ on the screen and waited for users to type commands. Figure 3-3 shows the DOS interface and C:\ prompt.

Figure
3-3

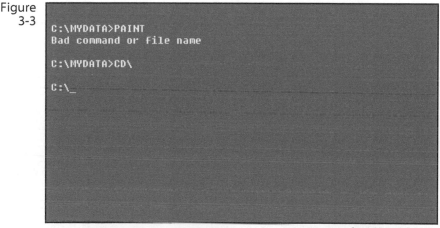

```
C:\MYDATA>PAINT
Bad command or file name

C:\MYDATA>CD\

C:\_
```

Source: Microsoft Corporation

Many people found it difficult to remember DOS commands, and computers did not gain widespread popularity until graphical user interfaces became available. Today's popular operating systems feature easy-to-use graphical user interfaces. A **graphical user interface** (abbreviated as GUI and pronounced as "gooey" or "gee you eye") displays controls and commands as pictures that users can manipulate with a touchpad, touchscreen, keyboard, mouse, or other input device.

Operating systems equip computers with a wide range of capabilities, including the ability to run multiple programs at the same time, a feature called **multitasking**. However, operating systems also establish limits. For example, DOS limits program names to eight characters, making it sometimes difficult to identify the contents of files by their names. Operating systems also limit the amount of memory that can be installed, and can limit the size of disk storage.

FAQ How do I recognize the Windows operating system?

Microsoft Windows is an operating system that was originally designed for desktop computers and has evolved through several generations. Windows 8 is the most recent version, but Windows 7, Windows Vista, and Windows XP are also still in use. The GUIs for these operating systems are similar, but the shape and placement of controls differ slightly. Windows 8 opens to a **Start screen** that displays a customizable array of colorful **tiles** representing applications, devices, and files (Figure 3-4).

TRYIT!

Figure
3-4

Source: Microsoft Corporation

Windows 7 and earlier versions have no Start screen. Instead, they feature a **Start button** in the lower-left corner of the screen that opens a **Start menu** containing a list of applications, devices, and files (Figure 3-5). The Start menu can be customized for quick access to frequently used files and programs.

Figure
3-5

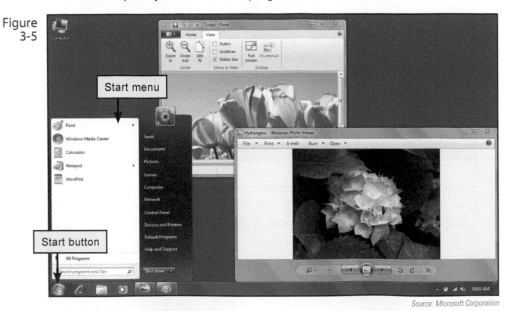

Source: Microsoft Corporation

The Windows operating system got its name from the rectangular work areas on the screen-based desktop. Each **window** can display a different document or program, which provides a visual model of the operating system's multitasking capabilities.

• How do I recognize the Windows operating system? (continued)

Microsoft offers several editions of Windows 8 designed for desktop and laptop computers. In addition to basic Windows 8, consumers can purchase Windows 8 Pro and Windows 8 Enterprise editions, which are designed for power users and businesses. Windows 8 Pro also runs on a select group of Intel-based tablet computers, offering the complete Windows 8 desktop plus the tiled Start screen, and access to the vast array of Windows software.

The number and variety of software applications that run on Windows 8 and its ancestors are unmatched by any other operating system. For the best selection of software, especially for games and business software, Windows is the operating system of choice. Speaking of software, the term "Windows software" is commonly used when referring to *applications*, not to the operating system. When referring to the operating system, just say "Windows" or "the Windows operating system."

The Windows user community is also an advantage of this operating system. Comprehensive tutorials and troubleshooting guides can be found online and on the shelves of most bookstores. Microsoft's official site, *www.microsoft.com*, includes thousands of pages of easily searchable information.

Windows has been criticized for two major weaknesses: reliability and security. The reliability of an operating system is usually gauged by the length of time it operates without glitches. Windows tends to become unstable more frequently than other operating systems.

Of the major personal computer operating systems, Windows has the reputation for being the most vulnerable to viruses, worms, and other attacks. One reason for Windows' vulnerability is because its huge user base makes it the biggest target for hackers. Although Microsoft is diligent in its efforts to patch security holes, its programmers are often one step behind the hackers; and while users wait for updates, their computers are vulnerable.

Microsoft Windows RT is a variation of Windows designed as a mobile operating system for tablet devices with ARM processors. It does not include a full-featured desktop and will not run Windows desktop applications, but it has a Start screen that looks essentially the same as the desktop versions of Windows 8 (Figure 3-6).

Figure
3-6

© MediaTechnics

Windows RT is optimized for a touch user interface, rather than one that uses a mouse pointing device. Like other mobile operating systems, Windows RT limits software to apps obtained through an authorized online store.

Microsoft also offers Windows Phone 8, an operating system designed for smartphones. It features a Start screen and live tiles similar to other versions of Windows 8.

FAQ How do I identify OS X?

OS X is the operating system designed for Apple's Macintosh line of computer systems. As an operating system designed to run on desktop and laptop computers, OS X features a GUI with beautifully designed graphics and multiple rectangular work areas to reflect multitasking capabilities.

Unique features of the Mac desktop include the Apple icon, the Dock, and an application menu bar fixed at the top of the screen. Figure 3-7 illustrates some basic features of the Mac user interface.

TRYIT!

Figure
3-7

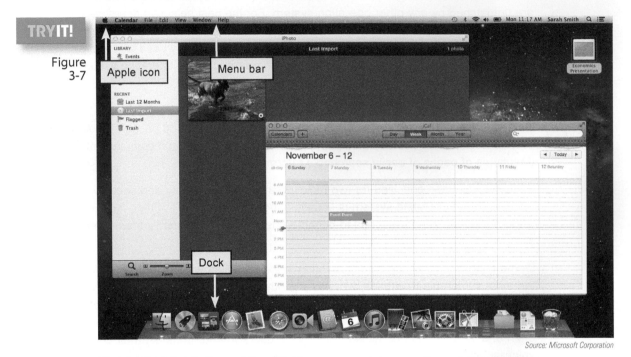

Source: Microsoft Corporation

The dock at the bottom of the OS X screen contains small graphics called **icons** representing programs, storage areas, and other items. Clicking a dock icon opens it and displays the associated item. Users can modify the dock to add programs and files for easy access.

The Apple icon leads to a menu containing options to set preferences, log off, and select shutdown options. The menu bar displays a list of command options for the active program. For example, when the Calendar program is active, the menu bar displays menu options such as File, Edit, and View that pertain to working with the appointment calendar.

Like Windows, OS X has been through a number of revisions. Version 10.8, sometimes called Mountain Lion, was released in 2012. Earlier versions include OS X version 10.4 (Tiger), version 10.5 (Leopard), version 10.6 (Snow Leopard), and version 10.7 (Lion).

OS X has a reputation for being an easy-to-use, reliable, and secure operating system. Back when PC owners were struggling with an inscrutable command-line operating system, Macintosh owners were breezing along with a point-and-click GUI. According to industry observers, Macintosh developers have always been in the lead when it comes to intuitive user interface design.

FAQ What devices use iOS?

Because OS X was designed for desktop and laptop computers, Apple developed **iOS** as an operating system for the Apple iPhone, which launched in 2007. iOS was subsequently used for the iPod Touch and iPad. All iOS devices use ARM-based microprocessors.

iOS is derived from OS X code, and both operating systems have a similar appearance and display a similar set of standard icons. iOS was the first operating system to offer routines to manage touchscreen gesture inputs, such as using your fingers to "squeeze" an on-screen graphic into a smaller size.

iOS displays a home screen containing application icons. At the bottom of the screen, a dock holds icons for frequently used apps. Touching an app launches it. Pressing the physical Home button located on the device returns the user to the home screen (Figure 3-8).

PLAY**IT!**

Figure
3-8

Home
button

© MediaTechnics

The iOS home screen is easily customized. Apps can be grouped into folders to save space on the Home screen. Touching and holding an app icon puts the device into "Jiggle mode" in which icons vibrate to indicate they are in a modifiable state. From Jiggle mode, icons can be deleted or dragged on top of each other to put them into a folder.

As a mobile operating system, iOS provides connectivity options. All iOS devices have wireless networking capability; iPhones and some iPads have cellular capabilities.

You won't find a desktop with application windows on an iOS device. Each app fills the entire screen. Background processes, such as music, voice calls, and notifications, provide very limited multitasking.

FAQ What devices use the Android operating system?

Android is a mobile operating system that is a popular platform for tablet computers, smartphones, and ebook readers. Android was developed by a company that was purchased by Google in 2005. It is an open source operating system, which means that it can be modified and distributed freely. As with other popular mobile operating systems, Android is designed for ARM processors.

Android displays a home screen containing icons that represent software applications. Touching an icon launches its app. Unlike iOS and Windows RT devices, Android devices have a screen-based home button rather than a physical button. Touching the on-screen home button recalls the home screen (Figure 3-9).

Figure
3-9

Source: Google, Inc.

In addition to touchscreen input, Android OS supports voice input for Google searching, voice dialing, navigation, and other applications. Worldwide, Android is the most popular smartphone operating system. As with other operating systems, Android is revised periodically. Android versions tend to be referred to by their code names: Gingerbread (released in 2010), Honeycomb (2011), Ice Cream Sandwich (2011), and Jelly Bean (2012).

The Android OS contains basic network and routing capabilities that allow Android devices to become Wi-Fi hotspots. For example, activating the Network utility on an Android-based smartphone transforms the phone into a network access device, and the phone's data connection can be used by a nearby desktop, laptop, or tablet computer to access the Internet.

Android gives you access to the file system and provides a utility that lets you view the files stored internally or on external SD cards. A third-party file manager utility is required to manipulate files.

FAQ Where is Linux used?

In 1991, a young Finnish student named Linus Torvalds developed the **Linux** (pronounced "LIH nucks") operating system. Linux was inspired by and loosely based on a UNIX derivative called MINIX, created by Andrew Tanenbaum. Linux is frequently used as an operating system for servers. It is less popular than Windows or OS X for computers owned by the average consumer.

Linux is distributed along with its source code under the terms of a GPL (General Public License), which allows everyone to make copies for their own use, to give to others, or to sell. This licensing policy has encouraged programmers to develop Linux utilities, software, and enhancements. Linux is primarily distributed over the Web.

Linux provides multitasking and multi-user capabilities, which account for its popularity as a server used in business networks accessed by many people. Linux is also secure and reliable. Android OS, iOS, and OS X are based on the program code used for UNIX and Linux.

Linux requires more tinkering than the Windows and Mac desktop operating systems. The comparatively limited number of programs that run under Linux also discourages many nontechnical users. A collection of high-quality open source software is available for the Linux platform, but many of these applications are targeted toward business and technical users.

A Linux distribution is a download that contains the Linux operating system, system utilities, a graphical user interface, applications, and an installation routine. Beginner-friendly Linux distributions include Fedora, Linux Mint, Debian, openSUSE, and Ubuntu. As you can see in Figure 3-10, the Linux user interface has icons, toolbars, and rectangular work areas similar to Windows and OS X.

TRYIT!

Figure 3-10

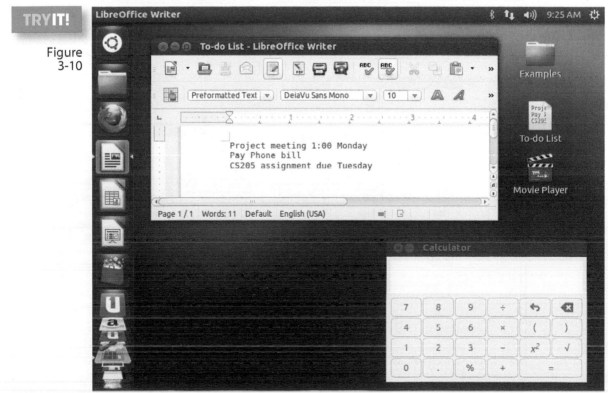

Source: Linux

FAQ What is document production software?

Document production software assists you with composing, editing, designing, printing, and electronically publishing documents. The most popular types of document production software are word processing and desktop publishing.

Word processing software, such as Microsoft Word and LibreOffice Writer, replaced typewriters for producing documents such as reports, letters, memos, papers, and manuscripts. Word processing software gives you the ability to create, spell-check, edit, and format a document on the screen before you commit it to paper.

Desktop publishing software (abbreviated DTP) takes word processing software one step further by helping you use graphic design techniques to enhance the format and appearance of a document. DTP software products, such as Microsoft Publisher, QuarkXPress, and Adobe InDesign, offer sophisticated features and produce professional-quality output for newspapers, newsletters, brochures, magazines, and books.

Whereas word processing software is document-based, DTP software is frame based. When you use word processing software, each page is basically one box into which you enter text and paste images. When the box becomes full, your software adds another page and the text flows onto it.

DTP software allows you to create a page using multiple frames; some frames can hold text, while other frames can hold titles, graphics, and tables. To achieve a pleasing layout, you can move, resize, and overlap frames. You can also link frames so that text flows seamlessly from one frame to another on the same page or over to a different page. Figure 3-11 gives you an idea of how a professional desktop publishing application works.

TRYIT!

Figure
3-11

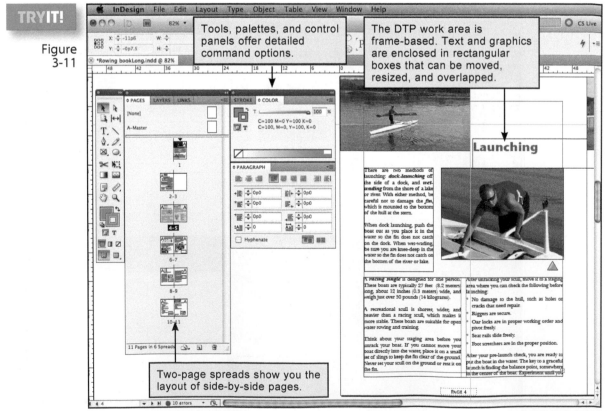

Source: Adobe Systems, Inc.

FAQ What is spreadsheet software?

A **spreadsheet** uses rows and columns of numbers to create a model or representation of a real situation, such as a checkbook, tax form, or gradebook. **Spreadsheet software**, such as Microsoft Excel and LibreOffice Calc, provides tools to create electronic spreadsheets, called worksheets. This type of software is ideal for projects that require repetitive calculations—budgeting, maintaining a grade book, balancing a checkbook, tracking investments, calculating loan payments, and estimating project costs.

A worksheet is like a "smart" piece of paper that automatically adds up the columns of numbers written on it. You can also use it to make calculations based on simple formulas that you enter, or more complex built-in functions. Worksheets can be grouped together into a workbook to share data. As an added bonus, spreadsheet software helps you turn your data into colorful graphs.

Spreadsheet software also includes basic data-handling features that allow you to sort data, search for data that meets specific criteria, and print reports. These data handling routines are suitable for simple lists of data, but they are not a replacement for the sophisticated data functions offered by database software. As a general rule, if your data can be arranged in a two-dimensional table, and you simply want to sort it in alphabetical or numeric order and pull out groups of similar data, you can use a spreadsheet rather than a database.

Because it is so easy to experiment with different numbers, spreadsheet software is particularly useful for what-if analysis. You can use what-if analysis to answer questions such as "What if I get an A on my next two Economics exams? But what if I get only Bs?" or "Can I afford monthly payments on a $15,500 car if I get $5,000 for my trade-in? But what if I get only $3,650 for my trade-in?" Figure 3-12 illustrates the components of a basic worksheet.

Figure
3-12

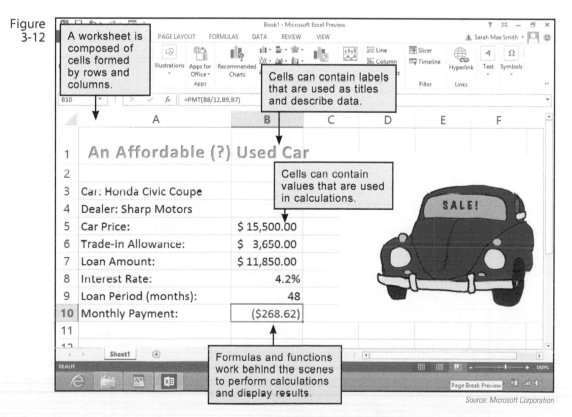

Source: Microsoft Corporation

FAQ What is database software?

The term "database" has evolved from a specialized technical term into a part of our everyday vocabulary. In the context of modern usage, a **database** is simply a collection of data that is stored on one or more computers. A database can contain any sort of data, such as university student records, a library card catalog, or customer e-mail addresses. Databases can be stored on personal computers, servers, mainframes, and supercomputers. Working behind the scenes, databases play an important role in maintaining data for e-commerce sites and other data-driven applications.

Database software, sometimes referred to as a database management system or DBMS, helps you enter, find, organize, update, and report information stored in a database. Microsoft Access is a well-known database software product for personal computers. It can be used for mailing lists and household inventories, but is more typically used in small business applications. SQLite, Oracle, and MySQL are popular server database software packages. These high-powered applications can manage large amounts of complex data for airline reservation systems and corporate accounting systems.

Database software stores data as a series of records, which are composed of fields that hold data. A **record** holds data for a single entity—a person, place, thing, or event. A **field** holds one item of data relevant to a record. Key fields contain unique identifiers, such as Social Security numbers, and are used to sort and quickly search for data. Most database software for personal computers and servers supports the **relational database** model in which records are grouped into tables and related to each other by common characteristics.

Most database software includes tools to create queries, electronic forms, and reports. A query is used to formulate search criteria. Electronic forms are used to enter information into the database. Reports gather, format, and present information in the database, and can typically be printed, published on the Web, or e-mailed to other people. Figure 3-13 shows how to name the fields for a database.

Figure 3-13

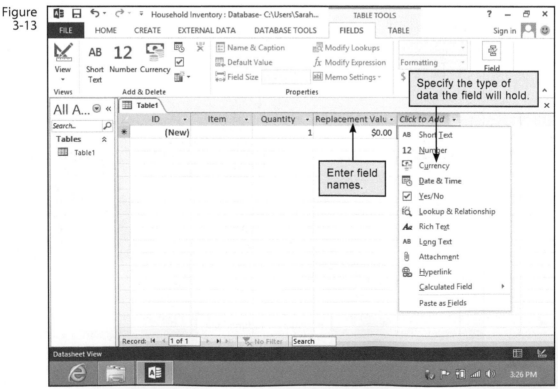

Source: Microsoft Corporation

FAQ What is presentation software?

Presentation software supplies tools for combining text, photos, clip art, graphs, animations, and sound clips into a series of electronic slides. You can display electronic slides on a monitor for a one-on-one presentation or use a computer projection device for group presentations. You can even post presentations on the Internet. Microsoft PowerPoint, Zoho Show, Google Slides, and LibreOffice Impress are popular presentation software applications, along with Internet-based apps such as Prezi.

Presentation software is used by instructors and students to create slides for classroom lectures and oral presentations. Instructors can use presentation technologies to create virtual classrooms for distance education courses. Businesspeople use presentation software to present and illustrate ideas at company meetings, conferences, and sales events. Presentation software includes templates, master slides, and themes that can be used to ensure that all presentations created by an organization, a person, or a department have a uniform style.

Presentation software also includes basic tools for creating line drawings, arrows, and other simple shapes. Digital photographs, animations, and videos can be incorporated into slides created with presentation software, but the presentation software itself does not include the necessary tools to create these types of content. Presentation software typically includes tools for creating speaker notes that help the presenter remember important information to supplement the slide display (Figure 3-14).

Figure 3-14

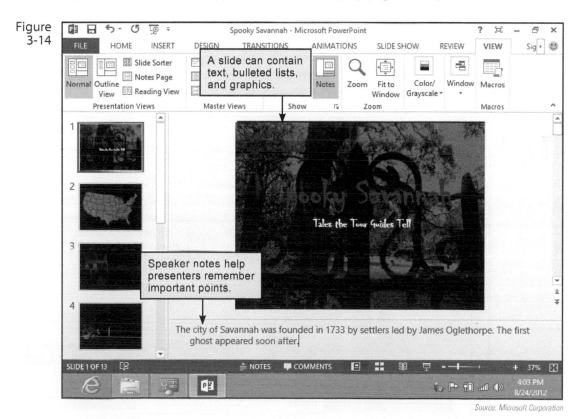

Source: Microsoft Corporation

PowerPoint's ability to work with text, charts, images, and tables illustrates how applications can interact and share data. You can paste data and charts from Excel worksheets onto PowerPoint slides. You can even create speaker notes using Word and pull them up with PowerPoint.

FAQ What about graphics software?

In computer lingo, the term **graphics** refers to pictures, drawings, sketches, photographs, images, or icons that appear on your computer screen. **Graphics software** is designed to help you create, manipulate, and print graphics. Some graphics software products specialize in a particular type of graphic, while others allow you to work with multiple graphics formats. Graphics software not only provides professional artists with the tools of their trade, but also promotes creativity for children and adults by encouraging the use of photos and art in documents, posters, and flyers.

Paint software (sometimes called image editing software) provides a set of electronic pens, brushes, and paints for painting images on the screen. A simple program called Microsoft Paint is included with Windows. Corel Painter and open source GIMP offer more full-featured graphics tools. Many graphic artists, Web page designers, and illustrators use paint software as their primary computer-based graphics tool to work with bitmap graphics file types such as JPEG, GIF, TIF, PNG, and BMP.

Photo editing software, such as Adobe Photoshop, includes features specially designed to fix poor-quality photos by modifying contrast and brightness, cropping out unwanted objects, and removing "red eye." Photos can also be edited using paint software, but photo editing software typically offers tools and wizards that simplify common photo editing tasks.

Drawing software provides tools for assembling lines, shapes, and colors into diagrams and corporate logos. The drawings created with tools such as Adobe Illustrator, Corel DESIGNER, and LibreOffice Draw tend to have a flat cartoon-like quality, but they are very easy to modify and look good at just about any size. **CAD software** (computer aided design) is useful for working with digital blueprints and schematic diagrams. CAD software and drawing applications such as the one in Figure 3-15 are designed to work with vector graphics file types such as EPS, WMF, and AI.

TRYIT!

Figure 3-15

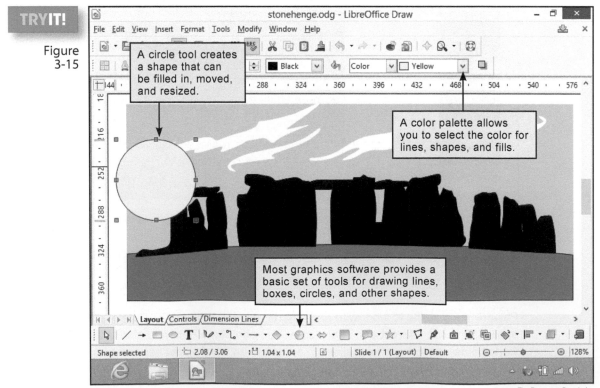

Source: The Document Foundation

FAQ What's available for working with videos, music, and other media?

Digital media is a term used for movies and other content that is stored digitally. Much of today's digital media, such as movies, music, and novels, is for entertainment, though some focuses on educational, political, and other serious topics.

Media is accessed by means of a player. A **player** is a type of system software that a computer uses to work with a specialized type of file, such as YouTube videos, iTunes tracks, or PDF documents. Players can be standalone software or they can be appended to other software, in which case they are referred to as **plug-ins**. Keep in mind that the term "player" can refer to a hardware device or software, such as the following:

- Software players include familiar media players, such as iTunes, Windows Media Player, and QuickTime.

- Hardware players include standalone devices such as CD players, VCRs, DVD players, Blu-ray players, ebook readers, and portable media players.

- Computer devices, such as CD, DVD, and Blu-ray drives, are also considered players, though they require software to play back content.

Most players offer a standard set of controls for playing media, so you can easily start, stop, pause, fast-forward, and rewind the music and movies you choose for entertainment, as shown in Figure 3-16.

Figure
3-16

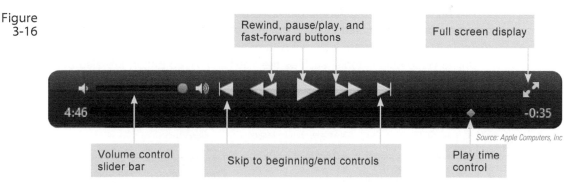

Rewind, pause/play, and fast-forward buttons

Full screen display

Source: Apple Computers, Inc

Volume control slider bar

Skip to beginning/end controls

Play time control

A media player works with one or more types of media, such as digital audio, MIDI, digital video, or digital animation.

Digital audio is music, speech, and other sounds represented in binary format for use in digital devices. Sounds can be digitized by a process called **sampling**, which converts a sound wave into digital bits and stores those bits in a computer file. Digital audio files can hold music tracks, narrations, and sound effects. They can be played on a personal computer, portable music player, or computer-based home entertainment center, and they can be incorporated into Web pages and digital videos. Digital audio is stored in a variety of file types, including WAV, MP3, M4P, and MIDI.

Computers also work with **MIDI** (Musical Instrument Digital Interface), which allows computers to communicate with music synthesizers. Thousands of MIDI files are available for downloading and can be played back through a computer speaker, an electronic keyboard, or another MIDI instrument. MIDI sequencing software and software synthesizers are an important part of the studio musician's toolbox.

• What's available for working with videos, music, and other media? (continued)

An **animation** is a series of still images, each slightly different, that creates the illusion of movement when displayed. Animations are used to create dynamic Web page elements, computer games, and movie special effects. Animations can be based on 2D bitmaps or vector graphics, or they can be based on 3D vector graphics.

Flash is a popular format for static graphics and animations. For many years, Flash was the gold standard for animations because it includes a scripting feature that allows users to interact with the action shown on the screen. This interaction is especially effective for instructional materials.

When iPads and iPhones shipped without Flash capability, developers began using HTML5 and JavaScript to create interactive animations. Animations that don't involve user interactions can be converted to digital video formats that don't require Flash Player and will run on iPads and iPhones.

Digital video is based on footage of real objects filmed and then stored as bits. It is used for consumer-level YouTube-style videos as well as professionally produced full-length films. Digital videos can be uploaded and downloaded over networks, such as the Internet, though files are large and require a fairly speedy connection.

Computers can work with several types of video files, including QuickTime (MOV), Windows Media Video (WMV), Flash Video (FLV), Audio Video Interleave (AVI), and Moving Picture Experts Group (MPEG). The growing popularity of computer-based video editing can be attributed to video editing software, such as Windows Movie Maker and Apple iMovie, which are included with new computers or available as free downloads. Online video editing tools, such as the YouTube Video Editor, are also available. Figure 3-17 walks you through the process of creating a video with Microsoft's Movie Maker software.

TRY IT!

Figure 3-17

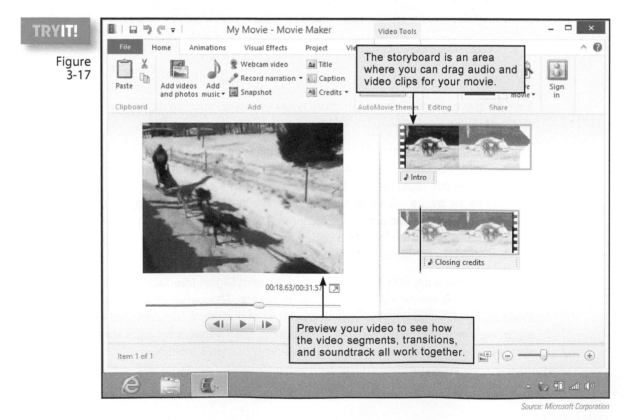

Source: Microsoft Corporation

QuickCheck A

1. [_____] software helps you perform a particular task; for example, writing a document or calculating car payments.

2. A computer's [_____] system is the master controller for all the activities that take place within a computer.

3. [_____] software is a good choice for projects that require repetitive calculations or what-if analysis.

4. True or false? Word processing software is a good choice if you want to keep track of a collection of data. [_____]

5. MOV, WMV, and FLV files typically store digital [_____] .

CHECKIT!

QuickCheck B

Based on the screen shown below, enter T if a statement is true; or F if a statement is false.

1. The software would be classified as utility software. [_____]

2. The software would be classified as paint software. [_____]

3. The image is a vector graphic. [_____]

4. This software would be a good choice for editing photos. [_____]

5. This software is designed to create gadgets, sometimes referred to as widgets. [_____]

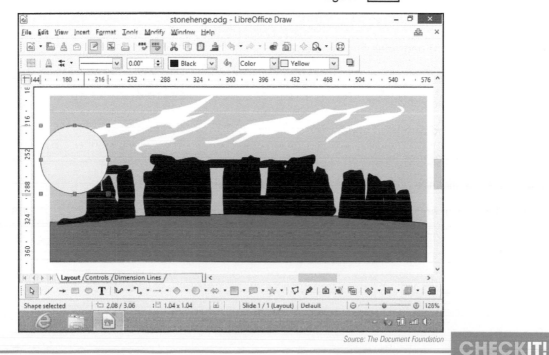

Source: The Document Foundation

CHECKIT!

4

Installing Software

What's Inside and on the CD?

It's surprising how quickly your collection of software can grow as you discover new ways to use your computer for school, work, and play. New software is distributed on CDs or DVDs; it also can be downloaded from the Web or obtained from an app store. Before you can use new software, it might have to be installed on your computer, and that is the focus of this chapter.

Installing new software involves some degree of risk. Viruses and other harmful software can be hiding on distribution disks and in downloaded files, so make sure your computer is protected by antivirus software. Sometimes newly installed software disrupts the normal functioning of your computer system, causing printer malfunctions or glitches in other software. It is prudent, therefore, to make sure you have a backup of your hard disk before you attempt to install new software.

If you're using a computer at work or at school, check with a supervisor to make sure that you're allowed to download and install software. Some organizations strictly control who is allowed to install software to avoid problems with unlicensed or destructive software.

To ensure that the installation process proceeds smoothly, check that your computer meets the software's system requirements and read all pertinent installation instructions on the software's packaging or Web site.

● **FAQs:**

● **Assessment**

FAQ How do I know which software will work on my computer?

Computers—and that includes desktops, laptops, tablets, and smartphones—usually come with a variety of preinstalled software. Your device will have an operating system and some system utilities. It might also include some application software. That's great for a start. But if you're like the majority of digital device owners, you want more applications and utilities than those supplied out of the box.

You'll find applications in a variety of places. Electronics stores carry a small selection of boxed application software for desktop and laptop computers. Software for these computers can also be found on software publishers' Web sites and download sites, such as Tucows and CNET Download.com. Tablet and smartphone owners usually obtain software from online app stores, such as iTunes, Amazon Appstore, and Google Play.

To discover if an application will work on your digital device, you can check the software's system requirements. **System requirements** specify the operating system and minimum hardware capacities necessary for a software product to work correctly. To find the system requirements, look on the software product box, on the software's download page, or in its app store description. Check the bulleted items listed in Figure 4-1.

Figure 4-1

System Requirements

Operating Systems: Windows 8/7/Vista/XP
Processor: Intel Core or equivalent
Memory: 1 GB or more
Hard Disk Space: 50 MB for installation
Screen Resolution: 1024 x 768 or better
Internet Connection

eCourse Internet Works
2014 eCourseWare Corp. All rights reserved. eCourse is a registered trademark of eCourseWare Corp.

- **Operating system.** First, check that the software is designed for your device's operating system: Windows, OS X, iOS, Android, or Linux.

- **Windows version and bit specs.** For Windows software, make sure the system specs are compatible with your version of Windows. A program designed for Windows 8 might not work on a device running Windows RT. When selecting Windows software, you might have to decide between the 32-bit and 64-bit version of the software. Search for System to determine which version of Windows is installed on your device.

- **Storage.** Applications installed on permanent storage within a device require storage space. System requirements usually specify how much space is required. Check your device to find out how much space is available. Even if you have enough space, you might decide not to install a big app that uses all the remaining storage space.

- **Mobile devices.** Apps from an app store don't necessarily work on all devices with a compatible operating system. For example, an app from the iTunes Store might work on an iPhone, but not on an iPad. Read the app store description carefully before you buy.

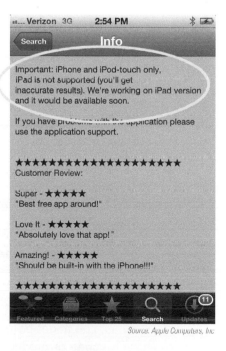

Source: Apple Computers, Inc

FAQ How do I install local software?

Some software applications have to be installed on your computer before you can use them. A software product that's installed on your computer's hard disk is referred to as **local software**. Local software requires hard disk space, but it tends to be full-featured and respond quickly to your commands. Local software is self-contained and does not require a network connection for operation.

Although a variety of applications are installed as local software, two categories of software—Web apps and portable apps—do not require installation on your computer's hard disk. You'll learn more about these software categories later in the chapter.

On a computer running the Windows operating system, the **installation process** copies files from a download site or distribution CD to your computer's hard disk, adds the software's name to the Start menu or Start screen, and provides Windows with technical information needed to efficiently run the new software.

Information about the program is stored on the hard disk in a special file called the **Windows Registry** that keeps track of all the hardware and software installed on your computer. Just as a hotel register keeps track of guests who check in and check out, the Windows Registry keeps track of software that you add and remove.

For most modern Windows software, the installation process is easy. Click the Try It! button in Figure 4-2 to step through the process of downloading and installing a local application.

TRYIT!

Figure 4-2

1. Download the distribution file containing the software. **DOWNLOAD** Ⓥ

2. If the download site is trustworthy, select Run when prompted.

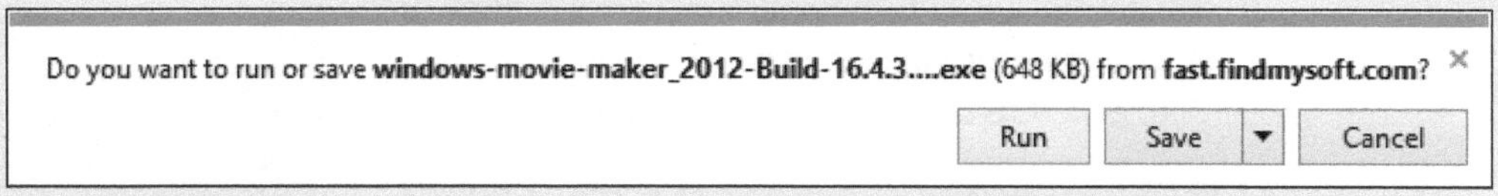

Do you want to run or save **windows-movie-maker_2012-Build-16.4.3....exe** (648 KB) from **fast.findmysoft.com**?   ✕

    Run   Save ▼   Cancel

Source: Microsoft Corporation

3. Windows will scan the software for viruses. You might be asked to approve the download to verify that you, rather than a remote hacker, initiated the installation.

4. The first thing downloaded is usually an installer that will handle any additional downloads and the installation process. Follow the instructions presented on your screen to download the remaining files.

5. You might be asked to select a location for the new software. You can simply select the location suggested by the installer.

6. When the setup is complete, look for the new application in the Windows Start menu or on the Start screen.

7. You might be required to activate the product by entering an activation code or product key. Cut and paste the code if possible; otherwise, type it carefully.

•How do I install local software? (continued)

A lot of action goes on behind the scenes when you install software on a Windows computer. Understanding the nuts and bolts of the installation process can help you troubleshoot problems and deal with older software that might not include automated installation routines.

1. Download. The first step in the process is to download the files to your computer. If you have to download a file manually, be sure to make a note of its file name and the folder in which you save it.

2. Locate. Downloads are generally stored in the Downloads folder on your computer's hard disk. If you need to find a download to unzip it, install it, or reinstall it, that is the place to look.

3. Extract. Software at download sites is usually compressed to make it as small as possible so that it downloads quickly. As part of the installation process, the software must be "extracted" to restore it to its original form. Extraction can be carried out manually if there is not an automated installation process.

4. Set up. Once extracted, the software is moved to its own folder, usually one that is within the Program Files folder. This process is typically handled by an installer or setup routine included in the download. When installing from a CD, insert the disc and wait a few seconds for the setup routine to begin. If you're installing downloaded software, look for a file named Setup in the Downloads folder on your hard disk. During the setup process, you might be given options such as the one shown in Figure 4-3.

Figure 4-3

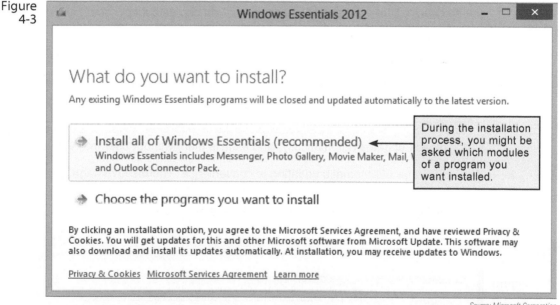

Source: Microsoft Corporation

5. Configure. Information about a new software application is added to the Windows Registry. The configuration process is handled by the installer and is not commonly carried out manually.

6. Create access links. Links make it easy for users to start applications. These links could appear as an entry on the Windows Start menu, as an icon on the desktop, or as a tile on the Windows Start screen. Links can be created manually if the installer does not create them or if additional startup links are desired.

FAQ What about software upgrades and updates?

Periodically, software publishers produce **software upgrades** designed to replace older versions. Upgrades are often designated by a **version number** (also referred to as a revision number), such as version 1.1 or version 2.0. A software upgrade usually offers enhanced features and performance. Upgrading to a new version normally involves a fee but is typically less costly than purchasing a completely new version.

If you've registered your current software, you're likely to receive e-mail notifications when new versions are available. Otherwise, you can keep informed about upgrades by periodically visiting the publisher's Web site. Before you decide to upgrade, make sure that you understand its features, purpose, and installation procedures. While an upgrade usually fixes some bugs, it might introduce new bugs. Upgrades can also introduce hardware or software compatibility problems, so make sure you have a recent backup before proceeding.

The procedure for installing an upgrade for a local application is usually similar to the process of installing the original version: The installation routine copies the upgrade to your computer's hard disk, extracts it, and makes the necessary modifications to the Windows Registry. The upgrade generally overwrites the old version of the application, but does not affect data files that you've created.

In between major new software upgrades, publishers often release **software updates**, sometimes referred to as patches, designed to fix bugs and update security. It is always a good idea to install updates when they become available.

Software updates are usually free. They are typically distributed over the Internet. Using the software's Preferences or Options menu, you can select how you'd like to handle updates:

- Manual. No updates are collected or installed until you manually check for them.

- Notification. The software notifies you when an update is available, and then you decide if and when you want to install it.

- Automatic. The software periodically checks its publisher's Web site for updates, downloads updates automatically, and installs them without user intervention.

The advantage of automatic updating is convenience. The disadvantage is that changes can be made to your computer without your knowledge. Learn more about software updates by clicking the Try It! button in Figure 4-4.

TRYIT!

Figure 4-4

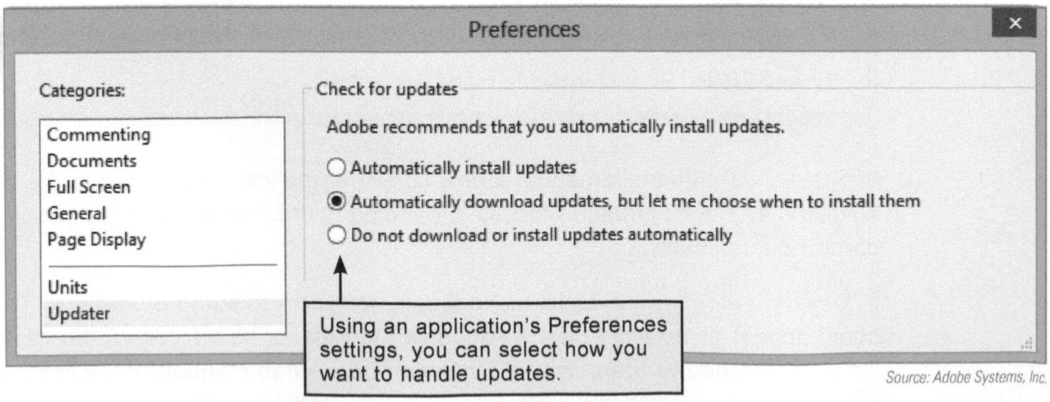

Using an application's Preferences settings, you can select how you want to handle updates.

Source: Adobe Systems, Inc.

FAQ How do I remove local software?

At some point, you might choose to remove a local software application from your computer, a process sometimes called uninstalling. You might want to remove an application to make room on the hard disk for other programs, documents, or graphics. You might no longer need some of your software or expired demoware. You might want to replace an application with one that has a better collection of features.

On some computers, it is possible to remove an application simply by tracking down the program file and deleting it. With Windows, however, the process is different because applications may consist of several program modules housed in various folders. Finding these modules is difficult because they may not have names associated with the application.

Another characteristic of program modules is that they can be shared by multiple programs. For example, both your word processing application and your graphics application might use the same program module containing a collection of clip art pictures. If you uninstall the graphics application, should your computer delete the clip art module from the disk and remove its entry from the Registry? No, because then the clip art would not be available when you use your word processor. Generally, your computer should not delete shared program modules when you uninstall software. When in doubt, don't delete!

In addition to the problem of shared program modules, removing software is complicated by the necessity of keeping the Windows Registry up to date. Remember that the Registry keeps track of all hardware and software in a computer system. When software is removed, the Registry files have to be modified accordingly.

To correctly uninstall a local application on a Windows computer, it is essential to use an uninstall utility. Some software includes its own uninstall utility. Windows also offers an uninstall utility that can be used to remove software from your computer. To access this uninstall utility, go to the Control Panel, and then select Uninstall a Program. When you see the list of programs, choose the one you want to remove (Figure 4-5).

TRY IT!

Figure 4-5

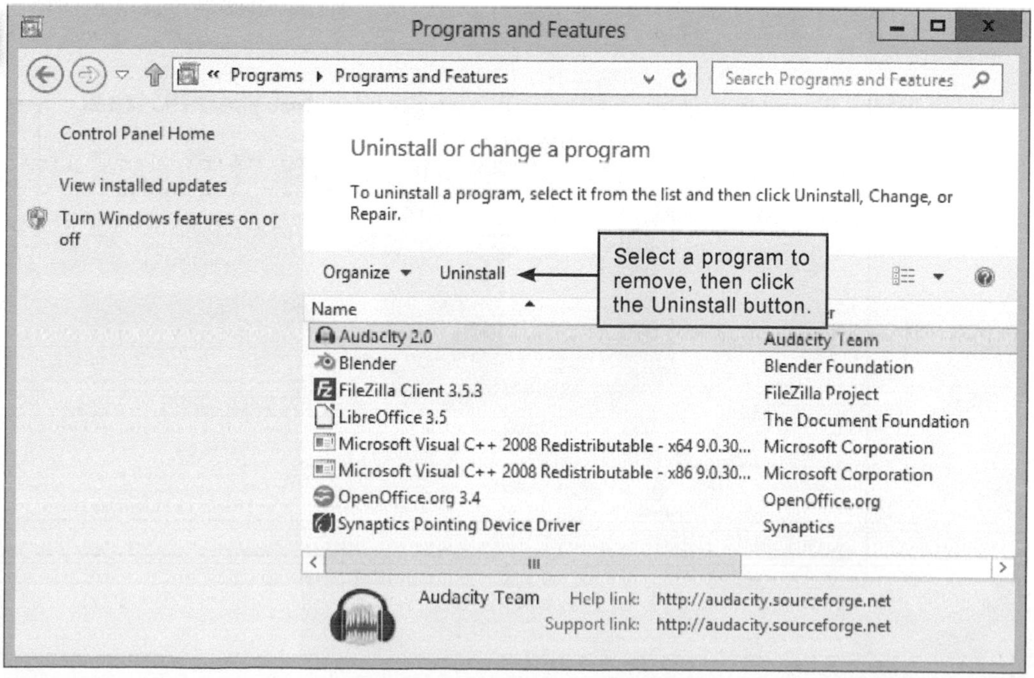

Source: Microsoft Corporation

FAQ What about portable software?

Portable software (sometimes referred to as portable apps) is designed to run from removable storage, such as a CD or USB flash drive. Program files do not exist on the hard disk, no configuration data is stored on the hard disk, and no entries need to be made in the Windows Registry. When the media containing portable software is removed from the computer, no trace of it is left on the hard disk or in the Registry.

The beauty of portable apps is that you can carry your software and your data on removable storage, such as a USB flash drive, and plug it into any computer. You won't have to worry if the computer contains software to open your data files because the software you need is also on the USB drive.

Your BookOnCD is an example of portable software. To use it, simply insert the CD containing the program files. Other examples of portable apps include LibreOffice Portable (office suite), Thunderbird (e-mail), Firefox (browser), and FileZilla (upload and download), which are designed to run from USB flash drives.

Portable software is so easy to install that it is sometimes referred to as install-free software. Installation is simply a matter of getting program files to the media on which they are supposed to run. For example, suppose that you want to access your productivity software at home, school, or work, and even at computers without an Internet connection. You can download the portable version of LibreOffice and then simply unzip it so that the programs end up on a USB flash drive that you can carry with you wherever you go. You can store your data files on the same USB drive so that you can work with them while you're out and about. Portable apps can be downloaded from several Web sites, including the popular site PortableApps.com (Figure 4-6).

Figure
4-6

A variety of popular applications are available as portable apps.

Source: Portable Apps

FAQ How do I get started with Web apps?

A **Web application** (or Web app) is software that is accessed with a Web browser. Instead of running locally, the program code for the software runs on a remote computer connected to the Internet or other computer network. Using software supplied over the Internet from a remote server is sometimes referred to as **cloud computing**.

Web apps are available for many of the same applications that run locally, such as e-mail, photo sharing, project management, maps, and games. In addition, Google, Microsoft, Zoho, and other software vendors offer popular spreadsheet and word processing Web apps that allow participants in multiple locations to collaborate on projects.

Many Web apps, such as Gmail and Facebook, require no installation at all on your local computer. Your device must, however, have a Web browser and an Internet connection. Web apps sometimes offer local versions that you can install and use when an Internet connection is not available. Google Docs (Figure 4-7) is an example of a Web application that has a corresponding client program for offline use.

TRY IT!

Figure
4-7

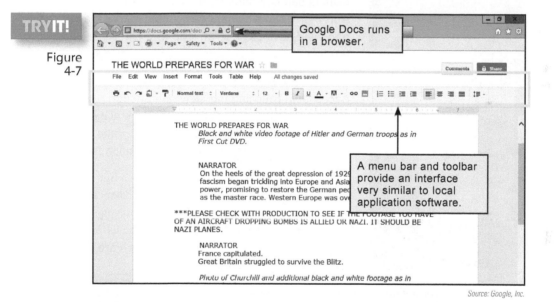

Source: Google, Inc.

Some Web apps are free, whereas others require a one-time registration fee or ongoing monthly usage fees. Web apps usually require users to register by supplying a bit of personal information, choosing a user ID, and selecting a password. Companies supplying software that runs from the Internet are referred to as **application service providers** (ASPs). The process of licensing fee-based software over the Internet is termed **Software as a Service** (SaaS) and is becoming increasingly popular. This software requires registration and is accessed by logging in with a user ID and password.

One advantage of Web-deployed software is that consumers don't have to worry about installing updates because the Web app site always carries the most current version. Web apps are available from any computer with a Web connection, and that is another advantage. However, Web apps and corresponding data files might not be accessible if the ASP service goes down, if you attempt to access the apps with an unsupported browser, or if security software blocks access to the Web app site.

Before registering to use Web apps, read the terms of use and privacy policy. Find out if you'll be subjected to advertising, if your personal information can be disclosed to third parties, and if anyone else can access data files that you store on the provider's site.

FAQ What about apps for mobile devices?

A **mobile app** is designed for a handheld device, such as a smartphone, a tablet computer, or an enhanced media player. This category of software consists of small, focused applications that are generally sold through an online app store. Many apps are free or cost less than US$5.00. There are lots of them, ranging from games to medical diagnostic tools used by health professionals. Some apps transform your device, turning your iPhone into a tape measure, for example, or your iPad into a piano.

Most handheld devices can use both Web apps and mobile apps. The difference between the two is that Web apps run on a remote computer, whereas mobile apps run from the handheld device so they have to be downloaded and installed. There are also some hybrid apps that run locally but access data stored on the Web. Mapping applications and apps that show your local weather operate in this way.

Figure 4-8

An icon provides access to the app store for a mobile device. The icon might also indicate if updates are available.

© MediaTechnics

To install a mobile app, the first step is to visit the app store for your device. iPhone, iPad, and iPod Touch owners can find apps for their devices at the online Apple App Store; Droid owners can go to Google Play. Most handheld devices have an icon that takes you directly to the app store for your device's platform (Figure 4-8).

At the app store, log in, select an app, and pay for it, if necessary. Touching the Download button retrieves the file and installs it automatically. The installation process places the app's program file on the storage device and creates an icon that you can use to launch the app.

Updates are accessed from an Updates button on the app store screen. Touching the button displays a list of updates. You might be asked for your user ID and password before continuing to a screen where you can touch the Update button. Some updates are large and take a few minutes to download and install.

The process of removing software on mobile devices varies by device. On the iPhone and iPad, touch and hold the program icon until it jiggles. Then touch the ⊗ and select the Delete option.

iPads, iPhones, and iPods are only allowed to download apps from the official iTunes App Store. Apps are available from other sources, but using them requires an unauthorized change to the device's software called a **jailbreak**.

Software that helps you jailbreak a device is available from several Web sites. After downloading and installing the jailbreak software, your device will be able to install apps from a variety of sources other than the iTunes App Store. The jailbreak lasts until you accept a software update from Apple. Updates wipe out the jailbreak software, forcing you to reinstall it.

Android phones are not limited to a single app store, so there is no need to jailbreak them to access more apps. There are various ways to make unauthorized modifications to any mobile device to overcome limitations imposed by mobile service providers. The process is called **rooting**, but most consumers have no need to root their mobile devices.

FAQ What's the significance of software copyrights and licenses?

After you purchase a software package, you might assume that you can install it and use it in any way you like. In fact, your purchase entitles you to use the software only in certain prescribed ways. In most countries, computer software, like a book or movie, is protected by a copyright.

A **copyright** is a form of legal protection that grants the author of an original work an exclusive right to copy, distribute, sell, and modify that work. Purchasers do not have this right except under the following special circumstances described by copyright laws:

- The purchaser has the right to copy software from distribution media or a Web site to a computer's hard disk in order to install it.

- The purchaser can make an extra, or backup, copy of the software in case the original copy becomes erased or damaged, unless the process of making the backup requires the purchaser to defeat a copy protection mechanism designed to prohibit copying.

- The purchaser is allowed to copy and distribute sections of a software program for use in critical reviews and teaching.

Most software displays a copyright notice, such as © 2014 eCourse Corporation, on one of its screens. This notice is not required by law, however, so programs without a copyright notice are still protected by copyright law.

In addition to copyright protection, computer software is often protected by the terms of a software license. A **software license**, or license agreement, is a legal contract that defines the ways in which you may use a computer program.

Software licenses can impose additional restrictions on software use, or they can offer additional rights to consumers. For example, most software is distributed under a **single-user license** (sometimes called a single-seat license) that limits use to one person at a time. However, some software publishers offer volume licenses for multiple users to schools, organizations, and businesses.

Figure
4-9

A **site license** (sometimes called a network license or volume license) is generally priced at a flat rate and allows software to be used on all computers at a specific location. A site license usually costs less than purchasing single-user licenses for a group of people, yet offers the software publisher a fair income stream. Site license users are obligated to follow the terms of the license and use it only at specified sites.

A **EULA** (end-user license agreement) is displayed on the screen when you first install software. After reading the software license on the screen, you can indicate that you accept the terms of the license by clicking a designated button—usually labeled OK, I agree, or I accept (Figure 4-9). If you do not accept the terms, the software does not load and you will not be able to use it.

Setup - SwordSpell

License Agreement
Please read the following important information before continuing.

Please read the following License Agreement. You must accept the terms of this agreement before continuing with the installation.

SwordSpell v2.0 is protected by United States Federal Copyright Law. LLC ("LLC" or the "Owner") retains the title to and ownership of SwordSpell v2.0 (the "Product"). LLC retains the copyright and trademark of the Product, as well as all rights not expressly granted. The licensee is defined as the individual or company utilizing the Product ("Licensee"). LLC grants the Licensee a non-transferrable license to use the Product under the following terms and conditions (the "Agreement"):

◉ I accept the agreement
○ I do not accept the agreement

< Back   Next >   Cancel

• What's the significance of software copyrights and licenses? (continued)

From a legal perspective, there are two categories of software: public domain and proprietary. **Public domain software** is not protected by copyright because the copyright has expired, or the author has placed the program in the public domain, making it available without restriction. Public domain software may be freely copied, distributed, and even resold. The primary restriction on public domain software is that you are not allowed to apply for a copyright on it.

Proprietary software has restrictions on its use that are delineated by copyright, patents, or license agreements. Some proprietary software is distributed commercially, whereas some of it is free. Based on licensing rights, proprietary software is distributed as commercial software, demoware, shareware, freeware, and open source software.

Commercial software is typically sold in computer stores, from Web sites, and at app stores. Although you "buy" this software, you actually purchase only the right to use it under the terms of the software license. Commercial software is also available as a rental for which you pay a monthly fee. Most licenses for commercial software adhere closely to the limitations provided by copyright law, although they might give you permission to install the software on multiple devices provided that you are the primary user of those devices.

Demoware is a version of commercial software that is distributed as a trial version. Demoware often comes preinstalled on new computers, but it is limited in some way until you pay for the full version. Commonly, demoware use is free for a limited period of time. At the end of the trial period, the software stops working if you don't pay for it. Most demoware alerts you when the trial period is coming to a close (Figure 4-10).

Figure 4-10

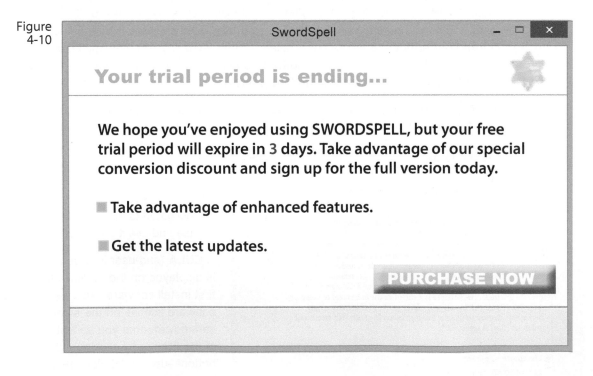

• What's the significance of software copyrights and licenses? (continued)

Shareware is another type of software licensed for free use during a trial period, after which users are supposed to pay a registration fee. Payment is on the honor system, however, so shareware authors collect only a fraction of the money they deserve for their programming efforts. Shareware users are encouraged to make copies of the software and distribute them to others. These shared copies provide a low-cost marketing and distribution channel.

Freeware is copyrighted software that—as you might expect—is available for free. Because the software is protected by copyright, you cannot do anything with it that is not expressly allowed by copyright law or by the author. Typically, the license for freeware permits you to use the software, copy it, and give it away, but does not permit you to alter it or sell it. Many utility programs and device drivers as well as some games are available as freeware. Some freeware displays annoying ads, which can be discontinued by purchasing an ad-free version of the app.

Open source software is often developed as a public, collaborative effort of volunteers. It is distributed for free or for a nominal charge under a license that permits users to view the source code, improve it, and redistribute the software. Linux is an example of open source software, as are LibreOffice, Thunderbird e-mail, and the Firefox browser.

Software vendors have a variety of ways to prevent unauthorized use of applications. The use of registration keys is common. A **registration key** is a unique set of letters and numbers used to activate a product. When you purchase software, you may be provided with a registration key on the screen or in an e-mail message. During the installation process, you'll be asked to enter your registration key. Only valid keys are accepted. They are usually checked against an online database of registration keys to make sure that keys are not passed around and shared by multiple users.

Figure 4-11

Enter your registration key when prompted. If the key is long, you might try to copy and paste it into the provided box; otherwise, type it carefully (Figure 4-11).

Before purchasing software, make sure the license allows you to use the software the way you want to. If you plan to install the software on more than one computer or introduce modifications, make sure the license allows you to do so. You can stay informed about product licensing, updates, and other matters by subscribing to the software publisher's e-mail notifications or by searching the publisher's Web site.

Some commercial software, such as security software, requires annual renewal. If you don't want to pay the fee every year, you might consider freeware or open source security software instead. Informed consumers tend to make better buying decisions. Just remember that many software programs exist and you can usually find alternatives with similar features offered under various licensing terms.

FAQ How do I deal with software installation and access problems?

Usually the installation process proceeds smoothly, but occasionally you'll encounter problems that require a bit of troubleshooting.

Installation stops before completion. When the setup program is unable to complete an installation, it usually displays an error message specifying a problem, such as running out of hard disk space or missing a file. If the error message does not suggest steps for resolving the problem, try an online search using the error message wording to discover what you can do to bypass this installation hurdle.

Installed program does not appear on the computer. Programs installed on a Windows computer should be accessible from the Start menu or Start screen. If not, look for the program's executable file in the destination folder you selected during the installation process. You can set up a shortcut to the program by right-clicking it.

Installed program fails to work. If an installed program does not open, consider uninstalling it and then trying the installation again. Reinstalling software can replace program modules that might have become corrupted and no longer function properly.

Other programs fail to work after a new product is installed. If a newly installed program disrupts other software, check the publisher's Web site to see if an update or a setting can return normal functionality. Otherwise, you might have to uninstall the new software.

Files cannot be read by the new application. New versions of software generally read files from previous versions, but sometimes a conversion process is necessary. The conversion process is usually automated so that as you open a file, it is converted into the right format for the new software. If you save the file in its new format, however, be aware that the old software might not be able to open it.

Access to online application denied. When you're denied access to online applications, the first step is to make sure you are using a valid user ID and password. Also, make sure your account has not expired or been cancelled for non-payment.

Online application not available. Technical problems sometimes make online applications unavailable. Make sure your Internet connection is working and that the application site is not being blocked by your computer's security software. If an online application is not working, make sure you are using a compatible browser and it is not out of date. Also make sure that your computer has all required auxiliary files, such as media players or plug-ins.

Defective distribution media. Suppose that you insert the distribution CD, and your computer's CD drive spins the disc but can't seem to load it. You might have a defective distribution disc. Before you return or exchange the CD, try it on another computer just to make sure that your computer's optical drive hasn't developed problems.

Installation program will not start. If you insert a distribution CD into the drive and the setup program does not automatically start, Windows security might be configured not to autorun programs from the CD. You can either change the security setting or use File Explorer to list the files on the CD. Look for a file called Setup.exe or Install.exe. Double-click it to get it started.

QuickCheck A

1. The Windows [_____] is a file that keeps track of all installed hardware and software within a computer system.

2. True or false? For best results, on a Windows computer you should uninstall software by locating the main program file, selecting it, then pressing the Delete key. [_____]

3. True or false? Portable software products, also referred to as Web apps, are supplied by companies called application service providers (ASPs). [_____]

4. Software [_____] are designed to fix bugs and patch security holes in existing software programs.

5. Two types of software allow you to "try before you buy": demoware and [_____] .

CHECKIT!

QuickCheck B

Answer each question with Y for Yes or N for No, based on the information provided in the software license agreement on the right:

1. Can I install the software and then decide if I agree to the license? [____]

2. Can I rent the software to my friends? [____]

3. Can I sell the software at my Web site? [____]

4. Can I install the software on two of my computers? [____]

5. If I sell my computer, can the buyer legally use the software if I no longer use it? [____]

Software License Agreement

Important - READ CAREFULLY: This License Agreement ("Agreement") is a legal agreement between you and eCourse Corporation for the software product, eCourse GraphWare ("The SOFTWARE"). By installing, copying, or otherwise using the SOFTWARE, you agree to be bound by the terms of this Agreement. The SOFTWARE is protected by copyright laws and international copyright treaties. The SOFTWARE is licensed, not sold.

GRANT OF LICENSE. This Agreement gives you the right to install and use one copy of the SOFTWARE on a single computer. The primary user of the computer on which the SOFTWARE is installed may make a second copy for his or her exclusive use on a portable computer.

OTHER RIGHTS AND LIMITATIONS. You may not reverse engineer, decompile, or disassemble the SOFTWARE except and only to the extent that such activity is expressly permitted by applicable law. The SOFTWARE is licensed as a single product; its components may not be separated for use on more than one computer. You may not rent, lease, or lend the SOFTWARE.

You may permanently transfer all of your rights under this Agreement, provided you retain no copies, you transfer all of the SOFTWARE, and the recipient agrees to the terms of this Agreement. If the software product is an upgrade, any transfer must include all prior versions of the SOFTWARE.

You may receive the SOFTWARE in more than one medium. Regardless of the type of medium you receive, you may use only one medium that is appropriate for your single computer. You may not use or install the other medium on another computer.

CHECKIT!

5 Getting Started with Windows

What's Inside and on the CD?

Microsoft Windows is the world's most popular operating system. Knowing how to use it efficiently gives you a head start in just about every computer-related task. Microsoft released Windows 8 in 2012. Despite some notable differences in the first screens it displays, Windows 8 has many of the same characteristics as Windows 7.

You can easily learn how to use both Windows 7 and Windows 8; this chapter walks you through the basics, including the difference between the Windows 7 Start menu and the Windows 8 Start screen. You'll learn how to log in, switch users, log out, launch applications, navigate the Windows taskbar, and arrange your Windows desktop. To assist you with troubleshooting, the chapter provides information about the Windows Help and Support Center. You'll also learn where to find information about your computer's Windows version and service packs.

FAQ Which version of Windows do I have?

Microsoft Windows has evolved through several versions, each one slightly different from the others in terms of features and appearance. Knowing which version of Windows is installed on your computer is useful, especially when troubleshooting hardware and software problems. Of the Windows versions listed in the time line in Figure 5-1, Windows 7 and Windows 8 have the largest user bases.

Figure
5-1

Windows Time Line							
Windows 3.1 1992	Windows 95 1995	Windows 98 1998	Windows Me 2000	Windows XP 2001	Windows Vista 2007	Windows 7 2009	Windows 8 2012

© MediaTechnics

Because Windows 8 and Windows 7 are in widespread use, this chapter covers both operating systems so that you can apply what you learn on whichever of the two operating systems is installed on the computers you use at home, work, or school.

There are several ways to discover which version of Windows is installed on a computer:

• Startup screen. The Windows logo and version might be displayed on the startup screen that appears when a computer powers up. You might also see version information displayed on the Windows login screen.

• Start screen or Start button. As you learned in a previous chapter, Windows 8 displays a Start screen, whereas Windows 7 and earlier versions display a Start button at the bottom of the screen.

• System information. Windows offers additional details about the operating system, such as whether it is the 32-bit or 64-bit version. You can discover these details and more by entering operating in the Windows Search box, selecting Settings, then selecting the option to show which operating system your computer is running. Windows displays a System screen similar to the one shown in Figure 5-2.

TRY IT!

Figure
5-2

FAQ How do I work with Windows 7?

To start Windows 7, simply turn your computer on. As your computer powers up and completes its boot process, Windows starts automatically.

Most computers are configured to collect login credentials before access is allowed. This security measure is helpful for protecting files and personal data. The Windows 7 login screen displays icons for each person who has an account on the computer. In a later chapter, you'll learn how to set up accounts. If you don't have an account on a computer, look for a Guest account icon that offers limited public access to a Windows computer. Figure 5-3 explains the main elements of the Windows 7 login screen.

Figure 5-3

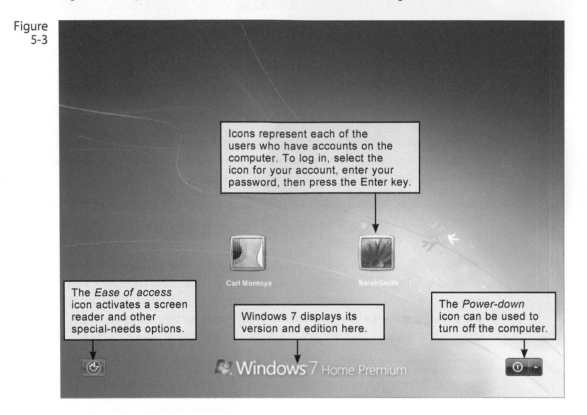

Icons represent each of the users who have accounts on the computer. To log in, select the icon for your account, enter your password, then press the Enter key.

Carl Montoya

SarahSmith

The *Ease of access* icon activates a screen reader and other special-needs options.

Windows 7 displays its version and edition here.

The *Power-down* icon can be used to turn off the computer.

Windows 7 Home Premium

- Your **Windows password** is associated with user rights that monitor who is allowed to access various programs and data files. Your user ID and password allow you to view, change, and delete stored files, such as those in your personal folders.

- When typing your password, you must use the correct uppercase and lowercase characters. As you type each character of your password, you will see an asterisk (*) or circle (•). These symbols are a security feature that hides your password from an onlooker.

- The Windows 7 login screen displays an *Ease of access* icon in the lower-left corner that provides options useful to special-needs users. You can use this link to turn on narration that reads the screen, activate an on-screen keyboard, or magnify text and objects displayed on the screen.

How do I work with Windows 7? (continued)

After you log in, Windows 7 displays a screen called the desktop, which is the backdrop for application windows and other graphical controls. The Start button is the main control for Windows 7. Clicking it produces the Start menu, which contains a handy collection of controls for starting programs, searching for files, getting help, adjusting system settings, and shutting down your computer. Click the Try It! button in Figure 5-4 to tour the Start menu.

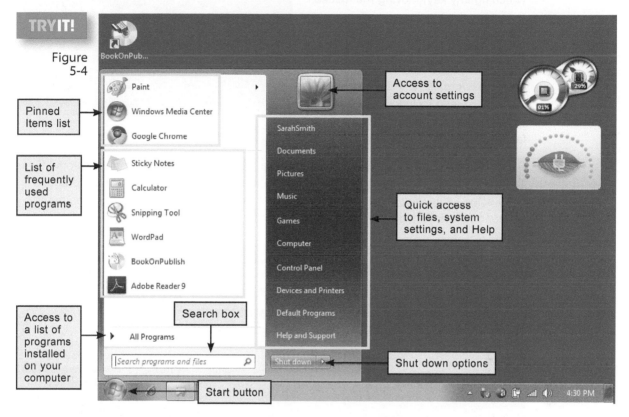

Figure 5-4

- The **Search box** helps you quickly find files and programs. Just above the Search box, the **All Programs option** produces a list of software installed on your computer. You'll refer to this list often to start programs.

- You can customize the **Pinned Items list** to show your favorite programs. To add a program to the Pinned Items list, you can right-click any program shown in the All Programs list, then click *Pin to Start Menu*. You can also drag any program or document icon to the Pinned Items area of the Start menu.

- Below the Pinned Items list, Windows displays the programs you've used most recently. These programs are automatically added by Windows as it monitors your program usage.

- The right side of the Start menu provides options for viewing files in your personal folders, accessing your account settings, adjusting system settings, getting help, and shutting down your computer.

- Hovering the mouse pointer over any program in the Start menu displays a **jump list**, which is a list of files that you recently opened using that program. This feature is especially handy if you can't recall the exact location of a file, but you remember which program you used to create it.

FAQ How do I work with Windows 8?

To start Windows 8, press the power button on your computer. In a few seconds you'll see the **Lock Screen**, which displays a colorful photo along with the date and time (right).

Touching any key, moving the mouse, or tapping the touchscreen closes the Lock Screen and displays the Windows 8 login screen where you can select your account icon and enter your password. As with Windows 7, the login screen includes an *Ease of access* icon for turning on accessibility features.

Once you're logged in, Windows 8 displays the Start screen with its array of colorful tiles. The Windows 8 Start screen is optimized for a touch interface, so tiles can be dragged or selected using your finger or a stylus as well as a mouse. Figure 5-5 explains the elements of the Windows 8 Start screen.

Figure 5-5

- To return to the Start screen from any application, press the ⊞ Windows key on your computer keyboard or the Windows button on a tablet computer's case.

- If your computer has a touchscreen, you can scroll by swiping right or left. You can also use pinch and zoom gestures to increase or decrease the size of the Start screen.

•How do I work with Windows 8? (continued)

In Windows 8, the Start screen includes a built-in Search function that takes the place of the Windows 7 Start menu. While looking at the Windows 8 Start screen, you can activate the Windows 8 Search box by typing the first few letters of the item you're looking for. Windows displays a list of matching items, which you can select and access with a mouse click or touch. Figure 5-6 illustrates the screen that appears when you type word while the Start screen is displayed.

TRYIT!

Figure 5-6

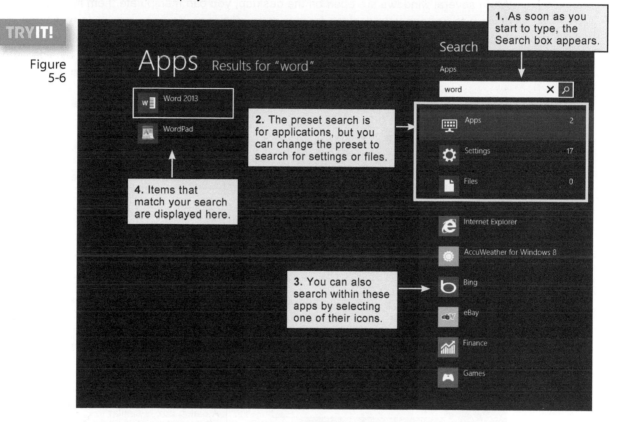

When using the Windows 8 Search box, keep in mind that you can alter the search for the following specific categories:

- **Apps.** The preset search for apps is useful if you want to start an application or utility for which there is no tile. Math Input Panel, Character Map, Magnifier, Steps Recorder, and QuickTime Player are just a few apps that you might want to access using Search.

- **Settings.** When you search in Settings, you can find useful system utilities that help you customize your computer's display, printers, security, and more. Use the search box to enter one or more keywords, such as change password, to access a utility that will help you view and change settings.

- **Files.** When you search in Files, you can find specific documents that you've created based on their titles or their contents. You can also locate photos, graphics, music, and other media by their titles.

- **Listed applications.** The Windows 8 Search box also works with listed applications, such as Internet Explorer, AccuWeather, and Bing. For example, you can enter a search for Savannah, GA and when you click AccuWeather, you'll see the current temperature in that city. Clicking the IE or Bing icon will display links to information about Savannah and its tourist attractions.

FAQ What's on the Windows desktop?

Whether you use Windows 7 or 8, the **Windows desktop** is the backdrop for many of the tasks you perform on your computer. It is the screen you see when the Windows 7 boot process is complete. In Windows 8, you can easily access the desktop by selecting the Desktop tile from the Start screen. The desktop can display application windows, message windows called **dialog boxes**, and icons.

When several windows are open on the desktop, you can manipulate them in a variety of ways to arrange your desktop for maximum efficiency. You can maximize a window so that it fills the screen and provides the largest amount of working space. When working back and forth between two windows, you might want to size them to fit side by side. Click the Try It! button in Figure 5-7 to explore ways to organize your desktop.

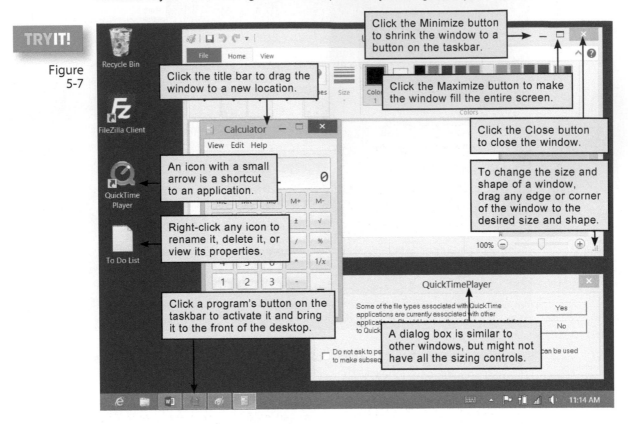

Figure
5-7

You can control the placement of icons that appear on your desktop. It is simple to rearrange icons so that those you use most often are easy to find. You can also create new folder and file icons for quick access to documents you frequently use.

- To create a new icon on the Windows desktop, right-click any empty area of the desktop and select New. Select an icon type from the list, then assign it a name.

- To delete an icon from the desktop, right-click it and then click Delete.

- To rename an icon, right-click the icon and select Rename.

- To display the properties of an icon, right-click the icon and select Properties.

- A **desktop shortcut** is an icon that displays a small arrow to indicate that it is simply a link to an application or file. If you delete a desktop shortcut, you are only deleting the icon, not the application or file it represents.

FAQ How do I use the taskbar?

The **taskbar** is located at the bottom of the Windows desktop and holds a variety of buttons. Except for the lack of a Start button in Windows 8, the taskbars for the Windows 7 and Windows 8 desktops are very similar (Figure 5-8).

Figure 5-8

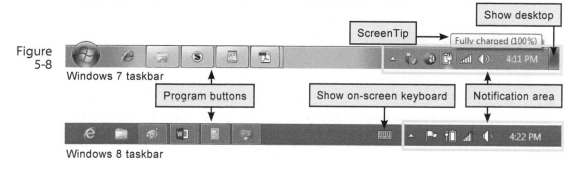

- To find out what each taskbar icon does, point to it and wait. In a second or two, a ScreenTip appears with the icon's title. A **ScreenTip** (also called a ToolTip) is a message that pops up to identify unlabeled buttons.

- **Program buttons** on the taskbar represent open, or "running," programs. If you don't see a window for the application you want to use, click its button on the taskbar.

- The **Notification area** displays buttons that provide status information and shortcuts to programs and utilities, such as volume control, power options, network strength, and antivirus software. If the Notification area contains more icons than can fit in the allocated space, the ⌃ button displays additional notification icons.

- A computer keeps track of the current date and time by using a battery-operated internal clock, and syncing with a standard clock on the Internet. If the date is not displayed, point to the time, and the date will appear after a second or two. Your computer uses the clock to record the date and time when files are created or modified, so it is important that the date and time are correct. To change the time or date, right-click the displayed time and select Adjust Date/Time.

- The taskbar's 🔊 Volume icon lets you quickly adjust the sound level emitted by your computer's speakers. Click the Volume icon to display the adjustment control.

- The taskbar's 📶 Internet access button displays the strength of your wireless connection. Clicking it lets you connect or disconnect from a network.

- The *Show desktop* button temporarily hides all open windows so that you can see the desktop. Clicking this button again reopens any windows you were using.

- On some computers, the taskbar is set to disappear when it is not in use. To reveal it, pass the mouse pointer off the bottom edge of the screen. You can also change the size of the taskbar to display more or fewer program buttons.

- To customize the taskbar, right-click it and then select Properties from the shortcut menu.

FAQ What do I need to know about basic Windows controls?

The Windows graphical user interface incorporates hardware and software. Hardware components of the user interface include a display device, mouse, keyboard, and perhaps a touchscreen that allow you to view and manipulate your computing environment. As described in Figure 5-9, the user interface also includes software elements, such as command buttons, split buttons, checkboxes, option buttons, sliders, lists, and menus.

Figure 5-9

A command button performs an action as soon as you click it. You'll often see these buttons in sets within dialog boxes.

A split button has two parts. Clicking the main part of the button carries out a command; clicking the arrow opens a menu with more options.

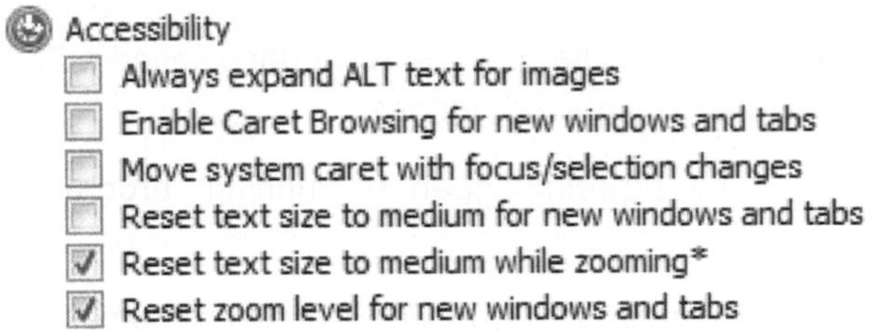

A checkbox is used to select options in situations where multiple options are allowed.

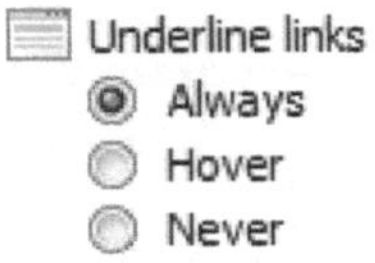

Option buttons are round; only one button in the set can remain selected.

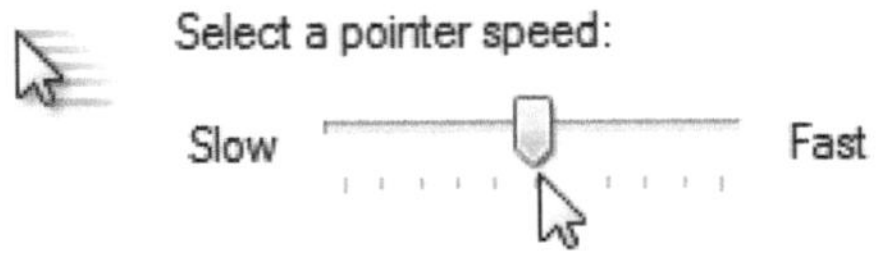

A slider can be dragged to select a value.

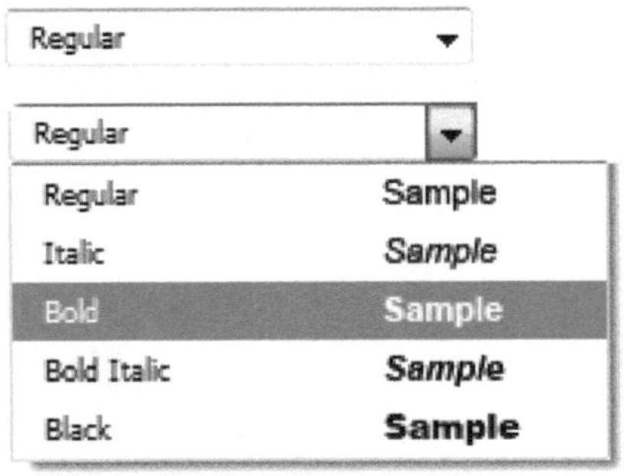

A list is similar to a menu; but instead of clicking a command, you click an option to select it.

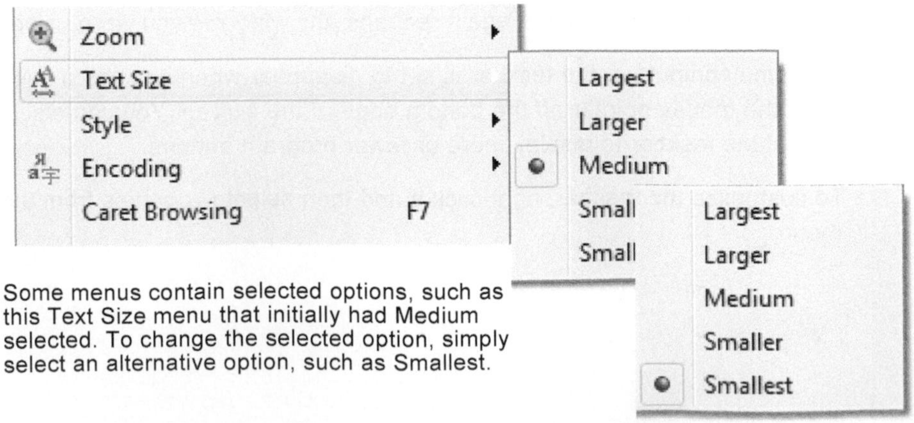

Some menus contain selected options, such as this Text Size menu that initially had Medium selected. To change the selected option, simply select an alternative option, such as Smallest.

FAQ What should I know about Windows updates?

In an earlier chapter, you learned the importance of application software updates for patching security holes and correcting program bugs that might cause system glitches. Updates are periodically available for operating systems, too. They are sometimes referred to as "patches." A group of updates, including those that have been previously released, is called a **service pack**.

Operating system updates become necessary to maintain compatibility with new equipment and technologies. Updates might also be necessary to address issues with applications, utilities, and plug-ins. Security holes in an operating system are one of the biggest threats to your data and to your privacy, so it is important to apply updates and service packs as they become available.

Windows has three categories of updates. Important and recommended updates can be installed automatically, whereas optional updates are installed manually.

- Important updates offer significant security, reliability, and privacy benefits. They should be installed as soon as they become available.

- Recommended updates pertain to non-essential problems and enhancements. Although installing these updates is not critical, they are typically installed at the same time as important updates.

- Optional updates include updated drivers and Microsoft applications, which are typically not required for secure and efficient operation of your computer system.

You can view a list of available updates and previously installed updates by typing Windows update in the Start screen or Start menu. Figure 5-10 explains important information that's available from the Windows Update panel.

Figure
5-10

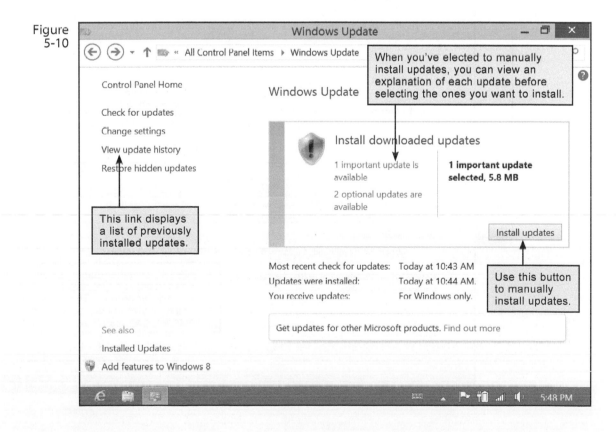

• What should I know about Windows updates? (continued)

Windows lets you choose how you want to receive and install updates. Your options are:

- **Install updates automatically.** All updates are downloaded automatically when they are available. Important and recommended updates are installed immediately. This option gives you the most security, at the expense of losing some control over what is installed on your computer.

- **Download updates, but do not automatically install.** All updates are downloaded automatically, but you can choose if and when to install them. Depending on your version of Windows and notification settings, you'll see a message or notification icon when updates are available.

- **Check for updates, but do not download them.** Windows can check for updates and notify you when they are available. You can decide if and when you want to download them and install them.

- **Do not update.** Windows will not check for updates or notify you of their availability. This option is a security risk and is not recommended for most consumers.

Figure
5-11

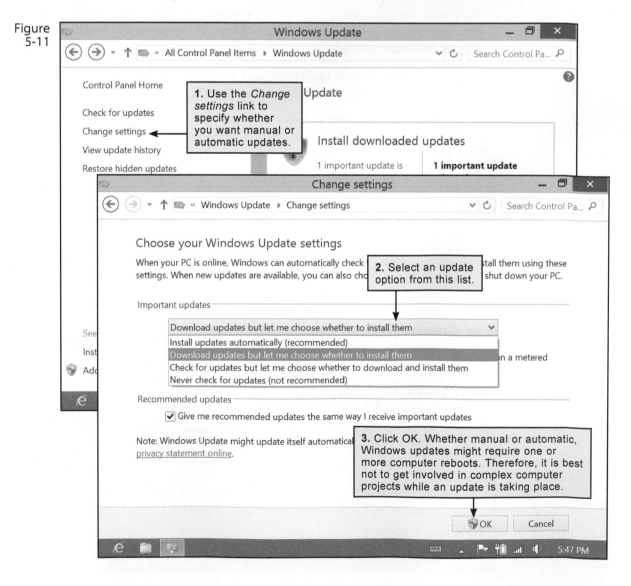

FAQ How do I access Windows Help?

To access information about Windows features, type Help at the Windows 8 Start screen or look for the Help and Support option on the Windows 7 Start menu. The Windows Help and Support Center is your gateway to Windows manuals, FAQs, and troubleshooting wizards. Basic help information is stored on your computer as part of Windows; additional help is supplied by Microsoft's online support center.

Computer manufacturers sometimes customize the Help and Support Center to include specific information about a particular brand of computer. This information can include troubleshooting tips, links to Internet-based help systems, and even links to brand-specific message boards and forums. Figure 5-12 explains basic tools for using Windows Help.

TRYIT!

Figure 5-12

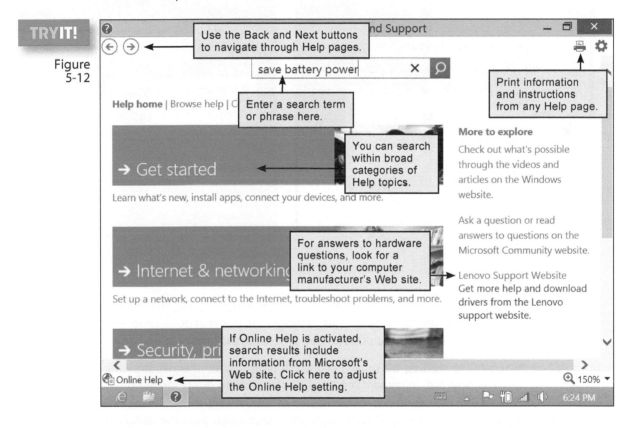

- If the Help and Support Center does not link you to the information you need, you can use a search engine, such as Google, to hunt for user groups, online forums, or articles containing relevant information. Be cautious, however, about information from online forums; some participants provide inaccurate advice.

- You might also consider asking local experts. For example, you might have a friend who has extensive Windows experience; your school might provide a student help desk; or your workplace might employ a staff of IT technicians.

- Help is a two-way street. As you gain expertise, consider sharing your knowledge in return for the help you received from others.

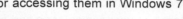 **How do I shut down Windows?**

When you want to turn your computer off from its fully awake state, Windows provides several shut down options. The process for accessing these options in Windows 8 differs from the process for accessing them in Windows 7, as shown in Figure 5-13.

Figure
5-13

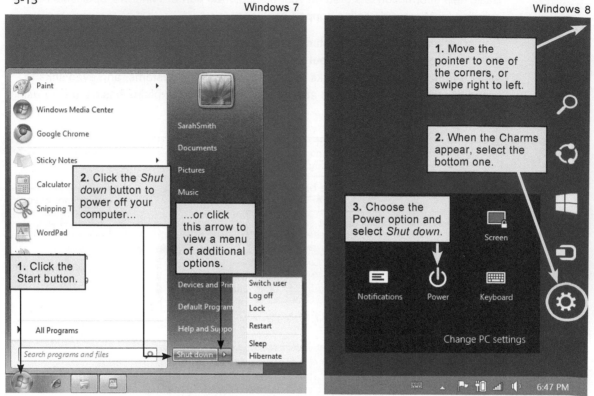

- Use the **Shut down option** to ensure that your work is saved, and temporary files created by the operating system are removed. As the shut down proceeds, Windows closes and your computer powers itself off or prompts you to do so.

- You can use the **Log off option** or **Switch user option** in situations where multiple users access the computer. The *Log off* option leaves the computer on, but closes your files so that the next person who logs on cannot access them. *Switch user* is applicable if you want to stay logged in while another person also uses the computer. These options are located on the *Shut down* menu in Windows 7, but in Windows 8 you would use your ▨ account icon on the Start screen to log out or switch users.

- Use the **Sleep option** when you're planning not to use your computer for a short time and want it to reactivate quickly. Sleep mode (sometimes referred to as "standby") keeps open programs and data files in memory, but puts the computer into a low-power state.

- The **Hibernate option** saves a record of the programs and files that you have open, but closes them before turning off the computer. The next time you turn on the computer, your session is restored.

- The **Restart option** powers your computer down and then reboots it. Use this option when you are troubleshooting and want to clear memory, then restart Windows.

QuickCheck A

1. The Windows [＿＿＿＿＿＿＿＿＿] includes a taskbar with buttons and a Notification area.

2. In Windows 8, you can log out or switch users using your account icon on the Start screen; but in Windows 7, you access these options from the [＿＿＿＿＿＿＿＿] button.

3. [＿＿＿＿＿＿＿＿] buttons are round; only one button in the set can remain selected.

4. A user [＿＿＿＿＿＿＿] is a combination of hardware and software that helps people and computers communicate.

5. True or false? Sleep mode keeps open programs and data files in memory, but puts the computer into a low-power state. [＿＿＿＿＿]

CHECKIT!

QuickCheck B

Indicate the letter of the desktop element that best matches the following:

1. Taskbar buttons [＿＿＿]

2. On-screen keyboard icon [＿＿＿]

3. Desktop shortcut [＿＿＿]

4. Application window [＿＿＿]

5. Notification area [＿＿＿]

CHECKIT!

Working with Windows Settings and Accounts

6

What's Inside and on the CD?

Your computer arrives with Windows preinstalled with a standard configuration of settings. The more you work with your computer, the more you'll identify aspects that could be better tailored to the way you work. Perhaps you wish the mouse could be zippier. Maybe the desktop background image seems distracting, or you're finding the text a little difficult to read. Possibly your computer seems sluggish and you're curious about its performance.

Windows offers a wide array of tools for customizing your computer and gauging its performance. In this chapter, you'll learn how to use tools such as the Control Panel and Task Manager to customize your screen-based desktop, designate printers, and get information that shows how well your computer is performing.

FAQ How do I access and change settings?

Operating systems are customizable, and Windows is no exception. You can change the color and size of many desktop elements, and specify which icons are shown and which remain hidden. In Figure 6-1, you can see two customized Windows desktops that look very different.

Figure
6-1

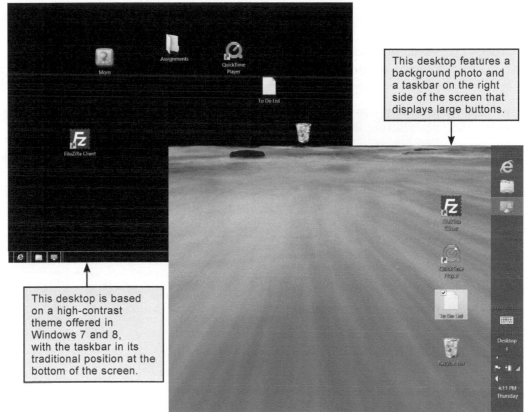

This desktop features a background photo and a taskbar on the right side of the screen that displays large buttons.

This desktop is based on a high-contrast theme offered in Windows 7 and 8, with the taskbar in its traditional position at the bottom of the screen.

In addition to customizing the look of your desktop, you can adjust the speed of your mouse, select a printer, check device drivers, gauge your computer's performance, and monitor system security. You can also change passwords, modify account status, adjust power settings, create networks, and more. Before you embark on customization experiments, however, keep the following important points in mind:

● Be careful when you change system settings. Changes to network settings can disable your Internet and e-mail connections. Incorrect hardware settings can make a peripheral device unusable. Before you change system settings, make sure you understand the effects of those changes on the computer.

● It is always a good idea to jot down original settings so that you can undo changes that cause problems.

● In businesses and in school computer labs, users are sometimes prevented from making changes to some or all system settings. If you work in such an environment and your settings don't seem to take effect, check with your system administrator.

● Some system settings require administrator rights. You'll learn more about this topic in the FAQ. *How do I set up and modify user accounts?*

• How do I access and change settings? (continued)

Windows offers several ways to access configuration settings. We'll cover the following methods in the next few pages:

- Windows 8 *Change PC settings* link

- Using the Search box in Windows 7 and Windows 8

- Accessing Control Panel in Windows 7 and Windows 8

Windows 8 has a unique, but limited, panel of settings that can be accessed from the **Charms menu** that appears when you move the pointer to one of the corners of the screen or when you swipe in from the right edge of a touchscreen (Figure 6-2).

Figure
6-2

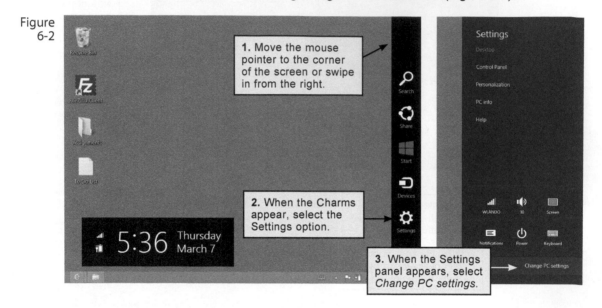

The *Change PC settings* options are primarily relevant for tablet users and for customizing the Start screen. Select the Try It! button in Figure 6-3 to get acquainted with the possibilities in the *PC settings* list.

TRYIT!

Figure
6-3

• How do I access and change settings? (continued)

The Windows Search box is handy for finding where to access a specific group of settings. In Windows 7, the Search box is displayed as part of the Start menu when you click the Start button, as shown in Figure 6-4.

Figure
6-4

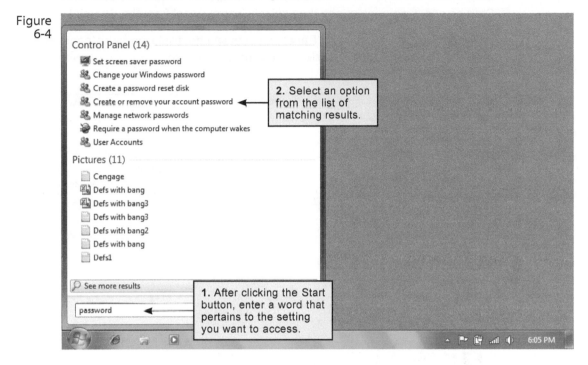

In Windows 8, the Search box appears whenever you start typing while the Start screen is displayed. Some settings are displayed in the results for Apps, but most settings appear only after you have selected the Settings option. As shown in Figure 6-5, list items with the ⚙ icon in front of them link to *PC settings* options. List items with color icons link to Control Panel options.

Figure
6-5

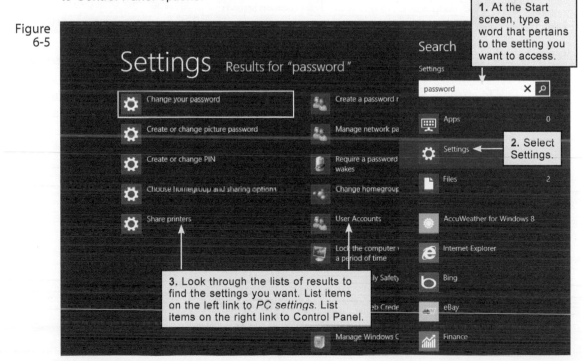

• How do I access and change settings? (continued)

The **Control Panel** is a collection of tools for customizing Windows system settings so that you can work more efficiently. To open the Control Panel in Windows 7, click the Start button and then select the Control Panel option. In Windows 8, when you're at the Start screen, type control and then select Control Panel from the Search list.

In Windows 7 or 8, the Control Panel contents can be displayed by category or as a list of icons. The list of icons is easiest to navigate. As shown in Figure 6-6, you can select the *Large icons* view.

Figure 6-6

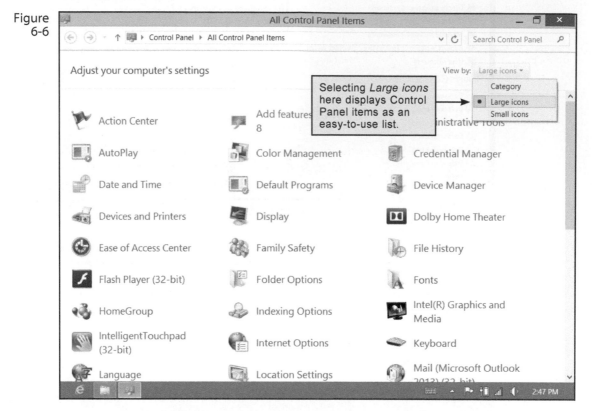

You can search within Control Panel using the Search box at the top of the screen. This search feature is useful if you can't figure out which icon leads to the settings you want to change. Suppose you want to find out if a device driver is up to date. There is no icon labeled "Device Driver" in Control Panel. Figure 6-7 illustrates the results of a search for "driver."

Figure 6-7

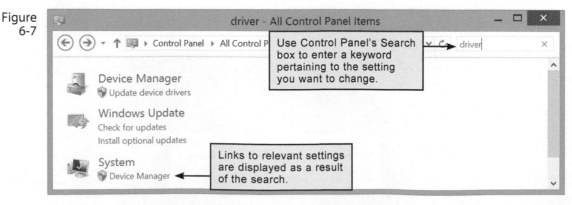

FAQ Can I adjust sleep and other power settings?

Computers use energy to power the screen, microprocessor, internal fan, status lights, hard disk drive, and assorted other components. Energy use varies from one computer model to another, and depends on what the computer is doing.

When actively running software or displaying videos, a computer is "under load" and is consuming power at close to its maximum rate. When a computer is on and displaying the Windows desktop but not performing other tasks, it is in idle mode and consuming less power. Computers consume less power when in sleep mode, and even less power in hibernate mode or when turned off. An average Dell laptop computer's energy use (shown in Figure 6-8) even when under load is about half that of a 100 watt light bulb.

Figure 6-8

Active	Idle	Sleep	Off	Annual
46 watts	13 watts	0.6 watts	0.3 watts	50 kWh

© MediaTechnics

Your computer's power consumption is important for two reasons. First, energy conservation is good for the environment. Second, energy conservation prolongs battery life and gives you more plug-free computing time. Windows offers three types of automated power plans to help you conserve power and make your laptop computer's battery last longer:

• Balanced. Gives you full performance when you need it and saves power when your computer is idle. Most computers are shipped with this option selected.

• Power saver. Reduces system performance and screen brightness to help you get maximum computing time on each battery charge.

• High performance. Allows maximum performance and screen brightness at the expense of battery-based run time.

In addition to selecting a power plan, Windows offers settings for what happens when you close the lid of your laptop and whether a password is required when your computer wakes up. By selecting the Power Options link from the Control Panel, you can view and modify power settings for your computer (Figure 6-9).

Figure 6-9

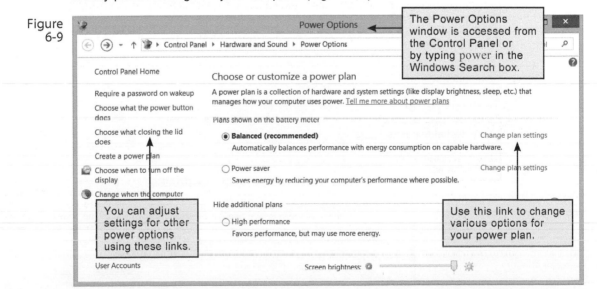

• Can I adjust sleep and other power settings? (continued)

If you have a portable computer, you can specify settings to use when the computer is operating on battery power and when it is plugged in. Typically the times specified for on battery will be shorter than for plugged in because when your computer is plugged into a wall outlet, you are not as concerned about battery drain. Typical settings for the Balanced power plan are shown in the top window of Figure 6-10. If you find that you're constantly waking up your computer, you might want to extend the times by a few minutes.

You can also control what happens when you shut the lid or press the power button. Your options are for the computer to do nothing, sleep, hibernate, or shut down. As shown in the bottom window of the figure below, most users prefer to use the Sleep setting because it is the fastest way to get the computer ready to use. Because hibernation uses less power than sleep modes, you might consider changing the lid-close setting to Hibernate if you tote your computer with you and have few opportunities to recharge it.

TRYIT!

Figure
6-10

Timing for power plan events can be adjusted to accommodate the way you work.

Regardless of the option you choose here, holding down the power button for several seconds turns the computer off.

Select what happens when you press the power button or close the lid.

You can select one of these options in each of the four categories.

FAQ How do I adjust the keyboard, touchpad, and mouse?

Windows allows you to adjust keyboard and mouse settings by using links in the Control Panel or by linking from the Start menu's Search box. From the Ease of Access Center, you can customize additional keyboard functions to make the computer easier to use for people with special needs.

Figure
6-11

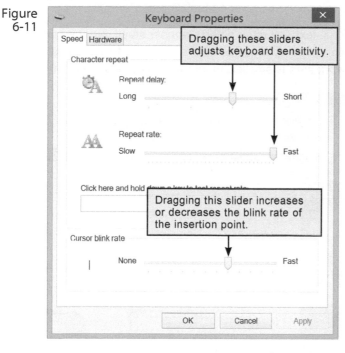

To adjust basic keyboard settings, type keyboard into the Windows Search box. From the Keyboard Properties box, you can increase or decrease the repeat delay, which is the time that elapses after you press a key until your computer starts displaying repeat characters. You can adjust the repeat rate, or speed at which the repeated characters appear. You can also change the rate at which the cursor (or insertion point) blinks (Figure 6-11).

You can customize your mouse and touchpad, too. Left-handers can reverse the touchpad or mouse buttons so that the right button is used to select items and the left button is used to display shortcut menus. You can also adjust the pointer speed. For example, when you increase your computer's screen resolution, you might want to increase the pointer speed so that it travels quickly across the large workspace.

To adjust settings for the mouse or touchpad, enter mouse in the Windows Search box. Click the Try It! button in Figure 6-12 to experiment with mouse and touchpad settings.

TRY**IT!**

Figure
6-12

Changing to the *Left-handed* option switches the way the mouse or touchpad buttons function.

Adjusting the double-click speed lets you click at a speed that's comfortable.

Selecting ClickLock allows you to click at the beginning and end of text that you want to highlight instead of holding the mouse button down while dragging over the text.

Each tab offers a group of settings.

Use this list to select a mouse or touchpad device before adjusting other settings.

FAQ How do I change display settings?

Windows provides all kinds of options for customizing the look of your on-screen desktop, including its size and background. The apparent size of your desktop depends on the resolution of your computer screen. Each dot of light on a computer screen is called a pixel, short for picture element. The number of horizontal and vertical pixels that a device displays on the screen is referred to as screen resolution.

Figure 6-13

At higher screen resolutions, text and other objects appear small, but the computer can display a large desktop work area. At lower screen resolutions, text and objects appear larger, but the apparent work area is smaller. Figure 6-13 illustrates this difference.

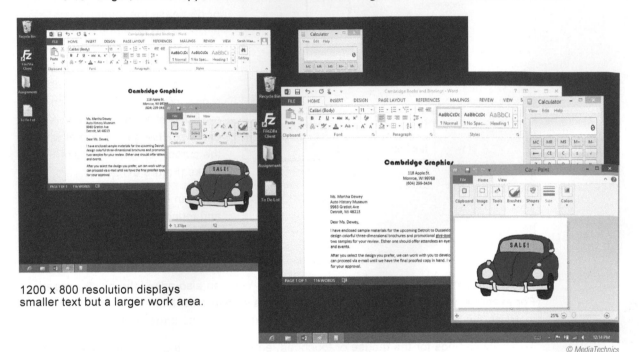

© MediaTechnics

1200 x 800 resolution displays smaller text but a larger work area.

1024 x 768 resolution displays larger text but a smaller work area.

TRY IT!

Figure 6-14

Right-click any blank area of the desktop and select *Screen resolution* to access resolution settings.

Screen Resolution

Change the appearance of your displays

Detect
Identify

Display: 1. Mobile PC Display
Resolution: 800 × 600   ← Select a resolution.
Orientation: Landscape
Multiple displays: Extend these displays

This is currently your main display.   Advanced settings

Connect to a projector (or press the ⊞ key and tap P)
Make text and other items larger or smaller
What display settings should I choose?

Choose this option to change the size of on-screen text.

Use advanced settings to adjust display color quality.

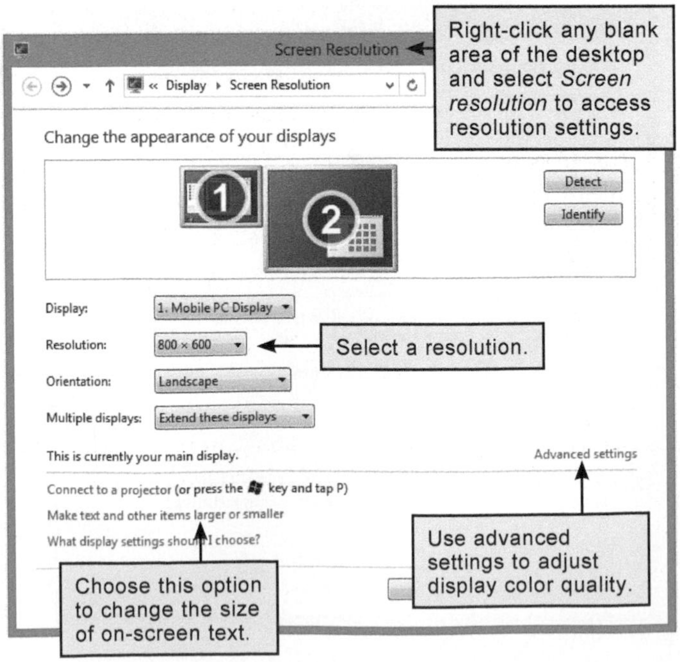

Most laptop computers have a recommended resolution that provides the best image quality. If this setting produces on-screen text that is uncomfortably small or distorts the aspect ratio, you can experiment with resolution settings to determine what's best for your work style.

You can also use the Screen Resolution window to activate multiple screens, in case you want to connect an external monitor to your laptop computer.

• How do I change display settings? (continued)

You can personalize the look of your Windows desktop by working with color schemes, backgrounds, and themes. A **desktop theme** is a predefined set of colors, sounds, and backgrounds that can transform your desktop from boring to brilliant (Figure 6-15).

Figure
6-15

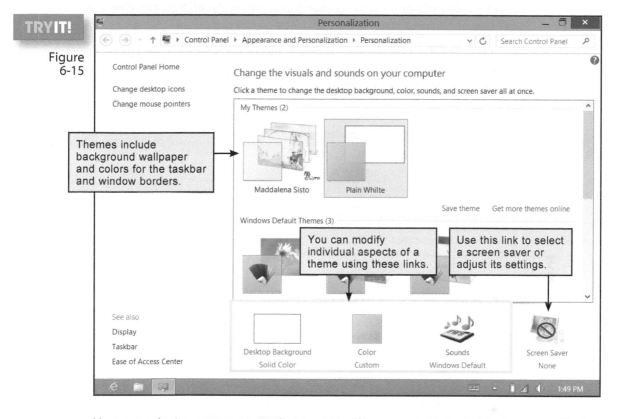

You can select a **screen saver** that appears after your computer is idle for a specified period of time. Screen savers were originally designed so that a static image displayed for a long period of time would not get "burned" into the screen.

Figure
6-16

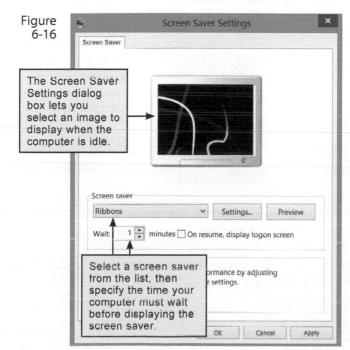

LCD display devices don't have a problem with screen burn-in, but screen savers are still popular because they are fun and they can hide work in progress while you are away from your desk.

When a screen saver is running, however, the display is consuming power. For energy efficiency and to prolong the life of a display device, it is more effective to turn off the screen when it is not in use. You can do so by applying power management settings that you learned about earlier in the chapter.

FAQ How do I control printers?

Your computer might have multiple printers attached, or you might have access to several printers on a network. To view a list of all the printers your computer can access, add new printers, create connections to network printers, and select a default printer, access the *Devices and Printers* option from Control Panel. You can also use the *Devices and Printers* option to view, pause, or cancel pending print jobs.

The printer you want to use automatically, unless you specify otherwise, is called the **default printer**. You can change your default printer if you replace your old printer or if your network provides access to a new printer. When you no longer plan to use a printer, you should delete it from the list of printers.

TRYIT!

Figure
6-17

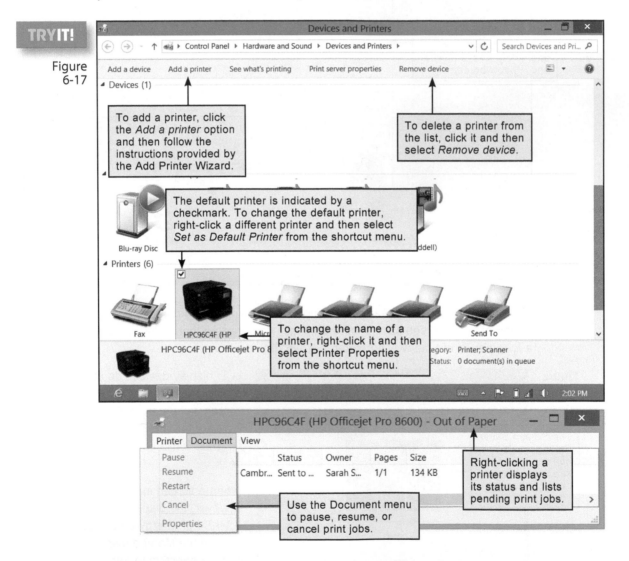

• When your computer has access to several printers, it is useful to name them by function. For example, you might name one printer "Photo Printer" and name another printer "Black and White Laser Printer." It is also useful to include the word "Network" with the names of printers you can only access when connected to a network. Although the icons for network and local printers are slightly different, in some views the icons can be small and hard to distinguish.

FAQ What's in the Ease of Access Center?

The Ease of Access Center provides links to all of the accessibility tools included with the Windows operating system. Accessibility tools can make a computer easier to use for people who have disabilities or special needs. You can select from tools that offer the following:

- Use the computer without a display by narrating what is on the screen.

- Make the computer easier to see by magnifying the display, increasing the contrast, and removing distracting backgrounds.

- Use the computer without a mouse or keyboard by activating an on-screen keyboard or setting up speech recognition that will recognize voice commands.

- Make the mouse easier to use by adjusting speed, enlarging the pointer, and activating additional hover features.

- Use text and visual alternatives for sounds by displaying text captions for the dialog in videos, and replacing system sounds with visual alerts.

- Make it easier to focus on tasks by automatically closing dialog boxes and turning off unnecessary animations.

You can change a computer's accessibility options by typing Access in the Windows Search box or looking for "Ease of Access Center" in Control Panel. Figure 6-18 illustrates the Ease of Access Center with narration turned on to read the screen.

Figure 6-18

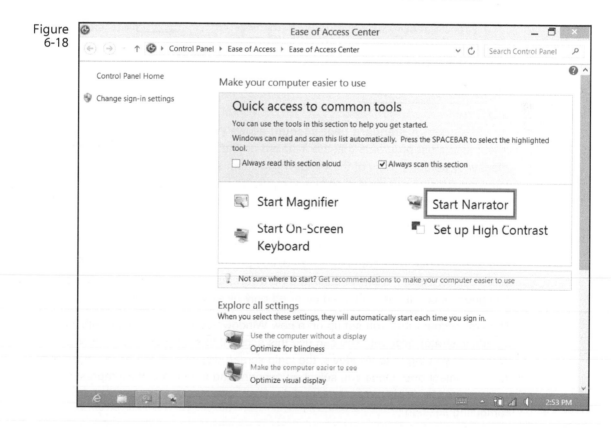

FAQ How do I set up and modify user accounts?

Credentials is a term that refers to user names, passwords, PINs, and other identifiers that can be used to log in to computers or Web sites. User accounts are an important set of credentials for accessing any computer on which Windows is installed. User accounts are weapons in the battle against unauthorized access and other surreptitious computer activity. A **user account** includes a user ID and password, plus specifications about which files can be accessed and what settings can be adjusted. Windows offers three types of user accounts: administrator, standard user, and guest.

Administrator. An **administrator account** lets you change any settings, access and change any other users' accounts, install software, connect hardware, and access all the files on a computer. Certain activities, such as uninstalling software, cannot proceed unless you are logged in as an administrator or can enter an administrator account name and password as shown in Figure 6-19.

Figure
6-19

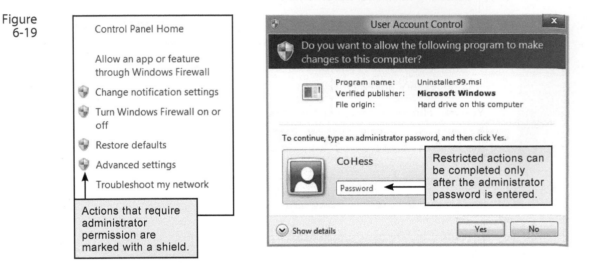

Standard user. A **standard user account** allows you to access folders and files that you create, use most programs that are installed on the computer, and adjust settings that affect your personal view of the Windows desktop. With this type of account, however, you cannot install or uninstall software, configure hardware, or change settings that affect other users unless you know an administrator password.

Guest. A **guest account** is designed for situations when you want to allow someone to use your computer without creating a user account. For example, you might have a visitor who wants to use your computer to go online and check e-mail messages. Guest account users cannot install software, configure hardware, change settings, or create accounts. The guest account can be turned on or off only by an administrator.

The first account that you set up on a new Windows computer automatically becomes an administrator account. You can use this account to set up additional user accounts. Whenever you log in to Windows, the login screen displays all the accounts so that you can select one. Once you select an account and log in, a picture representing your account is displayed at the top of the Start menu or Start screen throughout your computing session.

• How do I set up and modify user accounts? (continued)

The process for managing user accounts in Windows 8 differs a bit from the process in Windows 7. In Windows 7, all of the user management options are within the Control Panel's User Accounts screen. In Windows 8, however, account management tasks are divided between the User Accounts screen and the *PC settings* screen. Study Figure 6-20 to get an overview of the options available on these Windows 8 screens, then select Try It! to learn more.

TRYIT!

Figure
6-20

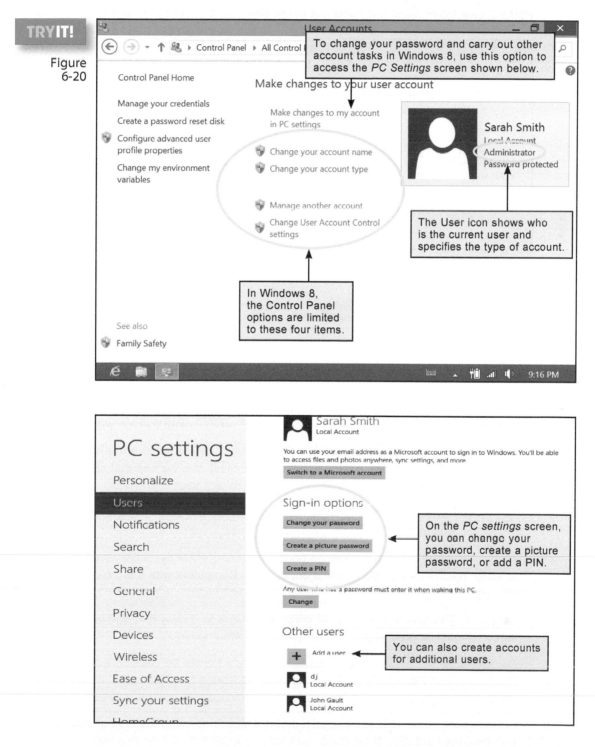

FAQ How well is my computer performing?

Have you ever wondered how well your computer is performing and how it stacks up against the computers used by your friends, at work, or in school labs? Is your machine hot, or is it just average? The Windows Experience Index rates your computer's performance in five categories. Scores in each category range from 1.0 to 7.9 in Windows 7. In Windows 8, scores range from 1.0 to 9.9. Higher scores mean better and faster performance. To view your computer's Windows Experience Index, look for the *Performance Information and Tools* link in the Windows Search box or the Control Panel.

Figure
6-21

Your computer's overall base score is the lowest subscore, not an average of the scores in all categories. Think of the base score as the weakest link; the one that constrains your computer's performance. Here's what the base score tells you:

- **Processor:** Scores less than 5.0 may indicate that the computer will underperform in tasks that require encryption, compression, or video processing.

- **Memory (RAM):** This score depends on the amount of RAM available, and the speed at which data is transferred into and out of RAM. Computers with 4 GB of RAM should score greater than 5.0.

- **Graphics:** The speed at which your computer is able to display text and images on the screen should be greater than 4.0 for average performance.

- **Gaming graphics:** This score measures how many frames per second a computer's graphics circuitry can handle. Computers with dedicated graphics cards should score greater than 8.0.

- **Primary hard disk:** This score is based on the speed at which data is transferred to and from the hard disk. Most computers score greater than 5.0 on this task.

FAQ What is Task Manager?

Task Manager offers yet another way to get information about your computer's performance. Unlike the Windows Experience Index, which shows you a performance summary, Task Manager's Performance tab shows you real-time performance graphs of CPU, memory, disk, and network usage. Task Manager plays an important role in troubleshooting hardware and software problems by helping you discover the source of performance bottlenecks.

To open Task Manager from Windows 8, type task in the Windows Search box or use the Ctrl Shift Esc key combination on your keyboard. Figure 6-22 explains the key points of information you can glean from Task Manager's Performance tab.

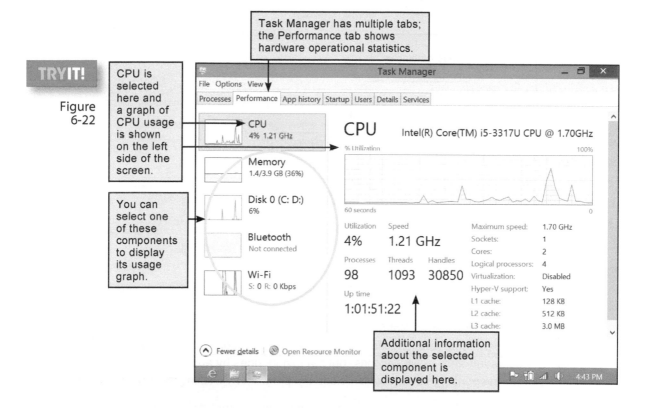

Figure 6-22

TRY IT!

Task Manager has multiple tabs; the Performance tab shows hardware operational statistics.

CPU is selected here and a graph of CPU usage is shown on the left side of the screen.

You can select one of these components to display its usage graph.

Additional information about the selected component is displayed here.

- To open Task Manager from Windows 7, look for *View running processes with Task Manager* in the Start menu's Search box. You can also start Task Manager by using the Ctrl Shift Esc key combination on your keyboard. The layout of Task Manager in Windows 7 differs slightly from its layout in Windows 8, but the information provided is similar.

- If you are simply curious about your computer's performance, you can open Task Manager from time to time.

- If the CPU Utilization statistic seems to be frozen at or near 100%, one or more applications might not be responding. You'll learn more about this topic on the next page.

- If your computer seems to be operating slowly, check memory usage. When memory use nears capacity, closing a few programs might get your computer back to normal operating speed.

• What is Task Manager? (continued)

Task Manager's Processes tab reports the name and status for each app, background process, and Windows process that is open and running. The apps listed should all be recognizable software applications. Background processes are routines launched by applications, device drivers, and utilities such as antivirus programs. Windows processes are routines launched by the operating system.

The processes list can come in handy when tracking down software problems and viruses (Figure 6-23).

Figure 6-23

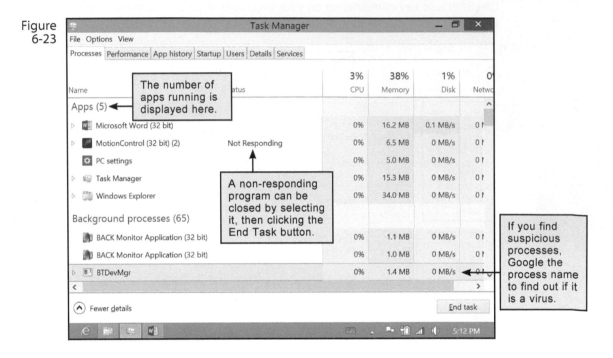

• Processes listed as Not Responding are "hung up" or "frozen" due to some kind of operational problem. Non-responsive programs sometimes return to normal operation after a few seconds; but if a minute goes by and a program remains in a non-responding state, you can close the program by clicking the End Task button.

• Programs closed with the End Task button usually shut down without giving you an opportunity to save your work; that's a good reason to make sure that you save your work every few minutes, or that your software's AutoSave feature is on.

• Most processes are legitimate; but if your computer has contracted a virus, it is likely to show up in the *Background processes* list. Processes that have suspicious names or that seem to utilize large amounts of CPU or memory might be viruses and should be investigated.

QuickCheck A

1. Computers consume the least amount of power in [   ] mode or when turned off.

2. True or false? The Control Panel and *PC settings* provide essentially the same options. [   ]

3. True or false? If you want objects to appear larger on the Windows desktop, you should increase the screen resolution. [   ]

4. The printer you want to use automatically, unless you specify otherwise, is called the [   ] printer.

5. For quick access to [   ] Manager, use the Ctrl Shift Esc key combination.

CHECKIT!

QuickCheck B

Enter the letter of the associated Control Panel option:

1. Administrator [   ]

2. Sleep [   ]

3. CPU usage [   ]

4. Themes [   ]

5. Narrator [   ]

a. Devices and Printers

b. Ease of Access Center

c. Power Options

d. User Accounts

e. Performance Information and Tools

f. Personalization

g. Mouse

CHECKIT!

What's Inside and on the CD?

All the documents, pictures, and music you create with your computer are stored as files. This chapter helps you understand how to best name your files, where to store them, and how to access them. It also emphasizes how to maintain an orderly set of files on your disks.

FAQ What is a computer file?

A **file** is a collection of data that has a name and is stored on a hard disk, CD, DVD, USB flash drive, network drive, or cloud storage device. Virtually all the information you can access from your computer is stored as files. Each document, graph, or picture you create with application software is stored as a file. The Web pages you view from the Internet are also stored as files, as are the applications that you download. Computer files can be divided into two categories: executable files and data files.

An **executable file** is a program module containing instructions that tell your computer how to perform specific tasks. Your computer "executes" these instructions to complete tasks such as sorting lists, searching for information, printing, or making calculations. For example, the word processing program that tells your computer how to display and print text is an executable file. When you select an application from the Start screen or Start menu, the computer runs the application's executable file.

A **data file** contains words, numbers, and pictures you can manipulate. For example, a document created using word processing software is a data file. You have several ways to access a data file, including the Open option on your application software's File menu and the Windows file management utility.

Files are stored in a variety of ways, based on whether they contain text, music, graphics, or programs. As shown in Figure 7-1, files often include additional embedded information that helps your computer identify, reconstruct, and display the file correctly.

Figure 7-1

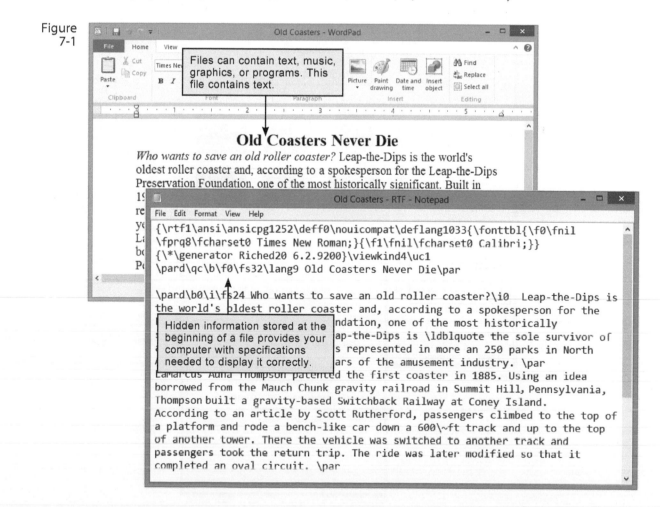

FAQ What are file properties and tags?

File properties describe file characteristics such as name, type, location, and size. A file's properties also include the dates when the file was created, modified, and last accessed.

Additional properties are assigned to certain types of files. For example, JPEG graphics files have a Dimensions property that indicates the picture's resolution, such as 1024 x 768. Music files don't have the Dimensions property, but they do have a Length property that indicates the music run time in minutes and seconds.

Some file properties, such as date and size, are assigned by Windows and cannot be directly changed by users. Other properties can be user-modified with customized **tags** that describe and categorize files. For example, a photographer might assign tags such as "Cropped from original" to a file containing a digital photo that has been cropped to change its size or shape.

Properties and tags can generally be viewed from the operating system's file manager. The utility included with Windows for managing files is called **File Explorer** in Windows 8, and **Windows Explorer** in Windows 7. You can open this utility by selecting the icon located on the taskbar of the Windows desktop. Figure 7-2 explains how to view file properties and tags in File Explorer.

TRY IT!

Figure 7-2

© MediaTechnics

FAQ What's important about file names, extensions, and types?

As you create documents, graphs, videos, and pictures, your computer holds the data in memory. When you're ready to save a file by transferring it to more permanent storage, you must give the file a unique name.

PC operating systems originally limited the length of a file name to eight characters or fewer. Also, a file name could not contain any spaces. These limitations made it difficult to create descriptive file names. For example, Orgch5 might be the name of a file containing the fifth draft of an organizational chart.

With current versions of Windows, you can use more descriptive file names such as Organizational Chart Draft 5. This capability, which came to be known as "long file names," makes it much easier to find a specific file based on its name.

Long file names also allow you to control capitalization. Most people tend to use the same capitalization for file names as they would use for a title, using uppercase for the first letter of every word except articles and prepositions. Windows is not case sensitive, however. Although you can use uppercase and lowercase, the file name Report is the same as report or REPORT.

Even in long file names, some symbols and file names are not allowed. When naming files, keep the following file naming conventions in mind:

Figure 7-3

Characters Not Allowed	File Names Not Allowed	Maximum Length
/ < > " \ : | * ?	Aux, Com1, Com2, Com3, Com4, Con, Lpt1, Lpt2, Prn, Nul	255 characters, including spaces

© MediaTechnics

A **file extension** is a set of characters added to the end of a file name to indicate the file's contents and origin. For example, in the file name Report.docx, the file extension .docx indicates the file is a Microsoft Word document. A file extension is separated from the main file name with a period, but no spaces. File extensions are typically three or four characters in length.

Hundreds of file extensions exist, and the situation would be pretty grim if you had to remember the extension for each program you use. Happily, you don't generally have to memorize file extensions—instead, your software automatically adds the correct one when you save a file. However, knowing the file types that correspond to common file extensions such as those in the table below can be handy when looking at file lists.

Figure 7-4

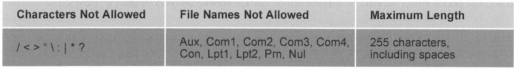

File Contents	File Extensions
Documents	.doc or .docx (Microsoft Word) .odt (LibreOffice Writer) .txt .rtf .wpd .wps
Databases	.mdb or .accdb (Microsoft Access) .dbf .odb (LibreOffice Base)
Spreadsheets	.xls or .xlsx (Microsoft Excel) .ods (LibreOffice Calc)
Graphics	.bmp .tif .gif .jpg .png .swf
Sound	.wav .mid .aif .mp3 .m4p .m4a .ogg
Video	.wmv .mpg .mov .avi .flv .WebM
Web pages	.htm .html
Programs	.exe .com .sys .dll .drv .ocx .app

© MediaTechnics

• What's important about file names, extensions, and types? (continued)

Executable files for applications that run on the Windows operating system have .exe extensions, whereas executable files for OS X have .app extensions. Operating systems tend to be shipped with file extensions hidden, but you can easily reveal them. Figure 7-5 illustrates how to reveal file extensions in Windows.

Figure
7-5

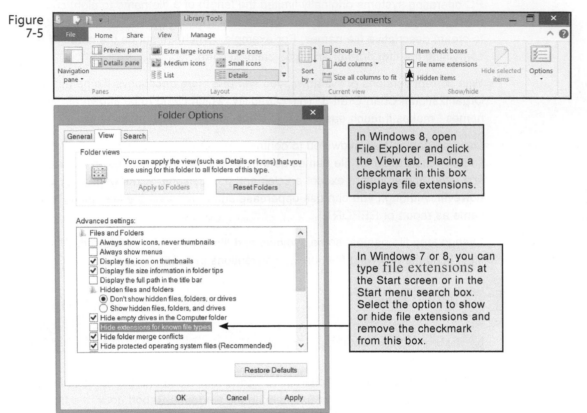

Regardless of whether extensions are hidden or shown, Windows displays a **file type** (also called a file format) based on the extension. A document created with Microsoft Word 2013 is labeled Microsoft Word Document. A document created with LibreOffice Writer would be classified as an OpenDocument Text file based on its .odt file extension. Before you open a file, pay attention to the file type to get an idea of what a file contains and which application is required to work with it.

Figure
7-6

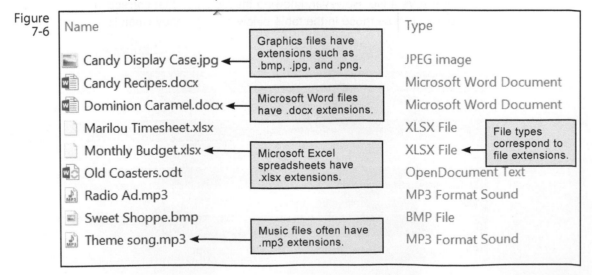

• What's important about file names, extensions, and types? (continued)

By looking at a file's extension or type, you can usually predict which application is required to view and edit the information contained in the file. So, if you see a file with a .docx extension, you know that you can use Microsoft Word to view and edit the file's contents.

Windows keeps a list of file types and their corresponding default programs. A **default program** is the one that Windows uses when you open a particular file type. The link between a file type and its default program is sometimes called a **file association**.

Often, the default program is the program that was used to create a file. So, as you might expect, Microsoft Excel is the default program for the XLSX file type. Whenever you open an XLSX file, Windows automatically opens Microsoft Excel so that you can view and edit the file.

In some cases, however, the default program is not so obvious. You can use Paint, Photoshop, Photo Viewer, and many other graphics applications to work with JPEG image file types. If you have several of these applications installed on your computer, how does Windows know which one to use? It uses the application from the default program list. In some cases, the default program is not the one you'd like to use.

You can open files using an application other than the one in the default program list in the following ways:

- Right-click (or touch and hold) the file name and select the *Open with* option. Windows displays a list of applications, and you can choose the one you want to use to view and edit your file. This method works well for occasional use.

- You can change the default programs list and choose the application that Windows automatically opens for a specific file type.

Click the Try It! button to find out more about changing the application that Windows uses to open various file types.

TRYIT!

Figure 7-7

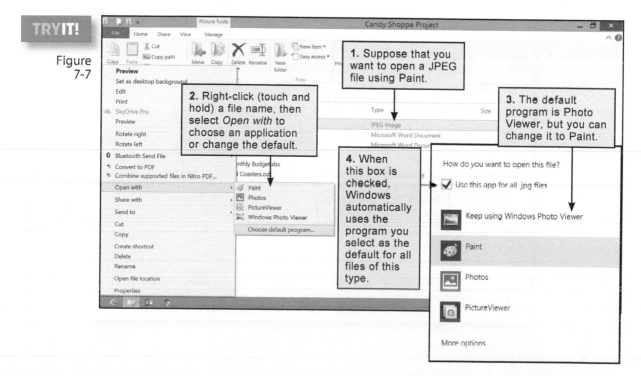

FAQ How do I find a specific file?

An easy way to find a file is to use the Windows Search box on the Start screen or Start button. Simply enter all or part of a file name and select Files, rather than Apps or Settings. Matches appear as you type. In Figure 7-8, entering "candy" locates files that include that word in the file name.

TRYIT!

Figure 7-8

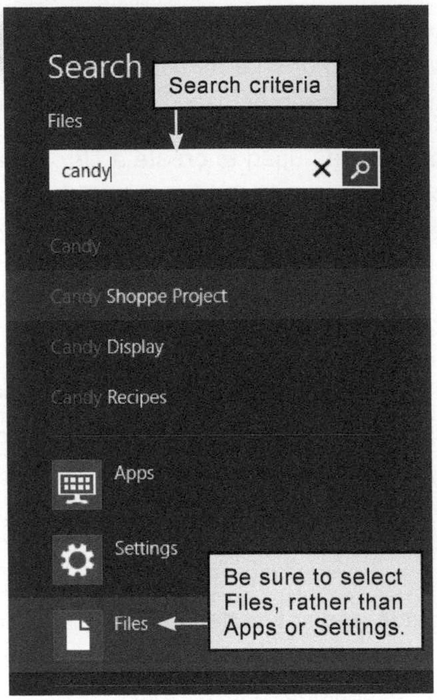

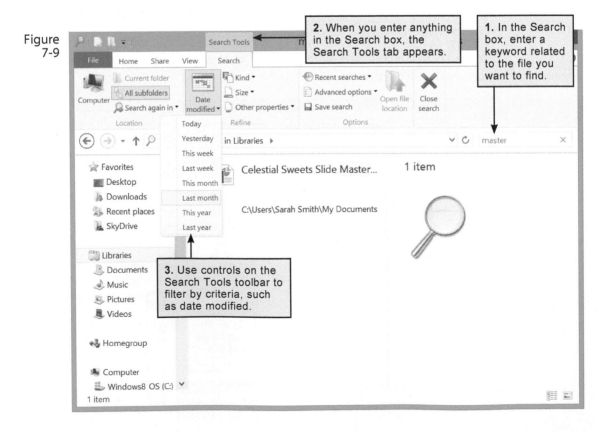

File Explorer offers more sophisticated ways to search than the Start screen or Start menu. You can search for files by date, author, size, type, rating, and other properties by using search filters.

Suppose you're looking for a PowerPoint slide master that you created a month ago. You remember that "master" was somewhere in the name, but you'd prefer that Windows didn't pull up the batch of slide masters you created this week.

When you click the Search box in the File Explorer window, a set of search tools appears. These tools are displayed slightly differently in Windows 8 than they are in Windows 7, but the functionality is similar. Figure 7-9 illustrates the way Windows 8 displays search tools and handles search filters.

Figure 7-9

FAQ How are files grouped?

Files are stored in a hierarchical arrangement of folders and subfolders. A **folder** (sometimes called a directory) groups files to keep them organized. Folders can hold other folders called **subfolders**. Windows groups folders into **libraries**, including four predefined libraries: Documents, Music, Pictures, and Videos.

You can get the big picture of files stored in all your computer's libraries and folders using File Explorer. The Explorer window is divided into several components. Understanding these components helps you find files and keep them organized. Study Figure 7-10 to familiarize yourself with Explorer's Navigation pane, file list, toolbar, and Details pane. Then click the Try It! button to learn how to sort the file list and change views.

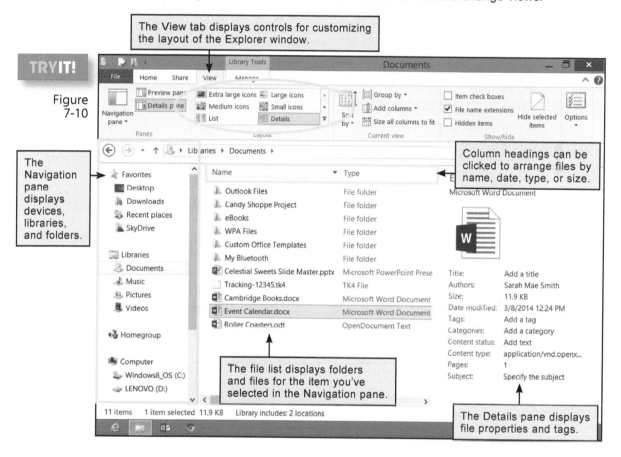

Figure 7-10

The View tab displays controls for customizing the layout of the Explorer window.

The Navigation pane displays devices, libraries, and folders.

Column headings can be clicked to arrange files by name, date, type, or size.

The file list displays folders and files for the item you've selected in the Navigation pane.

The Details pane displays file properties and tags.

- You can use the View tab (Windows 8) or *Change your view* button (Windows 7) to change the way the file list is displayed. Icon views display a picture to represent each file along with its name. **List view** displays the name of each file along with a small icon that indicates its type. **Details view** displays the file name, size, type, and date modified. The example above shows the Details view.

- Windows 7 has two views that are not available in Windows 8: **Tiles view** displays a large icon for each file, plus the file's name, type, and size. **Content view** displays the file's name, type, and icon.

- **Hidden files**, such as many of the system files essential for running Windows, are not displayed in the file list. To display hidden files in Windows 8, select the View tab, then put a checkmark in the *Hidden items* checkbox. To display hidden files in Windows 7, click the Organize button, select *Folder and search options*, then click the View button.

What are Explorer's main storage categories?

The Navigation pane on the left side of the Explorer window categorizes devices and folders for easy access. When you select a device, folder, or library from the Navigation pane, the contents of the item you've selected are shown in the file list.

Figure
7-11

When My Documents is selected in the Navigation pane...

▲ 📚 Libraries
  ▲ 📄 Documents
    ▷ 📁 My Documents
      📁 Public Documents
  ▷ 🎵 Music
  ▷ 🖼 Pictures
  ▷ 🎬 Videos

📁 Essays
📁 WPA Files
📄 Cambridge Books.docx   Microsoft Word Document
📄 Celestial Sweets Slide Master.pptx   Microsoft PowerPoint Presentation
📄 Database1.accdb   ACCDB File
📄 Event Calendar.docx   Microsoft Word Document
📄 Roller Coasters.odt   OpenDocument Text
📄 Tracking-12345.tk4   TK4 File

...its contents are displayed in the files list.

The Navigation pane is divided into groups for Favorites, Libraries, Homegroup, Computer, and Network. Review the navigation categories shown in Figure 7-12 and then read on for some tips on how to most effectively use Navigation pane categories to access and organize files.

Figure
7-12

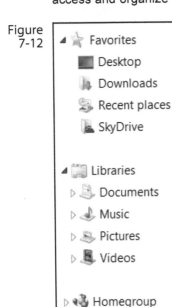

▲ ⭐ Favorites
  🖥 Desktop
  ⬇ Downloads
  📍 Recent places
  ☁ SkyDrive

▲ 📚 Libraries
  ▷ 📄 Documents
  ▷ 🎵 Music
  ▷ 🖼 Pictures
  ▷ 🎬 Videos

▷ 👥 Homegroup

▲ 💻 Computer
  ▷ 💾 Windows8_OS (C:)
  ▷ 💿 LENOVO (D:)
  ▷ 💿 USB DISK (E:)

▲ 🌐 Network

Favorites give you fast access to folders you use frequently. Simply drag a folder or file to the Favorites list, and you won't have to click through layers of folders to reach it. The Favorites list includes **SkyDrive**, an Internet-based storage location for saving files in the cloud.

Libraries are virtual folders that contain links to folders and files. Windows is preconfigured with four libraries, but you can make your own, for example, to hold a set of links to family history material that's stored in document and photo folders.

Homegroup offers access to shared folders, files, and printers on computers in a home network. When your computer joins a homegroup, the computers for other members of the group are listed under the Homegroup option.

Computer gives you access to folders on all devices connected to your computer. When accessing files stored on CDs or USB flash drives, use the Computer link.

Network provides a link to folders stored on local area network file servers and other network users' computers that you have permission to access.

FAQ How do I navigate to various folders and storage devices?

Most files are stored on your computer's hard disk. To transport a file, however, you might store it on a USB flash drive or CD. To share a file with others, you might store it on a network drive or a cloud storage drive. As you work with files, it is important to keep track of the device where a particular file is stored.

Figure
7-13

- Computer
- Windows8_OS (C:)
- LENOVO (D:)
- USB DISK (E:)
- Network
- SkyDrive
- Public Folder

Each local storage device on a Windows-based computer is identified by a unique **device letter**. The device letter for the hard disk drive is usually C. As shown in Figure 7-13, Windows displays a unique icon for each type of storage device, including your hard disk, USB flash drive, network file server, cloud storage, and local area network folders.

Folders in the Navigation pane are arranged in a hierarchy. You can expand the hierarchy to show subfolders or collapse the hierarchy to hide subfolders using the following techniques:

- Click a device or folder icon to display its contents in the file list.

- Double-click an icon or click the small ▷ arrow to display additional levels of folders in the Navigation pane, rather than the file list.

- To hide levels of folders, click the ◢ angled arrow.

A device letter, folder, file name, and extension specify a file's location. This specification is sometimes referred to as a **path**. When subfolders are written out in a file path, they are separated from folders with a \ backslash symbol. If you create a subfolder called Essays in the My Documents folder and use it to store a file called Macbeth, its path would be written C:\Users\YourName\Libraries\Documents\My Documents\Essays\Macbeth.docx. The Try It! for Figure 7-14 shows you how to navigate a file's path by expanding and collapsing the file hierarchy.

TRY IT!

Figure
7-14

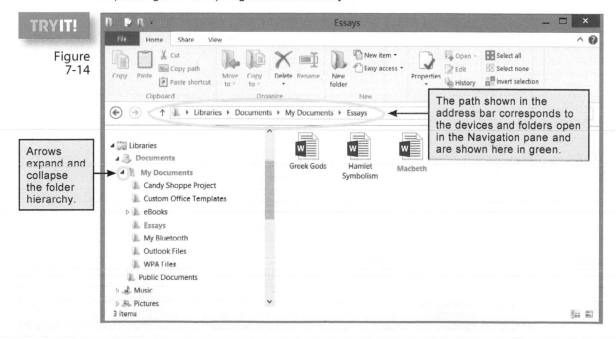

Arrows expand and collapse the folder hierarchy.

The path shown in the address bar corresponds to the devices and folders open in the Navigation pane and are shown here in green.

FAQ Can I create my own libraries and folders?

Windows provides each user account with a set of folders and libraries. To maintain well organized storage, you will certainly want to create additional folders. You might also decide to create additional libraries.

Let's consider folders first. Your predefined folders include My Documents, My Music, My Pictures, My Videos, and Downloads. That's a good start, but these folders can quickly accumulate many files that eventually become unwieldy to work with.

You can create subfolders and use them to divide files into more manageable groups. To do so, simply right-click a folder, select New, then select Folder. Enter a name for the subfolder. Once the subfolder is created, you can move files into it.

Next, consider libraries. Windows provides you with four predefined libraries: Documents, Music, Pictures, and Videos. These library names are deceptively similar to the names of your predefined folders, but libraries and folders are not the same.

A library is similar to a folder only in the sense that it can be used to group similar files; however, a library doesn't actually store files. Instead, it contains a set of links to files that are stored on various devices and in various folders.

To understand how you might use libraries, suppose you're working on a project that uses a variety of documents and music. You can create a library for the project that includes folders from My Documents and Public Music. These folders remain in their original locations, but the files they contain all appear in the listing for the new library.

The concept to understand is that a library such as Music is not a "real" location; it is more like an index in a book. If you try to create a subfolder by right-clicking the Music library, the subfolder will actually be created under My Music, which is a "real" folder. Click the Try It! button to learn more about creating and using folders and libraries.

Figure 7-15

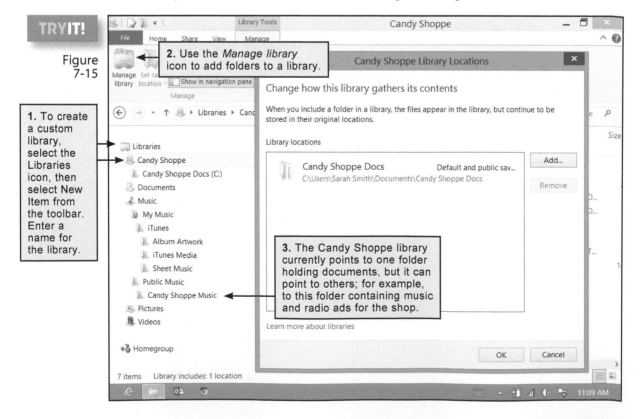

FAQ What's the best organization for my files?

The key to organizing your files is to create a clearly structured set of folders. Here are a few hints to help you improve the organization of your files:

- Use descriptive names for files and folders.

- Always store your data files in a folder. The first level under a device should contain only folders, not files.

- Whenever possible, store your files in your personal folders: My Documents, My Music, and so on.

- Create subfolders of your personal folders as necessary to group files logically by project or by type.

- Try not to store your data files in the folders that contain program modules for your application software.

- Delete unneeded files and folders.

In order to maintain logical groupings of files in your folders, you can move files from one folder to another. Consider moving files as necessary to group similar files into folders where you can easily find them.

You can move a file simply by dragging it from the File list to a folder in the Navigation pane. This procedure sometimes misfires, however. If you don't carefully position the file on the destination folder, the file can drop into an unintended folder where it could be difficult to find. To avoid this problem, use the cut and paste method.

When you use the cut and paste method to move a file, Windows removes or "cuts" the file from its current location and places it on the **Windows Clipboard**, which is a temporary holding area in your computer's memory. After you select a new location for the file, Windows pastes the selected folder or file from the Clipboard to its new location. Associating the process of moving files with "cut and paste" can help you remember the sequence of commands needed to move a file. Click the Try It! button to practice moving a few files.

TRY IT!

Figure 7-16

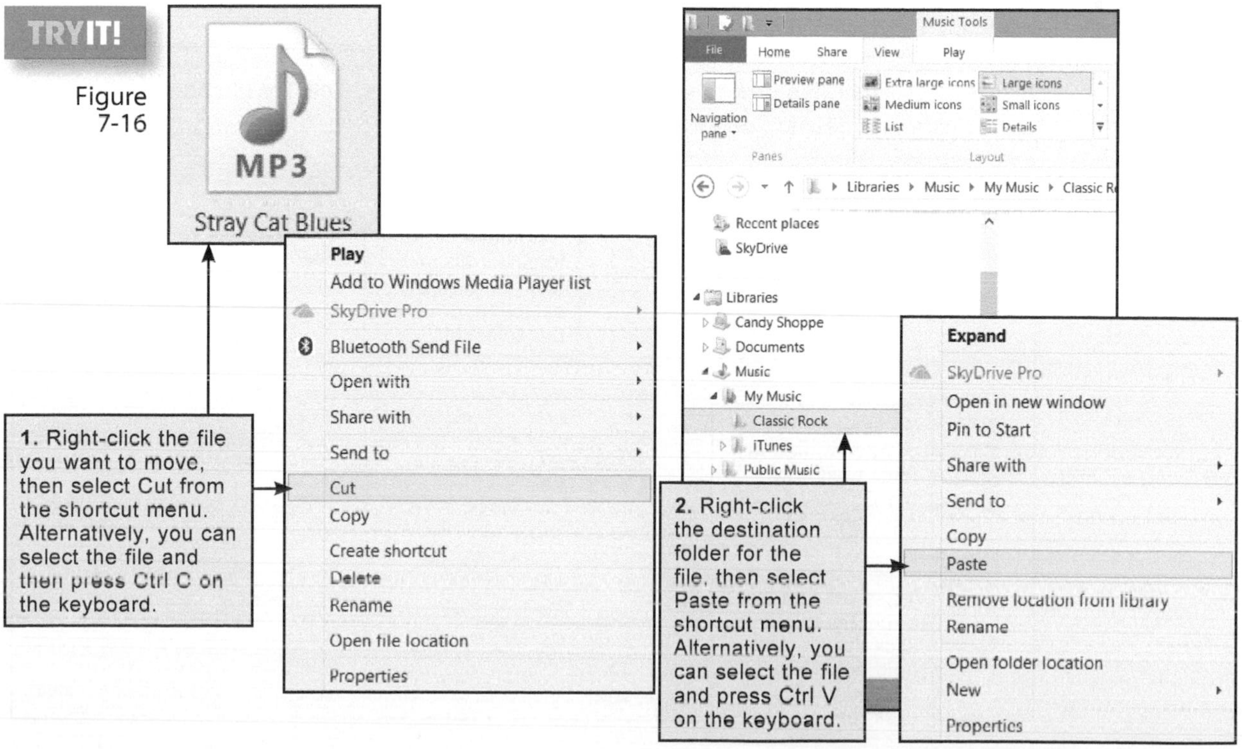

1. Right-click the file you want to move, then select Cut from the shortcut menu. Alternatively, you can select the file and then press Ctrl C on the keyboard.

2. Right-click the destination folder for the file, then select Paste from the shortcut menu. Alternatively, you can select the file and press Ctrl V on the keyboard.

• What's the best organization for my files? (continued)

Whereas you move files to improve the organization of files on a drive, you copy a file when you want to create a duplicate. You can copy a file into another folder before modifying it. You might copy a group of important files to a CD, which you could store in a secure location. You can also copy files to a USB flash drive if you want to access them on a computer other than your own. You can even copy files to an Internet-based cloud storage site to access them from a public computer while you're traveling.

To copy a file, Windows places a duplicate of the file on the Clipboard. The original file remains in its original location. After you select a location for the copy, Windows pastes the file from the Clipboard to the new location. Think of copying files as "copy and paste" to remember this sequence of commands.

In addition to copying a single file, you can copy groups of files using these techniques:

- To select a series of files, click the first file and then hold down the Shift key as you click the last file. All of the files in between will be selected. Continue holding down the Shift key as you right-click to view the shortcut menu and select Copy.

- If you want to select files that aren't listed contiguously, hold down the Ctrl key while you select each file. The Shift key and Ctrl key procedures work for moving files as well as copying them.

- You can use buttons on the toolbar to select all of the files in a folder or deselect them.

- The *Invert selection* button deselects the files that you've selected and selects the files that you did not select.

If you have a folder or file that you use frequently, you can pin it to the Start screen to create a tile, or you can send it to the desktop to create a desktop shortcut.

- To pin an item on the Start screen, right-click a file or folder, then select *Pin to Start*.

- To create a desktop shortcut, right-click a file or folder, select *Send to*, then select Desktop.

Figure 7-17 illustrates how to select multiple files or folders. The Try It! shows you how to create tiles and desktop shortcuts.

TRY IT!

Figure 7-17

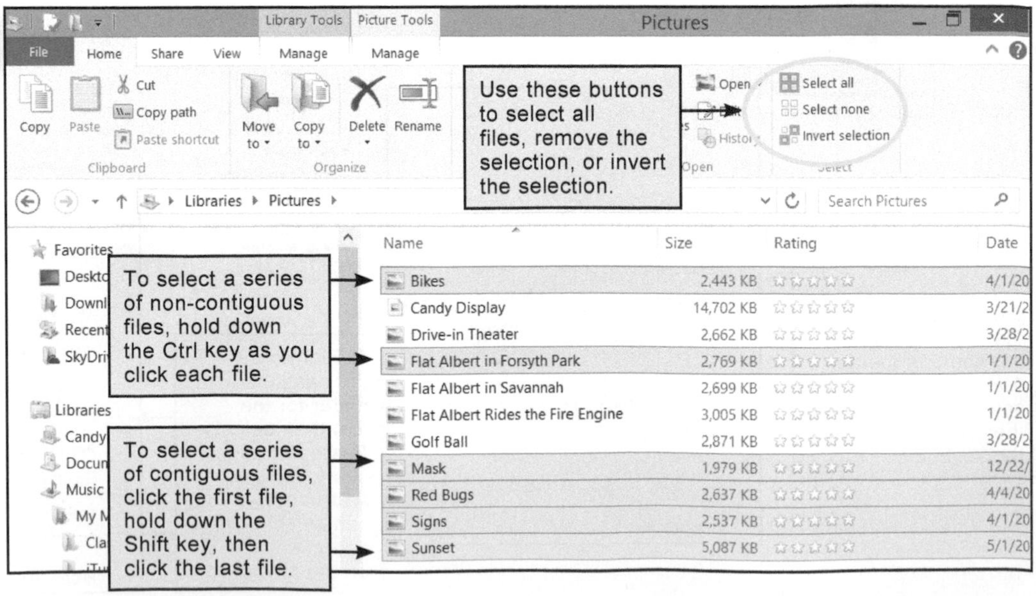

FAQ Can I change the name of a file or folder?

Once you have located a file or folder, it's easy to **rename** it so that its name better describes its contents. You can also use the Rename command to standardize the names of similar files, such as Playoff 2013, Playoff 2014, and Playoff 2015, so that they appear in sequence.

Renaming files is fairly straightforward, except for a little twist involving file extensions. When file extensions are hidden, it is not necessary to worry about them. As you rename a file, Windows automatically retains the old file extension for the new file name.

When file extensions are visible, however, you should be careful not to change them. Windows uses a file's extension to determine the application that opens it. If the extension is changed, Windows might not be able to open the selected file. For example, if you were to inadvertently change a document's extension from .docx to .bmp, Windows would no longer try to open it with Microsoft Word. Instead, it would try to open it with Paint, and that would produce an error because the file does not contain a graphic.

Windows offers several ways to change the name of a file:

- Right-click the file name, then select Rename from the shortcut menu.

- Click the file name, then click it again. After a brief pause, you'll be able to type the new name.

- Click the file name, then click the Rename button on the Home tab (Windows 8).

Renaming a folder follows the same general procedures as renaming a file. Figure 7-18 illustrates the right-click procedure for renaming a file and shows the location of the Rename button on the Home tab.

Figure 7-18

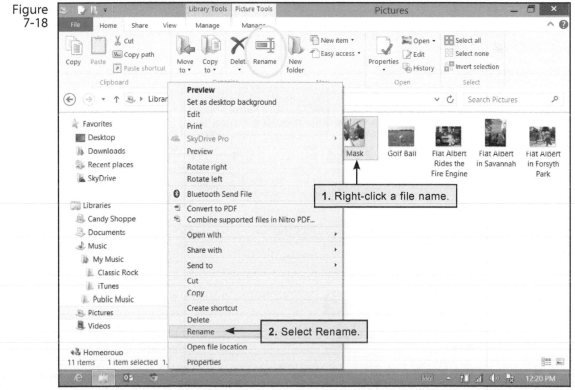

© MediaTechnics

FAQ How do I delete files and folders?

When you no longer need files or folders, you should delete them so that your computer's hard disk drive works more efficiently. Deleting unneeded files also pares down directory listings to avoid clutter. Deleting old versions of files helps you avoid revising an outdated version of a file when you meant to revise the current version.

To delete a file, select it and click the Delete button on the Home tab. Or right-click a file and select Delete from the shortcut menu. You can delete a folder using the same procedure; but be aware that when you delete a folder, you delete all the files it contains. You can use the Ctrl key, Shift key, or Select All option to delete more than one file or folder at a time.

If you run out of disk space, Windows displays a "Disk Full" message. This message usually means it's time for some PC housecleaning. If your hard disk is full, you might eventually have to delete old files and unneeded software. When removing software, remember to use an uninstall procedure rather than manually deleting program files.

Before you delete files and software, you can usually regain space by emptying your computer's Recycle Bin. The **Recycle Bin** is a holding area for the files you've deleted from your PC's hard disk. When you delete a file from the hard disk, its name is removed from Explorer's file list, but the file itself remains on the disk and continues to occupy disk space. This space is not released until you empty the Recycle Bin.

It is nice to know that a deleted file is not gone forever until you empty the Recycle Bin. You can retrieve files from the Recycle Bin and restore them to their previous folders. This feature is an excellent safety net if you mistakenly delete a file. Remember, however, that the Recycle Bin holds only hard disk files. It doesn't retain files you've deleted from USB flash drives and other storage devices. Click the Try It! button to find out how to delete a file and how to use the Recycle Bin.

TRY IT!

Figure
7-19

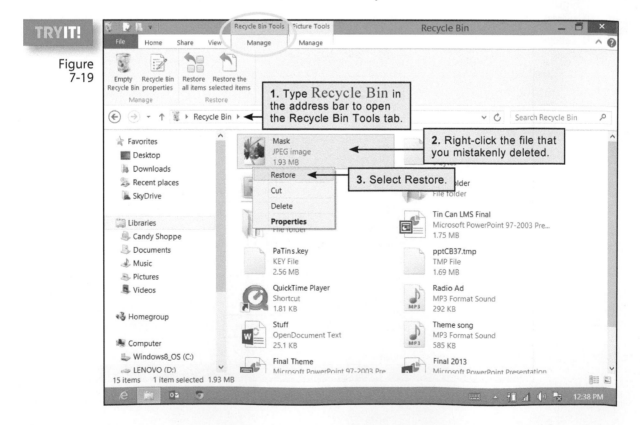

FAQ What is a compressed file?

File compression refers to any technique that recodes data in a file so that it contains fewer bits. Smaller files produced as a result of compression require less storage space and can be transmitted more rapidly than the larger, original files. Compressing files is sometimes called zipping. Windows includes a compression utility that you can use to compress a single file, multiple files, or a combination of files and folders.

Compression is typically used for files that are attached to e-mail messages and files that are uploaded to network servers. You might also consider compressing files when you want to share a group of documents, images, and videos for a project. Compressing these files keeps them together and in the same folder structure as they exist on your computer.

Graphics file formats such as TIFF, PNG, JPEG, and GIF automatically apply compression when you save the file. Video formats such as MPEG4 and AVI also apply compression, as do most audio formats such as MP3. Files stored in these automatically compressed formats won't get any smaller if you later try to compress them using the Windows compression utility. Files containing text, spreadsheets, databases, and presentations, however, usually get much smaller when you use a compression utility.

You can easily identify compressed files by their ⬛ zippered folder icon and .zip file extension. A compressed file should be unzipped before accessing its contents. Reversing the compression process is called unzipping or extracting. In Windows, you can click the compressed folder and use the Compressed Folder Tools, or you can right-click the zipped folder and select Extract All.

Figure 7-20 shows how you can zip a group of files by selecting them and using the Zip button, or using the right-click method. Work with the Try It! to learn more about zipping and unzipping files.

TRYIT!

Figure
7-20

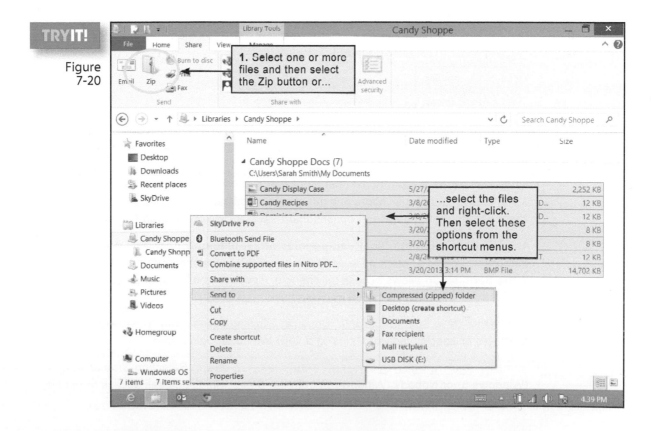

FAQ How do I share files?

Suppose that your computer is connected to a local area network and you'd like some of your files to be accessible to other network users. How can you make that happen? Windows offers several ways to share files:

Join a homegroup. A **homegroup** is a collection of trusted networked computers that automatically share files and folders. Access to the homegroup can be protected by password. To join a homegroup, double-click the Homegroup option in File Explorer's Navigation pane.

Use Public folders. A **Public folder** is similar to a drop box; it can hold files and folders that you want to share with other people on your network. Windows is preconfigured with several Public folders, including Public Documents, Public Music, Public Pictures, and Public Videos. When you want to share a file or folder, simply move it or copy it into one of these Public folders.

Designate specific files as shared. You can designate any file or folder on your computer as shared. Click the Try It! button to explore various ways to share files.

Figure 7-21

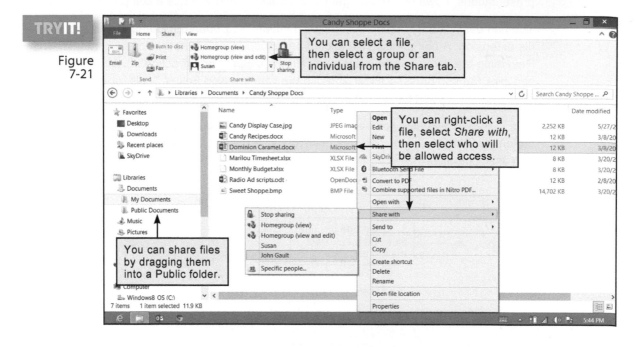

Sharing files poses a security risk that has several dimensions. Shared files are subject to misuse, inadvertent modification, and intentional modification by those who have access to them. Windows offers several options that help to keep your shared files secure:

- **Assign permission to files.** **Read permission** (or read-only permission) allows authorized people to open a file and view it, but they cannot modify it or delete it. **Read/ Write permission** allows access for opening, viewing, modifying, or deleting files. Permissions are sometimes referred to as user rights.

- **Limit sharing to specific people.** Consider allowing access only to homegroup members or specific individuals using a valid Windows login name.

- **Remove sharing from files you no longer want to share.** Selecting *Stop sharing* (Windows 8) or *Nobody* (Windows 7) from the *Share with* list closes access to the file.

• How do I share files? (continued)

In addition to specifying sharing rules for individual files and folders, Windows also provides several global file sharing settings, which you can access from the Network and Sharing Center. There you can:

- Turn your computer's file and printer sharing on or off.

- Turn sharing on or off for Public folders.

- Require a valid password to access shared files.

When you allow file sharing, it is like opening a doorway to your computer. You can try to limit the people who pass through the doorway and you can restrict what people are allowed to do once they enter the doorway, but just the fact that there is a doorway is an open invitation to pick the lock and gain access.

Security holes in file sharing routines are notorious for providing Internet-based hackers with unauthorized access to computers. You can use Control Panel's option for *Advanced sharing settings* to turn sharing off or on.

Figure
7-22

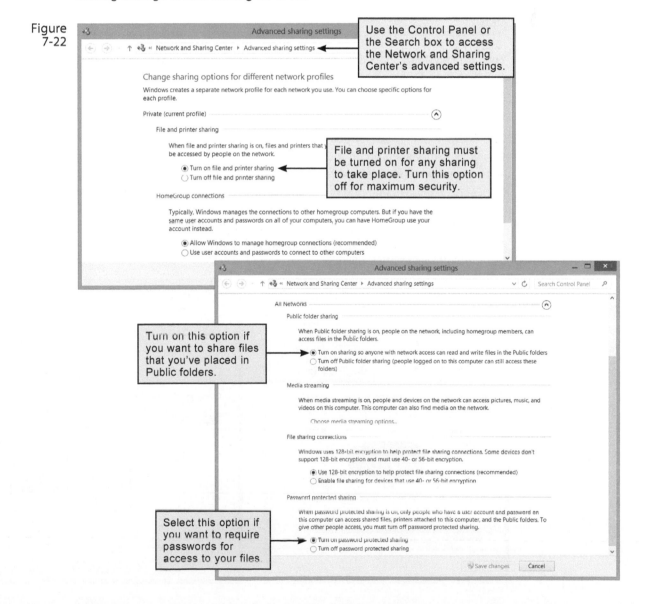

FAQ How much space do I have to store files?

You can store files on a USB flash drive or in the cloud; but for desktop and laptop computers, the primary storage device is a local hard disk. You can easily find out how much space is available on your computer's local storage devices by right-clicking the Computer listing in File Explorer's Navigation pane as shown in Figure 7-23.

Figure
7-23

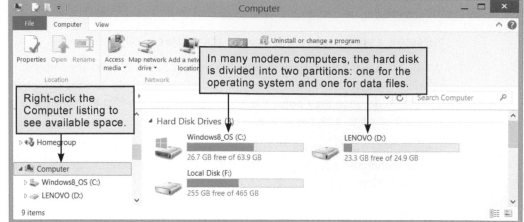

You can find additional information about a storage device by right-clicking it, or by selecting it and then selecting the Properties button on the toolbar. The Properties window shows you a pie chart depicting available space, and also contains tabs you can use to manage the efficiency and security of the storage device.

One useful tool is Disk Defragmenter, which arranges data on a hard disk for optimal efficiency. Data is stored on a disk in a series of clusters. When a file is large, it requires more than one cluster. If adjacent clusters are available, the file spills into those clusters; otherwise, Windows puts the remaining data in some other location and sets up a pointer to it. When files are not stored in adjacent clusters, they are referred to as fragmented. A **defragmentation utility** gathers these fragmented clusters together so they can be accessed more efficiently by the hard disk's read mechanism. Figure 7-24 shows how to use the defragmentation utility.

Figure
7-24

FAQ How do I back up important files?

A **backup** is a copy of one or more files that is made in case the originals become damaged. A backup is usually stored on a different storage medium than the original files. For example, you could back up files from your hard disk to an external hard disk, a writable CD or DVD, a USB flash drive, or an Internet-based cloud storage site.

One way to back up your important data files is to manually copy them to a CD, DVD, or USB flash drive. If you'd prefer to automate the process, you can use backup software. **Backup software** is a set of utility programs designed to back up and restore files on a computer's primary storage device. There are several types of backup software, each designed for a specific task. Some backup software is designed to back up data files, whereas other backup software recovers the operating system or customization settings.

File synchronization. **File synchronization** (sometimes referred to as mirroring) ensures that files in two or more locations contain the same data. Synchronization software designed for file backup monitors the files on your hard disk, watches for changes, and automatically makes the same changes to files on your designated backup device—preferably an external hard drive.

Windows 8 offers a synchronization utility called File History that you can use to back up files in your libraries, contacts, and favorites folders. It will also back up copies of files that you store on Microsoft SkyDrive cloud storage. To access File History, enter File History at the Start screen, then select it from the Settings list.

TRY IT!

Figure
7-25

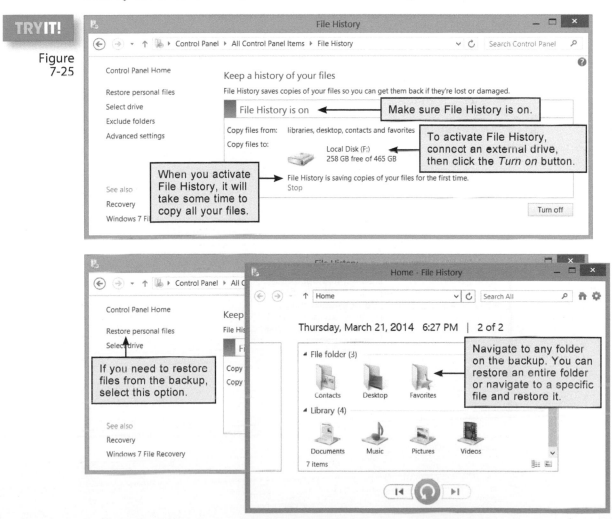

• How do I back up important files? (continued)

Recovery discs. File History backs up your data files, but does not back up programs or the operating system. If your computer's hard disk fails, you'll need a way to get the operating system installed on a new hard disk. Most computer manufacturers provide a way to create a **recovery disc** that you can use if your computer's hard disk fails. The contents and capabilities of recovery discs vary. Some are designed to restore your computer to its like-new state, but wipe out all your data. Others attempt to restore user settings, programs, and data. Before you depend on a recovery disc, make sure you know what it contains and how to use it in case of a system failure. You can find information and instructions by searching for Recovery at the Start screen.

Restore points. Windows offers a utility that creates restore points. A **restore point** is a snapshot of your computer settings, essentially a backup of the Windows Registry. If a hard disk problem causes system instability, you might be able to roll back to a restore point when your computer was operating smoothly. Restore points are set automatically when you install new software. You can manually set restore points, too. For example, you might want to set a restore point before setting up a network or installing new hardware.

Disk images. If you'd like to have a complete copy of your hard disk that contains the operating system, all your programs, and up-to-date data files, you need backup software with disk imaging capabilities. A **disk image** is a bit-for-bit mirror image of the entire contents of a storage device. The *Backup and Restore* utility provided by Windows 7 includes disk imaging, but File History, which is provided with Windows 8, does not. The old functionality is still in Windows 8, however, provided by a utility called Windows 7 File Recovery.

A disk image is the best insurance against a total hard disk failure because the backup image can be streamed onto a new hard disk, which restores your complete computing environment in one operation. Disk images take time to create, however, but disk imaging software can be programmed to run while your computer is not in use.

When using Windows 8, you can access the Windows 7 File Recovery utility from the Start screen by choosing Settings and typing File Recovery. In Windows 7, use the Control Panel to access *Backup and Restore*.

TRYIT!

Figure
7-26

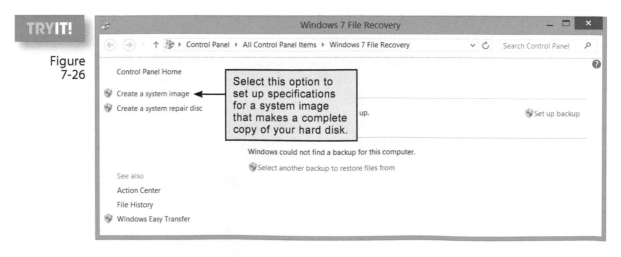

• How do I back up important files? (continued)

Cloud storage and backup. Cloud storage services such as Microsoft SkyDrive offer you remote storage space on an Internet-based "cloud" server. Most of these services have a setting that synchronizes files on your local hard disk with your files stored in the cloud. With the files in two places, you essentially have a backup for both. If your hard disk fails, you can access files from the cloud. If the cloud becomes inaccessible, you can access files from your computer's local hard disk.

With SkyDrive, any files you put in the SkyDrive folder will exist on cloud storage and on your local computer. Just remember to save files in the SkyDrive folder if you want them backed up in the cloud.

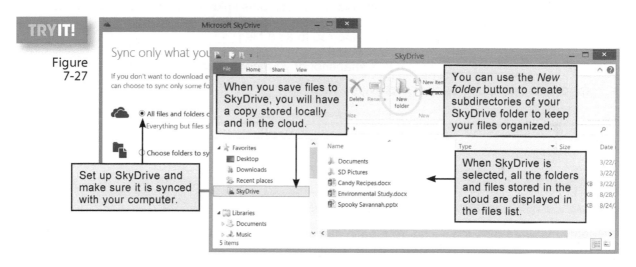

TRY IT!

Figure 7-27

Backups are an important safety net in case your primary storage device fails or, in the case of cloud storage, becomes inaccessible. Is one backup enough? Although most consumers are challenged to maintain even one backup, in the corporate world, backups are maintained according to strict versioning and recycling schedules.

Full backups. A backup made by copying the entire contents of a hard disk to a backup device is called a **full backup**. Full backups require lots of time and disk space. Alternatives to full backups include differential and incremental backups.

Differential backups. A **differential backup** makes a backup of only those files that were added or changed since the last full backup session. After making a full backup of important files, differential backups are scheduled at regular intervals. To restore all the files after a hard disk crash, files are first restored from a full backup, and then files are restored from the latest differential backup.

Incremental backups. An **incremental backup** backs up files that were added or changed since the last backup—not necessarily the files that changed from the last full backup, but the files that changed since any full or incremental backup. To restore a set of incremental backups, a full backup is installed, then each of the incremental backups is installed in succession.

As you can imagine, differential and incremental backups are a bit complex for most consumers. Thankfully, modern backup tools automate the process. Consumers, however, need to be aware of the purpose of backup options such as file synchronization, recovery discs, restore points, and disk imaging; and they need to make sure that these tools are set up and running on their computers.

QuickCheck A

1. A(n) [_____] file is a program module containing instructions that tell your computer how to perform a specific task, whereas a(n) [_____] file contains words, numbers, and pictures you can manipulate.

2. To select several files listed consecutively, click the first file, then hold down the [_____] key and click the last file.

3. A(n) [_____] is a virtual folder that contains links to other folders and files.

4. C:\JobSearch\Resume.doc would be referred to as a file [_____] .

5. A(n) [_____] point is a snapshot of your computer settings that can be used to roll your computer back to a previous state.

CHECKIT!

QuickCheck B

Supply the word that is missing from each numbered box in the image below:

1. [_____]   3. [_____]   5. [_____]

2. [_____]   4. [_____]

© MediaTechnics

CHECKIT!

Section II

Key Applications

What's in this Section?

GET IT?

When you complete Section II, use the digital textbook to take Practice Tests by selecting the Get It? button.

8 Getting Started with Application Software

What's Inside and on the CD?

Application software helps you use your computer to accomplish many useful tasks. Some of today's most popular application software is included in the Microsoft Office suite. The suite's flagship software is Microsoft Word—a word processing application that has become a worldwide standard. Microsoft Excel is the spreadsheet software of choice for many computer owners. Microsoft PowerPoint is top-rated presentation software. Microsoft Access is among the most frequently used PC database software packages.

Understanding the features common to most Windows applications makes it easy to learn new software. In this chapter, you'll take a look at features common to many Windows applications. You can use what you learn in this chapter as a foundation for working with Word, Excel, PowerPoint, and Access in later chapters.

FAQ How do I start and exit Windows applications?

Before you can start a Windows application, such as Microsoft Word, you should be logged on to your computer and viewing the Windows 8 Start screen, or the Windows 7 desktop. To start an application from the Windows 8 Start screen, click the application's tile. To start an application from the Windows 7 desktop, either double-click its icon or click the Start button and then select the application from the Start menu.

Office applications open to a preliminary screen where you can choose a recently viewed file, browse to open other files, or create a new file.

Figure 8-1

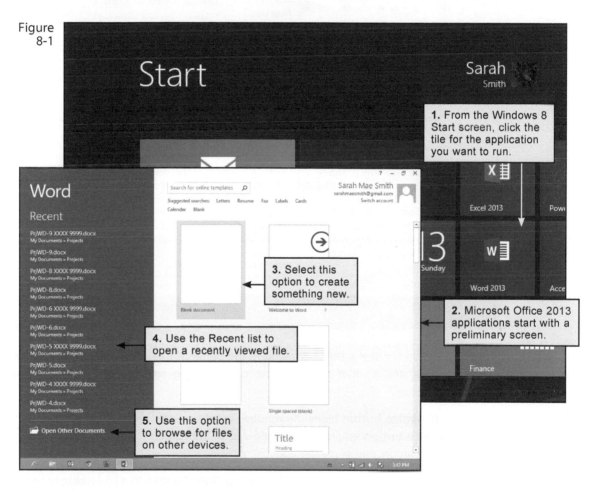

Windows allows you to run several applications at the same time, but it's best to close, or exit, an application when you're finished using it. To close an application, click the ☒ Close button. Closing unused applications frees up memory and helps your computer run more efficiently. Also, remember to close all applications before you initiate the shut down procedure to turn off your computer.

FAQ What are the basics of an application window?

Each application is displayed in a rectangular **application window** on the Windows desktop. The windows for Microsoft Office applications, such as Word and Excel, contain many similar elements. Let's look at those elements now, rather than covering them later when each application is introduced.

Figure
8-2

- An application window's **title bar** displays the name of the application, the name of the open file, and a set of sizing buttons for minimizing, maximizing, and closing the window.

- The ⊟ **Minimize button** hides the window, but leaves the application running. The ▢ **Maximize button** enlarges the window to fill the screen. The ☒ **Close button** closes the window and stops the application.

- When a window is maximized, the Maximize button changes to a ⊡ **Restore button**. Clicking the Restore button shrinks the window to the size it was just before it was maximized.

- You can adjust the width and height of an application window. When a window is not maximized, you can change its height or width by dragging any edge of the window frame right, left, up, or down.

- A **status bar** at the bottom of an application window contains information about the current condition of the application. Depending on the application, the status bar might display the current page number, the zoom level, or a Web page address.

- A **scroll bar** on the side of the window helps you move a document or graphic up and down within the window. A horizontal scroll bar might also appear at the bottom of an application window to help you scroll wide documents and graphics from left to right.

FAQ How do I switch between application windows?

You can have more than one application window open, or "running," on the desktop. This Windows feature is handy if you want to work on two projects at the same time, or if you want to copy a photo from your photo editing software to a document. Open application windows are represented by buttons on the taskbar. Clicking one of these buttons brings the window to the front of the desktop. Although multiple applications can be open at the same time, only one application can be active. The active application is indicated by a distinctly colored taskbar button.

Some applications also allow several data files to be open at the same time. For example, when using Microsoft Word, you could have your to-do list open at the same time you are working on a term paper. When you have multiple data files open using the same application, such as Microsoft Word, the application's taskbar button looks like several buttons are stacked on top of each other, representing multiple files. You can customize Windows if you prefer each data file to have its own taskbar button.

TRYIT!

Figure 8-3

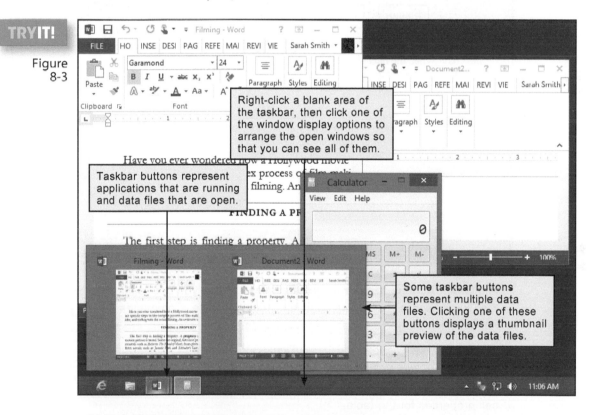

Right-click a blank area of the taskbar, then click one of the window display options to arrange the open windows so that you can see all of them.

Taskbar buttons represent applications that are running and data files that are open.

Some taskbar buttons represent multiple data files. Clicking one of these buttons displays a thumbnail preview of the data files.

- If an application window is open but hidden underneath another application window, clicking the application's button on the taskbar brings that window to the front, overlapping other windows on the desktop. You can also click any visible part of the hidden window to make it active.

- If an application window is minimized, clicking the application's button on the taskbar restores the window to its previous size and location.

- When multiple data files are open in a single application, such as Microsoft Word, you can hover the mouse pointer over the taskbar button to see a preview of the files and select the one you want.

FAQ How does the ribbon work?

Microsoft Office 2013 applications feature a **ribbon** that you can use to access all the commands for an application. The ribbon is divided into a hierarchy consisting of tabs, groups, and commands. The tabs are divided into groups. Each group contains related commands and options for performing various actions. For example, the HOME tab contains a Styles group with options for fonts to use for various levels of headings in a document.

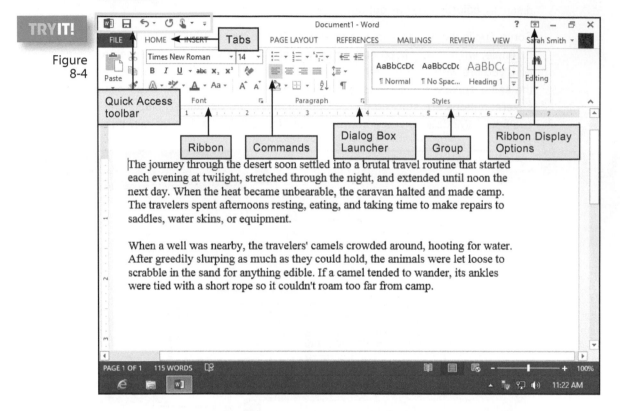

Figure
8-4

● The **Quick Access toolbar** contains commands that you use regularly. Elements of the Quick Access toolbar are completely customizable. Commands can be added by right-clicking the toolbar's down-arrow button.

● **Contextual tabs**, which contain formatting options for an object, appear when the object is selected. For example, after a table is inserted, the TABLE TOOLS tab appears. From this tab, you can change borders, insert or delete columns, and change cell properties for the table.

● Dialog boxes can be opened from the ◳ **Dialog Box Launcher** in the lower-right corner of a group. For example, in Figure 8-4, the Paragraph dialog box can be launched from the Paragraph group on the HOME tab.

● The Ribbon Display Options button can be used to hide the ribbon if you are working on a small screen. It also has an option to display just the tabs, in which case clicking a tab displays the rest of the ribbon.

FAQ How do I open a file from within an application?

Before you can work with a file, you must open it. There are several ways to open a file. One way is to first open an application, such as Microsoft Excel, and then use options on the FILE tab to select a file.

Office applications use file extensions to filter the list of files and display only those files that can be opened using the current application. So, when you are working in Excel, the file list displays only XLSX and other spreadsheet files that can be opened with Excel.

The application's FILE tab may display a list of recently opened files, making it easy to find files that you've been working on. If the file you want is not in the recent file list, then choose the Open option and proceed as shown in Figure 8-5.

Figure 8-5

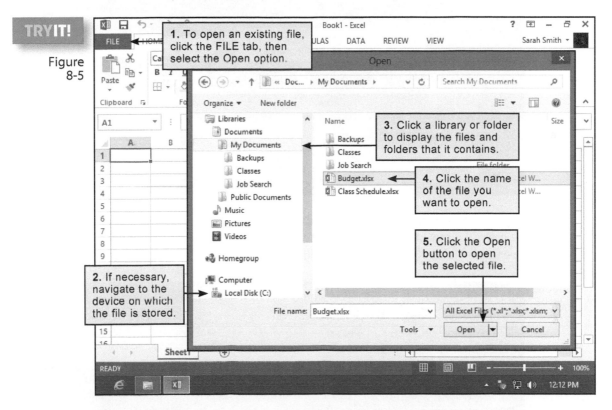

Microsoft Office can open files created using its Word, Excel, PowerPoint, and Access applications. It can also open files created with several other software applications. Files can be identified by their file extensions or by an icon. A file extension can be seen at the end of a file name if Windows is set to show extensions. If extensions are turned off, the icons in the table below can help you identify the type of data that a file contains.

Figure 8-6

File Type	Source	File Extension	Icon
Documents	Microsoft Word	.docx or .doc	
	Text files	.txt	
Spreadsheets	Microsoft Excel	.xlsx or .xls	
Presentations	Microsoft PowerPoint	.pptx or .ppt	
Databases	Microsoft Access	.accdb	

How do I open a file from the Start screen or desktop?

You can open files using the Start screen or from the Windows desktop. Using these methods, you can select a file without having to first start an application. Windows automatically opens the necessary application based on the file name extension.

For example, if you select a file containing a document called Filming.docx, Windows automatically opens Microsoft Word so that you can view and edit the contents of the Filming file.

Figure
8-7

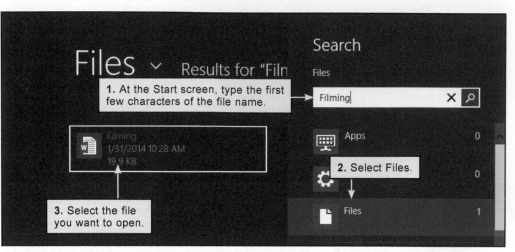

The Windows desktop may display shortcut icons for some files. Shortcuts are designated by a small arrow in the lower-left corner of the icon. Double-clicking a file's shortcut icon opens the file and its associated application.

Figure
8-8

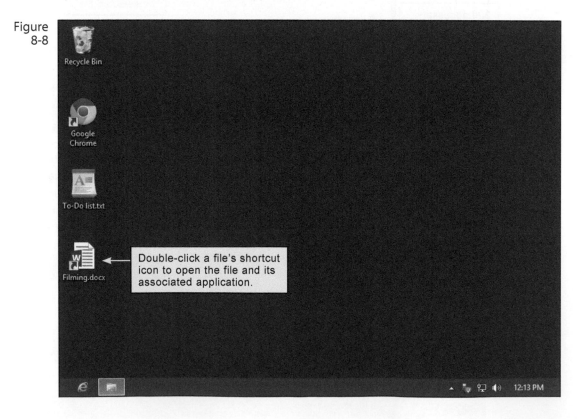

FAQ How do I open a file with the file manager?

File management utilities such as Windows Explorer (Windows 7) and File Explorer (Windows 8) help you navigate through storage devices, libraries, and folders to find files. You can access the file management utility by clicking the 📁 folder icon on the desktop taskbar.

Using the file manager, you can drill down through various devices, libraries, and folders to find a file. When you find the file you want to work with, simply double-click its name or icon.

Figure 8-9

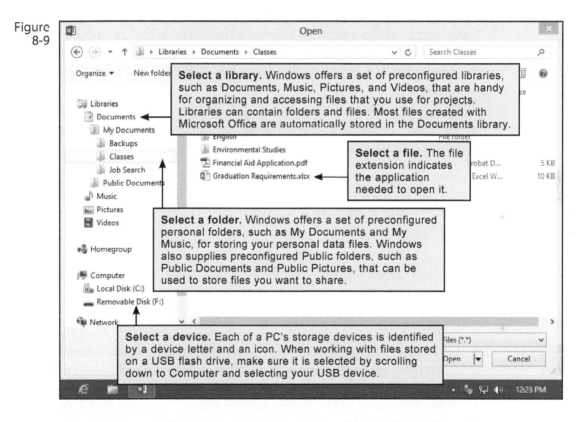

Select a library. Windows offers a set of preconfigured libraries, such as Documents, Music, Pictures, and Videos, that are handy for organizing and accessing files that you use for projects. Libraries can contain folders and files. Most files created with Microsoft Office are automatically stored in the Documents library.

Select a file. The file extension indicates the application needed to open it.

Select a folder. Windows offers a set of preconfigured personal folders, such as My Documents and My Music, for storing your personal data files. Windows also supplies preconfigured Public folders, such as Public Documents and Public Pictures, that can be used to store files you want to share.

Select a device. Each of a PC's storage devices is identified by a device letter and an icon. When working with files stored on a USB flash drive, make sure it is selected by scrolling down to Computer and selecting your USB device.

• Many Windows applications, including those in Microsoft Office, store files in your personal libraries and folders if no other drive or folder is specified. If you save a document, presentation, spreadsheet, or database and forget where it went, look in the Documents library. For photos, look in your Pictures library. For music, look in the Music library or Downloads folder.

FAQ What if a file doesn't open?

The process of opening files usually goes smoothly, but occasionally you'll encounter file problems. Here's a summary of common problems and their solutions:

- **Storage device not available.** Files can be accessed only if the device on which they are stored is connected to your computer. Before you attempt to open files from a USB flash drive, a LAN server, or Web-based online storage, make sure your computer can access the storage device. As necessary, plug in your USB drive, make sure your LAN connection is active, or make sure you have an Internet connection.

- **File not saved.** If you forgot to save a file before exiting, there's not much hope of retrieving it unless your software provides an AutoRecover feature. **AutoRecover** periodically saves a file as you're working on it. Check your software's settings to find out if AutoRecover is activated. If so, check Help to find out how to retrieve a file from AutoRecover.

- **File stored in the wrong folder.** If you can't find a file, it might have been inadvertently saved in an unexpected location. Use the application's search feature to find the file by name, date, or file type.

- **File moved.** If you moved a file from one folder to another, you won't be able to access it from your software or operating system's recently used files list because those lists point to the original file location. Use your software's Open dialog box to locate and open the file.

- **File is corrupted.** The file might have been damaged—a techie would call it "corrupted"—by a transmission or disk error. You might be able to use file recovery software to repair the damage, but it is usually easier to obtain an undamaged copy of the file from its original source.

- **Incompatible file type.** Most software applications work with a limited number of file types (also referred to as file formats) corresponding to the file extension. For example, Microsoft Paint opens file types such as Windows Bitmap (.bmp), GIF (.gif), and JPEG (.jpg). If you attempt to use Paint to open a Word document (.docx) file, however, your computer will display an error message: "Paint cannot read this file." To avoid this error, be sure to use the correct application software when you open a file.

- **Wrong association.** File Explorer maintains associations that list which file types can be opened by each application. If the association between an application and a file type is not correct, the file might not open. For example, if Paint is inadvertently set to be the default application for DOCX files, a file such as Report.docx won't open when you double-click it in File Explorer.

- **File has the wrong extension.** File extensions are sometimes inadvertently changed when a file is renamed. The most prevalent case is when a renamed file ends up with no extension and your computer does not know what software can open it. You can try to guess the file extension and add it. For example, if a file contains a graphic, chances are that it should have an extension such as .bmp, .gif, .jpg, .tif, or .png. If you can't guess the file type, you'll have to locate the original file with its extension intact.

- **Product or version incompatibility.** Some file formats exist in several variations, and your software might not have the capability to open a particular variation of the format. You might be able to open the file if you use different application software. For example, Photoshop might not be able to open a particular file with a .tif file extension, but Corel PaintShop Pro might open it.

FAQ How do I save a file?

When you create a file on your computer, you must save it if you want to be able to use it again in the future. Be sure to save files before you close their application windows; otherwise, you could lose the work in progress.

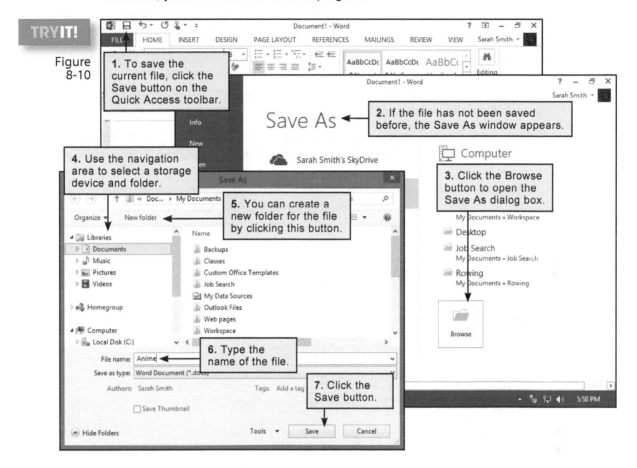

Figure 8-10

- When you first save a file, you must name it. File names can consist of letters, spaces, numbers, and certain punctuation symbols. File names cannot include the symbols / ? : = < > | and must not be longer than 255 characters. Each folder can contain only one file with a particular file name. However, different documents with the same name can be stored in different folders.

- Windows applications add the appropriate file extension automatically, so you don't have to type it when saving a file. In Office 2013, Word documents are usually saved with .docx extensions, Excel files with .xlsx extensions, PowerPoint presentations with .pptx extensions, and Access databases with .accdb extensions.

- Clicking the Save button automatically stores a file using the original name, drive, and folder where it was previously stored. If the file has not been saved before, clicking the Save button opens the Save As window so that you can navigate to the storage location where you want to save the file and enter a file name.

- If you've modified an existing file and want to save the new version under a different name, click the FILE tab, then click Save As to display options for saving the file. Navigate to the location where you would like to save the file, then enter a new name. The modified version of the file is saved under the new name, leaving the original version of the file unchanged under the original name.

• How do I save a file? (continued)

Although Microsoft Office is typically configured to save files in the Documents library, you have full control over the destination of your files. You can save to the desktop, or to any storage device connected to your computer, including the hard disk drive, CD/DVD drive, or USB flash drive. You can also save to a network or an Internet server, such as SkyDrive, if you have access rights and permission to save files in those locations.

You can create new folders for storing files, but you are more likely to keep files organized if you use the basic structure of folders that is provided by Windows. For example, if you want to create a new folder for your term papers, create a new folder as a subfolder of My Documents.

Each Office application has a default file type that it automatically uses when saving files. For example, Word adds a .docx extension to all its files. You can, however, change the format in which a file is saved by using the *Save as type* list provided by the Save As dialog box. For example, you might want to save a document as a template (.dotx) to be used in generating a series of similar documents. You might save a document in Rich Text Format (.rtf) or as plain text (.txt) so it can be opened by other word processing software.

Figure
8-11

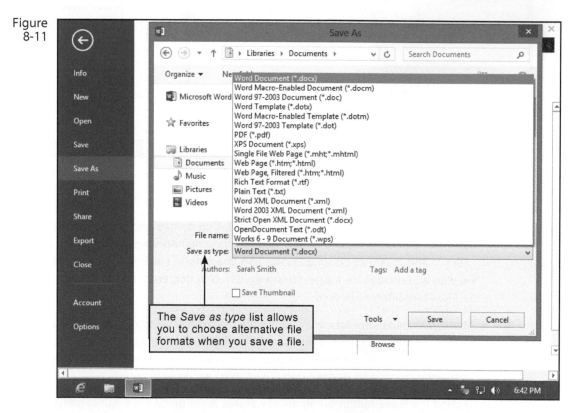

The *Save as type* list allows you to choose alternative file formats when you save a file.

• After you save a file, you can close it or exit the application. Simply closing a file leaves the application open so that you can work on a different file. Closing the application, sometimes referred to as exiting, closes the file and the application.

• To close a file but leave the application open, use the FILE tab to select the Close option.

FAQ How do I change the settings for Microsoft Office?

Microsoft Office is preconfigured with a set of **application options** (sometimes called preferences or default settings) that specify settings, such as where files are stored, which fonts are used to display text, how often files are autosaved, and which printer is used for output. You can modify these settings by clicking Options on the FILE tab.

TRYIT!

Figure 8-12

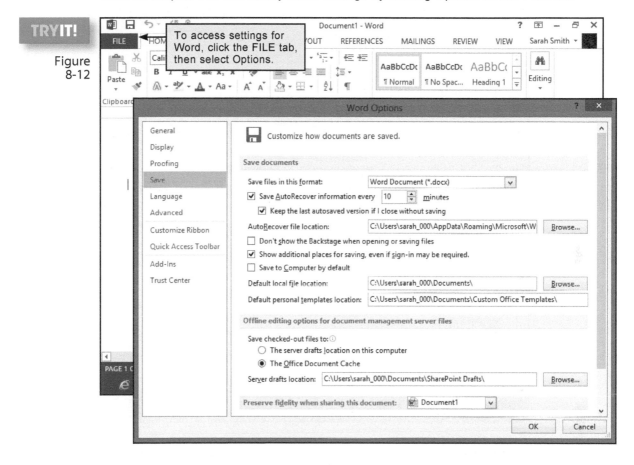

- Microsoft Office applications use your Documents library as the default location for storing files. It is a good practice to keep this default setting and simply navigate to an appropriate subdirectory when using the Save dialog box.

- AutoRecover can retrieve documents that would otherwise be lost as a result of system glitches or unplanned shut downs. To make sure AutoRecover is activated, click Options on the FILE tab. Customize the AutoRecover options on the Save tab.

- Be conservative when you change application settings. Some applications offer hundreds of settings, but the preset defaults usually work for most tasks. When reviewing application settings, just change a few at a time so that you can easily backtrack and reestablish the original settings.

FAQ How do I access help for Microsoft Office?

You can access help information about Microsoft Office from a variety of sources. The ? button opens a window with options for searching by keyword, scanning through popular searches, or perusing online tutorials.

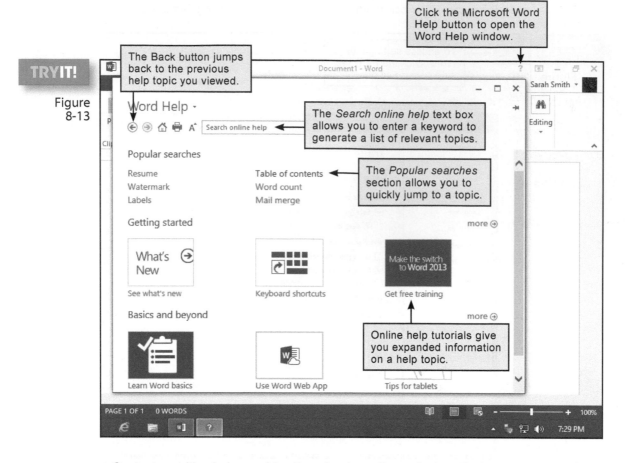

TRYIT!

Figure 8-13

* Context-sensitive help provides tips about a software feature that you are currently using. For example, when you click the Function button, Excel offers context-sensitive help for entering functions such as AVERAGE, COUNT, IF, and PMT. Context-sensitive help usually appears automatically, and some dialog boxes might include a help icon that offers tips on using its options.

* When built-in help does not provide answers, you can use a search engine such as Google to find answers from user groups and knowledge bases.

* When you use a search engine such as Google to get help, you'll get targeted results if you include the full title and version of the software you're using, along with keywords specifically related to your question.

* When seeking advice from online forums, use the advice judiciously. Some people who post advice are well intentioned, but pose solutions that can cause more trouble than the original problem.

* In addition to built-in and online help, you might have access to a help desk at school or at work. Help desks are staffed by people who have expertise in specific software applications. Be sure you follow help desk policies, which might require that you consult built-in help before asking trivial questions.

QuickCheck A

1. Before you close an application window, you should [_____] any work in progress.

2. The [_____] provides access to commands for accomplishing various tasks.

3. True or false? When you open a file, you have to know which file name extensions the application can work with. [_____]

4. True or false? Most applications save files in the Windows folder. [_____]

5. True or false? The first time you save a file, you will use the Save As dialog box to assign the file a name and specify its location. [_____]

CHECKIT!

QuickCheck B

Indicate the letter of the application window element that best matches the following:

1. The Save button [____]

2. The application window's taskbar button [____]

3. The Close button [____]

4. The horizontal scroll bar [____]

5. The Ribbon Display Options button [____]

CHECKIT!

9 Creating a Document

What's Inside and on the CD?

Microsoft Word is the component of Microsoft Office best suited for creating documents such as letters and reports. As word processing software, Microsoft Word provides a set of tools for entering and revising text, adding graphical elements such as color and tables, and then formatting and printing completed documents.

Most people use Microsoft Word more frequently than any other component of Microsoft Office. Microsoft Word is an excellent tool for creating documents of all sorts—from personal letters to business proposals.

In this chapter, you'll learn how to create documents using Microsoft Word. Then you'll learn how to select and edit text, check spelling, use the electronic thesaurus, and specify print options. You'll also learn how to use document templates to quickly generate common types of documents.

● **FAQs:**

FAQ What's in the Word program window?

You can open Word from the Windows 8 Start screen. Simply click the Word 2013 tile or type Word, then select it from the list of apps. In Windows 7, click the Start button and then select Microsoft Word from the Start menu.

When Word starts, a preliminary screen appears where you can select from a list of recently opened documents, browse to open a different document, or create a new document. After you've made a selection from the preliminary screen, the Word program window is displayed. Components of the Word program window include the title bar, Quick Access toolbar, ribbon, status bar, views, and zoom control.

TRY IT!

Figure 9-1

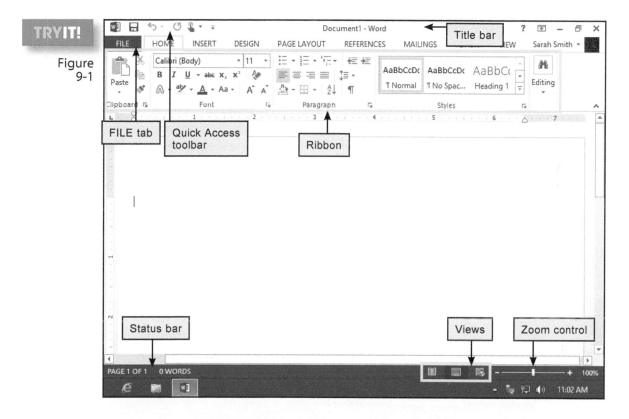

- The title bar indicates the name of the current document. If the current document has never been saved, the title bar displays the generic title Document1.

- Word's ribbon contains commands and tools that you can use to create and edit your document.

- There are different ways to view documents. The **Draft view** allows quick text editing and formatting; headers and footers are not visible. The **Web Layout view** shows how your document would look in a Web browser. The **Print Layout view** shows a preview of the printed page, complete with margins, headers, and footers. The **Read Mode view** displays your document with minimized toolbars at the top of the window. You can also work in **Outline view** to look at the structure of a document.

- The status bar provides information about the document displayed in the window and displays a Zoom control. The information can include page numbers and word count. If you right-click the status bar, you can customize the information displayed.

- You can increase or decrease the zoom level to view the document at various sizes by adjusting the Zoom level on the status bar.

FAQ What's in the document workspace?

Word's **document workspace** represents a blank piece of paper. Characters that you type on the keyboard appear in the document workspace. The document workspace is bordered by scroll bars and a ruler. The scroll bars help you quickly navigate through a document. The rulers help you gauge how the spacing of your on-screen document translates to the space on a printed page. The gray section on the ruler represents margin settings. The white section on the ruler represents space available for text and graphics.

The **I-bar pointer** is equivalent to the arrow-shaped mouse pointer you see when selecting items on the Windows desktop. You move the I-bar by moving the mouse. Use the I-bar to select text and reposition the insertion point.

Figure
9-2

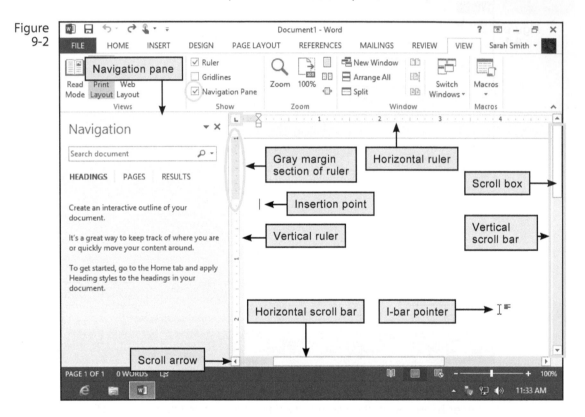

- You can set Word to display a ruler. Use the VIEW tab to display or hide the ruler. The vertical ruler is only visible in Print Layout view.

- The scroll bars offer several ways to navigate a document. Drag the scroll box to smoothly scroll to any part of the document. Click the scroll arrows to move up or down one line at a time.

- When working with lengthy documents, the Navigation pane lets you jump to various objects, such as comments, footnotes, tables, or headings. Use the Navigation Pane checkbox to display or hide the Navigation pane.

FAQ How do I create a document?

To create a new document, just click the blank document workspace and start typing. When typing a document, don't worry too much about spelling, formatting, or arranging the document. It is very easy to edit and format a document after you've entered the text.

TRYIT!

Figure 9-3

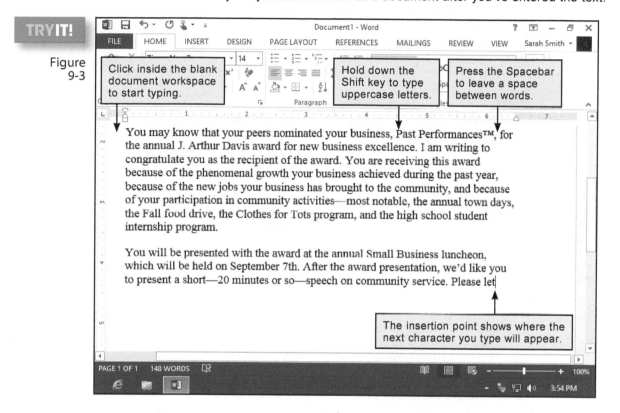

- The **insertion point** (or cursor) is a vertical bar that indicates your current location in the document. The insertion point is not the same as the I-bar. As you type, the insertion point moves to show where the next character will appear. Click anywhere in the document workspace to move the insertion point to that location.

- Through a feature known as **word wrap**, the insertion point automatically jumps down to the beginning of the next line when you reach the right margin of the current line. If the last word you type is too long for the line, it is moved down to the beginning of the next line. Press the Enter key only when you complete a paragraph.

- Press the Backspace key to delete the character to the *left* of the insertion point. You can also press the Delete key to delete the character to the *right* of the insertion point. These keys also work to erase spaces and blank lines.

- To add text in the middle of a line or word, use the mouse or arrow keys to move the insertion point to the desired location, then type the text you want to add.

- Use the Insert key on your keyboard to toggle between Overtype and Insert mode. Overtype mode causes new characters to be typed over existing characters. Insert mode causes new characters to be inserted at the current location in the document.

- Insert special characters, such as the trademark symbol, by clicking the INSERT tab, clicking Symbols, clicking the Symbol command, then clicking More Symbols. Select the symbol you want to insert, click Insert, then click Close to close the Symbol dialog box.

FAQ How do I select text for editing?

Many word processing features require you to select a section of text before you edit, change, or format it. When you **select text**, you are marking characters, words, phrases, sentences, or paragraphs to modify in some way. Selecting text doesn't do anything useful by itself; but combined with other commands, it enables you to use many of the other important features of Word. While text is selected, it is shown as highlighted with a gray background. Word provides several ways to select text.

TRYIT!

Figure
9-4

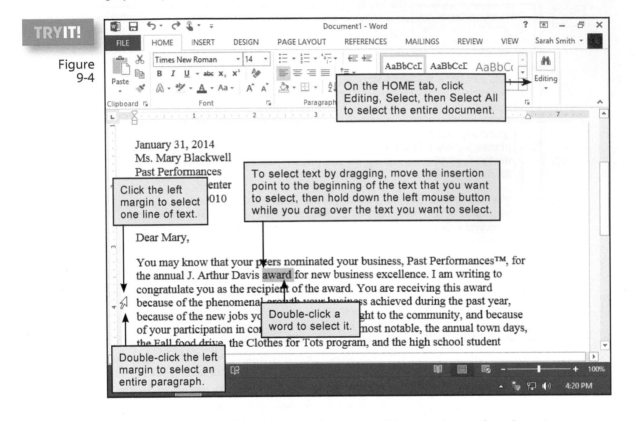

- Use the drag method to select short sections of text, such as a few characters or several words. Use one of the other selection methods when you need to select a single word, a line, a paragraph, or the entire document.

- When you point to a word, you can double-click to select only that word. You can triple-click to select the current paragraph.

- When you point to the left margin, the pointer changes to a white arrow. You can click once to select a line of text or double-click to select a paragraph.

- If you have trouble using the mouse, you can also use the keyboard to select text. Use the mouse or arrow keys to move the insertion point to the beginning of the text that you want to select. Hold the Shift key down while you use the arrow keys to select text.

- To deselect text, you should click away from the text that is currently selected. You can also press one of the arrow keys to deselect text.

- To select a section of text, such as several paragraphs, click at the beginning of the selection, then Shift-click at the end. You can also select non-contiguous text by selecting the first word or section, then using Ctrl-click to select subsequent sections.

FAQ How do I move, copy, and delete text?

As you create a document, you might want to move or copy sections of text—words, paragraphs, or even entire pages—from one part of the document to another. To copy or move text, you use the Clipboard, a special memory location that temporarily holds sections of your document.

TRYIT!

Figure 9-5

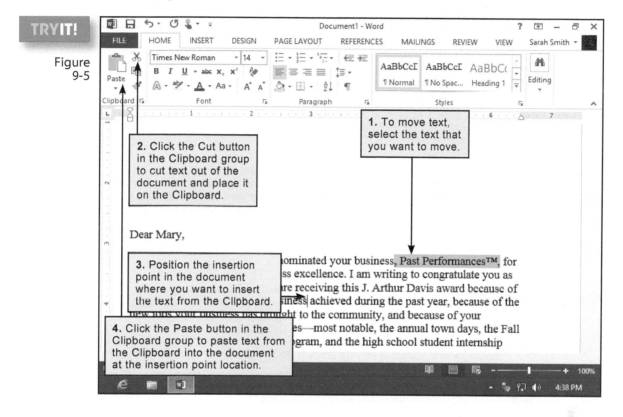

1. To move text, select the text that you want to move.

2. Click the Cut button in the Clipboard group to cut text out of the document and place it on the Clipboard.

3. Position the insertion point in the document where you want to insert the text from the Clipboard.

4. Click the Paste button in the Clipboard group to paste text from the Clipboard into the document at the insertion point location.

Dear Mary,

- To move a section of text from one part of your document to another, first select the text, then click the Cut button. The selected text is cut out of the document and placed on the Clipboard. To paste that text back into the document, move the insertion point to the place where you want to position the text, then click the Paste button. The text is copied from the Clipboard and placed into the document. This operation is known as **cut and paste**.

- You can also cut and paste using the drag-and-drop method. Select the text you wish to cut, then use the mouse to drag it to the new location.

- **Copy and paste** works much the same way as cut and paste, except that the text is not removed from its original location. Select the text you want to copy, then click the Copy button. The selected text is copied to the Clipboard, but the original text is not removed from the document. Move the insertion point to the place where you want to place the copy, then click the Paste button.

- After you cut or copy, the copied text remains on the Clipboard. You can use this feature when you need to put several copies of the same text into your document. Just move the insertion point to the location where you want to place the next copy, then click the Paste button. You can paste as many copies of the text as you like.

- You can cut and paste text, hypertext links, graphics, tables, and other objects between different applications, such as pasting Excel worksheet data into a Word document.

FAQ Can I undo a command?

If you perform an action and then change your mind, use the ↶ Undo button to undo the action. The Undo button has a counterpart—the ↷ Redo button—that allows you to repeat an action that you mistakenly undid. The ↻ Repeat button is used to repeat your last action.

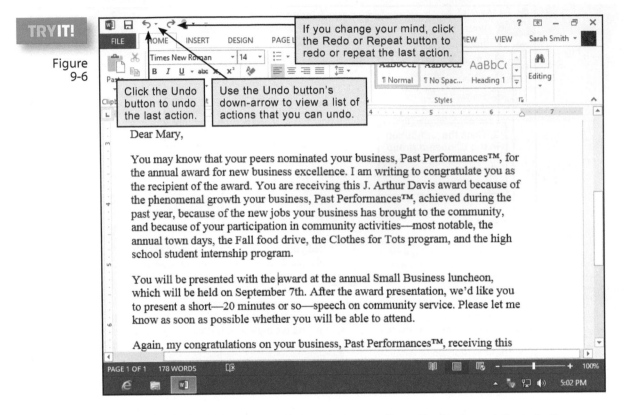

Figure 9-6

- If there are no actions that can be undone or redone, the Undo and Redo buttons are disabled—they appear grayed out and nothing happens if you click them.

- The Undo button works best when undoing an editing or formatting command. Actions such as saving and printing files cannot be undone.

- If you need to undo a series of actions, click the ⌄ down-arrow button on the right side of the Undo button to display a list of actions that can be undone. Drag over the list to highlight the actions you want to undo. You can also click a specific action to select it, but all the actions prior to that one will also be undone.

FAQ How do I check spelling, grammar, and readability?

Microsoft Word provides tools to help you check spelling and grammar in your documents. You should use these tools for all documents before printing or posting them—it only takes a few minutes and can help you catch embarrassing mistakes. However, you should also proofread your documents carefully. You can't depend on the spelling and grammar checker to identify all mistakes or to make sure your document says what you really mean it to say.

In addition to spelling and grammar, you can check the readability of a document by displaying **readability statistics** based on your document's average number of syllables per word and words per sentence. Readability statistics are summarized as a score between 1 and 100 (aim for a score of 60–70) or a grade level (aim for 7th or 8th grade).

TRYIT!

Figure 9-7

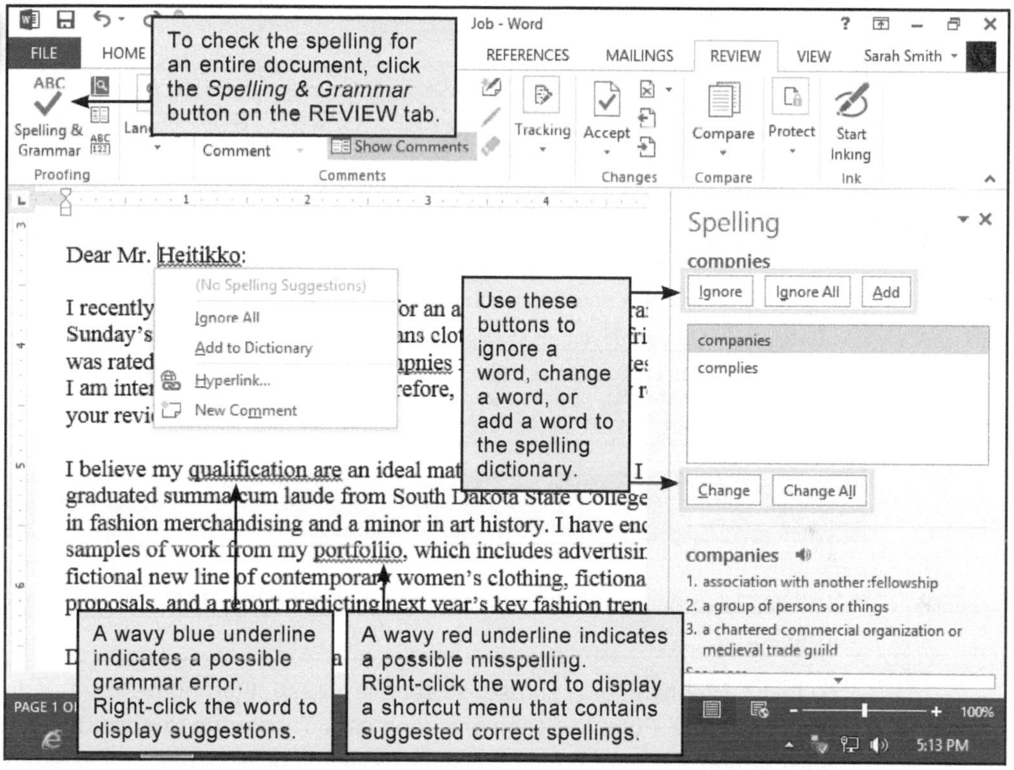

- If you don't see any wavy underlines, spelling and grammar checking might be turned off. Click the FILE tab, click the Options button, then click the Proofing button. Make sure there is a checkmark in the box for *Check spelling as you type*.

- You can also check the spelling and grammar of a complete document by clicking the *Spelling & Grammar* button on the REVIEW tab. Words that might be misspelled are shown in red. Possible grammar mistakes are shown in blue. You can click the appropriate buttons to ignore or replace each word or phrase.

- Readability statistics are shown at the end of a spelling and grammar check if the statistics feature is turned on. To turn on this feature, click the FILE tab, click the Options button, then click the Proofing button. Make sure there is a checkmark in the box for *Show readability statistics*.

FAQ How do I use the thesaurus and other research tools?

A thesaurus contains synonyms for words and some common phrases. When you are composing a document and can't think of the right word, you can type the closest word that comes to mind, and then use Word's thesaurus to search for words with a similar meaning.

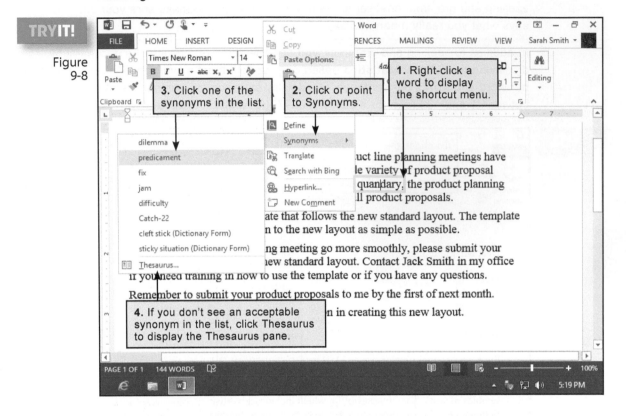

Figure
9-8

- You can also access Word's thesaurus by clicking the REVIEW tab, then clicking Thesaurus.

- To find a synonym for a phrase, select the phrase, then right-click it to display the shortcut menu. Point to Synonyms, then click Thesaurus to open the Thesaurus pane. A list of phrases appears. Sometimes you'll find an acceptable alternate phrase, but beware—some of the phrases listed might not be appropriate substitutes.

- Microsoft Word's REVIEW tab offers additional wordsmithing tools that are especially handy when working with multiple-language documents and when English is your second language. The Translate tool translates a word or sentence into another language.

FAQ Can I search for text and make global changes?

Suppose you've written a short story and just as you're about to wind up the plot, you decide to change the name of the main character. Or imagine that you discover you've misspelled the name of a pharmaceutical product that's the topic of a lengthy report. Will you have to carefully read through your document to locate every instance that needs to be changed? No, you can use Word's find and replace function.

TRYIT!

Figure 9-9

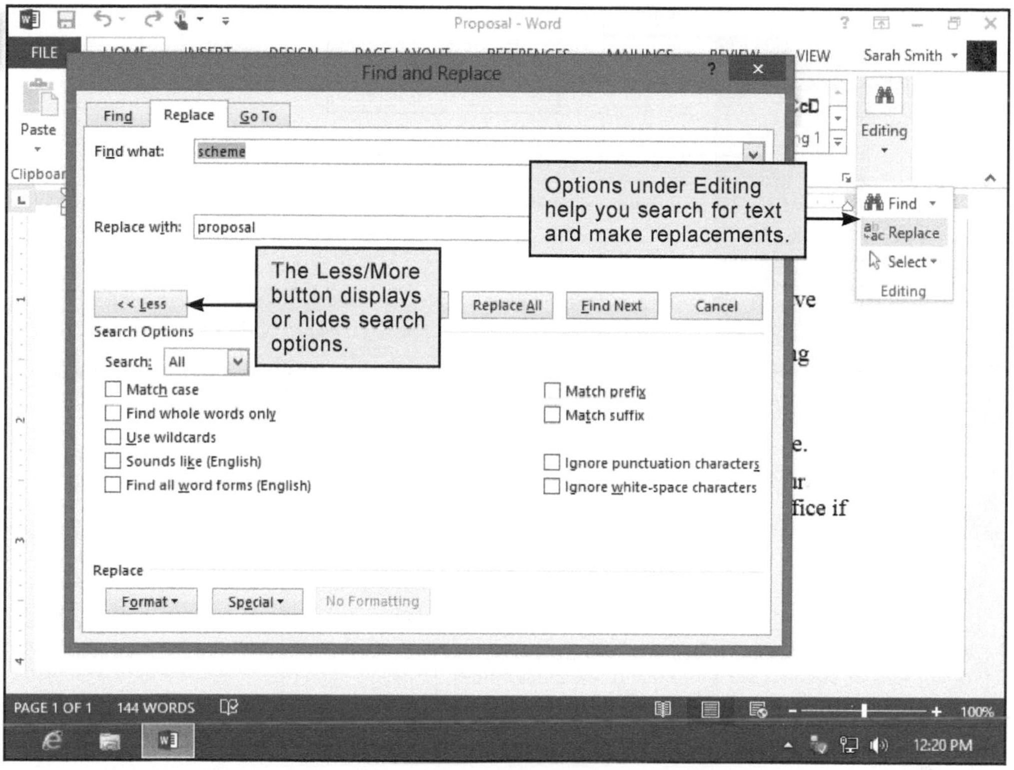

- When you enter replacement text, use capitalization only if you want all instances of the replacement text to be capitalized, as would be the case with proper names.

- If you enter the replacement text in all lowercase, Word will change the case to match the original text. Suppose that you want to replace scheme with proposal, as shown in Figure 9-9. In the *Replace with* box, you enter proposal in lowercase. If Word finds scheme it will replace it with proposal, and Scheme will be replaced with Proposal.

- Word looks for your search string in any part of a word, so searching for process will produce matches for microprocessor and processing. If you are simply looking for the word process, use the *Find whole words only* option in the *Find and Replace* dialog box.

- The *Sounds like* option lets you find words even if you are not sure how to spell them.

- You can use **wildcards** such as ? and *. For example, searching for b?n finds ban and bin. Searching for b*k finds beak, book, back, and so on. Refer to Word Help for more details about wildcards.

FAQ How do I use a document template?

You can create a document from scratch by entering text in the blank, new document workspace. As an alternative, you can use a **document template**, which is a preformatted document that can be used as the foundation for creating a new document. Word includes templates for many basic document types, such as letters, faxes, and resumes.

TRYIT!

Figure 9-10

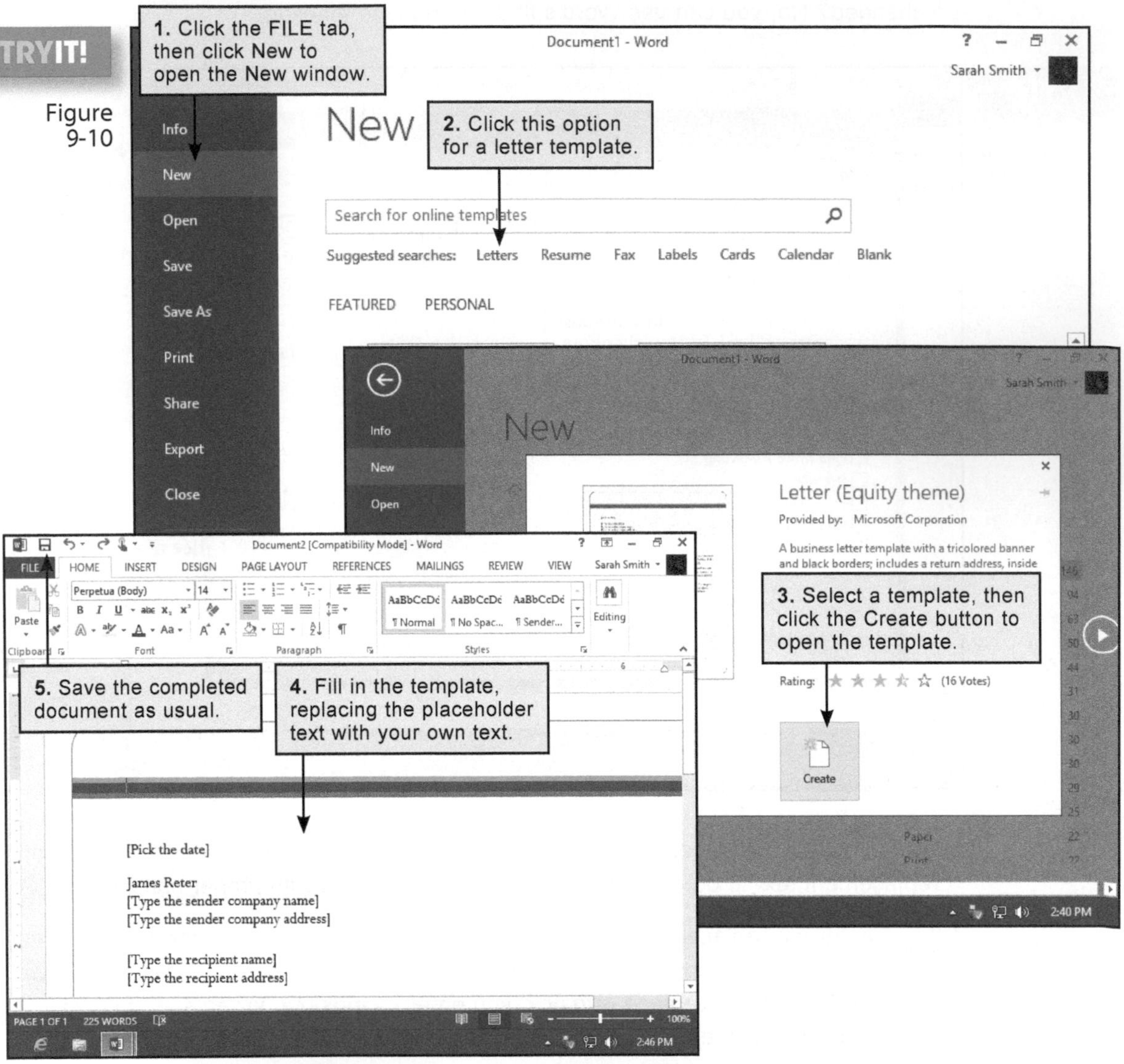

1. Click the FILE tab, then click New to open the New window.

Document1 - Word

Sarah Smith

Info
New
Open
Save
Save As
Print
Share
Export
Close

New

2. Click this option for a letter template.

Search for online templates

Suggested searches: Letters   Resume   Fax   Labels   Cards   Calendar   Blank

FEATURED   PERSONAL

Document1 - Word

Sarah Smith

Info
New
Open

New

Letter (Equity theme)

Provided by: Microsoft Corporation

A business letter template with a tricolored banner and black borders; includes a return address, inside

3. Select a template, then click the Create button to open the template.

Rating: ★ ★ ★ ☆ ☆ (16 Votes)

Create

Document2 [Compatibility Mode] - Word

FILE   HOME   INSERT   DESIGN   PAGE LAYOUT   REFERENCES   MAILINGS   REVIEW   VIEW   Sarah Smith

Perpetua (Body)   14

B I U abc x₂ x²

Paste

A Aa A A

Clipboard   Font   Paragraph

AaBbCcDc AaBbCcDc AaBbCcDc

¶ Normal   ¶ No Spac...   ¶ Sender...

Styles

Editing

5. Save the completed document as usual.

4. Fill in the template, replacing the placeholder text with your own text.

[Pick the date]

James Reter
[Type the sender company name]
[Type the sender company address]

[Type the recipient name]
[Type the recipient address]

PAGE 1 OF 1   225 WORDS   2:46 PM

- A **placeholder** is an element in a document template into which you enter text that personalizes your document. Common placeholders provide entry areas for today's date, your name, or your fax number. To use a placeholder, click inside it and type your own text. The placeholder disappears and your text is displayed.

- Word allows you to create your own document templates. After you're more familiar with Word, you might want to explore this feature to design templates for documents that you create on a regular basis. You can find more information about creating templates in Word Help and in the program documentation.

- If you work in a large business or organization, you might be required to use templates created by managers, supervisors, or designers. Some examples of document templates used in businesses are letterheads, fax cover sheets, memos, and reports. Requiring these official templates helps businesses maintain professional standards.

FAQ How do I save a document?

After you have created a document from scratch or personalized a document template, it's important to save the document properly so that you can find and use it again. The first time you save your document, be sure to store it in the correct location with the appropriate file type.

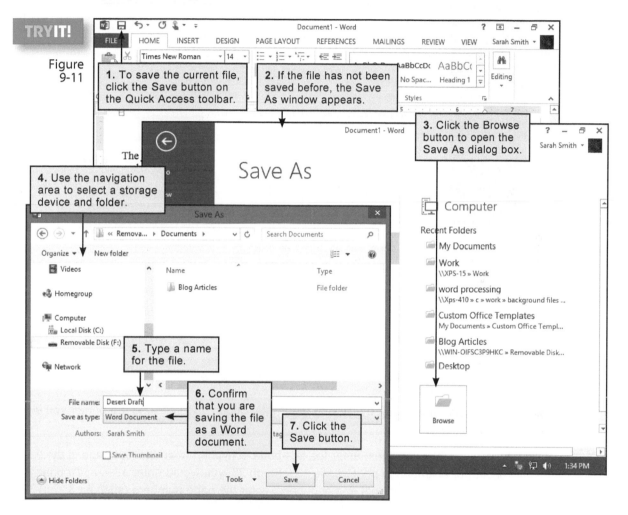

TRY IT!

Figure 9-11

1. To save the current file, click the Save button on the Quick Access toolbar.

2. If the file has not been saved before, the Save As window appears.

3. Click the Browse button to open the Save As dialog box.

4. Use the navigation area to select a storage device and folder.

5. Type a name for the file.

6. Confirm that you are saving the file as a Word document.

7. Click the Save button.

- The first time you save a document, the Save As dialog box appears. By default, Word saves your file in the My Documents folder as a Word document with a .docx extension. You can save the document in another location by selecting a different drive and folder.

- You can save your document as a different file type if you click the down-arrow button to the right of the *Save as type* text box. For instance, you might want to save the document in DOC format so it can be opened on a computer with an earlier version of Microsoft Office, such as Office 2007. You can also save a document in formats such as PDF, TXT, and RTF.

- After you save a document the first time, the next time you click the Save button, the document is automatically saved using the original file name and storage location. It's a good idea to save frequently as you work on a document to minimize the chance of losing data as a result of a power outage, software bug, or other unforeseen event.

FAQ How do I print a document?

You can print a document using the Print option available through the FILE tab. Before printing, you can select an alternate printer, or adjust settings to print multiple copies of a document, print selected pages, or collate the printed pages.

TRYIT!

Figure
9-12

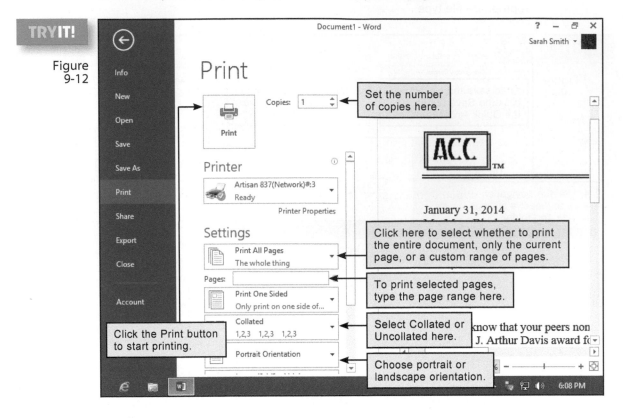

- You can select a printer by clicking the Printer button, then clicking the printer you want to use.

- To print a range of pages, enter the first page, a hyphen, then the last page in the range. For example, to print pages 13 through 28, you would enter $13-28$. To print specific pages that are not in a sequence, enter the page numbers (such as $3, 7, 12$) in the Pages text box, separated by commas.

- Portrait Orientation prints a page lengthwise so it is taller than it is wide. Landscape Orientation turns the page on its side so it is wider than it is tall.

- You can print on one side of the paper or set a duplex printer to print on both sides of the paper. You can simulate duplex printing using the *Manually Print on Both Sides* option and turning the paper when prompted to do so.

- When the Collated option is selected, each copy of a document prints in sequential page order so you don't have to collate it manually.

- In addition to providing print options, Word displays a preview showing how the printed document will look. The preview provides options for adjusting the magnification. If the print preview is acceptable, click the Print button to print the document. To return to the document without printing, click the arrow in the upper-left corner of the Print window.

FAQ How can I troubleshoot printing problems?

Suppose you try to print a document but nothing happens! Printing problems can be caused by the printer, by the software that controls the printer, or by installation glitches. Luckily, most printing problems are easily fixed. Your first step is to check the power light to make sure the printer is turned on. Also, verify that the printer is ready to print by pressing the appropriate buttons on the printer's control panel. You should also make sure the printer is loaded with the correct size and type of paper, and the printer's ribbon, ink cartridge, or toner cartridge is properly installed.

If the printer checks out, your next step is to check the print queue. A **print queue** manages multiple documents waiting to be printed. When one document is printed, the next document in the print queue is sent to the printer. Each printer connected to your computer has a separate print queue. You can use a print queue to display information about each print job; to pause, restart, or cancel print jobs; and to move documents higher or lower in the queue. If your computer is connected to more than one printer, use the print queue to make sure you sent the document to the correct printer.

Figure 9-13

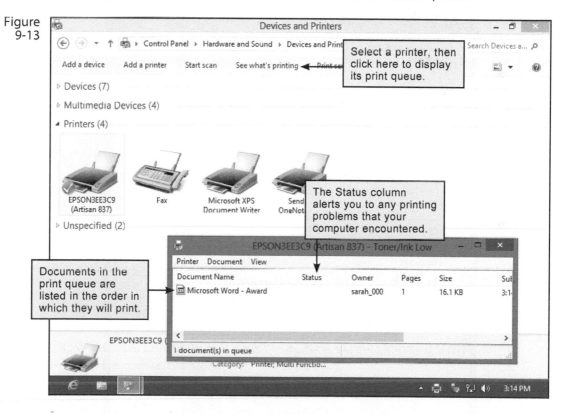

- You can view the print queue at any time. From the Windows 8 Start screen, type Printers, click Settings, click *Devices and Printers*, select a printer, then choose *See what's printing*.

- To pause, restart, or cancel a print job, open the print queue, click the name of the print job, then choose the desired option from the Document menu.

- If the printer is shared, other people might have documents in the print queue ahead of yours. Check the print queue to see if your document is waiting to be printed.

• How can I troubleshoot printing problems? (continued)

If the *Devices and Printers* window contains icons for several printers, only one of those printers can be designated as the default printer. All documents are sent to the default printer unless you specify otherwise. A common printing problem occurs when you connect a different printer to your computer but forget to change the default printer. When a printing problem occurs, make sure the default printer setting is correct.

To change the default printer, from the Windows 8 Start screen, type Printers, click Settings, then click *Devices and Printers*. Right-click the printer you want to set as the default printer, then choose *Set as default printer*.

The Printer Properties dialog box is another useful tool for troubleshooting printing problems. From the *Devices and Printers* window, right-click a printer and select Printer Properties. You can use this dialog box to change print settings, activate printer sharing, check the port used to connect your printer and computer, and even print out a test page. Printing a test page can help you determine if the printer is connected correctly.

Figure
9-14

EPSON3EE3C9 (Artisan 837) Properties

| Color Management | | Security | | Version Information |
| General | Sharing | | Ports | Advanced |

EPSON3EE3C9 (Artisan 837)

Location:

Comment:

Model: EPSON Artisan 837 Series

Features
Color: Yes
Double-sided: Yes
Staple: No
Speed: Unknown
Maximum resolution: Unknown

Paper available:

Letter (8

Click Print Test Page to test your printer settings after you modify print settings or install a new printer.

Preferences...   Print Test Page

OK   Cancel   Apply

A document might not print if the page settings are not specified correctly in the Page Setup dialog box. Some printers cannot print outside of certain page boundaries, or are limited to certain page sizes. Check your printer documentation for details, and verify that the margins and page size are correct by clicking the PAGE LAYOUT tab in Word, then clicking the Page Setup Dialog Box Launcher.

Another potential cause of printing problems is the printer driver software used by your computer to control the printer. If you can't find any other solution, check with your printer's manufacturer to see if an updated printer driver is available. Updated printer drivers are typically posted online and can be easily downloaded and installed.

QuickCheck A

1. True or false? In the document workspace, the insertion point is shaped like an I-bar.
   [   ]

2. Press the [   ] key to delete the character to the right of the insertion point.

3. When you copy text, the selected text is copied from the original location and placed on the [   ] .

4. True or false? If you accidentally delete the wrong text, you can click the Redo button to cancel the deletion and display the original text. [   ]

5. A document [   ] allows you to create a new document from a preformatted document.

CHECKIT!

QuickCheck B

Indicate the letter of the desktop element that best matches the following:

1. Selected text [   ]

2. The Copy button [   ]

3. The Paste button [   ]

4. The Cut button [   ]

5. The end of a line of text where the Enter key was pressed [   ]

CHECKIT!

Skill Tests

A Creating a document

B Selecting text

C Moving, copying, pasting, and deleting text

D Using document templates

10 Formatting a Document

What's Inside and on the CD?

In this chapter, you'll learn how to format your documents using features such as bold and italic text, different fonts and font sizes, line spacing, and paragraph alignment. You'll also learn how to use tables, bullets, and numbered lists to organize and present information.

Experienced word processing software users find that it's useful to apply formatting after writing the document. The idea is to focus initially on the content of the document, while adding, deleting, and moving text as needed. After you're satisfied with the content and organization of the document, you can go back and format the document as needed.

Appropriate formatting can increase the attractiveness and readability of your documents. However, it's important not to get carried away with formatting. Use different fonts, font sizes, and colors only where they add to the appearance or readability of the document. After all, you wouldn't want your documents to look like a ransom note pasted together with letters from a variety of newspaper stories!

FAQs:

FAQ How do I select different fonts, font sizes, and text colors?

You can use options on the HOME tab to select different text attributes for single characters, words, sentences, or paragraphs. The term **font** refers to the design or typeface of each character. Don't use too many fonts in one document—documents look more professional when limited to one or two basic fonts.

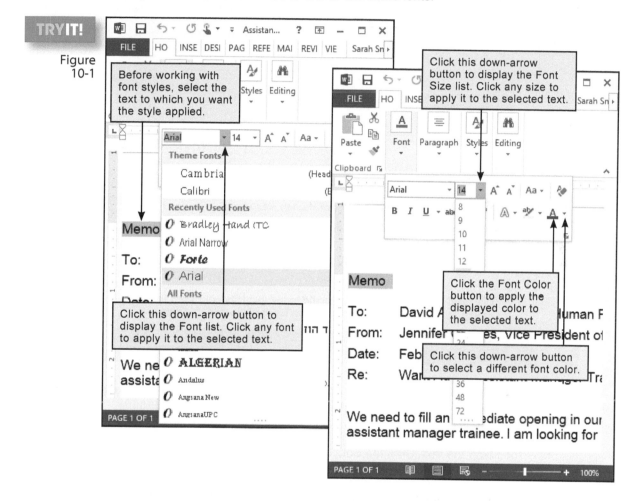

Figure 10-1

• **Text attributes** include font, font size, bold, italic, underline, and text color. Font size is normally 9–12 points, but you can select any font size up to 72 points. 72-point font is equal to one inch on a printed piece of paper. You can make text even larger by typing in a number up to 1638. This feature is useful for making signs and posters.

• Once you've selected text, you can change the font, font size, and color without reselecting the text. As long as the text remains selected, you can apply additional formatting options to it. After you've formatted the text, click anywhere outside of the highlighted area to deselect it.

• **Font effects** include superscript, subscript, strikethrough, small caps, and all caps. To apply font effects, select the text, then select the effect from the Font group. Additional font effects are available from the Font dialog box.

• If you want to change the font or font size for an entire document, click Editing, Select, then Select All on the HOME tab to select the entire document. Using Select All, you can apply any text attributes to all the text in a document, even to multiple pages.

FAQ How do I apply bold, italic, and underlining attributes?

You can use the options in the Font group to apply text attributes such as bold, italic, and underlining to text within your document.

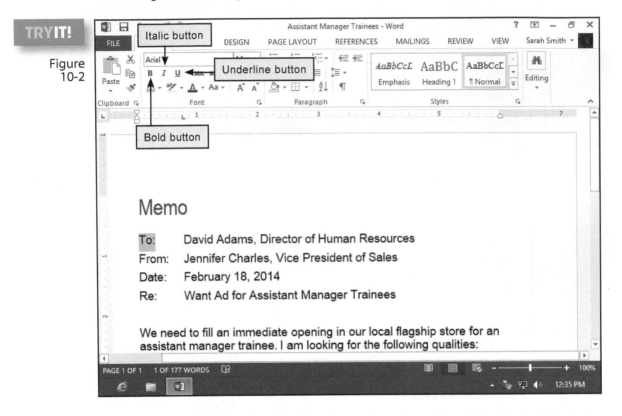

Figure 10-2

- Typically, you'll apply text attributes to text you've already typed. Just select the text, then use the desired button in the Font group to apply the text attribute.

- You can apply the bold text attribute before typing new text. Click the Bold button, then type the text. Click the Bold button again to discontinue bold and continue typing normal text. You can use a similar procedure to enter italic or underlined text.

- Text attribute buttons both apply and remove text attributes. For instance, if you apply the bold attribute but then change your mind and want to display the text as normal, select the text and then click the Bold button again to remove the bold attribute.

- If you select a section of text that includes both normal and bold text, the first time you click the Bold button, all of the selected text is displayed as bold. Click the Bold button again to display all of the selected text as normal text.

- Word automatically formats hyperlinks to Web pages such as www.facebook.com and displays them in underlined blue text. This is a special type of underlining; it is not controlled by the Underline button. To change the format of a hyperlink, right-click it and select an option from the shortcut menu that appears.

- **WordArt** offers fancy font effects that you can use for the text on posters and elsewhere. To add WordArt effects to selected text, click WordArt on the INSERT tab from the Text group, then select a style. You can apply additional formatting using the DRAWING TOOLS FORMAT tab.

FAQ How do I use the Font dialog box?

As you've already learned, you can apply some text attributes—such as bold, italic, and underlining—using the Font group on the HOME tab. But other text attribute options, such as character-spacing options, are only available from the Font dialog box.

You can also use the Font dialog box if you want to apply multiple formatting options to selected text. It's faster to use the Font dialog box to apply all the attributes in one operation than to apply the attributes one at a time using the buttons on the ribbon.

TRYIT!

Figure
10-3

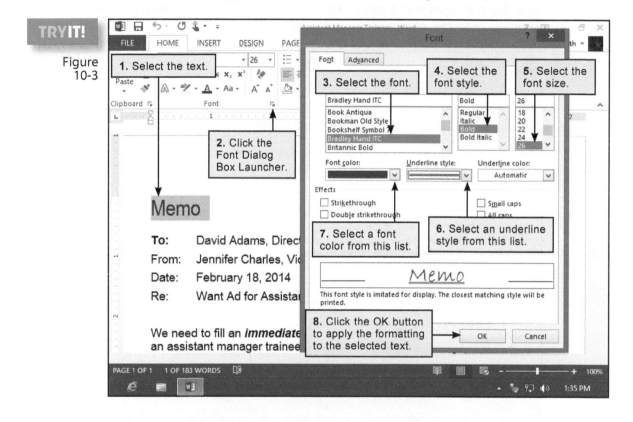

- Use the Advanced tab in the Font dialog box if you need to change the scale, spacing, vertical position, or kerning of selected text. Changing the **kerning**—the space between each letter—can be particularly useful when you need to make text fit into a limited space.

- The Preview area of the Font dialog box shows how your formatting affects the selected text. You'll see the selected font, font styles, colors, and effects before you click the OK button to accept your changes. If you don't like what you see in the Preview area, you can adjust the format settings or click the Cancel button to close the Font dialog box without applying the formatting options.

FAQ How do I center and align text?

The Paragraph group on the HOME tab provides options for centering, right-aligning, left-aligning, and justifying text.

Left-aligned text is positioned straight against the left margin, but appears uneven, or "ragged," on the right margin. **Centered text** is positioned between the margins and is typically used for titles. **Justified text** has both left and right margins aligned. You might want to use justified text in the body of a formal document to give it a more professional look. **Right-aligned text** is rarely used, but can be useful for headings in a paper, for example, or for the return address in a letter.

TRYIT!

Figure 10-4

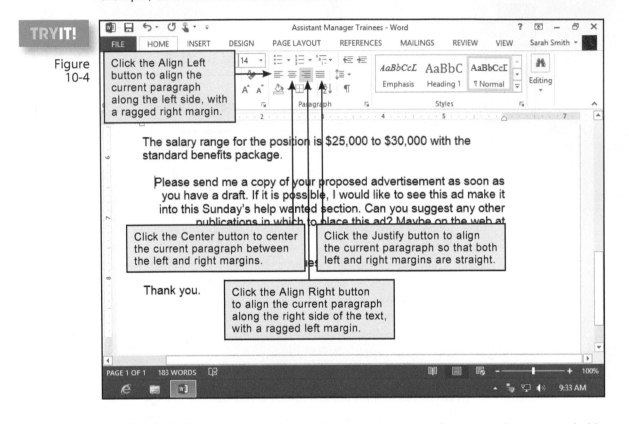

• Unlike bold, italic, and underlining, alignment options apply to an entire paragraph. You don't have to select the text to align it—just click in the paragraph you want to align, then click the appropriate alignment button.

• To center a title, press the Enter key at the end of the title so it becomes a separate paragraph. Click anywhere in the title, then click the Center button. Single lines, such as titles, are centered between the left and right margins. If the paragraph consists of multiple lines, every line in the paragraph is centered.

• To return a centered paragraph to left alignment, click in the paragraph, then click the Align Left button.

FAQ How do I use styles?

When formatting a document, select font and paragraph styles that fit the purpose of your document and the needs of the reader. A **style** consists of predefined formatting that you can apply to selected text. Word comes with several predefined styles. Using them will help you avoid design errors such as tight line spacing and ragged margins. Styles also allow you to be consistent in formatting text throughout a document.

In addition to predefined styles, you can create your own. If you find yourself regularly applying multiple format settings to sections of text, you can save time by defining your own style, then applying it as needed.

TRY IT!

Figure
10-5

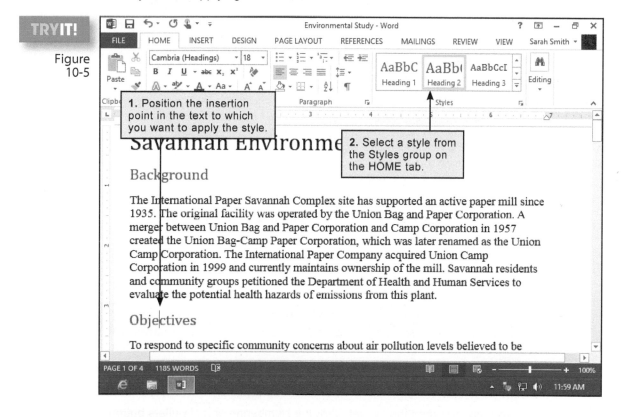

- To create a style, format a section of text using the desired font, font size, and font styles. Click the Styles Dialog Box Launcher to display the Styles dialog box. Click the New Style button to display the *Create New Style from Formatting* dialog box. Click the Name text box, then type the name for your new style. After you click OK and close the Styles dialog box, your new style is added to the Styles list. To apply the style to other text, select the text, then select your style from the Styles list.

- To remove a style from a section of text, select the text, then select the Normal style from the Styles list.

- To delete a style so that it no longer appears in the Styles list, click the Styles Dialog Box Launcher to display the Styles dialog box. Right-click the style you want to delete, then select Delete. Click Yes, then click the Close button to close the Styles dialog box.

FAQ How do I add numbering and bullets to a list?

Word's Paragraph group on the HOME tab contains buttons to format a list with bullets or numbers. A **bullet** is a symbol placed before each item in a list. You can use bullets when you want to set off the items in a list but don't want to imply a specific order. A numbered list is a list with a number in front of each item on the list, which implies the items are listed in order.

TRYIT!

Figure 10-6

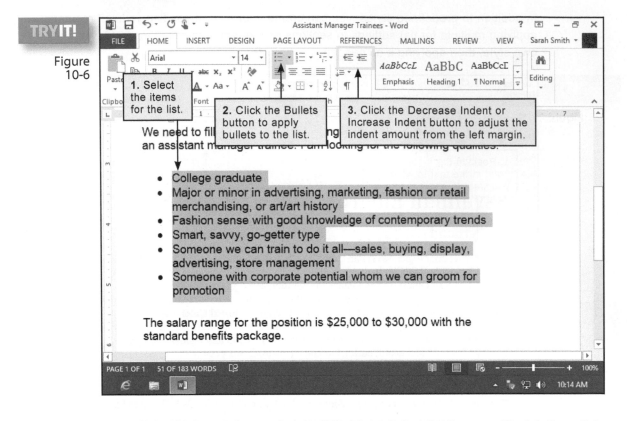

• Numbered lists work the same as bulleted lists. Select the items on the list, then click the ▤ Numbering button to add numbers to the list.

• If you haven't typed the list yet, click the Numbering or ▤ Bullets button, then type the items on the list. Each time you press the Enter key, a new number or bullet is inserted before the next list item. At the end of the list, press the Enter key and click the Numbering or Bullets button to discontinue the numbering for the next line of text.

• To remove numbering or bullets from a list, select the list, then click the Numbering or Bullets button.

• If you add, delete, or move the items in a numbered list, Word renumbers the list for you. If the numbering is incorrect, select the list, then click the Numbering button twice. This procedure removes and then reapplies the numbering, which usually corrects any problem with the numbers in the list.

• To change the numbered list style, select the list, click the arrow next to the Numbering button, then select a format. The style for a bulleted list can be changed in a similar manner.

• Lists can be sorted in alphabetic or numeric order using the ⇅ Sort button in the Paragraph group. Simply highlight the list items, then click the Sort button. Select Ascending or Descending, then click OK.

• How do I add numbering and bullets to a list? (continued)

A multilevel list displays list items in levels and sublevels. Common uses for multilevel lists include topic outlines and legal documents. Multilevel lists can be numbered, lettered, or bulleted using a variety of predefined or customized styles.

Although you can apply bullets or numbering to a multilevel list after entering the list, the more typical procedure is to activate the Multilevel List button before you enter the list items.

Figure 10-7

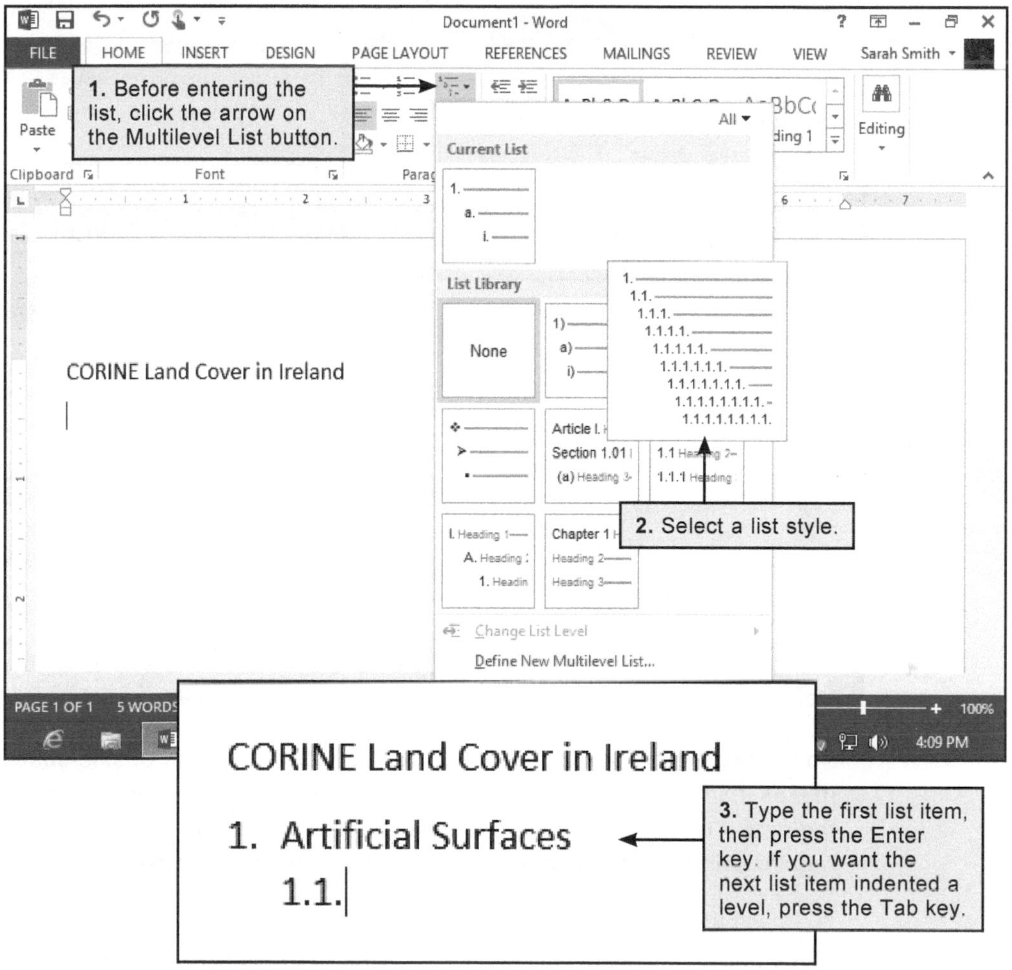

- Pressing the Enter key as you type a list automatically displays the next list number, letter, or bullet.

- Press the Tab key to change a list item to the next level down. Use Shift Tab to move a list item up a level.

- You can define custom styles for the text, numbers, and bullets in a list by clicking the arrow next to the Multilevel List button, then selecting Define New List Style. This option is especially handy for creating a list format that you want to reuse for multiple documents.

- When entering a list, you can change a number manually by right-clicking the number and selecting Set Numbering Value from the shortcut menu. The shortcut menu contains options for starting a new list and continuing the numbering from a previous list.

FAQ How do I adjust line spacing?

Your Word document is single-spaced unless you specify another spacing option, such as double- or triple-spacing. You can apply line-spacing options to a single paragraph, to a group of paragraphs, or to the entire document. You can also adjust the space between paragraphs. Single-spacing is appropriate for letters and memos, whereas double-spacing is often used for first drafts of manuscripts and reports.

Figure 10-8

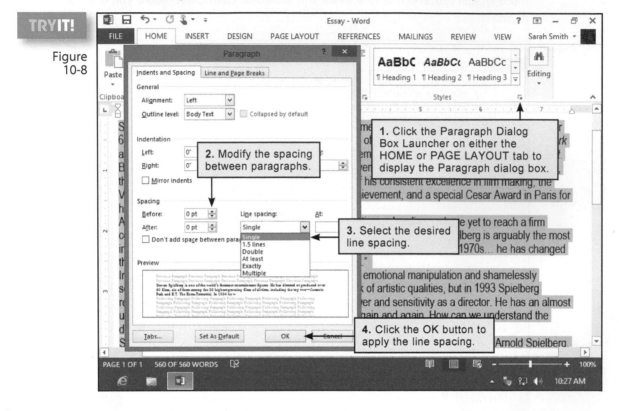

• Do not press the Enter key at the end of each line to create double-spaced text. This makes it difficult to edit your document because words won't wrap from one line to the next. The preferred way to double-space a document is to type the document as regular single-spaced text, then set the line spacing to double.

• To adjust the line spacing for one paragraph of text, position the insertion point in the paragraph, then click the Paragraph Dialog Box Launcher on the HOME or PAGE LAYOUT tab. Select the desired spacing from the *Line spacing* drop-down list on the *Indents and Spacing* tab. Single- and double-spacing are the most commonly used spacing settings.

• To adjust the line spacing for more than one paragraph, select the paragraphs, then adjust the line spacing as described above.

• To adjust the space between paragraphs, click the Paragraph Dialog Box Launcher on the HOME or PAGE LAYOUT tab. Select the desired paragraph spacing from the Before and After boxes on the *Indents and Spacing* tab.

• You can set the line spacing for the entire document before you begin typing. Click Editing, Select, then Select All on the HOME tab. Click the Paragraph Dialog Box Launcher on the HOME or PAGE LAYOUT tab. Select the desired line spacing, then click the OK button. As you type, the text appears on the screen with the selected line spacing.

FAQ How do I use tabs?

Setting a **tab** provides an easy way to align text in columns. Word provides default tab stops at 0.5" intervals, but you can change the default tab settings and add your own tab stops. The position of a tab stop is measured from the left margin.

TRYIT!

Figure 10-9

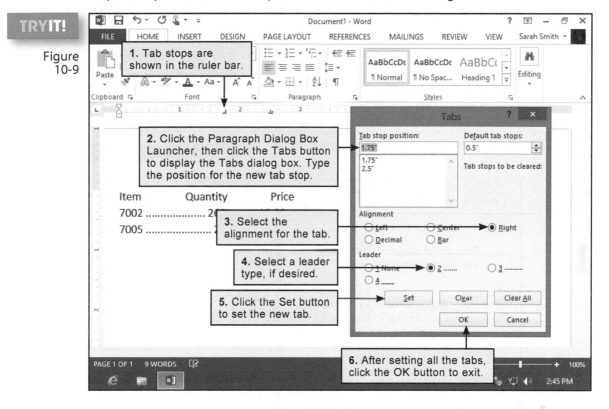

* There are many types of tab stops. A left tab stop means that text will be aligned on the left side of the tab. A right tab stop means that text will be aligned on the right side of the tab. A center tab stop centers text at that location, while a decimal tab stop aligns numbers with the decimal at the tab location. A bar tab stop places a vertical bar at the tab location.

* On the Word ruler bar, tab stops are represented by these small icons:

  └ Left tab   ┴ Center tab | Bar tab
  ┘ Right tab   ┵ Decimal tab

* To set tabs using the ruler, select the type of tab stop by clicking the icon at the left end of the ruler. Click a location on the ruler to set the tab stop. You can move a tab stop by selecting it, then sliding it right or left on the ruler bar.

* If the ruler bar is not displayed, click the VIEW tab and then select the Ruler option in the Show group.

* A **leader** is a line of punctuation characters, such as periods, that fills the area between text and a tab stop. Leaders are typically used in a table of contents to associate a page number with a chapter title or heading. To add a leader to a tab stop, click the option button to select the leader type. When you tab to that tab stop, the leader character—usually a series of periods—fills the area to the tab stop.

* To clear one tab stop, click that tab stop in the *Tab stop position* box, then click the Clear button. To clear all tab stops, click the Clear All button in the Tabs dialog box.

FAQ How do I indent text?

You can indent text from the left margin, from the right margin, or from both margins. You can also indent the first line of text differently from the rest of a paragraph. For example, you can indent the first line of a paragraph farther to the right than the rest of the paragraph. This **first-line indent** style is commonly used for college papers and manuscripts.

In contrast, the hanging indent style positions the first line of a paragraph farther to the left than the rest of the paragraph. **Hanging indents** are used for numbered lists, bulleted lists, and bibliographical citations. Word's Paragraph dialog box provides several options for indenting text.

TRYIT!

Figure 10-10

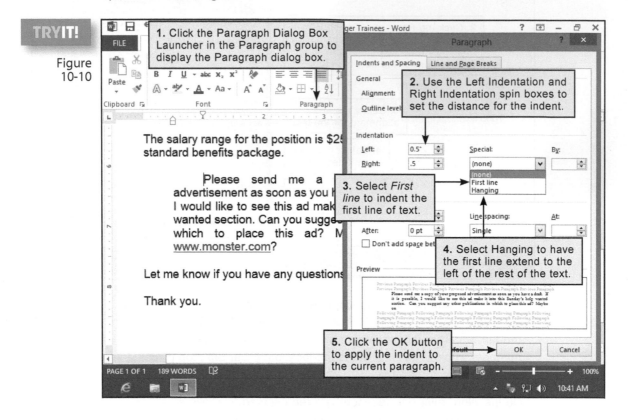

1. Click the Paragraph Dialog Box Launcher in the Paragraph group to display the Paragraph dialog box.

2. Use the Left Indentation and Right Indentation spin boxes to set the distance for the indent.

3. Select *First line* to indent the first line of text.

4. Select Hanging to have the first line extend to the left of the rest of the text.

5. Click the OK button to apply the indent to the current paragraph.

- To indent an entire paragraph from the left, click the spin box buttons in the Left Indentation box to increase or decrease the indent distance. Use the same process with the Right Indentation box to increase or decrease the right indentation.

- The Preview section shows how the paragraph will look after it is indented. As you change your selections, the Preview is updated.

- To indent the first line of text, select *First line* from the Special pull-down list. Select the amount of indentation for the first line of the paragraph from the By spin box.

- To create a hanging indent in which the first line of text extends more to the left than the rest of the text, select Hanging from the Special pull-down list. Select the amount of negative indent for the first line of the paragraph from the By spin box.

- Indent settings apply to the paragraph that contains the insertion point. To apply an indent to more than one paragraph, select the paragraphs, then use the Paragraph dialog box to set the indent.

FAQ How do I add footnotes or endnotes to a document?

Footnotes and endnotes are typically used to add comments to blocks of text or cite references to other documents. An asterisk or a superscript number appearing in the main text of a document indicates a footnote or an endnote. A **footnote** appears at the bottom of the page that contains the corresponding superscript number. An **endnote** appears at the end of a section or chapter.

TRY IT!

Figure
10-11

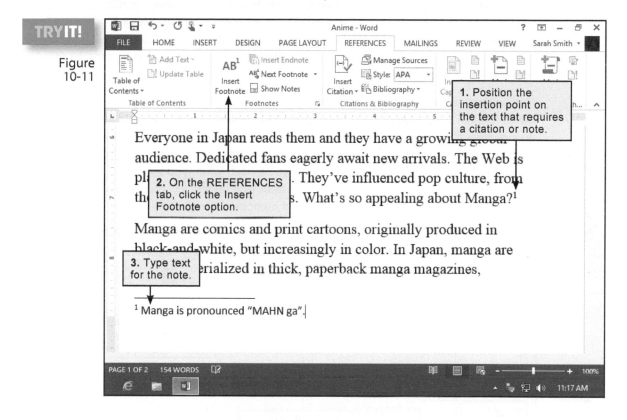

* To insert a footnote or an endnote, position the insertion point in the paragraph that contains the text needing a citation or comment. Click the REFERENCES tab. Click the Insert Footnote or Insert Endnote button. A text area appears on the bottom of your screen that allows you to type the note text.

* To modify the format of a footnote or an endnote, open the *Footnote and Endnote* dialog box by clicking the Footnote & Endnote Dialog Box Launcher.

* To delete a footnote or an endnote, select the superscript number that corresponds to the note in the text, then press the Delete key.

* The REFERENCES tab contains several tools for adding citations to a document. You can select a citation style, such as APA or MLA, and Word will automatically add the required formatting and punctuation to book titles and other materials you cite. Word can even produce a bibliography based on all the citations in a document.

FAQ How do I work with outlines and other document views?

Word provides several ways to view a document. You can display **format marks** to reveal hidden symbols that indicate paragraph breaks ¶, spaces ·, and tab stops →. To display hidden formatting marks, click the ¶ Show/Hide button in the Paragraph group on the HOME tab.

You can also change the document view to see how it will look when printed (Print Layout view), as a Web page (Web Layout view), or as an outline (Outline view). To change the document view, click the VIEW tab, then select one of the views. You can also change to Print Layout, Web Layout, or Read Mode by clicking one of the view buttons on the status bar.

Outline view is handy for organizing the content of a document. You can assign outline levels to each title, heading, and paragraph, and view any level of the outline to get an overview or include all details. In Outline view, it is easy to rearrange sections of a document to streamline its organization. Outline view is best used to work on the structure of a document, but it is not meant to be used when you want to create a document that displays paragraph numbers or outline levels. For tools to create multilevel outlines, refer to the FAQ about bulleted and numbered lists.

TRYIT!

Figure
10-12

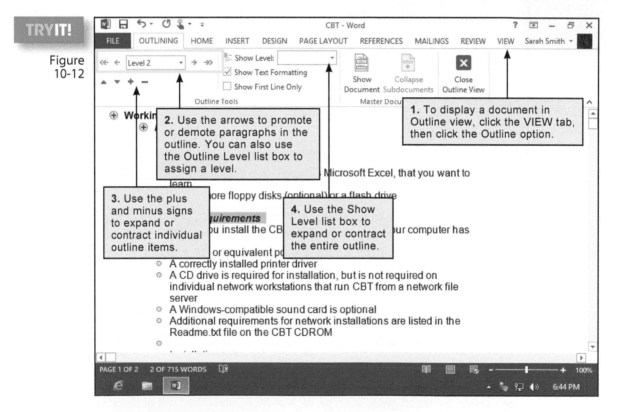

- Microsoft Word uses the following conventions to indicate outline levels:

  A plus sign ⊕ indicates a heading with subtext.

  A small solid circle ○ indicates body text at the lowest level of the outline.

  A gray line under a heading indicates subordinate text that is not displayed.

  A dash ⊖ indicates a heading without subordinate text.

FAQ How do I create a table?

A **table** is a grid consisting of rows and columns. The intersection of each row and column is called a cell. Each cell can hold text, numbers, or a graphic. You can format an entire table or individual cells.

TRYIT!

Figure
10-13

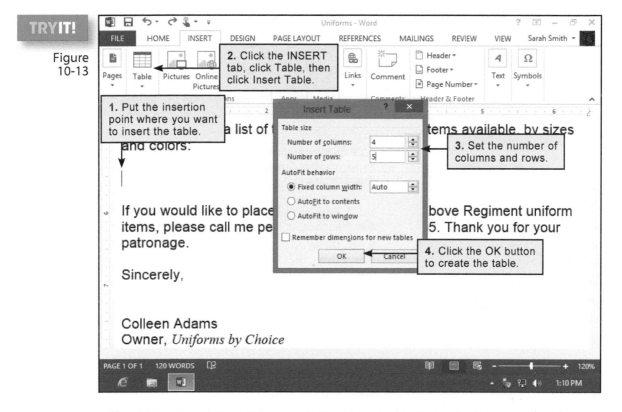

- To add text to a table, click any cell, then type text in that cell. The word wrap feature moves text down while you type and expands the size of the cell to make room for all of your text. To move to another cell, press the arrow keys, press the Tab key, or click the desired cell.

- To quickly format a table, make sure the insertion point is in the table, then click the TABLE TOOLS DESIGN tab. Select a table style from the Table Styles group. You can then modify the format to change the font or other table attributes.

- To insert a new row or column, place the insertion point in the cell closest to where you want the new row or column to appear. Click the TABLE TOOLS LAYOUT tab, then choose from among the options to specify the placement of the new row or column from the Rows & Columns group.

- To delete unused rows or columns, position the insertion point in the column or row you want to delete. Click the TABLE TOOLS LAYOUT tab, then click the Delete command in the Rows & Columns group. Select from among the options to specify what you want to delete.

- To adjust the width of a column, position the pointer over the dividing line between the columns. When the pointer changes to a ◄╫► shape, press the left mouse button and drag the column to the correct width.

- You can convert normal text into table text using the Table button on the INSERT tab. When converting text into a table, use commas to separate the text for columns, and use paragraph marks (Enter key) to separate the text that will become each row.

FAQ Can I format a document into columns?

There are three ways to format text into columns: tabs, tables, and columns. Tabs are most effectively used when you want to enter a single line of parallel text in each column. Tabs work well for short, multi-column lists:

Address	List Price	Days on Market
12 Main St.	$349,000	38
322 North Rd.	$149,500	36

Tables are effective when you want to enter parallel text, but some text requires multiple lines. A typical use of table-style columns is the text layout of a resume:

Work History	2008-present: Marketing & Graphics Assistant, Smith & Co., San Francisco: Created designs for consumer packaging using Adobe Illustrator and four-color processing; prepared designs for photo shoots
Education	M.F.A. Graphic Design & Marketing, 2010 San Francisco Art Institute, San Francisco, CA B.F.A. Marketing 2006 Emory University, Atlanta, GA

The third option, sometimes referred to as newspaper columns or newsletter columns, fills the left column entirely with text and then continues into the right column as shown below. Use newspaper-style columns when you want to format full paragraphs of text into columns.

TRYIT!

Figure 10-14

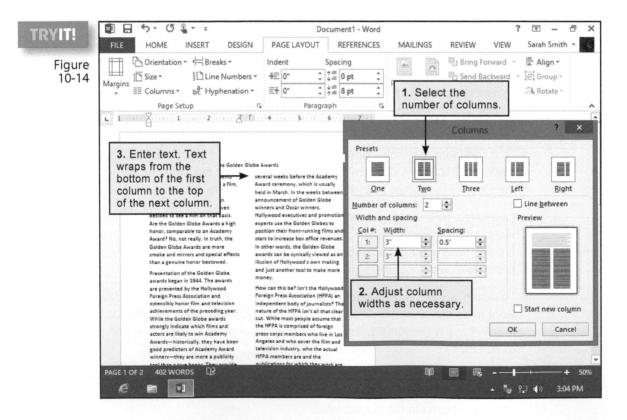

• If you want to jump to the next column before reaching the end, Ctrl Shift Enter inserts a column break into the text.

QuickCheck A

1. True or false? To create an active hyperlink in a document, select one or more words, click the Underline button, then change the font color to blue. ▭

2. Centering and alignment formats apply to an entire ▭ of text.

3. You should use the ▭ dialog box to apply multiple formatting options to text in a single operation.

4. A(n) ▭ is a symbol, such as a square or circle, placed before an item in a list.

5. True or false? To double-space a document, you should press the Enter key two times at the end of every line of text. ▭

CHECKIT!

QuickCheck B

Indicate the letter of the desktop element that best matches the following:

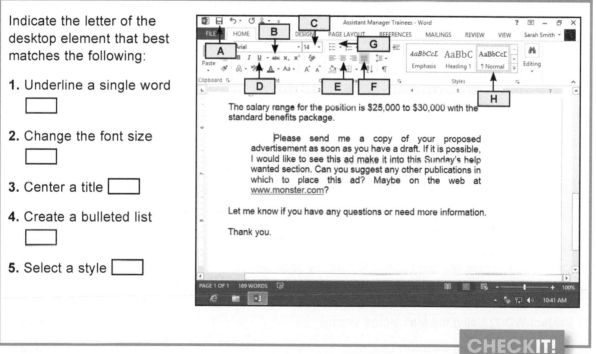

1. Underline a single word ▭

2. Change the font size ▭

3. Center a title ▭

4. Create a bulleted list ▭

5. Select a style ▭

CHECKIT!

Skill Tests

A Using text attributes and fonts

B Centering and aligning text

C Creating lists and setting line spacing

D Setting tabs and indenting text

CHAPTER **11**

Finalizing a Document

What's Inside and on the CD?

Writing a document is only half the battle. After you have checked spelling and grammar, applied formatting, and adjusted your wording, you can do even more. In this chapter, you'll learn how to add the finishing touches to prepare your document for printing or posting as a Web page.

Important features covered in this chapter include adding headers and footers, setting margins, and incorporating graphics. You'll learn how to save your document in HTML format so it can be posted as a Web page. Also, you'll find out how adding comments and tracking changes make it easy for multiple people to collaborate on a single document.

FAQ How do I create headers and footers?

A **header** is text that appears at the top of every page of a document. A **footer** is text that appears at the bottom of every page. Headers and footers typically contain information such as the title of the document, the date, the name of the author, and the current page number. Headers and footers are useful for keeping printed documents intact, for example, when a document is dropped or a part of it is misfiled.

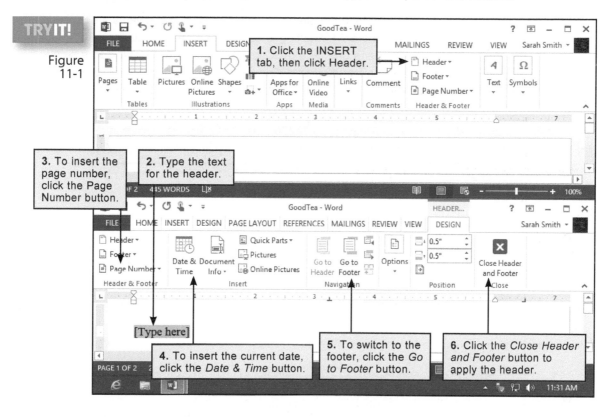

TRYIT!

Figure 11-1

1. Click the INSERT tab, then click Header.

2. Type the text for the header.

3. To insert the page number, click the Page Number button.

[Type here]

4. To insert the current date, click the *Date & Time* button.

5. To switch to the footer, click the *Go to Footer* button.

6. Click the *Close Header and Footer* button to apply the header.

- Headers and footers are displayed only in Print Layout view, on the Print window, and on printed pages.

- The header and footer have preset tabs—a center tab in the middle of the page, and a right tab near the right margin. Press the Tab key to move the insertion point to the next tab to enter text at that location.

- If you want to include text such as "Page 6" in your header or footer, click the Page Number button, then select the desired format. Page numbers are automatically updated when page content changes during editing.

- To insert the current date and time, click the *Date & Time* button in the Insert group, select the desired format from the *Date and Time* dialog box, then click OK. To have the date/time automatically update each time you open the document, place a checkmark in the *Update automatically* checkbox.

- Click the *Go to Header* or *Go to Footer* button to switch between the header and footer. You can edit the header or the footer, but not both at the same time.

- You can change the font and style of page numbers just as you would change any text by using the formatting options on the HOME tab.

FAQ How do I insert page breaks and section breaks?

A **page break** occurs within a document where one page ends and the next page begins. When a page is filled with text or graphics, Word automatically inserts a page break. You can also insert a manual, or "forced," page break at any point in the document. In Draft view, page breaks are shown as a horizontal dotted line. In Print Layout view, page breaks are displayed as the end of a sheet, or page, within the document.

A **section break**, displayed as a double dotted line in Draft view, divides a document into sections. You can apply different formatting to each section of a document. For example, you might define the title page of a term paper as a section, and format it as a single column with no headers. You could then define the body of the document as a separate section formatted with two columns and headers that contain page numbers.

TRYIT!

Figure 11-2

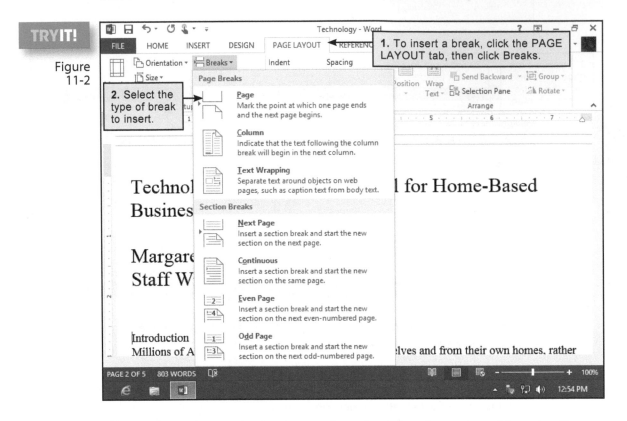

- Use sections when parts of a document require different page-based format settings for margins, borders, vertical alignment, columns, headers and footers, footnotes and endnotes, page numbering, and line numbers. Paragraph and text-based formatting options—such as line spacing, font, size, and bullets—are typically applied to selected text, rather than to sections.

- To insert a break, click the PAGE LAYOUT tab, click Breaks, then select the type of break you want. You can also insert a page break with the Page Break button in the Pages group on the INSERT tab or by using the keyboard shortcut Ctrl Enter.

FAQ Can I insert photos into a document?

You can use two types of graphics to enhance documents created with Microsoft Word: vector graphics and bitmap graphics. Both types of graphics can be used to add pizzazz to a page, draw interest to certain text selections, or illustrate important points. Don't overuse pictures, however. Too many can cause a page to look cluttered and confusing.

A **bitmap graphic**, referred to in Word as a picture, is composed of a grid of colored dots. Digital photos and scanned images are typically stored as bitmap graphics with extensions such as .bmp, .png, .jpg, .tif, or .gif. Word does not provide a feature to create bitmap graphics, but you can insert photos and other bitmaps stored in files on your computer.

To insert a bitmap graphic into a document, click the INSERT tab, then click Picture in the Illustrations group. Use the Insert Picture dialog box to navigate to the folder that contains the picture you want to insert, then click the Insert button.

TRY IT!

Figure
11-3

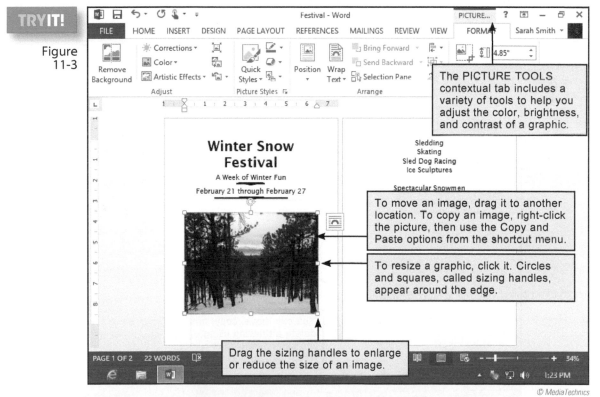

© MediaTechnics

- Word provides a PICTURE TOOLS contextual tab to help you adjust the color, contrast, and brightness of inserted bitmap graphics. You can also use this tab to crop or rotate a picture.

- To crop a picture, select the picture, click the Crop button in the Size group, drag the edges of the picture to frame the part of the image you want to display, then click the Crop button again to finalize the crop.

- Adjust the brightness, contrast, and color of a picture by selecting the graphic and choosing an option from the Corrections button in the Adjust group.

- You can control the way text flows around a picture in a document. Select the picture, click the Wrap Text button in the Arrange group, then select a text flow option from the list.

- To delete a picture, click it, then press the Delete key.

FAQ Can I insert line art into a document?

A **vector graphic**, sometimes called a drawing, is created with basic shapes, such as lines, curves, and rectangles. Clip art, logos, and organizational charts are often created using vector graphics, and have extensions such as .wmf and .ai. Microsoft Office includes a clip art collection you can access by clicking the INSERT tab, then clicking Online Pictures in the Illustrations group.

You can use the Shapes tool to create your own simple vector graphics within a document. You can also use it to enhance vector graphics you've obtained from other sources and inserted into a document.

You can create vector drawings by combining several shapes within a rectangular area called a canvas. To open a blank canvas, click the INSERT tab, click the Shapes button in the Illustrations group, then click New Drawing Canvas. When the canvas is selected, you can use the Insert Shapes group on the DRAWING TOOLS contextual tab to add shapes to the canvas.

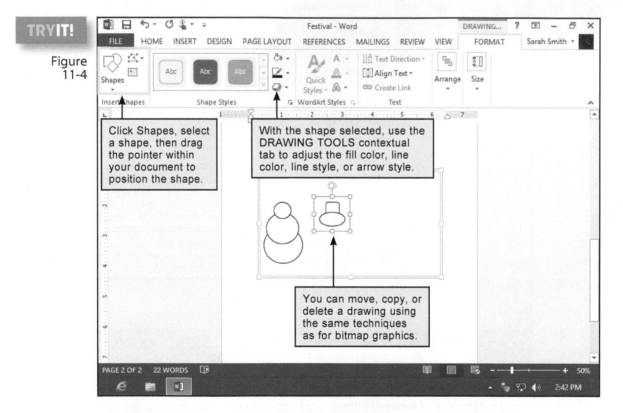

TRY IT!

Figure 11-4

Click Shapes, select a shape, then drag the pointer within your document to position the shape.

With the shape selected, use the DRAWING TOOLS contextual tab to adjust the fill color, line color, line style, or arrow style.

You can move, copy, or delete a drawing using the same techniques as for bitmap graphics.

- Multiple shapes can be grouped together so that they can be moved and resized as a single unit. To group objects, hold down the Ctrl key and select the shapes you want to group. In the Arrange group on the ribbon, click Group, then click Group. Shapes can be ungrouped using a similar procedure but clicking Ungroup instead of Group.

- You can use layers to make shapes appear to be stacked on top of one another or to appear in front of or behind text. To move a shape from one layer to another, in the Arrange group on the ribbon, click the bottom section on the *Bring to Front* or *Send to Back* button. Choose an order from the list.

- To control the way text flows around a vector graphic, click Wrap Text in the Arrange group, then select an option from the list.

FAQ How do I set margins?

Margin settings typically apply to an entire document and are changed using the Page Setup group on the PAGE LAYOUT tab.

In a Word document, the default margins are 1". Margin settings affect the amount of text that fits on a page. Small margins leave more room on a page for text than large margins.

TRY IT!

Figure
11-5

- Don't set the top and bottom margins too small if you're using headers and footers. Headers and footers do not print correctly if there isn't enough room in the top and bottom margins.

- Select Portrait orientation to print the page vertically. If you have a wide document, select Landscape orientation to print the page sideways.

- You can use the Paper tab in the Page Setup dialog box to set the paper size and control how paper feeds into your printer. Select the appropriate paper size from the *Paper size* list. You can find more information about printing options in the printer documentation.

- The Layout tab in the Page Setup dialog box is useful for creating different headers and footers on odd and even pages. Other layout options allow you to center text vertically on the page, insert line numbers, and add graphical elements, such as borders, to the document.

- Although margin settings are typically applied to an entire document, margins and other page formatting options can apply to the whole document, to selected sections of the document, or to the rest of the document that follows the current location of the insertion point. You can find more information about page setup options in Word Help.

FAQ How do I perform a mail merge?

A **mail merge** allows you to create multiple documents from a starting document and a data source. The starting document can be a letter, a label template, or an envelope template. For example, a starting document could be a form letter that you want individualized for a series of recipients. The recipient list contains information that will be merged into the starting document. After the information is merged, the final documents can be printed or saved for future use. The first step in a mail merge is to create or select a recipient list. After you've made that selection, you can create the text of your letter.

Figure 11-6

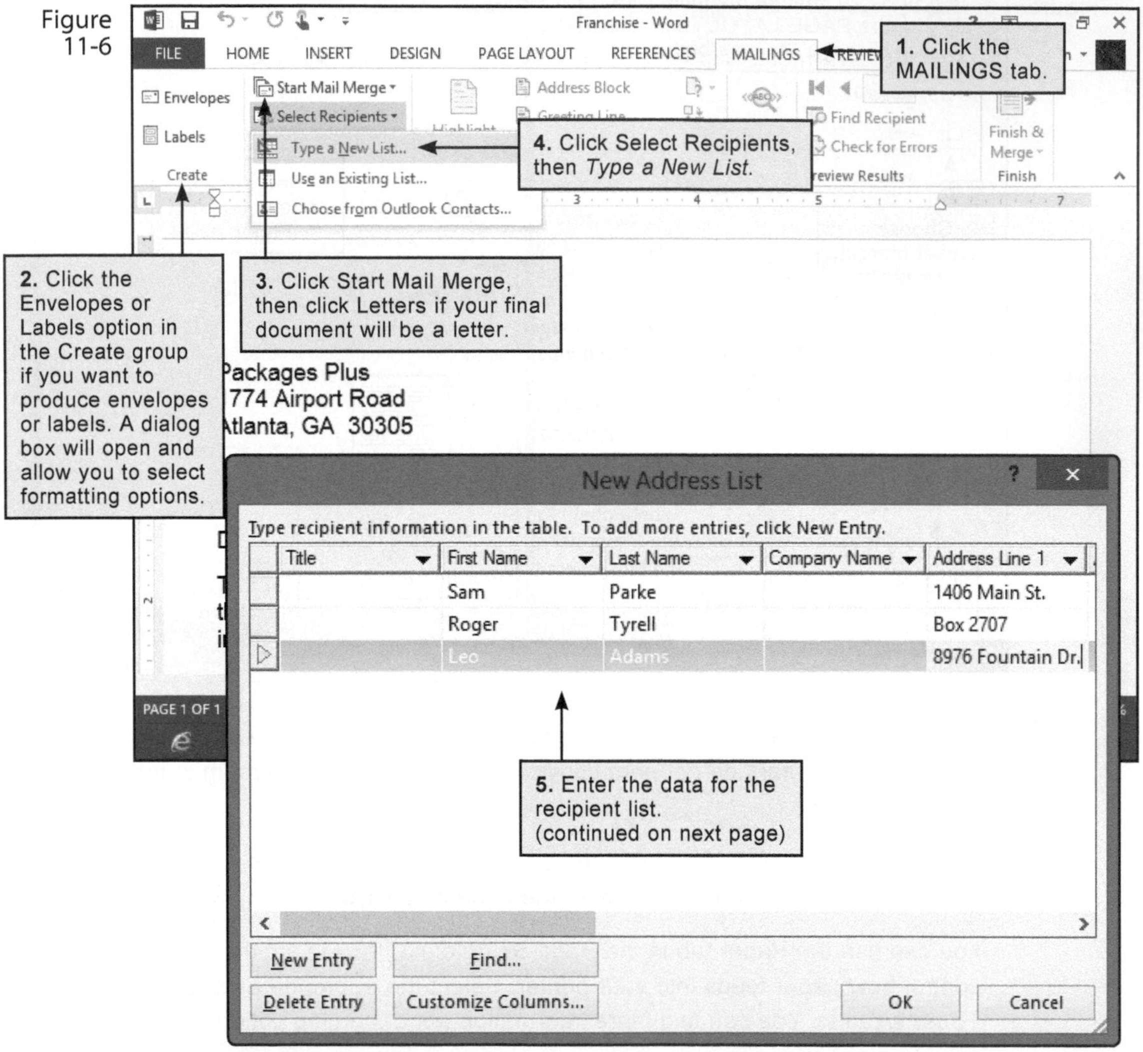

1. Click the MAILINGS tab.

2. Click the Envelopes or Labels option in the Create group if you want to produce envelopes or labels. A dialog box will open and allow you to select formatting options.

3. Click Start Mail Merge, then click Letters if your final document will be a letter.

4. Click Select Recipients, then *Type a New List*.

5. Enter the data for the recipient list. (continued on next page)

• When the recipient list is complete, save it. You can use it again for other mail merges.

• Although Word makes it easy to create a recipient list, you can also merge data from a database file, your Outlook address book, or an Excel spreadsheet. To do so, select *Use an Existing List* instead of *Type a New List* when you set up the merge.

• How do I perform a mail merge? (continued)

Recipient lists contain data such as names or addresses. Each item in a recipient list is considered a field. The data from a field can be inserted into a document during a merge. The location where data is to be inserted is specified by a merge field or merge block. A **merge field**, such as <<FirstName>>, contains one item of data. A **merge block**, such as <<AddressBlock>>, can contain multiple lines of data.

Merge fields are enclosed in angle brackets to show that they will not be printed in the final document. Instead, the data represented by the merge field, such as a person's first name, is inserted and printed during the merge.

Creating a document containing merge fields is easy. Simply type the document as usual, but use the Insert Merge Field button to indicate where you want individualized data to be merged.

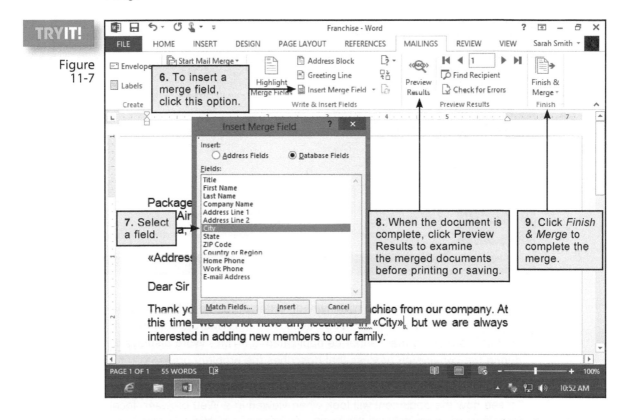

Figure 11-7

• You can insert preformatted merge field blocks or individual merge fields from the *Write & Insert Fields* group.

• Preview your final documents to make sure they look exactly the way you want before saving or printing them.

• When you merge an external database or data from a spreadsheet, the field names might not match the predefined merge fields offered by Microsoft Word. You can use the [Match Fields...] Match Fields button to assign temporary names that the mail merge can process.

FAQ How do I save a document as a Web page?

Instead of printing a document, you might want to post it on the Internet as a Web page. As with other Web pages, your document must be in HTML (Hypertext Markup Language) format to be accessible to Web browsers, such as Internet Explorer, Google Chrome, or Mozilla Firefox. You can use the Save As option accessed from the FILE tab to save a document in HTML format.

TRY IT!

Figure
11-8

1. Click the FILE tab, then click Save As.

2. Specify the drive, folder, and file name as you would during any save action.

3. Select Web Page from the *Save as type* list.

4. Click the Save button to save the document as a Web page.

- Word does a fairly good job of converting a document to HTML, but several formatting options available in Word cannot be duplicated in HTML documents. If a document contains formatting that cannot be duplicated in HTML, Word displays a message during the conversion process that describes the problem areas. You then have the option of canceling or continuing with the save.

- To see how the document will look when viewed in a Web browser, locate the file with File Explorer, then double-click the file to open it in a Web browser.

- Documents saved as Web pages are displayed as a single long page—sort of like a papyrus scroll—even though the original Word document consists of multiple pages. When viewing a long document in a Web browser, you can use the vertical scroll bar to move through the document.

- Contact your Internet service provider (ISP) or technical support person if you need instructions for posting your Web pages on the Internet.

FAQ How do I convert a document into a PDF?

PDF (Portable Document Format) was created by Adobe Systems and has become a universal standard for exchanging documents, spreadsheets, and other types of data files. Converting a file into a PDF ensures that when the file is viewed or printed, it retains the original layout. PDF is sometimes referred to as a fixed-layout format because once a document has been converted to a PDF, it cannot be edited.

Software for viewing PDFs is free and therefore most computers have the ability to display PDF files. You can convert Word documents into PDF files if you want to distribute them but you're not sure if the recipients have Microsoft Word.

To convert a document into a PDF file, save it first as a normal Word document. Then save it again by using the Save As command and selecting PDF from the *Save as type* list.

TRYIT!

Figure
11-9

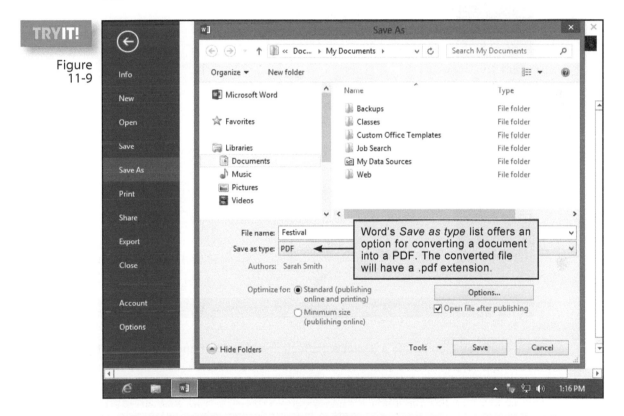

Word's *Save as type* list offers an option for converting a document into a PDF. The converted file will have a .pdf extension.

- Software for creating PDFs can be obtained in a number of ways. It is included with the Mac OS X operating system and Microsoft Office. You can download the free Adobe Reader from the Adobe Web site. Free PDF software usually allows you to create, read, and print PDF files.

- Some PDF software offers additional features. For the fullest feature set, Adobe offers Adobe Acrobat Pro. In addition to creating, viewing, and printing, Acrobat Pro allows you to annotate a PDF by inserting text, making line-out deletions, highlighting passages, and adding comments.

- **XPS** (XML Paper Specification) is a file format similar to PDF but created by Microsoft. XPS does not have the widespread popularity of PDF.

FAQ How do I work with electronic documents?

Whereas word processors were once used primarily to prepare documents for printing, today many documents remain in electronic formats that are transmitted by e-mail, sent directly to a fax machine, shared on an FTP site, or posted as Web pages and blogs.

Word has several built-in features that help you work with electronic documents. For example, the FILE tab's Share option can be used to attach a document to an e-mail message. The *Post to Blog* option is useful for creating blogs. Word even includes fax templates so you can easily create a fax cover sheet.

Figure
11-10

The way you plan to use a document affects the way you handle it. For most applications, you'll typically first save your document normally as a Word DOCX file. The table below contains recommendations for handling electronic documents.

Figure
11-11

E-mail attachment	Send DOCX files if you are certain the recipient has Word 2007, 2010, or 2013; otherwise, convert to DOC or PDF files. Large files might need to be zipped.
Web page	Save in HTM or HTML format. If your Web page includes graphics or links to other pages, make sure they are posted along with the document containing the primary content.
Blog	Save as a DOCX file if you are using Word's blog publishing feature.
Fax	Send any type of file that is accepted by the fax service.
FTP	Post DOCX files on the FTP site if you are certain the recipient has Word 2007, 2010, or 2013; otherwise, convert to PDF. Large files will transmit faster if they are zipped.

How do I work with electronic documents? (continued)

When working with electronic documents, remain alert to avoid the following problems:

- **Loss of information or formatting.** When files are converted from one file type to another, some aspects of the original document might be lost. In an earlier FAQ, you learned that a Word document converted into HTML loses its pagination when all the text is incorporated into a single long Web page. Other formatting that might be lost or garbled during conversion includes columns, tabs, highlighting, comments, and graphic placement. After converting a document into a different file type, compare the two versions for significant differences.

- **Necessary software not installed.** Before e-mailing or posting a file, consider the software that's needed to view it. Not everyone has Office 2007, 2010, or 2013, so DOCX is not a universal format. PDF is more universal and might be a better choice, especially if you're not certain of the software installed on your recipient's computer.

- **Missing linked data.** Word documents and e-mail messages can contain hyperlinks to Web sites, spreadsheets can be linked to document files, and Web pages can include links to graphics and other Web pages. When e-mailing or posting documents that incorporate links, be sure to also post all the data files referenced by the links.

- **Blocked file types.** Most computers are protected against viruses and other exploits, but the protective software and hardware can inadvertently block innocent files, too. E-mail attachments with extensions such as .scr, .bat, .hlp, and .exe are especially vulnerable to being blocked, but .doc and .docx files are sometimes blocked, too. To make sure your files haven't been blocked, ask for confirmation of their arrival. Compressed files with .zip extensions tend not to get blocked, so you might consider zipping documents and other files before you send them.

- **Large files.** File size and connection speed affect upload and download times when transferring electronic documents over the Internet. You can shrink the size of a file using a process called compression or zipping.

Figure
11-12

1. There are several ways to compress files, but one of the easiest is to save the document as a normal Word file, then open File Explorer.

2. Right-click the file that you want to compress.

3. Select *Send to*, then select *Compressed (zipped) folder.* Give the compressed file a name and it will be stored with a .zip extension as a smaller file than the original DOCX file.

FAQ Can I track changes and insert comments in a document?

As a document is revised, you might want to maintain a record of the original wording. This capability is especially important in the development of legal documents and when multiple people collaborate on a single document. Microsoft Word provides several features for such situations.

The **Track Changes** feature maintains all deleted, changed, and inserted text for a document and displays it in a contrasting font color. You can hide or display these changes and integrate them in the document by accepting them. Word's Comment feature allows you to insert the electronic version of "sticky notes" in your document. Comments are displayed as balloons in the margins and can be displayed or hidden as needed.

TRYIT!

Figure
11-13

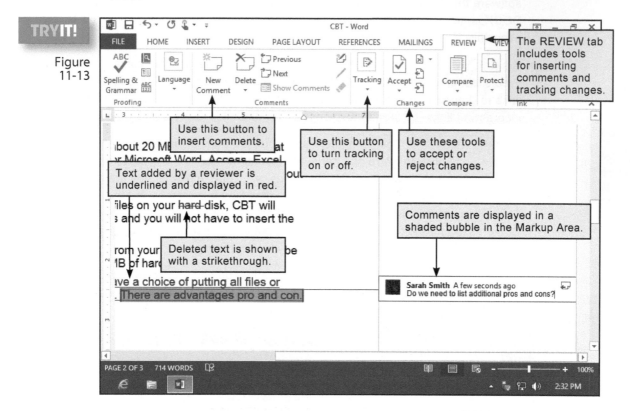

- To track changes, click the REVIEW tab, then click Track Changes under Tracking. As you edit the document, changes are indicated in a contrasting font color.

- To accept a change in an edited document, highlight the changed text, then click the Accept button in the Changes group. To reject a change, click the Reject button in the Changes group.

- To accept all changes in a document, click the arrow on the Accept button in the Changes group, then click *Accept All Changes*.

- To reject all changes in a document, click the arrow next to the Reject button in the Changes group, then click *Reject All Changes*.

- To insert a comment, click the New Comment button on the REVIEW tab. Type your comment in the comment bubble displayed in the Markup Area.

FAQ Is there a way to protect documents from unauthorized access?

You can protect your documents from unauthorized access in several ways. One option is to encrypt the document so that it can be opened only when a valid password is entered.

Figure
11-14

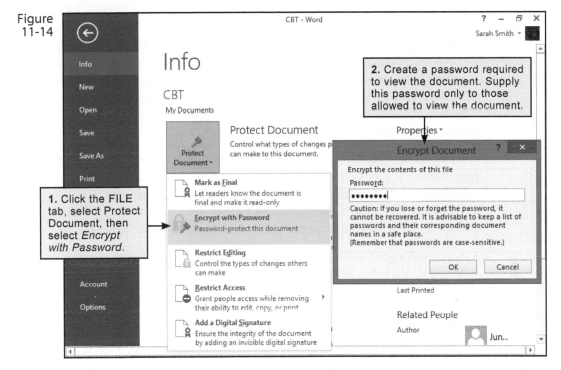

Another way to protect your documents is to allow anyone to open a document, but restrict the types of edits that can be made. You can set up these restrictions from the REVIEW tab as shown in Figure 11-15.

Figure
11-15

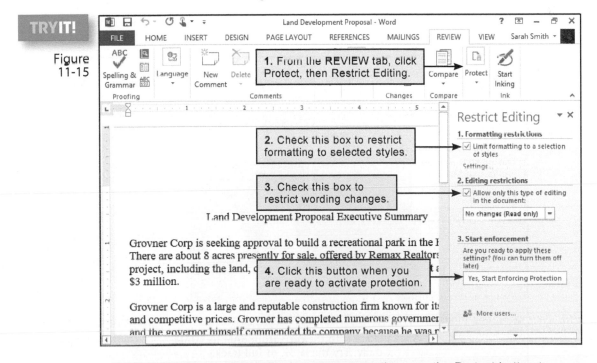

• If you would like to deactivate document protection, use the Protect button to access the Restrict Editing pane. Scroll to the bottom of the pane and click the Stop Protection button.

FAQ What other features can I use to finalize my documents?

Use the following tips and tricks to create more professional-looking documents, automate document formatting, or simply spruce up your existing documents:

- Borders and shading allow you to emphasize certain sections of text or parts of a table. A **border** is a line or graphic drawn around a page or section of text. Borders can be customized by width, color, number of lines, and type of graphic. **Shading** is a grayscale or color background applied to text or table cells. Borders and shading are often used together to highlight sections of text, differentiate cells and titles in a table, or create an eye-catching page or document. To apply borders and shading to a section of a document, use options on the Borders button and the Shading button in the Paragraph group on the HOME tab.

- Themes make it easy to create professional-looking documents without having to customize the style of every element in a document. A **document theme** is a predefined set of coordinated styles, colors, and text options designed to be applied to an existing document. Word includes themes such as Mesh, Wisp, and Office. To choose a theme for your document, click Themes on the DESIGN tab.

- **AutoFormat** allows Word to automatically format your document as you type. AutoFormat performs tasks such as replacing fractions (1/4 with ¼) and formatting Internet addresses as hyperlinks. To modify AutoFormat options, click the FILE tab, then click the Options button. Click the Proofing button, then click the AutoCorrect Options button.

- The **Format Painter** feature makes it easy to replicate formats from one text selection to another. Click any text that has the format you would like to replicate, click the Format Painter button in the Clipboard group on the HOME tab to capture the format, then click the text where you would like the format applied. If you double-click the Format Painter button, you can copy the format to several locations. When you are finished copying the format to the desired locations, simply click the Format Painter button to stop the paste process.

TRY IT!

Figure
11-16

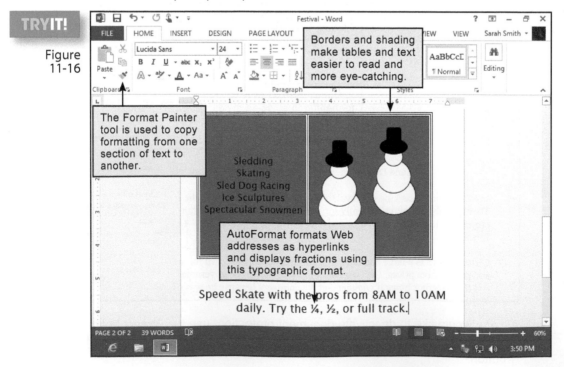

Borders and shading make tables and text easier to read and more eye-catching.

The Format Painter tool is used to copy formatting from one section of text to another.

AutoFormat formats Web addresses as hyperlinks and displays fractions using this typographic format.

Sledding
Skating
Sled Dog Racing
Ice Sculptures
Spectacular Snowmen

Speed Skate with the pros from 8AM to 10AM daily. Try the ¼, ½, or full track.

QuickCheck A

1. If you'd like a title page formatted separately from other pages in a document, add a(n) [＿＿＿＿＿＿＿＿＿＿] break.

2. You can use the Shapes tool to create simple [＿＿＿＿＿＿＿＿＿＿] graphics, such as line drawings, arrows, and stars.

3. A(n) [＿＿＿＿＿＿＿＿＿] is text placed at the bottom of every page of a Word document.

4. When you save a Word document as a Web page, it is converted to [＿＿＿＿] format. (Hint: Use the acronym.)

5. You can convert a Word document into a(n) [＿＿＿＿＿＿＿＿] file if you are going to send it to someone who might not have Word, but is likely to have Adobe Reader.

CHECKIT!

QuickCheck B

Indicate the letter of the desktop element that best matches the following:

1. Keep track of text inserted or deleted in a document [＿＿＿]

2. Text added by a reviewer [＿＿＿]

3. Comment added by a reviewer [＿＿＿]

4. Text deleted by a reviewer [＿＿＿]

5. Button for rejecting a suggested change [＿＿＿]

CHECKIT!

Skill Tests

A   Adding headers and footers

B   Inserting page breaks and changing margins

C   Performing mail merges

D   Creating Web pages and PDF files

CHAPTER 12

Creating a Worksheet

What's Inside and on the CD?

In this chapter, you'll learn the essentials of creating a worksheet with Microsoft Excel. **Microsoft Excel** is the component of the Microsoft Office suite best suited for working with numbers and formulas. As spreadsheet software, Microsoft Excel provides a set of tools for simple or complex calculations, such as creating a budget, estimating expenses, and creating an income and expense projection.

An electronic spreadsheet, often referred to as a worksheet, functions much like a visual calculator. You place each number needed for a calculation into a cell of the grid. You then enter formulas to add, subtract, or otherwise manipulate these numbers. The spreadsheet software automatically performs the calculations and displays the results.

FAQ What's in the Excel window?

You can open Excel from the Windows 8 Start screen. Simply click the Excel 2013 tile or type Excel, then select it from the list of apps. In Windows 7, click the start button and select Microsoft Excel from the Start menu. The Excel window is similar to the Microsoft Word window, but the Excel workspace is a grid of rows and columns.

TRYIT!

Figure 12-1

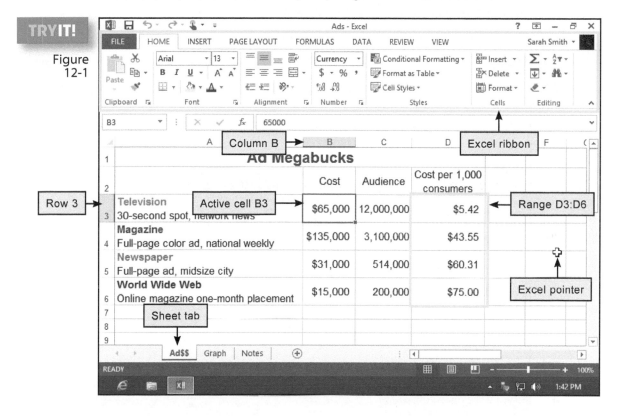

- A **worksheet** consists of a grid of columns and rows. The columns are typically labeled with letters, starting with A as the column farthest to the left. The rows are typically labeled with numbers, starting with 1 as the top row.

- Excel worksheets are saved in a three-dimensional **workbook**. A workbook contains one or more worksheets, each represented by a tab at the bottom of the Excel window. When you save or open a workbook, all worksheets in that workbook are automatically saved or opened. To switch to a different worksheet in the current workbook, click its sheet tab. Right-click a sheet tab to rename, insert, or delete a worksheet.

- A **worksheet cell** (or "cell" for short) is the rectangle formed by the intersection of a column and row. Each cell has a unique name consisting of the column letter and row number. For example, cell B3 is located in the second column of the third row.

- The **active cell** is the cell you can currently edit or modify, and it is marked with a green outline. You can change the active cell by clicking any other cell. You can also change the active cell by pressing the arrow keys.

- A **range** is a series of cells. For example, D3:D6 is a range that contains all cells from D3 through D6, inclusive. When specifying a range, use a colon to separate the first and last cells. To select a range of cells, click the cell in the upper-left corner of the range, then drag the mouse to the lower-right cell in the range.

FAQ How do I enter labels?

A **label** is any text entered into a cell of the worksheet. You can use labels for a worksheet title, to describe the numbers you've entered in other cells, and for text data, such as the names of people or cities. Any numerical data you do not intend to use in a calculation should be entered as a label. This data might be a telephone number, a Social Security number, or a street address.

TRYIT!

Figure 12-2

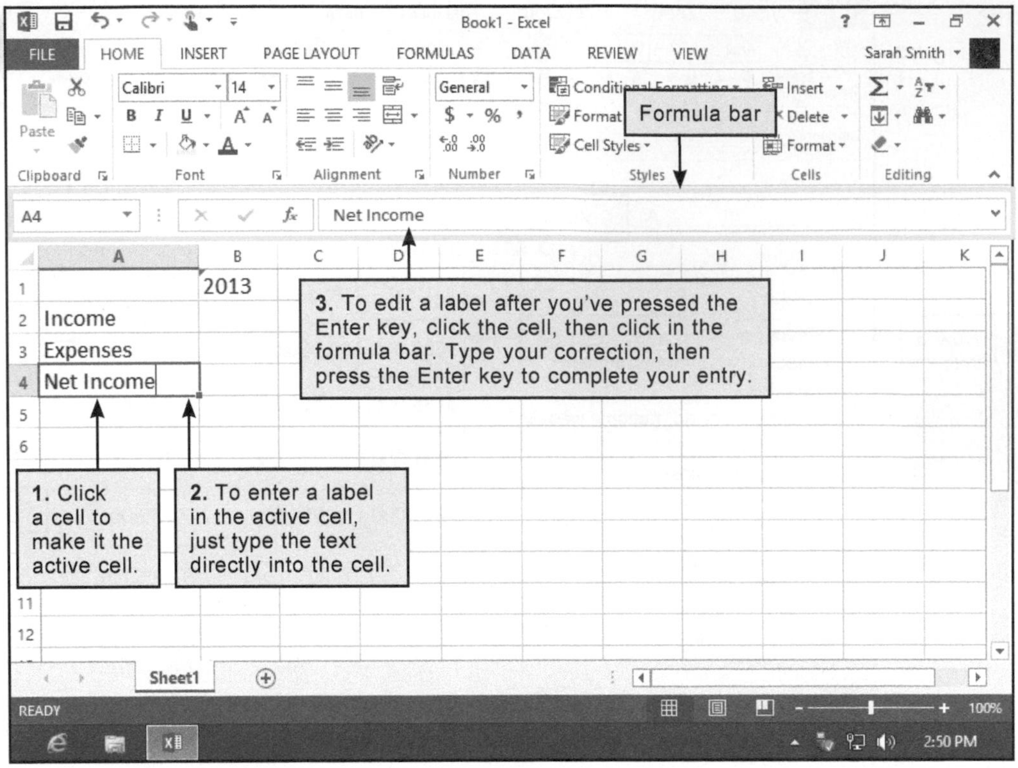

- If a label is too long to fit in the current cell, it extends into the cells to the right if they are empty. If the cells on the right are not empty, part of the label will be truncated, which means it will be hidden behind the adjacent cell's content.

- It's possible to make a long label wrap so that it is displayed in two or more lines of text inside the same cell. Select the cell or cells. On the HOME tab, click the Wrap Text button in the Alignment group.

- To edit a label after you've pressed the Enter key, click the cell, then click in the **formula bar**. Use the left and right arrow keys to move the insertion point in the formula bar, and use the Backspace and Delete keys to delete characters. Press the Enter key when you finish editing the label. You can also click the ☑ Enter button on the formula bar to complete your entry. Click the ☒ Cancel button to exit the formula bar without keeping any changes.

- It's possible to edit a label inside a cell. Double-click the cell to activate it, then edit the contents using the arrow, Backspace, and Delete keys. Press the Enter key when you finish editing the label. You can clear the entire contents of a cell by clicking the cell and then pressing the Delete key on your keyboard.

FAQ How do I enter values?

A **value** is a number that you intend to use in a calculation and that is entered into a cell of a worksheet. Cells containing values can be used in formulas to calculate results. As mentioned on the previous page, numbers that are not meant to be used in calculations, such as Social Security numbers, telephone numbers, and street addresses, should be entered as labels rather than as numbers.

TRY IT!

Figure 12-3

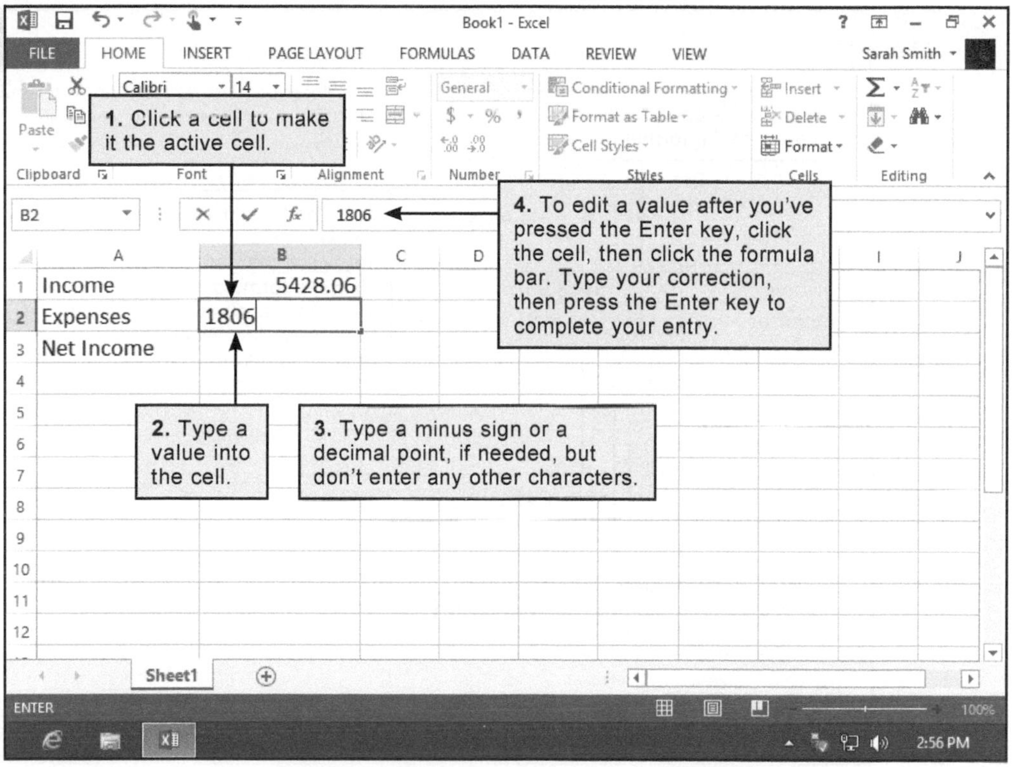

- Type a minus sign (-) before a number to enter a negative value. Although you can include the dollar sign and comma in values, it's best to just enter the unformatted number into a cell. You will learn how to format values in another chapter.

- After you've pressed the Enter key, you can edit a value just as you would edit a label—in the cell or in the formula bar.

- As you enter data, Excel tries to determine if it is a value or a label. When you want to specifically enter a number as a label, you can type an apostrophe (') before the number. For instance, type '555-1234 to enter the telephone number 555-1234 as a label.

- Values and labels can be entered automatically using the Fill handle and a technique called **drag-and-fill**. Enter the first two or three items for the series to establish a pattern. Select those cells, then point to the lower-right corner of the selected area. The pointer changes to a black cross ⊹ when you are in the right spot. Drag that pointer across or down several cells.

- There are several other ways to drag-and-fill data. Another option is to use the Fill button in the Editing group on the HOME tab. You can find more information about automatically filling cells in Excel Help.

FAQ How do I enter formulas?

A **formula** specifies how to add, subtract, multiply, divide, or otherwise calculate the values in worksheet cells. A formula always begins with an = equal sign and can use cell references that point to the contents of other cells. A **cell reference** is the column and row location of a cell. In the example below, the formula =B1-B2 subtracts the contents of cell B2 from the contents of cell B1 and displays the results in cell B3.

TRYIT!

Figure 12-4

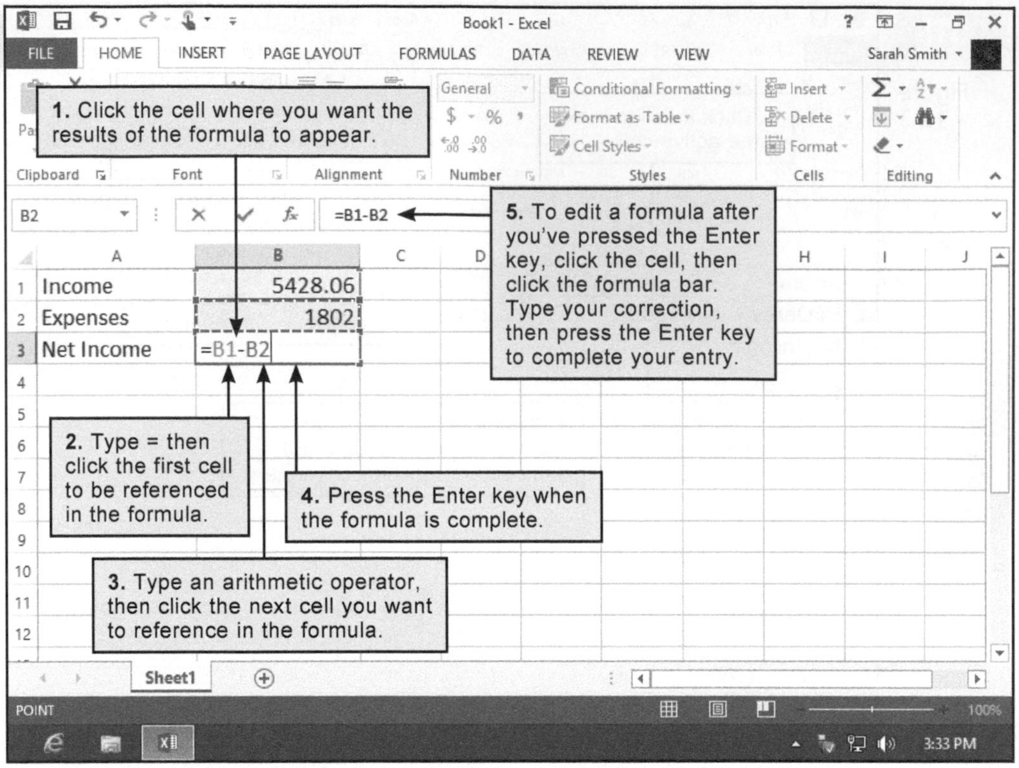

1. Click the cell where you want the results of the formula to appear.

2. Type = then click the first cell to be referenced in the formula.

3. Type an arithmetic operator, then click the next cell you want to reference in the formula.

4. Press the Enter key when the formula is complete.

5. To edit a formula after you've pressed the Enter key, click the cell, then click the formula bar. Type your correction, then press the Enter key to complete your entry.

- The most common arithmetic operators are - (subtraction), + (addition), * (multiplication), / (division), % (percent), and ^ (exponent). Note that an asterisk (*) instead of the letter "X" is used for multiplication.

- The easiest way to create a formula is to use the pointer method. Basically, this method allows you to click cells instead of typing the cell reference. After you click a cell for a formula, a rectangle of dashes called a **marquee** appears around that cell. To continue creating your formula, type an arithmetic operator (+, -, *, /), then click the next cell you want to reference. Continue until the formula is complete, then press the Enter key.

- You can also type a formula directly into a cell. For example, you could type =B1-B2 and then press the Enter key to complete the formula. The problem with this method is that it's easy to make a mistake and type an incorrect cell reference.

- You can edit a formula after you've pressed the Enter key in the same way you would edit labels or values—in the cell or in the formula bar.

FAQ How do I create complex formulas?

A worksheet can be used for more than simple calculations. You can build complex formulas to calculate statistical, financial, and mathematical equations by using the usual arithmetic operators, parentheses, and a mixture of both values and cell references.

TRY IT!

Figure
12-5

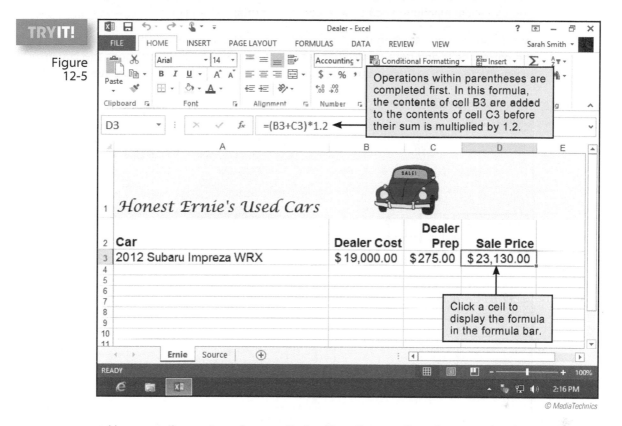

© MediaTechnics

- Use parentheses to make sure that arithmetic operations in a complex formula are executed in the correct order. If you don't use parentheses, Excel calculates the result using the standard mathematical order of operations, referred to as mathematical precedence. Multiplication and division are performed first, then addition and subtraction. For example, if you enter the formula =B3+C3*1.2, Excel first multiplies the contents of cell C3 by 1.2, then adds the result of the calculation to the value in cell B3. By using parentheses, you can specify a different order for a calculation. For example, if you would like to add the contents of cells B3 and C3 before multiplying by 1.2, you would enter this formula: =(B3+C3)*1.2.

- Formulas can include values, cell references, or both. For example, if the total price of an item is displayed in cell C18, you could calculate a 6% sales tax using the formula =C18*.06. Or, you could put the sales tax percentage in cell C19, then calculate the sales tax using the formula =C18*C19. The result would be the same either way.

- You should be aware that cell references in formulas can lead to unexpected results when you copy or move the formulas. You'll learn more about this topic in another FAQ in this chapter.

FAQ How do I use functions?

In addition to writing your own formulas, you can use predefined formulas called **functions**. Excel includes many financial functions such as payments and net present value, mathematical and trigonometric functions such as absolute value and arctangent, and statistical functions such as average and normal distribution.

Avoid common errors when using formulas and functions by verifying that they reference the correct cells and data. A **circular reference**—a formula that references the cell in which the formula resides—can produce erroneous results and should be avoided.

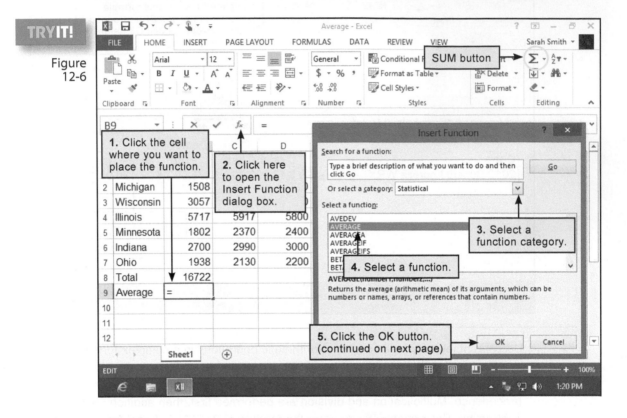

Figure 12-6

- You can use the Insert Function button to select a function from a list. Excel includes more than 250 functions from which you can choose. Commonly used functions, such as SUM, AVERAGE, MINIMUM, and MAXIMUM, are located in the Statistical category.

- Another useful function is the PMT function, which calculates the payments for a loan. You can use the PMT function to calculate all types of loan payments, such as those for a car or a house. Unfortunately, the PMT function is one of the more difficult functions to use, which is why it's covered in the Try It! on this page.

- Formulas can include multiple functions. For example, you could create a formula that uses both the AVERAGE function and the MINIMUM function to sum up a series of test scores, but first drop the lowest score.

- The SUM button can be used to quickly create a function to calculate the total of a column or row of cells. Excel examines the cells to the left of and above the current cell to determine which cells should be included in the total.

How do I use functions? (continued)

After you select a function, you'll specify the arguments. An **argument** consists of values or cell references used to calculate the result of the function. For example, the AVERAGE function requires an argument consisting of a series of numbers or a series of cells. When you complete the AVERAGE function, the result is calculated as an average of the values in the cells you specified.

Figure
12-7

- To select a range of cells for use as arguments in a function, click the upper-left cell that contains data you want to use in the function, then drag down to the lower-right cell. When you release the mouse button, the selected range of cells is displayed in the dialog box. Click the OK button to complete the function.

- Some functions use more than one argument, and those arguments can be required or optional. The PMT function, for example, has three required arguments (Rate, Nper, and Pv) and two optional arguments (Fv and Type).

- Excel can help you determine how to enter the arguments for a function. For the PMT function, you have to divide the annual interest rate by 12 if you're using monthly payments. If you need help with the arguments for a function, click the *Help on this function* link.

- Be careful when using functions you don't fully understand. If you're not sure how a function works, use the Excel Help window to find out more about it. When you use a new function, you should check the results with a calculator to make sure the function is working as you expected.

FAQ What happens when I copy and move cells?

You can use the Cut, Copy, and Paste buttons in the Clipboard group on the HOME tab to copy and move cell contents to a different worksheet location. Label data is copied or moved without changing. If you copy and paste cells that contain a formula, the copied formula is modified to work in the new location. A cell reference that changes when a formula is copied or moved is called a **relative reference**. Excel treats all cell references as relative references unless you specify otherwise.

TRY IT!

Figure 12-8

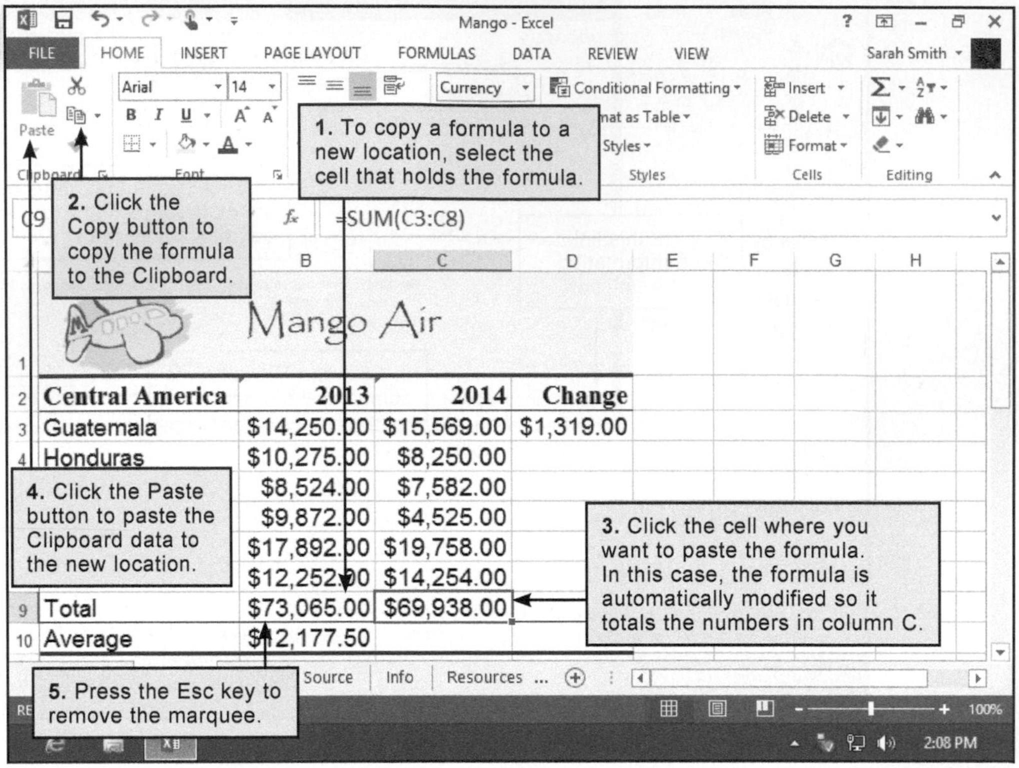

1. To copy a formula to a new location, select the cell that holds the formula.

2. Click the Copy button to copy the formula to the Clipboard.

4. Click the Paste button to paste the Clipboard data to the new location.

3. Click the cell where you want to paste the formula. In this case, the formula is automatically modified so it totals the numbers in column C.

5. Press the Esc key to remove the marquee.

© MediaTechnics

- To move the data in cells, select the cells, then click the Cut button. Click the cell where you want to paste the data, then click the Paste button. The data is moved from the original location to the new location.

- If you copy or move the data in a range of cells, the pasted data is positioned below and to the right of the active cell. In other words, click the cell in the upper-left corner of the new location before pasting the data.

- A formula that contains a relative reference changes when the formula is copied or moved. For example, assume cell B9 contains the formula =SUM(B3:B8). You then copy and paste that formula to cell C9. The formula will be changed to =SUM(C3:C8). The references B3 and B8 in the original formula were relative references. When the formula was originally located in cell B9, it actually meant "sum the numbers in the six cells above." When you copy the formula to cell C9, it still means "sum the numbers in the six cells above"—but those cells are now in column C instead of column B.

- Be careful when pasting, moving, and copying the contents of cells so that you maintain working formulas. For example, do not paste a value into a cell where a formula belongs.

FAQ When should I use absolute references?

Most of the time, you want Excel to use relative references; but in some situations, cell references should not be modified when moved to a new location. An **absolute reference** does not change, and will always refer to the same cell, even after the formula is copied or moved.

TRYIT!

Figure 12-9

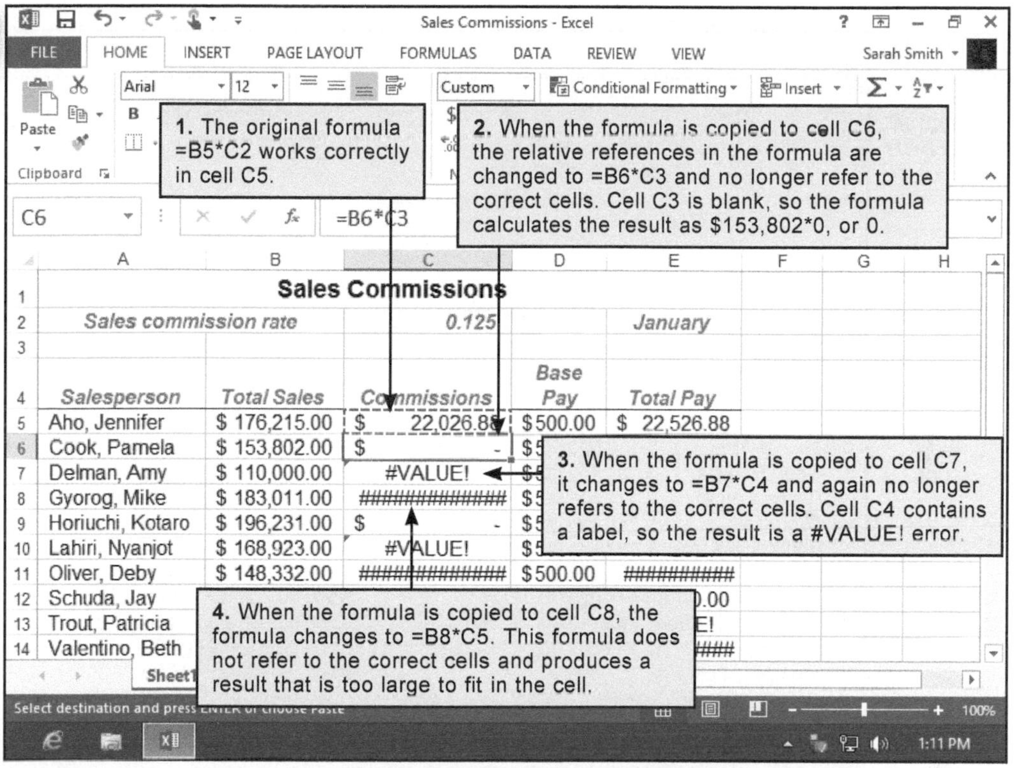

1. The original formula =B5*C2 works correctly in cell C5.

2. When the formula is copied to cell C6, the relative references in the formula are changed to =B6*C3 and no longer refer to the correct cells. Cell C3 is blank, so the formula calculates the result as $153,802*0, or 0.

3. When the formula is copied to cell C7, it changes to =B7*C4 and again no longer refers to the correct cells. Cell C4 contains a label, so the result is a #VALUE! error.

4. When the formula is copied to cell C8, the formula changes to =B8*C5. This formula does not refer to the correct cells and produces a result that is too large to fit in the cell.

- In the example above, cell C2 contains a commission rate. When you copy the formula in cell C5 to cell C6, the original formula =B5*C2 is changed to =B6*C3. The B6 part is fine, but C3 is an empty cell. The formula should still refer to the commission rate in cell C2.

- To create an absolute reference, insert a dollar sign ($) before the column reference and another dollar sign before the row reference. In the example above, you would modify the original formula to read =B5*$C$2. Using an absolute reference, no matter where the formula moves, Excel must always refer to the contents of cell C2 for the second part of the formula. When you copy the formula =B5*$C$2 to cell C6, the formula is changed to =B6*$C$2. The absolute cell reference is protected by the $ sign and will not be modified or adjusted.

- If you want to use an absolute reference in a formula, you can start typing, then press the F4 key after you click a cell to add it to the formula. Pressing the F4 key changes a cell reference to an absolute reference.

- You can also create mixed references by combining references so that only one of the column or row references is absolute. For example, $C2 creates an absolute column and a relative row reference. C$2 creates a relative column and an absolute row reference. The absolute identifier will not change, but the relative identifier will.

FAQ Can I access data from other worksheets?

A workbook—sometimes called a 3D workbook—is a collection of worksheets. Workbooks allow you to group related worksheets together in one file, and easily navigate from one worksheet to another. A worksheet can access data from other worksheets in the workbook. For example, a workbook might contain a Quarter1 worksheet, which accesses totals calculated from the January, February, and March worksheets.

TRY IT!

Figure
12-10

- The default workbook contains three worksheets, titled Sheet1, Sheet2, and Sheet3. Click the tabs at the bottom of the screen to navigate through the worksheets.

- You can rename worksheets, change the color of the tabs, or change the order of the worksheets by right-clicking a worksheet tab and making a selection from the shortcut menu.

- Insert a new worksheet by right-clicking the tab for the worksheet that should immediately follow the new worksheet. Select Insert from the shortcut menu, then select Worksheet from the Insert dialog box. You can insert a new worksheet by clicking the ⊕ New sheet button after the final worksheet tab.

- Delete an existing worksheet by right-clicking the worksheet's tab and clicking Delete.

- The Move/Copy option allows you to change the order of worksheets. For example, if you want to insert a new worksheet in front of Sheet1, simply insert the sheet after any tab, then use the Move/Copy option to position it as the first worksheet.

- To reference data from other worksheets, include the tab name before the row letter and column number. For example, the reference Sheet3!A1 indicates Column A, Row 1 on the worksheet called Sheet3. You can also reference data in other worksheets by navigating to the worksheet and clicking the desired cell while entering a formula or function.

QuickCheck A

1. The [   ] cell is the cell you can currently edit or modify.

2. B3:B12 is an example of a(n) [   ] of cells.

3. To edit a label, value, or formula after you've pressed the Enter key, click the cell, then click the [   ] bar.

4. The formula to subtract the contents of cell C3 from the contents of cell C2 is [   ] .

5. The $ signs make $C$5 a(n) [   ] reference.

CHECKIT!

QuickCheck B

Indicate the letter of the desktop element that best matches the following:

1. A cell containing a label [   ]

2. A cell containing a value [   ]

3. A cell containing a formula [   ]

4. The SUM button [   ]

5. The Insert Function button [   ]

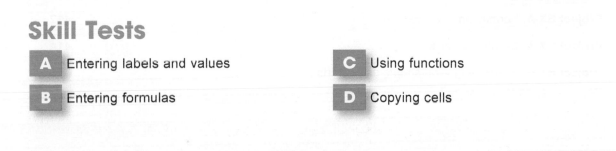

CHECKIT!

Skill Tests

| A | Entering labels and values | C | Using functions |
| B | Entering formulas | D | Copying cells |

CHAPTER 13

Formatting a Worksheet

What's Inside and on the CD?

In this chapter, you'll learn how to format worksheets created with Microsoft Excel. Formatting is not just for looks: An effectively formatted worksheet is more approachable and helps readers understand the meaning of values and formulas presented in the worksheet. For example, an accountant might use a red font for negative values in a large worksheet so that possible losses are easier to spot. A quarterly banking statement might use different colored backgrounds to help readers recognize the month in which each transaction took place.

In this chapter, you will learn that each type of data has special formatting characteristics that help to identify its purpose. Rather than typing dollar signs to identify financial values, for example, you will learn to format values as currency data.

One of the most powerful advantages of using spreadsheet software for calculations is that you can easily make changes to the data in order to see how they affect results. You will also learn how to create effective charts to present your data.

FAQ How do I add borders and background colors?

Borders and background colors define areas of a worksheet and call attention to important information. You can use the Borders button and the Format Cells dialog box to add borders and a colored background to one or more cells.

TRY IT!

Figure 13-1

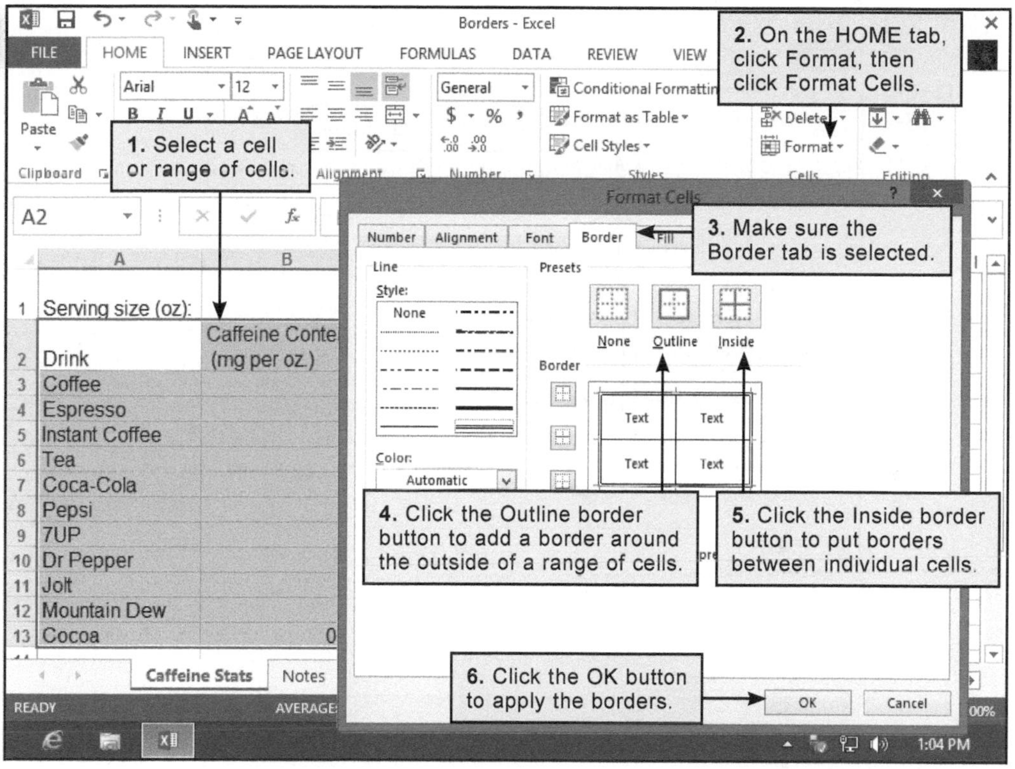

2. On the HOME tab, click Format, then click Format Cells.

1. Select a cell or range of cells.

3. Make sure the Border tab is selected.

4. Click the Outline border button to add a border around the outside of a range of cells.

5. Click the Inside border button to put borders between individual cells.

6. Click the OK button to apply the borders.

- To add borders around the outside and inside edges of selected cells, click both the Outline and Inside border buttons in the Presets section, as shown in the above figure. The Outline button puts a border around the outside edges of selected cells. The Inside button adds borders between individual cells.

- You can add and remove border lines by selecting any of the following border option buttons:

Top of range	Left of range	Diagonal to the left
Inside horizontal lines	Inside vertical lines	Diagonal to the right
Bottom of range	Right of range	

- Line options allow you to select a decorative line style or to make all the border lines appear in a selected color.

- To add a colored background to the selected cell or cells, click the Fill tab. Select a color, then click the OK button to apply the background color.

- You can quickly add simple borders using the ⊞▾ Borders button in the Font group on the HOME tab. For more complex borders, use the option for *More borders*. You can also specify border formats using the Format Cells dialog box shown above in Figure 13-1.

FAQ How do I format worksheet data?

You can use buttons in the Font group on the HOME tab to select different font attributes for any data in worksheet cells. Values and formula results can be formatted with the same font attributes used to enhance the appearance of labels.

TRY IT!

Figure
13-2

Font attribute buttons

Weekly Cash Flow Projection

Click the Font Color button to change the text in the cell to the indicated color—in this case, red.

Click this down-arrow button to select a different font color.

	A	B	C
1	Weekly Cash Flow Projection		
7			7537
8	Cash Disbursed		
9	Salaries and Wages		4289
10	Lease		925
11	Advertising		415
12	Office Supplies		208
13	Utilities		225
14	Repairs and Maintena		96
15	Total Disbursements		6158
16	End of Month Balance		1279

- You can apply multiple font attributes to any worksheet cell. Click the cell you want to format, then click as many font attribute buttons as you want. Click outside the cell to complete the process.

- To change the font for a range of cells, click the upper-left cell, then drag the mouse to select the cells. Release the mouse button, then apply font formatting options to the selected cells.

- Font attributes are typically applied to the entire contents of a cell, but it is possible to change the font attributes for selected text inside a cell. For example, to display one of the words in a cell in bold text, type the contents of the cell, then click the formula bar. Use the mouse or the arrow keys to select one word within the cell, then click the Bold button. You can use the same process to apply different fonts and attributes such as italic, underlining, and font sizes.

- For more formatting options, click Format in the Cells group, then click Format Cells.

- You can also use the ⌐ Format Cells Dialog Box Launcher in the Font group to display the Format Cells dialog box. Click the Font tab, if necessary. Select formatting options, such as Superscript or Subscript, then click the OK button to apply them.

FAQ How do I apply number formats?

In addition to font attributes, you can also apply number formats—currency, percent, commas, and decimals—to cells that contain values. The most commonly used number formats are available as buttons in the Number group on the HOME tab. In addition, the Format Cells dialog box provides some special number formatting options that can improve the readability of a worksheet.

TRYIT!

Figure 13-3

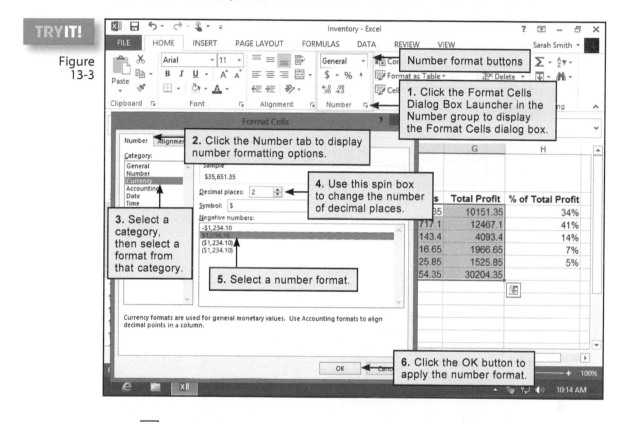

- The $ Accounting Number Format button displays cell contents in your local currency format. For example, if your copy of Windows is configured for use in the U.S., the currency option displays cell contents as dollars and cents with a leading dollar sign ($) and two digits to the right of the decimal point.

- The % Percent Style button displays cell contents as a percentage, which means .35 is displayed as 35%.

- The ' Comma Style button adds a comma to the values displayed in the cell. If your computer is configured for use in the U.S., the Comma Style button adds a comma every three digits to the left of the decimal point and displays two digits to the right of the decimal point.

- When you click the Decrease Decimal button, one fewer digit is displayed after the decimal point. When you click the Increase Decimal button, one more digit is displayed after the decimal point.

- To apply number formats to more than one cell, select a range of cells before clicking any of the number format buttons or before you open the Format Cells dialog box.

FAQ How do I adjust column and row size?

Narrow columns allow you to fit more information on the screen or on the printed page, but you might need to adjust the width of some columns in your worksheet to make all of your worksheet data visible.

If a label is too long to fit into a cell, it extends into the next cell on the right if that cell is empty. If the cell on the right contains data, the end of the label is cut off.

If a value is too long to fit into a cell, Excel displays a series of # characters in the cell. This is a signal that the cell contains a value that cannot fit within the current cell width. To see the number, simply increase the column width.

TRY IT!

Figure
13-4

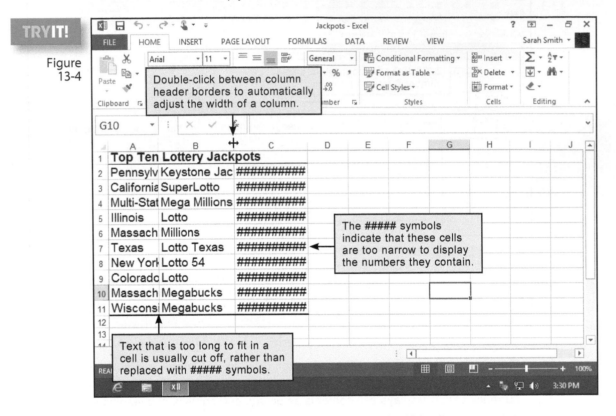

- To change the width of a cell, you must increase the width of the entire column. You can't make one cell in a column wider without affecting the other cells in that column.

- To manually adjust the width of a column, position the pointer over the vertical line between two column headings so that the pointer changes to a ✛ shape. Press and hold the left mouse button while you drag the vertical line left or right to manually adjust the width of the column.

- Excel automatically adjusts the height and width of selected cells when you use the AutoFit command located on the HOME tab's Format button.

FAQ How do I center and align cell contents?

By default, labels are aligned on the left edge of a cell while values and formulas are aligned on the right edge of a cell. Unfortunately, this means that a label at the top of a column of numbers is not aligned with numbers in the rest of the column. Typically, you'll want to center or right-align the headings for columns of numbers.

TRYIT!

Figure 13-5

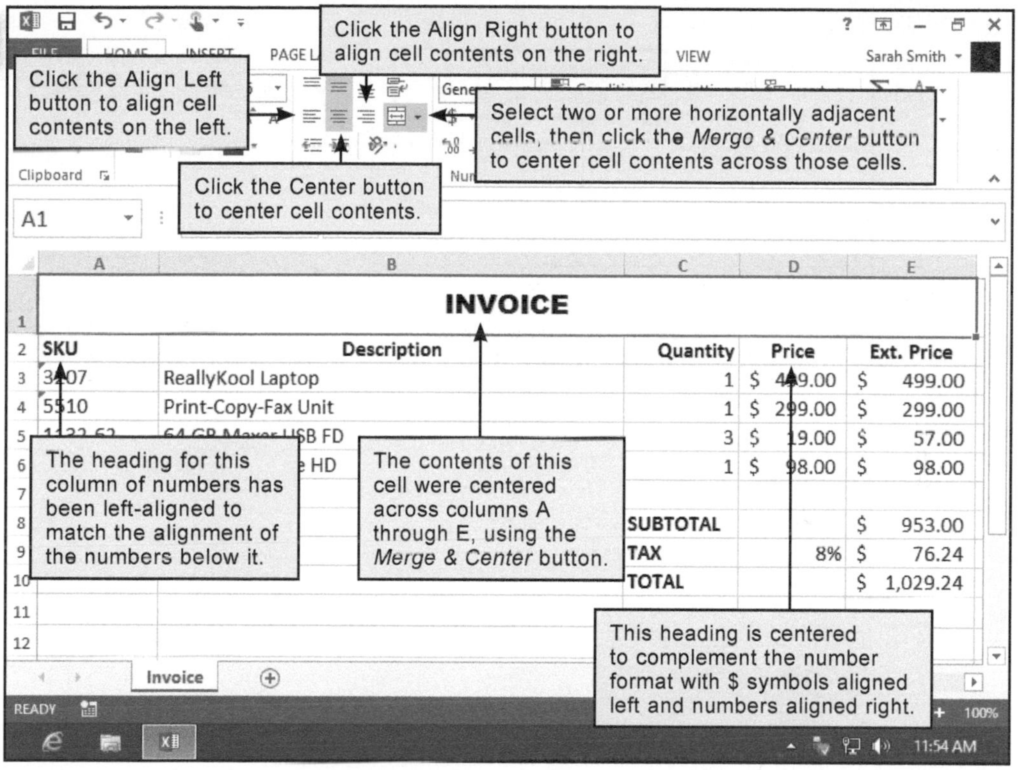

- If a cell containing label data is a column heading, select the cell, then click the Align Right button in the Alignment group on the HOME tab to move the label to the right side of the cell so that it aligns with the column of numbers.

- To change the alignment of a range of cells, select the range of cells, then click the desired alignment button in the Alignment group on the HOME tab.

- To quickly select all cells in a column, click the column header at the top of the column. To select all cells in a row, click the row header on the left side of the row.

- Sometimes you'll want to center a label across a number of columns. In the figure above, the title "INVOICE" is centered across columns A through E. To center text across columns, select the range of cells to be merged, then click the Merge & Center button in the Alignment group on the HOME tab.

- To merge a range of cells in a column, select the range of cells, then click the Merge & Center button in the Alignment group on the HOME tab. The down-arrow button next to the Merge & Center button allows you to unmerge cells as well as merge without centering.

FAQ How do I delete and insert rows and columns?

It is easy to delete a row or insert a blank row between rows that already contain data. You can also insert and delete columns. Excel even modifies your formulas as needed to make sure they refer to the correct cells each time you insert a new row.

TRY IT!

Figure
13-6

- To delete more than one row at a time, drag down over the rows you want to delete. Click the down-arrow button next to Delete in the Cells group, then click Delete Sheet Rows to delete the rows.

- To insert a row, click any cell in the row below where you want the new row to be inserted. You can also select a row by clicking the row identifier button on the left side of the window. Click the down-arrow button next to Insert in the Cells group, then click Insert Sheet Rows. The new row is inserted above the selected row.

- To insert more than one row at a time, drag down over the number of rows you want to insert. Click the down-arrow button next to Insert in the Cells group, then click Insert Sheet Rows to insert the new rows.

- Use the same procedures to insert and delete columns. To insert one or more columns, select the column or columns to the left of where you want the new column to be inserted, click the down-arrow button next to Insert in the Cells group, then click Insert Sheet Columns. To delete one or more columns, select the column or columns, click the down-arrow button next to Delete in the Cells group, then click Delete Sheet Columns.

- As you insert and delete rows and columns, Excel adjusts relative cell references in formulas to keep them accurate. For example, the formula =D3+D4 changes to =C3+C4 if the original column C is deleted. In the same way, the formula =D3+D4 changes to =D2+D3 if row 1 is deleted.

FAQ Can I use styles?

Like Word, Excel allows you to work with styles. You can use predefined styles or create custom styles. Predefined styles are built into the software, and include formats for displaying currency, percentages, and general numbers. You can also create your own styles to enhance the appearance of your worksheet.

TRY IT!

Figure 13-7

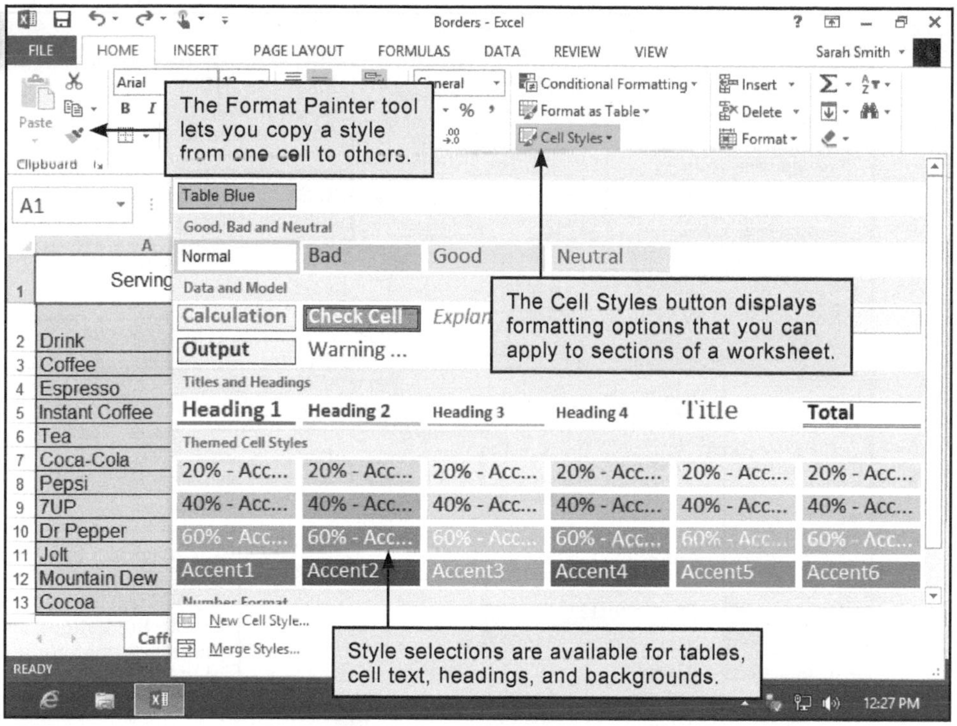

- Styles include text formatting, such as font, size, and color, as well as numeric formatting, such as comma placement, the number of decimal points, and the currency symbol.

- You can create your own styles for numbers or text. Click the Cell Styles button in the Styles group, then click New Cell Style. Type the new style name. If you want to modify characteristics of the new style, click the Format button to open the Format Cells dialog box. Click the OK button to accept the changes in the Format Cells dialog box, then click the OK button in the Style dialog box to create the style.

- The ✍ Format Painter button allows you to copy and paste formats from one cell to another. Click the cell containing the formats you want to copy, then click the Format Painter button in the Clipboard group. Click the cell where you want to apply the formats.

- Excel's PAGE LAYOUT tab offers a variety of predefined themes that improve the appearance of your worksheets. When you select a theme, its fonts and table styles are applied immediately. Once you've selected a theme, you can then choose from a collection of color-coordinated fonts and background styles that can be applied to worksheet cells.

FAQ How do I create a chart?

You can use the Charts group on the INSERT tab to chart or graph data in your worksheet. You should pick a chart type that suits the data. A **line chart** is used to show data that changes over time. A **pie chart** illustrates the proportion of parts to a whole. A **bar chart** (sometimes called a column chart) is used to show comparisons.

TRYIT!

Figure 13-8

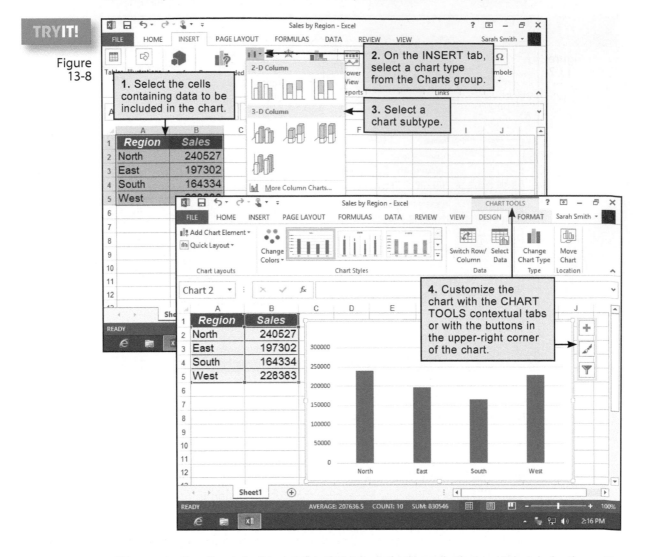

- When selecting the cells for a chart, if you include the cells that contain labels, they will be used to identify the lines, columns, or pie slices on the chart.

- If you are not certain which chart type to use, hover the pointer over any of the chart subtype buttons to display a description and usage recommendation.

- By default, the chart is inserted into the current worksheet. You can move the chart by clicking the Move Chart button on the DESIGN tab.

- When a chart is selected, you can move it or resize it by dragging the sizing handles.

- If you change the data in a worksheet cell, Excel updates the chart immediately after you press the Enter key.

FAQ How do I modify a chart?

Excel creates a chart based on the data and labels you select from a worksheet. You can modify this basic chart by changing the chart type and adjusting the chart data.

When making changes to a chart, make sure the chart is selected so that Excel displays the DESIGN and FORMAT contextual tabs as well as the Chart Elements, Chart Styles, and Chart Filters buttons.

TRYIT!

Figure 13-9

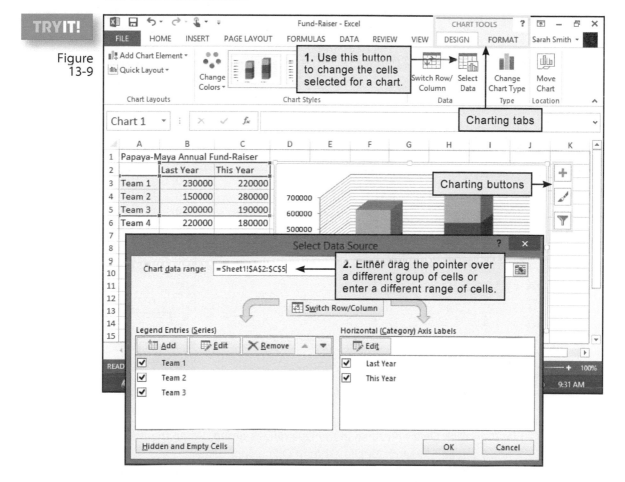

- You can select a different range of cells for a chart by clicking the Select Data button on the DESIGN tab. You can then drag over the cells directly in the worksheet, or you can type a range into the *Chart data range* box.

- To select a different chart type, click the DESIGN tab, then click the Change Chart Type button.

- If the chart doesn't seem to make sense, make sure the chart is selected and try clicking the Switch Row/Column button in the Data group. This button swaps the data plotted on the horizontal axis with the data plotted on the vertical axis.

- When you are satisfied that your chart displays the correct data using a meaningful chart type, you can turn your focus to improving the readability and appearance of the chart.

- In general, you begin most modifications by right-clicking the chart element you want to change. Excel displays a shortcut menu that contains options you can use to modify the chart element.

FAQ Can I add graphics to a worksheet?

Worksheet graphics can be used to highlight important sections, add interest or pizzazz to otherwise dull pages, or graphically illustrate spreadsheet data. Vector drawings can be created using Excel's drawing tools. Photographs or clip art can be inserted from a file or imported directly from imaging devices, such as scanners and digital cameras.

Figure 13-10

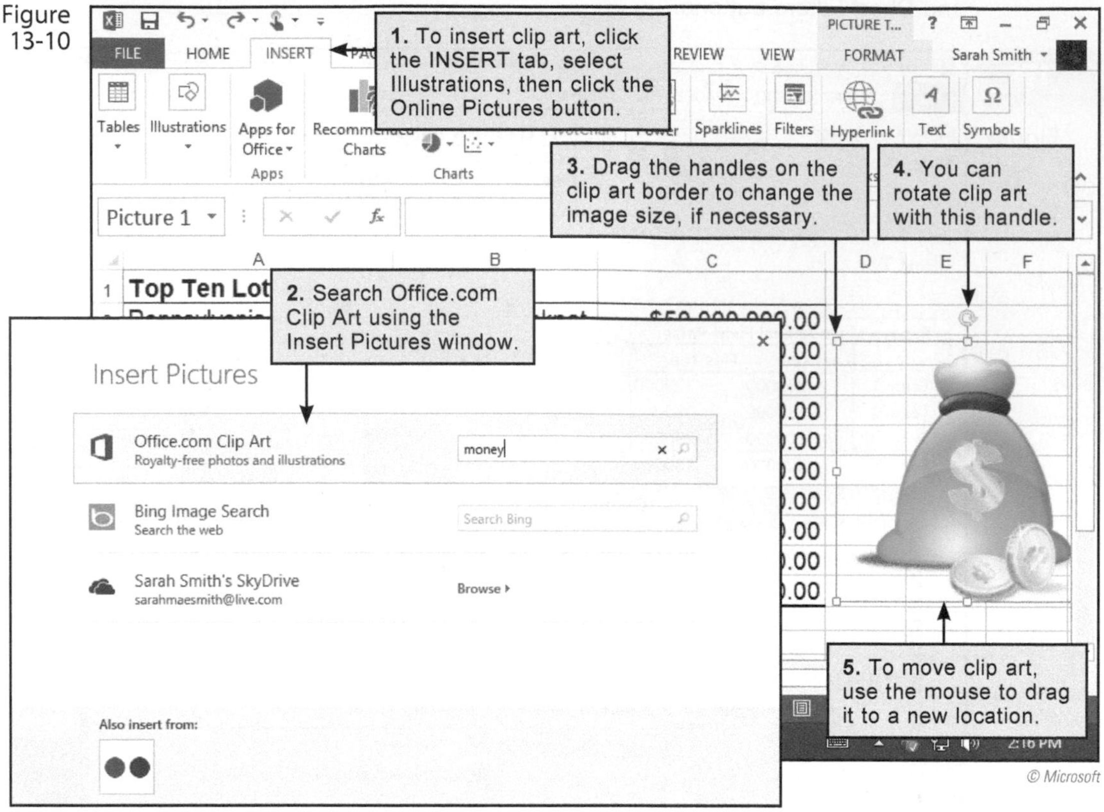

1. To insert clip art, click the INSERT tab, select Illustrations, then click the Online Pictures button.

2. Search Office.com Clip Art using the Insert Pictures window.

3. Drag the handles on the clip art border to change the image size, if necessary.

4. You can rotate clip art with this handle.

5. To move clip art, use the mouse to drag it to a new location.

Insert Pictures

Office.com Clip Art
Royalty-free photos and illustrations
money

Bing Image Search
Search the web
Search Bing

Sarah Smith's SkyDrive
sarahmaesmith@live.com
Browse ▸

Also insert from:

© Microsoft

- To insert clip art, click the cell where you want to place the graphic. Click the INSERT tab, then click Online Pictures in the Illustrations group. When the Insert Pictures window appears, search for clip art from Office.com Clip Art.

- Graphics can be resized using the square "handles" that appear on the edges of a selected graphic. For example, to enlarge a graphic, first select it by clicking anywhere on the graphic, then drag the handle in the lower-right corner down and to the right.

- To move a graphic, click the graphic to select it, then hold the mouse button down while dragging it to the new location.

- The round handle that appears at the top of a graphic allows you to rotate the graphic. To rotate a graphic, click to select it, then drag the green rotate handle right or left.

- The Shapes tools allow you to draw simple lines and shapes. To draw an arrow, click the INSERT tab, then click Shapes in the Illustrations group. Select ⬊ from the Lines group. Click the worksheet cell where you would like the arrow to start, then drag to draw the arrow.

- SmartArt is a collection of professionally designed graphics. To insert SmartArt, click the SmartArt button in the Illustrations group on the INSERT tab, select the shape you want to insert, then click the OK button. You can then drag the shape to any location on the worksheet.

QuickCheck A

1. True or false? When the contents of a cell are displayed as #####, that cell contains a number that is too long to display in the cell. [_____]

2. To center a label across several cells, select the horizontally adjacent cells, then click the [_____] & Center button.

3. True or false? The Format Painter tool allows you to copy cells from one location to another. [_____]

4. True or false? You need to press the Refresh Chart button to update a chart after changing chart data. [_____]

5. Use a(n) [_____] chart to show proportions of a part to a whole.

CHECKIT!

QuickCheck B

Indicate the letter of the desktop element that best matches the following:

1. The button used to add borders to a cell [____]

2. The *Merge & Center* button [____]

3. A cell formatted in the Currency style [____]

4. A cell formatted in the Percent style [____]

5. The Decrease Decimal button [____]

CHECKIT!

Skill Tests

A Applying borders and background colors

C Applying column widths and alignments

B Formatting text and numbers

D Creating charts

CHAPTER

14

Finalizing a Worksheet

What's Inside and on the CD?

In this chapter, you'll learn how to finalize your worksheets by sorting data and filtering it to view a subset of a worksheet's rows and columns. The chapter also explains how to check spelling and verify that formulas and calculations are correct. You'll learn how to prepare your worksheets for printing by adding page breaks, headers and footers, and gridlines. As an added bonus, you'll find out how to turn your worksheets into Web pages.

FAQ Can I sort data in a worksheet?

Excel provides tools that allow you to sort data in ascending or descending order. This feature gives Excel some of the basic data manipulation capabilities of database software. Data sorted in ascending order will be arranged in alphabetical order: Labels that start with "A" will be positioned above those that start with "B". Data sorted in descending order will be arranged in reverse alphabetical order: Labels that start with "Z" will be positioned above those that start with "Y".

TRY IT!

Figure 14-1

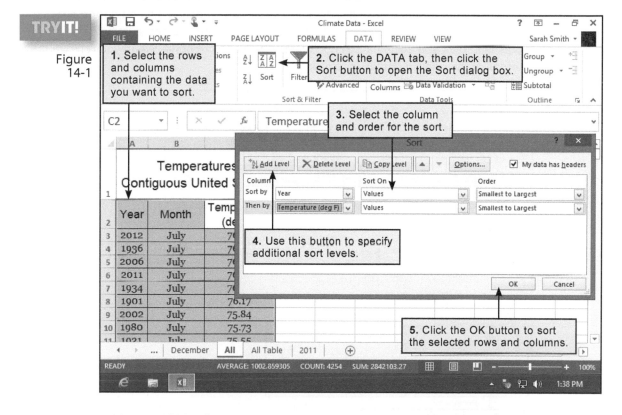

- It's a good idea to save your worksheet before performing a sort, just in case you forget to select all the necessary columns and end up scrambling your data.

- When selecting cells for a sort, make sure all the related columns are selected or the data will become scrambled. For example, if the sort in Figure 14-1 is performed with only columns A through B selected, the data will become scrambled and the temperatures in column C will no longer match the correct dates.

- If data becomes scrambled as a result of a sort, click the Undo button to undo the sort. Check the data carefully to make sure each row still contains the correct data, then select all columns of data and try the sort again.

- If you want to sort by the data in one column, you can use the ⬆ Sort A to Z or ⬇ Sort Z to A button in the Sort & Filter group on the DATA tab. Click a cell in the column before you click the desired sort button.

- If you want to sort by several columns, use the procedure shown in Figure 14-1. To perform a multilevel sort, you can add additional levels by clicking the Add Level button and designate the columns from the Then by list. You can set each level of the sort for either ascending or descending order. Click the OK button to apply the sort.

FAQ How do I filter data?

You can hide rows or columns of data in a worksheet if the data they contain is confidential or not relevant. Simply select the cells you want to hide, right-click the selected area, then click Hide. To display rows or columns that are hidden, select the rows or columns that border the hidden section. Right-click, then choose Unhide.

Filtering is a data management feature that allows you to focus on a subset of the data in a worksheet. You can, for example, filter data to view a specific year and hide the data for other years. You can filter data for specific price ranges, find data for a specific person, or locate data that matches multiple criteria. Filtering temporarily hides any worksheet rows and columns that don't match the search criteria. When you remove the filter, all of the original data is redisplayed.

TRYIT!

Figure 14-2

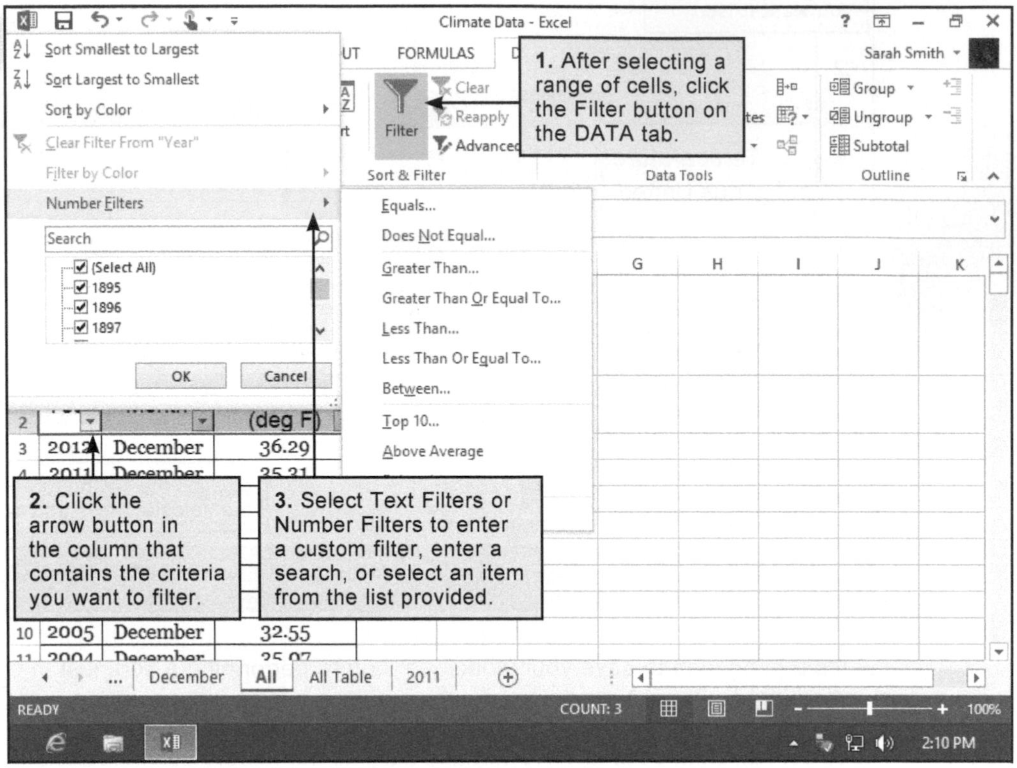

- When filtering numbers, you can use operators such as Greater Than, Less Than, or Equals. Select these operators from the Number Filters list.

- Use the Text Filters option to filter data based on the beginning or ending characters of the text contained in a row or column of cells.

- You can filter on multiple levels using a custom filter. For example, you can select data for the years between 1900 and 1910 (level 1), and for the month of July (level 2).

- Use filtering along with sorting to arrange your data in the most logical order. For example, sorting the climate data by temperature and filtering it by year might make the most sense when you want to see the 10 highest temperatures between 1900 and 1910.

- To clear the filter and redisplay all the worksheet data, click the [X Clear] Clear button on the DATA tab. To stop filtering, click the [Filter] Filter button.

FAQ How do I check spelling in a worksheet?

Excel can check the spelling of worksheet labels. Unlike Word's spelling checker, Excel doesn't show misspelled words with wavy underlines. Excel also doesn't provide a grammar checker. It is important for you to proofread your worksheets for grammar errors and spelling errors not caught by the spelling checker.

TRYIT!

Figure 14-3

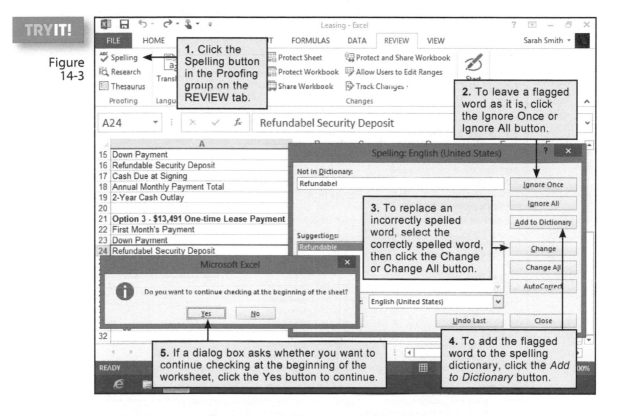

- You can begin to check the spelling with any cell selected. However, if you make cell A1 the active cell, you will avoid the question displayed in Step 5 above.

- If the correct spelling appears in the Suggestions list, click to select it, then click the Change button to correct the misspelled word.

- If no suggested spellings are displayed, click the *Not in Dictionary* text box, then type the correct word. Click the Change button to replace the misspelled word.

- If you're sure the word is spelled correctly, click the Ignore Once button to ignore this occurrence of the word. Sometimes a word—for example, a person's name—is not recognized by Excel. Click the Ignore All button if you want to ignore all other occurrences of this word throughout the entire worksheet.

- If the word is one you use frequently, click the *Add to Dictionary* button to add the current word to the spelling dictionary. For example, adding the city name "Ishpeming" to the Excel dictionary stops the spelling tool from identifying the name of this city as a misspelled word.

FAQ How do I test my worksheet?

You should always test your worksheets before relying on the results. Don't assume the result is correct just because it's generated by a computer. Your computer is almost certainly returning the correct results for the formulas and data you've entered, but it is possible you might have entered the wrong value in a cell, used the wrong cell reference in a formula, or made some other mistake in a formula. Figure 14-4 illustrates two common worksheet errors and how to troubleshoot solutions.

TRYIT!

Figure 14-4

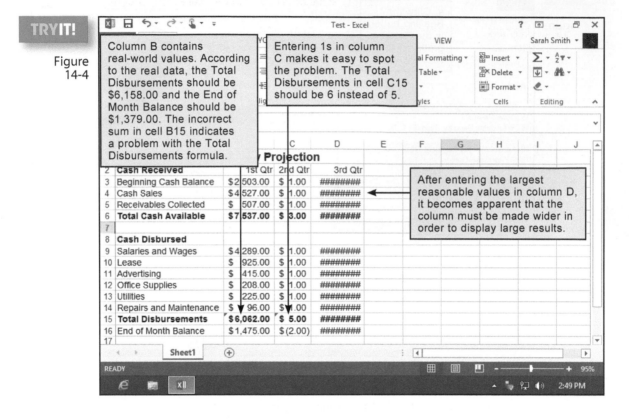

Column B contains real-world values. According to the real data, the Total Disbursements should be $6,158.00 and the End of Month Balance should be $1,379.00. The incorrect sum in cell B15 indicates a problem with the Total Disbursements formula.

Entering 1s in column C makes it easy to spot the problem. The Total Disbursements in cell C15 should be 6 instead of 5.

After entering the largest reasonable values in column D, it becomes apparent that the column must be made wider in order to display large results.

- It's a good idea to use the Save As option to rename and save an extra copy of your worksheet before testing, just in case your test significantly changes the worksheet.

- One way to test your worksheet is to enter a series of consistent and easily verified values, such as 1 or 10, into the data cells. If you enter 1s, you can quickly check the calculated results in your head and spot potential formula errors.

- Another way to test your worksheet is to enter a set of real-world values for which you already know the results. Compare the calculated result from the worksheet with the real-world result to make sure the worksheet is returning the correct results.

- It is also a good idea to test your worksheet by entering the largest and smallest values that would reasonably be expected in normal use of your worksheet. Small values, including zero, can lead to errors such as division by zero. The use of large values can lead to results that do not fit into the cell where the answer is to be displayed. In such a case, you'll need to make those columns wider.

FAQ How do I control the page layout for a worksheet?

Excel's Page Layout view helps you refine the appearance of a worksheet before you print it or post it as a Web page. You can adjust margins, change the page orientation, select the paper type, and adjust the layout settings.

To enter Page Layout view, click the VIEW tab, then select Page Layout. Once you are in Page Layout view, the worksheet is displayed as it will appear on a printed page. Also, some of the tools on the ribbon change to give you additional layout options.

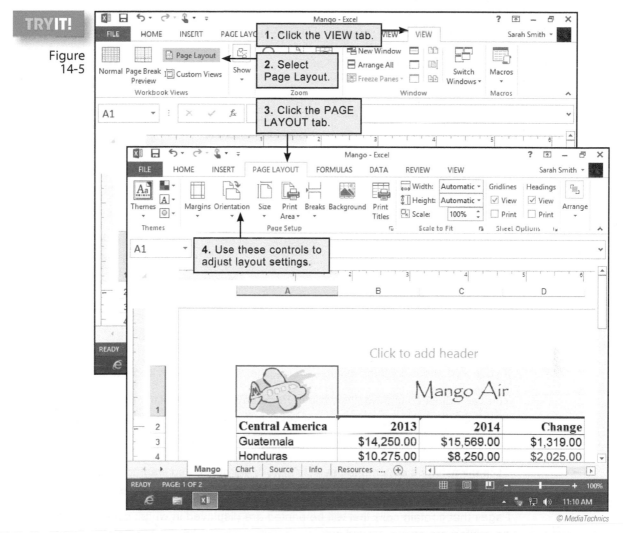

Figure 14-5

© MediaTechnics

- Orientation refers to the relative positions of the worksheet and the paper. **Portrait orientation** prints a worksheet on a vertically oriented page that is taller than it is wide. **Landscape orientation** prints a worksheet on the page sideways. Choose this option when your worksheet is wider than it is tall.

- You can select a specific area of a worksheet to print. When you use the Print Area button to select such an area, the setting is used every time you print. The Print Area button also allows you to clear the print area setting so that the entire worksheet prints.

FAQ How do I set margins?

Excel provides several ways to access margin settings, but one of the easiest ways is to drag directly in the margins while in Page Layout view. To get a good view of the entire worksheet before you change margins, you might want to reduce the zoom level to less than 100%.

Figure
14-6

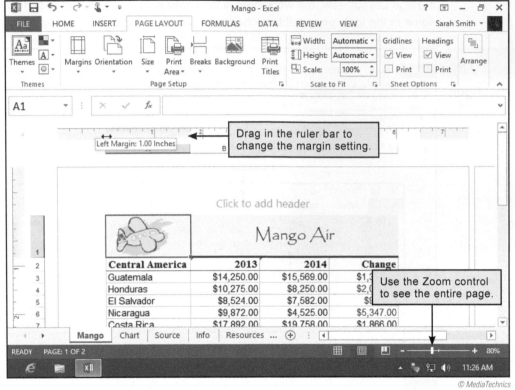

© MediaTechnics

- If your worksheet contains multiple pages, the margin settings apply to all the pages.

- You can adjust column widths while in Page Layout view. Making slight adjustments to column widths can help if the worksheet is just a bit too wide to fit on one page.

- Use the Margins button if you want to select preset margins.

- Click the Margins button, then select Custom Margins if you want to control the space allocated for headers and footers, or if you want to center a worksheet on the page.

- Pages that contain cells that will be printed are displayed in white; pages that will not be printed are shown grayed out.

FAQ How do I add headers and footers to a worksheet?

Like Microsoft Word documents, Excel worksheets can contain headers and footers. A header is text that appears at the top of every page. A footer is text that appears at the bottom of every page. Excel includes predefined headers and footers that contain information such as the worksheet title, current date, and page numbers. You can also create your own headers and footers.

TRY IT!

Figure 14-7

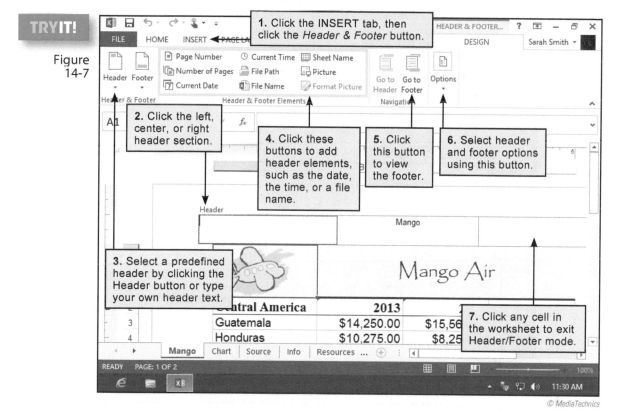

1. Click the INSERT tab, then click the *Header & Footer* button.

2. Click the left, center, or right header section.

3. Select a predefined header by clicking the Header button or type your own header text.

4. Click these buttons to add header elements, such as the date, the time, or a file name.

5. Click this button to view the footer.

6. Select header and footer options using this button.

7. Click any cell in the worksheet to exit Header/Footer mode.

© MediaTechnics

- The Options button offers several useful settings for headers and footers. Here are some suggestions on how to use them:

  Different First Page Because the worksheet title is visible on the first page, you can omit it from the page 1 header.

  Different Odd and Even Pages Specify page numbers on the left side of even numbered pages, but on the right side of odd numbered pages.

  Scale with Document Scale the headers and footers the same amount as the document scaling when printing.

  Align with Page Margins Align the header/footer text with page margins for a clean block style.

FAQ What options do I have for printed output?

You can use options on the ribbon to customize which elements of a worksheet will print. You can specify whether you want to print gridlines, column and row headings, formulas, and other worksheet elements. You can also specify scaling to reduce or enlarge a worksheet for printing.

TRY IT!

Figure
14-8

Click the Show Formulas button on the FORMULAS tab to display formulas.

Use these controls on the PAGE LAYOUT tab to adjust scaling.

Use these controls to print gridlines and headings.

© MediaTechnics

- **Gridlines** are the lines that separate one cell from another. In Page Layout view, gridlines are shown in light gray unless you turn them off by removing the checkmark from the Gridlines View box. If you do not want gridlines to print, make sure there is no checkmark in the Gridlines Print box.

- **Worksheet headings** are the column letters and row numbers. If you want headings displayed and printed, make sure there are checkmarks in the Headings View and Print boxes. Remove checks from these boxes if you don't want headings printed or if you don't want to see them on the screen.

- When you print a worksheet, typically only the results of formulas are displayed. It is useful to display formulas on a printout when troubleshooting or if the formulas are required to show the process behind the results of the worksheet. If you want formulas to print, click the Show Formulas button on the FORMULAS tab.

FAQ How do I set up a multipage worksheet?

Large worksheets sometimes require additional setup so that they print correctly. Before printing a multipage worksheet, use Page Layout view to preview the information that each page will contain.

You might want to insert a manual page break if a page ends with a row that should be grouped with data on the next page. You might also consider whether you would like to include row and column labels on every page to help readers identify the data presented after page 1.

Figure 14-9

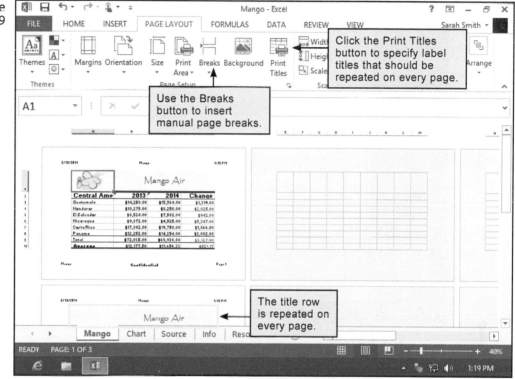

© MediaTechnics

- To specify the order in which pages of a multipage worksheet are printed, use the Sheet tab on the Page Setup dialog box. In the *Page order* section, choose *Down, then over* or *Over, then down*.

FAQ How do I print a worksheet?

Use the FILE tab's Print option to print a single copy of the current worksheet, to print multiple copies, to designate selected pages, or to use advanced print options. For example, you can print all the worksheets that make up a workbook. The default setting prints only the current worksheet.

TRYIT!

Figure 14-10

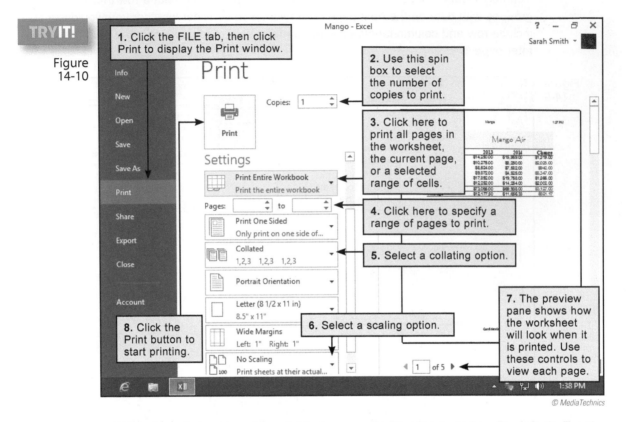

1. Click the FILE tab, then click Print to display the Print window.

2. Use this spin box to select the number of copies to print.

3. Click here to print all pages in the worksheet, the current page, or a selected range of cells.

4. Click here to specify a range of pages to print.

5. Select a collating option.

6. Select a scaling option.

7. The preview pane shows how the worksheet will look when it is printed. Use these controls to view each page.

8. Click the Print button to start printing.

© MediaTechnics

- Determine what you want to print before opening the Print window. By default, Excel prints the entire active worksheet. If you want to print only a section of the worksheet, select the range of cells before you click the FILE tab and select Print. You can then change Print Entire Workbook to Print Selection.

- To print only the current worksheet, select the Print Active Sheets option instead of the Print Entire Workbook option in the Settings section of the window.

- To print all worksheets in the current workbook, select the Print Entire Workbook option in the Settings section of the window.

- The scaling option is handy if you want to shrink the entire worksheet so that it fits on one page. Be aware, however, that scaling can produce a worksheet in tiny print. Check the print preview so you don't waste paper printing a worksheet that is unreadable.

- If your worksheet doesn't print, verify that the printer is online, and make sure you have specified the correct printer in the Print window.

FAQ What are my other output options?

Posting Excel worksheets provides an easy way to make them accessible to a large number of people without having to send each person a printed copy. You can output worksheets as PDF files using the Export option on the FILE tab. PDFs can be posted on a Web site, linked to your Facebook page, or e-mailed.

You can also use the FILE tab's Share option to save a worksheet in Excel format to Microsoft's Internet-based SkyDrive and allow others to view it. Another option is to save your worksheet as a Web page that you can post on the Internet.

TRYIT!

Figure 14-11

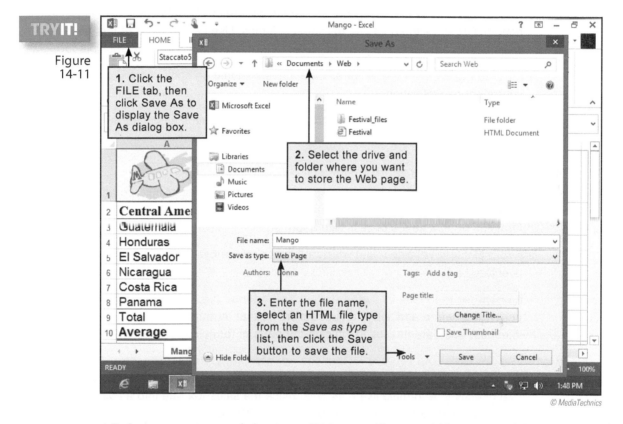

© MediaTechnics

- Before you save a worksheet as a Web page, it's a good idea to save it in normal Excel .xlsx format.

- Tables are a valuable formatting tool for creating Web pages. You can use Excel to create a table for this purpose. First, select the range of cells you want to include in the table, then follow the same steps to save as a Web page. In the Save As dialog box, choose an HTML file type, click the Selection option, name your file, then click Save.

- Some formatting options available in Excel cannot be duplicated in a Web page. If a worksheet contains formatting that isn't available in HTML, you'll be notified of the problem areas and will have the option of canceling or continuing with the save.

- Not all worksheets convert successfully to Web pages, so you should preview your worksheet in a Web browser to make sure the conversion is acceptable.

- After saving a worksheet in HTML format, follow your Web site host's instructions for posting it.

FAQ What makes a good worksheet?

Well-organized and well-formatted worksheets present data accurately, concisely, and in a format that is easy to understand. Consider the following recommendations for creating effective worksheets and avoiding common design errors:

- **Structure your data** so that the longest data sets go down the screen. For example, if you have 100 years of climate data for each of 12 months, put the labels for the years down the left side of the worksheet, and place the labels for each month across the top.

- **Arrange the information** on your worksheet so it reads from left to right and top to bottom. Organize the data into rows and columns. Use cells outside of the main data area to hold constants, such as sales tax rate, that are referenced by multiple formulas.

- **Provide meaningful labels** for all data. Labels should be spelled correctly and use consistent capitalization.

- **Make sure your data is entered accurately.** Double-check all numbers after entering them.

- **Enter formulas and functions carefully** and test them for accuracy.

- **Don't include labels in formula ranges.** Avoid the mistake of incorporating cells that contain labels into mathematical formulas, as sometimes happens when you copy formulas or fill a series of cells with a formula.

- **Avoid circular references** in which a formula references the cell in which the formula is entered.

- **Remember the rules of mathematical precedence** (i.e., multiplication and division are performed before addition and subtraction) so that formulas produce the results you intended; use parentheses to indicate the parts of formulas to be calculated first.

- **Use absolute and relative references appropriately.** In formulas, refer to cells that hold the data, rather than entering the data itself. For example, instead of using a tax rate directly in a formula like =.04*B12, place the sales tax rate into a cell such as D3. The formula to calculate sales tax becomes =D3*B12.

- **Avoid using too many fonts, font sizes, and colors in a worksheet,** but do use font attributes to highlight the most important data on your worksheet—typically totals and other summary data. By convention, red is the color used for negative values, overdrafts, and deficits.

- **Format numbers for easy reading.** For example, use commas in numbers and currency symbols for cells that hold numbers pertaining to money.

- **Use consistent formats for similar data.** For example, format all currency using the same number of decimal places and comma placement.

- **Format cells so that data fits into them** rather than spilling into neighboring cells. The exception to this rule is for worksheet titles that can be allowed to stretch over several cells.

- **Add documentation as necessary,** especially if other people will be entering data or modifying the worksheet.

QuickCheck A

1. True or false? Excel displays a wavy red underline under words that might be misspelled. [_____]

2. If the labels "banana", "peach", and "apple" are sorted in descending order, which label would be at the top of the sorted list? [_____]

3. True or false? Spreadsheet software always calculates correctly, so it's not necessary to test your worksheets before using them. [_____]

4. True or false? When printing with Excel, you can specify rows or columns to repeat on each page in a multipage printout. [_____]

5. True or false? A circular reference occurs when a formula references the cell where the formula is entered. [_____]

CHECKIT!

QuickCheck B

Indicate the letter of the desktop element that best matches the following:

1. The Spelling button [____]

2. The *Sort Smallest to Largest* button [____]

3. The button used to display a subset of data [____]

4. The button used to show formulas [____]

5. A column that is good for testing data because it contains easily verified values [____]

CHECKIT!

Skill Tests

A   Sorting and filtering

B   Checking spelling and testing worksheets

C   Preparing to print

D   Printing worksheets and saving as Web pages

CHAPTER 15

Creating a Presentation

What's Inside and on the CD?

Microsoft PowerPoint is the component of Microsoft Office best suited for creating visual backdrops for speeches and oral presentations. As presentation software, Microsoft PowerPoint provides a set of tools to help you script, organize, and display a presentation.

This chapter explains how good graphic design makes presentations visually compelling and easy to understand. A few simple bullets can be used to list key concepts. Numbered lists can present the steps in a process. Tables, charts, and graphics can simplify complex ideas and present numerical or statistical data creatively. To design effective presentations, avoid clutter and unnecessary graphical elements. Put common elements, such as the title of the presentation or the name of the author, on each slide to create consistency and tie the presentation together.

FAQ What's in the PowerPoint window?

A **PowerPoint presentation** consists of several slides. Each **presentation slide** contains objects such as titles, bulleted lists, graphics, and charts. Slides can even contain multimedia elements, such as video clips and sound bytes. Typically, slides are presented with a computer and a projection device. PowerPoint presentations can also be printed on transparent sheets for use with an overhead projector, printed on paper for handouts, shared in the cloud, or converted to movies that can be displayed on the Web.

You can open PowerPoint from the Windows 8 Start screen. Simply click the PowerPoint 2013 tile, or type PowerPoint and then select it from the list of apps. In Windows 7, click the Start button and navigate to the PowerPoint option on the Start menu.

From the preliminary PowerPoint screen, you can select a recent file, browse to open other presentations, or create a new presentation. After you've made a selection from the preliminary screen, the PowerPoint window appears. The PowerPoint window includes several work areas, in addition to controls on the ribbon, scroll bars, and status bar.

TRYIT!

Figure 15-1

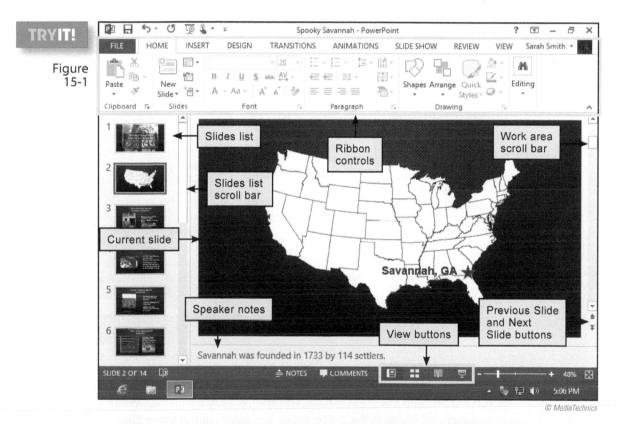

© MediaTechnics

- When a presentation is open in Normal view, the current slide is displayed in the center of the PowerPoint window. The Slides list is shown on the left, and speaker notes are shown near the bottom of the window.

- Use the scroll bar or the ⬆ Previous Slide and ⬇ Next Slide buttons to move from one slide to another in Normal view.

- You can also navigate through a presentation using the scroll bar next to the Slides list. Select a slide by clicking any slide that you want to view.

FAQ How do I create a presentation?

When PowerPoint opens, it displays a blank presentation and a slide that you can use as the title slide. Before you add more slides to your presentation, you can select a theme.

A **presentation theme** is a collection of professionally selected slide color schemes, fonts, graphic accents, and background colors. All the slides in a presentation should have a similar look, or design. Once you select a theme, PowerPoint automatically applies it to every slide in your presentation.

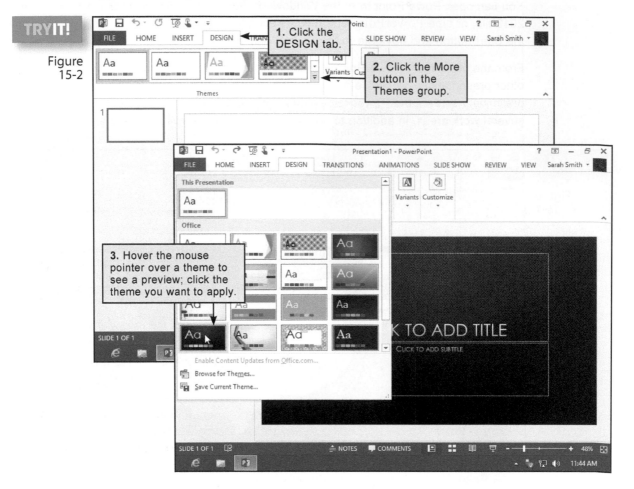

TRY**IT!**

Figure
15-2

1. Click the DESIGN tab.

2. Click the More button in the Themes group.

3. Hover the mouse pointer over a theme to see a preview; click the theme you want to apply.

- It's a good idea to save your presentation as soon as you have created the first slide and selected a theme. PowerPoint presentations are saved with a .pptx extension. As you are building the presentation, you should save frequently. When you save a presentation, all slides in the presentation are saved in the same file.

- If you change your mind about the theme you selected for a presentation, you can change it by clicking the DESIGN tab. Click any theme in the Themes group to apply the new theme to all slides in the presentation. You can also apply a theme to just one slide or to a group of slides by selecting the slide(s), right-clicking a theme in the Themes group, then selecting *Apply to Selected Slides*. All formatting applied before you changed the theme is replaced with the new design.

- Change the background color of a slide by clicking the DESIGN tab, selecting Format Background in the Customize group, then customizing the slide background using the Format Background pane. Additional background formatting is also available in the Variants group on the DESIGN tab.

FAQ How do I add a slide?

The New Slide button adds a slide to your presentation. When you add a slide, PowerPoint gives you a choice of slide layouts. Most slide layouts include at least one placeholder, in which you can enter text or graphics. You'll typically use the Title Slide layout for the first slide in your presentation, but you might want to also use the Title Slide layout to define sections of your presentation. Other slide layouts are set up for arranging bulleted lists, graphics, charts, tables, clip art, and videos.

TRYIT!

Figure 15-3

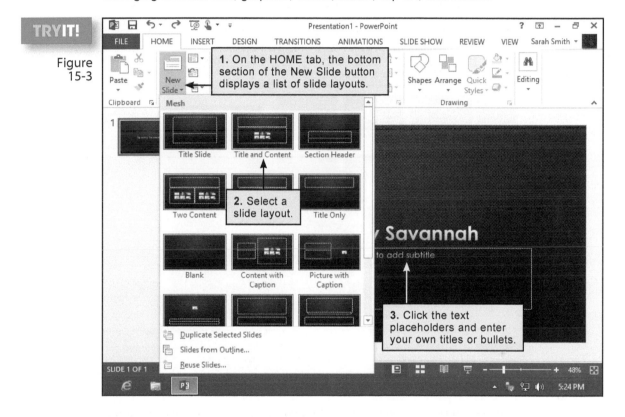

- If you don't like the predefined slide layouts, you can use the Blank layout, then use commands on the INSERT tab to add placeholders for text boxes, pictures, clip art, photos, shapes, or charts. For example, click the ▤ Text Box button in the Text group, click anywhere on the slide to create a text placeholder, then type your text.

- You can resize any placeholder or any slide object by using its sizing handles—the small circles and squares that appear on the object's borders.

- You can duplicate a slide in several ways. You can use the Copy and Paste buttons on the HOME tab. You can right-click a slide and use the shortcut menu's Copy and Paste options. When on the HOME tab, you can also click the arrow on the New Slide button, then select Duplicate Selected Slides. Before using any of these methods, click the slide you want to duplicate.

FAQ How do I add a bulleted list?

When you want to present a list of bulleted or numbered points, use one of PowerPoint's title and content layouts, such as Title and Content, Two Content, or Comparison. Bulleted lists focus the audience's attention on each point you are making. Each bullet should be a brief summary of what you are saying. Numbered lists help the audience to focus on sequences, priorities, and rankings.

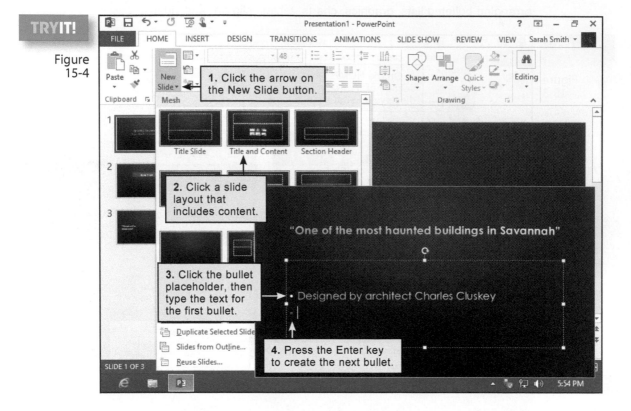

TRYIT!

Figure 15-4

- If you would like to change the list to a numbered list, use the ⊞ Numbering button located in the Paragraph group.

- Press the Enter key after typing each item in a list. Each time you press the Enter key, PowerPoint generates a new bullet or number. After you type the last item in the list, press the Enter key. Click the Bullets button in the Paragraph group to stop generating bullets. Or, click the Numbering button to stop generating numbers.

- You can press the Backspace key to remove a bullet or number.

- If you decide that you do not want bullet symbols in front of each list item, you can click the ⊞ Bullets button in the Paragraph group on the HOME tab to remove them.

- Use the ⊞ Increase List Level button to indent a bullet, or use the ⊞ Decrease List Level button to return a bullet to its previous level.

- You can add animation effects to a bulleted list to make the bulleted items appear one by one. You'll learn how to do this in the next chapter.

- Bullets effectively present an overview or summary of information, but you should limit their use to a maximum of five to seven per slide.

FAQ How do I add a graphic?

You can use graphics to add visual interest to your slides. The easiest way to insert a slide with a graphic is to select a slide layout that includes a content placeholder. After inserting the slide, you'll replace the Pictures, Online Pictures, or SmartArt placeholder with the graphic you want to use.

TRY IT!

Figure 15-5

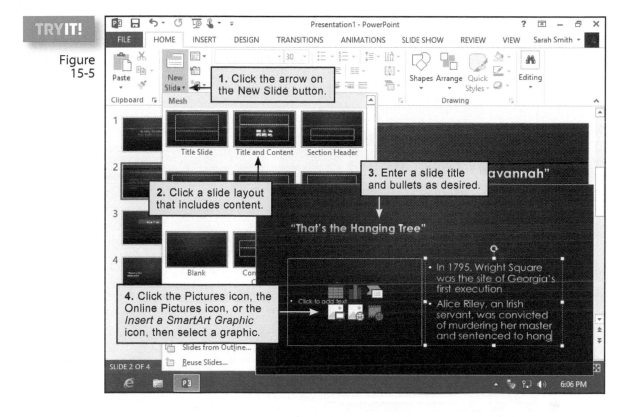

- To add clip art, click the ⊞ Online Pictures icon. The Insert Pictures window opens. The Insert Pictures window includes a tool that enables you to search for clip art online. Enter a search specification in one of the text boxes, then click the Search button. After you select a graphic, it is inserted in the slide, replacing the placeholder.

- To add a photo or scanned image instead of clip art, click the ⊞ Pictures icon displayed in the slide's placeholder. When the Insert Picture dialog box appears, navigate to the file you want to use, select it, then click the Insert button. The image is inserted in the slide, replacing the placeholder.

- SmartArt is a collection of graphical templates that can be used to depict organizational charts and processes. It can also provide a visually interesting backdrop for slide text and offer a modern alternative to the use of bullets. Clicking the ⊞ *Insert a SmartArt Graphic* icon displays PowerPoint's roster of SmartArt designs.

- Click any picture, clip art, or SmartArt to select it and display sizing handles. Use the sizing handles to change the position or size of any graphical element.

- To delete a graphic, select it, then press the Delete key.

- You can insert pictures, clip art, or SmartArt into any slide layout, even if it doesn't contain a graphic placeholder. Click the INSERT tab; click Pictures, Online Pictures, or SmartArt; then select a graphic. Use the sizing handles to position and size the graphic.

FAQ How do I add a chart?

PowerPoint provides several slide layouts containing chart placeholders. You can use the 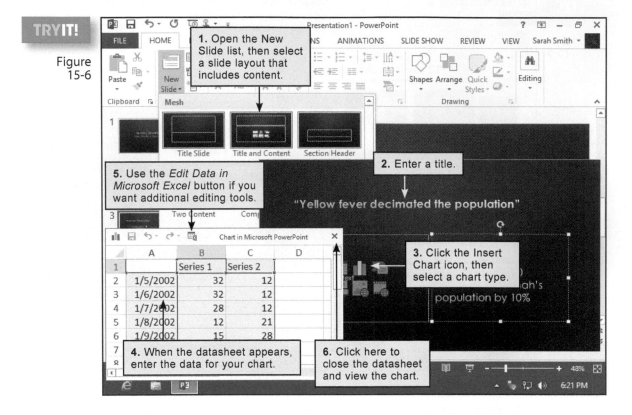 Insert Chart icon to add a bar chart, line chart, or pie chart. The chart comes complete with sample data in a datasheet, which you'll change to reflect the data you want to display on your chart. Some slide layouts provide an area for a large chart, while others are designed to accommodate a smaller chart plus bullets or other text.

TRYIT!

Figure 15-6

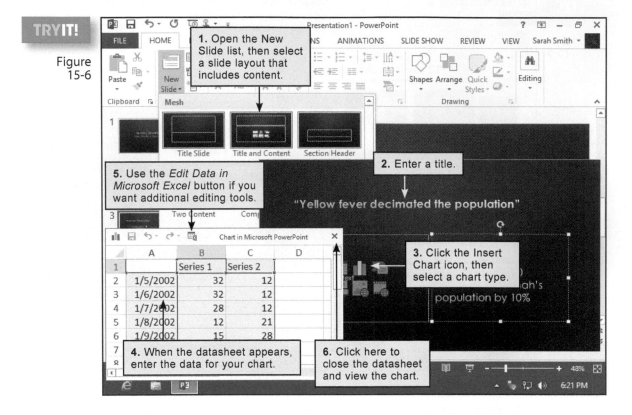

- You'll need to change the table of sample data by entering your own column headings, row labels, and data values. Click each cell containing sample data and replace it with your own labels or numbers.

- To delete sample data in the datasheet's columns or rows, select the cells, then press the Delete key.

- Use the scroll bars to view additional rows and columns.

- Click the 🖼 *Edit Data in Microsoft Excel* button on the sample table's title bar to access a complete set of tools for editing the table.

- To change the chart type, click the Change Chart Type button on the CHART TOOLS DESIGN contextual tab.

- You can use tools on the CHART TOOLS DESIGN and FORMAT contextual tabs to customize the elements of your chart.

FAQ How do I add a table?

You can add a table to a slide if you want to display text or graphics arranged in columns and rows. Select the ▦ Insert Table icon on any new slide layout with content to specify the number of columns and rows for your table. A blank table is displayed, and you can enter data into each cell.

TRY IT!

Figure 15-7

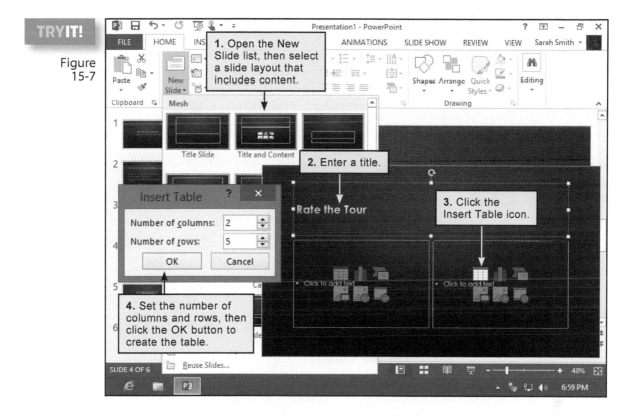

- When a table is inserted into a slide, the TABLE TOOLS DESIGN and LAYOUT contextual tabs appear. Using the buttons on these tabs, you can format table borders, add color shading to cells, and adjust the alignment of text in cells.

- To add text to a cell, click inside the cell, then type the text. You can edit and format text inside a table the same way as other slide text. You will learn more about formatting text in the next chapter.

- To add a graphic to a cell, click the cell, then click the INSERT tab. Select Pictures or Online Pictures from the Images group, depending on the type of graphic you want to insert.

- To adjust the height or width of cells, position the pointer over one of the dividing lines between cells. When the pointer changes to a ↔ or ↨ shape, drag the dividing line to the correct position.

- To insert rows, click the cell where you want to insert a row, then click either Insert Above or Insert Below in the Rows & Columns group on the TABLE TOOLS LAYOUT contextual tab. The steps to insert a column are similar to the steps to insert a row, except you click either Insert Left or Insert Right. The steps to delete a row or column are similar to the steps to insert them, except you use the Delete option in the Rows & Columns group on the TABLE TOOLS LAYOUT contextual tab.

FAQ How do I work with multimedia elements such as videos?

You can launch an audio clip or a video segment from a PowerPoint slide. Audio clips are most frequently added to slides as sound effects; this process is covered in the next chapter. You can easily insert videos stored in Flash Video, ASF, AVI, MPEG, and WMV formats. PowerPoint does not support clips from video DVDs, such as commercial films. MOV files can be played if Apple's QuickTime Player is installed. Refer to PowerPoint Help for details.

TRYIT!

Figure
15-8

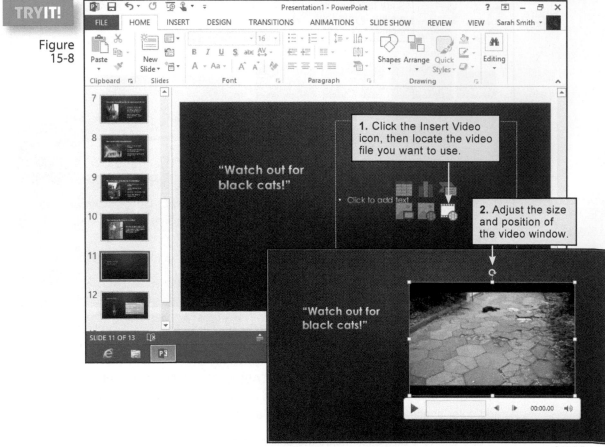

© MediaTechnics

- To stop a movie during a presentation, simply click the movie window.

- PowerPoint offers a set of Video Tools for adjusting the way movies appear on slides and play during presentations. To access Video Tools, click the movie window, then select the FORMAT or PLAYBACK tab.

- Movies play within the movie window displayed on the slide. You can change the size of the movie window by dragging its sizing handles.

- You can configure a movie to fill the screen when it plays, regardless of its size on the slide. Click the Play Full Screen checkbox on the PLAYBACK tab.

- You can hide the movie window so it does not appear on a slide during the presentation, but the movie still plays automatically when you reach the slide. Use the PLAYBACK tab to select Hide While Not Playing and Play Full Screen.

- Additional settings on the PLAYBACK tab allow you to set a movie to loop until you stop it or rewind after it is played.

FAQ Can slides include Web links?

PowerPoint slides can display several types of links, including links to Web sites. If you want to link to a Web site during a presentation, simply include the Web site's URL to create a hyperlink on a slide. Clicking the hyperlink automatically opens a browser and displays the specified Web page. Just make sure the computer at your presentation site has an Internet connection.

You can create more sophisticated links by using the Hyperlink button on the INSERT tab. The Insert Hyperlink dialog box lets you specify link text that appears on the slide instead of the actual URL, as shown in Figure 15-9.

TRY IT!

Figure
15-9

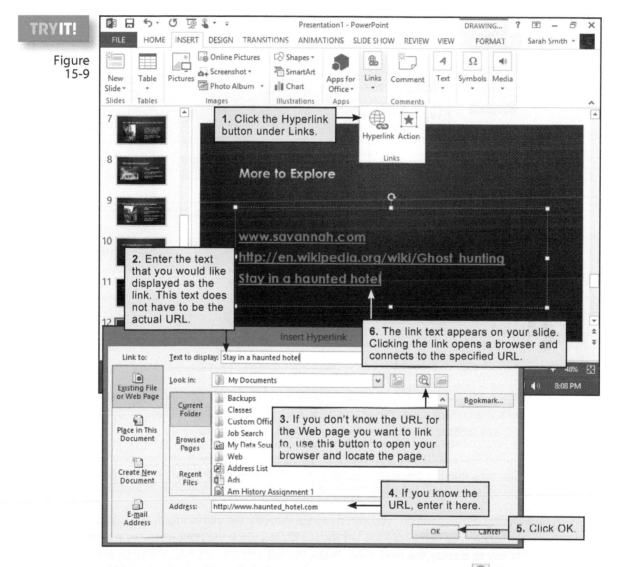

- When the Insert Hyperlink dialog box is open, you can click the 🔍 *Browse the Web* button to find a Web page and insert its URL. Using this method, you don't have to type lengthy URLs.

- Test hyperlinks before giving your presentation to make sure they work correctly.

- In addition to Web links, you can use the Hyperlink button to create links to other slides in your presentation so that you can quickly skip ahead or backtrack. You can also create links to slides in different presentations, to e-mail addresses, or to various files.

FAQ How do I view a slide show?

When you build a presentation, your screen contains the ribbon and other objects that should not be displayed when you deliver your presentation to an audience. In this chapter, you have seen how to create and modify a presentation in Normal view. When you are ready to see how your slides will look to your audience, switch to **Slide Show view**, which maximizes the slide pane so it fills the screen.

TRY IT!

Figure
15-10

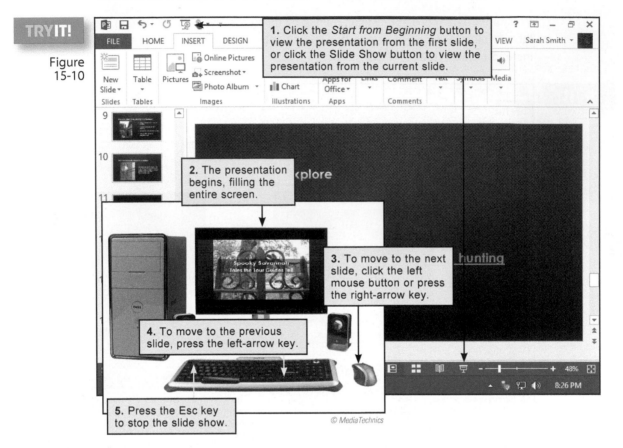

1. Click the *Start from Beginning* button to view the presentation from the first slide, or click the Slide Show button to view the presentation from the current slide.

2. The presentation begins, filling the entire screen.

3. To move to the next slide, click the left mouse button or press the right-arrow key.

4. To move to the previous slide, press the left-arrow key.

5. Press the Esc key to stop the slide show.

© MediaTechnics

- When you click the 🖵 Slide Show button on the status bar, the presentation starts with the current slide. When you click the 🔟 *Start from Beginning* button on the Quick Access toolbar, the presentation starts with the first slide.

- During a presentation, you can use the buttons in the lower-left corner of the slide to navigate through the slides, write on the slide with the PowerPoint pen or highlighter, or switch to another program.

- During a presentation, you can navigate through the slides in several ways. For instance, you can press the left mouse button, click the right-arrow key, or press the N key to display the next slide. Press the left-arrow key or the P key to move to the previous slide.

- Right-click a slide to display a shortcut menu that allows you to select a specific slide to display. Click Previous on the shortcut menu to go back one slide.

- Press the Esc key to end the slide show and return to the PowerPoint application.

- Before presenting to an audience, be sure to familiarize yourself with the content of each slide. Then, practice the timing of your presentation.

QuickCheck A

1. Microsoft PowerPoint is an example of [_____] software.

2. After adding a slide, you click the title text [_____] to replace it with your own title.

3. To add a new bullet to a bulleted list, press the [_____] key at the end of the previous bullet.

4. When you add a(n) [_____] to a presentation, you specify the number of rows and columns that will be displayed on the slide.

5. Before displaying a presentation, you should move to the [_____] slide in the presentation.

CHECKIT!

QuickCheck B

Indicate the letter of the desktop element that best matches the following:

1. A button that starts the slide show [____]

2. A contextual tab [____]

3. A slide layout with content [____]

4. The Insert Video icon [____]

5. The Insert Chart icon [____]

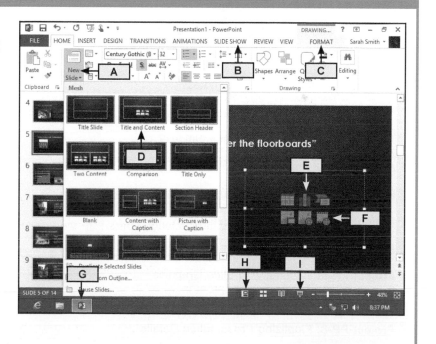

CHECKIT!

Skill Tests

A Creating presentations

B Adding titles and bulleted lists

C Adding graphics and charts

D Adding tables and viewing presentations

CHAPTER **16** # Finalizing a Presentation

What's Inside and on the CD?

In this chapter, you'll learn how to use the different views offered by Microsoft PowerPoint. In addition, you'll learn formatting techniques, as well as how to add animation and other visual effects to your slides. To finalize presentations, you'll learn how to print your presentation script, create handouts for your audience, save your presentation as a movie, and use an overhead projector if a computer projection device is not available.

FAQ What's the difference between Normal view and Outline view?

Microsoft PowerPoint provides different views that you can use to build, modify, and display your presentation. Most of the time, you will work in **Normal view**. Normal view is convenient for building the basic structure of your presentation and for adding speaker notes.

Outline view displays the text of your slides instead of slide thumbnails. You can enter text for your presentation in Outline view instead of entering it directly on the slide.

TRYIT!

Figure 16-1

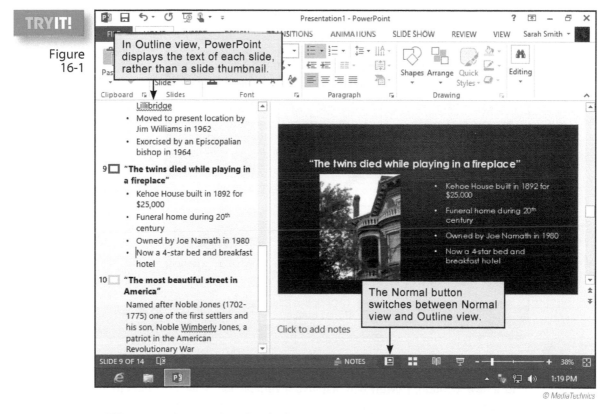

© MediaTechnics

- When entering text into the Outline panel, the following keys are useful:

  Enter: Takes you to the next slide, bullet, or placeholder

  Shift Tab: Promotes a level, as when you have been entering bullets and want to start a new slide

  Tab: Demotes a level, as when you want to add bullet points

- In addition to entering text into placeholders in Normal view, you can enter text for slides in the Outline list when the slide show is displayed in Outline view. You can edit this text using the editing keys, much like working with a word processor. You can also rearrange items by dragging them to new locations in the outline.

- If you have created an outline using Word or other software, the text can be imported into PowerPoint by selecting the arrow on the New Slides button and selecting *Slides from Outline*. Locate and select the document that contains the outline text, and it will be inserted based on its format. For more information on importing outlines, access PowerPoint Help.

FAQ How do I use Slide Sorter view?

Although you can rearrange slides using slide thumbnails in Normal view, PowerPoint offers a special view designed for this purpose. **Slide Sorter view** allows you to view miniaturized versions of all the slides in a presentation. In this view, it is easy to rearrange slides, delete slides, hide slides, and duplicate them.

TRY IT!

Figure 16-2

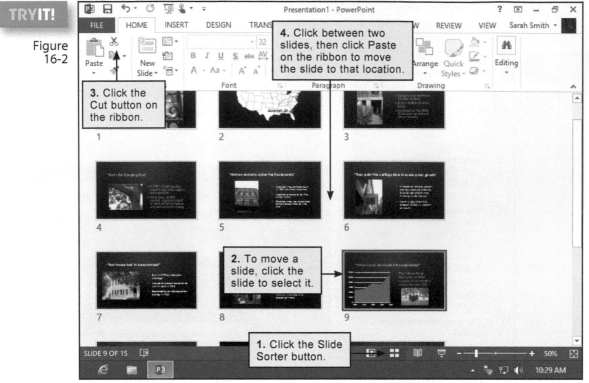

© MediaTechnics

- You can use the drag-and-drop method to move a slide. Select the slide, then drag it to a new location. PowerPoint displays a vertical line between slides to indicate the proposed slide position before you release the mouse button.

- To delete a slide, select it, then press the Delete key on your keyboard.

- You can hide a slide so that it won't appear when you show the presentation. While in Slide Sorter or Normal view, right-click the slide, then click Hide Slide on the shortcut menu. Repeat this procedure when you want to make the slide visible again. Hiding slides can be handy when you would like to give a shortened version of your presentation. Rather than showing slides without commenting on them, you can just hide the slides you won't have time to discuss.

FAQ How do I add transitions?

A **slide transition** is an effect that specifies how a slide replaces the previous slide during a presentation. Transitions include fades, wipes, and other effects. You can also select sound effects to go along with each transition. If you do not specify a transition, a new slide replaces the entire current slide all at once. Carefully selected transitions can make a presentation more interesting and help the audience pay attention, but overuse of transitions can become irritating and distract attention from the content of your presentation.

TRY IT!

Figure 16-3

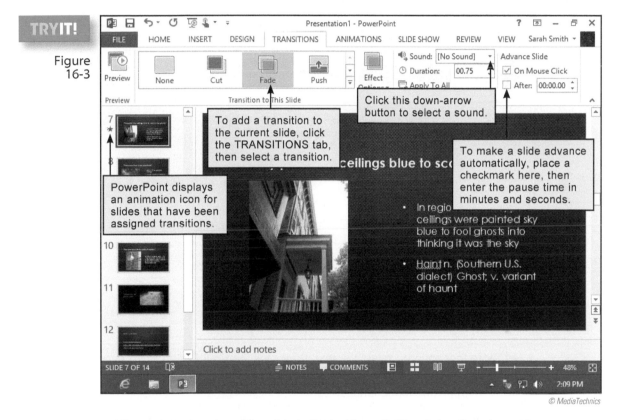

© MediaTechnics

- After you apply a transition, it is indicated by a ★ Play Animations icon. You can see the icon next to a slide in the Slides list in Normal view or in Slide Sorter view. While developing your slide show, you can click the icon any time you want to see how the transition looks.

- You can change a transition by selecting a slide, clicking the TRANSITIONS tab, then selecting a different transition from the *Transition to This Slide* group.

- In Slide Show view, a presentation advances from one slide to the next when you click the mouse or press a key. If you want a slide to advance automatically after a specified period of time, click the After checkbox in the Timing group on the TRANSITIONS tab. Use the spin box to set the display time. The time is displayed as mm:ss.ss, where the first two digits represent the number of minutes and the last four digits represent the number of seconds. To force the slide to advance after 1 minute and 30 seconds, for example, enter 01:30.00 in the After spin box.

FAQ How do I format text on a slide?

PowerPoint includes themes preformatted with fonts and font sizes specially selected to complement the background design. In most cases, these fonts work well; but sometimes you'll find it necessary to modify font attributes.

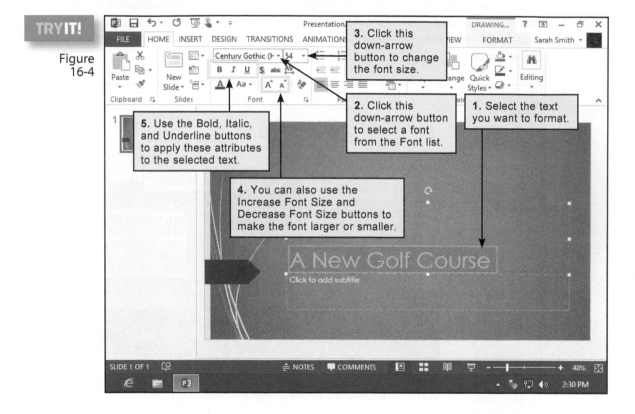

Figure
16-4

- For more font options, select the text, then click the Font Dialog Box Launcher in the Font group. Select the desired font, font style, size, color, and effect, then click the OK button to apply the font changes.

- When you select font sizes, you should consider the size of your presentation venue and use fonts that are visible from the back of the room. When using a large font, you might have to use fewer words on each slide.

- You also should consider the lighting in the room in which your presentation will be given. In a brightly lit room, slides are easier to read if you use a dark font color on a light background. In a dark room, you should use a dark background with light font colors. You can experiment with font colors to find the combination that works best in the room in which you will deliver the presentation.

- You can change the font attributes for all the slides in your presentation at the same time by using the slide master. The **slide master** is a template you can modify to create a consistent look for your presentation. Click the VIEW tab, then click Slide Master in the Master Views group. Select the text styles you want to modify, then change the font attributes using the Font dialog box. To close the slide master, click Close Master View on the SLIDE MASTER tab. Use Slide Sorter view to verify that the new font attributes are applied to the text on all of the slides in your presentation.

FAQ How do I add animation effects to a bulleted list?

The ANIMATIONS tab provides options for adding animation effects and sounds to items on a slide. **Animation effects** are typically used to draw attention to bullets as they appear on the slide during a presentation. For example, each bulleted item can "fly" in from the side when you click the mouse button. Animation effects can also be accompanied by sound effects to draw attention to each new bullet.

Figure 16-5

© MediaTechnics

- You can apply animation effects to any slide element, including text, graphics, charts, and tables. After you apply an animation effect, you can test it by clicking the ✶ Play Animations icon next to the slide in the Slides list. You can also select the slide and then switch to Slide Show view.

- After selecting Effect Options, you can use the *After animation* option to indicate whether the object should change to a different color or disappear after the animation. For example, you can change a bullet to a light font color just before the next bullet appears. The new bullet in a darker font will then become the focus.

- Use sounds sparingly—a sound effect can be humorous and effective the first time it's used, but it can become less amusing after 10 or 20 slides. If you use sounds for a presentation, make sure your presentation equipment includes a sound system with adequate volume for your audience.

FAQ How do I check spelling in a presentation?

PowerPoint's spelling checker is very similar to the one you use in Word. It provides an inline spelling checker that automatically indicates possible spelling errors with wavy red underlines. As with Word, simply right-click a word marked with a wavy red underline to view a list of correctly spelled alternatives. You can also use the Spelling button on the REVIEW tab to manually initiate a spelling check of the entire presentation.

TRYIT!

Figure 16-6

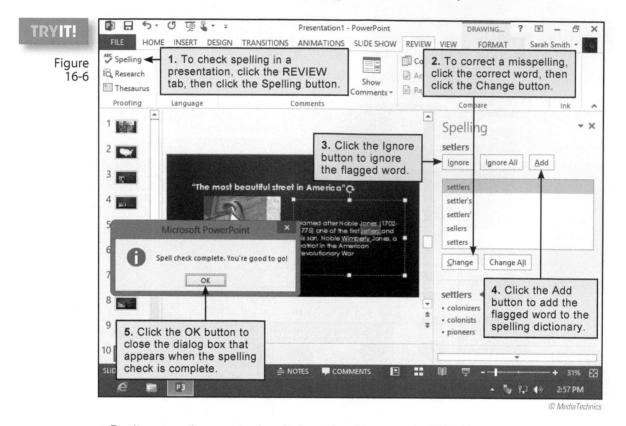

© MediaTechnics

- Don't worry—the wavy red underlines do not appear in Slide Show view when you display a presentation.

- You should always check spelling in a presentation before you save the final version. Misspellings can make your audience doubt the accuracy and validity of your statements.

- PowerPoint does not include a grammar checker, so make sure you proofread your presentation to eliminate grammar errors. Bulleted items are usually sentence fragments, but sometimes complete sentences are more appropriate. You should try to be consistent on each slide, using either complete sentences or only phrases.

- PowerPoint's AutoCorrect feature can automatically correct common typing errors as you work. Click the FILE tab, the Options button, the Proofing option, and then the AutoCorrect Options button. In the AutoCorrect dialog box, select any options that are useful to you. Options include automatically capitalizing the first word in a sentence and the names of days, changing two capital letters at the beginning of a word to a single capital letter followed by a lowercase letter, and correcting capitalization errors caused by accidental use of the Caps Lock key.

FAQ How do I work with speaker notes?

You can prepare **speaker notes** that remind you what to say about each slide. Speaker notes can be printed or they can be viewed on the computer you use at the lectern while the version of the presentation without speaker notes is projected for the audience.

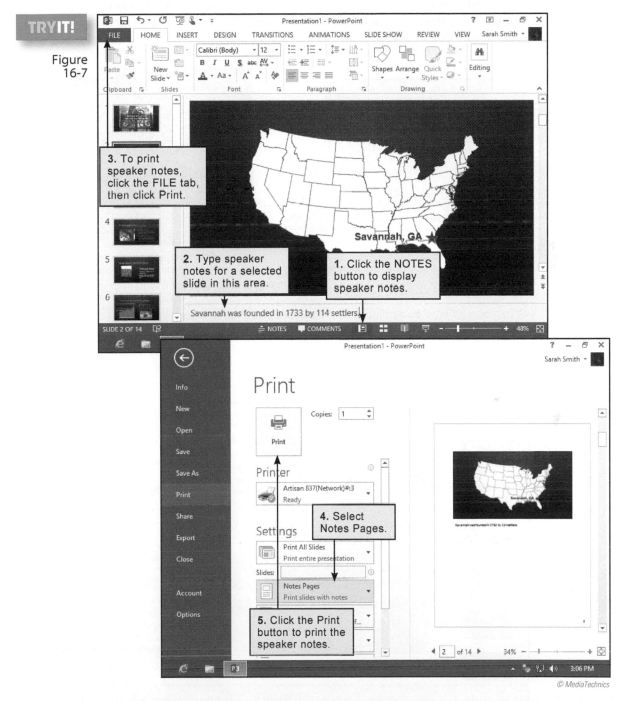

Figure
16-7

© MediaTechnics

• Speaker notes shouldn't include the exact text that appears on the slide. Use speaker notes for any additional comments you want to make.

• To print speaker notes, click the FILE tab, then click Print. Select Notes Pages in the Settings section. Click the Print button to print the speaker notes.

• How do I work with speaker notes? (continued)

PowerPoint offers **Presenter View**, which shows your speaker notes on the computer screen you use at the lectern while displaying the notes-free slides on the projected image that's seen by the audience. To use this handy feature, Windows must be configured to support two monitors. The signal for one monitor is sent to the projector. The signal for the display with speaker notes remains on the computer that's running the slide show. PowerPoint automatically detects the additional monitor.

Figure
16-8

PowerPoint displays speaker notes on the computer you use at the lectern.

PowerPoint projects the image without notes for the audience.

Give yourself time to configure and test your setup before your presentation begins.

Figure
16-9

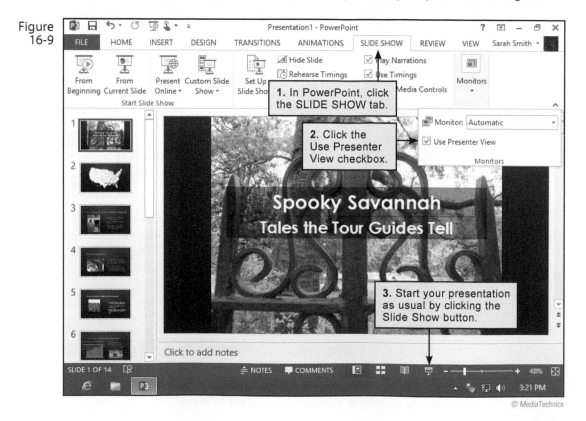

FAQ How do I print handouts?

Handouts help your audience remember the content of your presentation. Microsoft PowerPoint offers several print layouts for handouts. Choose the one that best fits the content and number of slides in your presentation.

TRY IT!

Figure 16-10

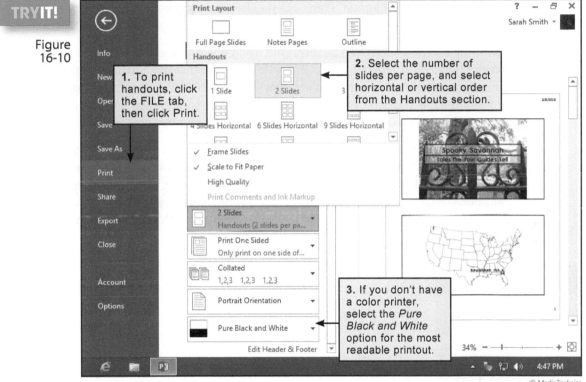

© MediaTechnics

- If your presentation is brief, you can print two or three slides per page for handouts. The two-slide layout prints each slide on one-half of the page. It is appropriate to use this layout when the graphics and bullets on the slides include most of the details of your presentation content. The three-slide layout prints blank lines to the right of each slide. It is appropriate to use this layout when you expect your audience to write notes about each slide.

- You can save paper by printing four to nine slides per page. You can select either horizontal or vertical order for all of these print layouts. Horizontal order prints multiple slides (in order) across the page; vertical order prints the slides (in order) down the page.

- The biggest advantage of using a PowerPoint presentation is the variety of colors and graphics you can use to enhance your slides. Your handouts can be printed in black and white or in color depending on your printer. Select the *Pure Black and White* option to convert the colors in your slides to the most readable grayscales for a black and white printer.

- The Frame Slides option gives your handouts a professional look by drawing a thin black line around each slide.

- You can print a text-only version of your presentation by selecting Outline in the Settings section. This handout is useful for very long presentations that include a number of bulleted items. Graphics do not print in the Outline version.

FAQ How can I distribute my presentations?

As an alternative to delivering a presentation to a live audience, you can distribute your presentation in several other ways. For example, you can output your slides as overhead transparencies by simply printing the presentation on transparency film. You can print your slides on paper and distribute them as handouts. PowerPoint presentations can also be converted into PDF format, which can be viewed on any computer with Adobe Reader installed.

PowerPoint presentations can be displayed using a viewer instead of the full presentation software product. A program called PowerPoint Viewer displays presentations on computers on which PowerPoint is not installed. PowerPoint Viewer can be downloaded for free from the Microsoft Web site. You can package your presentation on a CD along with PowerPoint Viewer for people who cannot attend your live presentation.

Some presentation software converts slides to HTML pages that you can post on the Web, but these pages typically do not incorporate transitions and animations. With PowerPoint 2013, however, you can save the presentation as a video that includes transitions, animations, and sounds. These PowerPoint videos can be posted on the Web. Click the Try It! button to find out how to turn a PowerPoint presentation into a video.

TRYIT!

Figure 16-11

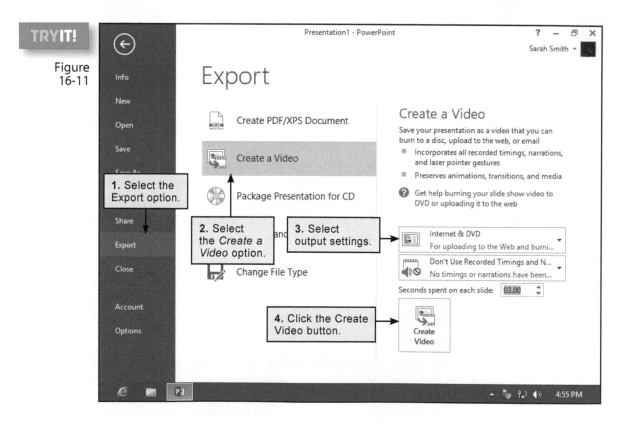

QuickCheck A

1. [_____] notes help you remember what to say when each slide is displayed during a presentation.

2. A(n) [_____] effect can make bullets "fly" onto the screen one at a time.

3. A slide [_____] controls the way a slide replaces the previous slide during a presentation.

4. True or false? PowerPoint has a feature that allows you to show your speaker notes on the computer screen you use at the lectern while displaying the notes-free slides on the projected image that's seen by the audience. [_____]

5. True or false? To package a presentation, including animations and sound, for display on the Web, simply convert the slides to HTML format. [_____]

CHECKIT!

QuickCheck B

Indicate the letter of the desktop element that best matches the following:

1. The Slide Sorter button [____]

2. Settings for displaying speaker notes at the lectern [____]

3. A slide with a transition [____]

4. The area for entering speaker notes [____]

5. The button that switches to Outline view [____]

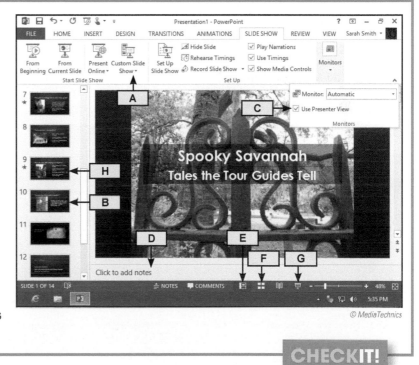

© MediaTechnics

CHECKIT!

Skill Tests

A Sorting slides and changing fonts

B Adding transitions and running the spelling checker

C Adding animation and sound to bullets

D Adding speaker notes

Creating a Database

What's Inside and on the CD?

Microsoft Access is the component of the Microsoft Office suite best suited for working with large collections of data called databases. As database software, Microsoft Access provides a powerful set of tools for entering and updating information, deleting information, sorting data, searching for specific data, and creating reports.

● **FAQs:**

FAQ How is data organized in a database?

Because it is useful for organizing many types of data, database software, such as Access, can be complex. A few simple concepts, however, should provide you with the background necessary to start working with this important data management tool.

Access is designed for creating and accessing relational databases. A relational database is very flexible because it can store data for several different but related categories. For example, a relational database could be used to store information about films and actors. Each category of data is stored in a **database table**. An Academy Awards database could have a table with information about Best Picture winners and another table containing biographical information about actors.

A table is composed of records and fields. A record contains information about a single entity in the database—a person, place, event, or thing. A field contains a single unit of information, such as the title of a film that won the Best Picture award.

Figure 17-1

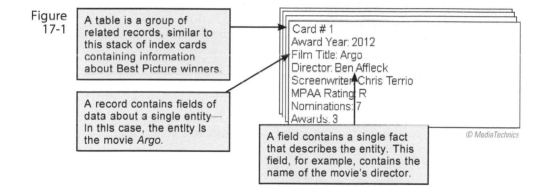

A table is a group of related records, similar to this stack of index cards containing information about Best Picture winners.

A record contains fields of data about a single entity—In this case, the entity is the movie *Argo*.

Card # 1
Award Year: 2012
Film Title: Argo
Director: Ben Affleck
Screenwriter: Chris Terrio
MPAA Rating: R
Nominations: 7
Awards: 3

© MediaTechnics

A field contains a single fact that describes the entity. This field, for example, contains the name of the movie's director.

The data in a table can be displayed in different ways. Most of the time, you'll work with the data arranged in rows and columns, such as in the figure shown below. Each row contains one record. Each cell in a row contains the data for one field.

TRYIT!

Figure 17-2

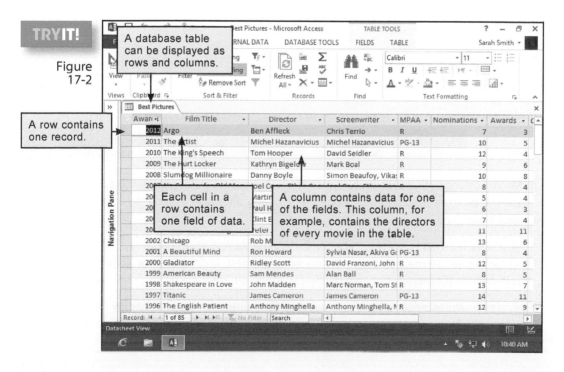

A database table can be displayed as rows and columns.

A row contains one record.

Each cell in a row contains one field of data.

A column contains data for one of the fields. This column, for example, contains the directors of every movie in the table.

FAQ What's in the Access window?

You can open Access from the Windows 8 Start screen. Simply click the Access 2013 tile or type Access, then select it from the list of apps. In Windows 7, click the Start button and navigate to Microsoft Access from the Start menu. A window appears where you can search for online templates, search for an existing database, or create a new database.

TRYIT!

Figure 17-3

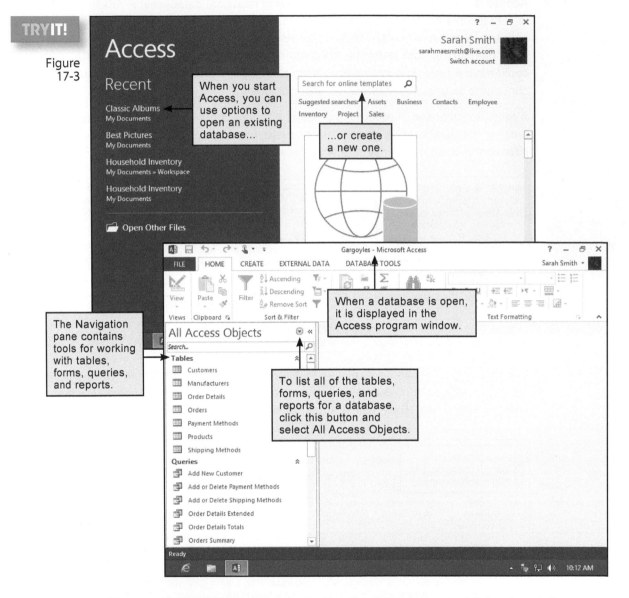

- When working with Access, you typically will not create a new database each time you use the program. Instead, you'll open an existing database in order to add to or edit the data it contains.

- As you've learned in previous chapters, documents and spreadsheets appear on the screen similar to the way they will look when printed. Databases are different—their data can be displayed and manipulated in many different ways.

- Access provides several tools you can use to create, modify, and display data in the database. These tools are contained in the Navigation pane on the left side of the database window.

FAQ How do I create a new database?

Creating a database is different from creating a document, worksheet, or presentation. With Word, for example, you typically enter text into a new document before you save it. With Access, first you save an empty database, then you create the elements that make up the database. These elements include tables, reports, forms, and queries.

TRY IT!

Figure
17-4

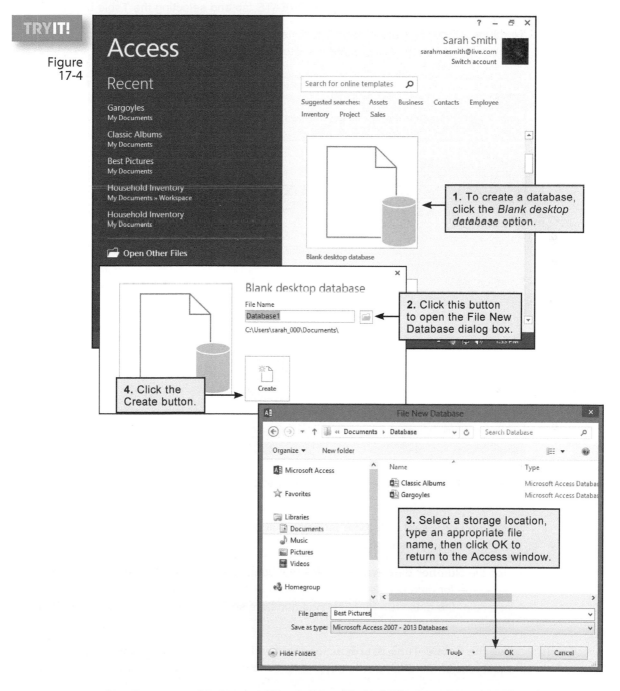

- Creating a new database simply makes a file that becomes the container for the tables, data, queries, and reports that you will eventually include in the database.

- Because a new database is essentially an empty shell, your next step is to create one or more tables and add data.

FAQ How do I create tables?

Before you can enter data in a database, you must specify the structure of the tables, records, and fields in your database. A table contains records. Each record consists of one or more fields, and each field contains a particular type of data, such as a name or date. When you create a new database, Access creates an empty table called Table1. You can create additional tables by clicking the CREATE tab and selecting the Table button.

To define a field for a table, you begin by selecting a **data type**, such as Short Text, Number, or Currency. You can then create a name for the field.

TRY IT!

Figure
17-5

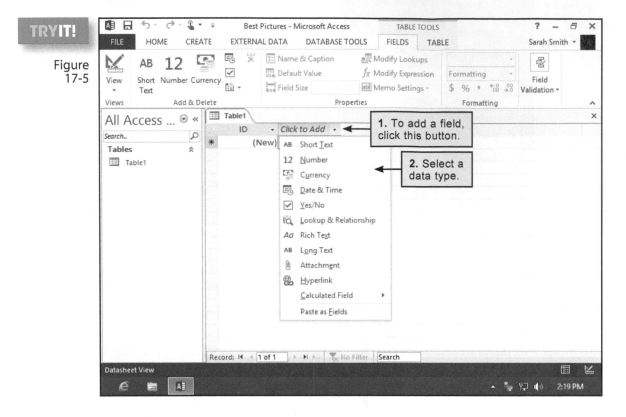

- Use the **Short Text data type** for fields that contain words and symbols of up to 255 characters in length.

- Use the **Long Text data type** for fields that contain variable length data, such as comments, notes, and reviews.

- Use the **Number data type** for fields that contain numeric data. Don't use the Number data type for data consisting of numerals that will not be used in calculations. For example, the data type for telephone numbers should be defined as Text rather than Number.

- Use the **Date & Time data type** for dates and times. This special data type makes it much easier, for example, to determine if one date occurs before or after another date.

- Access creates an ID field using the **AutoNumber data type**. A unique number is automatically entered in this field as you enter each new record.

- The **Yes/No data type** can be useful for fields designed to hold simple Yes/No or True/False data. For example, you might use a Yes/No data type for the field "Subtitled?"

• How do I create tables? (continued)

After you select a data type, Access waits for you to enter a field name. Simply type the field name, then press the Enter key.

Figure
17-6

Enter field names in the first row of a table.

- Field names can contain spaces, so "Film Title" is acceptable. To make documentation easier, some database designers prefer not to use spaces in field names, in which case the field name would be "FilmTitle". Whichever style you use for field names, try to use consistent spacing and capitalization for all fields.

- The maximum length for a field name is 64 characters, but in most cases try to limit the size of a field name to 20 characters or less.

- You can change the name of a field at any time, even after you've entered data into a table.

How do I create tables? (continued)

The empty table contains an ID field designed to be used as the primary key. A **primary key** is a field that uniquely identifies each record. It's very important that no two records are ever assigned the same value for this unique field. The ID field's data type is AutoNumber, which means that Access automatically assigns a unique value to each record, beginning with 1 for the first record.

You can modify the ID field to accommodate primary keys, such as SKUs, Social Security numbers, or telephone numbers, by changing the field name and data type as necessary. For example, in the Best Pictures database, only one movie receives the award each year, so the year can be used as the primary key.

Figure 17-7

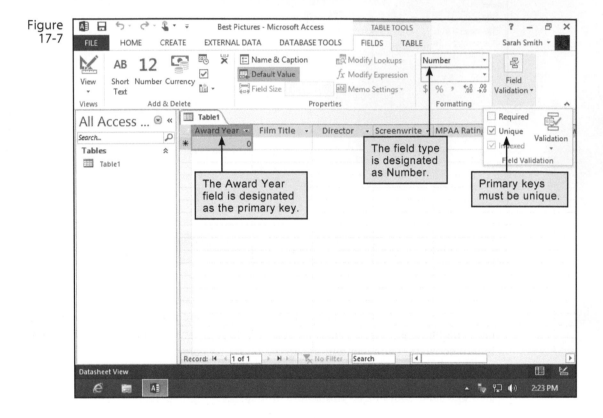

The Award Year field is designated as the primary key.

The field type is designated as Number.

Primary keys must be unique.

● The field you use for the primary key must contain unique data for each record. Make sure that the Unique box contains a checkmark for the field that you use as the primary key. Access will then make sure that the contents of the field are unique for each record. For example, if the table contains the Best Picture winner for 1964 and you mistakenly enter "1964" when adding a new record, Access will not save the new record until you correct the date.

FAQ How do I save tables?

You can save a table at any time as you are defining the fields or entering data. After saving a table, you can continue to edit; the save process is simply a way of saving work in progress as a precaution against power outages or hardware glitches.

The quickest way to save a table is to click the Save icon on the Quick Access toolbar. You'll be asked to supply a name for the table; and once the save is complete, the table name will appear in the Tables list.

TRYIT!

Figure
17-8

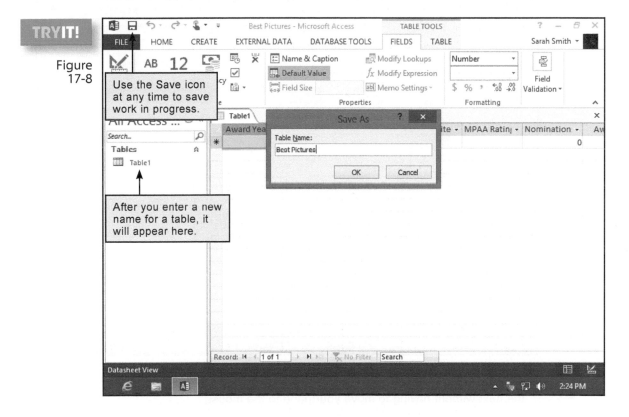

- Give each table a unique and descriptive name so that you can identify it easily.

- All tables in the database are stored in the same database file.

- To open a table the next time you start Access, open the database and then double-click the table name in the Navigation pane.

FAQ How do I enter and edit data in a table?

Once you've defined the fields for a table, you can enter data. If you have just created a table, the table is open. If the table is not open, double-click the name of the table in the Navigation pane. Access displays an empty record into which you can begin to enter data.

TRY IT!

Figure
17-9

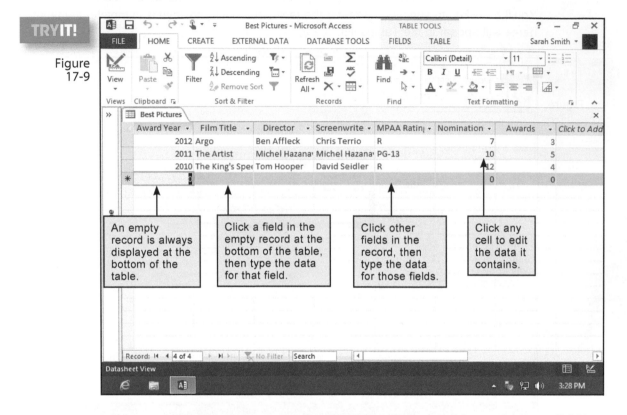

- When entering data, you can use the Tab key or Enter key to move from one field to the next without having to move your hand to the mouse.

- Be careful to enter data in a consistent manner. Do not, for example, enter "PG-13" in the MPAA Rating field for some records, but enter "PG 13" without the hyphen in other records. Without consistent entries, the search term "PG-13" won't find all of the films containing material that might be inappropriate for children younger than 13.

- To edit data, click the cell containing the data. Use the left-arrow and right-arrow keys to move the insertion point within the field. Use the Backspace and Delete keys to delete text to the left or to the right of the insertion point, respectively.

- To delete an entire record, right-click the row header containing the record. Click Delete Record on the shortcut menu, then click the Yes button.

- Access saves each record as you enter it; it is not necessary to click the Save button to record changes to the data as you complete the entry for each one.

FAQ Can I import data into a database?

As an alternative to typing data into a database table, you can import data from files created with other software, including worksheets created with Excel, databases created with older versions of Access, and e-mail address books created with Outlook. You can also import comma-delimited files created with a word processor or exported from other software.

A **comma-delimited file**, sometimes referred to as a **CSV file** (comma-separated values), is simply data separated by commas similar to the following:

2012,Daniel Day-Lewis,Lincoln
2012,Bradley Cooper,Silver Linings Playbook
2012,Hugh Jackman,Les Misérables
2012,Joaquin Phoenix,The Master
2012,Denzel Washington,Flight

Many software applications offer an export option that creates a comma-delimited file. You can use the export option to create a file that can then be Imported into Access. Import options are listed on Access's EXTERNAL DATA tab.

Suppose you have a list of actors nominated for the Best Actor Academy Award. To import the list, begin by clicking the Text File button in the *Import & Link* group on the EXTERNAL DATA tab, then select the file that currently holds the list.

TRY IT!

Figure
17-10

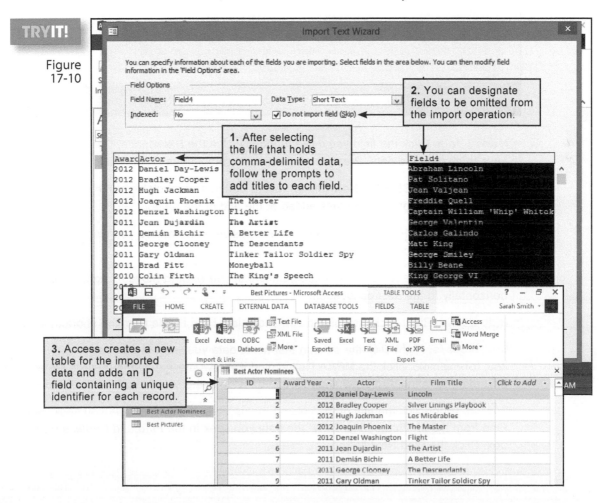

FAQ How do I work with tables?

Working with the data in an Access table is similar to working with data in an Excel worksheet. You can add, delete, move, and sort data, as well as search for specific data items. Controls for these operations are on the ribbon, but they can also be accessed by right-clicking the column or row you want to work with.

TRYIT!

Figure 17-11

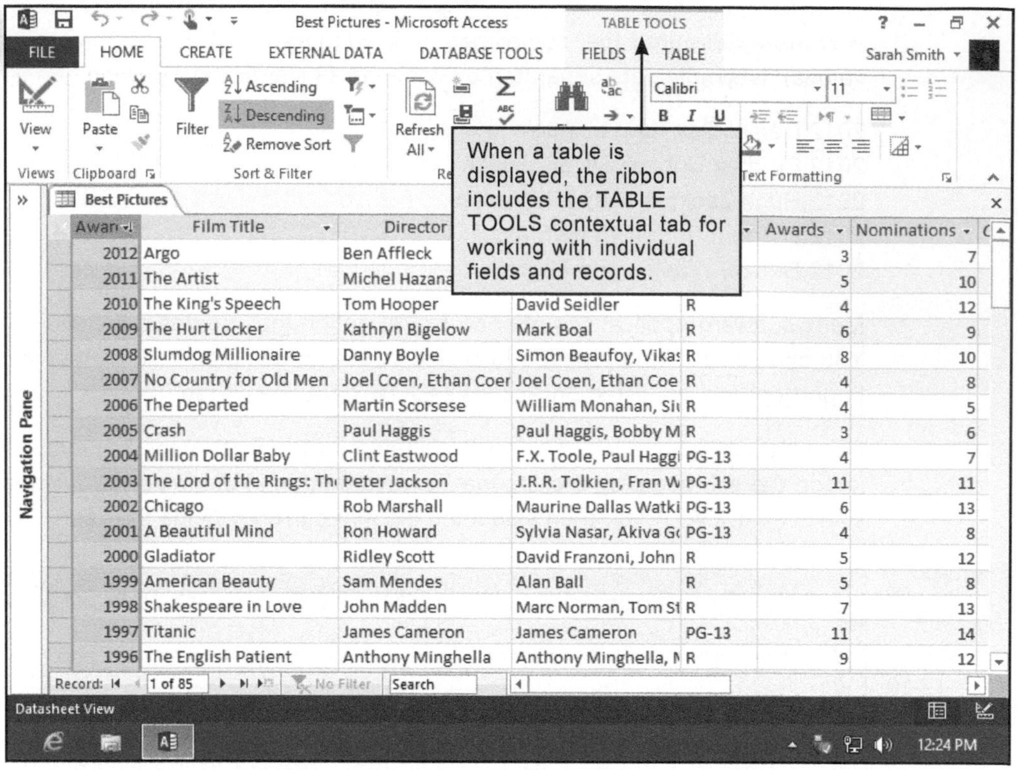

- **Modify data.** Click the field you'd like to modify. Use the Backspace, Delete, and typing keys to change the data. Press the Enter key to complete the modification.

- **Insert a record.** Click the New (blank) record button at the bottom of the database window. New records are always added at the end of the table.

- **Delete a record.** Right-click the box on the left side of the record you want to delete. Select Delete Record from the shortcut menu.

- **Move a field.** Select the column or columns that you want to move. Drag the column horizontally to the desired location.

- **Hide a field.** Right-click the column title and select Hide Fields from the shortcut menu.

- **Sort records.** Right-click the column that holds data you want to use as the sort key; for example, click the MPAA Rating field if you would like all the records sorted according to rating. From the shortcut menu, select either *Sort A to Z* or *Sort Z to A*.

- **Search.** Right-click the title of the column that is likely to hold the data you seek. Select Find from the shortcut menu. Enter the data you seek in the *Find and Replace* dialog box. Click the Find Next button.

FAQ How do I create a query using a wizard?

After you have organized your data into one or more tables, you can manipulate the data in many ways. For example, you can search a company database for all customers in a specific state or search the Best Pictures database for winners during the era of underground, independent cinema from 1960-1970.

You can create a **query** to search your database for records that contain particular data. A query contains criteria that specify what you would like to find. You can also use a query to display data for only selected fields. The Query Wizard offers a quick way to create simple queries and use them to locate data. Let's see how to create a query that shows only four fields: Award Year, Film Title, MPAA Rating, and Awards.

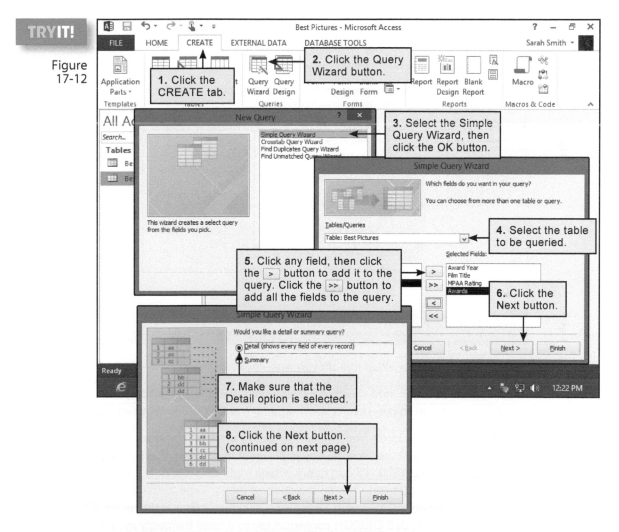

Figure 17-12

Simple Query Wizard - Which fields do you want in your query?

- The fields you select in this step will be included in the query results. Click a field, then click the > button to add an individual field. Click the >> button to add all fields. Click the < button to remove a field from the query. Click the << button to remove all fields.

Simple Query Wizard - Would you like a detail or summary query?

- Selecting the Detail option shows all of the specified fields for the records, whereas selecting the Summary option only displays the number of records that match your criteria.

How do I create a query using a wizard? (continued)

Figure
17-13

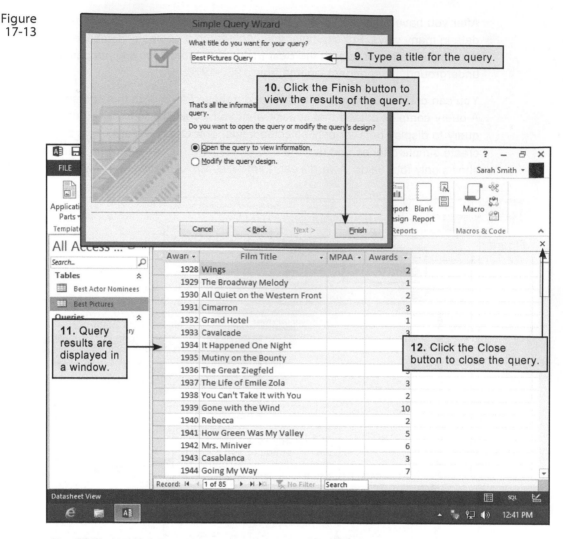

Simple Query Wizard - What title do you want for your query?

- After you enter a title and click the Finish button, the query results appear in a new window. In this example, results show data for the four fields specified by the query.

- To further refine a search, you can specify **query criteria**. For example, instead of a query that returns all the records, you might want to see only those records for films between 1960 and 1970. To add query criteria, right-click the query tab at the top of the window, then click Design View on the shortcut menu. Type >=1960 AND <=1970 in the Criteria row under the Award Year field. Click the ⊞ Run button in the Results group on the QUERY TOOLS DESIGN contextual tab to display the query results. Records that match the criteria are displayed in the query results window.

- If you have to change a query, you can click the FILE tab, then click Save As to save the query with a new name. Otherwise, when you close the query window after viewing the results of a query for which you specified query criteria, you will see a message saying *Do you want to save changes to the design of query 'Query Name'?* Click Yes if you would like to use the same query criteria every time you use this query.

- After a query is saved, you can run it repeatedly to display all the records—including new and updated data—that match the criteria you've specified.

QuickCheck A

1. True or false? A relational database contains information that is organized into tables containing columns and rows. [_____]

2. A(n) [_____] contains a single piece of information, such as a name or zip code.

3. A(n) [_____] contains fields of information about a single entity in the database, such as a person, event, or thing.

4. True or false? It is not important to be consistent when entering data into a table. For example, it does not matter whether you use "GA" or "Georgia" when entering data into a state field. [_____]

5. A(n) [_____] contains criteria that specify the data you want to find in a database.

CHECKIT!

QuickCheck B

Indicate the letter of the desktop element that best matches the following:

1. A text field [_____]

2. A number field [_____]

3. A primary key field [_____]

4. The button used to import a CSV text file [_____]

5. A blank field in a new record [_____]

CHECKIT!

Skill Tests

A Creating database files

B Creating tables

C Entering data

D Creating queries

CHAPTER 18

Finalizing a Database

What's Inside and on the CD?

In this chapter, you'll learn how to manipulate a database to create forms, generate reports, print reports, and convert reports into Web pages.

FAQ How do I create a form using a wizard?

You can organize your data into rows and columns using a table, which is the best way to view the data contained in a large number of records. Another way to display your data is with a form. A **database form** allows you to view your data one record at a time, with the fields of each record arranged on your computer screen as they might be arranged on a printed form. The Form Wizard helps you design an on-screen form in which you can enter and manipulate data for each record of a database.

TRY IT!

Figure
18-1

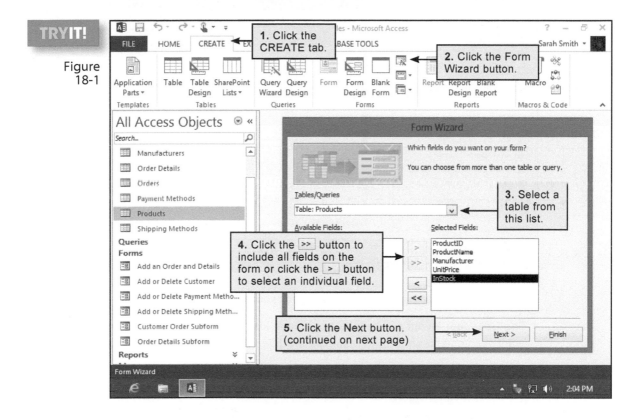

Form Wizard - Which fields do you want on your form?

- Most of the time, you'll want to include all fields on the form. To do so, click the `>>` button.

- As an alternative, you can select individual fields. For example, if you are going to enter specific data, such as today's purchases, you might use a form that shows only ID, FirstName, and LastName, along with a field for the purchase amount. You don't need to see the contact's address information while you are entering purchase data. To select a specific field, click it, then click the `>` button. Repeat these steps for each field you want to include on the form.

- You can remove an individual field from the Selected Fields list by clicking the `<` button.

• How do I create a form using a wizard? (continued)

Figure
18-2

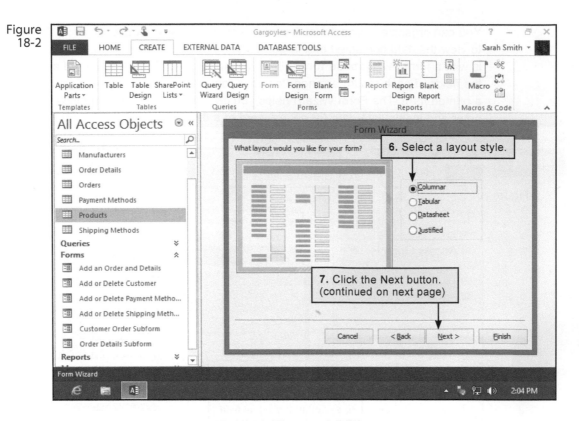

Form Wizard - What layout would you like for your form?

- The Columnar layout places labels next to fields, and lists the fields in columns. If you want your on-screen form to resemble a printed form, select the Columnar layout.

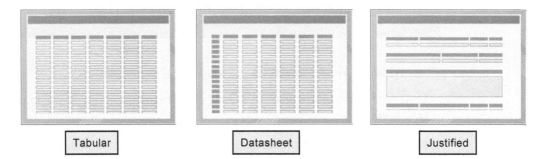

- You can experiment with other layouts to see how they work for different types of data. The Tabular layout places field labels at the top of a column, which makes it appear like a table. The Datasheet layout resembles a spreadsheet, with cells for entering data. The Justified layout displays fields across the screen in rows, with a label above each field.

• How do I create a form using a wizard? (continued)

Figure
18-3

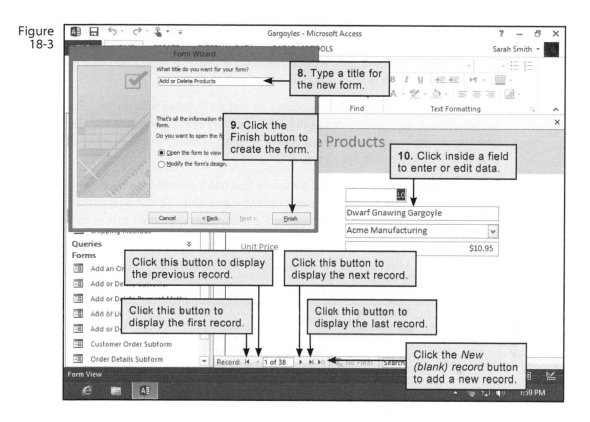

• Forms that you create are automatically saved in the database file, so you don't have to save a form separately.

• When you use a form to add or change the data in a record, you have to use the Refresh All button on the HOME tab to update the corresponding table.

• You can modify the design of any form by right-clicking the tab at the top of the form and selecting Design View.

• Click any label to edit it. To move a label and the associated data field, click to select the object, move the pointer over the edge of the object until the pointer changes to a ↔ shape, then drag the label and data field to a new location. To delete a label from the form, click the label, then press the Delete key on the keyboard. You can delete a data field the same way. Double-click an object to open the Property Sheet where you can modify additional attributes for the object.

• You can change the form layout by right-clicking the form's tab, selecting Layout View, and using the buttons in the Table group on the ARRANGE tab.

• As you become more familiar with Access, you might eventually want to create forms using Design View rather than the Form Wizard. Start with a blank form, then add labels and controls. Design View provides maximum flexibility for designing a form, but requires more time on your part.

FAQ How do I create a report using a wizard?

When you want to create a polished printout of some or all of the data in your Access database, you can create a report. A **database report** is typically a printed document containing data selected from a database. Like a query, a report can be based on criteria that determine which data is included in the report.

Reports often include totals and subtotals as well as detailed information. For example, suppose a company uses a report that lists inventory items sorted by manufacturer and item name. The report could be configured to simply display totals, or it could calculate and display the total value of the inventory.

When using a school or corporate database that has been created by a database professional, several predefined reports may be available. To run a report, simply click the report name, and Access will display the report based on data that is currently in the database.

You can also create your own custom reports using the Access Report Wizard as shown below.

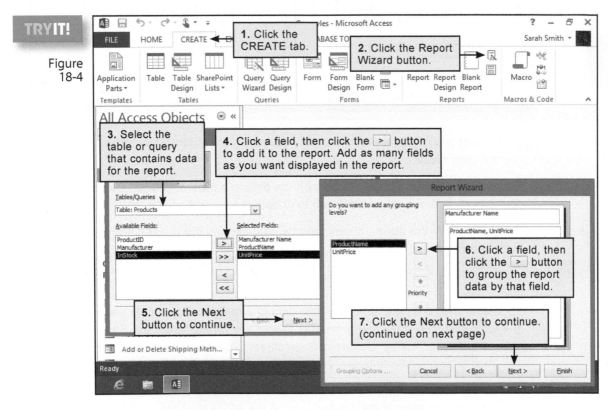

Figure
18-4

Report Wizard - Which fields do you want on your report?

- To add individual fields to the report, click a field, then click the > button. Click the >> button to add all available fields to the report.

Report Wizard - Do you want to add any grouping levels?

- When you add a grouping level, records are sorted according to entries in the group field. You can add several grouping levels to a report. For example, you might group a list of products by the manufacturer, then group them by item name. Grouping also helps arrange data when you want to produce a report containing subtotals.

• How do I create a report using a wizard? (continued)

Figure
18-5

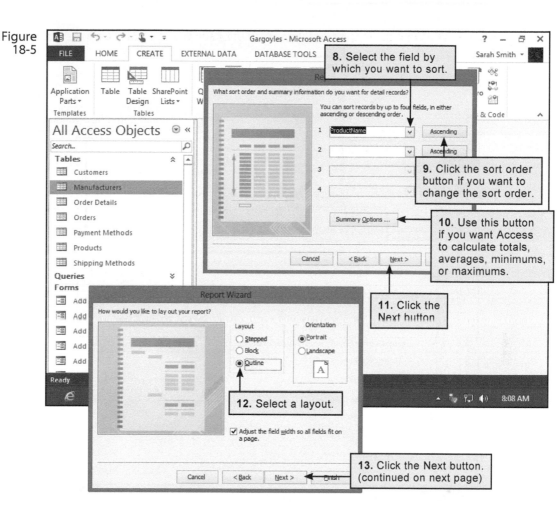

Report Wizard - What sort order and summary information do you want for detail records?

• To sort records within a group, click the down-arrow button and select the field by which you want to sort.

• Click the ☐ Ascending ☐ button to sort from A to Z (from low to high). Click the ☐ Descending ☐ button to sort from Z to A (from high to low).

• The Summary Options button can be used to display totals, averages, minimums, or maximums for fields containing numeric data.

Report Wizard - How would you like to lay out your report?

• Select an option button in the Layout section. The preview area helps you visualize the layout of the completed report.

• How do I create a report using a wizard? (continued)

Figure
18-6

14. Type a title for the report.

15. Click the Finish button to generate the report and open it in a new window.

16. The completed report is displayed.

17. Click the Close button to close the report.

• Type a report name, which is used to identify the report so that you can open it in the future. The report layout is automatically saved in the database file along with the tables, queries, and forms that you have already created.

• After you click the Finish button, the report is displayed. Use the vertical and horizontal scroll bars to view parts of the report that are not initially visible.

• You can modify the report layout at any time. Right-click the report name in the Navigation pane. Click Design View from the shortcut menu. You can use the options on the REPORT DESIGN TOOLS tabs to modify the report. Select an object on the report, then use the sizing handles to adjust their size. To move an object, click the object to select it, move the pointer over the edge of the object until the pointer changes to a ✛ shape, then drag the object to a new location.

FAQ How do I print a report?

Each time you display or print a report, the contents of the report are automatically updated to reflect the current data stored in the database. For example, suppose that you print a report today. Then over the next week, you add and change data in the database. If you display or print the report next week, it will include all of the updated data.

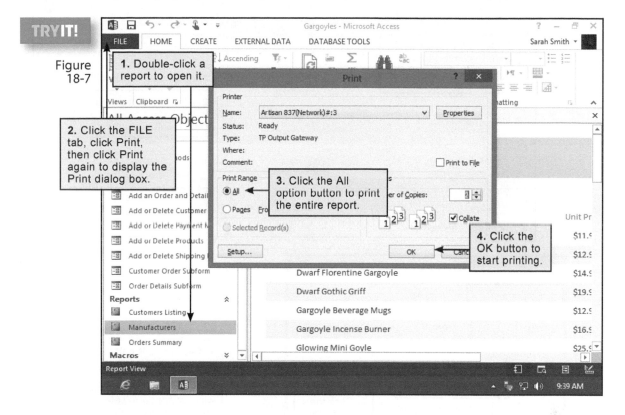

TRYIT!

Figure 18-7

1. Double-click a report to open it.

2. Click the FILE tab, click Print, then click Print again to display the Print dialog box.

3. Click the All option button to print the entire report.

4. Click the OK button to start printing.

- The data in a printed report is a "snapshot" that shows the status of your database at a particular point in time. When you edit or add data to the database, your report includes new and revised data. It is a good idea to include the date the report was printed on all pages to help readers determine if the data is current.

- To add the date or time as a report header, right-click the report name in the Navigation pane, then click Design View on the shortcut menu. Click the *Date and Time* button on the DESIGN tab. Select the date and time formats, then click the OK button. You can move the date and time fields to any location on the report. Select both fields by holding down the Shift key while you click each field. Move the pointer over the edge of the fields until the pointer changes to a ✛ shape, then drag the fields to the desired location in the report.

Figure 18-8

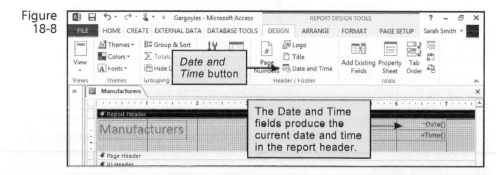

Date and Time button

The Date and Time fields produce the current date and time in the report header.

FAQ How do I save a report as a Web page?

Once you've created a report, you can print it or post it on the Web. As with other Web pages, your report must be in HTML format to be accessible to Web browsers.

TRYIT!

Figure 18-9

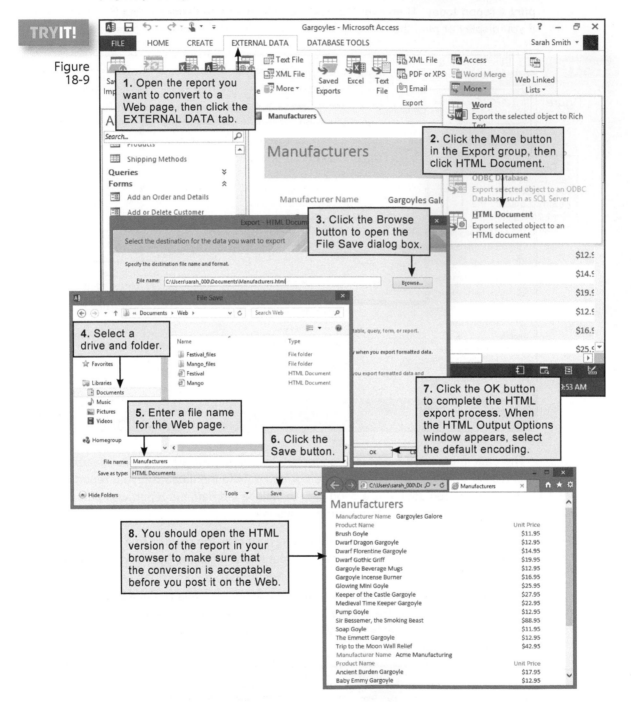

• Use a Web browser to preview the report as a Web page. Microsoft Access usually does a fairly good job when converting reports to Web pages, but you should check to make sure that the report layout and data appear to be correct.

• As the data in your database changes, the Web page version of the report will become increasingly out of date. Periodically, you should open the report and export it again as a Web page. This action ensures that all new data is included in the Web-based version of the report.

FAQ Do I need to specify relationships?

In a relational database, tables can be related to each other and you can use that feature to make data management more efficient. For example, suppose that you operate a small eBay store selling gargoyle merchandise. You maintain an Access database to keep track of your merchandise. You also would like to keep track of orders.

You quickly realize that it doesn't make sense to add fields for customer names and addresses to your table of merchandise. You also realize that because a customer can order more than one item at a time, you need some way to include several items in an order. To handle orders, you can create two additional tables: one table with information about who placed the order, and one table for the items in each order. You can create links between the data in the three tables to view the data as a single order form showing all the details about the customer and ordered items.

Figure 18-10

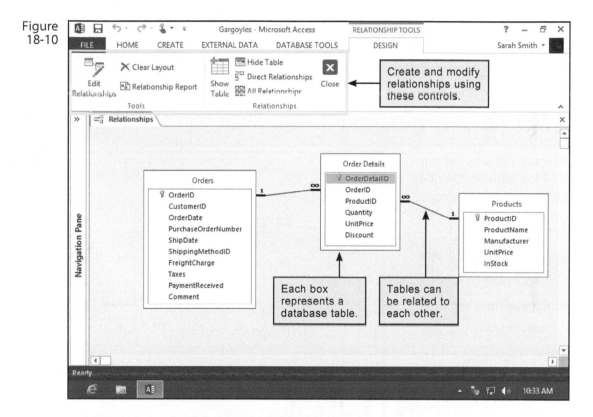

- In database terminology, a link between two tables is called a **relationship**. There are several types of relationships. In a **one-to-many relationship**, one record from a table is related to many records in another table, as when one order contains many items purchased by a customer.

- In a **many-to-many relationship**, a record in one table can be related to several records in another table and vice versa. This complex relationship exists between movies and actors. One movie can have many actors, but any of those actors can also have roles in many other movies. A **one-to-one relationship** means that a record in one table is related to only one record in another table. This type of relationship is rare in the world of databases.

- You can use the Relationships group on the DATABASE TOOLS tab to create, view, and modify relationships among the tables in a database. Projects AC-7 and AC-8 provide additional information about setting up and maintaining relationships within the tables of a database.

QuickCheck A

1. A database ▭ allows you to display one record at a time, rather than an entire table of data.

2. A database ▭ is typically a formatted printout of some or all of the data contained in a database.

3. True or false? You can use a form to view, edit, and add data to a table. ▭

4. True or false? Reports are updated each time you display them. ▭

5. True or false? Access automatically updates the data in Web pages every time you print a report. ▭

CHECKIT!

QuickCheck B

Indicate the letter of the desktop element that best matches the following:

1. A text field ▭

2. Add a record in Form view ▭

3. Access tools for relationships ▭

4. The *Last record* button ▭

5. Update the corresponding table ▭

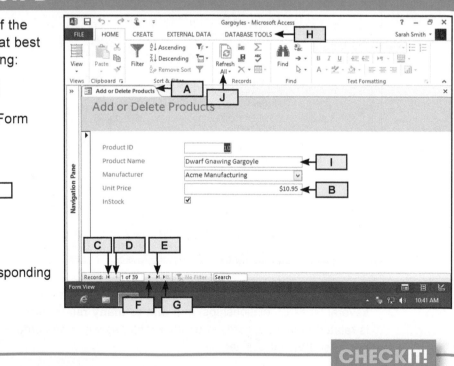

CHECKIT!

Skill Tests

| A | Creating forms | C | Printing reports |
| B | Creating reports | D | Generating Web page reports |

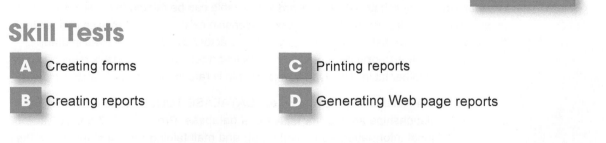

Online Connections

What's in this Section?

GETIT?

When you complete Section III, use the digital textbook to take Practice Tests by selecting the Get It? button.

CHAPTER

19 Networks

What's Inside and on the CD?

Today, networks are everywhere. Businesses, educational organizations, and government agencies all use computer networks to share information and resources. Home networks and public networks in coffee shops, airports, and other public places provide access to the largest network in existence—the Internet.

In this chapter, you'll learn basic network terminology, learn to identify network components, and learn about the variety of communications offered by local networks and the Internet.

FAQ What is a communications network?

A **communications network** is any collection of devices that have the ability to exchange signals and data with each other. Today, telephone, cellular phone, cable television, satellite television, and computer networks crisscross the globe and offer unprecedented access to information, people, and events.

Early communications networks, such as the telephone system, used a technology called **circuit switching**, which essentially established a dedicated, private link between one telephone and another for the duration of a call. This switching technique was the basis for the name "public switched telephone network" (PSTN), which was used to refer to the telephone system infrastructure.

In practice, circuit switching is rather inefficient. For example, when someone is on hold, no communication is taking place, yet the circuit is reserved and cannot be used for other communications. A more efficient alternative to circuit switching is **packet switching** technology, which divides messages into several packets that can be routed independently to their destination. A **packet** is simply a set of bits; it could be part of an e-mail message or part of a video download.

Packets from many different sources can share a single communications channel or circuit. Packets are shipped over the circuit on a first-come, first-served basis. If some packets from an e-mail message, for example, are not quite ready to send, the system does not wait for them. Instead, the system moves on to send packets from other sources. The end result is a steady stream of packets that take optimal advantage of the carrying capacity of a communications channel (Figure 19-1).

PLAYIT!

Figure 19-1

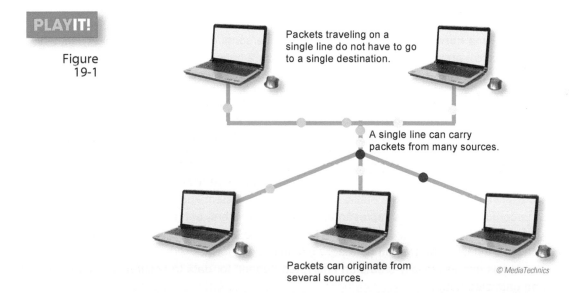

Packets traveling on a single line do not have to go to a single destination.

A single line can carry packets from many sources.

Packets can originate from several sources.

© MediaTechnics

Computer networks use packet switching technology to efficiently carry data. You can access computer networks using a personal computer, cell phone, computer game system, or other network-ready digital device. Network data is often stored on a **network server**, such as one that handles e-mail or movie downloads. When you access a network server, your computer acts as a **client** that receives data or other services. This arrangement of clients and servers is sometimes referred to as a client/server network.

• What is a communications network? (continued)

A **communications protocol** is a set of rules for efficiently transmitting data from one network device to another. Protocols allow diverse devices to communicate with each other. Communications protocols are also one of the factors that characterize various types of network standards, such as Ethernet, Wi-Fi, and Bluetooth.

- **Ethernet** is a popular network standard for businesses, school computer labs, and home networks. Ethernet is a wired network technology, requiring a cable to connect network devices.

- **Wi-Fi** (or WiFi) is a popular type of wireless network. Pronounced "Why Fhy," this type of network transmits data from one device to another using radio waves (also called RF signals). You're likely to encounter Wi-Fi networks in coffee shops, airports, and other public places. Wi-Fi is also a popular alternative to Ethernet for home, school, and business networks. Wi-Fi and Ethernet can coexist, too, so some networks include devices connected both wirelessly and with wires.

- **Bluetooth** is another wireless network technology, but it's reserved for short-range applications, such as transferring data between a mobile phone and a headset, or between a computer and peripheral devices.

A computer network can be as small as two PCs in a dorm room sharing a printer, or as large as the global Internet. A computer network can be categorized as a LAN or WAN.

A **wide area network** (WAN) covers a large geographical area and typically consists of several smaller networks, which might use different computer platforms and network technologies. Networks for nationwide banks and multi-location superstores can be classified as WANs. The Internet is the world's largest WAN.

A **local area network** (LAN) typically connects personal computers within a very limited geographical area—usually a single building. Home networks and computer labs are classified as LANs.

LAN and WAN technologies can merge and combine in a variety of ways to provide customized communications services. For example, an **intranet** is a scaled-down version of the Internet that links devices within an organization. An **extranet** is an intranet that allows access from outside an organization as well as from within it.

A **virtual private network** (VPN) is a type of extranet that allows remote users to connect to a private network using a public communications system such as the Internet. In the corporate world, sales representatives, telecommuters, and field workers can use their company's VPN server to access the corporate LAN without the risk of using a public connection that would be a possible entry point for hackers. VPNs use tunneling protocols that essentially create an encrypted "tunnel" for data to securely pass through an untrusted network.

Figure
19-2

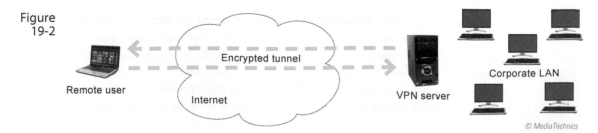

Remote user   Encrypted tunnel   Internet   VPN server   Corporate LAN

© MediaTechnics

FAQ How do I set up a local area network?

You can think of a network as a spiderweb with many interconnecting points. Each connection point on a network is referred to as a **network node**. A node typically contains a computer, but could also contain a network communication device, home entertainment equipment, or a network-ready printer. A typical local area network might include components like those in Figure 19-3.

Figure
19-3

© MediaTechnics

Setting up a local area network is not difficult. It involves the following steps that take only minutes to complete:

1. Purchase a router, unpack it, and plug it in.

2. Follow the router manufacturer's instructions to access the router setup utility.

3. In the setup utility, create a new router password that will be required to change network settings.

4. Enter an **SSID** (service set identifier) as the public name for your network. It is useful for a network to have a unique name, especially in neighborhoods where there are several overlapping networks.

5. Activate wireless encryption and select an encryption key that serves as the password required to connect to the network.

A **router** is a device that links two or more nodes of a network and is able to ship data from one network to another. Routers are handy for exchanging data between computers within a local area network and for connecting to the Internet. In a network configured with a router, all network data travels to the router before continuing to its destination.

PLAY**IT!**

Figure
19-4

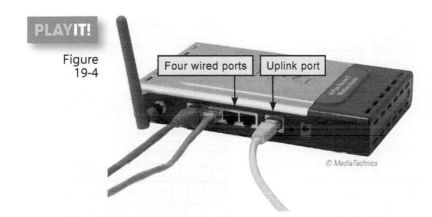

© MediaTechnics

Many routers can accept both wireless and wired connections. In Figure 19-4, the router's antenna transmits signals to Wi-Fi devices. Its four wired ports can connect to Ethernet devices, and the wired uplink port can connect to a modem for Internet access.

FAQ How do I connect to a local area network?

Windows automatically senses nearby networks and displays their SSIDs. To see a list of available networks when using Windows 7 or 8, click the  network icon, located in the notification area of the desktop. In Windows 8, you can also swipe from the right side of the screen and choose the network icon from there.

Some networks are secured, while others are open to the public. The icon that shows network strength also indicates if a network is secured.

Secured network icons

Unsecured network icons

Source: Microsoft Corporation; Google, Inc.; Apple Computers, Inc

The first time you want to connect to a secured network, you are required to enter the correct encryption key. When using a network that you did not set up, you can obtain the encryption key from the network administrator.

TRYIT!

Figure
19-5

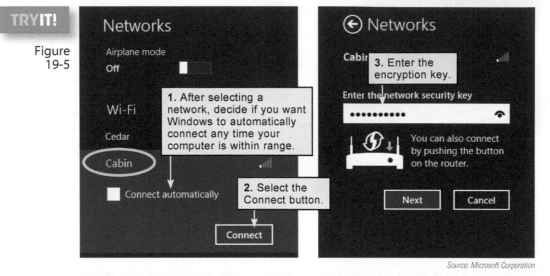

Source: Microsoft Corporation

Devices configured with iOS and Android operating systems can connect to LANs if they have Wi-Fi capability. The connection procedure is similar to the one you use with Windows. First, make sure that Wi-Fi is enabled, then wait for the device to sense the network. When asked, enter the encryption key as shown in Figure 19-6.

Figure
19-6

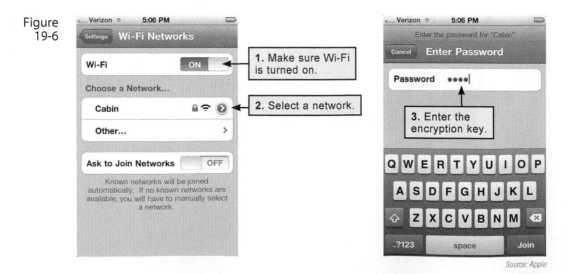

Source: Apple

FAQ How do I access files on a LAN?

When your computer is connected to a LAN, you have access to files designated as "shared" on other network computers. In a business setting or school lab, you might want to access files stored on a network file server. On a home network, you might want to move a photo from your tablet computer to your roommate's laptop.

When your computer is connected to a LAN, Windows automatically senses any devices that have been configured to be discoverable over the network. Discoverable devices are listed under the Network heading of File Explorer.

Windows also looks for users who are sharing their devices as part of your homegroup. You'll see 👤 user account icons under the Homegroup heading, rather than the 🖥 device icons displayed under the Network heading.

Figure 19-7

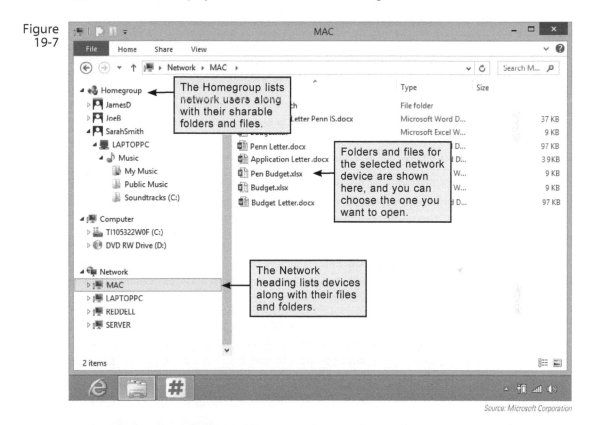

Source: Microsoft Corporation

- You can usually access the files stored in public folders listed under Network devices. However, to access other folders on these devices, you might have to enter a password.

- Homegroups are designed for computers with the Windows operating system, so they won't typically include computers running OS X, iOS, or Android. Computers with non-Windows operating systems can, however, appear under the Network heading. Therefore, if you are trying to access a Mac or an iPad, look for them there.

- When accessing files stored on other computers, be mindful of the changes you make and consider notifying the file's owner when you've made changes. When collaborating on projects, be sure to establish procedures so that one person in the group will not overwrite important changes made by other group members.

FAQ How does the Internet work?

The Internet is a global network that connects millions of smaller networks, computers, and other devices that exchange data using a standard communications protocol called **TCP/IP**. This protocol divides documents, e-mail messages, photos, and other digital files into standard-sized packets of data, which are shuttled to routers and on to their destination.

The Internet is not owned or operated by any single corporation or government. Instead, it has grown over time in a somewhat haphazard configuration as networks connected to other networks and to the core Internet infrastructure.

The Internet is maintained by **network service providers** (NSPs) such as AT&T, British Telecom, Sprint, and Verizon. NSP equipment and links are tied together by **network access points** (NAPs), so that, for example, data can begin its journey on a Verizon link and then cross over to a Sprint link, if necessary, to reach its destination. NSPs supply Internet connections to large Internet service providers, such as EarthLink, AOL, and Comcast. An **Internet service provider** (ISP) is a company that offers Internet access to individuals, businesses, and smaller ISPs.

Every device on the Internet has a unique **IP address** (also called an Internet address) that identifies it in the same way that a street address identifies the location of a house. When your computer is connected to any network that uses Internet protocols, it also has an IP address, which is attached to every packet of data you send or receive.

IPv4 (Internet Protocol version 4) addresses, such as 204.127.129.1, are divided by periods into four segments called **octets**. Longer **IPv6** addresses are divided by colons into eight segments, like this 2001:0db8:85 a3:0000:0000:8a2e:0370:7334.

A computer can have a permanently assigned **static IP address** or a temporarily assigned **dynamic IP address**. Typically ISPs, Web sites, Web hosting services, and e-mail servers that always need to be at the same address require static IP addresses. Most other network users have dynamic IP addresses.

Your computer can be assigned an IP address by a network administrator or an ISP. IP addresses can also be assigned by **DHCP** (Dynamic Host Configuration Protocol) servers. Figure 19-8 shows you how to find the IP address of your computer.

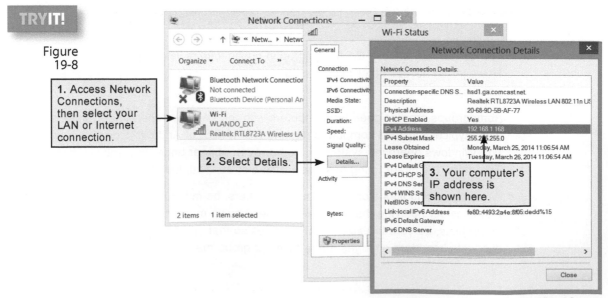

TRYIT!

Figure 19-8

1. Access Network Connections, then select your LAN or Internet connection.

2. Select Details.

3. Your computer's IP address is shown here.

Source: Microsoft Corporation

• How does the Internet work? (continued)

Although IP addresses work for communication between computers, people find it difficult to remember long strings of numbers. Therefore, many Internet servers also have an easy-to-remember name, such as nike.com. The official term for this name is fully qualified domain name (FQDN), but most people just refer to it as a **domain name**. By convention, you should type domain names using all lowercase letters.

A domain name is a key component of e-mail addresses and Web site addresses. It is the e-mail server name in an e-mail address and the Web server name in a Web address. For example, in the Web address www.msu.edu/infotech, the domain name is msu.edu.

A domain name ends with an extension, such as .com or .org, that indicates its **top-level domain**. For example, in msu.edu, edu is the top-level domain and indicates that the computer is maintained by an educational institution. Country codes also serve as top-level domains. For example, Canada's top-level domain is ca; the United Kingdom's is uk; and Australia's is au. Some of the most commonly used top-level domains are listed in Figure 19-9.

Figure 19-9

Domain	Description
biz	Unrestricted use; usually for commercial businesses
com	Unrestricted use; usually for commercial businesses
edu	Restricted to North American educational institutions
gov	Restricted to U.S. government agencies
info	Unrestricted use
int	Restricted to organizations established by international treaties
mil	Restricted to U.S. military agencies
net	Unrestricted use; traditionally for Internet administrative organizations
org	Unrestricted use; traditionally for professional and nonprofit organizations

© MediaTechnics

All of the Internet's domain names and corresponding IP addresses are stored on a system of computers called the **Domain Name System** (DNS). When an individual or a business registers a domain name for a Web site or an Internet service, records maintained by the DNS are updated. This process is autonomous and it sometimes takes 24 hours for the new domains to propagate through the system. Domain names can be registered for a small annual fee at sites such as register.com and networksolutions.com.

Figure 19-10

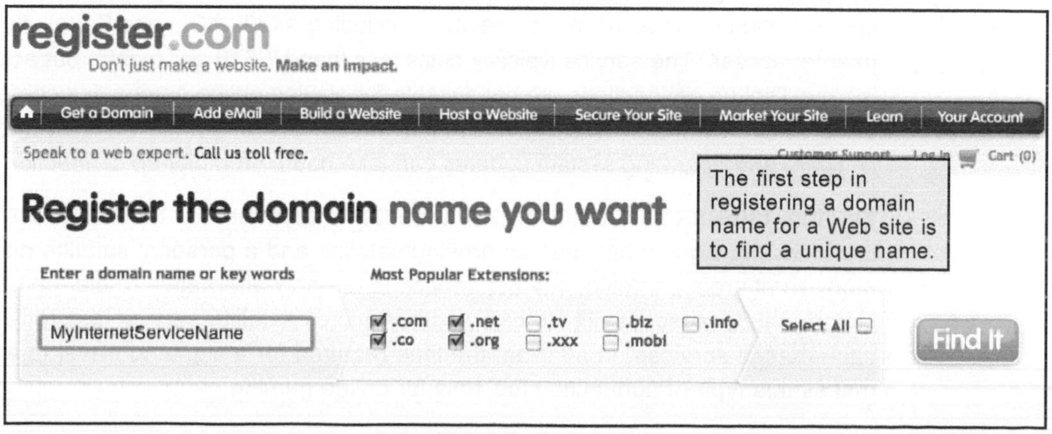

register.com
Don't just make a website. **Make an impact.**

| Get a Domain | Add eMail | Build a Website | Host a Website | Secure Your Site | Market Your Site | Learn | Your Account |

Speak to a web expert. **Call us toll free.**   Customer Support   Log In   Cart (0)

Register the domain name you want

The first step in registering a domain name for a Web site is to find a unique name.

Enter a domain name or key words   Most Popular Extensions:

MyInternetServiceName   ☑ .com ☑ .net ☐ .tv   ☐ .biz   ☐ .info   Select All ☐   **Find It**
                              ☑ .co   ☑ .org ☐ .xxx ☐ .mobi

Source: Register.com

FAQ How do I connect my computer to the Internet?

Computers can be connected to the Internet through telephone lines, cable television systems, satellites, cellular networks, wireless hotspots, and local area networks. Internet services vary in cost, speed, and reliability.

The capacity of an Internet connection is sometimes referred to as **bandwidth** and can be measured in bits per second. The slowest connections transmit a mere 56 Kbps (56 thousand bits per second), whereas fast connections, called **broadband**, blaze away at 100 Mbps (100 *million* bits per second) or more. Capacity is related to speed, and often the two are used interchangeably—though technically speeds would be measured in milliseconds (ms). Higher capacity and faster speeds are better if you want to play online games, use voice over IP, participate in Web conferences, or watch online videos.

Some Internet services offer **symmetrical connections**, in which data travels **upstream** from your computer to the Internet at the same speed as data traveling **downstream** from the Internet to your computer. However, **asymmetrical connections** are more common, with data traveling faster downstream than upstream. When using an asymmetric connection, for example, uploading a video typically requires more time than downloading it.

Internet connections are classified as **always-on connections** if they remain active even when you are not online. With an always-on connection, your IP address can remain the same for days, weeks, or even months. However, an active connection makes your computer more vulnerable to intrusions from online hackers.

Cable Internet service is a means of distributing broadband Internet access over the same infrastructure that offers cable television service. Cable companies, such as Comcast and Charter Communications, offer cable Internet service for a monthly subscription. Of all Internet services, cable Internet currently offers the fastest access speeds. However, advertised speeds are usually for downstream data transfer. Upstream speeds might be much slower. Cable Internet service uses a cable modem to transfer data from your computer to your home cable connection and then to the Internet.

DSL (digital subscriber line) is a broadband, Internet access technology that works over standard phone lines. It offers fast, affordable connections. DSL is available from local telephone companies and third-party DSL providers. DSL services can be symmetrical or asymmetrical. If you need lots of upstream speed, a symmetrical DSL connection could be the best choice.

Dial-up Internet service uses a **voiceband modem** and telephone lines to transport data between your computer and an ISP. The modem converts digital data that originates on your computer into an analog signal that can travel over the same frequencies as voices carrying on a telephone conversation. Several ISPs, including AT&T, AOL, and EarthLink, offer dial-up Internet access. The service typically costs less than US$10 per month, but access speed is slow. Dial-up connections are not suitable for playing online games, teleconferencing, using voice over IP, or watching videos that stream down from the Web. Even downloading software and operating system updates can take hours on a dial-up connection.

Satellite Internet service distributes broadband asymmetric Internet access by broadcasting signals between an orbiting satellite and a personal satellite dish. In many rural areas, satellite Internet service is the only alternative to dial-up access. Unfortunately, susceptibility to bad weather makes satellite service less reliable than cable-based services. In addition, the time required for a signal to travel to a satellite makes this type of connection too slow for online gaming.

• How do I connect my computer to the Internet? (continued)

Mobile broadband service transmits data from your computer to a nearby communications tower, which then links to the Internet. This service is offered by wireless cellular phone service providers, such as Verizon, AT&T, and Sprint. The speed and reliability of these connections can deteriorate as the distance to the tower increases. Signals can be disrupted by interference from electrical appliances and environmental factors such as hills, valleys, trees, brick walls, and concrete floors.

Local area networks also provide Internet access. Typically, the LAN's router is connected to a cable Internet or DSL provider and can pass the service along to any of the computers connected to the LAN. Many home networks are configured to allow one Internet connection to be shared by multiple computers.

Coffee shops, airports, hotels, libraries, school campuses, and many other locations offer public access to the Internet through a Wi-Fi hotspot. A **Wi-Fi hotspot** is basically a wireless local area network that provides access to guests using laptop computers or mobile devices. Some hotspots are free, whereas others require guests to register, pay a fee, and obtain a user ID and password to log in. Many hotspots are unsecured, so legitimate users should be cautious about sending and receiving sensitive data while connected to hotspots.

Because so many factors affect the speed of an Internet connection, you shouldn't be surprised if your connection speed varies from one day to the next. For example, your connection might seem slow if you're working with multiple browsers at the same time, or trying to use other Internet services while downloading a movie in iTunes.

Additional factors that can slow down a connection include the number of users logged in to your Internet service, environmental factors that affect the speed of wireless connections, the amount of traffic that's circulating on the Internet, rerouting caused by equipment failures, and bottlenecks caused by viruses. You can check the speed of your Internet connection using tools such as Ping or Speedtest.net (Figure 19-11).

TRY IT!

Figure 19-11

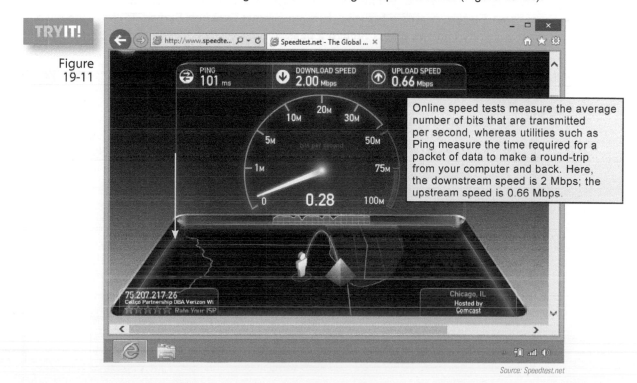

Online speed tests measure the average number of bits that are transmitted per second, whereas utilities such as Ping measure the time required for a packet of data to make a round-trip from your computer and back. Here, the downstream speed is 2 Mbps; the upstream speed is 0.66 Mbps.

Source: Speedtest.net

FAQ How do I access files stored in the cloud?

Suppose you are taking part in a group research project, and all the group members need access to the set of documents you're developing. Or, suppose that you want to store your photo collection in a location where it can be accessed while you are away from your desk. For situations in which you want to store files somewhere other than your local hard disk or USB drives, there are two popular options: cloud storage services and FTP.

Cloud storage services, such as iCloud and Microsoft SkyDrive, allow customers to store files on remote Internet servers and access these files as necessary, either directly from the server or by downloading them to a local device. Cloud storage services require registration and are generally fee-based. Software for accessing stored files can be a standalone utility, or it can be built into software applications and browsers. It is usually downloaded and installed automatically as part of the registration process.

In an earlier chapter, you learned how easy it is to store files on Microsoft SkyDrive, simply by saving them in the SkyDrive folder. Accessing those files is just as easy: Simply navigate to the SkyDrive folder and select the file you want to view and edit.

Figure
19-12

Source: Microsoft Corporation

FTP (File Transfer Protocol) provides a way to transfer files from one computer to another over any TCP/IP network. The purpose of FTP is to make it easy to upload and download computer files without having to deal directly with the operating system or file management utility of a remote computer. FTP sites can be accessed with FTP software, such as Filezilla, or with a browser, such as Internet Explorer. Some FTP sites are open to the public, whereas others require a password for access. FTP is an open technology, and FTP sites generally offer free access to approved users.

Figure
19-13

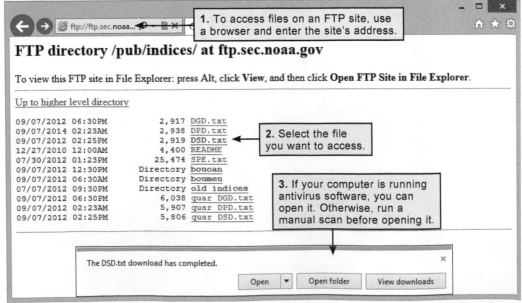

Source: Microsoft Corporation

FAQ What communications options does the Internet offer?

The Internet offers many tools for communicating and collaborating; and more are appearing every day. These tools can be classified using two sets of criteria: 1) synchronous or asynchronous; 2) public or private.

Synchronous. When a communications tool is **synchronous**, interchanges happen in real time and all parties must be online at the same time. This form of communication requires scheduling, and participants don't have much time to research or consider responses. With synchronous communication, however, participants can get feedback and responses immediately. Telephone calls are synchronous, as are video conferences.

Asynchronous. When communication is **asynchronous**, messages are held until the recipient is ready to view them. There is a convenience factor with this type of communication, and it affords time to research and consider messages before replying. E-mail is an example of asynchronous communication.

Public. Public communications can be accessed by individuals unknown to the person who has created a message. The word "posting" is associated with this type of communication because it is similar to posting a billboard, sign, or poster. Public communications can reach a wide audience, but messages are often viewed out of context. Therefore, it is important for posted messages to be clear and complete. Blogs and their comments would be considered public communications. Messages, files, and media posted on public sites originate from individuals, some of whom might be using false identities. Information might not be factual and images may have been altered. You should cross-check and verify facts from these sources.

Private. Communications for which you specify one or more recipients would be classified as private. Text messaging is a popular type of private communication. The advantage is that you can specify the initial recipients. They know you and have some context in which to interpret what you say or write. A limited audience can be an advantage or a disadvantage, depending on what you hope the message will accomplish. Be aware, however, that private messages can be forwarded by recipients, so they do not necessarily remain private.

Figure 19-14 lists today's most popular Internet-based communications technologies within a matrix based on public, private, synchronous, and asynchronous characteristics.

Figure 19-14

Public Asynchronous	Public Synchronous
RSS	Chat rooms
Blogs	
Podcasts	
Microblogs (Twitter)	
Forums and discussion groups	
Social media sites (YouTube, Pinterest)	
Private Asynchronous	**Private Synchronous**
Instant messaging (ICQ, AIM)	E-mail (Gmail, Outlook)
Text messaging services (SMS)	Voice over IP (Skype)
Multimedia messaging services (MMS)	Video conferencing (WebEx, Skype)
Social networking services* (Facebook)	

*Many social networking services offer several ways for participants to communicate, and not all are private and asynchronous.

© MediaTechnics

• What communications options does the Internet offer? (continued)

E-mail is one of the most well-known network-based tools, but many other tools operate on LANs, cellular networks, and the Internet. You'll read more about e-mail in later chapters, but the following communication and collaboration tools have their own unique uses.

Forums and **discussion groups** are two popular technologies for communicating and collaborating online. They typically offer a place where participants can post a message, which is read and responded to by other participants who log in later. Forums and discussion groups usually focus on a specific topic, and participants are required to subscribe to the group before they can log in. You might find yourself accessing a forum for solutions to technical support issues, but remember that participants are not necessarily experts and their advice is not always correct.

Instant messaging (IM) is a form of quick communication in which a message is typed, sent to one or more people, and received instantly. IM is typically computer-based and requires access to a network-based IM server that tracks who is logged in and delivers messages. Senders and recipients typically are both online during the exchange. ICQ was one of the original programs used for IM. AOL's AIM and Microsoft's Windows Messenger became popular with early adopters. Newer IM platforms include Google Talk and Facebook Messenger. Also referred to as online chat, IM offers a quick response to questions and allows people to coordinate activities and send short informational messages without getting involved in extended verbal communications.

TRYIT!

Figure
19-15

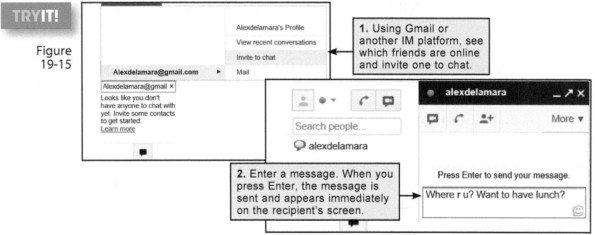

Source: Google

Text messaging (TM) refers to exchanging short messages usually sent over a mobile phone service. Text messaging is also called texting or SMS (Short Message Service). Text messaging is an asynchronous service; messages are delivered to a mobile device, where they are stored until viewed. In addition to its popularity for communicating with friends and colleagues, text messaging is used extensively to collect opinions and votes for reality shows such as American Idol. However, TM has also been misused for cheating on exams, and texting while driving can pose a public safety problem. An extension of this technology, Multimedia Messaging Service (MMS), can be used to send photo and video content to and from mobile phones.

Chat rooms provide a synchronous environment in which a group of participants share text-based information or voice chat. Pioneered by AOL and similar online services, chat rooms were an early form of social networking where people met and interacted in cyberspace. The popularity of chat rooms is declining as more sophisticated online environments for social networking have become available.

• What communications options does the Internet offer? (continued)

Voice over IP (VoIP) carries voice conversations over a computer network. VoIP software installed locally converts audio signals into digital data, divides it into packets, and ships it over the Internet through numerous routers to a specified destination where the packets are assembled into a coherent audio stream—all in less than a second. Although the technology sounds a bit complex, VoIP call quality is similar to that of a cell phone and offers substantial cost savings over cellular or landline phone service. Skype is one of the most popular VoIP technologies; and now with the option to transmit live video, it serves as a video conferencing platform, too.

Web conferencing and **video conferencing** technologies allow participants at two or more locations to interact through two-way video carried over the Internet or over the telephone system. Video conferencing applications, such as WebEx and GoToMeeting, offer substantial cost savings for business meetings, distance education, legal proceedings, and telemedicine because participants are spared the cost of travel. Conferencing software is usually installed locally, but mediated through a Web-based subscription service.

Social networking services, such as Facebook and LinkedIn, are designed for people to reconnect with old friends and coworkers, and make new social or professional contacts. Typically, a participant uses tools supplied by the service to create a profile that includes information about schools attended, hometown, friends, hobbies, and interests. A built-in referral system helps participants contact other participants with similar interests. Members can update and change their online status by modifying their profiles to bring them up to date, to enhance their privacy, or to discontinue their membership.

Social media sites, such as YouTube and Pinterest, provide a public forum for posting media such as photos and videos. People who access these sites can search for media related to various subjects. Much of the media is simply entertaining, but educational media also exist at these sites, which can be useful research tools.

A **blog** (short for "Web log") is a series of entries posted online similar to the entries in a diary or commentary expressed in a daily editorial column. Blogs are typically text-based, though videoblogs (vlogs) and photoblogs also exist. Software to create a blog using your computer or smartphone is free and readily available. The majority of blogs are personal and typically recount significant life events or opinions. These blogs often remain private, but many are open to the public. Blogs intended for public access sometimes focus on a particular topic; political, travel, and fashion blogs are popular. Blogs and similar content are sometimes delivered by an automated RSS (Really Simple Syndication) "feed" and read with an RSS reader or aggregator software.

A **podcast** is a series of audio files posted for public playback. Like radio shows, podcasts usually contain narrative commentary, sometimes combined with music.

Microblogs, such as Twitter and Tumblr, provide a platform for posting short text messages, small photos, or short videos.

Figure
19-16

Source: Twitter, Inc.

FAQ How do I configure my social networking sites?

Social networking sites, such as Facebook and LinkedIn, offer a variety of handy communications tools. Configuring your personal settings takes some care, however, to ensure that private communications and media are not broadcast over the site's public communications outlets.

Immediately after signing up for a social networking site, or any other site, check the site's privacy policy to find out how your personal information might be shared with other sites, advertisers, and other individuals. Then look for links to privacy and security settings. Review these settings carefully and consider the following tips for avoiding identity theft and embarrassing situations where private data becomes public:

- **Password.** Select a strong password and change it periodically to prevent interlopers from accessing and defacing your account.

- **Public profile.** Supply minimal information in your public profile. Avoid broadcasting your address and phone number, and never place your Social Security number or financial information on a social networking site.

- **Timeline and history.** On some social networking sites, other users can post entries in your timeline or personal history. If you activate this feature, be sure to check the entries frequently to make sure they are accurate.

- **Posts and lookups.** Make sure you know if your posts will be broadcast publicly, just to friends, just to family, or just to other groups you've set up in your networking circles.

- **Photo tagging.** When photos are uploaded to social networking sites, facial recognition utilities can automatically tag your name to a photo that resembles you. Mistaken identities can lead to sticky situations, so you might want to turn this feature off.

- **Blocking.** Social networking sites are full of lurkers who greet newbies with salacious photos and provocative proposals. You may also encounter undesirable friends of friends who post incessantly or get too personal. Knowing how to block these nuisances is a useful safety feature.

TRY IT!

Figure 19-17

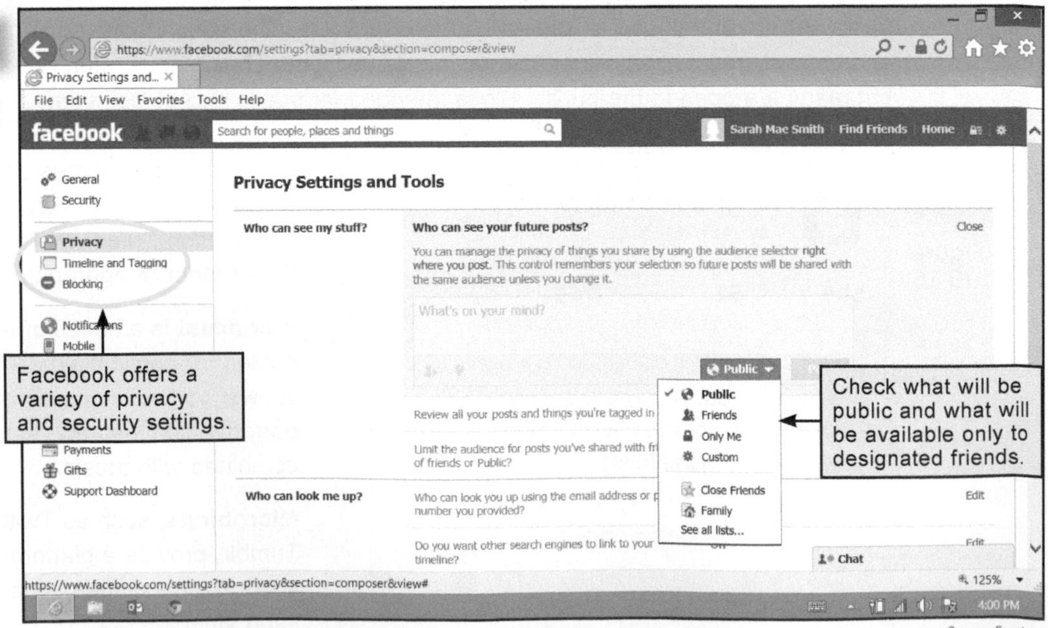

Facebook offers a variety of privacy and security settings.

Check what will be public and what will be available only to designated friends.

Source: Facebook

FAQ What is netiquette?

Electronic communications are just bits, but the messages they contain can be important. They can affect your job status. They can also affect other peoples' feelings and their reputations.

Netiquette is online jargon for "Internet etiquette." It is a series of customs or guidelines for avoiding misunderstandings, maintaining civilized discourse, and carrying on effective communication in online discussions, instant messages, text messages, and e-mail exchanges. The most important rules of netiquette include:

- Distinguish between business and personal. Make sure you consider the purpose of the correspondence and tailor your message accordingly. Business correspondence is more formal than casual messages to friends. Avoid using abbreviations, slang, smileys, and text message shorthand in business communications. **Smileys** are symbols that represent emotions. For example, the ;-) smiley means "just joking." Smileys can help convey the intent behind your words, but are most appropriate in casual correspondence; ditto for text messaging shorthand like "Where r u?" and "LOL" (laughing out loud).

- Respond promptly. Try to respond promptly to messages and make your replies concise and accurate.

- Proofread messages before you send them. Check spelling and grammar. Use uppercase and lowercase letters. A message that's typed in all uppercase means that you're shouting.

- Be cautious when using sarcasm and humor. The words in your messages and posts arrive without facial expressions or voice intonations, so a sarcastic comment can easily be misinterpreted.

- Be polite. Avoid wording that could sound inflammatory or confrontational. If you would not say it face-to-face, don't say it in electronic communications. **Flaming** is the practice of making deliberately hostile comments for the purpose of inciting emotionally heated discussions. Starting flame wars is considered bad netiquette. To avoid getting caught up in a flame war, do not respond to inflammatory comments. Even offering supportive comments to the flamee just adds fuel to the fire.

- Be respectful of people's privacy. Everyone has embarrassing incidents in their lives, but it is not appropriate to publicly broadcast those incidents without the person's permission. **Cyberbullying** is the repeated use of Internet-based communications technologies to deliberately harm other people through intimidation, humiliation, or embarrassment. You know it is wrong. Just don't do it.

- Be truthful. Spreading false information about a person verbally is called slander; spreading false information in written or pictorial form is called libel. Both are illegal, so be careful about posting a photo that's been altered to depict someone in an embarrassing situation.

- Avoid sexting. Make sure you follow school and company guidelines on the use of electronic communications. National, state, and local laws may also apply. Don't use e-mail or other electronic communications for illegal or unethical activities, such as cheating on exams or posting sexually explicit photos of yourself or others.

FAQ How do I troubleshoot network connectivity problems?

Networks sometimes fail and cut off users from important services, such as e-mail and Internet access. Network-wide system failures can occur on a local area network or on sections of the Internet. There is not much individuals can do to correct problems on the Internet. They can, however, troubleshoot problems with their local Internet connections and local area networks. If your Internet connection stops working, try the following:

- **Make sure wireless networking is on.** Many laptop computers have a physical switch on the keyboard or case that turns wireless networking off or on. To connect wirelessly to a network, the wireless switch must be on.

- **Check airplane mode.** Make sure your device is not in airplane mode, which disables all transmitting and receiving operations. In airplane mode, a device cannot make voice calls or connect to a network.

- **Check connection status.** Use the ▂▃▄ icon to make sure your device is connected to a network and the network has adequate signal strength. If signal strength is weak, move the device closer to the router, if possible.

- **Locate interference.** If you have intermittent network outages, look for sources of interference, such as cordless phones, baby monitors, or construction equipment.

- **Check the router.** Make sure the network router is functioning correctly. Its activity lights indicate if it is sending and receiving data. Rebooting a router can sometimes restore its connections. To reboot, unplug the router from the power source, wait about five seconds, and then plug it in again.

- **Use the Windows network troubleshooter.** Windows provides a set of troubleshooting utilities to identify and fix problems with Internet connections, homegroups, shared folders, network circuitry, and incoming connections. Enter network trouble in the Windows Search box, select Settings, then select the option *Identify and repair network problems*. You can then select a troubleshooting option, as shown below.

TRYIT!

Figure 19-18

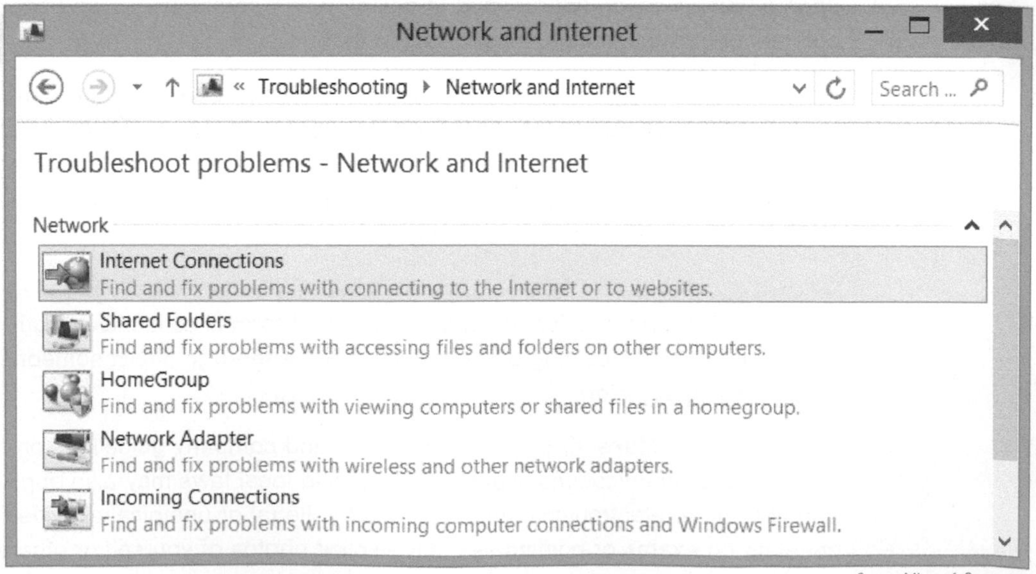

Source: Microsoft Corporation

QuickCheck A

1. A communications [   ] is a set of rules implemented by telecommunications software that is typically supplied with your computer's operating system.

2. [   ] is the transmission capacity of a communications channel.

3. A device called a(n) [   ] links two or more nodes of a network and can also link to the Internet.

4. When communication is [   ] , messages are held until the recipient is ready to view them.

5. True or false? All of the Internet's domain names and corresponding IP addresses are stored on a system of computers called DHCP. [   ]

CHECK**IT!**

QuickCheck B

Indicate the letter of the Explorer element that best matches the following:

1. A folder that holds shared files [   ]

2. A list of network users [   ]

3. A list of network devices [   ]

4. An Internet-based folder [   ]

5. A list of storage devices [   ]

SkyDrive ←— **A.**

◢ Libraries ←— **B.**
  ▷ Documents
  ▷ Music
  ◢ Pictures ←— **C.**
    My Pictures
    Public Pictures ←— **D.**
  ▷ Videos

▷ Homegroup ←— **E.**

▷ Computer ←— **F.**

▷ Network ←— **G.**

Source: Microsoft Corporation

CHECK**IT!**

CHAPTER 20

Working with E-mail

What's Inside and on the CD?

Billions of messages speed over the Internet every day. Electronic mail, which is usually abbreviated as "e-mail" or "email," has become an essential element of modern life. It is inexpensive and easy to use, delivers messages in a matter of seconds, and lets you broadcast the same message simultaneously to more than one person.

In the workplace, e-mail allows people in diverse locations to collaborate on projects and share ideas. Students use e-mail to communicate with instructors, submit assignments, and chat with other students. Home-based computer owners take advantage of e-mail to keep in touch with friends and relatives.

In this chapter, you'll learn the basics of e-mail. Examples and instructions are provided for Gmail and Microsoft Outlook—two of the most popular e-mail applications.

FAQ What is e-mail?

E-mail is an electronic version of the postal system that transmits messages from one computer to another, usually over the Internet. The term "e-mail" can refer to a single message or to the entire system of computers and software that transmits, receives, and stores e-mail messages.

An **e-mail message** is an electronic document transmitted over a computer network. E-mail messages arrive in your electronic **Inbox** where they can be stored for later use, forwarded to individuals or groups, and organized to create electronic audit trails that provide a record of messages and their replies. As you compose e-mail messages, they can be stored in an **Outbox** until you are ready to send them. Once messages are sent, a copy is usually stored in a folder called Sent Mail.

E-mail messages have a standard format that consists of two major sections: a header and body. An **e-mail header** is divided into fields that contain the sender's e-mail address, the recipient's address, a one-line summary of the message, and the date and time the message was written. Additional fields can contain addresses for sending copies, priority levels, and tracking information.

Information in the header fields is important. The From field can be used to sort messages according to the sender. Dates help you keep track of the order in which messages were received and sent. The Subject field can be used to arrange messages into "threads" or "conversations" so you can track the discussion process.

The body of an e-mail message contains the message itself and the data for any photos or supplementary files that are attached to the e-mail message. Figure 20-1 illustrates the main parts of an e-mail message.

Figure 20-1

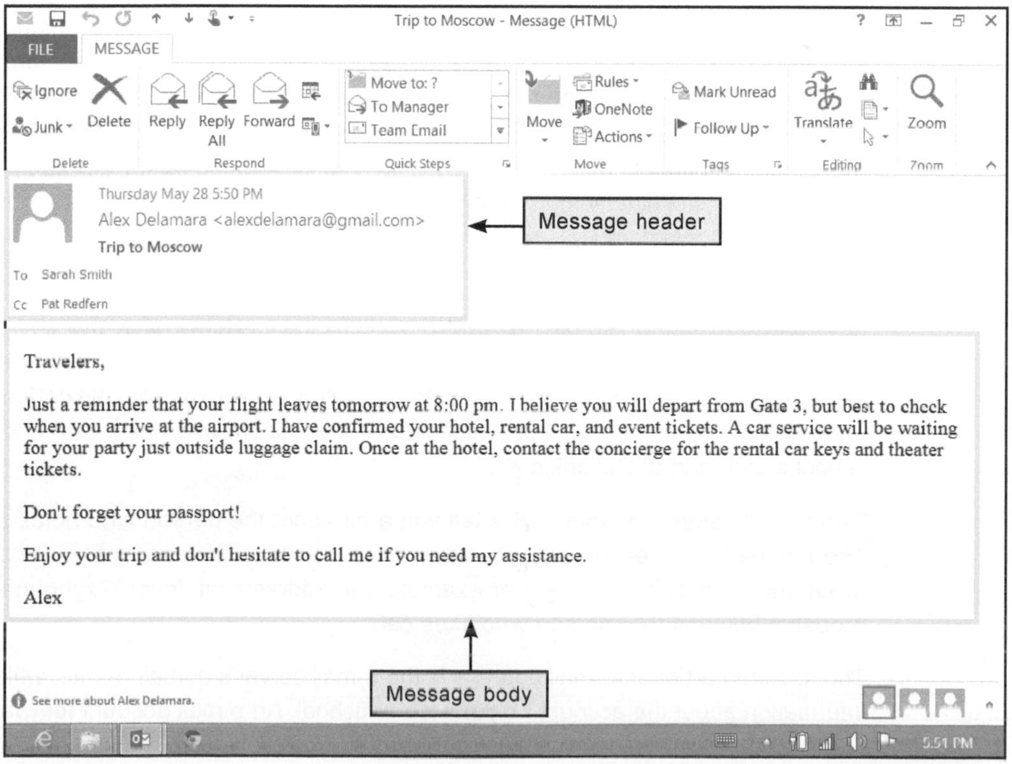

Source: Microsoft Corporation

• What is e-mail? (continued)

The computers and software that provide e-mail services form an **e-mail system**. At the heart of a typical e-mail system is an **e-mail server**—a computer that essentially acts as a central post office for a group of people. E-mail servers run special e-mail server software, which provides an electronic mailbox for each person, sorts incoming messages into these mailboxes, and routes outgoing mail over the Internet to other e-mail servers. To use an e-mail system, you need an Internet connection, an e-mail account, and software to compose e-mail messages.

Internet connection. As you learned in earlier chapters, Internet connections are available from telephone, cable, satellite, and cellular service providers. Wi-Fi hotspots and local area networks at home, school, or work can also provide Internet access. Any of these connections work for e-mail, though a dial-up connection will respond slowly when sending or receiving messages with photos or other large files attached.

E-mail account. Obtaining an e-mail account gets your electronic mailbox set up on an e-mail server. Your ISP might play the role of postmaster by establishing an e-mail account for you. You can also obtain an e-mail account from a Web-based e-mail service, such as Outlook.com, AOL Mail, Gmail, or Yahoo! Mail.

E-mail software. The software you use to send, receive, and manage messages is called **e-mail client software**. It is available for desktop computers, laptops, tablets, and smartphones. Some e-mail software can be installed on a local device such as a computer hard disk, whereas other e-mail software can be stored as a portable app on a USB flash drive, or accessed from the Web through a browser. E-mail systems based on client software that's installed locally are referred to as **local e-mail**. Systems that provide access to e-mail through a browser are called **Webmail**.

Whether you use local e-mail or Webmail, your e-mail account has a unique **e-mail address**. Like the address on a letter, an e-mail address provides the information necessary to route messages to a specified mailbox. An e-mail address typically consists of a user ID (also called a user name), followed by the @ sign and the name of the e-mail server that manages the user's electronic post office box. For example, the e-mail address john_smith@mtc.com refers to the e-mail account for John Smith on the e-mail server named mtc.com.

In order for e-mail to be routed correctly, each e-mail address must be unique. Gmail can have only one JohnSmith user ID, which explains the existence of e-mail addresses such as JohnSmith256@gmail.com and JSmithTraverseCity@gmail.com. You can, however, use the same user ID for e-mail accounts on different servers. For example, AlexV@msu.edu and AlexV@outlook.com are perfectly acceptable for a student who has e-mail accounts on a school server and at Outlook.com.

E-mail addresses can sometimes tell you a bit about the person who holds the account. The first part of an e-mail address often corresponds to the account holder's name, nickname, or online persona. For example, the address cat_lover32@hotmail.com probably belongs to a person who likes cats.

The second part of an e-mail address is the e-mail server's domain name, which can provide information about the account holder's job or school. An e-mail account for jwatson@ibm.com probably belongs to an IBM employee. An account for rbutler@uga.edu probably belongs to a student at the University of Georgia. An account for gijoe@centcom.mil might belong to a member of the U.S. military.

FAQ How does local e-mail work?

When you use local e-mail, an e-mail server stores your incoming messages until you launch your e-mail client and get your mail. Messages are then downloaded to a folder on a local storage device that serves as your e-mail Inbox. Once the messages are stored on your computer, the e-mail server removes them from your server-based mailbox.

Using your e-mail client, you can read your mail at your leisure. You can also compose new mail and reply to messages. This outgoing mail can be temporarily stored in an Outbox or it can be sent immediately.

The protocol **POP3** (Post Office Protocol version 3) is typically used to manage your incoming mail, whereas **SMTP** (Simple Mail Transfer Protocol) handles outgoing mail. Keep these two protocols in mind when setting up local e-mail because the server you specify for outgoing mail might be different from the server for incoming mail.

Figure
20-2

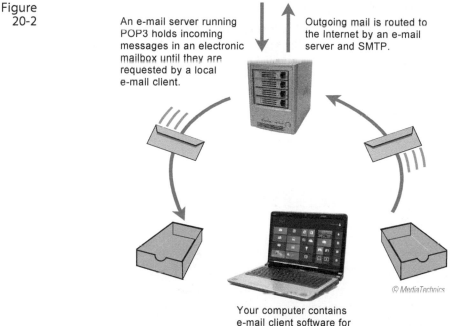

An e-mail server running POP3 holds incoming messages in an electronic mailbox until they are requested by a local e-mail client.

Outgoing mail is routed to the Internet by an e-mail server and SMTP.

© MediaTechnics

Your computer contains e-mail client software for reading and composing messages.

Because local e-mail stores your Inbox and Outbox on your computer, you can compose and read mail offline. You are required to go online only to transfer outgoing mail from your Inbox to the e-mail server, and to receive incoming messages. On a slow dial-up connection or in situations where you are charged for dial-up service by the minute, local e-mail might be preferable to Webmail.

Local mail also works well with broadband always-on connections, such as DSL, cable Internet, or satellite Internet. When using these connections, you can remain online throughout the entire process of collecting, reading, and sending mail. By configuring your e-mail client to send messages immediately, messages can be sent as they are composed instead of remaining in your Outbox and being sent as a batch.

The major advantage of local mail is control. Once your messages are transferred to your computer's hard disk, you can control access to them. With this control, however, comes the responsibility for maintaining backups of your important e-mail messages.

FAQ How do I set up local e-mail?

To set up local e-mail, the first step is selecting a local e-mail client. Microsoft Outlook is one of the most popular e-mail clients. Thunderbird, a free open source e-mail client, is another popular alternative, and several other very serviceable e-mail clients are available as shareware.

After installing an e-mail client, you can configure it for the e-mail service you're using. Your e-mail provider usually supplies the information needed for this task. That information can include the following:

- Your e-mail user ID, which is the first part of your e-mail address (For example, in AlexHamilton@gsu.edu, the user ID is AlexHamilton.)

- Your e-mail password, if required to access the e-mail server

- An address for the outgoing (SMTP) server, typically something like mail.viserver.net or smtp.mailisus.com

- An address for the incoming (POP3) server, typically something like mail.gsu.edu or pop.mailserver.net

To configure a local e-mail client such as Thunderbird, look for an Account Settings option on the Tools menu. When using Microsoft Outlook, click the FILE tab, then click the Add Account button.

TRY IT!

Figure
20-3

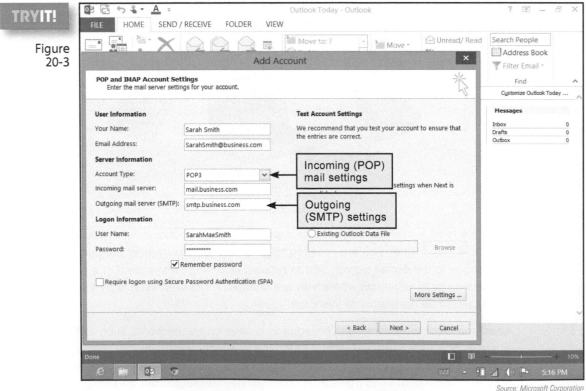

Source: Microsoft Corporation

FAQ How does Webmail work?

Webmail is typically a free service accessed using a browser. Most Webmail services also can be accessed using a local e-mail client, such as Microsoft Outlook, if you prefer a local client's feature set and do not want to remain online while reading and composing messages.

In a classic Webmail configuration, your Inbox is stored on the Web; and because messages are sent immediately, an Outbox is not needed. When you want to read or send mail, use a browser to go to your e-mail provider's Web site and log in. The controls for reading, composing, and managing messages are all presented in the browser window. While reading and composing mail, you typically must remain online. Figure 20-4 illustrates how Webmail works.

Figure 20-4

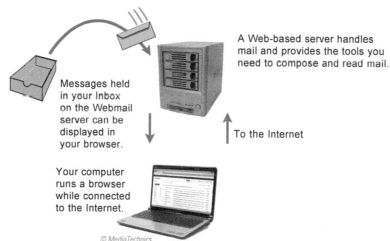

A Web-based server handles mail and provides the tools you need to compose and read mail.

Messages held in your Inbox on the Webmail server can be displayed in your browser.

To the Internet

Your computer runs a browser while connected to the Internet.

© MediaTechnics

Webmail can also be accessed from mobile devices when your computer is not handy. If you opt to use mail on a mobile device, read the options offered by your e-mail service provider and make sure you understand how to sync your mobile e-mail with the mail you view on your computer so that you don't miss an important message.

Free Webmail is supported by advertising, so expect to see advertisements. Today's sophisticated ad servers can search the content of an incoming message looking for keywords and then use them to display targeted ads in your e-mail window. For example, suppose you receive an e-mail message about a trip to Moscow. When viewing the message, you'll also be presented with ads about Moscow hotels, flights to Moscow, and similar promotions. Some Webmail services offer an ad-free option for a monthly fee.

Webmail is ideal for people who travel because accounts can be accessed from any computer connected to the Internet. Accessing e-mail from a public computer can be a security risk, however. If possible, reboot the computer before logging in to your e-mail account. Avoid entering sensitive information, such as your credit card number, in case your keystrokes are being monitored by malicious software lurking on the public computer. Be sure to log off when your session is finished. Log out of Windows and shut down the computer if you are allowed to do so.

Even when accessing Webmail from your home, security can be an issue. Unfortunately, Webmail services are the target of many malicious exploits, which can work their way into your computer through various security holes. When using Webmail, your computer must be protected by security software, and your computer will be more secure if you log out of your e-mail account when you are not using it.

FAQ How do I get a Webmail account?

Getting a Webmail account is an automated process that you can complete online. Begin by using a browser to access a Webmail site such as www.gmail.com, www.outlook.com, or www.yahoomail.com. Selecting the Sign Up or Register option produces an on-screen form like the Google Account screen shown in Figure 20-5. When you submit the completed form, your e-mail account is created and ready for immediate use.

Figure
20-5

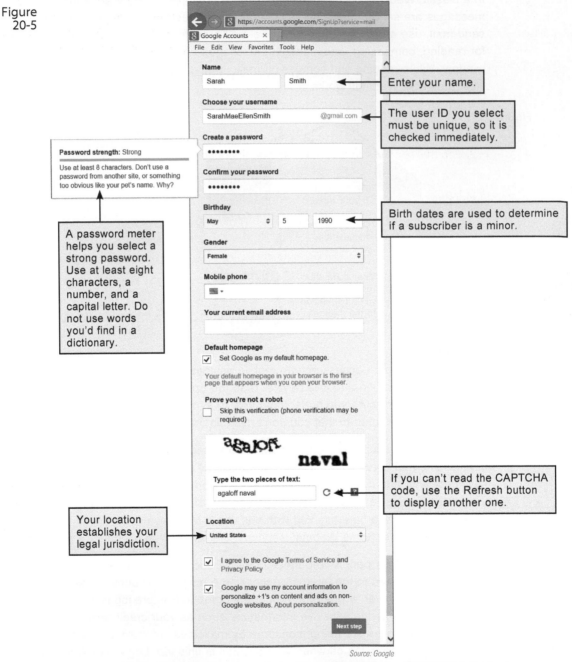

Enter your name.

The user ID you select must be unique, so it is checked immediately.

A password meter helps you select a strong password. Use at least eight characters, a number, and a capital letter. Do not use words you'd find in a dictionary.

Birth dates are used to determine if a subscriber is a minor.

If you can't read the CAPTCHA code, use the Refresh button to display another one.

Your location establishes your legal jurisdiction.

Source: Google

Most Webmail services display a goofy-looking code called a **CAPTCHA** that you must type in at the end of the registration process. CAPTCHAs are designed to block automated computer bots from creating e-mail accounts that are subsequently used for sending unsolicited e-mail called spam. The non-standard fonts used for CAPTCHAs require human intelligence to decipher. Automated computer bots with standard character-recognition systems cannot identify the letters, so CAPTCHAs help to ensure that e-mail accounts are given only to humans.

FAQ What's in the e-mail client window?

Whether you use a local e-mail client or a browser to access your mail, you need to be familiar with a basic set of controls for reading, composing, and sending messages. There are five basic areas.

Control panel. Control buttons for configuring your e-mail settings, sending mail, deleting messages, formatting text, and adding attachments can be displayed on a toolbar or ribbon. Some controls may appear only in certain modes, such as when you are composing new messages. Make sure you are familiar with the controls that appear in the main window and in subwindows provided for reading or composing messages.

Personal folders. Folders such as Inbox, Sent Messages, Deleted Messages, and Junk Mail are common across most Web-based and local e-mail clients. In addition, local clients usually have an Outbox folder, too.

Inbox list. When looking at your Inbox, messages are usually displayed as a list that includes the sender's name, date, and subject line.

Reading panel. The content of a selected message is displayed in a reading panel. Depending on your configuration settings, the reading panel might be displayed next to or below your Inbox list, or it might be a separate window that appears only when you click or touch one of the messages in the Inbox list.

Compose message panel. The area provided for you to compose new messages is generally presented as a separate window that you can move or enlarge on your screen.

Figure 20-6 illustrates the basic parts of Microsoft Outlook that you should be familiar with.

Figure 20-6

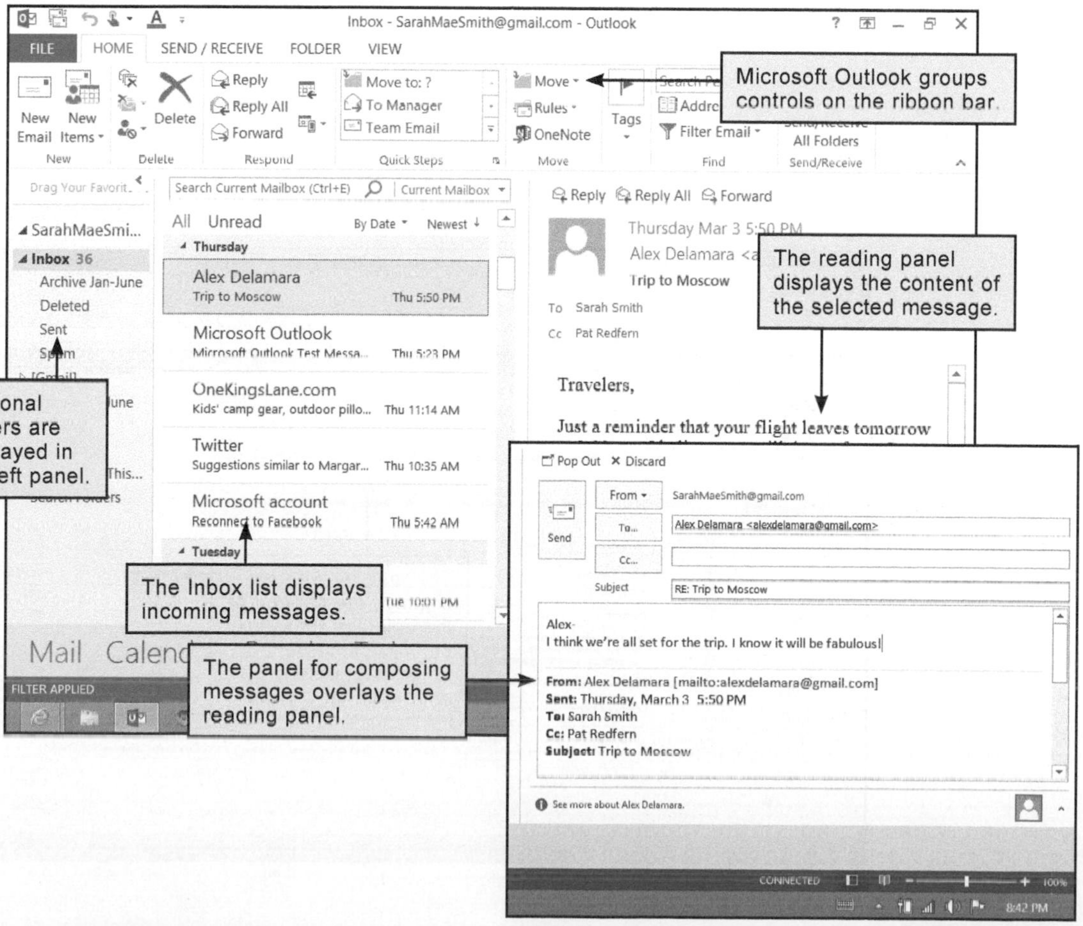

Microsoft Outlook groups controls on the ribbon bar.

The reading panel displays the content of the selected message.

Personal folders are displayed in the left panel.

The Inbox list displays incoming messages.

The panel for composing messages overlays the reading panel.

Source: Microsoft Corporation

• What's in the e-mail client window? (continued)

Gmail is similar to the Outlook e-mail client shown on the previous page. In Gmail, however, the controls and panels are arranged a bit differently. With Gmail, the Inbox list stretches across the entire window, as does the reading pane. The compose panel pops up over the Inbox list.

Figure 20-7

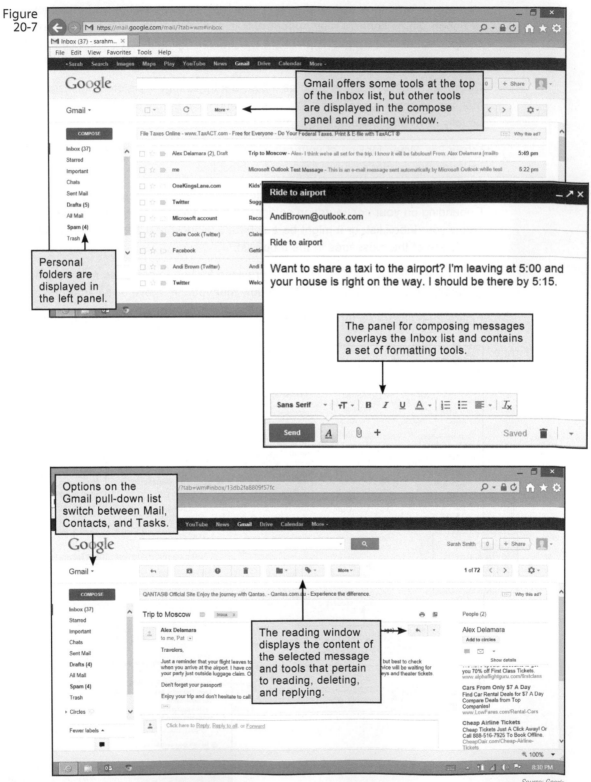

FAQ How do I write an e-mail message?

When you want to compose a message, look for a toolbar button or link labeled "Create Mail," "New Email," or "Compose Mail." Enter the recipient's address in the To: box. If you want to send a copy of the message to other people, you can include their e-mail addresses in the Cc: box. Use the Subject: box for a brief description of the message.

Most e-mail clients provide a sort of mini word processor for composing e-mail messages. You can type your message, edit it, and even check your spelling. Depending upon your e-mail settings, clicking the Send button either sends the message immediately, or places the message in your Outbox to be sent the next time you send and receive a batch of messages.

TRYIT!

Figure
20-8

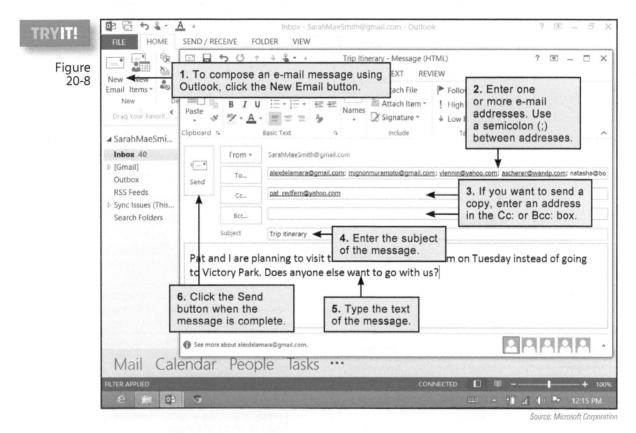

Source: Microsoft Corporation

- To send messages to more than one address, enter additional addresses in the To: box. You can use the Cc: box to "copy" a message to people who might be interested in the information, but who do not necessarily need to act on it. Remember that the message recipients will receive a header that lists all the recipients in the To: and Cc: lines.

- When you do not want some recipients' names to appear in the header, enter those recipients' e-mail addresses in the Bcc: box instead of the To: or Cc: box. If you don't see a Bcc: box, in Outlook select the Options tab and then select Bcc. In Gmail, select Bcc from the corner of the New Message box.

- Most e-mail clients provide controls similar to a word processor for formatting text. You'll find controls for bold, italic, underline, font style, font color, and highlighting.

- If you prefer the additional security offered by plain text messages that cannot carry malicious scripts, look for an ASCII, plain text, or non-HTML configuration option. When you select plain text, you will not have formatting options for bold, italic, and so on.

FAQ How do I read and reply to an e-mail message?

When new messages arrive, you'll want to read them and perhaps reply to some of them. To read a message using Outlook, click the message in the Inbox list. To respond to the message, click the Reply button, then type your response. To respond to everyone who received the message, click the Reply All button, then type your response.

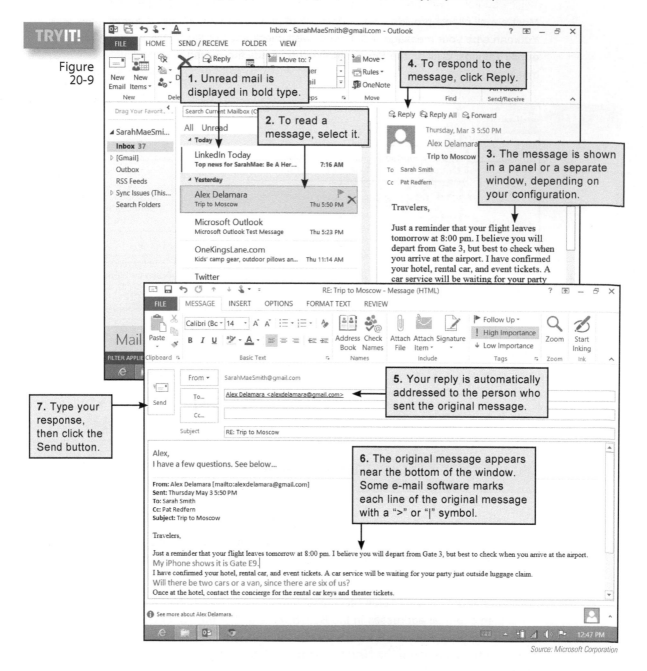

Figure 20-9

Source: Microsoft Corporation

- If the reply area is a small panel and you'd like more space, look for a Pop Out option to open a new window, which you can expand to full screen.

- If you want to respond to a number of points from the original message, the first line of your message might say, "See my comments below." Then, you can scroll down and intersperse your comments within the text of the original message. You can use an alternative font color or style to differentiate your comments from the original message.

FAQ How do I forward an e-mail message?

After you receive an e-mail message, you can pass the message on to other people—a process called forwarding. You might use forwarding if you receive a message that should be handled by someone else.

When you initiate the forwarding process, the original message is copied into a new message window, complete with the address of the original sender. You can then enter the address of the person to whom you are forwarding the message. You can also add text to the forwarded message to explain why you are passing it along.

Some e-mail software allows you to alter the text of the original message before you forward it. Because a message can be altered before being forwarded, you should be aware that forwarded messages you receive might not be entirely accurate versions of the original messages.

To forward a message using Outlook or Gmail, click the message, then click the Forward button. Enter the address of the person to whom you want to forward the message, then click Send to send the message.

Figure
20-10

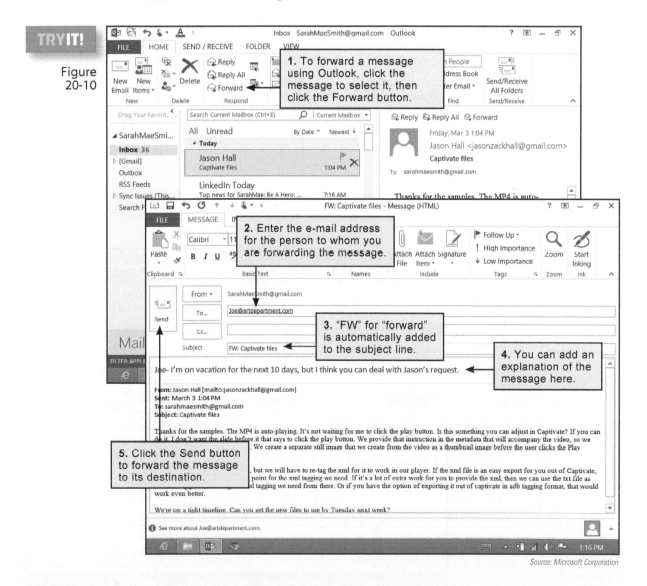

Source: Microsoft Corporation

FAQ How do I use the address book?

An **e-mail address book** (or contacts) contains a list of e-mail addresses for individuals and groups. You can set your e-mail client to automatically enter addresses for people the first time you reply to them. Addresses can be manually entered, too.

A **mail group** or mailing list is a list of e-mail addresses stored under a unique title. Groups are easy to set up and handy to use when you frequently send the same message to the same group of people.

TRY IT!

Figure
20-11

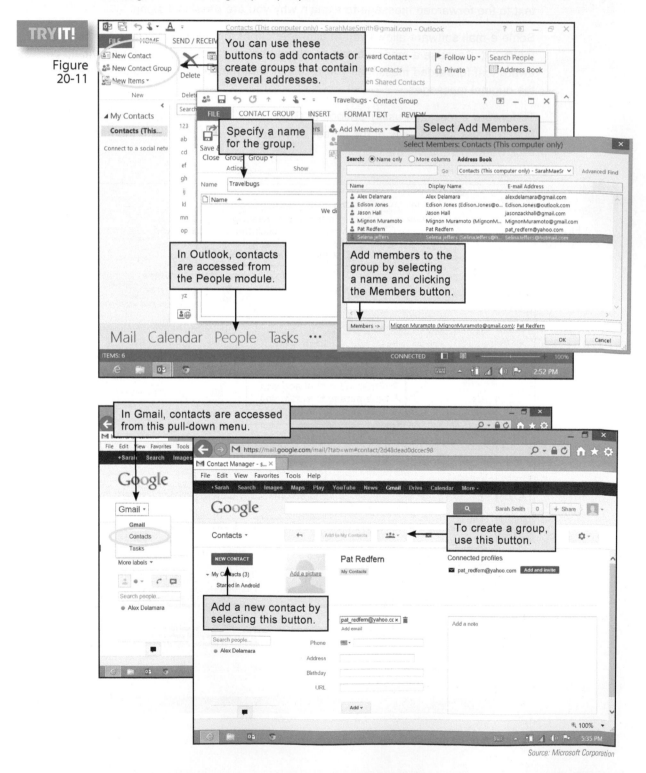

FAQ How do I send e-mail attachments?

An **e-mail attachment** is a file, such as a document, photo, music clip, or spreadsheet, that is attached to and sent along with an e-mail message. Attachments allow you to quickly, easily, and immediately share files with others. Consider compressing files larger than a megabyte before you attach them.

Attachments are a source of viruses, and savvy computer users are reluctant to open attachments unless they come from a trusted source. You can help reassure recipients that attachments are safe by briefly referring to the attachment in the body of your e-mail message.

TRYIT!

Figure 20-12

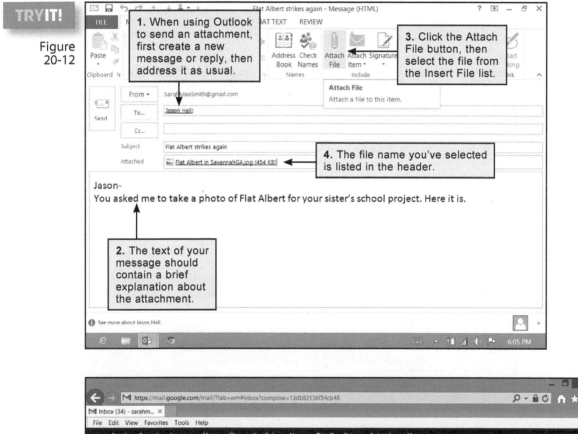

1. When using Outlook to send an attachment, first create a new message or reply, then address it as usual.

3. Click the Attach File button, then select the file from the Insert File list.

4. The file name you've selected is listed in the header.

2. The text of your message should contain a brief explanation about the attachment.

With Gmail, the process is similar. The attachment icon can be found here.

FAQ How do I view, save, and delete e-mail attachments?

Various e-mail clients work with attachments in different ways. Gmail automatically displays attachments containing photos, whereas Outlook does not. Many e-mail clients do not automatically display attachments containing documents, PDFs, worksheets, and other types of files. To display the contents of these attachments, look for a Preview button or View link.

TRYIT!

Figure 20-13

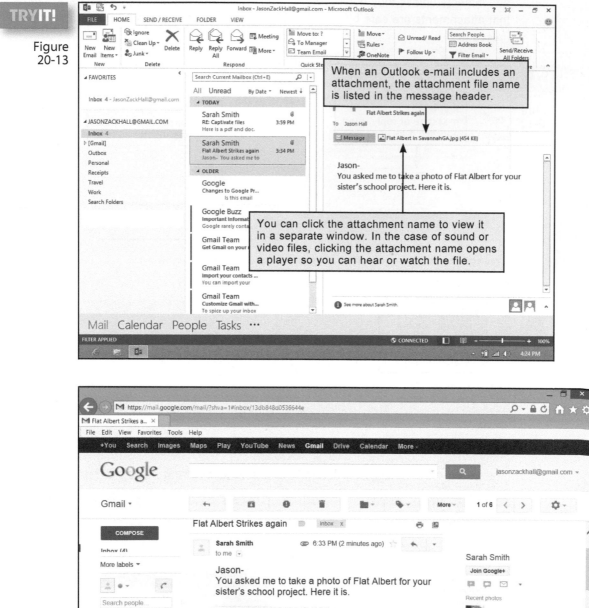

When an Outlook e-mail includes an attachment, the attachment file name is listed in the message header.

You can click the attachment name to view it in a separate window. In the case of sound or video files, clicking the attachment name opens a player so you can hear or watch the file.

Gmail displays most photos automatically. For other types of files, click the View button.

• How do I view, save, and delete e-mail attachments? (continued)

You can save an attachment on your hard disk for later use. The steps for doing so depend on the e-mail client you're using. In general, Webmail attachments are downloaded from the mail server if and when you save them. Attachments to local mail are stored in a temporary folder on your computer's hard disk; the process of saving an attachment moves it to one of your personal folders.

TRYIT!

Figure 20-14

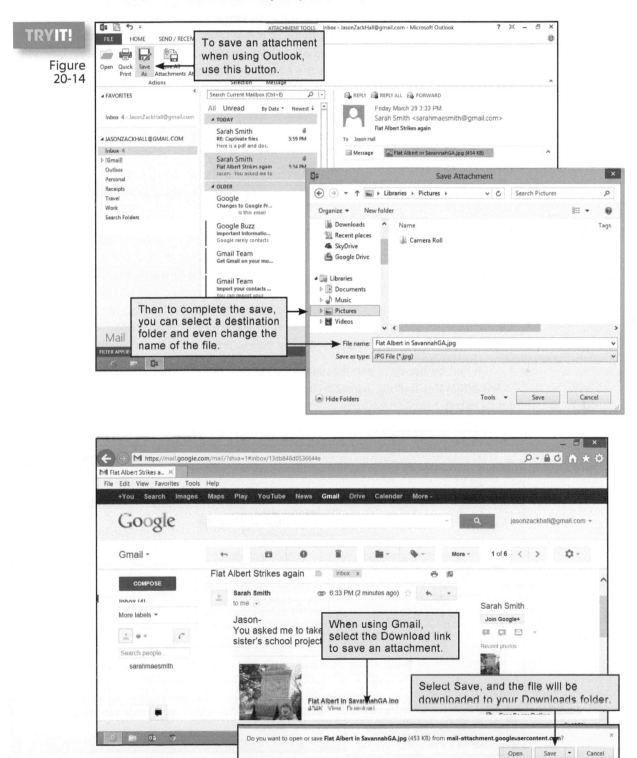

Source: Microsoft Corporation. © MediaTechnics

FAQ How can I organize my e-mail messages?

Sifting through thousands of messages in an unorganized Inbox is inefficient, so it pays to learn how to use the organizational tools your e-mail client offers. E-mail clients differ in their organizational tools, but most offer tools for the following organizational activities:

- **Mark as read or unread.** Unread mail is usually displayed in bold, and that feature helps to ensure that you've not missed an important message. Once you open a message, the bold font is removed and the message status becomes "read." You can manually change the read/unread status of a message. The most typical use of this feature would be when you've read a message but want to respond to it later. Using the Unread/Read option reinstates the bold font, putting the message visually in a category with unread messages.

- **Prioritize.** Your e-mail client might provide a way to prioritize messages, allowing you to deal with the most urgent correspondence first. For example, in Gmail, you can select the star icon or the ▭ important icon. Then you can group messages using those categories.

- **Search.** A targeted way to find a message is by searching for a word or phrase. For a quick search, limit the scope to the text in the subject line. Searching through the entire content of all your messages can take a bit longer.

- **Work with threads.** An **e-mail thread** (sometimes referred to as a conversation) consists of an original message and all of the replies and forwards that stem from it. The ability to pull up all the messages that pertain to a thread can be useful. Some e-mail packages automatically track threads according to the subject line. Other e-mail packages allow you to designate labels, such as "Moscow Trip," for similar messages. You can then use search filters to display messages with the same labels.

- **Sort.** It can be handy to sort messages by sender, rather than by date. If your e-mail client offers this feature, sorts can be carried out by clicking the column headings in the Inbox listing.

TRYIT!

Figure 20-15

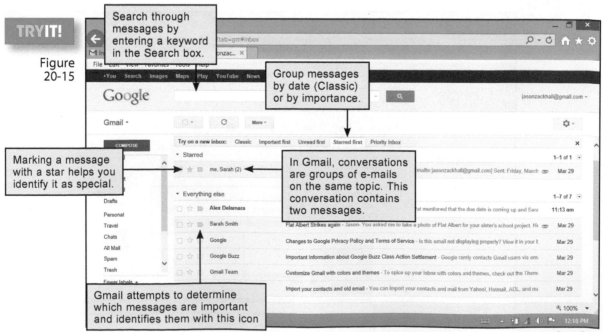

Search through messages by entering a keyword in the Search box.

Group messages by date (Classic) or by importance.

Marking a message with a star helps you identify it as special.

In Gmail, conversations are groups of e-mails on the same topic. This conversation contains two messages.

Gmail attempts to determine which messages are important and identifies them with this icon

Source: Google

•How can I organize my e-mail messages? (continued)

In addition to searching, sorting, adding priority markers, and working with conversations, you can also manage your e-mail messages using folders. Here are some tips:

• **Group mail into folders.** Most e-mail clients offer several predefined folders, such as Inbox, Drafts, Sent Mail, Spam, and Trash. You can create additional folders and move messages into those folders to group them by topic, by sender, or by any other criteria that helps you keep messages organized. Instead of manually moving messages, your e-mail client might allow you to create rules or filters for distributing messages into appropriate folders based on the sender or message subject line.

• **Empty the Trash folder.** The Trash folder holds e-mail messages that you've deleted. You might be able to set this folder to automatically purge messages based on how long they have been in the trash. Otherwise, you should manually empty the Trash folder periodically.

• **Check the Spam folder.** The Spam folder (also called Junk Mail or Junk) holds messages that your e-mail client has filtered out based on a set of rules for identifying mass mail advertising and e-mail originating from suspicious senders. Sometimes legitimate messages are placed in the Spam folder by mistake; it is a good idea to periodically check this folder so you don't miss an important message that was misplaced.

• **Move old mail to an archive folder.** You can use folders for archiving mail. For example, at six-month intervals, you can move all the mail out of your Inbox and into a folder with a title such as "Archive Jan-June." Moving a batch of messages to a secondary folder decreases the size of your Inbox and reduces the possibility that it will become corrupted. Outlook's AutoArchive feature takes care of this task automatically by moving messages to an archive folder after the message has been in your Inbox for a specified length of time.

Figure 20-16

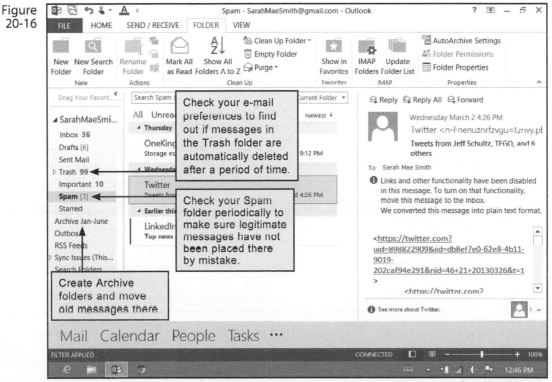

Source: Microsoft Corporation

FAQ What should I know about signatures and autoreplies?

Many e-mail clients offer automated features that attach a signature block to the end of e-mail messages, or autorespond to messages received when you are on vacation or away from your desk for an extended period of time.

Signatures. An **e-mail signature** is a block of text or graphics automatically added to the end of every e-mail message you send. For professional use, you could, for example, set up a signature that includes your name, title, and office telephone number.

Accountants and attorneys use the signature feature to add confidentiality notices to messages sent to clients. Standard confidentiality wording might be:

> This message is intended only for the use of the individual or entity to which it is addressed and may contain information that is privileged, confidential and exempt from disclosure under applicable law. If the reader of this message is not the intended recipient or the employee or agent responsible for delivering the message to the intended recipient, you are hereby notified that any dissemination, distribution, or copying of this communication is strictly prohibited. If you have received this Communication in error, please notify us immediately by replying to this message, and delete the original message you have received in error.

In Outlook, you can create a signature block by selecting the FILE tab, then selecting the Options, Mail, and Editor options. In Gmail, select the Settings icon and then follow the steps in Figure 20-17.

Figure
20-17

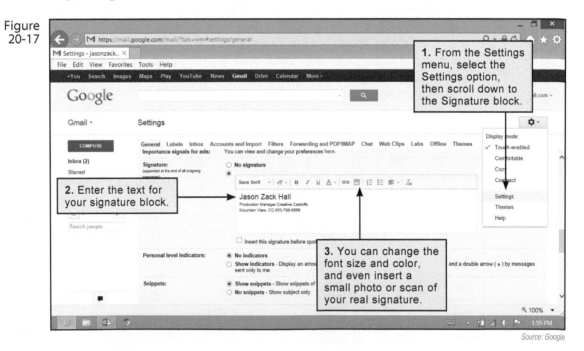

Source: Google

• What should I know about signatures and autoreplies? (continued)

Autoreply. Most e-mail clients can be configured to automatically reply to e-mail messages, a feature sometimes referred to as out of office response. Gmail refers to it as a vacation responder. Use this feature when you are away from your computer for an extended time, such as when you are on vacation.

When composing an out of office reply, carefully consider who will receive the message. If you are autoresponding to all your mail, your message will go to friends, colleagues, customers, and strangers. Don't include information that would reveal, for example, that your home will be vacant. And for work, it is not a good idea to broadcast all the fun you're planning to have on your Caribbean vacation. Figure 20-18 illustrates how to set an appropriate professional vacation responder in Gmail.

Figure
20-18
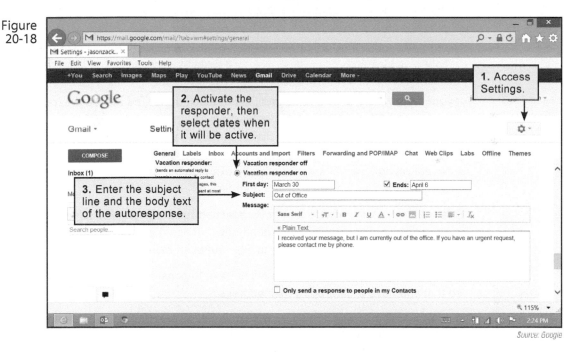

Source: Google

Autoforward. Autoforwarding allows you to forward messages to other e-mail addresses automatically. For example, while you are on vacation, you might want to forward your mail to an assistant. You can even set up filters to forward only certain messages, such as those pertaining to an ongoing project at work.

Figure
20-19
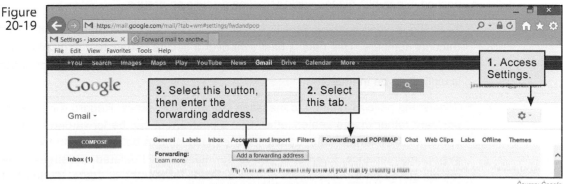

Source: Google

FAQ Is e-mail safe?

E-mail is patterned after paper-based letters sent through the ground-based postal service. The advantage of e-mail is that it arrives quickly and costs nothing. It also maintains an audit trail of messages and replies that can be useful in verifying decisions and approvals.

One of e-mail's main disadvantages is **spam**—unwanted electronic junk mail about medical products, low-cost loans, and software upgrades that often carries viruses and other malicious software. Today's proliferation of spam is generated by marketing firms that harvest e-mail addresses from mailing lists, membership applications, and casual Web browsing. Legislation to minimize spam has so far been ineffective.

To protect your computer and data from spam and other risks associated with e-mail, consider the following precautions:

- Never reply to spam when you receive it.

- Never open suspicious attachments or click links in dubious e-mail messages.

- If your e-mail provider offers a way to report spam, use it.

- If your e-mail client provides spam filters to block unwanted messages, put them to use. A **spam filter** automatically routes advertisements and other junk mail to the trash folder maintained by your e-mail client. Although spam filters can be very effective for blocking spam and other unwanted e-mail, they sometimes block legitimate messages. After activating spam filters, periodically examine the folder that holds your junk mail to make sure the filters are not overly aggressive.

- Spam filters usually include a set of predefined rules designed to filter out junk mail with subject lines such as "p()rn" and "d0n8 now!". If spam bypasses the predefined rules, you can construct additional rules to filter out even more spam.

- When spam gets out of hand, you might have to consider changing your e-mail account so that you have a different e-mail address.

- Use an e-mail provider that filters out spam at its server to block unwanted mail from reaching your Inbox.

- Make sure your antivirus software is configured to scan incoming mail and attachments for viruses and other malicious exploits.

- Provide your e-mail address only to people from whom you want to receive e-mail. Be wary of providing your e-mail address at Web sites, entering it on application forms, or posting it in public places such as online discussion groups.

- Be cautious when sending sensitive data, such as credit card numbers and Social Security numbers. This data is best sent over a secure connection or in an encrypted message. Sometimes a phone call is the best way to convey sensitive information as it is unlikely to be intercepted.

- Understand policies relating to message storage and access. Regard e-mail as a postcard rather than a sealed letter. Like a postcard, it can be forwarded to others, and it can be intercepted in transit. Your e-mail also can be read during the course of system maintenance. Even after you've downloaded and deleted messages, they can remain stored on e-mail servers and on backups for months or years. If you don't want your words made public, be cautious about enclosing them in an e-mail message.

QuickCheck A

1. Webmail is accessed using a(n) [_____] .

2. True or false? The To: field of an e-mail message can hold only one address; addresses for additional recipients must be placed in the Cc: or Bcc: box. [_____]

3. An e-mail [_____] is used to send word processing documents, spreadsheets, photos, and music clips along with an e-mail message.

4. [_____] is the term used to refer to electronic junk mail.

5. An e-mail [_____] consists of an original message and all of the replies and forwards that stem from it.

CHECKIT!

QuickCheck B

Indicate the letter of the screen element that best matches the following:

1. A message with an attachment [____]

2. The folder that holds a copy of all mail you've sent out [____]

3. A subject line [____]

4. An unread e-mail message [____]

5. The control you'd use to send the current message to another person [____]

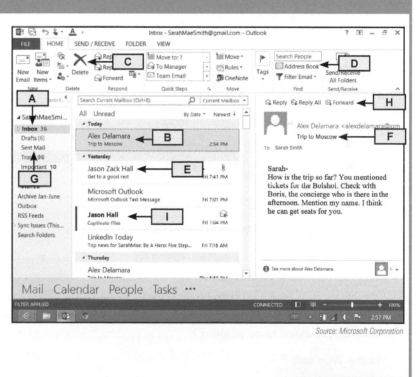

Source: Microsoft Corporation

CHECKIT!

21 Browsing the Web

What's Inside and on the CD?

The Web is a modern rendition of an idea first developed in 1945 by an engineer named Vannevar Bush, who envisioned a microfilm-based machine called the Memex that linked associated information or ideas through "trails." The idea resurfaced in the mid-1960s when Harvard graduate Ted Nelson coined the term "hypertext" to describe a computer system that could store literary documents, link them according to logical relationships, and allow readers to comment on and annotate what they read. Tim Berners-Lee made this idea a reality in 1991 when he wrote the first software to locate and link documents over the Internet. In this chapter, you'll learn how the modern Web works to link information from all corners of the globe.

FAQ What is the Web?

The **Web** (short for "World Wide Web") is a collection of data that can be linked and accessed using HTTP. **HTTP** (Hypertext Transfer Protocol) is the communications protocol that sets the standard used by every computer that accesses Web-based information. The Web is not the same as the Internet. The Internet is a communications system; the Web is an interlinked collection of information that flows over that communications system.

A **Web page** is the product or output of one or more Web-based files, which are displayed on your computer in a format similar to a page in a book. Unlike book pages, however, Web pages can dynamically incorporate pictures, videos, sounds, and interactive elements.

The computers that store Web pages are known as **Web servers**. Each Web server hosts one or more **Web sites** that contain information about a specific topic, company, organization, person, event, or place. The main page for a Web site is sometimes referred to as a **home page**.

Links between Web pages, technically called **hypertext links** (or hyperlinks), allow you to follow a thread of information from one Web page to another within a site or across to other sites. By clicking or touching a link, you are requesting the Web page indicated by the link. To fulfill your request, a Web server sends data for the Web page to your computer and the Web page can then be displayed on the screen.

Most Web pages are stored as HTML documents. **HTML** (Hypertext Markup Language) is a set of instructions that can be embedded into a document to produce specific effects, such as bold text, colored backgrounds, and underlined links. Embedded instructions are called **HTML tags** and they are encased in angle brackets. For example, when creating a title in an HTML document, you can specify that it will be displayed in bold by using the <b> HTML tag. HTML tags are also used to produce graphics on Web pages. Click the Try It! button to find out more about HTML tags.

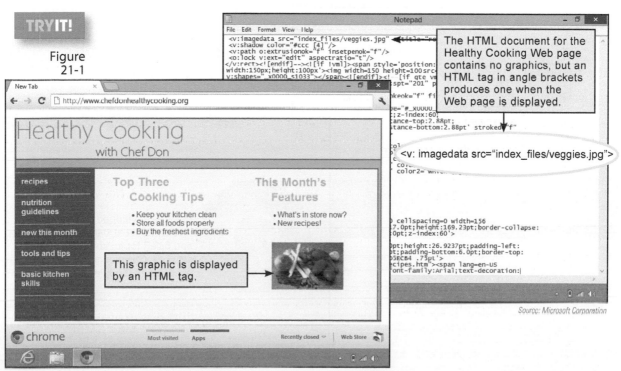

TRY IT!

Figure
21-1

The HTML document for the Healthy Cooking Web page contains no graphics, but an HTML tag in angle brackets produces one when the Web page is displayed.

<v: imagedata src="index_files/veggies.jpg">

This graphic is displayed by an HTML tag.

Source: Microsoft Corporation

© MediaTechnics

FAQ Which browsers are most popular?

A **Web browser**—usually referred to simply as a browser—is a program that runs on your computer to fetch and display Web pages. Browsers, such as Microsoft Internet Explorer, Mozilla Firefox, and Google Chrome, use HTTP to request Web pages and then interpret HTML tags to display the page on your computer screen.

Although many Web pages are stored as HTML documents, some are assembled from the data in databases or from XML (Extensible Markup Language) documents with the help of additional components, such as scripts and Cascading Style Sheets. Using these components, most browsers can display database data as well as HTML documents.

Figure
21-2

Microsoft Internet Explorer (IE) is included with the Windows operating system and can be accessed from the Windows 7 or Windows 8 desktop.

Source: Microsoft Corporation

Microsoft Internet Explorer RT can be started from a tile on the Start screen, and offers an alternate user interface for Internet Explorer. This version is optimized for touch and designed to function in a way that is similar to browsers on mobile devices.

Source: Microsoft Corporation

Mozilla Firefox is a descendant of the first graphical browser, Netscape Navigator. As open source software, Firefox is available for free and is easy to download and install.

Source: Mozilla Firefox

Google Chrome is one of the most recently developed browsers. Known for its streamlined design and billed for its speed and security, Chrome is free and available at Google's Web site.

Source: Google, Inc.

FAQ How do I start my browser?

You can start your browser by clicking a tile on the Windows Start screen or by clicking an icon on the desktop taskbar. In this chapter, we'll use the desktop version of Internet Explorer for examples because it is available in Windows 7 and Windows 8, plus it gives you full access to all personal and security settings. To open Internet Explorer, start at the Windows desktop and select the 🖉 icon. Key elements of the Internet Explorer browser window are shown in Figure 21-3.

Figure 21-3

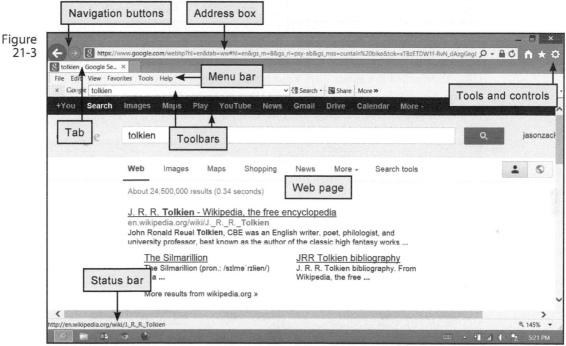

Source: Microsoft Corporation

When working with a new browser, make sure you can identify each of the following elements:

- **Web page.** The Web page appears in the main panel of the browser window.

- **Navigation buttons.** Forward and back buttons navigate from one page to another.

- **Address box.** The Address box displays the address of the current Web page and can be used to enter the addresses of other pages you would like to view.

- **Tools and controls.** Browsers provide icons for quick access to security settings and personal preferences.

- **Tabs.** Each tab provides access to a Web page when you have multiple pages open at the same time.

- **Menu bar.** The menu of browser commands may be presented on a toolbar or menu bar. In some browsers, these options are hidden unless you turn them on in settings or display them using a shortcut key such as Alt.

- **Toolbars.** Browsers can display various toolbars. For example, the Google toolbar provides a Search box so you can search the Web from any page.

- **Status bar.** The status bar typically displays the address of links when you hover the pointer over them.

FAQ How do I use a URL to go to a Web site?

A **URL** (Uniform Resource Locator) serves as an address to uniquely identify a Web page. Each URL specifies the Web server that stores the page, the folder (or folders) that hold the page, and the name of the page. You'll see URLs on everything from billboard ads to soup cans and business cards. URLs have several parts, as shown in Figure 21-4.

Figure 21-4

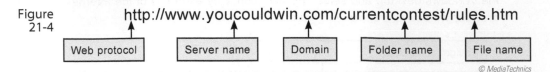

http://www.youcouldwin.com/currentcontest/rules.htm

| Web protocol | Server name | Domain | Folder name | File name |

© MediaTechnics

To enter a URL, first select the address box on your browser window. Next, type the URL, then press the Enter key. Your browser sends a request for this URL to the Web server, which transmits the requested Web page back to your browser. Your browser then formats and displays the page on your computer screen.

Figure 21-5

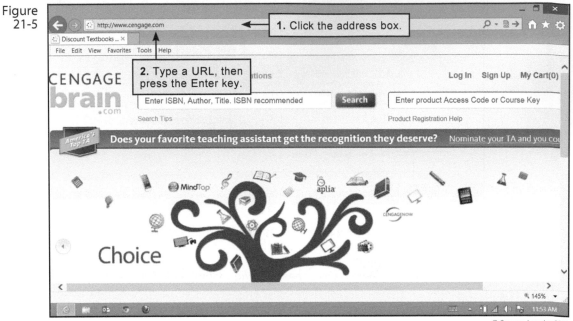

© Cengage Learning 2014

- You must be very precise when entering a URL. Don't use any spaces—even before or after punctuation marks—and make sure that you exactly duplicate uppercase and lowercase letters.

- A complete URL usually starts with http:// as in http://www.ibm.com. However, you usually don't have to type the http:// part of the URL.

- Folder names are separated from other parts of the URL by forward slashes (/), not backward slashes (\) as are used in Windows file paths.

- The part of a URL that appears after the dot, such as .com, .edu, and .gov, indicates the top-level domain of the URL. As you know from the previous chapter, educational institutions use the .edu domain. The domain for U.S. government agencies is .gov. The U.S. military, the original sponsor of the Internet, uses the .mil domain. International Web sites might use .int, or an abbreviation indicating a specific country such as .ca for Canada or .fr for France.

FAQ How do I use links on a Web page?

A hypertext link is a connection, or path, between two Web pages. It contains the URL of a Web page, and so it can be used to "jump" from one Web page to another. Links are usually displayed on a Web page as underlined text or as a graphic. When positioned over a link, the arrow-shaped pointer turns into a 🖑 **link pointer**. When you click a link, the requested Web page is transmitted from the Web server and displayed on your computer. When working with a touch interface, you can simply tap a link to jump to its page.

Figure 21-6

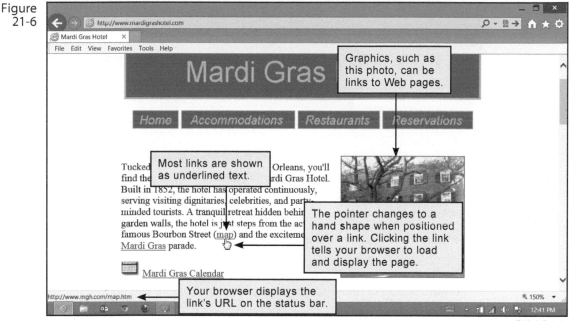

© MediaTechnics

- Text links typically change color after you click them. The color change makes it easy to see which links you have already clicked and viewed.

- To discover if a graphic is a link, move the pointer over the graphic. If the pointer changes to a hand shape, then the graphic is linked to another Web page or media element.

- If your browser is configured to display a status bar, when you move the pointer over a link, the link's URL is displayed in the status bar. For example, in the figure above, the hand is pointing to the map link. On the status bar, you can see the URL for this link.

- By being aware of what's shown in the status bar, you can get an idea of a link's destination before you click it. This information can be important for your security. It might help you avoid fake Web sites designed to fool visitors into providing private information or downloading viruses.

- When working with a touch interface, touching and holding a link displays the link destination in a nearby box.

- Most Web sites contain additional links that you can use to drill down to more and more specific material. In the figure above, the Mardi Gras Calendar link might display a monthly calendar with days that you can select to see a list of events for a particular date.

FAQ How do I use browser navigation tools?

Forward and Back buttons. Whereas hyperlinks help you jump to new Web pages, navigation buttons help you jump back to pages that you've already viewed. Your browser maintains a list of Web pages displayed during the course of a session. A session starts when you open your browser and ends when you close it. Navigation buttons help you navigate through the Web pages you view during a session. The universal symbols for the Back and Forward buttons are arrows. If you'd like to return to pages you viewed during other sessions, use the Favorites or History lists as explained later in the chapter.

Figure
21-7

Back button

Forward button

http://mardigrashotel.com

Mardi Gras Hotel   ×

File   Edit   View   Favorites   Tools   Help

Source: Microsoft Corporation

- When you first start your browser, the Back and Forward buttons are disabled or "grayed out." The Back button becomes enabled when you go to a new page. The Forward button becomes enabled after you use the Back button to go back to a previously viewed page.

- Contrary to what you might expect, the Forward button does not take you to new pages that you haven't yet viewed. Instead, the Forward button essentially counteracts the Back button. If you click the Back button to go back to a page, you can then click the Forward button to return to the page you viewed before you clicked the Back button.

Home button. The Home button displays your home page—the page that appears when you first start your browser. Clicking this button at any time during a session returns you to your home page. Set your home page to a Web site that you use frequently. A search engine such as Google or Bing works well if you do a lot of Web searches. You might instead want to set your home page to your favorite social networking site.

Figure
21-8

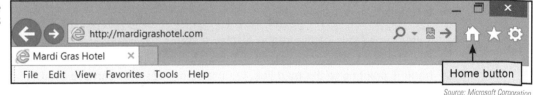

http://mardigrashotel.com

Mardi Gras Hotel   ×

File   Edit   View   Favorites   Tools   Help

Home button

Source: Microsoft Corporation

- Although the page that appears when you first start your browser is called your home page, that term is also applied to the main page of a Web site, such as the page you see when you connect to www.cnn.com or www.msn.com. To clarify the difference, most books use the term "your home page" for the page you set in your browser. References to "a site's home page" usually mean the main page of a Web site.

- To change your home page, first make sure your browser is displaying the page you'd like to designate as your home page. Right-click (or touch and hold) the Home button and select *Add or Change Home Page*.

•How do I use browser navigation tools? (continued)

Refresh button. Some Web pages contain content that changes periodically. For example, bids for eBay items change as the bidding escalates. Changes may not automatically appear on Web pages, however, because the pages have been downloaded to your computer's storage device.

If you've had a Web page open for a long period of time and suspect that it might have changed, you can use the Refresh button to reload the page. Reloading a page forces your browser to contact the Web site, re-download all of the content, and display it on your screen.

Figure
21-9

W http://en.wikipedia.org/wiki/Frodo

W Frodo Baggins - Wi... ×

Refresh button

Source: Microsoft Corporation

Tabs. Sometimes you might find it useful to work with more than one Web page at a time. For example, when researching a topic, there might be material on two or more pages that you want to cross-reference. Or, you might want to keep one page open while following links to other pages.

Browsers provide several ways to work with multiple Web pages:

• **Open more than one instance of the browser.** You can select the browser icon on the taskbar or desktop to open a second browser window. You can then resize and position the windows to view them both at the same time.

• **Open a new page.** In mobile browsers, going to a new Web page creates a "stack" of pages. You can access these pages by going to the stack and selecting the one you want to view. Mobile browsers generally don't allow you to view more than one Web page at time, however.

• **Open a new tab.** When you first open your browser, your home page is displayed on a tab. Subsequent pages are also displayed on this tab unless you specify that you'd like them displayed on new tabs. When using tabs, you can view only one Web page at a time, but you can quickly switch back and forth from the page on one tab to a page on another tab. You can configure tab settings using the Settings icon and selecting Internet Options.

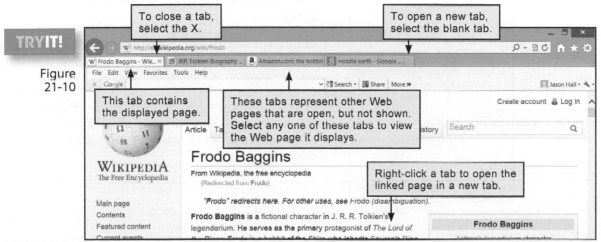

To close a tab, select the X.

To open a new tab, select the blank tab.

Figure
21-10

This tab contains the displayed page.

These tabs represent other Web pages that are open, but not shown. Select any one of these tabs to view the Web page it displays.

Right-click a tab to open the linked page in a new tab.

Source: Wikipedia

FAQ How does the Favorites list work?

As you continue to use the Web, you'll visit some pages on a regular basis. For example, you might frequently visit www.wunderground.com to check your local weather. Or, you might periodically check football scores at http://oncampussports.com/category/football/.

Rather than typing the URL every time you want to visit a particular Web page, you can add it to a **Favorites list** or create a **Bookmark**. Favorites and bookmarks work in a similar way; the terminology just varies from one browser to another. After you've added a Web page to your list of favorites, you can then simply open the Favorites list and select the page you want to view.

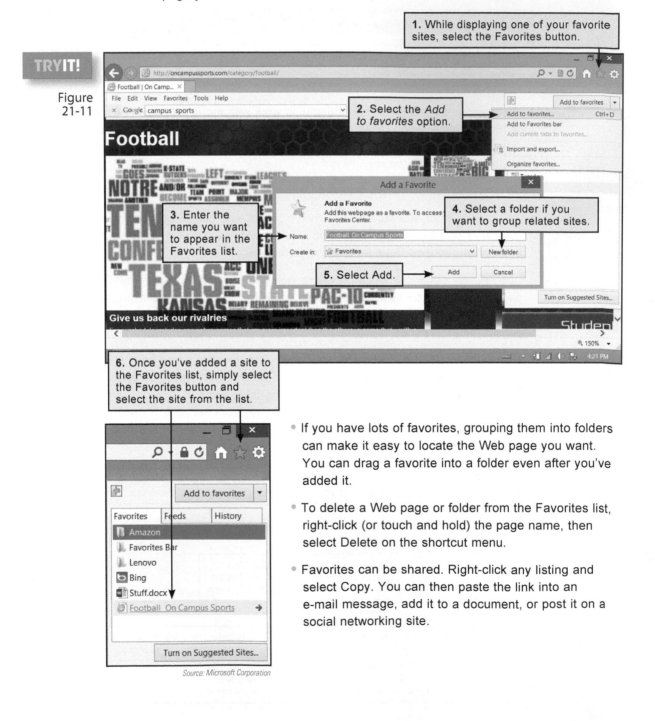

Figure
21-11

Source: Microsoft Corporation

- If you have lots of favorites, grouping them into folders can make it easy to locate the Web page you want. You can drag a favorite into a folder even after you've added it.

- To delete a Web page or folder from the Favorites list, right-click (or touch and hold) the page name, then select Delete on the shortcut menu.

- Favorites can be shared. Right-click any listing and select Copy. You can then paste the link into an e-mail message, add it to a document, or post it on a social networking site.

FAQ How does the History list work?

A **History list** displays the titles or URLs of individual Web pages you visited in the past. The list is maintained by your browser, so it typically includes every Web site and every Web page that you visit. In IE, the History list can be accessed from the Favorites button.

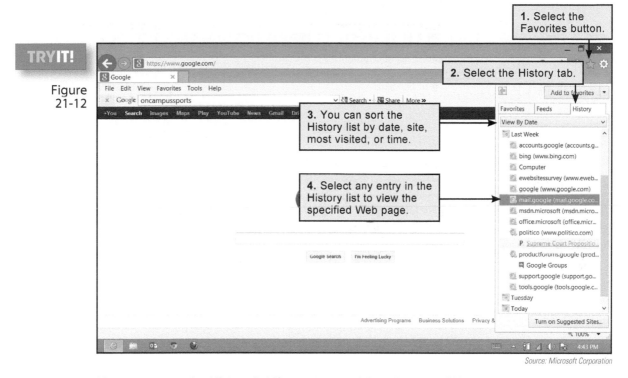

Figure
21-12

1. Select the Favorites button.

2. Select the History tab.

3. You can sort the History list by date, site, most visited, or time.

4. Select any entry in the History list to view the specified Web page.

Source: Microsoft Corporation

You can empty the History list if you want to delete the trail of Web sites you've visited. When using a public computer, emptying the History list will prevent the next person who uses the computer from discovering which sites you viewed.

Figure
21-13

1. To delete browser history, select the Settings button.

On your own computer, you might simply want to delete the items checked here. Before signing off from a public computer, you might want to check the remaining boxes, too, to delete all traces of your browsing history.

2. Select these options from the Settings menus.

Source: Microsoft Corporation

FAQ How do I find information on the Web?

The most popular way to find information on the Web is by using a **search engine**, such as Google, Ask.com, Yahoo! Search, or Bing. Depending on the search engine, you can look for information by entering keywords, filling out a form, or clicking a series of links to drill down through a list of topics and subtopics.

TRYIT!

Figure 21-14

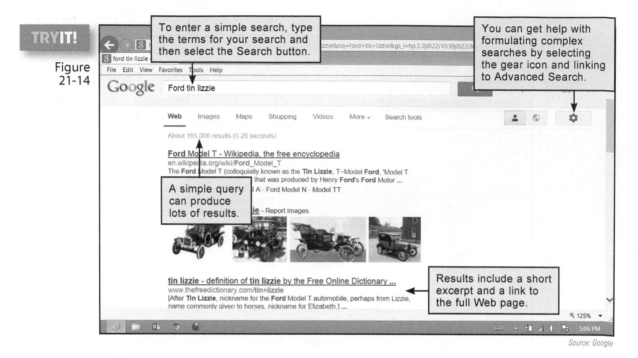

To enter a simple search, type the terms for your search and then select the Search button.

You can get help with formulating complex searches by selecting the gear icon and linking to Advanced Search.

A simple query can produce lots of results.

Results include a short excerpt and a link to the full Web page.

Source: Google

- When entering keywords, be as specific as possible. A keyword search for "Ford" produces millions of links to pages about Ford automobiles, as well as pages about former president Gerald Ford and actor Harrison Ford. "Ford Tin Lizzie" would result in a much more targeted search and return a more manageable number of results.

- As a general rule, the more keywords you use, the more targeted your search becomes. You can often refine your search by looking at the short descriptions presented by the search results and using keywords from those results that seem most pertinent to your search.

- Search engines provide tools for advanced searches. These tools vary somewhat, depending on which search engine you're using, but are explained in detail somewhere on the search engine Web site. In general, advanced search tools help you formulate searches based on exact phrases, Boolean operators, dates, and file types.

- An exact-phrase search requires the search engine to find pages that include a particular phrase with the words occurring in a specified order. To specify an exact-phrase search, you typically surround the phrase with quotation marks.

- A Boolean search uses the operators (or symbols) AND (+), OR, and NOT (-) to specify how your keywords are to be combined. For example, if a search for Model T automobile turns up a lot of pages about car clubs that don't interest you, refine your search by entering Model T automobile -club. Using the minus sign before the word "club" indicates you don't want to see links to any pages containing that word.

• How do I find information on the Web? (continued)

Search engines, Web sites used for research, and most commercial sites promote advertising as part of their business model. Ad revenues help to support free services, such as searches, maps, and Webmail.

Ads, which are also called sponsored links, are displayed based on search terms that you enter or the content of pages you are viewing. Advertisers pay host Web sites to display their ads.

Consumers need to be able to detect which links are advertisements. Reputable search engines, such as Google, clearly indicate ads and sponsored links. Selecting one of these links displays information furnished by the advertiser. Like any advertising, claims may be exaggerated or misleading.

Figure 21-15

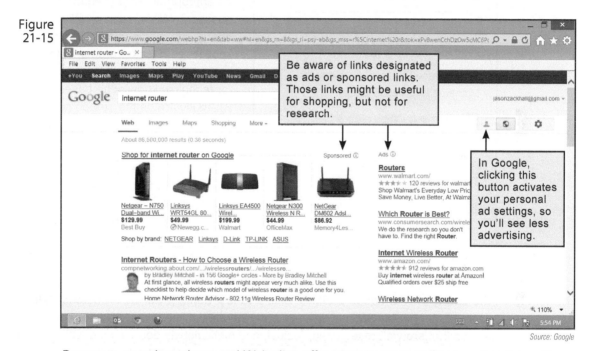

Source: Google

Browsers, search engines, and Web sites offer ways to opt out of some advertising. For example, Google's opt-out settings allow you to reject interest-based ads that reflect your browsing history. To adjust your personal ad settings for Google searches and Gmail, go to www.google.com/ads/preferences and follow the instructions.

When opting out of advertising, keep the following points in mind:

• You might not be able to eliminate all ads or sponsored links.

• Your opt-out selections apply only to the browser in which you set them. If you switch to a different browser, you'll have to opt out again.

• Your opt-out settings are stored in files called cookies on your computer. If you delete cookies when clearing browser history, you'll have to go through the opt-out process again.

• You can also block ads from specific advertisers. This technique is useful for annoying ads that appear despite your opt-out settings.

• Ads may still appear as you browse to other sites. For example, if you opt out of Google ads, you may still see ads when you are at sites such as About.com or Bing.

FAQ How do I separate online facts from fiction?

The Web includes a staggering amount of information, but not all of it is necessarily reliable or accurate. You might need to access several sites to gather sufficient information to solve a problem, form an opinion based on facts, or collect data to complete a research project.

Figure 21-16

Source: Microsoft Corporation

A human-readable knowledge base is a collection of information on a particular subject. The information is searchable by using keywords, drilling down through a hierarchical classification scheme, linking to related documents, or selecting an appropriate FAQ (frequently asked question). Wikis, such as Wikipedia, offer a commonly used platform for knowledge bases. Forums, help menus, and customer support links are platforms for technical knowledge bases. Figure 21-16 illustrates the search screen for the Microsoft Knowledge Base, which contains problem-solving tips for consumers.

Knowledge bases are just one source of online information. Blogs, Twitter feeds, news sites, personal Web sites, government Web sites, academic journals, and sites sponsored by various organizations all can be accessed to gather information.

The quality of information available online varies. Some is accurate and complete, whereas other information is erroneous, deliberately misleading, or false. You may find articles that are well researched, factual, and meticulously documented. Other articles may be based entirely on opinion, rumors, or made-up statistics.

High-quality information is accurate, unbiased, complete, and up to date.

Accurate. Accurate information is based on facts and free from error. It can be verified and cross-checked. Accurate information tends to exist in primary source documents, whereas the information in secondary or tertiary sources may be incorrectly restated or interpreted.

Unbiased. Unbiased information is free from prejudice and favoritism. It is objective, rather than being distorted by opinion and personal feelings. Most information is biased but may still be useful as long as you recognize the viewpoint it contains.

Complete. Quality information should address a topic without omitting important details. Omitting details can introduce bias; and though a slice of information may be accurate, it can be misleading when taken out of context.

Up to date. The world changes. People modify their opinions, scientific research reveals new facts, inventors create new products, witnesses step forward with new testimony. High-quality information reflects the most up-to-date data available.

• How do I separate online facts from fiction? (continued)

There are numerous guidelines for evaluating the quality of information you find online. The following tips should prove useful. Try applying them to the Web page shown in Figure 21-17 to give it a quality rating of 1 (low) to 5 (high).

Who produced the content and what are their credentials? Look for the names of authors, photographers, designers, and others who produced content. Google their names to link to their biographies, social pages, or other work.

What is the top-level domain? Recognizing .edu, .com, .org, and other top-level domains helps to classify the person, organization, or business that is responsible for the site.

What else can the URL tell you? The Web page title or site name can help you identify whether the information is provided by a Web site, blog, tweet, forum, news aggregator, or social network post.

Who sponsors the site? Check the site's copyright or About page to determine who or what is the site sponsor.

Is the material date-appropriate? Check the date when the material was created or posted.

Has the information been peer reviewed? Articles reviewed by topic experts are usually more accurate than articles that have not been reviewed. If an article includes public comments, those comments may provide insight into the accuracy or bias of the author.

Are there ads on the page? Sites with advertising might not publish content that is unfavorable to its advertisers.

Did the material originate at the site, or was it re-posted, republished, or retweeted? Redistributed material might be altered; you can refer to the original material to ensure its accuracy.

Is the material a mashup or derivative work? Stay alert for doctored photos and parodies.

What is the site's access policy? Sites that require a subscription or registration may have higher quality information, or information that is tailored to a specific clientele.

Figure 21-17

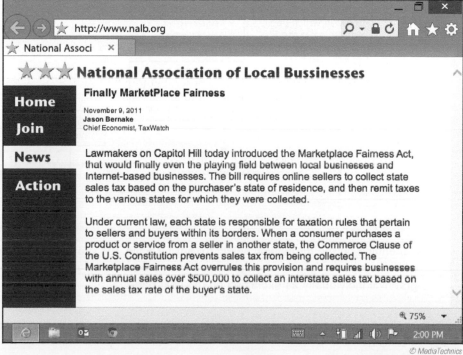

© MediaTechnics

FAQ Can I save Web pages, graphics, and text?

You can easily save a Web page on your computer's hard disk so that you can view it while you are offline. Use the Save As option on Internet Explorer's Page menu to initiate the save.

Most browsers give you the option of saving a Web page as an HTML file or as a plain text file. You should save the page as an HTML file if you want to share or modify it. The saved file includes all the HTML tags present in the original Web page document.

Alternatively, you can save the page as a plain text file without embedded HTML tags. A plain text file is easier to read if you open it with word processing software. It also works better than an HTML file if you want to later cut and paste text from the file into your own documents. Click the Try It! button to explore how to save Web page content.

TRY IT!

Figure
21-18

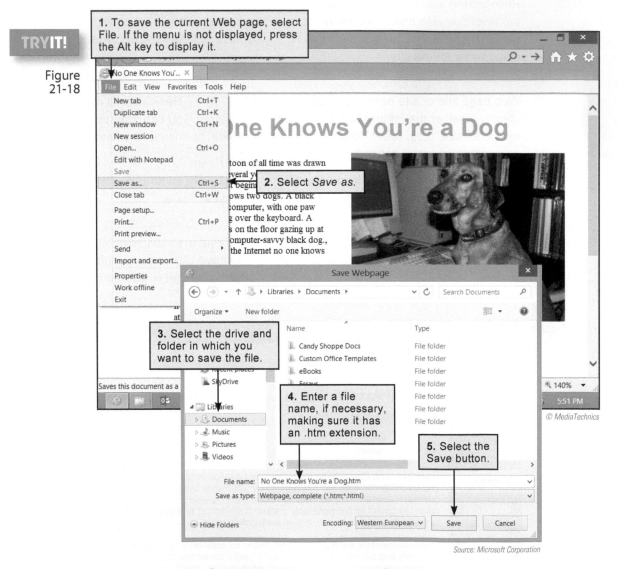

Source: Microsoft Corporation

© MediaTechnics

- Depending on the format you select for saving a file, the graphics might not be included with the saved page. If the graphics are not saved with the page, you can save the graphics individually as explained on the next page.

• Can I save Web pages, graphics, and text? (continued)

From time to time, you'll run across graphics or photos that you'd like to save individually for future reference. You don't have to save the entire page on which the graphic appears; you can save just the graphic, storing it in its own file on your computer's hard disk. Right-click (or touch and hold) the Web page graphic you want to save. A shortcut menu provides options for checking the graphic's file size and saving it.

Figure 21-19

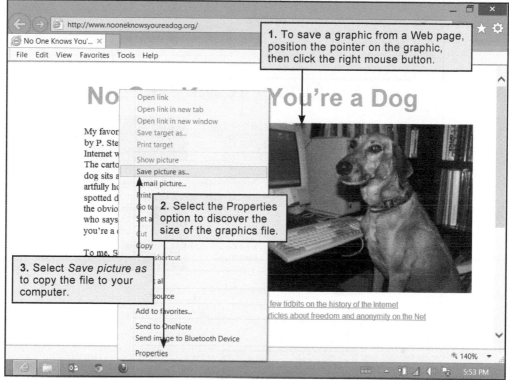

© MediaTechnics

• Most photos and pictures on the Web are copyrighted. You can usually save them for personal use, but you should not use them in any commercial product or in your own Web pages unless you obtain permission from the copyright holder.

• The graphics you see on Web pages typically exist as either JPEG, GIF, or PNG files. If graphics files are fairly small in size, they travel quickly over the Internet and appear in your browser without much delay. You can use the Properties option on the shortcut menu to determine the size of a graphic.

• Once you've saved a file on your computer, you can access it while offline by using your browser or any graphics software that works with the type of file you've saved.

• You can also copy a graphic and paste it directly into your favorite graphics software. To do so, right-click the graphic and select the Copy option. Start your graphics software and use the Edit menu's Paste option. After pasting the graphic, be sure to save the file.

• Can I save Web pages, graphics, and text? (continued)

Suppose that you're searching the Web for information about a specific topic and taking notes for a research paper. It might be very useful to snip out a passage of text from a Web page and then paste it into the document that contains your notes. Later, when you compose the paper, you can incorporate the ideas from the passage or you can quote the passage in its entirety—including, of course, a reference citation to its source.

Figure 21-20

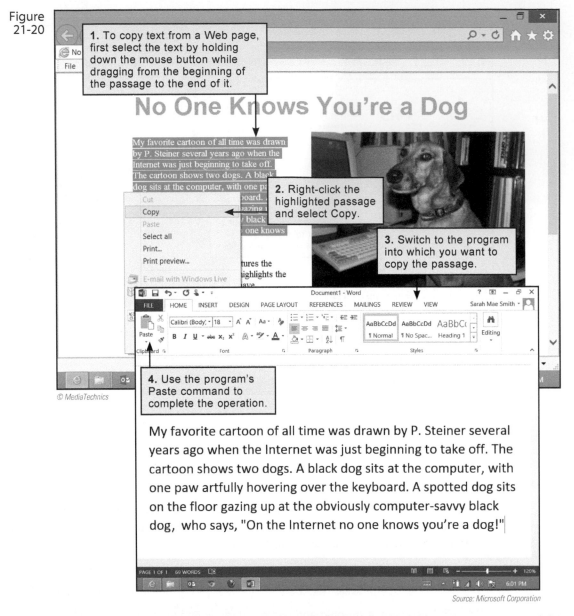

© MediaTechnics

Source: Microsoft Corporation

• Like material in printed books, content published on the Web is protected by copyrights. Be sure to provide a citation for any material you copy from the Web and then incorporate into your own work. Style guides such as *The Chicago Manual of Style* provide guidelines for formatting Web citations.

• After you copy a section of text from the Web, move the pointer up to your browser's address box and select the URL. Copy the URL and paste it into the document that contains your notes. Using the URL as a reference, you'll be able to return to the original site whenever you need additional data to complete a citation.

FAQ How do I print a Web page?

Once you locate a Web page with relevant information, you might want to print it for future reference. For example, when you complete an online purchase, you might want to print your order confirmation. Most browsers make it easy to print a Web page using a toolbar button or menu option.

Figure
21-21

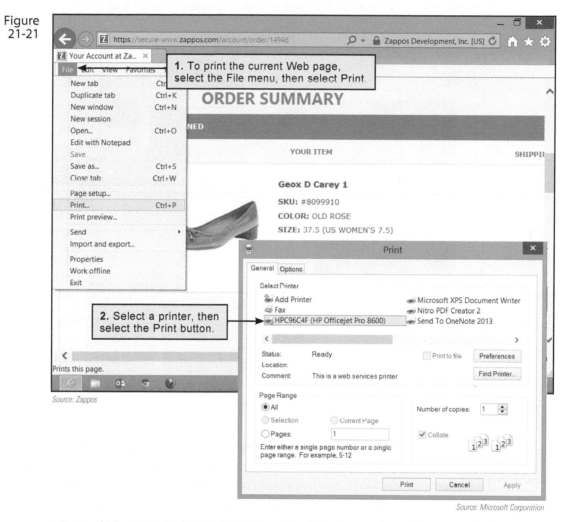

Source: Zappos

Source: Microsoft Corporation

- Some Web pages include a link to a printer-friendly version of the page, designed to print on standard size paper. This version is also designed to use color in such a way that a single page won't use all of your printer ink. Look for the "printer-friendly" link before you start a printout.

- Many Web "pages" are very long—the equivalent of 10 to 20 printed pages. Some browsers divide long Web pages into a series of printable pages and let you select which of those pages you want to print. Other browsers do not have this capability. To print a part of a long Web page, you can use the copy and paste technique described in the previous FAQ.

- You might find it useful to include both the Web page's URL and its title on your printout. Today's browsers do this for you automatically.

FAQ How do I access digital media from the Web?

"Digital media" is a term used to refer to photos, drawings, videos, animations, music, and narrations. Today's digital media is accessed via the Internet from Web sites such as iTunes, YouTube, Flickr, Pinterest, and Hulu. To find media, you can use media filters at a generalized search engine such as Google. Another way to find media is to access a media repository such as YouTube and use its built-in search tool.

Figure
21-22

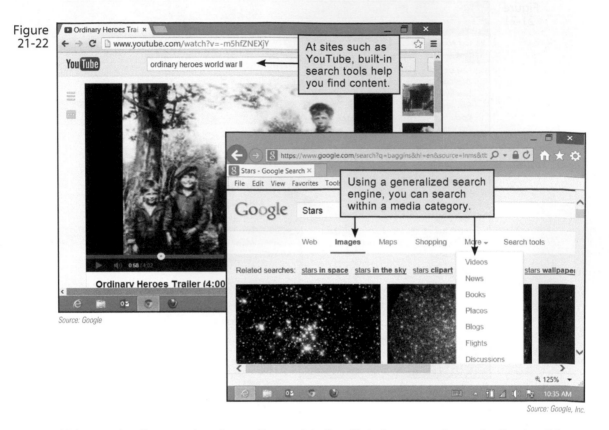

Source: Google

Source: Google, Inc.

Videos, animations, and audio media consist of multiple frames and sounds. To play this type of media, your computer requires a continuous flow of data. That data can flow from your local device after it has been downloaded, or it can stream over the Internet in real time as you are watching or listening.

Downloading media. When you download a media file and save it on your computer, you can access it whenever you like. You have to wait, however, for the file to download before you can open it. With large media files, such as full-length movies, that can be a disadvantage. When you buy a movie from iTunes to watch offline, you have to wait for it to download.

Streaming media. Streaming is a delivery method that plays music or displays video in real time as it arrives from the Web to your computer. Sites such as YouTube, Hulu, and iTunes Match offer streaming music and video clips for sample tracks, trailers, TV shows, and video shorts.

While streaming takes place, parts of the media file might be temporarily stored on your computer. However, the music or video is not stored in a format that you can use to replay the music or video when you are offline. This limitation helps to protect the media from unauthorized use and distribution. For example, music that you stream from iTunes Match is not stored on your computer, so it cannot be copied and sent to a friend.

FAQ Why do browsers need plug-ins?

A plug-in (or add-on) is a software component that adds functionality to a browser. Some plug-ins add toolbars, such as the Google Toolbar. Other plug-ins are designed to play media within the browser window. When you access the YouTube site with a browser and play a video, your browser interacts with the HTML5 plug-in or the Flash Player plug-in to stream the video to your computer.

Browsers usually come equipped with a set of commonly used plug-ins, and additional plug-ins can be added to access media supplied in other file formats. Plug-ins are available on the Web. They are downloaded and installed much like any other software. Popular plug-ins include Adobe Flash Player, Microsoft Silverlight, and Apple QuickTime.

You can view the plug-ins that are installed for your browser. With Internet Explorer, select the Settings control, and then select Manage Add-ons. Using the window shown in Figure 21-23, you can make sure the plug-ins you want to use are enabled and you can disable those that you prefer not to use. You can also configure plug-ins not to run on specific sites that might contain suspicious media.

TRYIT!

Figure
21-23

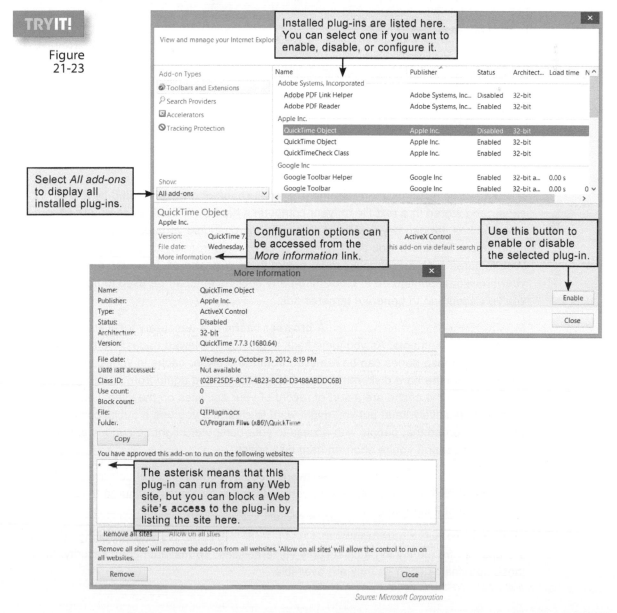

Select *All add-ons* to display all installed plug-ins.

Installed plug-ins are listed here. You can select one if you want to enable, disable, or configure it.

Configuration options can be accessed from the *More information* link.

Use this button to enable or disable the selected plug-in.

The asterisk means that this plug-in can run from any Web site, but you can block a Web site's access to the plug-in by listing the site here.

FAQ Is the Web safe?

Among the millions of businesses and individuals that offer products, services, and information on the Web, some are unscrupulous and try to take advantage of unwary shoppers, chat group participants, and researchers. Internet-borne viruses and online credit card fraud are regularly featured on news reports. However, security tools and some common sense can make using the Web as safe as, or safer than, paying with a credit card at your local mall or favorite restaurant.

Use a secure connection for sensitive data. Most commercial Web sites encrypt sensitive information sent to and from the site during the payment phase of an e-commerce purchase. URLs for secure Web connections begin with https instead of http. Before submitting credit card numbers, Social Security numbers, or other sensitive data, look for https in the URL and a padlock icon in the browser window.

Figure
21-24

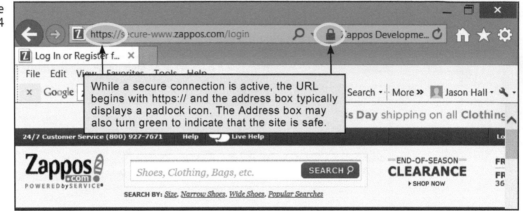

While a secure connection is active, the URL begins with https:// and the address box typically displays a padlock icon. The Address box may also turn green to indicate that the site is safe.

Source: Zappos

Block third-party cookies. A **cookie** is a small chunk of data generated by a Web server and stored in a text file on your computer's hard disk. Cookies can be used to keep track of the pages you view at a site, the merchandise you select, and other profile information. Therefore, you don't want to block cookies from legitimate sites because Web features such as shopping carts require them. You should, however, make sure your browser is configured to block third-party cookies that can be used to track the sites you've visited and to generate targeted ads.

Monitor temporary Internet files. A **browser cache** is a temporary local storage area for Web page elements. As you jump back to previously viewed pages, the text and graphics for those pages can be retrieved from the browser cache in your computer's memory or on the hard disk, rather than being downloaded again from a Web server. Web pages in the cache are a sort of record of your activities on the Web. Like cookies, a cache is relatively safe; but you might want to clear it if you use a public computer, if you're concerned that people with access to your computer might be curious about your Web activities, or if you're short on hard disk space.

Run antivirus software. Antivirus software modules contain several defensive tools that block Web-based exploits. Make sure your antivirus software is configured to run at all times and that it is up to date.

Keep your browser and operating system updated. Browsers and operating systems are updated frequently to patch security vulnerabilities. To maintain good security, apply these updates as soon as they are available.

QuickCheck A

1. A(n) [_____] , such as www.yahoo.com/automobiles or www.msu.edu/fac, uniquely defines a particular Web page. (Hint: Use the acronym.)

2. When you start a browser, it automatically loads and displays a page from a Web site. This starting page is known as your [_____] page.

3. Assume that you type a URL in order to go to Web page A, then you click a link to go to Web page B. If you click the Back button, then click the Forward button, Web page [_____] will be displayed on your screen.

4. True or false? The History list shows only Web pages you visited during the current computing session. [_____]

5. A(n) [_____] is generated by a Web server and then stored on your computer to keep track of the pages you view at a site, the merchandise you select, and other profile information.

CHECKIT!

QuickCheck B

Indicate the letter of the browser element that best relates to the following:

1. Toolbar [____]

2. Settings [____]

3. Tabs [____]

4. Link URL [____]

5. Media search [____]

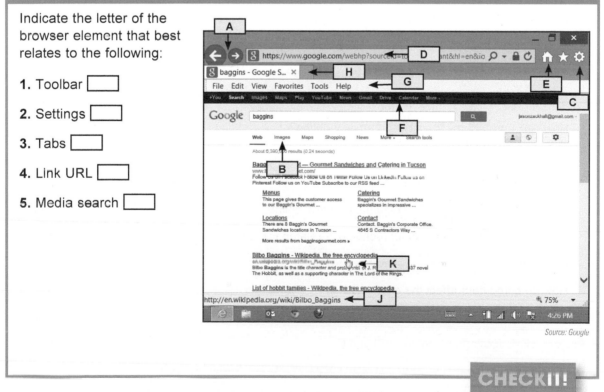

Source: Google

CHECKIT!

What's Inside and on the CD?

For most of us, computers are indispensable tools for storing data, crunching numbers, and producing written work. We use them for formal and informal e-learning. Online shopping at e-commerce sites is convenient and gives us a chance to compare prices and features before we purchase. E-government sites provide easy access to official forms, offer a channel for corresponding with our representatives, and provide information about important voter issues.

The importance of computers and their widespread use raise issues about their safety, security, and ethical application. In this chapter, you'll learn how computers affect privacy, security, health, and the environment. As you read, you'll find many tips for protecting your privacy, avoiding scams, spotting hoaxes, and thwarting identity thieves.

FAQ How do computers benefit society?

Computers have become an important part of society, helping us with mundane tasks as well as contributing to the complex dynamics of business, politics, the economy, and personal relationships. Computers, the Web, and the Internet have done more than simply facilitate life-as-usual; they have transformed many aspects of the way we live.

Socializing. The social scene has evolved in some surprising directions. Online dating became popular when sites like Matchmaker.com and eHarmony opened. The online scene is now supplemented by online social networking with Facebook, Google+, Twitter, and similar sites.

News. At one time, daily newspapers and televised news were the main sources of information about current events. Today, a wide-ranging group of citizen journalists use blogs, vlogs, and podcasts to disseminate news and opinions. Citizen reporters and commentators present a diverse range of opinions and cover events that are often ignored by mainstream media.

Education. Today, many students take online classes instead of commuting to campus. E-learning opportunities abound for formal and informal learning. Assisted by online tutorials and learning management systems (LMSs) such as Blackboard and Moodle, access to education is much more convenient than in the past—and that's especially useful for single parents and individuals with physical challenges.

Business. Digital technologies make it possible for workers to telecommute, attend Web conferences instead of traveling to meetings, collaborate using Web apps, and communicate using e-mail. Using tools like WebEx and GoToMeeting, time previously devoted to commuting can be spent more productively, and travel costs are eliminated. Though a possible disadvantage of telecommuting is reduced human contact, teleworkers may be able to focus without interruptions from meetings and other workplace distractions. Flexible schedules can enhance family life, and corporations may be able to reduce costs associated with office space.

Manufacturing. Factories have changed, too. Hazardous jobs can now be handled by computer-controlled robots and automated systems. In addition to increased worksite safety, these systems can also increase efficiency, and those efficiencies help to maintain reasonable product prices by offsetting increases in labor and material costs.

Figure 22-1

© MediaTechnics

Banking. Our financial system, once based on paper currency and checks, has gone digital. Trips to the bank have been replaced by access to ATMs in malls and other handy locations. E-banking, income tax filing, and PayPal transactions happen from your computer keyboard. Point-of-sale systems connect to worldwide credit card processing systems that reduce paperwork and create an electronic paper trail of transactions.

Shopping. E-commerce is, perhaps, one of the most transformative digital technologies. Not only can shoppers purchase merchandise using their computers, but they can access stores far distant from home and use shopping aggregators like PriceGrabber and Nextag to find the best deal. Businesses use similar online tools to locate suppliers for raw goods, parts, and services.

FAQ How can I protect my computer from viruses?

The term **malicious code** refers to any program or set of program instructions designed to surreptitiously enter a computer, disrupt its normal operations, or gather sensitive data. The most prevalent types of malicious code include viruses, Trojan horses, and worms.

Viruses. The term "virus" is commonly used to refer to any type of intrusive program, but technically a computer virus is only one type of malware. A **computer virus** is a set of program instructions that can attach itself to a "host" executable software program, such as a game or an office suite component. When the host program runs, the virus code is also executed, enabling the virus to reproduce itself, spread to other files, and carry out disruptive activities.

Viruses can corrupt files, destroy data, display an irritating message, or otherwise disrupt computer operations. A common misconception is that viruses spread themselves from one computer to another. On the contrary, they can replicate themselves only on the host computer. Viruses are spread from one computer to another by human actions, such as sharing infected USB flash drives, downloading infected software, and opening infected e-mail attachments.

A key characteristic of viruses is their ability to lurk in a computer for days or months, quietly replicating themselves. While this replication takes place, you might not be aware that your computer has contracted a virus; therefore, it is easy to inadvertently spread infected files to other people's computers. After several days or months go by, a trigger event, such as a specific date, can unleash a virus payload. Payloads can be as harmless as displaying an offensive message, or as devastating as erasing all the data on your computer's hard disk.

Trojan horses. A **Trojan horse** is a computer program that seems to perform one function while actually doing something else. Technically, it is not the same as a virus because, unlike a virus, a Trojan horse is not designed to make copies of itself. Trojan horses are notorious for stealing passwords, but they can also delete files and give remote hackers access to a computer system. A Trojan horse might allow a hacker to see the contents of your screen, control your Webcam, or capture your login keystrokes.

Some Trojan horses contain a virus or a worm, which can replicate and spread. Virus experts call this a blended threat because it combines more than one type of malicious code. In addition to Trojan-horse/virus combinations, worm/virus combinations are also prevalent.

Computer worms. With the proliferation of network traffic and e-mail, worms have become a major concern in the computing community. A **computer worm** is malicious software designed to spread from computer to computer over local area networks and the Internet. Unlike viruses, computer worms are not attached to host programs and run independently.

Worms deliver payloads that vary from harmless messages to malicious file deletions. A **mass-mailing worm** makes use of information on an infected computer to mail itself to everyone listed in a user's e-mail address book. Other worms deliver denial of service attacks. A **denial of service attack** is designed to generate a lot of activity on a network by flooding it with useless traffic—enough traffic to overwhelm the network's processing capability and essentially bring all communications to a halt.

• How can I protect my computer from viruses? (continued)

Most malicious code is stored in executable files, usually with .exe, .com, .bat, and .scr file name extensions. Viruses are sometimes hidden in files with two extensions—for example, Shakira.mp3.com or FinancialAid.docx.exe. When Windows is set to hide file extensions, users see only the first harmless-looking extension.

Malicious code can slip into your computer from a variety of sources. Be cautious of homemade CDs and disreputable Web sites that offer pirated games and other supposedly fun stuff. They are a common source of viruses and Trojan horses.

E-mail attachments are also a common source of malicious code. Typically, infected attachments look like executable files, usually with .exe file name extensions. These files infect your computer if you open them.

Malware can also slip into your computer when you click links embedded in e-mail messages. Those links can connect your computer to a malicious Web site where downloaded files contain malware.

Antivirus software is a set of utility programs that looks for and eradicates viruses, Trojan horses, worms, and other malware. Typically, computer owners configure their antivirus software to run constantly in the background to check files and e-mail messages as they are downloaded.

Modern antivirus software attempts to locate viruses by watching for virus signatures. A **virus signature** is a section of the virus program, such as a unique series of instructions, that can be used to identify a known virus, Trojan horse, or worm, much like a fingerprint is used to identify an individual.

The information that your antivirus software uses to identify and eradicate malicious code is stored in one or more files usually referred to as virus definitions. New malware is unleashed just about every day. To keep up with these newly identified pests, antivirus software publishers offer virus definition updates, which are usually available as Web downloads. Most antivirus software can be configured to automatically check for updates and download them when available. Click the Try It! button in Figure 22-2 to learn more about using antivirus software.

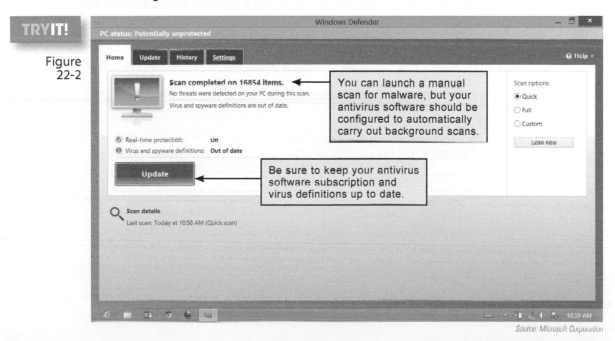

TRY IT!

Figure 22-2

Source: Microsoft Corporation

•How can I protect my computer from viruses? (continued)

Avoiding viruses, Trojan horses, and worms is preferable to trying to eliminate these pesky programs after they have taken up residence in your computer. Once malware infiltrates your computer, it can be difficult to eradicate, even with antivirus software. The process of eradicating a virus—sometimes called disinfecting—usually includes deleting the virus code from files or deleting infected files.

If your computer contracts a virus, check your antivirus software publisher's Web site for information on identifying the virus and eradicating it. To protect your computer against malicious code, you can take the following steps:

- Install antivirus software. Windows Defender is included with Windows 8. Third-party antivirus software brands such as Norton, McAfee, and avast! offer protection for desktop computers, laptops, tablets, and smartphones.

- Keep your antivirus software running full-time in the background so that it scans all files as they are opened and checks every e-mail message as it arrives. If you do not use antivirus software, your computer is very likely to get a virus, fall under the control of a hacker, or become vulnerable to data theft.

- Keep your antivirus software up to date by allowing it to automatically download updates when they become available.

- Before you download a file—especially a file containing software—make sure the file's source is reputable. Stay away from Web sites that offer pirated software. Do not open a downloaded file unless your antivirus software is active.

- Whenever you receive a CD or USB flash drive, use your antivirus software to scan the files it contains before you copy them to your hard disk, run them, or open them.

- Never open an e-mail attachment unless you know whom it is from, you have an idea what it contains, and you were expecting to receive it.

- Do not click links in e-mail messages that originate from unknown sources.

- Watch for information about the latest virus threats. Many threats make headline news. You can also find out about threats at antivirus software publisher Web sites.

- Set Windows to display file extensions so that you don't inadvertently download a virus file because you could see only the first innocent-looking extension. Figure 22-3 reminds you how to configure File Explorer so that file extensions are displayed.

Figure 22-3

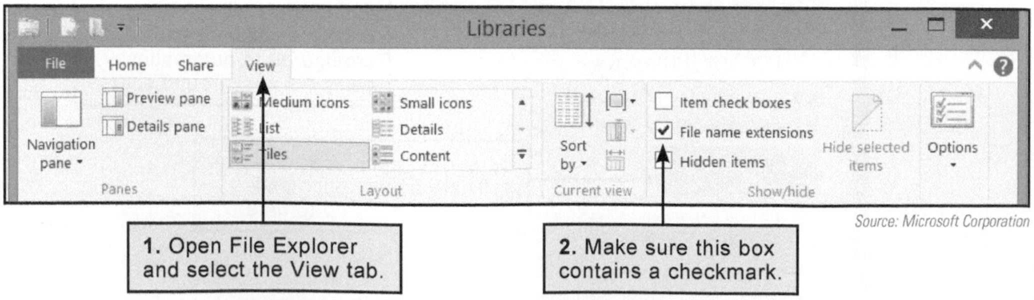

Source: Microsoft Corporation

1. Open File Explorer and select the View tab.

2. Make sure this box contains a checkmark.

FAQ How does a router protect my computer from intrusions?

Intruders don't have to enter your premises to access your computer. Hackers use various schemes to gain unauthorized access to computers via networks. The practice of searching the Internet for unprotected computers is called a **port probe**. You learned in an earlier chapter that computers have external ports for connecting peripheral devices. Computers also have virtual ports that can be opened or closed to accept various types of transmitted data. For example, port 110 is used to accept e-mail and port 80 is used to collect data from the Web.

Hackers use port scanning software to transmit port probes to random IP addresses looking for unsecured computer systems. If a probe discovers that your computer is vulnerable, hackers can surreptitiously copy your data or use your computer as a base of operations for sending out viruses, spam, and other disruptive programs. Routers effectively hide your computer's ports because they block unsolicited port scans coming from the Internet.

In a typical LAN, the router is a single point of contact between local devices and the Internet. Two networks can interconnect using a device called a **gateway**. The routers used on local area networks contain gateway circuitry that allows the LAN to exchange data with the Internet. As shown in Figure 22-4, all packets coming from the Internet go to the router, where they are forwarded to devices within the LAN.

Figure
22-4

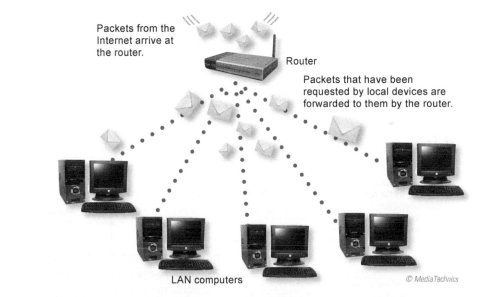

Packets from the Internet arrive at the router.

Router

Packets that have been requested by local devices are forwarded to them by the router.

LAN computers

© MediaTechnics

The router's IP address is the only one that can be accessed directly from the Internet. The rest of the devices in a LAN have non-routable IP addresses that cannot be accessed directly from the Internet. Routers offer network security because they allow external data into the LAN only if a local device specifically requests the data for a download, Web page, or other service. Data that is not specifically requested is blocked, which prevents hackers from randomly choosing an IP address and successfully sending port probes and malware to it.

FAQ How does firewall software protect my computer from intrusions?

Firewall software (sometimes referred to as a personal firewall) is designed to analyze the flow of traffic entering your computer from a network. It makes sure that incoming information was actually requested and is not an unauthorized intrusion. It blocks activity from suspicious Internet addresses, and it reports intrusion attempts so that you know when hackers are trying to break into your computer.

Firewall software is the opposite of a gateway. Whereas a gateway is designed to allow data to flow, a firewall is designed to limit the flow of data.

Firewall software is essential for computers that are connected directly to the Internet. If you don't have a router, then make sure firewall software is installed and running at all times. The Windows operating system includes a utility called Windows Firewall that you can use to block intrusion attempts. Your computer should have only one firewall active at any given time. If your antivirus software or security suite includes a firewall, then Windows Firewall can be deactivated.

To access Windows Firewall, type Firewall in the Windows Search box, select Settings, then select the Windows Firewall option. Using the window shown in Figure 22-5, you can turn the firewall on or off, and you can adjust settings to allow or block specific programs and services.

TRYIT!

Figure 22-5

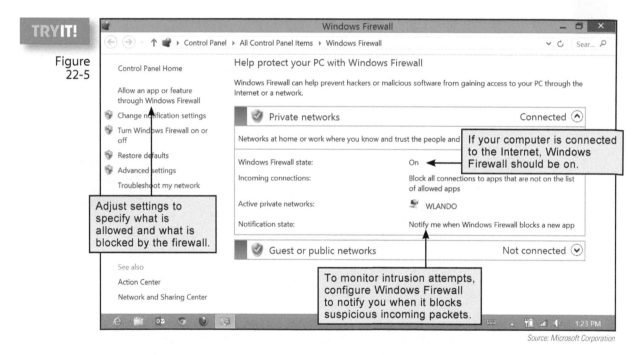

Source: Microsoft Corporation

FAQ How does encryption protect my network from intrusions?

Wireless networks broadcast signals that can be picked up by any device within the coverage area. Airborne transmissions are easily captured by hackers or by innocent neighbors who just happen to be within the range of your wireless network. The data carried by Wi-Fi signals can be encrypted with WEP, WPA, or PSK.

The original wireless encryption was called **WEP** (Wired Equivalent Privacy) because it was designed to provide a level of confidentiality similar to that of a wired network. WEP is very easy to bypass. It does, however, protect a wireless network from casual hacks and inadvertent crosstalk from nearby networks.

WPA (Wi-Fi Protected Access) and its follow-up version, WPA2, offer stronger protection by making sure that packets have not been intercepted or tampered with in any way. **PSK** (pre-shared key), also referred to as personal mode, is a type of WPA used on many home networks.

When setting up wireless encryption, you create an **encryption key**, which works like a password. When a computer tries to join the network, the encryption key will be required. To activate encryption for your wireless network, open the router's configuration software as explained in Figure 22-6.

Figure 22-6

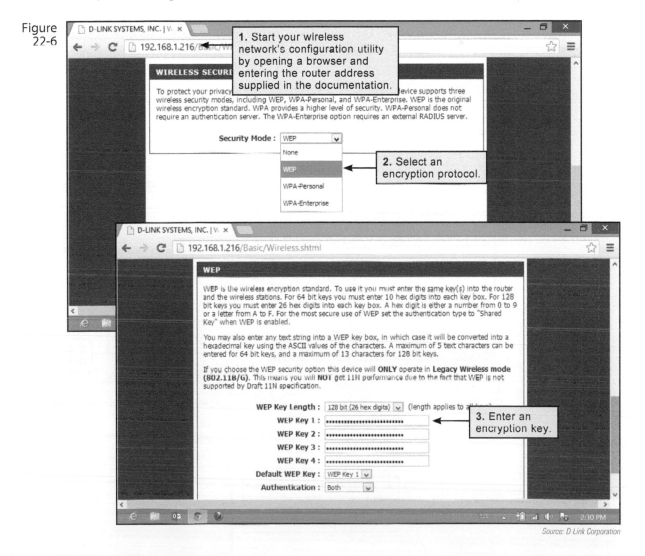

Source: D-Link Corporation

FAQ Can I use encryption to hide the contents of files?

On networks, encryption works by scrambling data as it leaves your computer so that data is in encrypted format while in transit. Encryption is applied only to the copy of your data that is transmitted. The data that is stored on your computer remains in unencrypted format. The data in those files is open to anyone who gets access to your computer from its keyboard, from another computer on your network, or from a remote Internet connection.

Encryption is not the same as compression. Compressed files use a public algorithm to perform the compression, and anyone has the capability to uncompress them without a key or password.

If you have files stored on your computer that contain confidential, personal, or sensitive data, you can protect the contents of those files by encrypting them. Even a successful hacker or intruder will not find the scrambled contents of encrypted files to be of much use.

Encryption utilities scramble the data in a file by using a multi-digit key. A key is also necessary to decrypt the data into a usable format. The password you assign to an encrypted file acts as the key. Do not forget the password. Without it, you won't be able to open the file.

Applications such as Microsoft Word provide utilities for saving files in encrypted format. You learned about this utility in the word processing chapters. Some versions of Windows also include an encryption utility called EFS (Encrypting File System). If your version of Windows has this capability, you can access it from File Explorer by right-clicking the file you want to encrypt, selecting Properties, then selecting the Advanced button.

Figure 22-7

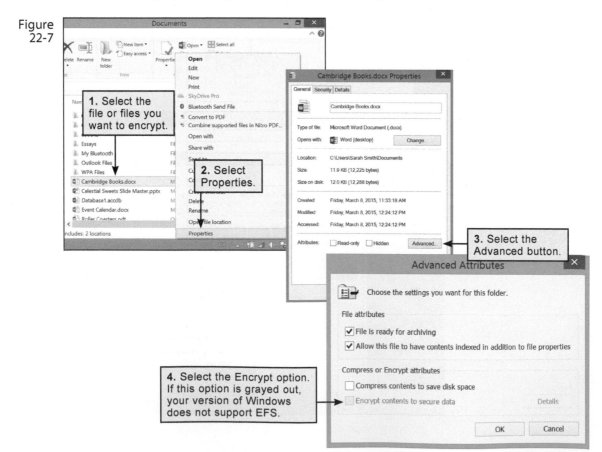

Source: Microsoft Corporation

FAQ Should I worry about identity theft?

Identity theft occurs when someone obtains your personal information and uses it without your permission to commit fraud or other crimes. An identity theft victim might be refused loans, jobs, and educational opportunities. Victims might even get arrested for crimes they didn't commit. A person whose identity has been stolen can spend months or years trying to restore a favorable reputation and credit record.

Identity thieves obtain personal information using a variety of high-tech and low-tech schemes. They rummage through your trash and mail looking for pay stubs and credit card receipts. They might ransack your home, steal your purse, or pilfer your wallet to obtain credit cards and your driver's license. High-tech thieves can hack into your personal computer, or the computer databases of your employer, bank, or credit card company.

Thwarting identity thieves requires vigilant supervision of your identity data, such as Social Security number, credit card numbers, driver's license, passport, pay stubs, credit card receipts, and medical records. Consider these tips for protecting your identity:

Don't divulge personal information. Before you divulge any personal information on the phone, through the mail, or over the Internet, confirm that you're dealing with a legitimate representative of a reputable organization. Double-check by calling customer service using the number on your account statement or in the telephone book.

Shred your trash. Use a shredder or tear up your charge receipts, pay stubs, copies of credit applications, insurance forms, physician statements, cancelled checks, and bank statements. Cut up expired credit cards.

Guard your mail. Deposit sensitive outgoing mail in a post office collection box instead of an unsecured mailbox. For incoming mail, use a post office box or a mail slot, rather than trusting mail to a mailbox on your porch or curb.

Protect your identification documents. Keep your Social Security card and passport in a secure place. Keep a list of credit cards that you carry, along with the customer service number to call if a card is lost or stolen. Keep your driver's license in a clear window of your wallet, so that you don't have to hand it to clerks.

Divulge your Social Security number only when absolutely necessary. Before you supply your Social Security number, find out why it is needed, how it will be used, and how it will be secured.

Keep track of computer data. Before you dispose of an old computer or storage device, use file shredder software to delete any personal information stored on it. **File shredder software** overwrites a hard disk or USB drive with random 1s and 0s to make data unrecoverable.

Use strong passwords. Passwords should be long; more than eight characters. They should contain letters and numbers, and uppercase and lowercase letters. They should not be composed of words that can be found in a dictionary.

Keep passwords secret. Do not allow friends or coworkers to use your passwords to log in and use your e-mail account, network account, iTunes account, or Web site account.

Keep informed. Check www.consumer.ftc.gov/ for additional information on protecting your identity, and to learn what to do if you think your identity has been stolen.

FAQ How can I protect my identity and privacy online?

Privacy violations take place when your personal information is distributed or your online activities are tracked without your permission. Unscrupulous organizations can use your personal information to inundate you with ads and marketing offers, while criminals can use this data to stalk you or steal your identity. Despite legislation, a number of quasi-legal schemes exist for collecting your personal data. These schemes have flourished online. Currently, spyware is a major online privacy threat.

Spyware is any technology that surreptitiously gathers information. In the context of the Web and e-commerce, spyware secretly gathers information and relays it to advertisers or other interested parties. Web-based marketers use several spyware techniques, including third-party cookies and Web bugs.

When you connect to a Web site, you expect it to store an innocuous cookie on your computer's hard disk. Some Web sites, however, feature banner ads supplied by third-party marketing firms. If you click the ad, this third party can create a **third-party cookie** and use it to track your activities at any site containing its banner ads.

A **Web bug** (also called a clear GIF or pixel tag) is an object, such as a tiny graphic, embedded on a Web page that sets a cookie to third-party Web sites. Unlike third-party cookies that are produced when you click an ad, Web bugs can set cookies automatically whenever the page they are on is opened by your browser.

Marketing firms claim that third-party cookies are simply used to select and display ads that might interest you, but privacy advocates are worried that these cookies can be used to compile shopper profiles, which can be sold and used for unauthorized purposes. To protect your privacy, you can configure your browser to block third-party cookies. Figure 22-8 explains how to do so for Internet Explorer.

Figure 22-8

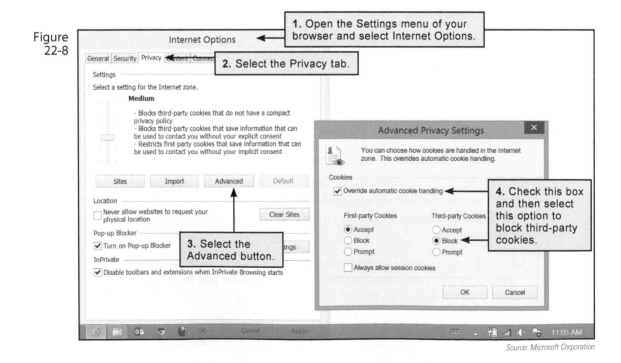

Source: Microsoft Corporation

• How can I protect my identity and privacy online? (continued)

You can violate your own privacy by unintentionally releasing information about yourself that can be exploited by aggressive marketing companies, hackers, and criminals. For example, to gain access to some sites, you might be asked for your name and other personal information. You must consider whether access to a Web site is worth the information you are required to divulge.

You might also inadvertently supply personal information in e-mail messages sent using a computer at school or at work. Although most schools and businesses usually refrain from reading your e-mail messages, under certain circumstances it is legal for them to do so. Read computer use policies at your school or workplace to learn your e-mail privacy rights.

To protect your privacy online, keep the following guidelines in mind:

- Do not reveal your e-mail address to any organization unless you want to receive correspondence from it.

- Never reply to spammers.

- Be wary about sharing information about your family and friends.

- Use an alias when participating in chat rooms and do not divulge personal information to other chat room participants.

- Be wary of online surveys, sweepstakes, and contests, especially those that ask for information about your job, finances, and income.

- When registering for access to a Web site, supply a minimum amount of information.

- Regard e-mail more like a postcard than a sealed letter, especially if your e-mail account is supplied by your school or employer.

- Configure your browser to block third-party cookies.

- Don't post photos online that you would not want your grandmother, children, or prospective employer to see.

- Keep track of your privacy settings for social networking sites; check them periodically to make sure they have not been inadvertently changed.

- After using a public computer, make sure you sign out, log off, delete temporary Internet files, and shut down Windows. You can also take advantage of **private browsing** offered by browsers such as Internet Explorer (Figure 22-9).

Figure 22-9

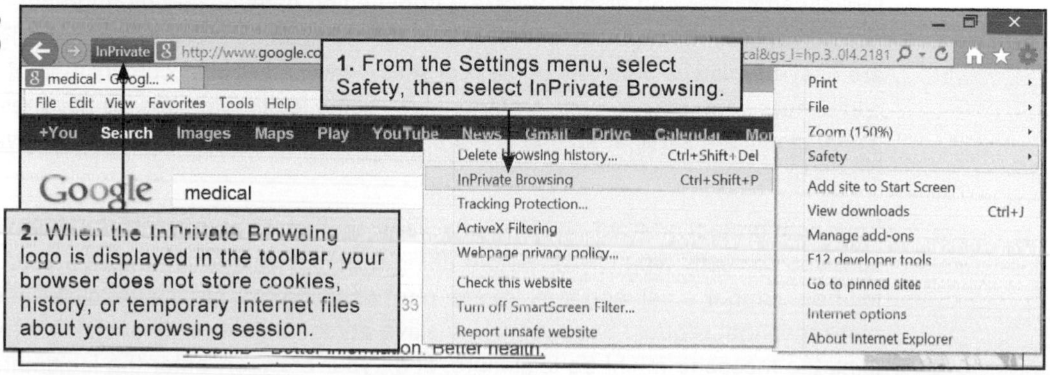

1. From the Settings menu, select Safety, then select InPrivate Browsing.

2. When the InPrivate Browsing logo is displayed in the toolbar, your browser does not store cookies, history, or temporary Internet files about your browsing session.

Source: Microsoft Corporation

FAQ How can I avoid scams and hoaxes?

Scam artists fooled unsuspecting victims long before computers were invented. Today, scammers take advantage of the Internet to reach across borders and access millions of potential victims. The most pervasive scams include phishing exploits, fake Web sites, and fraudulent e-mail messages.

Phishing is the use of fraudulent Web sites and e-mail links to trick people into revealing sensitive, personal, and financial information. A typical phishing scam begins with an e-mail message that seems to be an official notice from a trusted source, such as a credit card company, online payment service, software vendor, or bank. Under the guise of updating your password, reactivating your credit card, or confirming your address, the e-mail message offers a handy link to a supposedly legitimate site. However, the link leads to a fake site; and if you enter your password, credit card number, bank account number, or Social Security number, you're handing it over to a hacker.

Fake sites often look similar to real sites. They include corporate logos and they may even offer a secure connection when you enter sensitive information. Identifying these sites is not easy. Most browsers include built-in antiphishing features that compare URLs you might visit with a list of known phishing sites. Unfortunately, phishing sites spring up faster than the list can be updated, so don't depend on your browser as your only defense against phishing attacks.

Digital certificates offer another layer of protection. A **digital certificate** is issued by a certificate authority that essentially vouches for the certificate holder's identity. The certificate contains the holder's name, a serial number, an expiration date, and an encryption key. Digital certificates can be attached to e-mail messages, documents, and software, but they are useful antiphishing tools when attached to Web sites. If a site has a digital certificate, selecting it should display the certificate holder's name and other details.

Figure 22-10

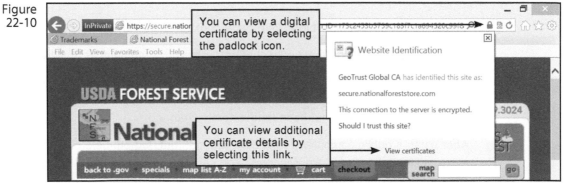

Source: US Forest Service

Digital certificates can also protect you from getting bamboozled by a fraudulent Web site masquerading as a well-known merchant. Sometimes these sites have URLs that are easy-to-mistype versions of the real sites—www.ediebauer.com instead of www.eddiebauer.com, for example. Unfortunately, some legitimate sites do not subscribe to a digital certificate service, so that is not a security feature you can rely on to evaluate every Web site you visit.

Your best protection from phishing attacks is caution. First, pay careful attention to make sure you correctly type URLs. Before doing business with an unknown company, give its toll-free number a call and look for site reviews using Google. Never click links in e-mail messages that request passwords, sensitive personal data, or financial information. If you think the message might be legitimate, open your browser, enter the legitimate URL for the business, and use links at the site to check if your account needs any maintenance.

• How can I avoid scams and hoaxes? (continued)

The number and variety of phishing schemes are uncountable, but the following list includes samples of the most prevalent e-mail scams that are currently circulating. Don't be tempted to click the links they contain.

PayPal account problem. We have detected one or more attempts to log in to your PayPal account from a foreign IP address. Click here to reinstate your account.

Funds transfer from offshore bank. Mr. Mbembke from Nigeria is escaping political persecution and needs to temporarily transfer U.S. $10 million to an offshore bank, if you would be so kind as to furnish your bank account number for this purpose, he will reward you with 10% of its value.

LinkedIn account blocked. Your LinkedIn account has been blocked due to suspicious activity. To remove the restriction please click this link.

Stolen travel documents. I am overseas working with a Volunteer Training Program and my bag was stolen from me with my passport, credit cards, and mobile phones in it. Can you loan me some funds to get back home?

Parcel delivery failure. We couldn't deliver your parcel. Please print the attached label and show it at your local post office to retrieve the package.

Driver license renewal. Thank you for your payment of $109.38 to the Florida Department of Highway Safety and Motor Vehicles. To review this transaction, click here.

Greeting card. Joe Blow has sent you a greeting card! Click this link to see it.

Microsoft Windows login. Dear Windows User, It has come to our attention that your Microsoft Installation records are out of date. Click the Verify button below and enter your login information to confirm your records.

In addition to scams designed to collect personal information and spread malware, a variety of e-mail messages about nonexistent viruses circulate on the Internet. A typical **virus hoax** warns of a devastating new virus, describes some outlandish procedure for eradicating it, and encourages you to notify all your friends.

The e-mail warning might itself contain a virus. Or, a virus might lurk in the file you are instructed to download for eradicating the non-existent virus. If you send panicked e-mails to all your friends, you invariably end up with egg on your face. Before you take any action based on an e-mail virus notification, check one of the many antivirus sites, such as www.symantec.com, www.f-secure.com, www.mcafee.com, or www.hoaxbusters.org.

Figure
22-11

Watchout For This   Standard Header ▾

Alex Delamara <ale... View   Monday, January

To: Pat Redfern <pat_redfern@yahoo.com>

Dbugexe (8KB)

Pat-

I thought I should pass this warning on to you. It looks like a new virus. ◀——

Hello, my name is Matthew Thomas and I am a computer analyst at GEC. I h
who works at IBM and this morning he told me about a new virus that has be
discovered. This is very damaging and it is carried over the e-mailing systems.
ability to completley format your hard drive, however it takes a few days to fully do this. It
is vital that you install this program into your computer first. I have already installed it so the

Messages about virus hoaxes often mention a reputable organization and contain links or attachments. They also encourage you to immediately forward the message to everyone in your e-mail address book.

FAQ What about filtering and censorship?

Censorship is the suppression of speech, writing, or other public communication that is thought to be objectionable or offensive. In situations such as protecting military secrets in time of war, censorship can have benefits. It does, however, limit freedom of speech, which is a basic tenet of democracy.

Internet filtering is the technical method used to carry out electronic censorship by blocking Web sites, blogs, forums, or other Internet content from reaching certain audiences. Filtering is controversial, but it is practiced by concerned parents, litigation-averse librarians, and repressive governments.

The Web contains all kinds of information, music, and images. Some of its less savory content includes pornography, information on bombs and poisons, extremist propaganda, and ads for quack medicines. Balancing online freedom of speech with restrictions that ensure safety, security, and cultural ethics is becoming increasingly complex.

Parents are especially concerned with maintaining their children's privacy and safety online. Many sites are not suitable for children. Even at sites sponsored by reputable child-centered organizations, participants in chat rooms may not all have good intentions. Parents should consider the following guidelines for keeping their children safe online:

- **Supervise.** Spend time with your children online. Let them show you their favorite sites and meet some of their chat buddies. Don't let your child remain online for long periods of time without supervision. Drop in and check the screen occasionally.

- **Keep the computer public.** Your child should understand that the computer is public equipment and you or other family members might use it. Periodically, you might want to check for any potentially inappropriate activity by looking at your child's e-mail, the History list, and the list of sites stored in the Web cache.

- **Use filtering software.** Windows Parental Controls (Figure 22-12) offer tools for establishing time limits and blocking access to specific programs. Specialized filtering software, such as Net Nanny, offers similar tools and also includes tools for blocking access to Web sites that are not child friendly.

Figure
22-12

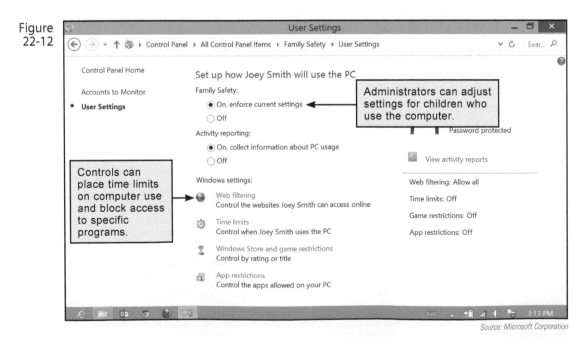

Source: Microsoft Corporation

FAQ What should I know about intellectual property online?

Intellectual property refers to intangibles, such as ideas, music, art, photos, logos, movies, and programs, that are the result of creativity and intellectual effort. Although intellectual property can be fixed in tangible media—CDs, DVDs, film, and sheet music—the underlying "property" is not necessarily tied to a particular media. It is the content that is important, rather than a particular format of the content. Trademarks, patents, and copyrights are important legal protections for intellectual property.

Trademarks typically protect corporate logos and product names. They are important tools for businesses that want to maintain corporate reputations and prevent shoddy imitations from being sold by unscrupulous vendors.

Patents usually protect inventions from being used without permission from the inventor. In the digital world, encryption algorithms and file formats have been patented. The MP3 file format, so popular for digital music, was patented in 1991, which forced companies that distributed MP3 players to pay royalties to the patent holder.

Copyrights typically protect works such as software, photos, movies, and music. Many copyrighted works include a copyright notice, such as "Copyright 2014 eCourse Inc." This notice is not required by law, however; so works without a copyright notice may still be protected by copyright law.

Copyright law makes it illegal to copy and distribute protected works without the permission of the author or the author's representative. Circumventing copyright law and illegally copying, distributing, or modifying protected works is sometimes referred to as **piracy**. Illegal copies have an economic impact. Content creators are not compensated for their work, and legal users may be forced to pay higher prices to make up for revenues lost from pirated copies.

Figure 22-13

© MediaTechnics

Copy protection refers to any physical method used to prevent works from being copied. Copy protected software CDs are designed to be used a limited number of times for installation purposes. They might also include technology that makes copies of the CD unusable. Music CDs and movie DVDs can also be copy protected, so that even with two writable CD or DVD drives, the disks produced do not work.

Because copy protection methods can be hacked and circumvented, a consortium of ISPs rolled out the "Six Strikes" Copyright Alert System in 2013. Customers who are suspected of illegal downloading and file sharing receive notices from their ISPs, and repeat offenders are subject to penalties such as suspension of service. The Software & Information Industry Association (SIIA) also works to stop illegal software distribution with a piracy hotline and anti-piracy music videos.

You can become a victim of piracy if you inadvertently download or purchase an illegal copy of a book, movie, music track, or software application. To avoid getting caught in the Six Strikes net, be sure to download content from reputable sources, even when you have to pay for it.

What should I know about intellectual property online? (continued)

The material published on Web sites, in blogs, and in other online forums is protected by copyright. When you publish your own material online, it is automatically covered by copyright.

Copyright law does not prohibit all copying. It is legal to make copies under **fair use** regulations, which allow you to copy small excerpts of copyrighted works for use in educational materials and critical reviews. Fair use allows you to insert fragments of literary works in research papers without first gaining permission from their authors. You should, however, always cite the source of such material. To determine whether you can use material under the fair use regulations, make sure it fits the following criteria:

- You are using the material for educational purposes or for critical review.

- You are not using a substantial part of the entire work.

- Your use does not provide a level of functionality that replaces the work so that consumers would not need to purchase it.

It is easy, of course, to cut and paste large sections of someone else's material into your own reports and essays. Failure to cite your source or pretending the material is your own is plagiarism. Not only is plagiarism unethical, it is unlawful. In educational environments, plagiarism is considered especially egregious. Penalties, typically set forth in the student code of conduct, can be severe.

When your intended use of copyrighted material is not covered by fair use, you should obtain the author's permission. If you want to use a photo or music clip on your Web site, for example, contact the copyright holder. You can often do so via e-mail. You should also be aware that many clip art collections and other products billed as "copyright free" actually contain copyrighted material. If you read the small print, you might discover that you can use the material without permission only for personal, non-commercial use.

You might also consider using content with a Creative Commons (CC) license that allows you to use another person's work without asking for permission. Content with CC licenses can be found on Web sites such as Flickr, Google Images, YouTube, Europeana, and SoundCloud. The works remain copyrighted, but a CC license relaxes some copyright restrictions. Open sharing helps artists gain wider recognition for their work and fosters creativity by allowing content to be reused and remixed.

Creative Commons licenses may contain any of the rights or limitations shown in Figure 22-14. Make sure the license allows your intended use.

Figure 22-14

(BY)	Attribution (BY)	Requires you to cite the original author.
(SA)	Share Alike (SA)	Allows you to create derivative works as long as they are distributed under the Creative Commons Share Alike license.
(NC)	Non-Commercial (NC)	Allows the work to be used for personal but not commercial purposes.
(ND)	No Derivative Works (ND)	Allows the work to the used, but not altered.

FAQ How can I keep informed about technology-related issues?

Whether you're buying a computer, working in a computer career, investing for retirement, or just casually browsing the Internet, it pays to keep informed about current technology. As you might expect, numerous sources provide access to such information.

Computer publications. Popular computer magazines include *Computer Power User (CPU)*, *Wired*, and *PCWorld*. Two of the most prominent online sources for computer news are CNET News and Ars Technica.

Figure 22-15

Source: Conde Nast

Mailing lists and RSS feeds. Subscribing to a mailing list or RSS feed from Computer Weekly or InfoWorld can bring computer news and commentary right to your desktop.

Professional organizations. If you have a professional interest in computers, you should consider joining a professional organization such as the Association for Computing Machinery. Membership typically provides access to professional libraries, online or print journals, computer conferences, job listings, and special interest groups.

Corporate sites. Computer company Web sites often contain valuable information about corporations, products, and employment. Investors can find plenty of financial data in corporate reports. When you have a problem with a product, the first place to look for solutions is the manufacturer's customer support Web page or knowledge base.

Consumer reviews. If you're interested in purchasing computer equipment, check out consumer sites such as www.epinions.com, www.consumerreports.org, and www.consumersearch.com. Also check computer-related blogs. These sites carry hundreds of reviews and ratings for computers, printers, and other peripheral devices.

School and work policies. Make sure you're aware of computer-use policies at your school or workplace. These policies typically specify what kinds of personal activities are allowed on school-owned or company owned computers. They also should indicate the level of privacy you can expect with respect to e-mail and electronic communications over school or business networks.

• How can I keep informed about technology-related issues? (continued)

Figure 22-16   **Laws and regulations.** Computer use is governed by many laws and regulations. The most significant U.S. laws pertaining to computers are described briefly in Figure 22-16.

United States Copyright Act (1976) extends copyright protection beyond print media to "original works of authorship fixed in any tangible medium of expression, now known or later developed, from which they can be perceived, reproduced, or otherwise communicated, either directly or with the aid of a machine or device."

Fair Use Doctrine, a part of the U.S. Copyright Act, generally allows copying if it is for educational or personal use, if only a portion of the original work is copied, and if it does not have a substantial effect on the market for the original work.

Sony Corp. v. Universal City Studios (1984) sets a precedent that companies are not liable for user infringements, such as using VCRs to make unauthorized copies of videotapes, so long as the technology has valid, non-infringing uses, such as copying personal home videos. In recent cases, the defense for peer-to-peer file sharing networks was based on this decision.

Computer Fraud and Abuse Act (1986 amended in 1994, 1996, 2001, and USA PATRIOT Act) makes it a criminal offense to knowingly access a computer without authorization; transmit a program, information, code, or command that causes damage; or distribute passwords that would enable unauthorized access.

Electronic Communications Privacy Act (1986) extends telephone wiretap laws by restricting government agents and unauthorized third parties from tapping into data transmissions without a search warrant. The law does not apply to data, such as e-mail, transmitted on employer-owned equipment.

Health Insurance Portability and Accountability Act (1996) requires health care providers to take reasonable procedural and technical safeguards to ensure the confidentiality of individually identifiable health information.

Digital Millennium Copyright Act (1998) makes it illegal to circumvent copy-protection technologies, such as those used to prevent unauthorized copying of software CDs, music CDs, and movie DVDs. In addition, it is illegal to distribute any type of cracking software technology that would be used by others to circumvent copy protection. Protects ISPs against copyright infringement by subscribers if the ISP takes prompt action to block the infringement as soon as it discovers illegal activity.

Communications Decency Act (1996) protects ISPs from liability for defamatory statements made by customers. Prohibits material deemed offensive by local community standards from being transmitted to minors. The latter section was overturned in 2002.

Children's Online Privacy Protection Act (1998) attempted to protect children from Internet pornography. Overturned in 1999.

Gramm-Leach-Bliley Act (1999) requires financial institutions to protect the confidentiality and security of customers' personal information.

Children's Internet Protection Act (2000) requires schools and libraries that receive federal funds to implement filtering software that protects adults and minors from obscenity and pornography.

USA PATRIOT Act (2001) enhances the authority of law enforcement agents to preempt potential terrorist acts by various means, such as monitoring electronic communications without first obtaining a search warrant in situations where there is imminent danger. Offers safe harbor to ISPs that voluntarily disclose potentially threatening activities of users. Increases maximum penalties for hackers.

Homeland Security Act (2002) establishes a Department of Homeland Security with an agency to monitor threats to the communications infrastructure, including the Internet, and exempts from the Privacy Act any information about infrastructure vulnerabilities to terrorism submitted by individuals or non-federal agencies.

Sarbanes-Oxley Act (2002) establishes financial reporting regulations to prevent corporate fraud. Requires full disclosure in accounting systems and protects corporate whistleblowers.

CAN-SPAM Act (2003) establishes national standards for sending commercial e-mail by requiring senders to use a valid subject line, include the sender's legitimate physical address, and provide an opt-out mechanism.

Green v. America Online (2003) interprets sections of the Communications Decency Act to mean that ISPs are not responsible for malicious software transmitted over their services by hackers.

MGM v. Grokster (2005) refines the precedent set in the 1984 Sony Corp. v. Universal City Studios case. Companies that actively encourage infringement, as seemed to be true of peer-to-peer file-sharing networks such as Grokster, can be held accountable for user infringement.

FAQ How can I avoid computer-related health risks?

Many people in today's information society spend long hours gazing at computer screens and typing on keyboards. Computers are an important part of the work environment—not only for people with traditional desk jobs, but also for telecommuters. A **telecommuter**, or "teleworker," uses a home-based computer and telecommunications equipment to perform work-related tasks. Today, telecommuters often work for call centers that provide technical support, take reservations for hotels, or process catalog orders.

Telecommuters and on-site employees who work with computers for most of the workday sometimes experience health problems related to computer use, such as eye strain caused by screen glare or small fonts. Computer users are also susceptible to musculoskeletal strain, such as back pain related to improper arrangement of desk, chair, and computer equipment. Long hours at the computer and prolonged typing sessions can also contribute to repetitive motion injuries, such as carpal tunnel syndrome.

To avoid computer-related health hazards, it is important to take frequent breaks to rest your eyes and move your muscles. You should also be aware of the ergonomics of your work areas. **Ergonomics** is the study of work environments. Results of ergonomics research have produced guidelines for making work environments safer and healthier.

Studies have found links between computer use and eye problems. A large screen can reduce eye strain, and lighting is important. Position your screen so it doesn't reflect glare from lights or windows.

Prolonged mouse, keyboard, and trackpad use can take a toll on hands and wrists. Be sure to use a keyboard that is a comfortable size and shape. Position your mouse where it is easy to reach.

Doctors and physical therapists commonly use the term "flex-forward posture" to describe the sitting posture shared by many computer users. The layman's term "computer slump" refers to the same thing: sitting hunched over a computer keyboard with your neck craned forward.

Habitual slouching can lead to stiffness and muscle tenderness. Left uncorrected, the problem can cause nerve irritation that spreads down the arms and back.

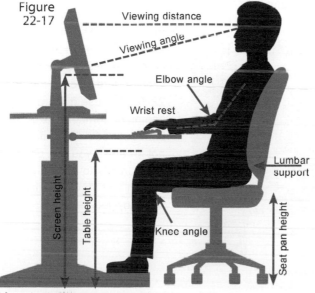

Figure 22-17

Viewing distance
Viewing angle
Elbow angle
Wrist rest
Lumbar support
Knee angle
Screen height
Table height
Seat pan height

© Cengage Learning 2014

Adjustable chairs and desks allow you to position equipment and maintain good posture. For example, Figure 22-17 illustrates how to set up a desktop computer, table, and chair to avoid potentially disabling musculoskeletal injuries.

In addition to taking steps to avoid health risks, computer owners should make sure their work areas are safe. Equipment should rest on a secure surface and have adequate air circulation. Cables should be stowed where they cannot become tangled in feet and arms, or cause a fire hazard. It is also important not to overload electrical circuits.

FAQ How do computers affect the environment?

Keeping up with technology means replacing your computer every few years. But what should you do with your old, outdated computer? Millions of computers are discarded every year. Billions of printer ink cartridges, floppy disks, CDs, and DVDs end up in landfills. Computers contain toxic materials, such as lead, phosphorus, and mercury, which can contaminate groundwater if not disposed of properly. Discarded disks and toner cartridges add materials to overburdened landfills. Computer owners can take some simple steps to have a positive effect on the environment:

• Recycle consumable products such as paper. If possible, use the back of discarded printouts for notes or bundle them up and send them to your local recycling center.

• Use electronic documents whenever possible to reduce the use of paper.

• Refill or recycle printer ribbons, ink cartridges, and toner cartridges. Check your local office store for reinking and refill supplies. Also check your ink and toner packaging for disposal instructions. Many manufacturers provide mailing labels so that you can return these items for recycling.

• Donate your old computer, monitor, and printer to a charitable organization. By doing so, you not only keep equipment out of the waste stream for several more years, but you help others by providing opportunities to use empowering technologies. Just make sure to remove the hard disk or use shredder software to delete personal data from the hard disk before sending your computer to a charity.

• Dispose of malfunctioning equipment at a facility designed to handle electronic waste. Some manufacturers accept old and out-of-service equipment. Check their Web sites for details. Your community recycling center usually accepts electronic components, too.

• Recycle used CDs and DVDs when possible. Media that contains personal data should be destroyed, however.

• Computers use electricity, but they are becoming more and more efficient. Laptop computers typically consume less power than desktops. To reduce power consumption, you can configure your computer to enter standby mode when not in use. Depending on the settings you select, standby mode can turn off the monitor, power down the hard disk, or power down the entire computer.

Figure 22-18

Recycled Computer Creations by Gregory Steele, Marquette, MI

• Be creative. The Web contains lots of information about great craft projects, such as the circuit-board clock in Figure 22-18, that use discarded computer components and storage media. Even if you are not an artist, you can donate components to a creative person and support artists who use recycled materials.

QuickCheck A

1. Technically, a computer [_____] replicates itself when its host program runs, whereas a computer [_____] can spread and replicate autonomously.

2. WEP and WPA are used to [_____] data traveling on wireless networks.

3. To prevent unauthorized access to your data by hackers, install and activate [_____] software that can analyze and control the flow of traffic entering your computer.

4. [_____] use regulations allow you to legally copy small excerpts of copyrighted works for use in educational materials and critical reviews.

5. [_____] guidelines help you position your computer, desk, and chair to avoid potentially disabling musculoskeletal injuries.

CHECKIT!

QuickCheck B

Based on the screen displayed at right, answer T if the statement is true or F if the statement is false.

1. Antivirus software is installed. [____]

2. Your computer has been given a digital certificate. [____]

3. You don't have to worry about fake e-commerce sites. [____]

4. Virus signatures will be automatically updated. [____]

5. You can assume incoming e-mail attachments are safe. [____]

PC Security Pending	
Items	**Status**
Auto-Protect	On
Your PC is protected from viruses, spyware, and other risks.	
Firewall	On
Your PC is protected from intrusions and hacker attacks.	
LiveUpdate	Off
Your PC is protected from the latest known viruses, spyware, and other risks.	
Email Scanning	Off
Your incoming email attachments are protected	

Source: Microsoft Corporation

CHECKIT!

Projects

© VLADGRIN/Shutterstock

Introduction to Projects

The projects in this section are designed to help you review and develop skills you learned by reading the chapter material and working with Try It! and assessment activities. Projects serve as a valuable intermediate step between the *Practical Computer Literacy* learning environment and working on your own. Even if you are not required to complete the projects for a class, you'll find that trying some of the projects can enhance your ability to use Windows, Microsoft Office, e-mail, and the Web.

Required Software. Although not required for interacting with the Try It! activities in Chapters 1–22, Microsoft Office 2013 must be installed on the computer you use to complete the projects in this section. For projects in Chapter 20, you'll need an e-mail account. For projects in Chapter 21, you'll need access to the Internet and a browser, such as Internet Explorer, Firefox, or Chrome.

To discover if Microsoft Office 2013 software has been installed on your computer, from the Windows 8 Start screen or the Apps screen, simply type Word, Excel, PowerPoint, or Access, then click the corresponding program tile. When using Windows 7, click the Start button; type Word, Excel, PowerPoint, or Access in the Search box; then click the corresponding program link.

Project Help. If you don't remember how to complete a task for a project, refer to Chapters 1–22. They are designed to provide a quick reference to the skills you've learned. Keep the printed book handy as you work on the projects and when working on your own.

Project Files. For many of the projects, you'll start by copying project files from the CD supplied with this book. You can copy a project file from the CD using the Copy It! button on the first page of a project. As another option, you can use File Explorer to copy the files directly from the CD to a USB flash drive or to your computer's hard disk. We suggest keeping all of the project files together in one location. We will refer to this location as your Project folder.

How to Submit Assignments. At the completion of each project, you will have created a file that demonstrates your ability to apply your skills. To submit a completed project to your instructor, use one of the methods indicated in the instructions at the end of the project. Most projects can be printed, submitted on a USB flash drive, or sent as an e-mail attachment. Your instructor might have a preference for one of these methods. You'll find additional information about printing, saving, and e-mailing projects on the next two pages.

Submitting an Assignment as a Printout or on a Removable Storage Device

You can print or save your Microsoft Office project files using the FILE tab, as shown in the figure below.

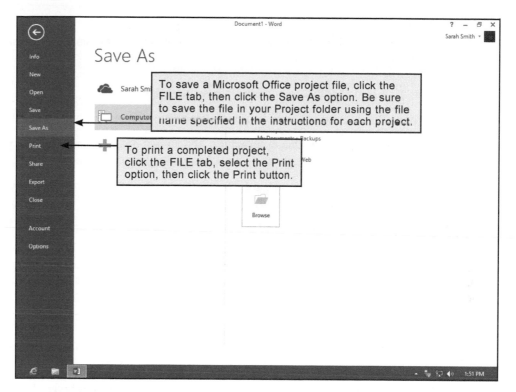

- To print a project file:

1. Make sure that a printer is attached to your computer and that it is turned on.

2. In Microsoft Office, select the FILE tab, choose the Print option, then select the Print button.

3. If the printout doesn't already include your name, student ID number, class section number, date, and project name, be sure to write this information on the printout.

- To save your file on a removable storage device, such as a USB flash drive:

1. While the file is open, select the FILE tab, then select the Save As option.

2. When the Save As window appears, navigate to the removable storage device.

3. In the *File name* box, enter the name specified by the project instructions.

4. Click the Save button to complete the process.

5. Before submitting a USB flash drive to your instructor, make sure that it is labeled with your name and class section number.

Note: If you save your file on your computer's hard disk, you can use the Copy command in File Explorer to copy it to a USB flash drive.

Submitting an Assignment as an E-mail Attachment

You can typically use either Method 1 or Method 2, as explained below, to submit most projects. Access projects, however, require Method 1.

● **Method 1—Add Attachments Manually**

With Method 1, you'll send your project file using your local e-mail client or Webmail account.

1. Make sure that you have saved the project file.

2. Start your e-mail software and start a new message.

3. Address the new message to your instructor.

4. Click the Attachment button or select the Attachment option from a menu. If you don't see an Attachment option, look for a File option on the Insert menu.

5. When prompted, navigate to the folder that holds the attachment—usually your Project folder—and select the project file.

6. Select the Send button to send the e-mail message and attachment.

● **Method 2—Use Microsoft Office 2013's Send Feature**

If Microsoft Office 2013 is set up in conjunction with your e-mail software, you can send your project file directly from Word, Excel, or PowerPoint by using the following steps:

1. After saving your project, keep your application (Word, Excel, or PowerPoint) window open.

2. Select the FILE tab, then select the Share option. Choose Email, then select *Send as Attachment*.

3. Enter your instructor's e-mail address in the To: box, enter the body of the e-mail, then send it.

● **Getting an E-mail Account**

You can obtain a free Webmail account from e-mail providers such as Google (www.gmail.com), Outlook.com (www.outlook.com), or Yahoo! (www.yahoo.com). Use your Web browser to connect to the Webmail site and register for an account. You'll be able to use it as soon as you complete the registration process.

When you use a Webmail account, complete your project offline. Next, connect to your Webmail account, create a new message addressed to your instructor, then attach your project file to the message before sending it.

If you prefer to use local e-mail, you'll need to set up an account with an ISP or some other provider, such as your school. To set up a local e-mail account, you might need to obtain the following information from your ISP:

- The Internet access phone number (dial-up service only)

- Your e-mail address (such as hfinn5678@verizon.net)

- Your e-mail password (such as huck2finn)

- The incoming mail server type (usually POP3)

- Your incoming mail server's name (often the part of your e-mail address that comes after the @ symbol, such as aol.com)

- Your outgoing SMTP mail server's name (such as mailhost.att.net)

- The primary and secondary domain name server (DNS) numbers (such as 204.127.129.1)

Microsoft Office 2013 Configuration

Microsoft Office 2013 provides many ways to configure and modify how its applications look and operate. While this adaptability can be a positive feature, it can cause confusion if your version of Microsoft Office 2013 is not configured to look or work the same way as the version used for the examples in *Practical Computer Literacy*. Here's how to configure your software to match the settings that were used for the instructions and figures in this book.

- **To configure Microsoft Word, Excel, and PowerPoint:**

1. Select the FILE tab, then choose Options. With the General category selected, make sure *Show Mini Toolbar on selection* and Enable Live Preview are selected.

- **To configure Microsoft Access:**

1. The entire ribbon should be visible. If it is not, choose the Ribbon Display Options button on the right side of the title bar, then choose *Show Tabs and Commands*.

The sample screens were produced on a screen with 1024 x 768 resolution. If your computer's screen resolution is different, the images might appear slightly different, though they will not be incorrect.

- **To configure your screen resolution:**

1. Right-click any blank area of the Windows desktop.

2. Select *Screen resolution*.

3. Choose 1024 x 768 resolution, then select the OK button.

Project HW-1: Buying a Computer

In this project, you'll compare the specifications and prices for two computers to decide which one would be best for you.

Requirements: This project requires an Internet connection and a browser for researching various computer brands and models.

Project file: No project file is required.

1. Assess your computing needs. Which of the items in this list pertain to you?

Usage Plan	Purchase Recommendation
You plan to use your computer for popular activities such as e-mail and Facebook, browsing the Web, playing a few games, managing your finances, downloading digital music, and writing school papers.	A mid-priced computer with standard features might meet your needs.
You're on a budget.	A budget-priced computer will handle the same applications as a mid-priced computer, but some tasks might run more slowly.
You plan to work on accounting and budgeting for a small business.	Consider one of the business systems offered by a local or an online computer vendor.
You spend lots of time playing computer games.	Buy a computer with the fastest processor and graphics card you can afford.
You plan to work extensively with video editing or desktop publishing.	Select a computer system with a fast processor, lots of hard disk capacity, and a graphics card loaded with memory.
Someone who will use the computer has special needs.	Consider purchasing appropriate adaptive equipment, such as a voice synthesizer or one-handed keyboard.
You plan to use specialized peripheral devices.	Make sure the computer you purchase can accommodate the devices you plan to use.
Your work at home overlaps your work at school or on the job.	Shop for a computer that's compatible with the computers you use at school or work.
You want to work with specific software, such as a game or graphics tool.	Make sure you select a computer that meets the specifications listed on the software box or Web site.
You're buying a new computer to replace an old one.	If you have a big investment in software, you should select a new computer that's compatible with the old one.
You want a 3D display for games and movies.	Make sure the monitor is rated for 3D display.
You need a computer that is easy to transport.	Consider a tablet computer or small laptop computer.

© MediaTechnics

• Buying a Computer (continued)

2. Decide on a form factor. Do you want a desktop, an all-in-one, a laptop, a tablet, or a smartphone? Explain why.

3. Select a platform. Which operating system do you prefer: Windows 7, Windows 8, Windows RT, Windows Phone, OS X, iOS, or Android?

4. Use the Internet to locate two computers that meet your needs. For each computer, record the following information:

Computer manufacturer

Computer model

Processor type

Processor speed

Memory capacity

Drive capacity

Screen size

Number and type of expansion ports

Price (excluding shipping and taxes)

5. List any additional characteristics of the computers that might be important to your purchase decision. Factors you might consider include laptop weight, camera resolution, battery life, bundled software, and available accessories.

6. Create a side-by-side comparison of the two computers you've selected for consideration.

7. Write a paragraph explaining which computer you would select and why.

8. Submit your needs assessment, side-by-side comparison, and explanatory paragraph as an e-mail message, as an e-mail attachment, as a printout, on a USB flash drive, or in any other format specified by your instructor.

Project WI-1: Taking Screenshots

In this project, you will learn how to take a snapshot of your computer screen.

Requirements: This project requires Microsoft Windows 7 or Windows 8, and Paint.

Project file: No project file is required.

Many of the projects in this section of *Practical Computer Literacy* require you to submit a screenshot showing your work. The process involves the following easy steps:

1. Make sure that your computer screen shows the windows, messages, and menus that you want to include in the snapshot. Here are a few hints:

- The pointer will not be included in the snapshot, so it doesn't matter where it is located.

- The insertion point will appear in the snapshot, so make sure it is located where you want it to be.

- If you have more than one window on the screen, one of them will be the active window. Make sure you have selected the window you want to be active.

2. Press the PrtSc or Print Screen key on the computer keyboard. Doing so places a copy of the screen on the Clipboard.

3. Open Paint. To open Paint in Windows 8, type Paint at the Start screen, then choose the Paint option. In Windows 7, click the Start button, choose All Programs, then select Paint.

4. Paste the Clipboard contents into Paint. To do so, hold down the Ctrl key and press V. Alternatively, you can click the Paste button on Paint's ribbon bar.

5. Save the file. Click File, then select Save As. Select a file format; PNG or JPEG are the best options. You can put the screenshot in the Pictures library.

• Taking Screenshots (continued)

For this project, do the following:

1. Prepare for the screenshot by displaying the Windows desktop. Make sure all the desktop icons are neatly aligned. Feel free to choose an attractive desktop background photo, texture, or theme.

2. Take a screenshot of the Windows desktop.

3. Use Paint's Text tool to label the following:
Taskbar
Notification area
Program buttons
Desktop icon
Shortcut icon (if one is shown in the screenshot)

4. Your screenshot might look like the following, though your desktop background might be different.

5. Save the screenshot as a PNG file.

6. Name the file PrjWI-1 [Your Name].

7. Submit the file as an e-mail attachment, as a printout, on a USB flash drive, or in any other format specified by your instructor.

Project WI-2: Identifying Windows Versions and Updates

In this project, you'll apply what you have learned about identifying Windows versions and checking for updates.

Requirements: This project requires Windows 7 or 8.

Project file: No project file is required.

As you learned in Chapter 5, Windows 7 displays the desktop after you log in, whereas Windows 8 typically displays the Start screen. However, this difference might change with subsequent updates to Windows, so you need a more definitive way to locate information about the version of Windows installed on a computer. Let's make sure that you can find the Windows version information you might need for troubleshooting or upgrading.

1. Start Windows and log in.

2. Access Control Panel using one of the following methods:

   Windows 8: Click the Start button and select Control Panel from the Start menu.

   Windows 7: From the Start screen, type Control Panel and then select it from the list.

   Windows RT: Swipe from the right to view the Settings panel and then select Control Panel.

3. Make sure the Control Panel view is set to *Large icons*.

4. Select the System icon. From the System window, record the Windows edition and the System type.

5. Click the Windows update link. Record how many important updates are available.

6. In the lower-left corner of the screen, click the Installed Updates link. Record the KB number and the date for the most recent Microsoft Windows update.

7. Using the information you recorded, answer the following questions that might be asked when you contact technical support with a hardware or software problem:

   7a. Are you using Windows 7 or Windows 8?

   7b. Do you have the Home, Professional, or Enterprise edition of Windows?

   7c. Have all current Windows updates been installed?

   7d. What is the KB number of the most recent update?

8. Submit your responses to the questions in Step 7 in an e-mail, as a printout, or in any other format specified by your instructor.

Project WI-3: Organizing the Desktop

In this project, you'll extend what you've learned about the Windows desktop to customize the Notification area, create desktop shortcuts, and add icons to the taskbar's pinned list.

Requirements: This project requires Windows 7 or 8.

Project file: No project file is required.

1. Log in and view the desktop. With Windows 8, you can view the desktop by selecting the Desktop tile from the Start menu.

2. Begin by looking at the icons in the Notification area in the lower-right corner of the desktop. Hover the mouse over all icons and record their names.

3. Select the arrow that's labeled *Show hidden icons*. The icons shown in the box are available but not displayed in the Notification area.

4. Click the Customize link.

5. Notice that the icons labeled *Show icon and notifications* are displayed in the Notification area. Icons labeled *Only show notifications* appear in the Notification area only if there is a status change, such as an update or error.

6. Let's change one of the icons so that it is always displayed. If *Safely Remove Hardware and Eject Media* is labeled *Only show notifications*, choose it. Otherwise, select any other icon.

7. Use the arrow to display a list of options as shown below, then select *Show icon and notifications*. Click the OK button and the icon should appear in the notification area.

• Organizing the Desktop (continued)

8. Next, take a look at the icons located in the main desktop area. You can create a shortcut icon to easily access your favorite application, folder, or file.

9. Right-click the desktop and select New. Then select Shortcut from the pop-up menu.

10. Click the Browse button, then select Libraries. Drill down through the Documents listing to select a file.

11. Select the Next button. You're given a chance to revise the file name, but just click the Finish button to create the shortcut.

12. Remember, a shortcut is simply a link. If you delete the shortcut, you will not delete the actual application, file, or folder.

13. Now that you have created a shortcut, you can turn your attention to the pinned list. In Windows 8, pinned icons are displayed on the taskbar. In Windows 7, pinned items are displayed on the Start menu. Let's pin the Paint application to the taskbar or Start menu.

14. The first step is to locate the Paint application or its shortcut. To do that:

Click the ▨ Explorer icon in the taskbar.

Select the (C:) icon as shown on the right.

In the Search box, enter Paint. (Hint: In Windows 7, search for MSPaint.)

Right-click the ▨ Paint icon. (Hint: If there is more than one Paint item, select the one located in C:\Windows.)

Select *Pin to taskbar* (Windows 8) or *Pin to Start menu* (Windows 7).

The Paint icon should appear on the taskbar or the Start menu.

Close the Explorer windows so the desktop is displayed.

15. Take a screenshot showing your notification icons, shortcut icon, and pinned item. (Hint: Windows 7 users should click the Start button so the menu is shown in the screenshot.) Be sure to include your name and project number on the screenshot.

16. Submit your screenshot as an e-mail attachment, as a printout, on a USB flash drive, or in any other format specified by your instructor.

Project WI-4: Personalizing Windows

In this project, you'll extend what you've learned about Microsoft Windows to view and adjust customization settings.

Requirements: This project requires Microsoft Windows.

Project file: No project file is required.

As you complete each step, write your answers to the questions.

1. Arrange the icons on your desktop by type. (Hint: Begin by right-clicking the desktop and choosing *Sort by*.) What is the name of the first icon?

2. Check the date and time. Is your computer set to automatically adjust for Daylight Saving Time?

3. Check the Speaker volume. As you reposition the Volume slider bar, a chime from your computer's speaker lets you hear the volume. Is the volume level appropriate for your work setting?

4. Select the Control Panel's Personalization option to check your desktop and screen settings. What is the current theme?

5. What is the desktop background?

6. Change the color of your desktop background to dark purple, then change the toolbar to light purple. How do you like that color scheme?

7. Does your computer have a screen saver activated? If so, what is its name and what is the wait period?

8. What is the screen resolution? (Hint: Begin by right-clicking the desktop or using the Control Panel's Display icon.)

9. Change the screen resolution. Are there some resolutions in which the desktop does not fill the entire screen? If so, what are they?

• Personalizing Windows (continued)

10. Use Control Panel to access keyboard settings. Try adjusting the repeat rate, repeat delay, and cursor blink rate. What are your preferred settings for each?

11. Select the Mouse icon from Control Panel. Does the Mouse Properties dialog box allow you to adjust settings for a mouse, a touchpad, or both?

12. Use Control Panel to access Power Options. What are your computer's settings for the options in the following table?

	On battery	Plugged in
Dim the display		
Turn off the display		
Put the computer to sleep		

© MediaTechnics

13. After you record the current power settings, click the link to *Restore default settings for this plan*. Were your settings the same as the default settings? If you want your original settings, adjust them before continuing.

14. Use Control Panel to access *Devices and Printers*. What are the names of printers that are available to your computer? Indicate which printer is the default, and also indicate if any printers are accessed over a network.

15. Submit your answers to the questions in Steps 1–14 as an e-mail message, as an e-mail attachment, as a printout, on a USB flash drive, or in any other format specified by your instructor. Be sure to include your name and project number with your answers.

Project WI-5: Experimenting with Accessibility Options

In this project, you will apply accessibility settings that are designed for people with audio and visual disabilities.

Requirements: This project requires Windows 7 or 8.

Project file: No project file is required.

1. Access Control Panel and select the icon for the Ease of Access Center.

2. Select Start Magnifier.

3. Move the pointer to the lower-right corner of the screen. How would you describe what happens?

4. Click the magnifying glass to display the Magnifier control window. Experiment with the controls in the Magnifier window. Describe the purpose of each control shown below.

5. Close the Magnifier window to turn magnification off.

6. Next, click the Start Narrator option to turn narration on.

7. Click the Control Panel Home link in the upper-left corner of the screen to access the Control Panel. Then close your eyes and try to use the Narrator instructions to locate the link to Mouse controls. Describe your experience.

8. Click the Narrator icon in the taskbar to display the Narrator menu. Select Exit to stop the narration.

9. Which accessibility setting is designed for people who cannot easily hear warning sounds that signal error conditions?

10. Compile your answers to the questions in Steps 3, 4, 7, and 9. Submit them as an e-mail message, as an e-mail attachment, as a printout, on a USB flash drive, or in any other format specified by your instructor. Be sure to include your name and project number with your answers.

Project WI-6: Setting Up User Accounts

In this project, you will check your account settings and set up a user account.

Requirements: This project requires Microsoft Windows, and Step 7 requires administrative rights.

Project file: No project file is required.

1. Log in as usual and check the options offered by your account icon. In Windows 8, select your account icon from the upper-right corner of the Start screen. In Windows 7, click the Start button and select your account icon in the upper-right corner of the Start menu. Make a list of the options.

2. If you are using Windows 8, list the account options offered by PC Settings. To complete this step:

   Swipe from the right (or move the pointer to the lower-right corner of the screen) to display the Charms menu.

   Select Settings.

   Select Change PC Settings.

   Select Users.

3. Using Windows 7 or 8, access the Control Panel and then select User Accounts. List the options available for working with user accounts.

4. What type of account do you have?

5. Is your account password protected?

6. List the steps necessary to change your password.

7. If you have administrative rights, set up an account for a standard user named B. MyGuest by doing the following:

   Select *Manage another account*.

   Select options for adding another user.

   If given a choice, set up a local account.

   Enter Guest as the user's name and password.

   Follow the rest of the prompts to complete the process.

8. Compile your answers to the questions in Steps 1–6 and submit them in the format specified by your instructor. Be sure to include your name and the project number with your answers.

Project WI-7 : Working with Task Manager

In this project, you will apply your knowledge of Task Manager to monitor your computer's performance.

Requirements: This project requires Windows 7 or 8.

Project file: No project file is required.

1. Start Task Manager by using the Ctrl Shift Esc key combination. Maximize the Task Manager window.

2. Using information from the Details or Processes tabs, answer the following questions:

2a. How many apps are running?

2b. How many processes are running?

2c. Which app requires the most memory?

2d. How much memory is being used by the largest app?

2e. Which background process requires the most memory?

2f. Is any process using more than 10% of the CPU resources?

2g. What is the overall CPU usage?

3. Using the Performance tab, display a graph of CPU usage and answer the following questions:

3a. Would you describe the graph as even or spiky?

3b. Would you describe CPU usage as high or low?

4. Open a browser, such as Internet Explorer or Chrome, and arrange your desktop like the one shown below so that you can monitor CPU usage while you access Web sites.

5. Approximately how much CPU usage is required for a typical Google search?

6. Change the Task Manager view so that it displays a chart of memory usage, then try some additional Google searches. Does memory usage follow the same pattern as CPU usage?

7. Compile your answers for steps 2, 3, 5, and 6, then submit them in the format specified by your instructor. Be sure to include your name and project number with your answers.

Project WI-8: Organizing Directories and Folders

In this project, you will apply what you have learned about Windows file management to organize your personal files. Take notes on paper as you complete the steps. You'll compile and submit your notes at the end of the project.

Requirements: This project requires Microsoft Windows and Microsoft Word.

Project file: No project file is required.

Note: If you are using a lab or work computer, make sure that you have permission to modify files and folders in the My Documents folder.

1. Open File Explorer (Windows 8) or Windows Explorer (Windows 7). Expand the Computer option so that you see all the devices connected to your computer. List the storage devices attached to your computer and take note of the icons that represent them.

2. Use Explorer's Search box to search your entire hard disk for files that contain the word sample in the file name. (Hint: If your hard disk is partitioned into Drive C: and Drive D:, search both of them.) How many files were found?

3. Open the Pictures library. How many folders are included in the library and what are their names?

4. Create a new folder by clicking the *New folder* button on the Explorer toolbar. Name the folder WI-8 Pictures. Where does Explorer automatically place the new folder?

5. Take a screenshot of the Pictures library. Save the file as WI-8 Library Exercise. Close the Paint window. Where does Windows automatically save the file?

6. Move the file to the WI-8 Pictures folder by dragging it to the folder or by cutting and pasting it into the folder. Does the file show up in the Pictures library list?

7. Open the Documents library so that its subfolders and files are displayed in the Files pane. Make sure the View is set to Details. How many subfolders are in the My Documents folder? (Hint: Look at the Details pane.)

8. Make sure the Documents library is displayed in the Files pane, then arrange its contents by type. How many files of each type are there?

• Organizing Directories and Folders (continued)

9. Arrange the files by size. What are the name and size of the largest file? What are the name and size of the smallest file?

10. Arrange the files by date. What are the name and date of the most recent file? What are the name and date of the oldest file?

11. Take a screenshot showing the subfolders for My Documents. Name the file PrjWI-8 [Your Name].

12. List three ways you could improve the folder structure.

13. Carry out your plan from the previous step. Create, rename, and delete folders as necessary, then move files into them.

14. Take a screenshot of the new directory structure. Save the screenshot and name it PrjWI-8 Improved [Your Name].

15. Use the Views button on the Explorer toolbar to experiment with various Views, such as Tiles, Icons, List, and Details. Which view do you prefer?

16. Compile your answers for the questions in Steps 1–10, your responses for Steps 12 and 15, and your two screenshots. Submit this material in the format specified by your instructor.

Project WI-9: Compressing Files

In this project, you will learn how to compress files using the Windows compression utility.

Requirements: This project requires Microsoft Windows and Paint.

Project file: PrjWI-9.zip

COPYIT! 1. Copy the file PrjWI-9.zip to your Project folder using the Copy It! button on this page in the *Practical Computer Literacy* digital book.

2. The file PrjWI-9.zip contains four graphics that were zipped using the Windows compression utility. Use File Explorer to display the list of files in your Project folder. Double-click the PrjWI-9.zip file. Your application window might look slightly different, but you should see the four files shown in the figure below.

3. To unzip the files, click the *Extract all* button on the File Explorer toolbar.

4. When prompted to select a destination for the extracted files, just press the Enter key to accept the suggested folder name.

5. The unzipped PrjWI-9 files should be displayed. Double-click one of the files to view it.

6. Close the application window after you view the file.

• Compressing Files (continued)

7. Suppose you want to create several graphics and compress them into one object that you can send as an e-mail attachment. Begin by opening the Paint application.

8. Create a simple shape and then use the Text tool to add your name to the shape.

9. Save your graphic in JPEG format in the Pictures library. Name the file Picture1-[Your Name].

10. Add a second shape to the first one and use the Save As option to save the revised graphic as Picture2-[Your Name]. Close Paint.

11. Navigate to the Pictures library. Make sure the two files that you created are located in this library.

12. Hold the Ctrl key down while you select both of the files you created for this project. Select the Share tab and use the Zip button to compress the two files. A zipped folder with a temporary name is created.

13. Enter FYI-[Your Name] for the folder name.

14. Now, open Paint and create a third graphic. Save it as Picture3-[Your Name]. Close Paint.

15. Back in File Explorer, drag Picture3 into the FYI.zip folder.

16. To check that the FYI zipped folder contains your files, double-click it. Your three graphics files should be listed.

17. Send the FYI compressed folder to your instructor as an e-mail attachment. Be sure to include the project number and your name in the Subject line of the message.

Project AP-1: Working with Application Windows

In this project, you'll apply what you've learned about application windows to start several programs and arrange your desktop.

Requirements: This project requires Microsoft Windows, WordPad, and Paint.

Project file: No project file is required.

You can write your answers to the questions on a sheet of paper with your name and the title AP-1 Answers. The number for each answer should correspond to the number of the step that contains the question. For example, your first answer will be for Step 5.

1. Start the Paint program. Make sure that the Paint window is maximized.

2. Use the Lightning icon in the Shapes group to draw a large lightning bolt anywhere in the workspace. Complete the shape by clicking any blank area of the screen.

3. Select the ▣ Restore Down button.

4. Minimize the Paint window, reopen it by selecting its button on the taskbar, then maximize the window.

5. Select the ▣ button in the upper-left corner. What are the menu options?

6. What are the other buttons on the left side of the title bar?

7. What happens when you select the down-arrow labeled Customize Quick Access Toolbar?

8. How many tabs are there in the Paint window and what are their names?

9. Draw a heart in the center of the screen. Complete the shape by clicking any blank area of the screen.

10. Type someone's name inside the heart using the Text tool. Click any blank area of the screen to close the text box.

11. Minimize the Paint window, then hover over the taskbar to view the thumbnail of the window.

12. Start the WordPad program and enter your answers for Steps 5, 6, 7, and 8.

13. Right-click a blank area on the taskbar and select *Cascade windows*.

14. View the windows side by side.

15. View the windows stacked.

16. Maximize the Paint window. Add a five-point star beneath the lightning shape.

17. Open Microsoft Word and Microsoft PowerPoint.

18. View the four windows side by side.

• Working with Application Windows (continued)

19. Using the Paint window's Zoom control and scroll bars, position all three shapes in the window so you can view them. Your screen should look similar to the one below. Use WordPad's Zoom control so you can view all of the answers in the WordPad window.

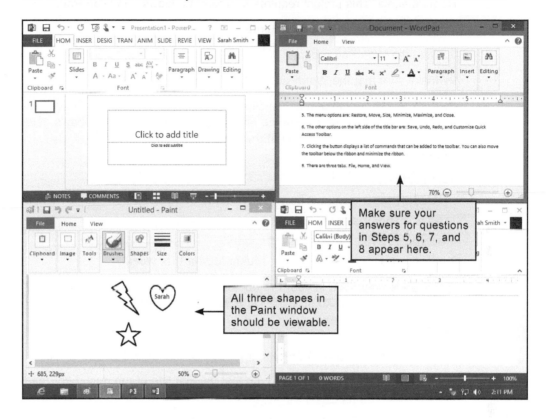

20. Press the PrtSc or Print Screen key on your keyboard.

21. Maximize the Paint window, then paste the screenshot.

22. Save the screenshot as a JPEG file in your Project folder and name it PrjAP-1 [Your Name].

23. Close all open windows.

24. Submit your project on a USB flash drive, as a printout, as an e-mail attachment, or in any other format specified by your instructor.

Project AP-2: Working with Files

In this project, you'll apply what you've learned about Windows applications to create, save, open, and delete a file.

Requirements: This project requires Microsoft Windows and WordPad.

Project file: No project file is required.

1. Start the WordPad program.

2. Make sure that the WordPad window is maximized.

3. Click anywhere in the blank section of the document window and type the following short memo. Type your own name on the FROM: line and type today's date on the DATE: line. (Hint: Press the Enter key at the end of each line.)
MEMO
TO: Professor Greer
FROM: [Student's name]
DATE: [Today's date]
SUBJECT: This week's lesson
I will not be able to attend my music lesson this week.

4. Save the document in your Project folder as PrjAP-2.txt. (Hint: Use the *Save as type* list if necessary to make sure the file is saved as a Text Document.)

5. Close WordPad.

6. Start WordPad again. Open the file PrjAP-2.txt from your Project folder.

7. Type the word IMPORTANT so that the first line of the document reads IMPORTANT MEMO. Your document should now look like the one shown on the next page.

‣ Working with Files (continued)

8. Save the new version of your document under a different name in your Project folder. Use PrjAP-2 [Your Name].

9. Submit the project file as an e-mail attachment, on a USB flash drive, or in any other format specified by your instructor.

10. Delete the original file, PrjAP-2.txt, from your Project folder.

Project AP-3: Configuration and Navigating Basics

In this project, you'll explore how to use the Word Options dialog box to configure user information and file location settings. You'll also explore some efficient ways to navigate within documents. You'll find out how to use Ctrl End to move to the end of a document in one jump. You'll experiment with the Page Up, Page Down, Home, and End keys, then use the Go To command to jump to a specified page.

Requirements: This project requires Microsoft Word.

Project file: PrjAP-3.docx

COPY IT!

1. Copy the file PrjAP-3.docx to your Project folder using the Copy It! button on this page in the *Practical Computer Literacy* digital book.

2. Start Microsoft Word.

3. Open the file PrjAP-3.docx from your Project folder.

4. Select the FILE tab, then choose Options. When the Word Options dialog box appears, select the Save category on the left and notice the default location set to hold your documents when you save them. Select the Browse button to view the dialog box that allows you to change this location. Unless you want to change the location now, select the Cancel button to return to the Word Options dialog box.

5. Select the General category. Enter your name in the *User name* text box if it is not already there.

6. Select the OK button to save your user information and close the Word Options dialog box.

7. Select the VIEW tab, then make sure that the Print Layout button is selected.

8. Press Ctrl End to move to the end of the document. (Hint: Make sure Num Lock is off if you are using the End key on the numeric keypad.)

9. Press Ctrl Enter to insert a page break.

10. Make sure the insertion point is at the top of the new page. Insert the text below, placing a blank line between the title and the paragraph that follows:

Breakout Session Evaluation

Please provide comments on the effectiveness of each breakout session. Do not sign your evaluation.

11. Use the scroll bar to scroll to the beginning of the document.

12. Press the Page Down key a few times and notice how this key changes the position of the insertion point. Press the Page Up key to return to the top of the document.

13. Click in the middle of any full line of text in the document. Press the Home key and notice how this key changes the position of the insertion point. Press the End key to see what it does.

14. Select the HOME tab and use the Editing group's GoTo command to jump to page 5. When page 5 is displayed, close the *Find and Replace* dialog box.

• Configuration and Navigating Basics (continued)

15. Add the following line to the end of the memo:

Drop it off on the table at the conference room door before you leave.

The last page of your document should now look like the one shown below.

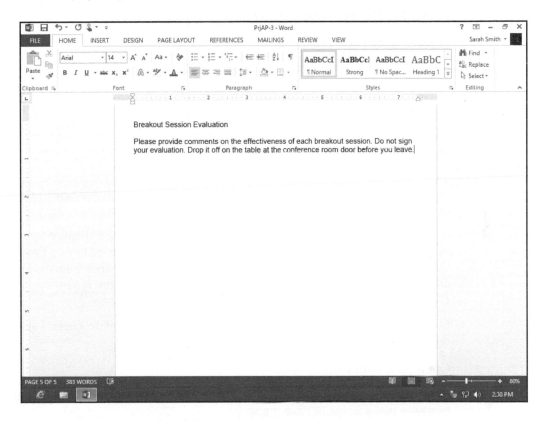

16. Save the new version of your document under a different name in your Project folder. Use PrjAP-3 [Your Name] as the new file name.

17. Submit the project file as an e-mail attachment, as a printout on a USB flash drive, or in any other format specified by your instructor.

Project WD-1 : Creating a Word Document

In this project, you'll apply what you've learned about Microsoft Word to create a document, modify it, and insert a hyperlink.

Requirements: This project requires Microsoft Word.

Project file: No project file is required.

1. Start Microsoft Word.

2. Create a new document containing the text below, placing a blank line between each paragraph:

Dear Marjorie,

Hi! I was happy to receive your letter and learn that all is going well with you, Bob, and the kids. I really miss you all!

Your new job at the bookstore sounds great! How do you manage to keep your mind on work where there are so many fascinating books and magazines just begging to be read?

You mentioned that your first big assignment is to create a display appropriate for the month of February, but without featuring Valentine's Day or Presidents' Day. Did you know that I keep a database of offbeat events, like International Tuba Day and National Accordion Awareness Month? Let me know if you're interested and I'll create a query and send you a list of interesting events.

Sorry for the shortness of this note, but I have to run off to class. I promise to write more soon.

Good luck with the new job!

3. Compare the text that you typed with the text shown above and correct any typing mistakes that you might have made.

4. Use the Delete key to delete the phrase "create a query and" from the last sentence of the third paragraph. The Delete key deletes text without copying it to the Clipboard.

5. Copy the phrase "for the month of February" from the third paragraph. Paste the copied phrase before the period at the end of the sentence that ends with "send you a list of interesting events." Make sure that the spacing is appropriate before and after the pasted text.

6. Select the sentence "I really miss you all!" in the first paragraph. Drag and drop the sentence after the sentence "Good luck with the new job!" at the end of the document. Make sure that the spacing is appropriate before and after the pasted text.

7. Delete the fourth paragraph of the document.

8. Use the Undo button to restore the deleted paragraph.

9. While holding down the mouse button, drag the pointer over the phrase "International Tuba Day" to select it.

10. Right-click the selected phrase and select Hyperlink from the shortcut menu. Make sure the *Text to display* box contains "International Tuba Day."

11. In the Address box, enter www.tubaday.com, then select the OK button.

• Creating a Word Document (continued)

12. You've created a hyperlink in your document. To test it, hold down the Ctrl key and select the link. Once you've connected to the International Tuba Day site, you can close your browser and complete the remaining steps in the project.

13. Compare your letter with the document below. Don't worry if the sentences in your document break in different places at the right margin.

Dear Marjorie,

Hi! I was happy to receive your letter and learn that all is going well with you, Bob, and the kids.

Your new job at the bookstore sounds great! How do you manage to keep your mind on work where there are so many fascinating books and magazines just begging to be read?

You mentioned that your first big assignment is to create a display appropriate for the month of February, but without featuring Valentine's Day or Presidents' Day. Did you know that I keep a database of offbeat events, like International Tuba Day and National Accordion Awareness Month? Let me know if you're interested and I'll send you a list of interesting events for the month of February.

Sorry for the shortness of this note, but I have to run off to class. I promise to write more soon.

Good luck with the new job! I really miss you all!

© MediaTechnics

14. Add your name as the last line of the letter.

15. Save your document in your Project folder as PrjWD-1 [Your Name].

16. Submit the project file as an e-mail attachment, as a printout, on a USB flash drive, or in any other format specified by your instructor.

Project WD-2: Cutting, Copying, and Pasting

In this project, you'll apply what you've learned about Microsoft Word to copy and paste text, and automatically insert special symbols as well as the date and time.

Requirements: This project requires Microsoft Word and Microsoft Excel.

Project file: PrjWD-2.xlsx

COPYIT!

1. Copy the file PrjWD-2.xlsx to your Project folder using the Copy It! button on this page in the *Practical Computer Literacy* digital book.

2. Start Microsoft Word.

3. Create a new document containing the text below, placing a blank line between each paragraph:

MEMO

To: All Staff

Date:

Congratulations to Maria, winner of our quarterly sales bonus! Maria has sold over 1,000 SuperWidgets this year!

Sales totals are as follows:

4. Press the Enter key twice.

5. Start Microsoft Excel.

6. Open the file PrjWD-2.xlsx from your Project folder.

7. Highlight cells A1 through D9.

8. Copy the cells using the Copy button in the Clipboard group on the HOME tab. As an alternative, you can use the Ctrl C key combination.

9. Switch back to Microsoft Word.

10. Make sure the insertion point is positioned below the last line of the document.

11. Use the Paste button in the Clipboard group on the HOME tab (or press Ctrl V) to paste the spreadsheet data into the document. Make sure the spreadsheet is aligned to the left.

12. Switch back to Microsoft Excel. Copy the Congratulations graphic from the spreadsheet. Switch to Microsoft Word and paste the graphic into the document. Use the Wrap Text options on the PICTURE TOOLS contextual tab to size and position the graphic just to the right of the memo heading lines containing MEMO, To, and Date.

13. If the Paste operation was successful, switch back to Microsoft Excel and close it.

14. In your Microsoft Word document, position the insertion point after the word "Date" on the third line of the memo. If necessary, press the Spacebar to create a space after the colon.

• Cutting, Copying, and Pasting (continued)

15. Click the INSERT tab, then click the *Insert Date and Time* button in the Text group. Choose the third option to insert the date in the format March 28, 2014.

16. Position the insertion point at the end of the word "SuperWidgets."

17. On the INSERT tab, use the Symbol button to insert the ^{TM} trademark sign.

18. Your memo should look similar to the one below. Don't worry if the gridlines around the spreadsheet data do not appear on your document.

© MediaTechnics

19. Save your memo in your Project folder using the file name PrjWD-2 [Your Name]. Submit your project on a USB flash drive, as a printout, as an e-mail attachment, or in any other format specified by your instructor.

Project WD-3: Troubleshooting Printing Problems

Sometimes documents fail to print. In this project, you'll experiment with various techniques to troubleshoot common printing problems.

Requirements: This project requires Microsoft Word.

Project file: No files are needed.

1. Start Microsoft Word.

2. Create a new document containing the title below. As you go along, you can add to the document your answers for questions posed in Steps 4–8.

Exploring Printing Problems

3. Before printing, it is important to make sure your printer is plugged in, turned on, and online. On a separate sheet of paper, draw a diagram of the printer currently connected to your computer and label the power switch, power light, online light, and control panel.

4. What is the brand name and model of the printer that is connected to your computer?

5. One of the most common causes of printing problems is selecting the wrong printer. Use the FILE tab to select Print. What is the name of the printer displayed in the Printer box? Is it the same as the printer you worked with in Step 3? If not, select the correct printer in the Printer box.

6. Microsoft Windows provides help for troubleshooting printing problems. Open *Windows Help and Support* by typing Help while on the Windows 8 Start screen, then selecting the *Help and Support* tile. Enter printer problems in the Search box, then press the Enter key. Start the *Printer troubleshooter*. What is the first question asked by the troubleshooter? After you answer this question, what happens?

7. Printers are ultimately controlled by the Windows operating system. Open the *Devices and Printers* window. What are the names of all the installed printers and faxes? Which device is the default? (Hint: Arrange your open windows side by side so that you can see the *Devices and Printers* window at the same time as the Word window.)

8. Check the print queue for the default printer. How many documents are in the print queue? What is their status?

9. You can print a test page to make sure the printer is working properly. Right-click your printer, then select *Printer properties*. From the General tab, select Print Test Page. The test page might look similar to the figure on the next page.

• Troubleshooting Printing Problems (continued)

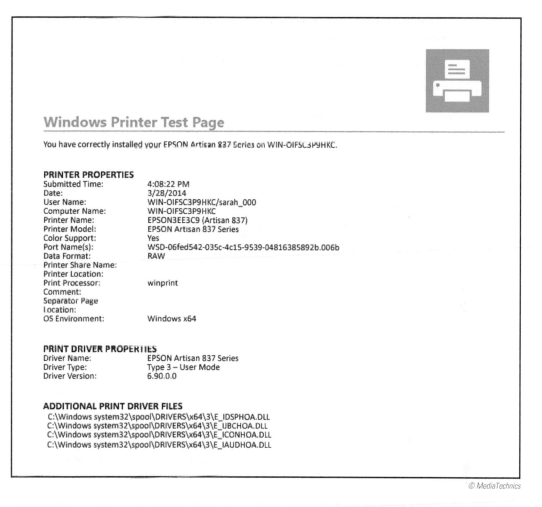

Windows Printer Test Page

You have correctly installed your EPSON Artisan 837 Series on WIN-OIFSC3P9HKC.

PRINTER PROPERTIES
Submitted Time:	4:08:22 PM
Date:	3/28/2014
User Name:	WIN-OIFSC3P9HKC/sarah_000
Computer Name:	WIN-OIFSC3P9HKC
Printer Name:	EPSON3EE3C9 (Artisan 837)
Printer Model:	EPSON Artisan 837 Series
Color Support:	Yes
Port Name(s):	WSD-06fed542-035c-4c15-9539-04816385892b.006b
Data Format:	RAW
Printer Share Name:	
Printer Location:	
Print Processor:	winprint
Comment:	
Separator Page Location:	
OS Environment:	Windows x64

PRINT DRIVER PROPERTIES
Driver Name:	EPSON Artisan 837 Series
Driver Type:	Type 3 – User Mode
Driver Version:	6.90.0.0

ADDITIONAL PRINT DRIVER FILES
C:\Windows system32\spool\DRIVERS\x64\3\E_IDSPHOA.DLL
C:\Windows system32\spool\DRIVERS\x64\3\E_IJBCHOA.DLL
C:\Windows system32\spool\DRIVERS\x64\3\E_ICONHOA.DLL
C:\Windows system32\spool\DRIVERS\x64\3\E_IAUDHOA.DLL

© MediaTechnics

10. Save your Exploring Printing Problems document in your Project folder using the file name PrjWD-3 [Your Name].

11. Print your Exploring Printing Problems document and submit it along with your printer sketch and the test printout. Write your name, student ID number, class section number, date, and PrjWD-3 on all the submitted papers.

Project WD-4: Formatting a Document

In this project, you'll apply what you've learned about Microsoft Word to format an existing document.

Requirements: This project requires Microsoft Word.

Project file: PrjWD-4.docx

COPYIT!

1. Copy the file PrjWD-4.docx to your Project folder using the Copy It! button on this page in the *Practical Computer Literacy* digital book.

2. Start Microsoft Word.

3. Open the file PrjWD-4.docx from your Project folder.

4. Apply the bold text attribute to the line "Memorandum - Novel-Tea & Coffee, Inc."

5. Apply italic to the phrase "air-tight" in the sentence that begins with "Please don't forget."

6. Apply bold and underlining to the phrase "number one" in the last sentence.

7. Select the Memorandum line, then change its font to Book Antiqua, size 18.

8. Center the Memorandum line.

9. Select the word "Memorandum." Use the Change Case button in the Font group on the HOME tab to select UPPERCASE.

10. Select the list of items starting with "Bean quality," then format the list as a bulleted list.

11. Indent the first line of the main paragraphs by .4". The three paragraphs that you'll indent begin with "Just a reminder," "Please don't forget," and "Thanks for helping."

12. Change the line spacing to 1.5 lines for the paragraphs that begin with "Just a reminder," "Please don't forget," and "Thanks for helping."

13. Remove the underlining from the phrase "number one" in the last sentence.

14. Justify the paragraphs that begin with "Just a reminder," "Please don't forget," and "Thanks for helping" so that both the left and right margins are straight.

15. For justified paragraphs, hyphenation can reduce some of the extra spacing added between words. On the PAGE LAYOUT tab, use the Hyphenation button in the Page Setup group to access the Hyphenation dialog box. Place a checkmark in the box for *Automatically hyphenate document*. Uncheck the box for *Hyphenate words in CAPS*.

16. Enter the number 1 in the *Limit consecutive hyphens to* box. Professional publishers prefer not to have more than one consecutive line ending with hyphens.

17. Click the OK button to close the Hyphenation dialog box, then compare your document with the document in the figure on the next page.

• Formatting a Document (continued)

MEMORANDUM - Novel-Tea & Coffee, Inc.

To: Tea n' Coffee Shop Managers
From: Food and Beverage Director, Novel-Tea & Coffee
RE: Reminder – Fundamentals of Coffee-making

Just a reminder to all Tea n' Coffee Shop managers that it takes more than our fine beans to make a quality cup of coffee. Sometimes our employees are so busy frothing cream or sprinkling cinnamon that they can forget the five key factors to creating the best possible cup of coffee. Listed below are the five fundamentals of superb coffee creation:

- Bean quality
- Water purity
- Elapsed time from roasting beans to perking
- Cleanliness of equipment
- Elapsed time from grinding beans to perking

Please don't forget to store all beans in clean, glass, *air-tight* containers to retain the freshness and aroma of the coffee beans. Beans from your weekly shipment that you don't anticipate using within the week must be kept in the refrigerator or freezer. This retains flavor by preventing chemical reactions in the beans.

Thanks for helping to make Tea n' Coffee Shops **number one** in the tri-state area.

© MediaTechnics

---

18. Save your document in your Project folder using the file name PrjWD-4 [Your Name].

19. Submit the project file as an e-mail attachment, as a printout, on a USB flash drive, or in any other format specified by your instructor.

Project WD-5: Using Tabs and Paragraph Alignment

In this project, you'll focus on font formats and tab settings.

Requirements: This project requires Microsoft Word.

Project file: PrjWD-5.docx

COPYIT!

1. Copy the file PrjWD-5.docx to your Project folder using the Copy It! button on this page in the *Practical Computer Literacy* digital book.

2. Start Microsoft Word.

3. Open the file PrjWD-5.docx from your Project folder.

4. Select the document title "How Much Lead is in Your Cup?," then use the Font dialog box to change the title font to size 26, dark blue, bold italic with a shadow effect of Offset Right. (Hint: Click the Text Effects button in the Font dialog box to locate options for the shadow effect.)

5. Select the list of items starting with "Perked coffee 90-150 mg" and ending with "Tea 30-70 mg." Use the Paragraph Dialog Box Launcher to open the Tabs dialog box and set a left tab at the 1" position. Set another left tab at the 3" position, with a dotted leader. Close the Tabs dialog box.

6. Position the insertion point to the left of "Perked coffee," then press the Tab key to move it to the first tab position. Place the insertion point to the left of "90-150 mg," then press the Tab key to move it to the second tab position and display the dotted leader. Use a similar process with the remaining two list items.

7. Position the insertion point at the end of the line that ends with "30-70 mg," then press the Enter key to create a new line. Add this fourth list item, with appropriate tabs: Colas 30-35 mg.

8. Select the ¶ Show/Hide button in the Paragraph group on the HOME tab to display non-printing characters. Notice that the locations in which you pressed the Tab key are indicated by arrows. The locations where you pressed the Enter key are indicated by the ¶ symbol.

9. Position the insertion point to the left of any ¶ symbol in the document. Press the Delete key to delete it. By removing this line break symbol, you joined two lines together.

10. To reestablish the original line break, click the Undo button on the Quick Access toolbar. Hide the non-printing characters by selecting the ¶ Show/Hide button.

11. At the top of the document, replace the reporter's name with your own name.

12. Compare your completed document with the document in the figure on the next page.

• Using Tabs and Paragraph Alignment (continued)

Novel-Tea News
Reporter: [Student's Name]

How Much Lead is in Your Cup?

Caffeine is a product found in many popular beverages. Yet most people are trying to curb their daily caffeine intake. After all, the effects of excessive caffeine have recently received a lot of press coverage.

As employees of Novel-Tea & Coffee, you will often get caffeine-related questions from customers. The following list of common drinks paired with their caffeine content may help you answer many of those questions.

Perked coffee ....90-150 mg
Instant coffee ....60-80 mg
Tea ....30-70 mg
Colas ....30-35 mg

Most customers also associate caffeine with chocolate. A typical chocolate bar contains 30 mg of caffeine. Yes, a cup of perked coffee does have three to five times the caffeine of a chocolate bar, but doesn't a chocolate bar have a few more calories than a cup of perked coffee?

So hopefully this information will help you answer commonly asked questions about caffeine and help us better serve our customers.

© MediaTechnics

13. Save your document in your Project folder using the file name PrjWD-5 [Your Name].

14. Submit the project file as an e-mail attachment, as a printout, on a USB flash drive, or in any other format specified by your instructor.

Project WD-6: Creating a Table

In this project, you'll apply what you've learned about Microsoft Word to create a table in a document.

Requirements: This project requires Microsoft Word.

Project file: PrjWD-6.docx

COPY IT!

1. Copy the file PrjWD-6.docx to your Project folder using the Copy It! button on this page in the *Practical Computer Literacy* digital book.

2. Start Microsoft Word.

3. Open the file PrjWD-6.docx from your Project folder.

4. Insert a table before the paragraph that starts with "Because of the special nature." The table should consist of four columns and seven rows.

5. Enter the following four labels into the first row of the table:

COFFEE (16 oz.)   TOTAL CALORIES   CALORIES   FROM FAT

6. Select all of the cells in the leftmost column. Resize the column by using the TABLE TOOLS LAYOUT contextual tab. Change the Table Column Width to 2.5". Center just the label using the Align Top Center button in the Alignment group.

7. Combine the cells containing the labels "CALORIES" and "FROM FAT" by using the Merge Cells button in the Merge group.

8. With the merged cell selected, create a new cell next to the merged cell by using the Split Cells button in the Merge group. Select 2 for number of columns and 1 for number of rows.

9. Enter the label FAT (grams) in the new cell.

10. Your labels should look similar to the example below. Enter the following data into the cells of the table, under the appropriate labels:

COFFEE (16 oz.)	TOTAL CALORIES	CALORIES FROM FAT	FAT (grams)
Black Coffee	0	0	0
Café Latte (non-fat milk)	126	0	0
Café Latte (whole milk)	204	99	11
Cappuccino (non-fat milk)	75	0	0
Cappuccino (whole milk)	120	54	6
Café Mocha (non-fat milk)	174	18	2

11. Insert one more row into the table and enter the following data:

Café Mocha (whole milk)	234	90	10

12. You can split a table if you need to. Select the cell in the first column, fifth row, then select the Split Table button in the Merge group. Use the Undo button on the Quick Access toolbar to consolidate the rows back into a single table.

13. Using the TABLE TOOLS LAYOUT contextual tab, delete the row containing "Black Coffee."

• Creating a Table (continued)

14. Use the Sort button in the Data group on the TABLE TOOLS LAYOUT contextual tab to sort the data in ascending order, first by TOTAL CALORIES, then by COFFEE (16 oz.). Select the number type for TOTAL CALORIES and the text type for COFFEE (16 oz.).

15. Select the TABLE TOOLS DESIGN contextual tab. Highlight all the labels in the top row, choose the Shading button in the Table Styles group, then select the Light Green Standard Color.

16. With all the top-row labels still highlighted, use the Borders button in the Table Styles group to select No Border.

17. To automatically format the table, use the Table Styles group on the TABLE TOOLS DESIGN contextual tab. Select the Grid Table 2 - Accent 2 format.

18. If needed, insert a blank line so that the table is separated from the paragraphs above and below it.

19. At the top of the document, replace the reporter's name with your own name.

20. Compare your document to the figure below.

Novel-Tea News
Reporter: [Student's Name]

How Much Fat Is in Your Cup?

As employees of Novel-Tea & Coffee, you may be asked about the calories and the fat content of some of our standard and specialty drinks. The following list of standard drinks with their caloric and fat contents may help you answer those questions.

COFFEE (16 oz.)	TOTAL CALORIES	CALORIES FROM FAT	FAT (grams)
Cappuccino (non-fat milk)	75	0	0
Cappuccino (whole milk)	120	54	6
Café Latte (non-fat milk)	126	0	0
Café Mocha (non-fat milk)	174	18	2
Café Latte (whole milk)	204	99	11
Café Mocha (whole milk)	234	90	10

Because of the special nature of our monthly spotlight drinks, they are likely to be higher in both calories and fat content than any of the above drinks. We'll try to get you the data on a spotlight drink when we announce the drink.

If a customer is troubled by the calories or fat content of a particular drink, suggest a drink that's similar, but with fewer calories or less fat. For example, suggest a cappuccino instead of a café latte, or recommend using non-fat milk instead of whole milk. Hopefully this information will help you answer commonly asked questions and help us better serve our customers.

© MediaTechnics

21. Save your document in your Project folder using the file name PrjWD-6 [Your Name]. Submit your project on a USB flash drive, as a printout, or as an e-mail attachment, according to your instructor's directions.

Project WD-7: Using the Mail Merge Wizard

In this project, you'll use Microsoft Word's Mail Merge Wizard to create an address list and perform a mail merge.

Requirements: This project requires Microsoft Word.

Project file: No project file is required.

1. Start Microsoft Word and select the *Blank document* template.

2. Select the MAILINGS tab. Use the Start Mail Merge button in the Start Mail Merge group to select the *Step-by-Step Mail Merge Wizard*.

3. In the Mail Merge pane, select Letters as the type of document, then select the *Next: Starting document* link.

4. In the Mail Merge pane, select *Start from a template*, then choose the *Select template* link. In the Select Template dialog box, choose the *Letters* tab. Select the *Adjacency letter* template, then click the OK button. Click the *Next: Select recipients* link.

5. In the Mail Merge pane, select the *Type a new list* option, then click the Create link. Enter the following information in the New Address List dialog box:

First Name	Last Name	Address Line 1	City	State
Jim	Gallagos	1420 Elm Pass	Springfield	IL
Ed	Zimmerman	1562 River Way	Springfield	IL
Alice	Wegin	523 West Ave	Oak Grove	IL

Use the New Entry button to insert new rows. When you've entered all three names, close the New Address List dialog box.

6. Save the list as Address List in your Project folder. Close the Mail Merge Recipients dialog box. Click the *Next: Write your letter* link.

7. Select today's date for the date placeholder.

8. Replace the sender company placeholder and sender company address placeholder with the following information:

Perfect Pizza
1320 W. Oak Grove Rd.
Springfield, IL

9. Delete the placeholders for the recipient's address and name. Select the *Address block* link from the Mail Merge pane. Verify the format for the address in the Preview pane, then close the Insert Address Block dialog box.

10. Delete the placeholder for the salutation. Use the *Greeting line* option from the Mail Merge pane to select any salutation format.

11. Replace the placeholder for the letter's text with:

I'm pleased to announce that Perfect Pizza has opened a new branch in your neighborhood! Stop by any time this week for a free slice of pizza!

12. Delete the placeholder for the sender's title in the closing. Modify the closing placeholder at the bottom of the page so it becomes:

Sincerely,

• Using the Mail Merge Wizard (continued)

13. From the Mail Merge pane, select the *Next: Preview your letters* link. Use the Forward and Back buttons on the Mail Merge pane to view the merged letters.

14. From the Mail Merge pane, select the *Next: Complete the merge* link. Select the *Edit individual letters* link. Choose All, then select the OK button. The mail merge is complete. Scroll down the document. You should have three individually addressed letters.

15. Compare the first letter to the document shown below. Don't worry if the date is different.

4/18/2014

Sarah Smith
Perfect Pizza
1320 W. Oak Grove Rd.
Springfield, IL

Jim Gallagos
1420 Elm Pass
Springfield, IL

Dear Jim Gallagos,

I'm pleased to announce that Perfect Pizza has opened a new branch in your neighborhood! Stop by any time this week for a free slice of pizza!

Sincerely,

Sarah Smith
Perfect Pizza

© MediaTechnics

16. Save both documents in your Project folder. Save the initial document using the file name PrjWD-7 [Your Name] and the final document as PrjWD-7A [Your Name].

17. Submit the two project files as e-mail attachments, as printouts, on a USB flash drive, or in any other format specified by your instructor.

Project WD-8: Using SmartArt Graphics

In this project, you'll use the SmartArt Graphics options to customize a document.

Requirements: This project requires Microsoft Word.

Project file: PrjWD-8.docx

COPY IT!

1. Copy the file PrjWD-8.docx to your Project folder using the Copy It! button on this page in the *Practical Computer Literacy* digital book.

2. Start Microsoft Word.

3. Open the file PrjWD-8.docx from your Project folder.

4. Position the insertion point in the text box that contains the text "SmartArt," then delete the text.

5. With the insertion point still in the text box, choose the INSERT tab, then select the SmartArt button in the Illustrations group.

6. From the List category, select the Basic Block List option, then click the OK button.

7. Insert the following items in the text boxes:

   Sledding
   Skating
   Sled Dog Racing
   Ice Sculptures

8. Delete any extra text boxes by selecting them, then pressing the Delete key on your keyboard.

9. From the Layouts group on the DESIGN tab, select the Vertical Box List layout. Adjust the size of the SmartArt so it fits properly in the text box.

10. From the SmartArt Styles group, select the Subtle Effect style.

11. Compare your document to the one on the next page.

• Using SmartArt Graphics (continued)

© MediaTechnics

12. Save your document in your Project folder using the file name PrjWD-8 [Your Name].

13. Submit the project file as an e-mail attachment, as a printout, on a USB flash drive, or in any other format specified by your instructor.

Project WD-9: Finalizing a Document

In this project, you'll apply what you've learned about Microsoft Word to check a document for errors, correct mistakes, set margins, use styles, display document statistics, add headers, and add footers. You'll also add footnotes, endnotes, and citations, plus find out how to assemble citations into a bibliography.

Requirements: This project requires Microsoft Word.

Project file: PrjWD-9.docx

COPYIT!

1. Copy the file PrjWD-9.docx to your Project folder using the Copy It! button on this page in the *Practical Computer Literacy* digital book.

2. Start Microsoft Word.

3. Open the file PrjWD-9.docx from your Project folder.

4. Use the Margins button on the PAGE LAYOUT tab to set the right and left margins of the document to 1.25".

5. Select Options from the FILE tab. Select the Proofing category and make sure that the boxes for checking grammar and showing readability statistics are checked. Close the Options window before continuing.

6. Start the spelling and grammar checker, and correct any errors it finds.

7. If the spelling checker catches any proper names that you'd like to add to your custom dictionary, choose the Add button.

8. Use the thesaurus to select a more appropriate word to replace "serious" in the first line of the third paragraph.

9. Add a left-justified header to the document that includes your name and your student ID number on one line; add your class section number and PrjWD-9 on a second line.

10. Add a right-justified footer that shows the word Page followed by the page number.

11. Apply the Heading 1 style to the first line in the document.

12. Use the Find button on the HOME tab to locate the word "BAR." Select the REFERENCES tab, then add the endnote Browning Automatic Rifle.

13. Position the insertion point at the end of the paragraph on the first page that ends with "...shot as spies." Use the Insert Citation button to add the following citation to the book: Insights into History by Jefferson MacGruder, published in 2008 by Random House (New York).

14. Go to the end of the document and right-click the endnote. Select *Convert to Footnote*, which moves it to the bottom of the page on which it is referenced.

15. Position the insertion point at the end of the document once again. Press the Enter key, then select the Bibliography button on the REFERENCES tab. Select the Works Cited option. Make sure that the Works Cited section of your document looks like the sample on the next page.

• Finalizing a Document (continued)

> In the big picture of World War II, Art and Ron were part of a desperate effort to repulse a last-ditch German attack that began on December 16. Many historians (Jones, 1998) now note that the Axis was on the brink of collapse and further struggle simply prolonged the course of the war and needlessly increased the number of casualties on both sides of the struggle.
>
> **Works Cited**
>
> Jones, G. (1998). *World War II Reconstructed.* Boston: Little Brown.
> MacGruder, J. (2008). *Insights into History.* New York: Random House.

16. Review your document. Make sure it contains citations in parentheses for MacGruder on page 1 and Jones on page 4, a footnote at the bottom of page 1, and a Works Cited section at the end of the document.

17. Save your document in your Project folder using the file name PrjWD-9 [Your Name].

18. Submit the project file as an e-mail attachment, as a printout, on a USB flash drive, or in any other format specified by your instructor.

Project EX-1: Creating a Worksheet

In this project, you'll apply what you've learned to create a worksheet using Microsoft Excel.

Requirements: This project requires Microsoft Excel.

Project file: No file is required.

1. Start Microsoft Excel and open a blank workbook.

2. Select the FILE tab, then choose Options to open the Excel Options dialog box. Use the General and Save categories to make sure the user name and default local file locations are correct. Save these settings if you have permission to modify them. Otherwise, cancel and return to the worksheet.

3. Enter the labels and values shown below. Adjust column widths if necessary.

	A	B	C	D	E	F
1	Phone Charges Per Roommate for February					
2	Basic Monthly Service Rate			20.44		
3	Long Distance Charges for Each Roommate:					
4			Jamesson	Coleman	Depindeau	Struthers
5			5.65	0.25	1.35	3.75
6			0.45	0.65	2.15	0.88
7			1.68	0.56	3.78	1.23
8				4.15	5.77	0.95
9				1.25		0.88
10				3.67		1.95
11						3.88
12	Total Long Distance					
13	Share of Basic Rate					
14	Total Phone Charges					

4. In cell C12, use the SUM button to calculate the sum of the cells in column C. Use a similar procedure to calculate the long distance call totals for Coleman, Depindeau, and Struthers in cells D12, E12, and F12, respectively.

5. In cell C13, create a formula to calculate Jamesson's share of the $20.44 basic monthly service rate by dividing the contents of cell D2 by 4. Create a similar formula for each roommate in cells D13, E13, and F13.

6. In cell C14, create a formula to calculate Jamesson's share of the total phone bill by adding the contents of cell C12 to the contents of cell C13. Create a similar formula for each roommate in cells D14, E14, and F14.

7. Change the contents of Cell A1 to Feb Phone.

8. Use the Undo button to change the label in cell A1 back to the original wording.

9. Compare your worksheet to the one shown in the figure on the next page.

• Creating a Worksheet (continued)

Excel spreadsheet showing:

	A	B	C	D	E	F
1	Phone Charges Per Roommate for February					
2	Basic Monthly Service Rate			20.44		
3	Long Distance Charges for Each Roommate:					
4			Jamesson	Coleman	Depindeau	Struthers
5			5.65	0.25	1.35	3.75
6			0.45	0.65	2.15	0.88
7			1.68	0.56	3.78	1.23
8				4.15	5.77	0.95
9				1.25		0.88
10				3.67		1.95
11						3.88
12	Total Long Distance		7.78	10.53	13.05	13.52
13	Share of Basic Rate		5.11	5.11	5.11	5.11
14	Total Phone Charges		12.89	15.64	18.16	18.63
15						
16						
17						
18						
19						

10. Save your worksheet in your Project folder using the file name PrjEX-1 [Your Name].

11. Submit the project file as an e-mail attachment, as a printout, on a USB flash drive, or in any other format specified by your instructor.

Project EX-2: Using Functions

In this project, you'll apply what you've learned about SUM plus the MAX, MIN, AVERAGE, and IF functions to complete a Microsoft Excel worksheet.

Requirements: This project requires Microsoft Excel.

Project file: PrjEX-2.xlsx

COPYIT! 1. Copy the file PrjEX-2.xlsx to your Project folder using the Copy It! button on this page in the *Practical Computer Literacy* digital book.

2. Start Microsoft Excel.

3. Open the file PrjEX-2.xlsx from your Project folder. When completing the rest of the steps for this project, you can use the f_x Insert Function button on the formula bar, or you can use the Function Library buttons on the FORMULAS tab. You might want to experiment a bit with both methods to discover the one you like best.

4. Use the SUM button to display the total number of flights in cells B11 and C11.

5. In cell B12, use the MIN function to display the smallest number of Mango Air flights from the list that begins in cell B4 and ends in cell B10. Enter a similar function in cell C12 for Econo Air flights.

6. In cell B13, use the MAX function to display the largest number of Mango Air flights from the list that begins in cell B4 and ends in cell B10. Enter a similar function in cell C13 for Econo Air flights.

7. In cell B14, use a function to display the average number of Mango Air flights from the list that begins in cell B4 and ends in cell B10. Enter a similar function in cell C14 for Econo Air flights.

8. In cell D3, enter the label Most Flights and adjust the column width so the label fits in a single cell.

9. In cell D4, use the IF function to compare the number of flights for Mango Air and Econo Air, based on the numbers that appear in cells B4 and C4. The IF function should display Econo Air in cell D4 if that airline has the most flights for Costa Rica. It should display Mango Air in cell D4 if that airline has the most flights. (Hint: Place quotation marks around "Econo Air" and "Mango Air" when you create the function, and remember that the Insert Function dialog box provides help and examples.)

10. Use the Fill handle to copy the IF function from cell D4 down to cells D5 through D10.

11. In cell B16, use the COUNTA function to display the number of destination countries for Mango Air flights from the list that begins in cell A4 and ends in cell A10. Enter a similar function in cell C16 for Econo Air flights.

12. Enter your name in cell E1.

13. Change the number in cell C9 to 85.

14. Compare your worksheet to the one shown in the figure on the next page.

• Using Functions (continued)

© MediaTechnics

15. Save your worksheet in your Project folder using the file name PrjEX-2 [Your Name].

16. Submit the project file as an e-mail attachment, as a printout, on a USB flash drive, or in any other format specified by your instructor.

Project EX-3: Using Absolute and Relative References

In this project, you'll apply what you've learned about absolute and relative references to complete a sales commission worksheet.

Requirements: This project requires Microsoft Excel.

Project file: PrjEX-3.xlsx

COPYIT!

1. Copy the file PrjEX-3.xlsx to your Project folder using the Copy It! button on this page in the *Practical Computer Literacy* digital book.

2. Start Microsoft Excel.

3. Open the file PrjEX-3.xlsx from your Project folder.

4. Notice that cell B2 contains a sales commission rate. Each salesperson receives a commission equal to his or her total sales multiplied by the commission rate. The commission rate changes periodically. The worksheet is set up so that if the sales manager changes the rate in cell B2, all the sales commissions will be recalculated.

5. Create a formula in cell B10 to calculate the sales commission for column B by multiplying the Total Sales in cell B9 by the Commission Rate in cell B2. (Hint: You must use an absolute reference for the Commission Rate in the formula.)

6. Copy the formula from cell B10 to cells C10 through E10.

7. Check the results of the copied formulas to make sure that they are correct. If cells C10 through E10 contain zeros, you did not use the correct absolute reference for the formula that you entered in Step 5. If necessary, modify the formula in cell B10, then recopy it to cells C10 through E10.

8. Compare your worksheet to the one shown in the figure on the next page, but don't save it until you complete Steps 9 and 10.

• Using Absolute and Relative References (continued)

Commission Worksheet

Salesperson	Renfrew, Steven	Anderson, Jane	Cole, Michael	James, Ron
Commission Rate:	0.02			
Week 1	$ 14,283.00	$ 11,020.00	$ 13,477.00	$ 12,405.00
Week 2	$ 17,808.00	$ 12,381.00	$ 1,100.00	$ 12,889.00
Week 3	$ 12,302.00	$ 14,830.00	$ 13,747.00	$ 14,700.00
Week 4	$ 13,100.00	$ 19,787.00	$ 18,483.00	$ 15,806.00
Total Sales	$ 57,493.00	$ 58,018.00	$ 46,807.00	$ 55,800.00
Sales Commission	$ 1,149.86	$ 1,160.36	$ 936.14	$ 1,116.00
Base Salary	$ 500.00	$ 501.00	$ 502.00	$ 503.00
Salary Plus Commission	$ 1,649.86	$ 1,661.36	$ 1,438.14	$ 1,619.00

9. Change the contents of cell B2 to 0.03.

10. Enter your name in cell B4.

11. Save your worksheet in your Project folder using the file name PrjEX-3 [Your Name].

12. Submit the project file as an e-mail attachment, as a printout, on a USB flash drive, or in any other format specified by your instructor.

Project EX-4: Formatting a Worksheet

In this project, you'll apply what you've learned about Microsoft Excel to complete and format a worksheet.

Requirements: This project requires Microsoft Excel.

Project file: PrjEX-4.xlsx

COPY IT!

1. Copy the file PrjEX-4.xlsx to your Project folder using the Copy It! button on this page in the *Practical Computer Literacy* digital book.

2. Start Microsoft Excel.

3. Open the file PrjEX-4.xlsx from your Project folder.

4. Click the ☐ empty block between the "A" and "1" labels in the upper-left corner of the worksheet to select the entire worksheet.

5. Change the font size of the entire worksheet to 14 point.

6. Use the Fill handle to copy the formula from cell C6 to cells D6 and E6.

7. Copy the formula from cell C15 to cells D15 and E15.

8. Copy the formula from cell F4 to cells F5 through F6, and cells F9 through F15.

9. Insert a new, empty row before row 15.

10. Change the color of the text in cell A1 to dark blue.

11. Change the font in cell A1 to Times New Roman, size 20, bold.

12. Use the *Merge & Center* button in the Alignment group to merge the contents of cells A1 through F1 so that the title is centered across those columns.

13. In cell A2, enter today's date.

14. Click cell A2 and use the Dialog Box Launcher in the Number group to open the Format Cells dialog box. Select a date format that displays dates in the format Wednesday, March 14, 2014.

15. Merge the contents of cells A2 through F2 so that the date is centered.

16. Format cells A3 through F3 as bold text. Format cells A8 and A16 as bold text.

17. Format the numbers in cells C4 through E16 as currency.

18. Format the numbers in cells F4 through F16 as percentages with no decimal places.

19. Right-align the labels in cells C3 through F3.

20. Add both inside and outside borders (All Borders) to two cell ranges: B4 through F5 and B9 through F13.

21. Adjust the width of all columns so that all labels and values fit within the cells.

22. Now, explore what happens when you align some of the worksheet labels at a 90-degree angle. Select cells C3 through F3. Use the Orientation button in the Alignment group to select Rotate Text Up.

• Formatting a Worksheet (continued)

23. Aligning column headings at a 90-degree angle is useful for worksheets that have many narrow columns. On this worksheet, however, the labels looked better at the normal angle, so use the Undo button on the Quick Access toolbar to undo the 90-degree angle.

24. Compare your worksheet to the one shown below.

25. Save your worksheet in your Project folder using the file name PrjEX-4 [Your Name].

26. Submit the project file as an e-mail attachment, as a printout, on a USB flash drive, or in any other format specified by your instructor.

Project EX-5: Creating Charts

In this project, you'll apply what you've learned about Microsoft Excel to create a column chart and a pie chart for an e-commerce worksheet.

Requirements: This project requires Microsoft Excel.

Project file: PrjEX-5.xlsx

COPYIT!

1. Copy the file PrjEX-5.xlsx to your Project folder using the Copy It! button on this page in the *Practical Computer Literacy* digital book.

2. Start Microsoft Excel.

3. Open the file PrjEX-5.xlsx from your Project folder.

4. Select the data in cells B3 through C6. Use the INSERT tab to create a 3-D Pie chart. Select Layout 6 in the Chart Layouts group on the DESIGN contextual tab. Enter Which Activities Lead? in the Chart Title box. Move the chart to a new sheet and name the sheet Comparison Chart.

5. Change the style of the chart to Style 9.

6. Change the Chart Area (the chart background) to Subtle Effect - Red, Accent 2 in the Shape Styles group on the FORMAT tab.

7. On the E-commerce worksheet, select the data in cells H4 through H9. Use the INSERT tab to create a Clustered Column chart.

8. If necessary, move the chart so you can view the data in columns F and G, then add the labels for each year to the chart. Select the DESIGN tab, then choose the Select Data button. Click the Edit button for the Horizontal (Category) Axis Labels. Select cells G4 through G9, then close both of the dialog boxes. The dates should now be displayed under each bar of the graph.

9. Enter the chart title U.S. Projections. Use the ⊞ CHART ELEMENTS button to add the vertical Y-axis title $ Billions. Move the chart to a new sheet and name the sheet Growth Chart.

10. Change the chart type to *Line with Markers*. Change the Chart Area to Subtle Effect - Blue, Accent 1 in the Shape Styles group on the FORMAT tab.

11. Examine the charts to ensure that the spreadsheet data is accurately represented. One easy verification technique is to identify a data trend and see if the trend is shown both in the data and on the chart. A trend in this data is the trend for projected growth to increase from one year to the next. Verify that the line chart corresponds to this trend by making sure the line moves up as it moves to the right.

Use care when identifying trends; make sure the conclusions you draw are accurate. Be aware of what can and can't be concluded from data. For example, although this data shows that 52% of e-commerce business activity is from business to consumer, it would be incorrect to assume that 52% of monetary transactions on a given day are between businesses and consumers.

12. Copy both charts to the E-Commerce tab.

• Creating Charts (continued)

13. Size and position the pie chart so that the upper-left corner of the chart is in cell A10 and the lower-right corner is in cell D23.

14. Size and position the line chart so that the upper-left corner of the chart is in cell F11 and the lower-right corner is in cell J23.

15. Click a blank cell in the worksheet, then display a print preview. Use Settings options to change the page orientation to Landscape and center the worksheet horizontally on the page. The worksheet preview should look like the one shown in the figure below.

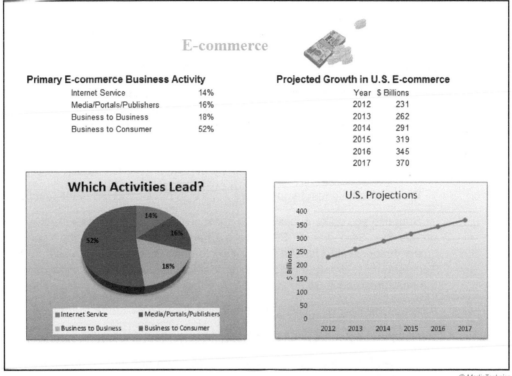

16. Save your worksheet in your Project folder using the file name PrjEX-5 [Your Name].

17. Submit the project file as an e-mail attachment, as a printout, on a USB flash drive, or In any other format specified by your instructor.

Project EX-6: Interpreting Worksheets and Charts

In this project, you'll practice identifying simple trends and drawing conclusions based on tabular information and charts. You'll also try your hand at sorting, ranking, and filtering data.

Requirements: This project requires Microsoft Excel.

Project file: PrjEX-6.xlsx

COPY IT!

1. Copy the file PrjEX-6.xlsx to your Project folder using the Copy It! button on this page in the *Practical Computer Literacy* digital book.

2. Start Microsoft Excel and open the file PrjEX-6.xlsx from your Project folder.

3. The worksheet contains raw data from the National Climatic Data Center. It is a 100-year record (1910–2009) of mean temperatures in the U.S. for the month of January. Examine the data. What would you guess is the average temperature for this 100-year period? Can you tell if temperatures seem to be increasing or decreasing?

4. To make it easier to analyze the data, highlight cells A3:B102 and use the DATA tab's Sort button to arrange the temperatures in order from smallest to largest. The lowest temperature should be 22.58 in 1979. If your results are different, undo the sort and try it again, making sure to highlight both columns A and B.

5. Which year had the highest January mean temperature, and what was it?

6. Do all of the highest temperatures appear to have occurred in the last 50 years?

7. Suppose you'd like to answer the question "In which years was the average temperature greater than 34 degrees?" Select cells A2 and B2, which contain the Year and Temperature labels, respectively. Use the Filter button to enter filter mode, then use the arrow next to Temperature to create a Number Filter that is "Greater Than 34." How many years had temperatures above 34 degrees?

8. Clear the filter by clicking the Filter button again.

9. Now, sort columns A and B by year from earliest to most current.

10. In cell E3, calculate the average temperature and write it down. Do temperatures before 1920 appear to be above or below average?

11. To identify trends in the temperatures, enter formulas in column E to compute the average January temperatures for each of the ten-year intervals listed in the Decade column. Which decade appears to have had the highest average January temperatures?

12. Excel can automatically rank the decades so that you can easily see which decade was the warmest, which was the second warmest, and so on. Select cell F6 and enter the formula =RANK(E6, $E$6:$E$15). That formula should produce the number 8 to indicate that 1910–1919 was the eighth warmest decade. Copy the formula down through row 15. Which decade is ranked ninth?

13. Create a pie chart of the data in cells D6 through E15. Does that chart make sense? Change the chart type and look at the data formatted as a column chart, a scatter chart, and a line chart. Which chart best shows the temperature trends over time, and which one best lets you compare temperatures from one decade to the next?

• Interpreting Worksheets and Charts (continued)

14. Select the Clustered Column chart type. Add the chart title Average January Temperatures Per Decade above the chart.

15. Add the vertical Y-axis title Degrees Fahrenheit. Remove the "Series 1" legend from the chart. Format the vertical axis so the temperatures are displayed without decimal places. (Hint: Start by right-clicking the vertical axis, then select Format Axis.) Compare your chart to the example below.

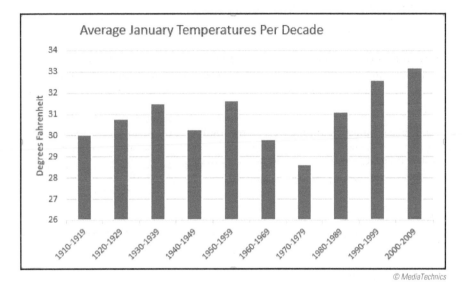

© MediaTechnics

16. Place the chart on Sheet2 and rename Sheet2 Chart by Decade.

17. Examine the chart to ensure that the spreadsheet data is accurately represented. One easy verification technique is to identify a data trend and see if the trend is shown both in the data and on the chart. A trend in this data is the trend for the lowest temperatures in the 1960s and 1970s, and the highest in the last 20 years. Verify that the column chart corresponds to this trend.

18. You can add a trendline to your chart by selecting the [+] CHART ELEMENTS button, then selecting the Trendline option. Select Linear. According to this trendline, how would you characterize the temperature differences now compared to 100 years ago?

19. To forecast trends based on your chart, right-click the line, then select Format Trendline to display the Format Trendline dialog box. Under Forecast, enter 2 in the Forward box. Based on the result, what would you expect as the average temperature for the decade 2020–2029?

20. Add your name to cell G1 on the Sheet1 worksheet. Save your project using the file name PrjEX-6 [Your Name].

21. Submit the project file as an e-mail attachment, as a printout, on a USB flash drive, or in any other format specified by your instructor.

Project EX-7: Finalizing a Worksheet

In this project, you'll apply what you've learned about Microsoft Excel to complete a worksheet, freeze its titles, and finalize it for printing.

Requirements: This project requires Microsoft Excel.

Project file: PrjEX-7.xlsx

COPY IT!

1. Copy the file PrjEX-7.xlsx to your Project folder using the Copy It! button on this page in the *Practical Computer Literacy* digital book.

2. Start Microsoft Excel and open the file PrjEX-7.xlsx from your Project folder.

3. Notice that when you scroll the worksheet, the title and column headings are no longer visible. To freeze the titles at the top of the screen, select cell A3. You've selected this cell because you want the titles above row 3 to remain fixed in place when you scroll.

4. Select the VIEW tab, then use the Freeze Panes button to select Freeze Panes. Now scroll the worksheet and make sure that rows 1 and 2 remain in view.

5. Scroll down the worksheet and notice that data for the miniature gargoyles is not complete. Select cells B43 and B44, then use the Fill handle to consecutively number the products. (Hint: To check your work, make sure that the Miniature Dragon Gargoyle has a product number of 359, and the Miniature War Horse has 381.)

6. All of the miniatures are the same size, weight, price, and shipping cost. Use the Fill command to duplicate the information from cells C43 through F43 for all miniature gargoyles.

7. Right-justify the data in column C. Center the titles in columns B through F.

8. Select cell B2. Use the Wrap Text button in the Alignment group on the HOME tab to wrap the text.

9. Use tools on the DATA tab to sort the data in cells A3 through F68 in A to Z order by Description.

10. Check the spelling of the worksheet and correct misspellings as needed.

11. Unfreeze the panes so that you can scroll the entire worksheet.

12. Use tools on the INSERT tab to add a right-justified header to the worksheet that includes your name, your student ID number, your class section number, today's date, and PrjEX-7.

13. Add a centered footer to the worksheet that includes the word Page followed by the page number. (Hint: If you can't see header and footer elements such as Page Number, select the DESIGN tab.) Select any cell in the worksheet to exit the *Header & Footer* mode.

14. Excel is in Page Layout view, and you can see how this worksheet is set up to print. Does it print all the miniature gargoyles? What's printed on the second page?

15. The print area is currently set at A1:I43, which does not include all of the miniature gargoyles. To clear the print area so the entire sheet will be printed, use the Print Area button on the PAGE LAYOUT tab to select Clear Print Area.

16. Use the FILE tab's Print settings to adjust the scaling option so that the worksheet will be printed on a single sheet of paper. Print your worksheet.

• Finalizing a Worksheet (continued)

17. The text on the single-page printout is quite small. Change the scaling setting back to No Scaling.

18. Let's suppose that you don't want to print the Discount Schedule. In Normal view, select cells A1 through F68. Using the PAGE LAYOUT tab, designate this range as the print area so that the Discount Schedule is not printed.

19. Use the Print Titles button to designate rows 1 and 2 as the title to print on every page.

20. Specify that you want to print gridlines and headings so that you can see the row numbers and column letters on the printout.

21. Set the orientation to Landscape and center the worksheet horizontally on the page.

22. Look at a print preview of your worksheet. It should look similar to the pages below.

Page 1

[Student's Name]
[Student's ID]
[Section Number]
[Date]
[PrjEX-7]

	A	B	C	D	E	F
1	Gothic Gargoyle Collection					
2	Description	Product Number	Size	Weight	Price	Shipping
3	Ancient Burden Gargoyle	872	4"Wx2"H	16	$32.95	$5.95
4	Dwarf Dragon Gargoyle	551	3"Wx5"H	4	$12.96	$5.05
5	Dwarf Dragon Gargoyle	731	3"Wx7"H	5	$19.95	$5.95
6	Dwarf Florentine Gargoyle	810	2"Wx4"H	9	$14.95	$5.95

Page 2

[Student's Name]
[Student's ID]
[Section Number]
[Date]
[PrjEX-7]

	A	B	C	D	E	F
1	Gothic Gargoyle Collection					
2	Description	Product Number	Size	Weight	Price	Shipping
21	Medium Elf with Bow	895	3"Wx3"H	1.5	$29.95	$4.95
22	Medium Fang Gargoyle	886	3"Wx3"H	1.5	$29.95	$4.95
23	Medium Female Warrior	897	3"Wx3"H	1.5	$29.95	$4.95
24	Medium Fire-Breathing Gargoyle	887	3"Wx3"H	1.5	$29.95	$4.95
25	Medium Florentine Gargoyle	879	3"Wx3"H	1.5	$29.95	$4.95

Page 3

[Student's Name]
[Student's ID]
[Section Number]
[Date]
[PrjEX-7]

	A	B	C	D	E	F
1	Gothic Gargoyle Collection					
2	Description	Product Number	Size	Weight	Price	Shipping
39	Medium Warrior with Axe	899	3"Wx3"H	1.5	$29.95	$4.95
40	Medium Warrior with Pike	898	3"Wx3"H	1.5	$29.95	$4.95
41	Medium Warrior with Sword	896	3"Wx3"H	1.5	$29.95	$4.95
42	Miniature Dragon Gargoyle	359	1"Wx1"H	0.5	$10.98	$3.95
43	Miniature Dragon Rampant Gargoyle	369	1"Wx1"H	0.5	$10.98	$3.95

Page 4

[Student's Name]
[Student's ID]
[Section Number]
[Date]
[PrjEX-7]

	A	B	C	D	E	F
1	Gothic Gargoyle Collection					
2	Description	Product Number	Size	Weight	Price	Shipping
57	Miniature Keeper of the Castle Gargoyle	363	1"Wx1"H	0.5	$10.98	$3.95
58	Miniature Le Roi Gargoyle	364	1"Wx1"H	0.5	$10.98	$3.95
59	Miniature Lion Gargoyle	370	1"Wx1"H	0.5	$10.98	$3.95
60	Miniature Mounted Knight	372	1"Wx1"H	0.5	$10.98	$3.95
61	Miniature Ring-Bearer	373	1"Wx1"H	0.5	$10.98	$3.95
62	Miniature Smaug Gargoyle	366	1"Wx1"H	0.5	$10.98	$3.95
63	Miniature Troll	374	1"Wx1"H	0.5	$10.98	$3.95
64	Miniature War Horse	381	1"Wx1"H	0.5	$10.98	$3.95
65	Miniature Warrior with Axe	380	1"Wx1"H	0.5	$10.98	$3.95
66	Miniature Warrior with Pike	379	1"Wx1"H	0.5	$10.98	$3.95
67	Miniature Warrior with Sword	377	1"Wx1"H	0.5	$10.98	$3.95
68	The Emmett Gargoyle	735	3"Wx4"H	11	$12.95	$5.95

23. Save your worksheet in your Project folder using the file name PrjEX-7 [Your Name].

24. Submit the project file as an e-mail attachment, as a printout, on a USB flash drive, or in any other format specified by your instructor.

Project PP-1: Creating a Presentation

In this project, you'll apply what you've learned to create a PowerPoint presentation about extreme sports.

Requirements: This project requires Microsoft PowerPoint.

Project file: Bungee.gif

COPYIT!

1. Copy the file Bungee.gif to your Project folder using the Copy It! button on this page in the *Practical Computer Literacy* digital book.

2. Start Microsoft PowerPoint. Create a new presentation using any theme. The example on the next page shows the Berlin theme.

3. The layout of the first slide should be Title Slide. Enter Extreme Sports as the title. Enter Taking it to the Limit as the subtitle.

4. Add a *Title and Content* slide. Enter What are Extreme Sports? as the slide title. Enter the following items as bullets:

> Beyond traditional sports
> High level of physical exertion
> Inherent danger
> Adrenaline rush
> Young demographic
> Individuals rather than teams

5. Add another *Title and Content* slide. Enter History of Extreme Sports as the slide title. Add the following items as bullets:

> Might be traced back to rock climbing and marathon running in the 1970s, but opinions vary
> Evolved from traditional sports due to advances in sports technology
> A modern rite of passage, according to some sociologists
> Popularized by media attention and marketing trends
> Guaranteed to continue to evolve

6. Add another *Title and Content* slide. Enter Extreme Sports Examples as the slide title. Add the following items as bullets:

> Vert skating
> Hang gliding
> Barefoot skiing
> Bungee jumping

7. Add the photo Bungee.gif to the slide. Resize and position the image on the slide so that it is about as wide as the slide title.

8. Experiment with changing the slide background with the options on the DESIGN tab. Click the Format Background button. Set the FILL option to *Solid fill*. Change the background color to Purple. Close the Format Background pane.

9. Use the Undo button on the Quick Access toolbar to display the original background.

10. Compare your slides to those shown in the figure on the next page.

• Creating a Presentation (continued)

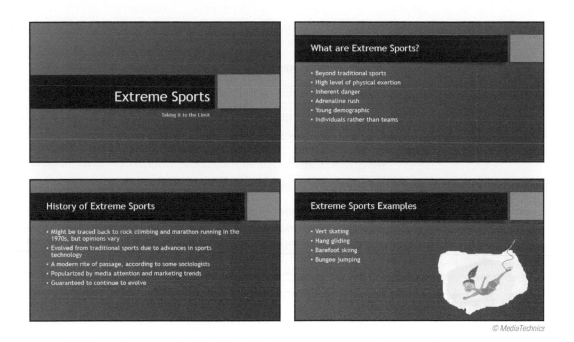

© MediaTechnics

11. Save your presentation using the file name PrjPP-1 [Your Name].

12. Submit the project file as an e-mail attachment, as a printout, on a USB flash drive, or in any other format specified by your instructor.

Project PP-2: Creating Slides with Charts and Tables

In this project, you'll apply what you've learned about charts and tables to create PowerPoint slides for a fitness center.

Requirements: This project requires Microsoft PowerPoint.

Project file: PrjPP-2.pptx

COPY IT!

1. Copy the file PrjPP-2.pptx to your Project folder using the Copy It! button on this page in the *Practical Computer Literacy* digital book.

2. Start Microsoft PowerPoint.

3. Open the file PrjPP-2.pptx from your Project folder.

4. Add a *Title and Content* slide. Enter Target Heart Rates as the slide title. Add a table consisting of three columns and four rows. Select the table style called Medium Style 1 - Accent 2.

5. Enter the following data into the table:

Age	Minimum Rate	Maximum Rate
20	120	170
30	114	162
40	108	163

6. Using tools on the LAYOUT tab, set the height of each row to 1".

7. Select the slide you just made in the pane that contains the Slides list. Right-click the slide, then select Duplicate Slide in the shortcut menu. Suppose you realize that you need a slide without a table for the next slide. Use the Undo button to remove the duplicate slide.

8. Add a *Title and Content* slide. Enter Caloric Expenditures by Body Weight as the slide title.

9. Create a clustered column chart that shows the following data:

	Jogging	Swimming
125 Lbs.	7.3	6.9
175 Lbs.	10.4	9.8

Make sure you have the weight categories as the labels for the X-axis at the bottom of the chart. Enlarge the font to 18 pt. for both axes and the legend so it is easier to read. Delete the Chart Title placeholder.

10. Compare your slides to those shown in the figure on the next page.

• Creating Slides with Charts and Tables (continued)

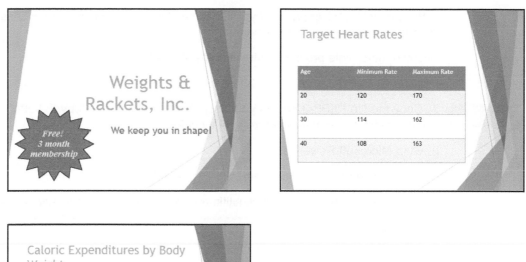

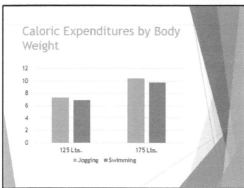

11. Save your presentation in your Project folder using the file name PrjPP-2 [Your Name].

12. Submit the project file as an e-mail attachment, as a printout, on a USB flash drive, or in any other format specified by your instructor.

Project PP-3: Using Animations, Transitions, and Sounds

In this project, you'll apply what you've learned to add animations, transitions, and sounds to a PowerPoint presentation.

Requirements: This project requires Microsoft PowerPoint.

Project file: PrjPP-3.pptx

COPYIT!

1. Copy the file PrjPP-3.pptx to your Project folder using the Copy It! button on this page in the *Practical Computer Literacy* digital book.

2. Start Microsoft PowerPoint.

3. Open the file PrjPP-3.pptx from your Project folder.

4. On the first slide, change the subtitle text "The time is right!" to size 44, bold, and italic.

5. Add the Uncover transition to the second slide.

6. Suppose you want the second slide to appear from the bottom of the first slide instead of from the right side, which is the default. Use the Effect Options pull-down list to achieve your desired effect.

7. Add the Shred transition to the third slide.

8. Add the Drum Roll transition sound effect to the same slide.

9. Add the Fly In animation (coming from the left) to the bulleted list on the third slide in the presentation. (Hint: Use Effect Options to specify the direction.)

10. Notice that the bullets appear in two groups. Suppose you want the bulleted items to appear one at a time when the presenter clicks the mouse. Use the arrow button of the Start box in the Timing group to select On Click.

11. View the presentation to see how the transition and animation effects work together. Click the mouse, press Enter, or select the right-arrow button to display each bulleted item.

12. Do you think the combination of the Drum Roll sound effect and the Shred transition is more distracting than effective? Perhaps removing the sound effect would be better. Switch back to Normal view and remove the sound effect from the transition on the third slide.

13. View the presentation once more to see if you're satisfied with the new combination of transition and animation effects.

• Using Animations, Transitions, and Sounds (continued)

14. When you're done, switch to Slide Sorter View. You should see ✷ Play Animations icons under slides 2 and 3, as shown below.

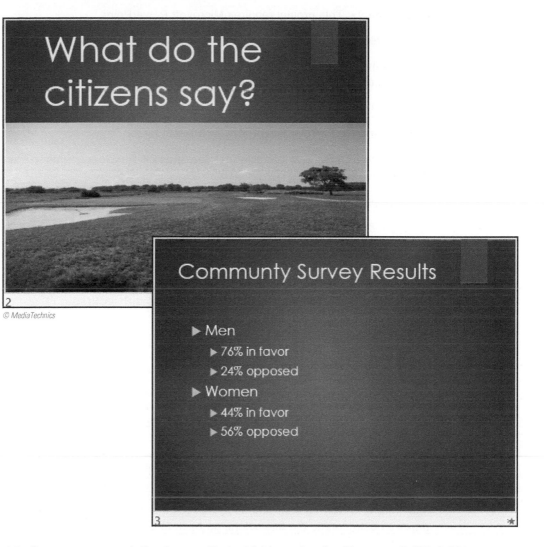

© MediaTechnics

15. Save your presentation in your Project folder using the file name PrjPP-3 [Your Name].

16. Submit the project file as an e-mail attachment, as a printout, on a USB flash drive, or in any other format specified by your instructor.

Project PP-4: Finalizing a Presentation

In this project, you'll apply what you've learned as you finalize a version of the Microsoft PowerPoint presentation that you worked with in Project PP-3.

Requirements: This project requires Microsoft PowerPoint.

Project file: PrjPP-4.pptx

COPYIT!

1. Copy the file PrjPP-4.pptx to your Project folder using the Copy It! button on this page in the *Practical Computer Literacy* digital book.

2. Start Microsoft PowerPoint.

3. Open the file PrjPP-4.pptx from your Project folder.

4. Use Slide Sorter view to move the "Questions & Answers?" slide to the end of the presentation.

5. Move the "Best Site" slide so that it comes immediately after the "Potential Sites" slide.

6. In Normal view, add the following speaker note to the first slide in the presentation: Introduce team members Jill Smith, David Byrne, and Tom Woods.

7. Add the following speaker note to the "Questions & Answers" slide: Let's get a general idea of your reaction to the proposed golf course... raise your hand if you would like the project to proceed.

8. Delete the slide titled "We need to proceed as quickly as possible!"

9. Check the spelling of all slides and make any necessary corrections.

10. Select the VIEW tab, then choose the Slide Master button. Select the first (and largest) master slide. Select the text *Click to edit Master title style*. Go back to the HOME tab and change the font color for the title text to Gold, Accent 3. Change the font style to bold.

11. Look through the list of master slides and make sure that all the title colors have been changed.

12. Return to Normal view and double-check the color of all the titles. If you need to make adjustments to the title colors, go back to Slide Master view.

13. Bullets should use consistent grammar and sentence structure. Modify the bullets on slide 5 so that all are either full sentences with periods at the end, or sentence fragments with no periods.

14. In Slide Sorter view, compare your presentation to the one shown on the next page.

● Finalizing a Presentation (continued)

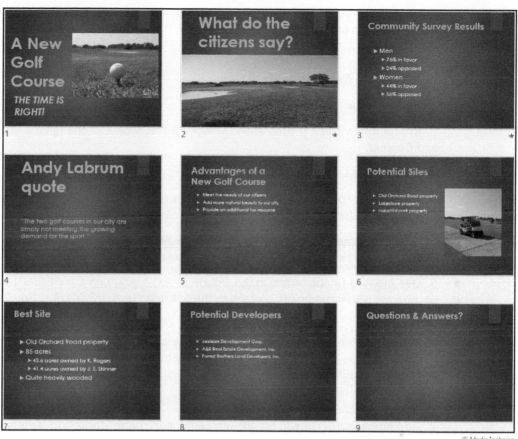

© MediaTechnics

15. Save your presentation in your Project folder using the file name PrjPP-4 [Your Name].

16. Submit the project file as an e-mail attachment, as a printout, on a USB flash drive, or in any other format specified by your instructor.

Project PP-5: Creating an Organization Chart

In this project, you'll explore the graphics capabilities of PowerPoint to create a presentation that includes an organization chart.

Requirements: This project requires Microsoft PowerPoint.

Project file: No file is required.

1. Start Microsoft PowerPoint.

2. Create a new blank presentation. Select the first slide and change the layout to *Title and Content*.

3. Add the title Company Hierarchy.

4. In the center of the slide, select the *Insert a SmartArt Graphic* content icon. Select the Organization Chart option from the Hierarchy category.

5. Delete all boxes except the top tier by selecting the box, then pressing the Delete key. Add the title President to the top of the organization chart.

6. Use the Add Shape button in the Create Graphic group on the DESIGN tab to create a second tier with three boxes containing the following text: VP Marketing, VP Research, and VP Operations.

7. Select the President box. If you see an insertion bar, try again until the entire box is selected, not the text inside the box. Use the arrow on the Add Shape button to create an assistant for the President.

8. Add the text Administrative Assistant to the new box.

9. Add four subordinates to the VP Marketing box. Type Marketing Rep in each subordinate box.

10. Select the VP Marketing box, select Layout in the Create Graphic group, then select Right Hanging.

11. Remove one Marketing Rep box by selecting it, then pressing the Delete key.

12. Compare your slide to the one shown in the figure on the next page.

• Creating an Organization Chart (continued)

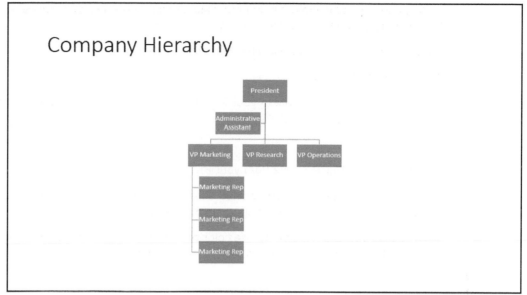

13. Add your name as a second line in the President box.

14. Use the SmartArt Styles group to change the style for the organization chart to Subtle Effect.

15. Save your presentation in your Project folder using the file name PrjPP-5 [Your Name].

16. Submit the project file as an e-mail attachment, as a printout, on a USB flash drive, or in any other format specified by your instructor.

Project PP-6: Working with Slide Graphics

In this project, you'll explore how to use Microsoft PowerPoint to add simple graphical elements to slides and change existing slide graphics.

Requirements: This project requires Microsoft PowerPoint.

Project file: PrjPP-6.pptx

COPYIT!

1. Copy the file PrjPP-6.pptx to your Project folder using the Copy It! button on this page in the *Practical Computer Literacy* digital book.

2. Start Microsoft PowerPoint.

3. Open the file PrjPP-6.pptx from your Project folder.

4. Display the first slide, which is titled "Nitrogen Cycling." Select the chart area, then use tools on the FORMAT tab to change the Chart Area to a solid fill color of Dark Red.

5. Suppose you want to change the color of the Ammonia line to Light Blue. With the Format Chart Area pane still open, select the Ammonia line and format the data series to make it Light Blue.

6. Switch to the slide titled "Losses in Fish Hatch." Suppose you decide that a different chart type would be more appropriate for displaying the information. Select the chart and use tools on the DESIGN tab to select a 3-D Pie Chart. Change the Chart Style to Style 8 to show the slices and their labels.

7. Suppose you want to position the pie chart toward the center of the slide. Move the chart down so that it is centered vertically on the slide. (Hint: Make sure the entire chart area is selected, then drag the border.)

8. Now, suppose you want to duplicate this chart on another slide. Make sure the chart is selected. Select the Copy button in the Clipboard group on the HOME tab. Switch to the slide titled "Causes of Mortality," then use the Paste button to paste the chart on the slide. Position and size the chart on the right side of the slide so it visually balances the bullets. Resize any data labels as necessary so that no words break to the next line.

• Working with Slide Graphics (continued)

9. You can use elements in the Drawing group on the HOME tab to draw your own graphics that tie slide elements together. Switch to the slide titled "Biological Cycling." You can follow the next set of steps to make the slide look like the one below.

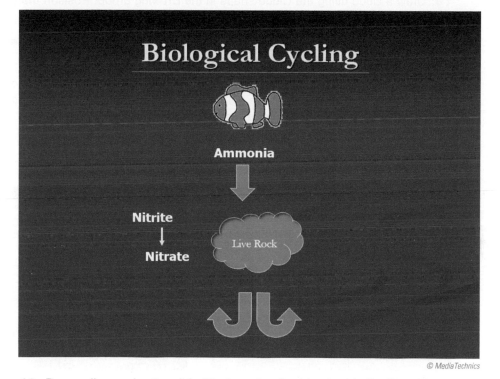

© MediaTechnics

10. Draw a line under the slide title by using the Line tool in the Drawing group.

11. Draw an arrow that points down from "Ammonia" by using the Block Arrow shape. Resize and reposition the arrow so it looks like the one in the slide above.

12. Now, add the thin arrow between "Nitrite" and "Nitrate" by using the Arrow tool in the Drawing group. Position the arrow so it points from "Nitrite" to "Nitrate."

13. Suppose you want to change the format of the thin arrow. Select the arrow, then use the Shape Outline tool to select Yellow. You can also change the line thickness using the Shape Outline option. Select Weight from the pull-down list, then select the 3 pt option.

14. Suppose you want to duplicate a drawn object. Select the U-Turn arrow, then use the Copy button. Next, use the Paste button to paste the duplicate U-Turn arrow on the slide. To flip the arrow, use the Arrange tool on the HOME tab to select Rotate, then select Flip Horizontal. Position the flipped arrow so it is next to the original arrow, as illustrated above.

• Working with Slide Graphics (continued)

15. Add the text Live Rock to the slide, just above the two U-Turn arrows, using the Text Box tool on the INSERT tab.

16. Draw a cloud using the Cloud shape in the Drawing group. Position the cloud over the text box containing "Live Rock."

17. The cloud is covering the text box. To move the cloud behind the text, select the cloud, then use the Arrange tool to send it backward.

18. Suppose you want to change the style of the cloud. To apply a shadow effect, make sure the cloud is selected, then use the Shape Effects tool on the FORMAT tab. Select Shadow, then select Inside Diagonal Top Left.

19. Make sure the slides in your presentation look like the slides below, then save the presentation in your Project folder using the file name PrjPP-6A [Your Name].

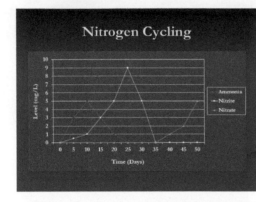

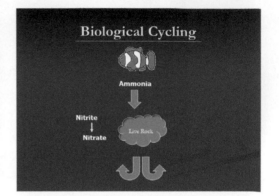

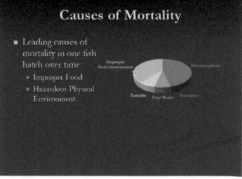

• Working with Slide Graphics (continued)

20. Now, create a new presentation using any theme you like. The presentation should contain one title slide and one blank slide. Enter Biological Cycling as the title for slide 1.

21. Next, copy the objects from slide 2 of the PrjPP-6A presentation to slide 2 of the new presentation. To do so, switch to the PrjPP-6A presentation and display slide 2. Click the slide background, then press Ctrl A on the keyboard. All of the items on the slide are now selected. Copy the selected items. Switch to slide 2 of the new presentation, then paste the items on the blank slide.

22. Make any adjustments to the title and objects, if necessary.

23. Save the new presentation in your Project folder using the file name PrjPP-6B [Your Name].

24. Submit the two project files as e-mail attachments, as printouts, on a USB flash drive, or in any other format specified by your instructor.

Project PP-7: Working with Slide Text

In this project, you'll explore how to zoom in or zoom out to view a slide; explore how to copy, cut, and paste graphics and text; experiment with text formatting; and explore how to use the PowerPoint Options dialog box to configure user information and file location settings.

Requirements: This project requires Microsoft PowerPoint.

Project files: PrjPP-7.pptx, Clubs.jpg, and Scenic.jpg

COPY IT! 1. Copy the file PrjPP-7.pptx to your Project folder using the Copy It! button on this page in the *Practical Computer Literacy* digital book.

COPY IT! 2. Copy the file Clubs.jpg to your Project folder using the Copy It! button on this page in the *Practical Computer Literacy* digital book.

COPY IT! 3. Copy the file Scenic.jpg to your Project folder using the Copy It! button on this page in the *Practical Computer Literacy* digital book.

4. Start Microsoft PowerPoint and open the file PrjPP-7.pptx from your Project folder.

5. Let's explore what happens when you adjust the magnification level. Use the Zoom control in the lower-right corner of the PowerPoint window to view the maximum zoom level. Depending on your computer's screen resolution, the slide might now be too big to fit in the window. Use the button to the right of the Zoom control to select the most practical zoom level.

6. To explore how to configure a presentation's author information, select the FILE tab, then choose Options. When the PowerPoint Options dialog box appears, enter your name and initials in the boxes provided.

7. To adjust the Save options, click the Save category. Typically, PowerPoint is configured to save presentations in the My Documents folder. If you want to change this setting, use the *Default local file location* box to do so now.

8. To apply your new settings and close the PowerPoint Options dialog box, select the OK button.

9. Add a new slide at the end of the presentation. Select the *Title and Content* layout. Enter Top Three Sponsors as the slide title. Add the following items as three bullets:

Titleist

PepsiCo

PGA

10. Select the bullets and change them to a numbered list using the Numbering button in the Paragraph group on the HOME tab.

11. With all of the list items selected, use the Line Spacing button to double-space the list.

12. Add the image Scenic.jpg from your Project folder to the slide. Adjust the size and position of the image so that it looks visually pleasing.

13. Switch to the slide titled "We need to proceed as quickly as possible." Suppose you would rather have this image on the slide titled "Questions and Answers?" Move the image to the slide titled "Questions and Answers?" Adjust the position of the graphic so that it looks visually pleasing.

• Working with Slide Text (continued)

14. Switch to the slide titled "What do the citizens say?" To explore the best alignment for the quoted text, position the insertion point at the beginning of the text, then select the Justify button in the Paragraph group. Next, select the Align Right button. Finally, select the Center button.

15. Make sure the rectangular quote text box is selected, then move the entire text box to the "Top Three Sponsors" slide.

16. Select the quoted text, then decrease the font size to 24 pt. Reposition and resize the objects on the slide so that it looks similar to the one shown in the figure below.

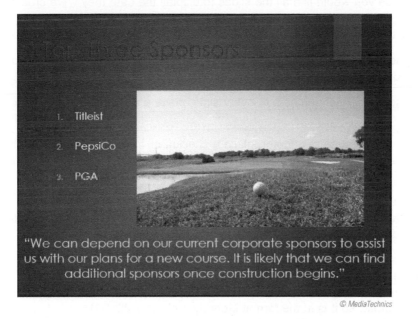

© MediaTechnics

17. Switch to the "We need to proceed as quickly as possible" slide. Add the image Clubs.jpg from your Project folder to the slide. Adjust the image on the slide so that it is visually pleasing.

18. Save the presentation in your Project folder using the file name PrjPP-7 [Your Name].

19. Submit the presentation for this project as an e-mail attachment, as a printout, on a USB flash drive, or in any other format specified by your instructor.

Project PP-8: Finalizing Presentation Details

In this project, you'll explore how to add footers to slides.

Requirements: This project requires Microsoft PowerPoint.

Project file: PrjPP-8.pptx

COPY IT! 1. Copy the file PrjPP-8.pptx to your Project folder using the Copy It! button on this page in the *Practical Computer Literacy* digital book.

2. Start Microsoft PowerPoint and open the file PrjPP-8.pptx from your Project folder.

3. Suppose you would like all the slides to display the date they were created, slide numbers, and your name. Select any slide, then select the *Header & Footer* button on the INSERT tab. When the *Header and Footer* dialog box appears, click the Slide tab.

4. To add the date the slides were created, click the *Date and time* checkbox. Make sure the Fixed option is selected, then type today's date in the box.

5. To add sequential numbers to every slide, place a checkmark in the *Slide number* checkbox.

6. To add your name to a footer, place a checkmark in the Footer box and type your name in the box. Place a checkmark in the *Don't show on title slide* box. This step prevents the footer from appearing on the title page.

7. Select the *Apply to All* button to add the footer to all the slides and close the *Header and Footer* dialog box. Look through the slides to make sure your footer appears on every slide except the title slide.

8. Suppose that you want to display the current date on the title slide each time the presentation is given. Select the title slide, then use the *Header and Footer* button to put a checkmark in the *Date and time* checkbox, and to select *Update automatically*. Change the date format so it is in the format Monday, February 22, 2014.

9. Remove the checkmarks from the *Don't show on title slide* checkbox. Use the Apply button to close the dialog box. Today's date now appears in the lower-right corner of the title slide.

• Finalizing Presentation Details (continued)

10. Now, suppose you want to print the presentation on 8.5" x 11" paper and you would like to stretch each slide to fit the entire page. Select the DESIGN tab, then under Slide Size, choose the Custom Slide Size option. When the Slide Size dialog box appears, use the arrow button in the *Slides sized for* box to select *Letter Paper (8.5 x 11 in)*. Change the orientation of the slides to Portrait, click the OK button, then select the Ensure Fit button. Your title slide should look similar to the one shown in the figure below.

11. Save your presentation in your Project folder using the file name PrjPP-8 [Your Name].

12. Submit the project file as an e-mail attachment, as a printout, on a USB flash drive, or in any other format specified by your instructor.

Project AC-1: Creating a Database Table

In this project, you'll apply what you've learned about Microsoft Access to create a database, create a table, and enter data into the table. You'll also explore data formats and validation rules.

Requirements: This project requires Microsoft Access.

Project file: No project file is required.

1. Start Microsoft Access.

2. Create a new blank desktop database in your Project folder. (Hint: Click the folder on the right side of the File Name box to select your Project folder.)

3. Name the database PrjAC-1 [Your Name]. Click the Create button under the File Name box to complete the operation.

4. Suppose you have a personal library filled with books that you like to lend out to friends. You can keep track of your books by creating a simple library database.

5. In Table 1, enter the following fields: Title, Author, Publisher, Quantity, Lend Date, Borrower, and E-mail. Specify the Short Text data type for all the fields except Quantity and Lend Date. Specify Number as the data type for the Quantity field. Specify the *Date & Time* data type for the Lend Date field.

6. Change the name of the ID field to ISBN and change the data type to Short Text. (Hint: The data type setting is in the Formatting group on the FIELDS tab.)

7. Select the Quantity field, then set its default value to 1. (Hint: Look for the Default Value button in the Properties group.)

8. Select the Lend Date field, then use the Format option in the Properties group to change the field's format to Short Date.

9. Delete the Quantity field.

10. Add a field called Book Value and specify Currency as its data type. Drag the field so it is between the Publisher and Lend Date fields.

11. Choose any five books that you own and fill in all the fields except Lend Date, Borrower, and E-mail. If you can't see the full text for a field, drag the dividing line between field headers to resize the column.

12. Sort the records by Author in A to Z order.

13. Select two records and add data for the Borrower, Lend Date, and E-mail fields.

14. Sort the data by the Borrower field in Z to A order.

• Creating a Database Table (continued)

15. The fields in your table should be arranged like those in the figure below.

16. Close the table, save it, and name it Book List.

17. Use one of the following options to submit your project on a USB flash drive, as a printout, or as an e-mail attachment, according to your instructor's directions:

● To submit the project on a USB flash drive, close Access, then copy the file PrjAC-1 [Your Name] from your Project folder to a USB drive. Make sure your name is on the USB drive.

● To print the file, make sure that the Book List table is open. Select the FILE tab, choose the Print option, then select Quick Print. Write your name, student ID number, class section number, date, and PrjAC-1 on the first page of the printout.

● To submit the project as an e-mail attachment, exit Access and start your usual e-mail program. Type your instructor's e-mail address in the To: box. Type PrjAC-1, your student ID number, and your class section number in the Subject: box. Attach the file PrjAC-1 [Your Name] from your Project folder to the e-mail message and send it.

Project AC-2: Creating Queries

In this project, you'll apply what you've learned about Microsoft Access to find specific records and create queries for finding specific information in a database.

Requirements: This project requires Microsoft Access.

Project file: PrjAC-2.accdb

COPYIT!   1. Copy the file PrjAC-2.accdb to your Project folder using the Copy It! button on this page in the *Practical Computer Literacy* digital book.

2. Start Microsoft Access.

3. Open the file PrjAC-2.accdb from your Project folder.

4. Open the Products table. Sort the items by the Product Number field in ascending order.

5. Sort the items by price from largest to smallest. Save the table, then close it. (Hint: To save the table, click the Save button on the Quick Access toolbar.)

6. Use the Query Wizard button on the CREATE tab to create a simple query that includes all fields from the Products table. Name the query Products Under $10. Specify that you want to modify the query design before you click the Finish button that closes the Simple Query Wizard.

7. Add <10 to the Criteria cell of the Price field to limit the query results to products that cost less than $10. Click the Run button in the Results group to view your results. Compare your results to those shown in the figure below.

ID	Product Number	Description	Price
1	72838	8 oz Coffee Mug	$3.45
2	82892	12 oz Coffee Mug	$4.15
3	18372	Cup Holder	$2.85
5	83827	Auto Trash Bag	$7.95
7	23702	Lock De-icer	$2.89
8	37027	Windshield Scraper	$3.25
* (New)	0		$0.00

8. Save the query, then close it.

9. Use the Query Wizard button to create a simple query that includes only the State/Province and EmailName fields from the Contacts table. Name the query Ohio E-mail Addresses. Specify that you want to modify the query design before you close the wizard.

• Creating Queries (continued)

10. Add criteria to limit the query results to records of people located in the state of Ohio (OH). Run the query and compare your results to those shown in the figure below.

Ohio E-mail Addresses	
State/Province ▾	EmailName ▾
OH	jmc@cnet.net
OH	ynaka@cnet.net
OH	
*	

11. Save the query, then close it.

12. Save your database in your Project folder using the file name PrjAC-2 [Your Name].

13. Use one of the following options to submit your project on a USB flash drive, as a printout, or as an e-mail attachment, according to your instructor's directions:

- To submit the project on a USB flash drive, close Access, then copy the file PrjAC-2 [Your Name] from your Project folder to a USB drive. Make sure your name is on the USB drive.

- To print the project, make sure that the Products Under $10 query is open. Select the FILE tab, choose the Print option, then select Quick Print. Close the Products Under $10 query, then open the Ohio E-mail Addresses query. Follow the previous instructions for printing a query. Staple the pages together, then write your name, student ID number, class section number, date, and PrjAC-2 on the first page.

- To submit the project as an e-mail attachment, exit Access and start your usual e-mail program. Type your instructor's e-mail address in the To: box. Type PrjAC-2, your student ID number, and your class section number in the Subject: box. Attach the file PrjAC-2 [Your Name] from your Project folder to the e-mail message and send it.

Project AC-3: Creating Forms

In this project, you'll apply what you've learned about Microsoft Access to create forms that would allow a data entry person to easily update the Products and Contacts tables.

Requirements: This project requires Microsoft Access.

Project file: PrjAC-3.accdb

COPYIT!

1. Copy the file PrjAC-3.accdb to your Project folder using the Copy It! button on this page in the *Practical Computer Literacy* digital book.

2. Start Microsoft Access.

3. Open the file PrjAC-3.accdb from your Project folder.

4. Use the Form Wizard button on the CREATE tab to create a form containing all the fields from the Products table. Specify the Columnar layout. Enter Product Inventory as the form title.

5. Click the Finish button and compare your form to the one shown below.

6. Use the Product Inventory form to add a new record for product number 54431, which is Fix-a-Flat priced at $1.89. (Hint: Click the ▶* New (blank) record button on the navigation bar at the bottom of the window.) Note that the ID field is automatically filled in for you.

7. Close the Product Inventory form.

8. Open the Products table and use the Refresh All button to make sure the new record for Fix-a-Flat has been added to the table. Close the Products table.

9. Use the Form Wizard to create a form containing the following fields from the Contacts table: LastName, FirstName, and EmailName. Use the Justified layout. Enter E-mail List as the form title.

10. Compare your form to the one shown below.

• Creating Forms (continued)

11. Suppose you would like the date and time on a header for each form. Switch to Layout View. Select the *Date and Time* button in the Header/Footer group on the DESIGN tab. In the *Date and Time* dialog box, check the format you prefer, then click the OK button. The form should now have the date and time in its upper-right corner.

12. Switch to Design View and edit the title so that it says E-mail Address List instead of "E-mail List." Resize the text box so that the title is displayed on one line. Save the changes to your form and return to Form View to view the new form with the revised title.

13. Forms are usually displayed on the screen for data entry and editing. You can print one or more forms. For example, you might print and mail a form to a client so that he or she can verify the data it contains. To print the form you are viewing, click the FILE tab, select the Print option, then click Quick Print.

14. When working with small forms, such as the E-mail Address List, you might want to print all the forms on a single page. To do so, select the Print option instead of Quick Print, then make sure the Print dialog box has the Print Range set to All.

15. Add the e-mail address of a friend or relative to the E-mail Address List form, then close the form. Open the Contacts table, then use the Refresh All button to make sure the new record is added to the Contacts table. Close the Contacts table.

16. Save your database in your Project folder using the file name PrjAC-3 [Your Name].

17. Use one of the following options to submit your project on a USB flash drive, as a printout, or as an e-mail attachment, according to your instructor's directions:

• To submit the project on a USB flash drive, close Access, then copy the file PrjAC-3 [Your Name] from your Project folder to a USB drive. Make sure your name is on the USB drive.

• To print the data as it appears in the form, make sure that the Product Inventory form is open. Select the FILE tab, choose the Print option, then select Quick Print. Close the Product Inventory form and open the E-mail Address List form. Follow the previous instructions for printing a form. Staple the pages together, then write your name, student ID number, class section number, date, and PrjAC-3 on the first page.

• To submit the project as an e-mail attachment, exit Access and start your usual e-mail program. Type your instructor's e-mail address in the To: box. Type PrjAC-3, your student ID number, and your class section number in the Subject: box. Attach the file PrjAC-3 [Your Name] from your Project folder to the e-mail message and send it.

Project AC-4: Creating Reports

In this project, you'll apply what you've learned about Microsoft Access to generate printed reports.

Requirements: This project requires Microsoft Access.

Project file: PrjAC-4.accdb

COPYIT!

1. Copy the file PrjAC-4.accdb to your Project folder using the Copy It! button on this page in the *Practical Computer Literacy* digital book.

2. Start Microsoft Access.

3. Open the file PrjAC-4.accdb from your Project folder and make sure that all the database objects are displayed on the left side of the Access window. To do so, click the ⊙ button in the Navigation pane and make sure that All Access Objects is selected.

4. Use the Report Wizard to create a report containing only the LastName, FirstName, and EmailName fields from the Contacts table. Do not add any grouping levels. Sort the records by last name in ascending order. Use the Tabular layout for the report. Enter Contact E-mail Addresses for the report title.

5. Compare your report to the one shown in the figure below, then close the report.

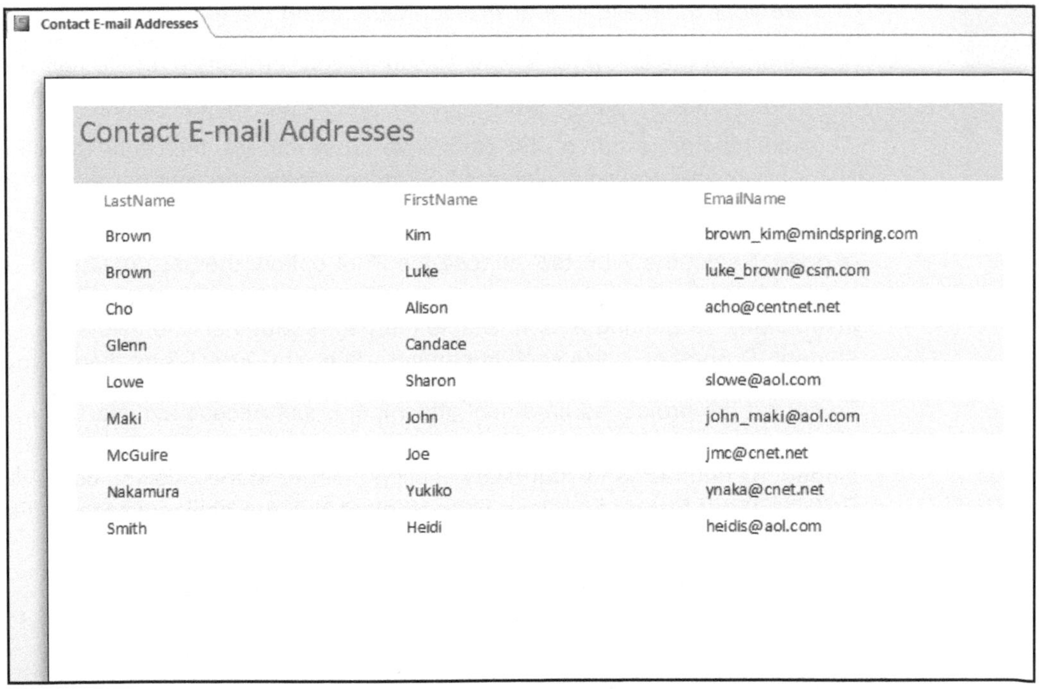

Contact E-mail Addresses

LastName	FirstName	EmailName
Brown	Kim	brown_kim@mindspring.com
Brown	Luke	luke_brown@csm.com
Cho	Alison	acho@centnet.net
Glenn	Candace	
Lowe	Sharon	slowe@aol.com
Maki	John	john_maki@aol.com
McGuire	Joe	jmc@cnet.net
Nakamura	Yukiko	ynaka@cnet.net
Smith	Heidi	heidis@aol.com

• Creating Reports (continued)

6. Use the Report Wizard to create a report for the Products Under $10 query that contains all fields except the ID field. Group by Department. Sort the records by Description in ascending order. Use the Stepped layout for the report. Enter Products Under $10 by Department for the report title.

7. Compare your report to the one shown in the figure below, then close the report.

Products Under $10 by Department

Products Under $10 by Department

Department	Description	Product Number	Price
Automotive			
	Auto Trash Bag	83827	$7.95
	Cup Holder	18372	$2.85
	Fix-a-Flat	54431	$1.89
	Lock De-icer	23702	$2.89
	Windshield Scraper	37027	$3.25
Floral			
	Herb Garden	77543	$3.49
Housewares			
	12 oz Coffee Mug	82892	$4.15
	8 oz Coffee Mug	72838	$3.45
	Plastic Hangers/12	78662	$3.99
	Rock Key Safe	986443	$5.99
	Votive Candles	887611	$0.99

8. Make sure all database tables and reports are closed. Save your database in your Project folder using the file name PrjAC-4 [Your Name].

9. Use one of the following options to submit your project on a USB flash drive, as a printout, or as an e-mail attachment, according to your instructor's directions:

• To submit the project on a USB flash drive, close Access, then copy the file PrjAC-4 [Your Name] from your Project folder to a USB drive. Make sure your name is on the USB drive.

• To print the project, open the Contact E-mail Addresses report, select the FILE tab, choose the Print option, then select Quick Print. Close the Contact E-mail Addresses report and open the *Products Under $10 by Department* report. Follow the previous instructions for printing a report. Staple the pages together, then write your name, student ID number, class section number, date, and PrjAC-4 on the first page.

• To submit the project as an e-mail attachment, exit Access and start your usual e-mail program. Type your instructor's e-mail address in the To: box. Type PrjAC-4, your student ID number, and your class section number in the Subject: box. Attach the file PrjAC-4 [Your Name] from your Project folder to the e-mail message and send it.

Project AC-5: Indexing and Filtering

In this project, you'll explore how indexes can be used to make databases more efficient. You'll also find out how to use filters to create a quick query by example.

Indexes are used to find and sort records quickly. The field used as a primary key should always be indexed. It is a good idea to index any other fields commonly used for searching and sorting. In Access, index settings can also be used to restrict fields to unique values. For example, a customer number field must contain only unique customer numbers because no two customers can share a customer number. An index restricts values entered into the field to only unique values.

Requirements: This project requires Microsoft Access and Paint.

Project file: PrjAC-5.accdb

COPY IT!

1. Copy the file PrjAC-5.accdb to your Project folder using the Copy It! button on this page in the *Practical Computer Literacy* digital book.

2. Start Microsoft Access.

3. Open the file PrjAC-5.accdb from your Project folder. Open the Contacts table, then click the FIELDS tab on the ribbon so that you can modify the fields.

4. Suppose you'd like to create an index on the State/Province field to speed up sorts and searches. Select the State/Province column, then choose the Indexed checkbox in the Field Validation group.

5. Remember, because the ID field is the primary key, it is automatically indexed. Now that the State/Province field and ID field are indexed, sorts and searches on these fields will require less time—especially in databases that contain thousands of records. You can't tell the difference with a small database, but keep this important database design technique in mind for your own large databases.

6. Access includes filters that help you quickly sift through a table to find records. Select the arrow button on the column header in the State/Province field. Remove the checkmarks from all of the boxes except OH, then select the OK button.

7. Compare your results to the example below.

• Indexing and Filtering (continued)

8. With the filter applied, press the PrtSc or Print Screen key on your keyboard.

9. Open Paint, then paste the screenshot.

10. Save the screenshot as a JPEG file in your Project folder and name it PrjAC-5A XXXXX 9999, where XXXXX is your name or student ID number and 9999 is your class section number.

11. Close Paint.

12. Cancel the OH filter by clicking the State/Province arrow button and selecting *Clear filter from State/Province*.

13. Now use a filter to display only contacts located in Canadian provinces. Compare your results to those shown below.

14. With the filter applied, press the PrtSc or Print Screen key on your keyboard.

15. Open Paint, then paste the screenshot.

16. Save the screenshot as a JPEG file in your Project folder and name it PrjAC-5B [Your Name].

17. Close Paint. Close all the objects in your database.

18. Save your database in your Project folder using the file name PrjAC-5 [Your Name].

19. Use one of the following options to submit your project on a USB flash drive, as a printout, or as an e-mail attachment, according to your instructor's directions:

• To submit the project on a USB flash drive, close Access, then copy the database file PrjAC-5 [Your Name] from your Project folder to a USB drive. Copy the JPEG files PrjAC-5A [Your Name] and PrjAC-5B [Your Name] from your Project folder to the USB drive. Make sure your name is on the USB drive.

• To print the project, open the PrjAC-5A [Your Name] file. Select the FILE tab, then choose Print. Open the PrjAC-5B [Your Name] file, select the FILE tab, then choose Print. Staple the pages together, then write your name, student ID number, class section number, date, and PrjAC-5 on the first page.

• To submit the project as an e-mail attachment, exit Access and start your usual e-mail program. Type your instructor's e-mail address in the To: box. Type PrjAC-5, your student ID number, and your class section number in the Subject: box. Attach the files PrjAC-5 [Your Name], PrjAC-5A [Your Name], and PrjAC-5B [Your Name] from your Project folder to the e-mail message and send it.

Project AC-6: Working with Lookup Fields

Access includes a Lookup data type that can be used to streamline and standardize data entry. Let's suppose you are working with two tables that pertain to the work of artist Jackson Pollock. One table contains a list of his significant paintings. The other table contains a list of art galleries that sometimes display his work.

A gallery curator uses two tables for this data because some galleries own more than one Pollock painting. You can use a lookup field to easily enter the name of the gallery that displays or owns each Jackson Pollock painting.

Requirements: This project requires Microsoft Access.

Project file: PrjAC-6.accdb

COPYIT!

1. Copy the file PrjAC-6.accdb to your Project folder using the Copy It! button on this page in the *Practical Computer Literacy* digital book.

2. Start Microsoft Access.

3. Open the file PrjAC-6.accdb from your Project folder. Open the two tables and familiarize yourself with the fields each one contains.

4. Suppose you want to keep track of the galleries in which these paintings are located. The Paintings table will need an additional field. To avoid entering long gallery names, you can create a lookup field based on the galleries that are listed in the Galleries table.

5. Select the *Click to Add* button in the Paintings table.

6. Select the *Lookup & Relationship* data type to start the Lookup Wizard.

7. Choose the option for *I want the lookup field to get the values from another table or query*, then select the Next button to continue.

8. Select Table: Galleries, then click the Next button.

9. Add the Gallery field to the Selected Fields list, then click the Next button.

10. Sort by Gallery in ascending order.

11. Skip the option for column width by selecting the Next button.

12. Replace Field 1 with Gallery as the label for the lookup field, then click the Finish button.

13. Double the width of the Gallery column.

14. When you click a cell in the Gallery field, a Lookup button appears so that you can view a list of galleries and select one.

15. Click the Lookup button in the Gallery field for the painting *Easter and the Totem*, then select *Museum of Modern Art*.

16. Use the Lookup button in the Gallery field to enter these galleries for the next three paintings:

Enchanted Forest	Peggy Guggenheim Collection
Eyes in the Heat	Peggy Guggenheim Collection
Full Fathom Five	Museum of Modern Art

• Working with Lookup Fields (continued)

17. Pollock's Mural painting is at the University of Iowa Museum of Art, which is not one of the galleries in the lookup list. To add this gallery, switch to the Galleries table, then add the following record:

University of Iowa Museum of Art   Iowa City

18. Make sure you've pressed the Enter key or Tab key so that the record is added.

19. Now switch back to the Paintings table and use the Refresh All button on the HOME tab.

20. Use the Lookup button in the Gallery field to enter University of Iowa Museum of Art for the Mural painting.

21. Add the Museum of Fine Arts to the Galleries table.

22. Complete the Paintings table by entering the following galleries:

Number 10	Museum of Fine Arts
Number 7	National Gallery of Art
One: Number 31, 1950	Museum of Modern Art
Shimmering Substance	Museum of Modern Art
Stenographic Figure	Museum of Modern Art
Summertime: Number 9A	Tate Modern
The She-Wolf	Museum of Modern Art

23. Compare your table with the figure below.

Painting Name	Price	Painting Date	Gallery	Click to Add
Easter and the Totem	$200,000.00	1953	Museum of Modern Art	
Enchanted Forest	$800,000.00	1947	Peggy Guggenheim Collection	
Eyes in the Heat	$1,000,000.00	1946	Peggy Guggenheim Collection	
Full Fathom Five	$200,000.00	1947	Museum of Modern Art	
Mural	$200,000.00	1943	University of Iowa Museum of A	
Number 10	$300,000.00	1949	Museum of Fine Arts	
Number 7	$850,000.00	1951	National Gallery of Art	
One: Number 31, 1950	$200,000.00	1950	Museum of Modern Art	
Shimmering Substance	$500,000.00	1946	Museum of Modern Art	
Stenographic Figure	$150,000.00	1942	Museum of Modern Art	
Summertime: Number 9A	$2,000,000.00	1948	Tate Modern	
The She-Wolf	$500,000.00	1943	Museum of Modern Art	

24. Save your database in your Project folder using the file name PrjAC-6 [Your Name].

25. Use one of the following options to submit your project on a USB flash drive, as a printout, or as an e-mail attachment, according to your instructor's directions:

• To submit the project on a USB flash drive, close Access, then copy the file PrjAC-6 [Your Name] from your Project folder to a USB drive. Make sure your name is on the USB drive.

• To print the project, print the Galleries table and the Paintings table. Staple the pages together, then write your name, student ID number, class section number, date, and PrjAC-6 on the first page.

• To submit the project as an e-mail attachment, exit Access and start your usual e-mail program. Type your instructor's e-mail address in the To: box. Type PrjAC-6, your student ID number, and your class section number in the Subject: box. Attach the file PrjAC-6 [Your Name] from your Project folder and send the e-mail message.

Project AC-7: Creating Relationships

In this project, you'll learn how to create and use relationships. A relationship links a record from one table to one or more records in another table. For example, suppose a college offers a series of workshops for students. A many-to-many relationship exists between students and workshops. Each workshop can be attended by many students; and a student can attend more than one workshop.

To complete this project, you'll create a relationship between the Students table and the Workshops table so that you can use the data from both tables in a single report. Many-to-many relationships require a third table containing links between the two tables in the relationship. The database contains a table called Rosters that contains the student ID for each student who is enrolled in each workshop.

Requirements: This project requires Microsoft Access.

Project file: PrjAC-7.accdb

COPYIT! 1. Copy the file PrjAC-7.accdb to your Project folder using the Copy It! button on this page in the *Practical Computer Literacy* digital book.

2. Start Microsoft Access. Open the file PrjAC-7.accdb from your Project folder.

3. The database contains three tables. Open each table and familiarize yourself with the data in each table. From the data in these tables, can you find the name of at least two students who are enrolled in the Volunteering workshop? The process becomes much easier when you establish relationships between tables.

4. Select the DATABASE TOOLS tab, then choose the Relationships button. The Relationships tab now displays three field lists—one for each of the tables.

5. Note that the Workshops table and the Rosters table both include a WorkshopID field. To create a relationship between these tables, drag WorkshopID from the Workshops table and drop it on WorkshopID in the Rosters table.

6. When the Edit Relationships window appears, make sure it says *One-to-Many* as the Relationship Type, then click the Create button. If the window says *One-to-One*, cancel the operation, then repeat Step 5, making sure to drop on the word "WorkshopID."

7. Next, create a one-to-many relationship between the Rosters table and the Students table using the StudentID field.

8. Close the Relationships window.

9. With the relationships created, you can generate a query to easily see the names of students enrolled in each workshop. To begin, select the Query Wizard button on the CREATE tab.

10. From the Workshops table, add the WorkshopTitle field to the Selected Fields list. From the Students table, add the LastName and FirstName fields. Name the query Students Enrolled in Each Workshop.

11. Scroll down to view the ten students enrolled in the Volunteering workshop. If your query does not produce the expected results, delete it and try Steps 9 and 10 again.

• Creating Relationships (continued)

12. You can also create a database report for the workshop rosters. Use the Report Wizard to create a report with the following specifications:

- Fields: Add all fields from the Workshops table, and only the LastName and FirstName fields from the Students table.

- View data: Select *by Workshops* for the data view.

- Grouping levels: Do not add any.

- Sort order: Sort the records by LastName in ascending order.

- Layout: Use the Outline layout for the report.

- Title: Enter Workshop Rosters for the report title.

13. Compare your results to the report shown below. Be sure to look at page 2 of the report. Is it now easier to determine the names of students enrolled in the Volunteering workshop?

Workshop Rosters	
WorkshopID	1
WorkshopTitle	Conquering Test Anxiety
Location	West Hall 510
Time	W 4-5 pm
LastName	**FirstName**
Butler	Sheila
Chappell	Daniel
Davis	Jeff

14. Save your database in your Project folder using the file name PrjAC-7 [Your Name].

15. Use one of the following options to submit your project on a USB flash drive, as a printout, or as an e-mail attachment, according to your instructor's directions:

- To submit the project on a USB flash drive, close Access, then copy the file PrjAC-7 [Your Name] from your Project folder to a USB drive. Make sure your name is on the USB drive.

- To print the Workshop Rosters report, open it, use the FILE tab to select the Print option, then select Quick Print. Close the report. To print the relationships, open the Relationships window. Select the Relationship Report button in the Tools group on the RELATIONSHIPS TOOLS DESIGN contextual tab. Select the Print button in the Print group on the PRINT PREVIEW tab, then click the OK button. Close the Print Preview. Save and close the relationships report using the default report name. Write your name, student ID number, class section number, date, and PrjAC-7 on the printouts.

- To submit the project as an e-mail attachment, exit Access and start your usual e-mail program. Type your instructor's e-mail address in the To: box. Type PrjAC-7, your student ID number, and your class section number in the Subject: box. Attach the file PrjAC-7 [Your Name] from your Project folder to the e-mail message and send it.

Project AC-8: Managing Tables and Relationships

In this project, you'll explore basic database management techniques, such as viewing tables in different ways and deleting old or obsolete items from the database.

Requirements: This project requires Microsoft Access.

Project file: PrjAC-8.accdb

COPYIT!

1. Copy the file PrjAC-8.accdb to your Project folder using the Copy It! button on this page in the *Practical Computer Literacy* digital book.

2. Start Microsoft Access and open the file PrjAC-8.accdb from your Project folder.

3. Open the Student Names table and the Students table. Use the Switch Windows button in the Window group on the HOME tab. Select Tile Horizontally to arrange both tables as shown below so that they do not overlap.

4. Does data in one of these tables duplicate data in the other table? The Student Names table seems to include only students from Alabama. To more easily see if the same students are in the Students table, sort the Students table in A to Z order by State.

5. Examine the data in the two tables. The records in the Student Names table also appear to be in the Students table. Are their Student ID numbers the same? Students in the Student Names table are sorted in descending order by Student ID. To match this order, sort the Students table in descending order by Student ID.

• Managing Tables and Relationships (continued)

6. It is still a bit difficult to compare the data. You can apply a filter to show only the students in Alabama in the Students table. In the Students table, select any State field that contains "AL." Choose the Selection button in the *Sort & Filter* group on the HOME tab. Select Equals "AL". Now Access displays only students who live in Alabama, sorted by Student ID. Compare the two tables. The data in the Student Names table is already stored in the Students table.

7. Remove the filter on the Students table by using the Filter button in the *Sort & Filter* group. Select *Clear filter from State*.

8. Close both tables. Select the No button if you are asked if you want to save the changes.

9. Assume you've seen enough to convince yourself that the Student Names table is not needed. You can delete the table, but first you should check if the table is related to any other tables. Select the Relationships button on the DATABASE TOOLS tab. Select the All Relationships button. Notice the relationship between the Student Names table and the Students And Courses table. Right-click the relationship, then select Delete. Click the Yes button when prompted to delete the relationship. Close the Relationships window.

10. The Student Name query is based on data from the table you want to eliminate. To delete the query, right-click the Student Name query, then select the Delete option. Click the Yes button to complete the deletion.

11. Now that you have deleted the relationships and queries associated with the Student Names table, you can delete the table itself. Right-click the Student Names table, then select the Delete option. Click the Yes button to complete the deletion.

12. Save your database in your Project folder using the file name PrjAC-8 [Your Name].

13. Use one of the following options to submit your project on a USB flash drive, as a printout, or as an e-mail attachment, according to your instructor's directions:

• To submit the project on a USB flash drive, close Access, then copy the file PrjAC-8 [Your Name] from your Project folder to a USB drive. Make sure your name is on the USB drive.

• To print the relationships, open the Relationships window. Click the All Relationships button. Select the Relationship Report button in the Tools group on the DESIGN tab. Select the Print button in the Print group on the PRINT PREVIEW tab, then click the OK button. Close the Print Preview. Save the relationships report using the default report name, then close it. Write your name, student ID number, class section number, date, and PrjAC-8 on the first page.

• To submit the project as an e-mail attachment, exit Access and start your usual e-mail program. Type your instructor's e-mail address in the To: box. Type PrjAC-8, your student ID number, and your class section number in the Subject: box. Attach the file PrjAC-8 [Your Name] from your Project folder to the e-mail message and send it.

Project AC-9: Creating Grouped Reports

In this project, you'll explore how to use Microsoft Access to create reports containing "control breaks" that group, summarize, and total data.

Requirements: This project requires Microsoft Access.

Project file: PrjAC-9.accdb

COPYIT!

1. Copy the file PrjAC-9.accdb to your Project folder using the Copy It! button. Start Microsoft Access and open the file PrjAC-9.accdb from your Project folder.

2. Open the Mutual Fund table. Notice that it contains a list of funds, such as American Value, that are managed by various companies, such as Dean Witter. Each record includes the fund's current value, and its performance over the past year and past five years.

3. Print this table by clicking the FILE tab, selecting the Print option, then choosing Quick Print.

4. Next, highlight just the Dean Witter records. To print just these records, select the FILE tab, choose Print, select Print Selected Record(s), then select the OK button. Close the Mutual Fund table. Printing the raw data contained in a table does not provide much flexibility for formatting and organizing report data, so it is rarely done. The reporting features provided by Access offer much more flexibility.

5. Use the Report Wizard to create a report based on data in the Mutual Fund table. Respond to the wizard prompts with the following specifications and compare your report to the one shown in the figure below:

- Tables/Queries: Mutual Fund
- Fields: Company, Fund Name, and Net Asset Value
- Grouping: Company
- Sort: Fund Name in ascending order
- Summary Options button: Sum
- Layout: Stepped
- Title: Net Asset Value by Company

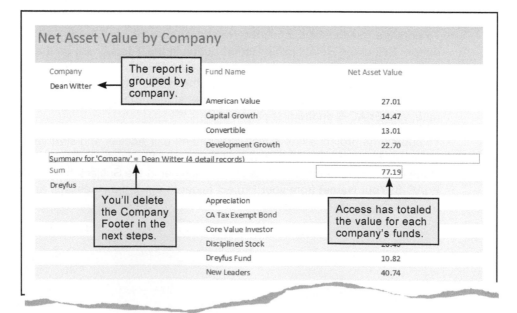

• Creating Grouped Reports (continued)

6. The report contains a Company Footer that starts with "Summary for 'Company.'" This footer detracts from the readability of the report, so it should be deleted. Close the Print Preview. The report should now be displayed in Design View. Locate the block containing the Company Footer and delete it.

7. Select the View button on the DESIGN tab to make sure the Company Footer has been removed. Use the Quick Print option to print the report. Save the report, then close it.

8. Now, suppose you want to create a report that contains the average, minimum, and maximum 1-year and 5-year statistics for each fund management company. Use the Report Wizard to create a report based on data in the Mutual Fund table. Respond to the wizard prompts with the following specifications:
- Tables/Queries: Mutual Fund
- Fields: Company, One Year, and Five Years
- Grouping: Company
- Summary Options button: Avg, Min, and Max for One Year and Five Years
- Summary Options button: Summary Only
- Layout: Stepped
- Title: 1-Year and 5-Year Fund Performance Summary

9. Close the Print Preview. The report should now be displayed in Design View. Locate the block containing the Company Footer, then delete it.

10. Switch back to Report View and compare your report to the one shown in the figure below. Print it. Save the report, then close it.

1-Year and 5-Year Fund Performance Summary		
Company	One Year	Five Years
Dean Witter		
Avg	12.6	11.0
Min	10.5	5.0
Max	17.0	15.1
Dreyfus		
Avg	17.1	12.1
Min	-2.6	5.5
Max	25.7	15.3
Evergreen		

11. Save your database in your Project folder using the file name PrjAC-9 [Your Name].

12. Write your name, student ID number, class section number, date, and PrjAC-9 on the printouts. Submit the printouts for this project according to your instructor's directions.

Project AC-10: Exporting Information

In this project, you'll practice exporting Access data to a spreadsheet, to a Word document, and into comma-delimited format.

Requirements: This project requires Microsoft Access, Microsoft Excel, Microsoft Word, WordPad, and Notepad.

Project file: PrjAC-10.accdb

COPYIT!

1. Copy the file PrjAC-10.accdb to your Project folder using the Copy It! button on this page in the *Practical Computer Literacy* digital book.

2. Start Microsoft Access and open the file PrjAC-10.accdb from your Project folder.

3. Open the Products table.

4. Take a moment to become familiar with the fields and records in the Products table. Suppose you'd like to work with this data in a spreadsheet. You can export the data from Access to Excel.

5. Select the EXTERNAL DATA tab, then choose the Excel button in the Export group. (Hint: Make sure you select the button in the Export group, not the Import group.)

6. Click the Browse button, navigate to your Project folder, enter the file name PrjAC-10A, then save it.

7. Select the export options *Export data with formatting and layout* and *Open the destination file after the export operation is complete*, then select the OK button.

8. When the export is complete, the Excel file is displayed. Compare your spreadsheet with the spreadsheet shown in the figure below.

• Exporting Information (continued)

9. Close Excel. In the Access window, select the Close button in the Export - Excel Spreadsheet dialog box without saving the export steps. Close the Products table.

10. Use the Report Wizard to create a report containing the LastName, FirstName, BusinessPhone, City, and State/Province fields from the Contacts table. Group the report by State/Province. Sort the records by LastName in ascending order. Use the Stepped layout. Enter Phone Contacts for the report title, then select the Finish button.

11. You can export reports to Microsoft Word, where you can add explanatory text. You can also export tables, queries, and forms to Word. All data is exported to Word in Rich Text Format (rtf). To export the Phone Contacts report, switch to Report View, select the EXTERNAL DATA tab, then choose the More button in the Export group. Select Word.

12. Select the Browse button, navigate to your Project folder, then enter the file name PrjAC-10B. Select the Save button. Select the export option *Open the destination file after the export operation is complete*, then select the OK button. Your Word document should look very similar to the Phone Contacts report.

13. Close Word. In the Access window, close the Export - RTF File dialog box, then close the Phone Contacts report.

14. You can also export Access data for processing by programs such as Notepad that work with ASCII text In comma-delimited format. Open the Contacts table, select the EXTERNAL DATA tab, then select Text File in the Export group.

15. Select the Browse button, navigate to your Project folder, then enter the file name PrjAC-10C and save it.

16. Do not select any of the export options. Select the OK button.

17. The Export Text Wizard opens and displays a preview of your data. Notice that fields are separated by commas. Select the Next button.

18. Make sure Comma is selected as the choice of delimiter, then select the Next button. Select the Finish button. Close the Export - Text File dialog box. Close the Contacts table.

19. Your file has been saved. To view its contents, use File Explorer to locate the PrjAC-10C file in your Project folder. Double-click the file and it will open in Notepad or WordPad.

20. Use one of the following options to submit the three project files on a USB flash drive, as printouts, or as e-mail attachments, according to your instructor's directions:

• To submit the project files on a USB flash drive, close Access, then copy the files PrjAC-10A, PrjAC-10B, and PrjAC-10C from your Project folder to a USB drive. Make sure your name is on the USB drive.

• To print each project file, double-click each file to open it. The correct application program should start. In Excel, Word, or WordPad, select the FILE tab, choose the Print option, then select Print. In Notepad, select the File menu, choose Print, then select the Print button. Staple the pages together, then write your name, student ID number, class section number, date, and PrjAC-10 on the first page.

• To submit the project files as e-mail attachments, exit Access and start your usual e-mail program. Type your instructor's e-mail address in the To: box. Type PrjAC-10, your student ID number, and your class section number in the Subject: box. Attach the project files PrjAC-10A, PrjAC-10B, and PrjAC-10C. Click the Send button or perform any additional steps required by your e-mail software to send an e-mail message.

Project NW-1: Finding Your Computer's IP Address

In this project, you will find your computer's IPv4 LAN address and the address that's broadcast as your computer's public Internet address.

Requirements: This project requires Microsoft Windows and a browser, such as Internet Explorer or Firefox.

Project file: No project file is required.

1. Access Control Panel and make sure the view is set to *Large icons*.

2. Select the *Network and Sharing Center*.

3. Look for the active network that provides Internet as the access type.

4. Select the network listed for Connections. (Hint: If more than one connection is listed, select the Wi-Fi connection.)

5. In the Status window, select the Details button.

6. The Network Connection Details window lists your computer's IP address on the IPv4 line.

7. Write down your computer's IPv4 address.

• Finding Your Computer's IP Address (continued)

8. To determine whether your computer's IP address is public or private, check to see if it falls within the range of these private IP address blocks:

10.0.0.0 to 10.255.255.255

172.16.0.0 to 172.31.255.255

192.168.0.0 to 192.168.255.255

9. Now, start your browser to find the IP address that's used to route your computer's data over the Internet.

10. Use a search engine such as Google to search for What's My IP Address?

11. Select one of the results to learn more details.

12. Write down the IP address and other relevant information.

13. Compare your computer's public IP address to its IPv4 address. Are they the same?

14. Compile the following information and submit it in an e-mail message, as an attachment, or in any other format specified by your instructor:

Your name

The location of your computer (home, school, office, etc.)

Your computer's IPv4 address

Whether the IPv4 address is public or private

Your computer's public IP address

Your Internet service provider (ISP)

Your public IP address location (city, state)

How well did the What's My IP Address? search query pinpoint the location of your computer?

Is your computer's IPv4 address the same as its public IP address; why or why not?

Project NW-2: Exploring Your Internet Connection Speed

In this project, you will test your Internet connection using Ping, Traceroute, and Speedtest.net tools. You will also view Internet connection speeds worldwide.

Requirements: This project requires Microsoft Windows, word processing software, and a browser, such as Internet Explorer or Firefox.

Project file: No project file is required.

1. Use your word processing software to create a project document called PrjNW-2 [Your Name]. As you complete the steps for the project, add your responses to this document, which you'll submit to your instructor.

2. To check your Internet connection speed, you can ping an Internet address, such as www.yahoo.com. Enter command prompt at the Windows 8 Start screen or in the Windows 7 Start menu's Search box. A Command Prompt window should appear.

3. Type ping www.yahoo.com and then press the Enter key. (Hint: If you make a typing error, you can use the Backspace key to correct your mistake as long as you have not pressed the Enter key. If you press the Enter key and receive an error message, simply re-enter ping www.yahoo.com.)

4. Study the Ping results. The Ping utility automatically pings www.yahoo.com four times, and then reports the minimum, maximum, and average times for data to make a round trip between your computer and the Yahoo! Web site. Ping sometimes displays "request timed out" messages, which mean that the Web site you specified is down or is not accepting pings for security reasons.

5. Switch to the project document and create a heading for Ping Stats. Record the minimum, maximum, and average times shown on the Ping report.

6. Next, run the Traceroute utility to gather more information about your Internet connection. At the next command prompt, type tracert www.yahoo.com and press the Enter key.

7. Compare your results to the example below.

```
Tracing route to www.yahoo-ht3.akadns.net [69.147.114.210]
over a maximum of 30 hops:

 1   30 ms    2 ms    2 ms   c-24-271-294-232.ma.comcast.net [24.271.294.232]

 2    9 ms                   4.8.1
 3    *                      40-ur01.ma.comcast.net [68.87.156.201]

 4   11 ms                   1-ur01.     t.net [68.87.144
 5   23 ms                   1-ur01.ma.comcast.net [68.87.144

 6   15 ms   10 ms   11 ms   te-7-1-ar02.ma.comcast.net [68.87.145.53]

 7   10 ms   24 ms   11 ms   po-11-ar01.ma.comcast.net [68.87.146.37]

 8   29 ms   13 ms   15 ms   po-10-ar01.ma.comcast.net [68.87.146.22]

 9   23 ms   15 ms   16 ms   po-11-ar01.ma.comcast.net [68.87.146.26]

10   18 ms   25 ms   17 ms   68.86.90.69
11   20 ms   18 ms   20 ms   te-9-2.car1.NewYork1.Level3.net [4.71.172.117]
12   25                 ms   ae-31-53.ebr1.NewYork1.Level3.net [4.68.97.94]
13         ms   ae-3.ebr1.Washington1.Level3.net [4.69.132.89]
14   24 ms        ms   ae-11-51.Washington1.Level3.net [4.68.121.18]

15   29 ms   25 ms   25 ms   4.79.228.2
16   25 ms   25 ms   32 ms   ge-3-1-0-p140.re1.yahoo.com [216.115.108.5]

17   36 ms   25 ms   31 ms   ge-1-42.bas-a2.re3.yahoo.com [66.196.112.203]
18   24 ms   24 ms   26 ms   f1.www.vip.re3.yahoo.com [69.147.114.210]
```

An asterisk indicates that a router along the route did not respond to the ping.

ISP URL

ISP IP address

Hop number

• Exploring Your Internet Connection Speed (continued)

8. Switch to the project document and add a heading for Traceroute Stats. Enter the number of hops listed on your Traceroute report.

9. Add the URL and IP addresses for the first hop to the project document.

10. Type exit at the next command prompt to close the Command Prompt window.

11. You can also test connection speed using an online speed test. To get started, open a browser, such as Internet Explorer or Firefox.

12. In the browser Address bar, enter www.speedtest.net and then press the Enter key.

13. Click the Begin Test button.

14. When the test is complete, add a Speedtest.net heading to your project document. List the results shown for Ping, Download Speed, and Upload Speed.

15. Also, write down the origination IP address shown in the lower-left corner, and the location of the destination host shown in the lower-right corner.

16. Next, add the heading Comparison to your project document.

17. Under the Comparison heading, indicate if your connection speed was better when tested with the Ping utility or Speedtest.net. Explain your results. (Hint: Look at the IP addresses and think about the origin and destination for each of the tests.)

18. If you want to compare your Internet connection speed to the rest of the country, you can look at the Internet Traffic Report. In your browser's Address bar, type www. internettrafficreport.com and press the Enter key.

19. Click your region of the world in the table to view detailed statistics. Look at the average response time. Add this value to the project document under the heading Traffic Report.

20. Explain how the average response time differs from your Ping and Speedtest.net results.

21. Save your project document and then submit it as an e-mail attachment, a printout, or a file, according to your instructor's guidelines.

Project EM-1: Exploring Webmail

In this project, you will use your e-mail account to send a message, identify key components of your e-mail client, and send a message containing an attachment.

Requirements: This project requires Microsoft Windows and a browser, such as Internet Explorer.

Project file: No project file is required.

1. Start your browser.

2. If you already have a Gmail account, sign in and proceed to Step 13. If not, enter accounts.google.com/signup in your browser's address bar to display a page where you can sign up for a Google account.

3. Enter your first name and last name, then choose a user name.

4. If the user name you've selected is unavailable, a list of available names similar to the one you've selected is displayed. Click a user name from the list if your original user name is unavailable.

5. Enter a password and pay attention to the Password Strength message to make sure that your password is classified as "Strong." Retype the password in the Confirm password box.

6. If you do not want to set Google as your default home page, remove the checkmark from the corresponding checkbox.

7. Enter your birthday and other requested information.

9. In the Word Verification box, type the characters exactly as you see them.

10. Read the Google Terms of Service at the bottom of the page, then click the *I agree* checkbox.

11. Click the *Next step* button.

12. On the Google Profile page, click the *Next step* button, then on the next page, click *Get started*.

13. If necessary, log in by entering your username and password. Select Gmail.

• Exploring Webmail (continued)

14. You should now be viewing the contents of your mailbox. Compose an e-mail message to yourself with the following attributes:

To: [Yourself]

Cc: Pat_Redfern@yahoo.com

Subject: Reminder

Contents: Remember to send [Your Name]'s assignment EM-1 to instructor.

15. Send the message.

16. Wait for a minute or so, then check your Inbox for the reminder.

17. Open the reminder and take a screenshot.

18. Open the screenshot in Paint, then use the Text tool to label the following items:

Reply icon or link

Reply subject line

Body of original message

Attachment icon

Trash

Inbox

Outbox (Sent mail)

19. Save the screenshot as PrjEM-1 [Your Name] in the Pictures library.

20. Forward the Reminder e-mail to your instructor, adding the PrjEM-1 screenshot as an attachment.

Project EM-2: Working with Automated E-mail Features

In this project, you'll customize your e-mail account to add your signature, create an out-of-office/autoresponse reply, set up autoforwarding, and create a group contact.

Requirements: This project requires Microsoft Windows, a browser, and an e-mail account.

Project file: No project file is required.

1. Log in to your e-mail account.

2. Access your account settings. In Gmail, use the gear-shaped ⚙ Settings icon in the upper-right corner of the window, then select Settings from the menu.

3. Find the Signature setting and use it to create a distinctive signature, keeping in mind the following points:

• You can choose a font, size, and color for your name.

• In a business situation, you should add your title and company name.

• You may also add a tag line such as "Have a great day!" But remember that your signature and tag line are attached to all of your messages, so make sure they are appropriate for all recipients.

4. Activate the signature feature. In Gmail, the *No signature* button should not be selected.

5. Next, scroll down to the Vacation Responder. You can use Gmail's Vacation Responder to set up out-of-office replies or generalized autoresponse messages.

6. Set up a Vacation Responder with the following properties:

First day: [Today's date]

Ends: [Tomorrow's date]

Subject: I'll get back to you soon.

Message: I'm away from my computer right now, but I'll respond to your message as soon as I can.

7. You can forward your mail to another account—for example, if you want to use a local e-mail client to collect your Webmail. In Gmail, access Settings and select *Forwarding and POP/IMAP*.

Source: Google

8. Click Add forwarding address.

9. The address you add here will be used as your forwarding address. If you want to add one now, you can do so. If you want to keep your messages in Gmail, click the X close button.

10. Click the link for creating a filter.

11. Use this form to specify the characteristics of messages that you want to forward. For example, entering your instructor's e-mail address will automatically forward all messages from your instructor to the forwarding address you specified in Step 9.

12. Close the forwarding window.

• Working with Automated E-mail Features (continued)

13. Save the settings you've made for your signature and autoresponse message. In Gmail, you can do so by scrolling down and selecting the Save Changes button.

14. Now, create a group for some of your contacts. Access your contacts list in Gmail by clicking the Gmail logo in the left navigation pane, then selecting Contacts.

Source: Google

15. Make sure that you have at least five contacts in your address book. You can add contacts by clicking the ⚭⁺ *Add To "My Contacts"* button and entering each contact's e-mail address.

16. If your instructor is not listed as a contact, add his or her e-mail address.

17. Next, create a group called Tutoring Circle. To do this in Gmail, click New Contact, click the ⚭⁻ Groups icon, click Create new, then enter Tutoring Circle. Click the OK button to complete the process.

18. Add your instructor and two other contacts to the Tutoring Circle group. To do so in Gmail, click My Contacts, then select a contact. Click the ⚭⁻ Groups icon and select Tutoring Circle. Repeat for the remaining two contacts.

Source: Google

19. Now, send the following message to the Tutoring Circle group:

To: Tutoring Circle

Subject: Our next meeting with [Your Name] as tutor

Message: Our next tutorial session will be this Wednesday at 7:00 pm in West Science 101. Everyone in this group has that time free. Be there. No excuses!

20. Make sure that your signature was automatically added to the end of the message. Send the message.

Project EM-3: Managing E-mail Folders

In this project, you'll work with e-mail folders for archiving and organizing e-mail, and dealing with trash and spam.

Requirements: This project requires an e-mail account. Specific instructions are given for Gmail users.

Project file: No project file is required.

1. Log in to your e-mail account and view your Inbox.

2. Some e-mail clients allow you to sort mail by sender, subject, or date simply by clicking the column headings. Find out if your e-mail client offers this feature.

3. Gmail does not offer sorting, but you can use the Search box to filter messages to a specific sender, date, or subject. In the Gmail Search box, enter from:me and press the Enter key. Messages that you've sent to yourself are displayed.

4. To clear the search and view all the messages in your Inbox, click the Inbox link.

5. Archiving moves messages into another folder, which removes clutter from your Inbox without deleting important messages. Put a checkmark in the box on the left side of any message in your Inbox.

6. Click the Archive icon.

Source: Google

7. To view the archive, select All Mail from the navigation links on the left side of the Gmail window.

8. You can also create folders to hold a specific group of messages, such as messages from a range of dates or messages that pertain to a specific topic. Click the *Create new label* link in the Gmail navigation panel.

9. Type Jan-June as the new label name.

• Managing E-mail Folders (continued)

10. Click the Create button. Now Jan-June is listed in the Navigation panel.

11. Move a message into the Jan-June folder by selecting the message, selecting the Labels icon, then selecting Jan-June.

Source: Google

12. Click the Jan-June folder in the Navigation panel to make sure the message was moved there.

13. Click More labels, if necessary, to access the Trash folder.

14. Look through the messages in the Trash folder to ensure that you do not want to save any of them.

15. Click the Empty Trash Now link to delete all the messages in the Trash folder.

16. Let's see how the Spam folder works. Go back to your Inbox and mark one of your messages by selecting its checkbox.

17. Select the [!] Report spam icon. The checked message is moved into the Spam folder.

18. Click More labels, if necessary, to access the Spam folder.

19. The Spam folder holds messages that you mark as spam or those that are automatically classified as spam by your e-mail service provider. If a message does not belong in the Spam folder, you can move it back to the Inbox. To do this in Gmail, select the message's checkbox, then click the Not spam link.

20. To complete this project, take a screenshot of your e-mail window showing the Jan-June folder that you created, which contains one message. Name the screenshot PrjEM-3 [Your Name] and e-mail it to your instructor.

Project WW-1: Working with Browsers

In this project, you'll check basic browser settings, work with tabs, and create bookmarks.

Requirements: This project requires Windows, Paint, and a browser. Internet Explorer is recommended.

Project file: No project file is required.

1. Open a browser, such as Internet Explorer. Maximize the browser window.

2. If Google is not your home page, navigate to it by entering www.google.com in the Address box, then pressing the Enter key.

3. Check the browser window display settings. To complete this step in Internet Explorer, right-click the background at the top of the screen and make sure that the three menu items shown below are checked.

4. Select the ⌂ Home icon. The page displayed is your home page.

5. Change your home page to the WolframAlpha search engine. In Internet Explorer, navigate to www.wolframalpha.com. Right-click the Home icon, then select *Add or change home page*. Select *Use this webpage as your only home page*, then click the Yes button.

6. Add Wikipedia (www.wikipedia.org) to your Favorites list. To complete this step in Internet Explorer:

   Select the ★ Favorites icon.

   Select *Add to favorites*.

   Select the Add button.

7. Experiment with tabs to make sure you know how to add, select, and delete them. In Internet Explorer, do the following:

   Navigate to the Wikipedia page about the telephone. Make a note of the number of tabs you have open.

   Hold down the Ctrl key and click the link in paragraph two to Alexander Graham Bell. Note how many tabs you have open now.

   View the Alexander Graham Bell page.

   Open a third tab for one of the links on the Alexander Graham Bell page.

   Open a blank tab by clicking the tab stub, as shown below.

• Working with Browsers (continued)

Navigate to www.corp.att.com/history so the AT&T history site is displayed by the fourth tab.

Delete the third tab by clicking its X button.

Take a screenshot showing the browser windows with the three remaining tabs.

Save the screenshot as Tabs [Your Name].

8. Navigate to the CIA World Factbook by going to www.cia.gov, then clicking the World Factbook link.

9. Add the CIA World Factbook to your Favorites list in a new folder called Research Sites. To do this step in Internet Explorer:

Select the ⭐ Favorites icon, then select *Add to favorites*.

Select the New folder button, then enter Research Sites.

Select the Create button.

Select the Add button.

10. Add the INFOMINE site (infomine.ucr.edu) to the Research Sites folder of your Favorites list.

11. Move the Wikipedia Favorites link to the Research Sites folder. To do this step in Internet Explorer:

Select the ⭐ Favorites icon.

Click the arrow on the *Add to favorites* button to display a menu of options.

Select *Organize favorites*.

Drag the Wikipedia link to the Research Sites folder.

Select Close.

12. Open the Favorites list and make sure the Research Sites folder is expanded to show the Web sites it contains.

13. Take a screenshot and save it as Research Sites [Your Name].

14. Check your browser history by clicking the ⭐ Favorites Icon, then selecting the History tab.

15. Use a link from your History list to go to a Web page that you've previously visited.

16. Use your browser's ↻ Refresh icon to make sure that all the page elements are up to date.

17. Display your History list again.

18. Expand the oldest entry to display its links.

19. Delete any links in the History list that you would rather not share with your instructor.

20. Take a screenshot of your History list and save it as History List [Your Name].

21. Submit the three screenshots as an e-mail attachment, as a printout, or in any other format specified by your instructor.

Project WW-2: Exploring Browser Security

In this project, you will review procedures and settings for safe and secure Web browsing.

Requirements: This project requires Windows and a browser. Internet Explorer is recommended.

Project file: No project file is required.

1. Open a browser, such as Internet Explorer. Your browser's toolbar provides information to help determine if a site is safe and secure, or if it is a fake.

2. Navigate to the Bank of America Web site at www.bankofamerica.com. The Address bar includes three things that indicate this is a secure and legitimate site. What are those three things?

3. Cookies can be used to track your browsing habits, and third-party cookies are frequently used to compile your shopping profile and display targeted advertising. Check your browser settings to make sure it is blocking third-party cookies. To do this step using Internet Explorer:

Select the ⚙ Settings icon.

Select *Internet options*.

Select the Privacy tab.

Select the Advanced button.

Make sure that first-party cookies are marked Accept.

Make sure that third-party cookies are marked Block.

Click the OK button, then close the Internet Options window.

4. You can keep your location private, whether you are using a desktop computer or a mobile device. Turn your browser's location services off. To do this step using Internet Explorer:

Select the ⚙ Settings icon.

Select *Internet options*.

Select the Privacy tab.

Select the option *Never allow websites to request your physical location*.

Click the OK button, then close the Internet Options window.

5. Browsers store information about the sites you've visited in the History list and browser cache. Make sure that you know how to delete the browser history. To delete the browser history in Internet Explorer:

Select the ⚙ Settings icon.

Select Safety.

Select *Delete browsing history*.

When using a public computer, you should check all the boxes so that your browsing history is completely deleted.

• Exploring Browser Security (continued)

At home you may choose not to delete some of the history data. For example, you might want to retain the saved passwords that you use for sites such as Facebook and Gmail.

Clear any history items if you would like to do so.

Close the Delete Browsing History window.

6. If you are using a public computer and you would like your browser to automatically delete history information when you close it, activate private browsing. To start Internet Explorer's InPrivate Browsing feature:

Select the ⚙ Settings icon.

Select Safety.

Select InPrivate Browsing.

Read the information supplied on the screen so that you know how InPrivate Browsing works.

7. Test the InPrivate Browsing feature to make sure it works. To do this step using Internet Explorer:

Navigate to www.oldtowncanoe.com and make sure that InPrivate Browsing is still active.

Navigate to your home page.

Look at your History list for today.

Make sure that Old Town Canoe is not listed.

Close your browser window.

Reopen your browser window. Because you have started a new browser session, InPrivate Browsing should no longer be active.

Look at your History list. As before, Old Town Canoe should not be included.

8. Close your browser.

9. Thinking about the activities in this lab, how do you expect each of the following settings to be configured when you start your browser again?

First-party cookies

Third-party cookies

Location Services

InPrivate Browsing

10. Submit your answers for the question in Step 9 as an e-mail message, as an e-mail attachment, as a printout, on a USB flash drive, or in any other format specified by your instructor.

Project WW-3: Searching the Web

In this project, you will work with search engines and other Web-based tools to create and refine searches using keywords, search operators, and search tokens.

Requirements: This project requires Windows, a browser, and a word processor or an e-mail client.

Project file: No project file is required.

1. Open any word processing software and create a blank document titled Project WW-3 [Your Name]. Use this document to record information about your search results for each step of the project.

2. Open a browser and navigate to a search engine, such as Google. Suppose you are a gardener living in Jacksonville, Florida, and you'd like to know if your local climate would support the kind of palm trees that produce dates. Which search engine are you using?

3. Enter the keyword palms. How many results does the search engine produce?

4. Modify the search to date palms. Did adding a keyword produce more or fewer results?

5. Click the search engine's Image link to see photos of date palms. List two of the Web sites on which the photos were found.

6. Click the search engine's Video or YouTube link to see a list of videos about date palms. Which video seems most valuable for a gardener who wants to grow date palms?

7. If you click the search engine's Map link, does it show growing areas for date palms?

8. Select the search engine's Web link, then change the search to date palms growing zone. What are the U.S. growing zones for date palms?

9. Formulate a search to find the growing zone in which Jacksonville, Florida, is located. What was your search string? What is its growing zone?

10. Search engines allow you to enter search operators, such as AND, OR, and NOT, to refine your search criteria. Enter the following searches, record the number of results, and look at the search results to characterize the kind of information found:

   date AND palms

   date OR palms

   date NOT palms

   palms NOT dates

• Searching the Web (continued)

11. Search engines also provide tokens to locate results by date, within a range of numbers, within a specific site, or for a specific phrase. Enter the following searches, record the number of results, and look at the search results to characterize the kind of information found:

date palms $100..135

site:ehow.com growing dates

"date palms"

"palm dates"

12. Search engines such as Google and Bing display ads related to search results. When you search for medjool dates, what kinds of ads are displayed?

13. When you want personal opinions and experiences, rather than encyclopedia information, you can search topic forums. Enter a search for date palm growers forum. Can you find a forum where participants have tried to grow trees from the dates they've purchased at a grocery store?

14. Knowledge bases provide a good source of information on specific topics. Navigate to the EDIS knowledge base at http://edis.ifas.ufl.edu. Can you find out how mealy bugs affect palm trees and how to eradicate them?

15. Save the document containing your answers, then submit it as an e-mail attachment, on a USB flash drive, or in any other format specified by your instructor.

Project SE-1: Exploring Computer Security

In this project, you will work with three fundamental aspects of computer security: passwords, antivirus software, and firewalls.

Requirements: This project requires Windows, a browser, and a word processor or an e-mail client.

Project file: No project file is required.

1. Log in to Windows. Many aspects of computer security depend on passwords, starting with the password you use to log on to your computer.

2. Check the strength of your logon password. To check password strength, do the following:

   Open a browser.

   Use a search engine to navigate to Microsoft's Check Your Password Web site.

   Enter your current password.

3. If your password is not strong, then you should select a better one. To create a strong password, try this method:

   Select a sentence that is at least nine words long and contains a number—for example, "The first house I lived in was located on 522 Front Street."

   Combine the first letter of each word, maintaining its case, into a password string—for example, TfhIliwlo522FS.

4. To change your login password:

   Type pass at the Windows Start screen or in the Start menu.

   Select Settings if you are using Windows 8.

   Select the option *Change your password*.

   Select the *Change your password* button.

   Enter your current password.

   Enter your new, strong password.

   Re-enter your new password.

5. To combat computer viruses, worms, and other malware, it is essential for your computer to run antivirus software. To check the status of antivirus software on your computer, do the following:

   Access the Control Panel and make sure the view is set to *Large icons*.

   Select the Action Center link.

   Expand the Security section by clicking the circled arrow as shown in the figure below:

• Exploring Computer Security (continued)

6. Look at the Security list to find the name of the software that is installed for virus protection.

7. Access your antivirus software. To do so, enter the name of your antivirus software at the Start screen in Windows 8 or select it from the Start menu in Windows 7.

8. Use the menus, tabs, and toolbars of your antivirus software to answer the following questions:

What is the name of your antivirus software?

What is the status of this software? For example, is it on or off?

Is it providing real-time protection by running while your computer is on?

Are the virus definitions up to date?

When were the virus definitions last updated?

What does the antivirus software do with suspicious files?

Can you adjust settings for scanning incoming and outgoing e-mail?

Can you adjust settings for scanning files on removable drives?

9. Close your antivirus software.

10. Firewall software protects your computer from unauthorized intrusions. The Control Panel Action Center window should still be open on your computer. Look for the name of your firewall software.

11. Access your computer's firewall software. To do so, enter the name of the firewall software at the Start screen in Windows 8 or select it from the Start menu in Windows 7.

12. Answer the following questions about your computer's firewall software:

What is its name?

What is its status?

Does it contain a list of allowed or approved applications?

What happens when the firewall senses a suspicious application that could be an intrusion?

13. Compile your answers to the questions in Steps 8 and 12 into a document, an e-mail message, or any other format specified by your instructor, then submit them.

Project CP-1 : Word Processing

In this project, you'll apply all that you've learned about Microsoft Word.

Requirements: This project requires Microsoft Word.

Project files: Capstone1.docx and Marquee.jpg

COPYIT! 1. Copy the file Capstone1.docx to your Project folder using the Copy It! button on this page in the *Practical Computer Literacy* digital book.

COPYIT! 2. Copy the file Marquee.jpg to your Project folder using the Copy It! button on this page in the *Practical Computer Literacy* digital book.

3. Start Microsoft Word and open the file Capstone1.docx from your Project folder. You will use the file Capstone1.docx as the basis for this project, making the modifications shown on pages 477–479. The following steps will help you implement the modifications.

4. Add The History of the Drive-In Theater as a left-justified header, and your name as a right-justified header.

5. Add page numbers as centered footers on all pages, including the title page.

6. Search for theatre and replace it with theater.

7. Format the title with the Heading 1 style. Format the line containing the author's name with the Heading 2 style. Center the title and the author's name.

8. Insert Marquee.jpg between the title and byline, and center it.

9. Set a right-justified tab at 6" and use it to align the numbers in the Table of Contents.

10. Format the heading "Table of Contents" as white, bold, 14 pt. font with a dark gray background. Format all the headings in the same style using the Format Painter.

11. Delete and move paragraphs as shown on page 477.

12. Add a footnote as shown on page 477.

13. Insert page breaks as shown on pages 477–479. Remove any blank lines of text at the top of each page.

14. Highlight all the text in Figure 1 and adjust the margin to 1" from the left.

15. In Figure 1, use the Show/Hide Characters button and modify the list so that instead of spaces, there is only one tab between each item. Set a right-justified tab at 2". Set a left-justified tab at 2.5". Format the text as 9 pt. font.

16. Change the text in Figures 2 and 3 to tables. Format the column headings as white, 12 pt., bold text with a dark gray background. Adjust the columns so the cells all contain only one line of text. Format the text as 9 pt. font.

17. Format the figure titles using the Heading 6 style at 8 pt., centered.

18. In the Unusual Drive-In Theaters section of the document, find synonyms for the words "occupy," "gaudy," and "necessities."

19. Make the wording changes indicated on page 478.

20. Add the Wikipedia reference shown on page 479. Make sure all links are active hyperlinks.

• Word Processing (continued)

21. Set the top margin to 1", the bottom margin to .75", and the right and left margins to 1.25".

22. Check your work against the document shown on pages 480 and 481. Save the project as Capstone1-[Your Name]. You will use parts of this project again when you work on the third Capstone project.

23. Submit your project on a USB flash drive, as a printout, or as an e-mail attachment according to your instructor's preference.

Header with document title left justified

Header with your name right justified

Search and replace "theatre" with "theater"

The History of the Drive-In Theatre

> Insert Marquee.jpg and center it

Apply Heading 1 style and center the title

Prepared by Raj Shakur ← *Apply Heading 2 style and center it*

Table of Contents ← *Apply dark gray shading, font color = white, bold, 14 pt.*

Introduction 3

The Inventor 3

The First Drive-In Theatres 3

Unusual Drive-In Theatres 1

Sources 5

Insert page breaks

Right justify page numbers at 6 inches, but leave headings left justified. Hint: Use tabs.

Use Format Painter to apply the same style as "Table of Contents" to all circled headings.

Introduction

Richard M. Hollingshead, Jr., an auto products salesman, noticed that movie attendance in the 1930s was not a family affair. Children went to matinees in the afternoons, and adults went to the movies in the evening. Dads hated getting dressed up to go out, Moms hated the bother of getting a baby sitter, and nobody enjoyed the hassle of parking the car.

Move paragraph

The drive-in movie theatre is one of America's last great icons. The concept was a natural— combining Americans' love for cars with their love for movies. Perhaps you're too young to have enjoyed the weekly ritual of being dressed in your pajamas right after dinner, watching your parents rush around gathering towels and napkins and pillows and snacks and then packing them plus all the kids into the family car and heading off to the drive-in theatre. If so, then you really missed something. But ask your parents about it, and see if Mom doesn't get a faraway look in her eyes. And check out that silly smile that Dad gets on his face.

Delete paragraph

Jenny Valentina recalls her first drive-in experience: "We went to see Fantasia, a Disney production. The feature didn't start until very late, it seemed to me. But I was only 6 and usually went to bed at 7:30. I managed to keep my eyes open for maybe a half hour of the movie, and then drifted off into a kind of half sleep. I remember Mickey Mouse as the sorcerer's apprentice. There were also some dancing hippopotamuses. And a big volcano."

So let's take a trip down memory lane (or, for most of you, a history lesson—but a painless one, we promise you) and learn about the history of a piece of Americana: the drive-in theatre.

The Inventor

Hollingshead's idea was to create a movie theatre where you could watch movies from your car. After experimenting in his own driveway to figure out the optimum arrangement of cars—all the necessary spacing, angles, inclines, and ramps—Hollingshead applied for a patent on his idea. Patent #1,909,537 was granted to Richard Hollingshead on May 16, 1933. ① *Add footnote shown at bottom of page*

The First Drive-In Theatres

The first drive-in theatre opened in Camden, New Jersey on June 6, 1933. Its $30,000 construction cost was financed by Hollingshead and three other investors. Its name was simply "Drive-In Theatre."

Footnote > ① The patent was invalidated by the Delaware District Court in May 1950.

1 < *Add centered page numbers*

© MediaTechnics

• Word Processing (continued)

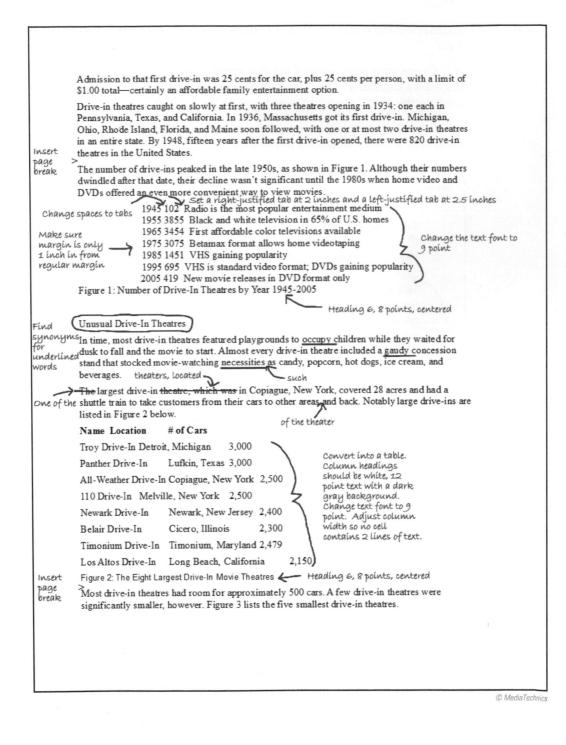

Admission to that first drive-in was 25 cents for the car, plus 25 cents per person, with a limit of $1.00 total—certainly an affordable family entertainment option.

Drive-in theatres caught on slowly at first, with three theatres opening in 1934: one each in Pennsylvania, Texas, and California. In 1936, Massachusetts got its first drive-in. Michigan, Ohio, Rhode Island, Florida, and Maine soon followed, with one or at most two drive-in theatres in an entire state. By 1948, fifteen years after the first drive-in opened, there were 820 drive-in theatres in the United States.

[Insert page break]

The number of drive-ins peaked in the late 1950s, as shown in Figure 1. Although their numbers dwindled after that date, their decline wasn't significant until the 1980s when home video and DVDs offered an even more convenient way to view movies.

[Set a right-justified tab at 2 inches and a left-justified tab at 2.5 inches]

[Change spaces to tabs]
[Make sure margin is only 1 inch in from regular margin]

1945 102 Radio is the most popular entertainment medium
1955 3855 Black and white television in 65% of U.S. homes
1965 3454 First affordable color televisions available
1975 3075 Betamax format allows home videotaping
1985 1451 VHS gaining popularity
1995 695 VHS is standard video format; DVDs gaining popularity
2005 419 New movie releases in DVD format only

[Change the text font to 9 point]

Figure 1: Number of Drive-In Theatres by Year 1945-2005

[Heading 6, 8 points, centered]

Unusual Drive-In Theatres

[Find synonyms for underlined words]

In time, most drive-in theatres featured playgrounds to <u>occupy</u> children while they waited for dusk to fall and the movie to start. Almost every drive-in theatre included a <u>gaudy</u> concession stand that stocked movie-watching <u>necessities</u> as candy, popcorn, hot dogs, ice cream, and beverages. *theaters, located*   *such*

[One of the] The largest drive-in ~~theatre, which was~~ in Copiague, New York, covered 28 acres and had a shuttle train to take customers from their cars to other areas and back. Notably large drive-ins are listed in Figure 2 below.   *of the theater*

Name	Location	# of Cars
Troy Drive-In	Detroit, Michigan	3,000
Panther Drive-In	Lufkin, Texas	3,000
All-Weather Drive-In	Copiague, New York	2,500
110 Drive-In	Melville, New York	2,500
Newark Drive-In	Newark, New Jersey	2,400
Belair Drive-In	Cicero, Illinois	2,300
Timonium Drive-In	Timonium, Maryland	2,479
Los Altos Drive-In	Long Beach, California	2,150

[Convert into a table. Column headings should be white, 12 point text with a dark gray background. Change text font to 9 point. Adjust column width so no cell contains 2 lines of text.]

Figure 2: The Eight Largest Drive-In Movie Theatres   *[Heading 6, 8 points, centered]*

[Insert page break]

Most drive-in theatres had room for approximately 500 cars. A few drive-in theatres were significantly smaller, however. Figure 3 lists the five smallest drive-in theatres.

• Word Processing (continued)

Name Location	# of Cars
Harmony Drive-In	Harmony, Pennsylvania	50
Highway Drive-In	Bamberg, South Carolina	50
Ponce de Leon Drive-In	Ponce de Leon, Florida	60
Twilite Drive-In	Nakina, North Carolina	60
Norwood Drive-In	Norwood, Colorado	64

Convert to a table with the same format as previous table

Figure 3: The Five Smallest Drive-In Movie Theatres ⟵ *Heading 6, 8 points, centered*

According to Wikipedia, 2001 marked the beginning of "Do-It-Yourself Drive-ins" and "Guerrilla drive-ins" where films are unofficially shown in parking lots and other vacant urban or rural venues using DVDs and LCD projectors. Any blank wall can serve as a screen. Film showings are often organized online via e-mail, Twitter, or social networking sites.

So the drive-in theatre lives on. Perhaps not in all its former glory, but in a modern mashup version made possible by today's technology.

(Sources)

"After Sunset: The Life & Times of the Drive-In Theatre" (updated 1 Nov., 1996) http://www.janson.com/rights/2009/05/06/after-sunset-the-life-times-of-the-drive-in-theater

Segrave, Kerry. *Drive-In Theatres: A History from Their Inception in 1933*. McFarland & Company, 1992.

"Welcome to the Drive-In Theatre: The Drive-In Theatre History Page" (updated 24 Oct., 1996) http://www.driveintheatre.com

> *Wikipedia http://en.wikipedia.org/wiki/Drive-in_theater*

Final margins:
Top 1 inch
Left 1.25 inch
Bottom .75 inch
Right 1.25 inch

• **Word Processing (continued)**

© MediaTechnics

The History of the Drive-In Theater   [Student's Name]

The History of the Drive-In Theater

NOW SHOWING

JOHN WAYNE

in

The History of the Drive-In Theater   [Student's Name]

Table of Contents

The History of the Drive-In Theater   [Student's Name]

Introduction

The drive-in movie theater is one of America's last great icons. The concept was a natural—combining Americans' love for cars with their love for movies. Perhaps you're too young to have enjoyed the weekly ritual of being dressed in your pajamas right after dinner, watching your parents rush around gathering towels and napkins and pillows and snacks and then packing them plus all the kids into the family car and heading off to the drive-in theater. If so, then you really missed something. But ask your parents about it, and see if Mom doesn't get a faraway look in her eyes. And check out that silly smile that Dad gets on his face.

So let's take a trip down memory lane (or, for most of you, a history lesson—but a painless one, we promise you) and learn about the history of a piece of Americana: the drive-in theater.

The Inventor

Richard M. Hollingshead, Jr., an auto products salesman, noticed that movie attendance in the 1930s was not a family affair. Children went to matinees in the afternoons, and adults went to the movies in the evening. Dads hated getting dressed up to go out, Moms hated the bother of getting a baby sitter, and nobody enjoyed the hassle of parking the car.

Hollingshead's idea was to create a movie theater where you could watch movies from your car. After experimenting in his own driveway to figure out the optimum arrangement of cars—all the necessary spacing, angles, inclines, and ramps—Hollingshead applied for a patent on his idea. Patent #1,909,537 was granted to Richard Hollingshead on May 16, 1933.[1]

The First Drive-In Theaters

The first drive-in theater opened in Camden, New Jersey on June 6, 1933. Its $30,000 construction cost was financed by Hollingshead and three other investors. Its name was simply "Drive-In Theater."

Admission to that first drive-in was 25 cents for the car, plus 25 cents per person, with a limit of $1.00 total—certainly an affordable family entertainment option.

Drive-in theaters caught on slowly at first, with three theaters opening in 1934: one each in Pennsylvania, Texas, and California. In 1936, Massachusetts got its first drive-in. Michigan, Ohio, Rhode Island, Florida, and Maine soon followed, with one or at most two drive-in theaters in an entire state. By 1948, fifteen years after the first drive-in opened, there were 820 drive-in theaters in the United States.

---

[1] The patent was invalidated by the Delaware District Court in May 1950.

3

• Word Processing (continued)

The number of drive-ins peaked in the late 1950s, as shown in Figure 1. Although their numbers dwindled after that date, their decline wasn't significant until the 1980s when home video and DVDs offered an even more convenient way to view movies.

Year	Number	Note
1945	102	Radio is the most popular entertainment medium
1955	3855	Black and white television in 65% of U.S. homes
1965	3454	First affordable color televisions available
1975	3075	Betamax format allows home videotaping
1985	1451	VHS gaining popularity
1995	695	VHS is standard video format; DVDs gaining popularity
2005	419	New movie releases in DVD format only

Figure 1: Number of Drive-In Theaters by Year 1945-2005

Unusual Drive-In Theaters

In time, most drive-in theaters featured playgrounds to entertain children while they waited for dusk to fall and the movie to start. Almost every drive-in theater included a flashy concession stand that stocked movie-watching essentials such as candy, popcorn, hot dogs, ice cream, and beverages.

One of the largest drive-in theaters, located in Copiague, New York, covered 28 acres and had a shuttle train to take customers from their cars to other areas of the theater and back. Notably large drive-ins are listed in Figure 2 below.

Name	Location	# of Cars
Troy Drive-In	Detroit, Michigan	3,000
Panther Drive-In	Lufkin, Texas	3,000
All-Weather Drive-In	Copiague, New York	2,500
110 Drive-In	Melville, New York	2,500
Newark Drive-In	Newark, New Jersey	2,400
Belair Drive-In	Cicero, Illinois	2,300
Timonium Drive-In	Timonium, Maryland	2,479
Los Altos Drive-In	Long Beach, California	2,150

Figure 2: The Eight Largest Drive-In Movie Theaters

Most drive-in theaters had room for approximately 500 cars. A few drive-in theaters were significantly smaller, however. Figure 3 lists the five smallest drive-in theaters.

Name	Location	# of Cars
Harmony Drive-In	Harmony, Pennsylvania	50
Highway Drive-In	Bamberg, South Carolina	50
Ponce de Leon Drive-In	Ponce de Leon, Florida	60
Twilite Drive-In	Nakina, North Carolina	60
Norwood Drive-In	Norwood, Colorado	64

Figure 3: The Five Smallest Drive-In Movie Theaters

According to Wikipedia, 2001 marked the beginning of "Do-It-Yourself Drive-ins" and "Guerrilla drive-ins" where films are unofficially shown in parking lots and other vacant urban or rural venues using DVDs and LCD projectors. Any blank wall can serve as a screen. Film showings are often organized online via e-mail, Twitter, or social networking sites.

So the drive-in theater lives on. Perhaps not in all its former glory, but in a modern mashup version made possible by today's technology.

Sources

"After Sunset: The Life & Times of the Drive-In Theater" (updated 1 Nov., 1996) http://www.janson.com/rights/2009/05/06/after-sunset-the-life-times-of-the-drive-in-theater

Segrave, Kerry. *Drive-In Theaters: A History from Their Inception in 1933*. McFarland & Company, 1992.

"Welcome to the Drive-In Theater: The Drive-In Theater History Page" (updated 24 Oct., 1996) http://www.driveintheater.com

Wikipedia http://en.wikipedia.org/wiki/Drive_in_theater

Project CP-2: Spreadsheets

In this project, you'll apply all that you've learned about Microsoft Excel.

Requirements: This project requires Microsoft Excel.

Project files: Capstone2.xlsx and DIClipArt.bmp

COPYIT!

1. Copy the file DIClipArt.bmp to your Project folder using the Copy It! button on this page in the *Practical Computer Literacy* digital book.

COPYIT!

2. Copy the file Capstone2.xlsx to your Project folder using the Copy It! button on this page in the *Practical Computer Literacy* digital book.

3. Start Microsoft Excel and open the Capstone2.xlsx file from your Project folder.

4. Look at the worksheet on the next page as a guide for constructing your worksheet and completing the rest of the steps.

5. Use the picture DIClipArt.bmp for the image in the upper-left corner of the worksheet. Shrink it to 1" in size using the tools on the PICTURE TOOLS FORMAT tab. Expand row 1 to the bottom of the picture.

6. Use WordArt to enter the title Drive-In Theaters.

7. In row 3, enter the column headings shown on page 483 and format the text as bold, 14 pt., and with a Dark Red Standard Color. Make the text wrap to a second line in the cells. Adjust the column width and row height.

8. In row 3, "Year" should be left justified. The other headings should be right justified.

9. Format the years in column A as text, not numbers.

10. Format the numbers in column B to display numbers with commas, but no decimal places. Format the numbers in column C as dollars and cents.

11. In cell C19, use a function to calculate the average for column C. In cell D19, enter the label Average in bold.

12. Create a 3-D Area chart showing the number of operating drive-ins from 1945–2010.

13. Title the chart U.S. Drive-Ins (18 pt. bold). Add the title Number in Operation for the vertical axis (9 pt. bold).

14. Display vertical and horizontal gridlines in the chart area. (Hint: Look for the Gridlines option on the ⊞ CHART ELEMENTS button.)

15. Right-click the data series to format it with a gradient fill. Select Top Spotlight - Accent 2 from the *Preset gradients* button.

• Spreadsheets (continued)

16. Create a 3-D Line chart showing the trend in drive-in admission prices.

17. Title the chart Admission Price per Car (18 pt. bold).

18. Format the data series with a similar gradient as you used for the first chart.

19. Format the plot area of both charts with a light tan color.

20. For both charts, delete the text "Series 1" from the baseline. Also, make sure the horizontal axis labels contain the values from the Year field. (Hint: Use the Select Data Source button.)

21. Resize and reposition both charts so they are similar to the image below

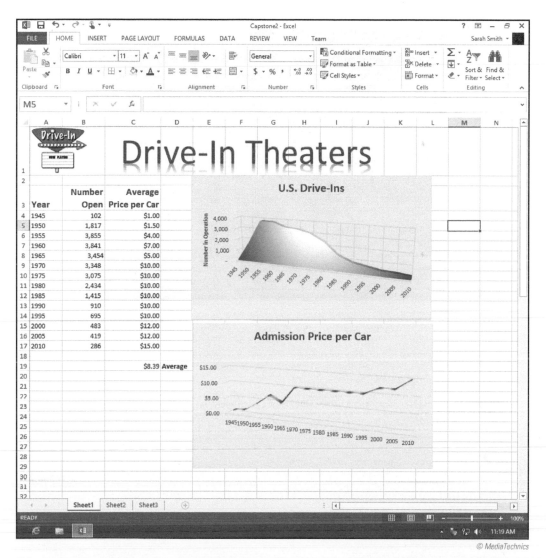

© MediaTechnics

22. Save the worksheet as Capstone2-[Your Name]. You will use parts of this project again when you work on the third Capstone project.

23. Submit your project on a USB flash drive, as a printout, or as an e-mail attachment according to your instructor's preference.

Project CP-3: Presentations

In this project, you'll apply all that you've learned about Microsoft PowerPoint.

Requirements: This project requires Microsoft PowerPoint.

Project files: Drivein1.jpg and Snackbar.jpg

 1. Copy the file Drivein1.jpg to your Project folder using the Copy It! button on this page in the *Practical Computer Literacy* digital book.

 2. Copy the file Snackbar.jpg to your Project folder using the Copy It! button on this page in the *Practical Computer Literacy* digital book.

3. Start PowerPoint and create a presentation containing seven slides, as shown below and on the next pages.

Slide 1:

• Use the Mesh theme.

• Add the title and subtitle as shown.

PowerPoint (continued)

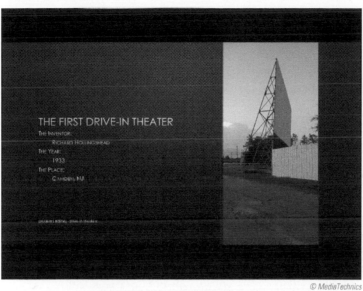

© MediaTechnics

Slide 2:

- Use the *Picture with Caption* layout.

- Use the photo Drivein1.jpg.

- Add the text as shown.

- Add a footer containing your name and "Drive-In Theaters", which will appear on all slides except the title slide.

© MediaTechnics

Slide 3.

- Use the Two Content layout.

- Add the title and bullets as shown.

- Add the image Snackbar.jpg and position it as shown.

• PowerPoint (continued)

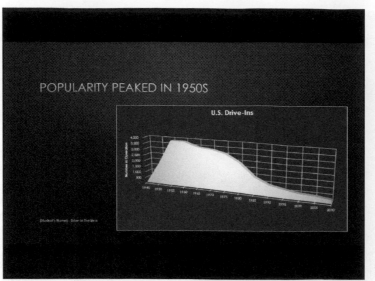

Slide 4:

- Use the Title Only layout.
- Add the title shown.
- Copy the chart from Capstone Project 2 and paste it onto the slide.
- Adjust the size and position of the chart.

Slide 5:

- Use the Title Only layout.
- Add the title shown.
- Copy the table in Figure 2 from Capstone Project 1. (Hint: Select the box with the plus sign that hovers just above the upper-left corner of the table to copy the entire table.)

- Paste the table onto the slide.
- Enlarge the font for the column headings to 20 pt. Enlarge the font for the rest of the table text to 16 pt.
- Center the text vertically in the cells. (Hint: Vertical centering places the text equidistant between the top and bottom of the cell; it is not the same as centering from left to right.)

• PowerPoint (continued)

(C) MediaTechnics

Slide 6:

- Use the Blank layout.

- Search the Web for photos and clip art pertaining to drive-in theaters.

- Copy and paste several photos to create a collage.

- List the Web sites where you obtained the photos under the "Photo Credits:" heading.

Slide 7:

- Use the *Title and Content* layout.

- Add the title shown.

- Add the Continuous Arrow Process SmartArt from the Process group.

- Change the SmartArt Style to the Flat Scene style.

- Change colors by selecting one of the options from Accent 6 variations.

- Add the following Web links:
  Wikipedia: http://en.wikipedia.org/wiki/Drive-in_theater
  Drive-In Theater: www.driveintheater.com
  Drive-in Movie: www.driveinmovie.com

4. Save the project as Capstone3-[Your Name].

5. Submit your project on a USB flash drive, as a printout, or as an e-mail attachment according to your instructor's preference.

Note: Page numbers in boldface indicate
    key terms.